BONUS
FIELD GUIDE
WITH YOUR
FAVORITE
BIRDS

The COMPLETE BOOK for
BACKYARD
BIRD LOVERS

EVERYTHING YOU NEED TO KNOW ABOUT
ATTRACTING AND FEEDING BIRDS IN YOUR YARD

SALLY ROTH

RODALE

This book is a compilation of *The Backyard Bird Feeder's Bible* (© 2000 Sally Roth)
and *The Backyard Bird Lover's Field Guide* (© 2007 Sally Roth), previously published by Rodale Inc.

Mention of specific companies, organizations, or authorities in this book does not imply
endorsement by the author or publisher, nor does mention of specific companies, organizations,
or authorities imply that they endorse this book, its author, or the publisher.

Rodale books may be purchased for business or promotional use. For information, please write to:
Special Markets Department, Rodale Inc., 733 Third Avenue, New York, NY 10017

Printed in the United States of America
Rodale Inc. makes every effort to use acid-free ♾, recycled paper ♻.

Cover design by Susan Eugster
Cover photograph by © iStockphoto

ISBN-13 978–1–59486–989–1
ISBN-10 1–59486–989–8

2   4   6   8   10   9   7   5   3   1   hardcover

We inspire and enable people to improve their lives and the world around them
For more of our products visit **rodalestore.com** or call 800-848-4735

the BACKYARD
Bird Feeder's
B·I·B·L·E

© 2000 by Sally Roth
Illustrations © 2000 by John Burgoyne

First published 2000
First published in paperback 2003

The information in this book has been carefully researched, and all efforts have been made to ensure accuracy. Rodale Inc. assumes no responsibility for any injuries suffered or for damages or losses incurred during the use of or as a result of following this information. It is important to study all directions carefully before taking any action based on the information and advice presented in this book. When using any commercial product, *always* read and follow label directions. Where trade names are used, no discrimination is intended and no endorsement by Rodale Inc. is implied.

Printed in the United States of America on acid-free ∞, recycled paper ♲

We're always happy to hear from you. For questions or comments concerning the editorial content of this book, please write to:

Rodale Book Readers' Service
33 East Minor Street
Emmaus, PA 18098

Look for other Rodale books wherever books are sold. Or call us at (800) 848-4735.

For more information about Rodale Organic Living magazines and books, visit our Web site at:

www.organicgardening.com

Editor: Deborah L. Martin
Contributing Editors: Susan B. Burton and Sarah S. Dunn
Cover and Interior Book Designer: Nancy Smola Biltcliff
Interior Illustrator: John Burgoyne
Cover Photographers: Mitch Mandel (hardcover and paperback), Robert P. Carr/Bruce Coleman Inc. (hardcover), and John Sorensen (paperback)
Photography Editor and Cover Photo Stylist: Lyn Horst
Layout Designer: Keith Biery
Researchers: Diana Erney, Sarah Wolfgang Heffner, Pamela R. Ruch
Copy Editor: Nancy N. Bailey
Manufacturing Coordinator: Mark Krahforst
Indexer: Lina Burton
Editorial Assistance: Kerrie Cadden

RODALE ORGANIC LIVING BOOKS

Executive Editor: Margot Schupf
Art Director: Patricia Field
Content Assembly Manager: Robert V. Anderson Jr.
Copy Manager: Nancy N. Bailey
Editorial Assistant: Sara Sellar

Library of Congress Cataloging-in-Publication Data

Roth, Sally.
    The backyard bird feeder's bible : the A-to-Z guide to feeders, seed mixes, projects, and treats / Sally Roth.
          p.   cm.
    Includes bibliographical references (p.   ) and index.
    ISBN 0–87596–834–1 hardcover
    ISBN 0–87596–918–6 paperback
    1. Bird feeders.   2. Birds—Feeding and feeds.   I. Title.
QL676.5 R6683   2000
639.9'78—dc21   00–009063

Distributed to the book trade by St. Martin's Press

| 6 | 8 | 10 | 9 | 7 | 5 | hardcover |
| 6 | 8 | 10 | 9 | 7 | | paperback |

In memory of Rachel Carson,
in hope of never a silent spring

Rodale
Organic Gardening Starts Here!

Here at Rodale, we've been creating organic gardens for more than 50 years—ever since my grandfather J. I. Rodale learned about composting and decided that healthy living starts with healthy soil. In 1940 J. I. started the Rodale Organic Farm to test his theories, and today the nonprofit Rodale Institute Experimental Farm is still at the forefront of organic gardening and farming research. In 1942 J. I. founded *Organic Gardening* magazine to share his discoveries with gardeners everywhere. His son, my father, Robert Rodale, headed *Organic Gardening* until 1990, and today a fourth generation of Rodales is growing up with the magazine. Over the years we've shown millions of readers how to grow bountiful crops and beautiful flowers using nature's own techniques.

In this book, you'll find the latest organic methods and the best gardening advice. We know—because all our authors and editors are passionate about gardening! We feel strongly that our gardens should be safe for our children, pets, and the birds and butterflies that add beauty and delight to our lives and landscapes. Our gardens should provide us with fresh, flavorful vegetables, delightful herbs, and gorgeous flowers. And they should be a pleasure to work in as well as to view.

Sharing the secrets of safe, successful gardening is why we publish books. So come visit us at the Rodale Institute Experimental Farm, where you can tour the gardens every day—we're open year-round. And use this book to create your best garden ever.

Happy gardening!

Maria Rodale

Maria Rodale
Rodale Organic Gardening Books

Contents

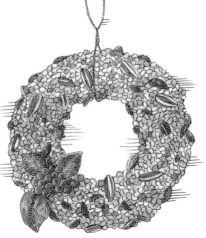

Acknowledgments

Thank you first of all to my tolerant son, David— I'm so glad you're a nature lover, too, even if it isn't cool for a teenager to admit it. And thank you to my daughter, Gretel, and granddaughter, Erica, who find joy in the world every day.

Thanks to my understanding friends, who remind me there's more to life than birds but who never argue with "I'm working."

Dear Deb, what would I have done without the endless Diet Coke breaks and discussions of human nature? Dear Pauline, thanks for sharing the joy of God and love. Dear Jim, thanks for the always-entertaining political conversations. Dear Heidi, thanks for your painstaking work in matters of science, but even greater thanks for your kindred spirit that makes nature walks—a very private time—so much fun to share. I'll never forget stumbling through the dark to find the *Xanthopastis* caterpillars! Dear Paul, thanks for always being yourself— but Indian bikes still rule. Dear Lynn, thanks for ever-patient listening, high-energy dancing, and that wild-woman insight. Dear Randy, thanks for sharing yourself through your songs—the Taylor sounds beautiful in your hands. Dear Paul, thanks for pondering the big questions and offering shelter from the storm. Dear Ben, thanks for Vangelis and for coming to the rescue of the cecropia moth at 4:00 A.M. Dear Beth, Jill, Barbara, Tracey, Jane, and Peggy, thanks for the shared voices and shared strength of good women. Dear Larry, thanks for loving music as much as I do and for taking me back to my roots. Dear Pati, thanks for being part of this wonder-filled world. I am truly blessed.

Thanks to Nancy Bailey and Sue Burton for polishing my language and organizing my thoughts with incredible patience and inexhaustible goodwill.

Finally but foremost, a big bear hug to Deb Martin, my editor, whose sense of humor let us both survive the creation of this book—you made working fun! You and GI Joe will always be my heroes.

The Best Part of Bird Watching

I was exploring a local birding hot spot with my friend Heidi last year when both of us were taken completely by surprise by a couple of bald eagles that came flapping out of a little woods to soar over our heads. We stood spellbound in the open field where we'd been hunting for rocks.

"That's the way it is with birds," I remarked. "Go look for an eagle and you won't find one. Look for rocks, and you get an eagle."

We laughed about what terrible birders we were, having spent the beautiful sunny day looking at everything around us and totally forgetting to watch for the birds that draw "real" bird watchers to this area. We'd admired prairie grasses bent from the November winds, common-as-dirt song sparrows singing in the weeds, delicate pearly shells glinting in a drought-stricken lake bed, red hawthorn berries glowing in the sun, clouds forming and re-forming in the impossibly blue sky.

"I figure I just skipped a few steps in that old joke," said Heidi. "The one about the stages of a birder, you know, like the stages of man?"

I hadn't heard it, so she filled me in. Bird watchers begin by watching birds, goes the story: They watch them singing from a bush, pecking at seeds on the ground, pulling a worm from the lawn.

Then they take the next step and start learning their names; soon they are making lists and searching for species to fill the gaps. Once they reach the next stage, they are obsessed, traveling far distances to focus binoculars on their quarry, thinking "Ah, number 527! Number 528!" Lost in the thrill of the hunt, they no longer see the birds as birds but as quests—they forget to watch them. Eventually, though, bird watchers return to their beginnings, enjoying the birds without caring whether they're the rarest of the rare or the most common of backyard residents.

The joke is an exaggeration, of course, because many life-listers still watch the birds, but I like it because it emphasizes what to me is the best part of being a bird watcher. It's not how many you've seen, or what rarities you have notched in your belt—it's the wonder of watching a bird, any bird, as it lives its perfect natural life.

Although I love a beautiful bird as much as anybody—seeing a bluebird can make my whole day!—I still enjoy watching the antics of the ill-mannered house sparrows that congregate at my feeders. (Of course, I did travel 2 hours to see a big rare gyrfalcon that had strayed from the Arctic to a Pennsylvania quarry, but only because I love hawks and Audubon's print of gyrfalcons has hung over my bed for half my life.)

I can't imagine a yard without birds, and that's why I do everything I can to make my place tempting to them. It's a win-win proposition for both of us: I get the pleasure of watching them at their daily lives, and they get a reliable and constant source of food as well as the added attractions of fresh water and a safe and sheltered place to rest or nest.

I've been lucky to have been a country girl for most of my life, but I live in town now, and I've learned that the same tricks that brought birds to my feeders when I was surrounded by wild space are just as effective in a small yard amid neighbors. It's not all house sparrows and starlings, either: More than 40 different kinds of birds have visited here in just 2 short years (but who's counting?).

Food Brings in the Birds

Food is the number one attraction for birds because most of their everyday life is given over to finding the food to stoke their high-metabolism bodies. "She eats like a bird" means something very different to birds than it does to us: If we ate like they do, we'd be at the table all day long.

I learned about feeding birds at my mother's knee. I helped her toss bread crumbs and leftovers out the door to hungry cardinals and blue jays. We had no feeder, but the birds didn't care; they'd descend in minutes to vacuum up the offerings. Only potato peelings went untouched, and I remember asking my mother why. "Birds don't eat potatoes," she told me, "but the bunnies will."

Those were my first lessons in what birds like to eat—and don't. Watching birds in the natural world as I explored the woods and fields and setting up my own feeding station taught me a lot more about bird diets. I laughed the first time I read about scientists' inventories of the contents of bird stomachs—what a job!—but I've realized that other than firsthand observation, that is the only way to get a handle on who's eating what. Now I'm in awe of the botanic skills of those scientists, who had to be able to recognize the seeds of hundreds of plants. But I also recognize the limitations of the method: What was in the stomach depended upon where the bird was

American goldfinches sparkle in the spring when the males trade their drab winter feathers for bright yellow plumage trimmed tidily in black. These birds go for a tube feeder filled with sunflower or niger seed.

collected and what the wild crops were like that year. While stomach inventories are a good starting place to tailor-make a menu, they're not the final word.

My science has always depended on my own observations. With so much variation in the plants of this wonderfully diverse country of ours, what my birds are eating may not be the same as what yours are dining on. Luckily, a few seeds are so welcomed by so many birds that they function as "one seed fits all." It's no secret why millet and sunflower are top sellers everywhere: Birds eat them with relish. Fill your feeders with these seeds, and you're guaranteed a steady stream of customers.

That's the great thing about bird feeding. You can keep it that simple: Go out and buy just two kinds of seed, never read a "how to attract birds" book, and enjoy a lifetime of birds at your feeder.

Or you can go the route I've chosen, and learn what foods are preferred by birds and what foods will lure birds that aren't interested in the standard fare. You can fill your yard with practically every kind of bird that lives nearby or passes through your area. You can thrill to a brilliant tanager at your window feeder or a shy thrush in your garden. You can call the kids to see their first bluebird, and you can invite your neighbor for tea and chickadees. It's a wonderful life!

What You'll Find in Here

This book includes just about everything I've learned in four decades of watching birds every day, in every season, in every kind

---

Key to the Symbols

Plants for Food
Fruits and flowers, tall shade trees, twining vines, and blooming bushes—they all say "Stop here!" to birds seeking a spot to dine or a place to nest. Grow your own bird-welcoming and beautiful landscape!

Bird Foods
Out of bird seed? What's in your cupboard to offer the birds instead? Create custom seed mixes and whip up tasty treats from your kitchen to entice your favorite birds to your yard. These entries make it easy.

Birds
Learn more about the common—and uncommon—birds that show up at feeders across North America. Each of these bird-focused entries features a quick-reference list of "Feeder Foods" that are most likely to attract that bird.

Bird Behaviors
The more you watch the birds in your yard the more bird activities you'll see: communication, competition, mating, mimicry, and more. These entries explain what it means when birds behave the way they do.

of weather. The eastern birds of my childhood are in here as are the northwestern friends that visited my feeders in Oregon and the Midwest birds that keep me company here in Indiana. So are all the northern, southern, and western birds I've met on travels and at friends' feeders.

You'll learn about the birds themselves and what their behaviors mean. You'll find the tricks to supplying their favorite feeder foods. You'll discover plants that they prefer. You'll find out how to make your yard a safe haven. As you browse through this book, look for the little symbols at the beginning of each entry. There are eight different ones, and they serve as a key to the general subject of an entry (the symbols are defined below).

Sample the entries in any order you like, according to what you're most curious about. I guarantee that your feeders will entertain more birds than ever once you start putting the suggestions in this book into practice.

One caution before you dig in: Bird watching and bird feeding are lifelong passions. You'll spend more time outside or looking out the window than ever before. You'll start watching birds while you're stuck in traffic jams or in the parking lot at school, waiting for your kids. You'll become an evangelist even without trying, as friends and family get hooked on the lively action at your feeders. Before you know it, you'll be thinking like a bird as you work in the yard and choosing plants and designs because the birds will like them. And, of course, the chair by the bird-feeder window will become the most popular seat in the house.

Bird Watching	**Animal Visitors**	**Feeders and More**	**Seasonal Subjects**
Take your backyard-bird viewing to a new level with techniques from these entries. Choose the most useful binoculars and field guides, find out more about bird photography, or participate in your first bird count.	Who else visits bird feeders? Discover the other critters that dine on seeds, suet, fruit, nectar, and other bird foods. Find out how to enjoy the extra wildlife in your yard—and how to thwart unwelcome feeder raiders.	From making your own tube feeder to cleaning the bird bath, these entries describe all the best equipment—homemade and store-bought—to put the food and feeders right where birds are most likely to find them.	What do birds do when it rains? What kind of foods should you offer in the middle of summer? Find out how you can get the most out of your bird-feeding efforts every season of the year.

Accessories

MANUFACTURERS OF BIRD FEEDERS are making it easy for consumers to jump on the bird-feeding bandwagon. Of course, all you need to make the birds happy is a supply of seed and a tray to put it in. But if you feed birds on a regular basis and have a feeding station that includes several types and sizes of feeders, you'll appreciate the new labor-saving devices. You can buy gizmos that clean or hang your feeders, contraptions to keep out squirrels, and technological marvels to bring the bird world closer to you inside. Here are some of the accessories I've found most useful. Look for them in well-stocked bird-supply stores, home improvement stores, or discount stores, or order from catalogs such as those listed in "Resources" on page 348.

Scrub-brush hose attachment. This short-handled brush attaches directly to your garden hose. A stream of water travels through a narrow tube in the handle and loosens grime and stuck-on seed from your birdbath or feeder.

Brush for plastic tube feeders. Slide this long brush into your tube feeder and rotate to clean out old seed in a jiffy. Soft bristles won't scratch plastic.

Niger seed bags. Add extra feeding places for finches in a snap by hanging seed-stuffed pouches brimming with niger. Birds cling to the mesh and extract the seeds through the small openings.

Add-on trays for tube feeders. Cut down on spilled seed by attaching a plastic tray to the bottom of your tube feeder to catch niger or other seeds that fall from openings. *Bonus:* The tray adds perching room for cardinals and other customers.

Bell-shaped ant guard. Hook this plastic bell above your nectar feeder, coat the inside with petroleum jelly, and prevent ants from raiding your sugar water supplies. Longer lasting, more effective, and much less messy than smearing petroleum jelly on the feeder hanger itself.

Shepherd's crooks. Easy to push into any soil, these low-cost metal posts let you install feeders quickly and easily by stepping onto the anchoring

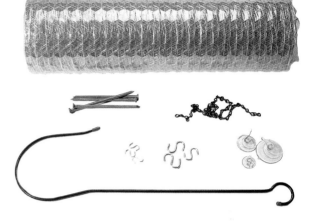

Accessories make your feeders more versatile: Suction cups with screws or hooks let you put a feeder right on your window. Use large nails to skewer citrus fruit or apples; chicken wire is handy for shaping a temporary cover or squirrel guard around a feeder.

support. Some feature more than one curved hook, for multiple-feeder capacity.

Extra arms for feeder poles. A simple clamp lets you add extra hooked arms—and that means extra feeders—to poles up to 1¼ inches in diameter.

Steel feeder stand. Heavy, tip-proof, flat base accepts a metal post, such as a shepherd's crook, so you can enjoy feeders on your deck or patio.

Tree-mount feeder bracket. Never have to pound a nail into living wood again. This stretchy cord wraps snugly around a tree to hold the included feeder-supporting hook. To avoid inadvertently girdling your tree, use this type of support for a winter-time feeder that you remove—along with the stretchy cord—when spring arrives.

Bird monitor system. Bring the sounds of the feeder area indoors with this wireless monitor system. It works like a waterproof baby monitor. The sensitive microphone picks up chirps, songs, and even the sounds of cracking seeds and rustling wings.

Accidents

BIRDS REPRODUCE IN BROODS to compensate for the many individuals lost to predators, disease, and accidents. Sad to say, human activity causes most bird accidents. The leading causes of bird fatalities include collisions with vehicles, fatal encounters with glass windows, knockouts at tall radio, television, or cell phone towers during migration flights, and bashes with big city buildings. Lighthouses, ocean oil slicks, and chemicals also take their toll on birds. Add the predations of our feline friends to the list, and you can see what a danger our human habits are to wild birds.

Apart from the widespread dangers birds face, there is a long list of other accidents that may befall them. Songbirds may become trapped in garages and other outbuildings. Quail, pheasants, and other game birds have had unfortunate entanglements with barbed wire. Lawn mowers and farm equipment endanger ground-nesting field birds.

Even water can pose a problem to swallows, which skim low across the surface to collect insects. One wing beat too low, and the bird may be unable to regain the air. In the feeder area, most accidents happen when birds fly into windows. Use fruit-tree netting, stretched tightly so it's barely visible to human eyes, to break up reflections and keep the birds in your yard safe.

Tribulations of Being Tiny

Hummingbirds are particularly prone to accidents due to their small size. They may become fish food or frog dinner at ponds. A friend of mine found a hummer hanging by its beak from her screen door. Bird watchers have found the little birds trapped in the sticky threads of orb weaver spiders.

> Even spider webs may prove to be hazardous for hummingbirds and other tiny birds.

Acorns

Attract chickadees, jays, nuthatches, quail, titmice, wild turkeys, woodpeckers

PACKED WITH PROTEIN, acorns are a huge hit with all nut-eating birds, including chickadees, jays, nuthatches, titmice, and woodpeckers. They're also tops with game birds like wild turkeys and quail. Lacking the necessary whacking power to get at acorn nutmeats themselves, smaller birds such as buntings, finches, juncos, and sparrows will clean up crumbs dropped by larger birds or acorns smashed by the bird-feeder filler (that's you).

Oak (*Quercus* spp.) trees of any kind are magnets for birds when the acorns are ripe for picking, which may be late summer to fall, depending on the oak species. Beating the birds to the harvest may sound a little mean, but you're really just stockpiling acorns for winter feeding when acorns can be hard to find.

Meaty acorns taste bitter to us, but they are beloved by birds, from chickadees to wild turkeys. Stockpile a few in the fall to offer as winter feeder treats.

Plant for the Future

MATURE OAKS add majesty to a landscape, but even young oak trees are of great value to birds. Many oaks begin producing acorns when they're 5 to 7 years old, and the crop only gets better as the trees mature. Even before they start to bear acorns, young oaks provide homes for tasty caterpillars and other bird-nourishing insects.

Before you plant, make sure you have room for an oak. Squint your eyes and picture a 100-foot-tall giant in your site, not that 4-foot nursery specimen you've been looking at. To keep maintenance to a minimum, choose an oak species that's native to your region rather than a nonnative species that may struggle in your local soil and climate.

Check your local nursery or refer to "Resources" on page 348 for nurseries that specialize in native plants. Or you can go the freebie route and simply plant a few of the acorns you've collected. Wrap the acorns loosely in a little cage of ½-inch-mesh hardware cloth to protect them from squirrels, then set them in the ground about 3 inches deep. Cover with a thin layer of fall leaves, and mark the spot with a plant label stake as a reminder to watch for sprouts in the spring.

Harvesting, Storing, and Serving Acorns

It doesn't take a lot of effort to gather a supply of acorns for winter bird feeding. Just fill your pockets whenever you notice the fallen nuts on your nature hikes or while strolling your yard. Although some acorns taste sweet to human palates and others are extremely bitter, birds seem to appreciate all of them.

Some acorns begin to germinate soon after hitting the ground, while others need a rest period over winter before they sprout. To keep your acorns fresh, store them outdoors or in an unheated garage in a moisture-proof metal container with a secure lid, so that squirrels don't help themselves to your hoard. When you want to give your feeder birds a treat, put a handful of acorns in an old sock, fold over the top, and use a hammer to split open the acorns. Pour the broken nuts into a tray feeder and sit back to watch the show.

Age

OUR STUDIES OF CAPTIVE BIRDS indicate that if a bird manages to avoid predators, disease, accidents, and starvation, it can achieve a ripe old age of 10 years or more. Sheltered from natural disaster, robins have been reported to live as long as 15 years, and a captive cardinal reached the rather incredible age of 28 years!

Unfortunately, in the wild, birds rarely achieve their potential life span. Many of them live a very short life: from 6 months to a year or two, with an estimated two-thirds of birds that reach flying stage never making it to their first birthday. Records retrieved from banded birds show that representatives of many species, from chickadees and goldfinches to grosbeaks and jays, manage to notch 5 years or more, with some lasting into their teens. In general, very small birds such as warblers have shorter lives than larger birds. Hawks, owls, geese, and gulls and other seabirds hold the old-age records for birds: Some individuals have thrived for more than 40 years.

If you can distinguish an individual bird in your backyard, perhaps because of albinism or unusual behavior or song, you can keep track of its age yourself. A tufted titmouse with a white tail feather visited my feeder for 6 years, then disappeared in year 7. A blue jay that produced a distinctive imitation of a red-tailed hawk scream was a feeder patron and a nesting resident for 4 years.

> About two-thirds of the birds that reach flying stage never make it to their first birthday.

Albinism

Birds of a feather flock together, and those birds that display the white feathers characteristic of albinism may not be accepted among their species. A flock of birds may harass or shun a mostly white bird, perhaps because its high visibility draws the attention of predators.

Partially albinistic birds are an oddity but not a real rarity. Once you begin watching the birds around you, you're likely to spot a robin or house sparrow or other bird with white feathers where there should be color. Stress or shock, injury, environmental factors, or genetics may cause the lack of pigment in the colorless plumage. Complete albinos, which lack pigment even in their bill, legs, and eyes so that these features show up as pink, are much rarer than partial albinos.

Identifying a bird with mostly or totally white feathers is tricky. Bird watchers must rely on body shape, song, or behavior clues to provide enough information to pinpoint the species.

Birds that normally are brown or black like this robin are more likely to display albinistic feathers than brightly colored birds such as goldfinches and tanagers.

Aloes and Agaves

Attract hummingbirds, orioles

Spiky, stiff-leaved aloes (*Aloe* spp.) and agaves (*Agave* spp.) hail from desert country, and so they make great garden plants in warm, dry climates. Agaves are American plants and are a familiar sight in the Southwest, where their tall flowering stalks attract thirsty hummingbirds. Aloes, including the well-known *Aloe vera,* come from Africa.

Separating aloes from agaves can be a challenge because the plants look similar. Some agaves even go by the common name "aloe," like the American aloe (*Agave americana*), better known as century plant.

These plants are a prickly bunch overall. They grow in a cluster of spearlike, succulent leaves armed with sharp spines to deter thirsty desert animals from munching on the juicy leaves. At bloom time, a flow-ering stalk arises, bearing clusters of tubular flowers. In some species, the main plant dies after flowering, and new plants form around the "parent."

Agaves and aloes are at home in desert gardens, where their nectar-rich blooms draw crowds of hummingbirds and orioles. Outside of USDA Zone 8 or 9, treat them as indoor-outdoor plants: Keep them on a sunny windowsill in winter, then move them outside in summer. To encourage flowering, withhold water for 6 to 8 weeks in winter and early spring, then water well to mimic desert rains.

Some large agaves such as the century plant may take 20 years or more to bloom.

Altruism

BIRDS LOOK OUT FOR EACH OTHER in fascinating ways. A covey of quail usually posts a lookout bird, who alerts the others if danger threatens. The sentry may choose an elevated perch, the better to see its surroundings. Although this conspicuous watch post increases the danger for the individual bird (from hawks, particularly), it provides safety for the flock. Doves and pigeons, too, may keep watch for others of their kind when feeding.

Jays and crows act like the police officers of the bird world, alerting all within hearing when a predator threatens. Of course, jays aren't above using their raucous alarm call to clear a feeder area so that they can have it all to themselves.

During nesting season you may see one of the most amazing acts of bird altruism in action. Tree-climbing snakes and squirrels, which have a hearty appetite for bird eggs and nestlings, often run into a full-bird defense when approaching a nest. Usually the nest owner raises the initial alarm, and every nesting bird in the area quickly joins in the attack. With loudly flapping wings and dive-bombing threats, the birds try to deter the snake, and they are often successful. This is an example of reciprocal altruism: The adult birds, no matter what species, vigorously defend the endangered young, and should the need arise, their young will also be guarded by this band of protective parents.

Learn to recognize the alarm calls of your local birds, and hurry to the scene when you hear them. You may witness a fascinating life or death struggle or even help deter a predator in search of avian prey.

> Adult birds will band together to protect nestlings—even of other species—that are in danger.

Amaranth

Attracts juncos, tree sparrows, and many other seed eaters

BIRD BRAINS NEVER HAVE TO WORRY about making grain into flour, which is why amaranth remains a favorite food crop with our avian pals. When a beak is your main utensil, tiny amaranth seeds will do just as well as fat kernels of wheat. (Humans have a different perspective, which is why ancient amaranth, once a widespread grain crop in hot, dry places of the world, lost favor to easier-to-handle grains.)

Pigweed (*Amaranthus retroflexus*) is perhaps the most well-known amaranth. Tough and hardy, it pops up everywhere—much to the delight of small birds that feast upon its prolific seeds all winter long.

You're likely to spot pigweed sprouting near your bird feeder, thanks to deposits from your feeder guests. If you let a few plants grow, you'll find they're as popular with birds as your feeder. And the tough, densely branched plants make great shelter for small birds, all the way through winter. Let frost-killed pigweed stems stand and you'll see juncos, tree sparrows, and other seed eaters amid the plants.

If you prefer a more refined amaranth for you and the birds, try the dramatic love-lies-bleeding (*A. caudatus*), with hot pink drooping tassels that look like fat, fuzzy yarn. Or go for bold with the multi-colored foliage of 'Joseph's Coat', 'Molten Fire', and other showy cultivars of *A. tricolor*. All amaranths are easy to grow as annuals in any zone, but they take their time coming into flower. Start them indoors early if your growing season is short.

> If your growing season is short, start amaranth indoors to give it time to produce flowers.

Amelanchier

Attracts bluebirds, catbirds, great crested flycatchers, jays, mockingbirds, orioles, tanagers, thrashers, thrushes, waxwings

BIRDS SHOW GOOD TASTE when it comes to their favorite shrubs and trees—many of the most popular plants with birds are also beautiful in a garden. Among the best for birds and gardens is amelanchier, also known as Juneberry, shadblow, shadbush, or serviceberry. This group of shrubs and small trees bursts forth in a flurry of snowy white flowers in early spring. Deep blue-purple berries follow the flowers and are so tasty that you may find yourself enjoying them right along with the birds. The good looks and the (literal) good taste of amelanchiers make them a great foundation for a bird-feeding station *and* a handsome addition to your landscape.

Versatile and Attractive

Various amelanchier species are native to just about every part of North America, from the cold North to the mild Northwest to the hot desert regions. Depending on your garden style, you can choose plants that grow by suckering roots to form a tall hedge (*Amelanchier alnifolia, A. canadensis,* or *A. ovalis*), or low ground-covering shrubby species (*A. stolonifera*) that look wonderful on hillsides. The single-stemmed, small-tree types (*A. arborea, A. asiatica, A. × grandiflora, A. laevis,* or *A. lamarckii*) are as pretty as a dogwood in the landscape. In addition to their spring floral display and bird-pleasing berries, most amelanchiers develop colorful fall foliage. Most amelanchiers are hardy through Zone 4.

Plant amelanchiers in full sun to shade, in average, well-drained garden soil. When the berries ripen from red to blue-purple, watch for bluebirds, catbirds, great crested flycatchers, jays, mockingbirds, orioles, tanagers, thrashers, thrushes, and waxwings to visit in search of the mild-flavored, blueberry-like fruit. You may like fruit so much that you want to plant an extra bush or two for yourself. A bit seedier than blueberries, amalanchier berries taste great atop a bowl of cereal and make a delicious filling for pies or crisps.

Shadblow gets its name from its habit of blooming when fish called shad move from the ocean into rivers to spawn. "Blow" is an old word that means bloom.

Beautiful berries that ripen from red to purple don't stay on the tree for long. Birds can strip a tree of its fruit before you get a taste of the blueberry-like flavor.

Best Small-Tree Amelanchiers

DO YOUR part to lift amelanchiers out of undeserved anonymity and enjoy the benefits these plants have to offer: pretty spring flowers, bird-pleasing (and people-pleasing) fruits, and attractive fall foliage color. Here are several selections that form excellent small trees, worthy of any landscape. Except where noted, most will reach a mature height of 12 to 15 feet.

'Alta Glow' (*A. alnifolia* cv.): Columnar form, to 18 feet tall; unusual cream-colored fruit; yellow, cream, and maroon fall foliage colors

'Autumn Brilliance' (*A. × grandiflora* hybrid): More upright form than others; larger-than-usual white flowers; gorgeous red fall color

'Ballerina' (*A. × grandiflora* hybrid): Strong grower; lots of flowers and thus lots of good-size, sweet fruit; purple-bronze to red fall foliage

'Cumulus' (*A. laevis* cv.): Upright and oval-shaped with clouds of flowers; good for fruit, too; orange-red fall color

'Prince Charles' (*A. laevis* cv.): Vigorous grower, to 25 feet tall; abundant flowers bloom before the leaves open in spring; flavorful fruits; orange-red fall foliage

'Princess Diana' (*A. × grandiflora* hybrid): Very graceful form; loads of white flowers; good red fall foliage color

'Robin Hill' (*A. × grandiflora* hybrid): Upright rather than spreading; pink buds open to white flowers that yield small red fruit; yellow-red fall foliage

'Strata' (*A. × grandiflora* hybrid): Elegant horizontal branching habit with a substantial floral display; looks beautiful growing in perennial beds

'Tradition' (*A. canadensis* cv.): Oval form to 20 feet tall with graceful branching; early blooming; produces abundant fruit; brilliant orange-red fall color

Ants

Attract jays, robins, woodpeckers

WHEN YOU SPOT AN ANTHILL in your yard, count yourself lucky to host insects that birds love. Jays, robins, and woodpeckers are especially fond of ants, but lots of other birds eat ants, too. The critters are plentiful, apparently delectable, and easy for birds to find and eat.

Ants also figure in one of the more bizarre bird behaviors: anting, in which a bird uses an ant like a bath sponge to wipe down its feathers, especially under the wings. Ant bodies contain formic acid, which ornithologists think acts like a natural pesticide to keep feather lice and mites in check. Watch for jays and other birds lolling directly on top of anthills and contorting their bodies as they rub the ants among their feathers.

There's no need to attract ants to your garden—they're already there, going about their busy subterranean lives and venturing out to collect morsels of food for the storehouse.

You may also find ants herding aphids in your garden. The ants feed on the sticky sweet "honeydew" that the aphids secrete; in exchange, they protect aphids from predators and may actually carry the aphids to your plants. This fondness for sweets means that ants may seek out nectar feeders. If they do, deter ants by smearing petroleum jelly on the hanger or by using a commercial bell-shaped ant guard or a plastic water-filled moat to prevent access. Such solutions are easy, quick, and cheap—less than $5 for permanent nectar protection.

> Many feeder and backyard birds enjoy a meal of ants. Some birds freshen their feathers with them, too.

Apples

Attract bluebirds, chickadees, jays, mockingbirds, robins, starlings, thrashers, titmice, towhees, Carolina wrens

AN APPLE A DAY may deter the doctor, but it will bring birds flocking to your feeder in fall and winter. Roughly chop an apple into chunks, spread them in your feeder, and you'll soon have jays, mockingbirds, and Carolina wrens nibbling away at the treasure. Scatter some chopped apple on the ground and robins, brown thrashers, and towhees may also partake of the feast. If bluebirds are in the area, they too may fly in to enjoy a regular offering of apple.

Apples for birds needn't be perfect—they'll eagerly gobble up mushy or wormy fruit. Chopping an apple makes it easier for smaller beaks to eat, but slicing the fruit in half will attract customers, too, who will carefully eat every bit of flesh and leave just the hollowed-out skin behind.

Apples are also tops with starlings. Slice a couple of apples in half, place them on the ground, and you'll get a starling circus outside your window, as the birds joust and squabble over the sweet flesh. Kids love to watch the activity!

If you're trying to deter starlings from your feeding area, save your apples for feeders they can't frequent. A coffee can hung horizontally, with a small entrance hole that allows titmice and chickadees to enter but bars starlings, is a good place to put a small amount of chopped apple. Weighted feeders that deter larger birds will also prevent starlings from getting your apple offerings. But since apples, especially those past their prime, are usually easy to come by (just ask your grocer), you can also include starlings in this feast. Slice whole fruits in half and place them in a decoy feeder, away from those that your more desirable birds frequent.

If you find yourself with an abundance of apples and no room in the fridge for storage, take time to

A vertical feeder keeps apples in easy reach of agile wrens and other desirable fruit eaters but helps keep crowds of starlings from gobbling your offerings in one sitting.

slice and dry them for later use. There's no need to remove the cores—birds like the seeds, too. Just slice the apples thinly with a sharp knife, and loosely string the slices with a heavy-duty carpet needle and thread. Hang to air-dry. Or spread the slices on cookie sheets, and bake at 200°F. How long they take to dry in the oven depends on the moisture content and thickness of the apple slices. Check the slices after 15 minutes, then increase the time as needed by 10-minute intervals. Store dried apples in resealable plastic bags. Chop or serve whole in feeders, or use strings of dried apple slices to decorate outdoor evergreens or a discarded Christmas tree.

Baby Birds

MANY BIRDS WILL TAKE UP RESIDENCE near a reliable food source such as your well-stocked feeder, as long as your yard holds the plants or nest boxes they need to raise a family. That means you may get to see fledglings at your feeder, a sight that will bring a smile to even the grouchiest curmudgeon. With their fuzzy heads and stubby bodies, baby birds are delightful.

Should you come upon a baby bird in your yard, the best advice is to leave it alone. Nearly all songbirds leave the nest a few days before they can fly. The parents bring them food as they hop about and flap from one place to another, trying out their wings. The best thing you can do for these not-yet-airborne babies is to keep your cat inside. If a baby bird moves so fast that you have trouble catching it, it does not need your help. If, however, you find an obviously helpless nestling on the ground, you may be able to save it. Fill a berry box or shoe box with facial tissues, and add a 20-ounce soda-pop bottle filled with very warm water to provide vital heat. Nestle the baby in the makeshift nest, cover with a hand towel to preserve the heat, and get the baby to a bird rehabilitator as fast as possible. Your veterinarian or local nature center should be able to supply the name and phone number of one of these dedicated, experienced, and legally licensed people. In spite of your good intentions, it is very difficult—and illegal—to raise a baby songbird.

> If you discover a baby bird in your yard, leave it alone—and keep the cat indoors.

Bacon

Attracts bluebirds, crows, jays, ravens, starlings, woodpeckers, Carolina wrens

IN THE OLD DAYS when bacon was a regular part of breakfast, cooks were happy to share the leftover grease with their feathered friends. In today's fat-conscious society, many people have sworn off bacon, but birds don't need to fight fat! Bacon grease is still a great food for backyard birds.

The simplest way to package bacon grease for bird feeding is in metal tuna or cat-food cans. Punch a hole in the side wall of the can with a nail. Use pliers to bend the tip of a wire into a knot that won't slip through the hole, and thread the wire through the can for hanging. Fill the can to the brim with cooled, but still-liquid bacon grease, then stick it in the refrigerator to solidify. Once the grease is no longer runny, hang the can from a branch.

Bluebirds, jays, woodpeckers, and Carolina wrens readily accept this source of fat, whether you offer it straight or use it in bird-treat recipes. Bacon grease also draws crows, starlings, and even ravens.

Pour cooled but still-liquid bacon fat into empty tuna or cat food cans. After it solidifies, punch a hole in the side, and run a wire through it for easy hanging.

Baffles

Squirrels, raccoons, and similar animals may be welcome guests in your yard, but most birders prefer that these critters stick to their own feeders and leave the bird feeders alone. Not only do they tend to clean out a bird feeder in a hurry, but a resident squirrel will also deter most birds from visiting the feeder while it dines. For reasons unclear to us humans, squirrels will almost always go for the bird feeders first. To prevent them from hogging feeders intended for birds, it's time for that ounce of prevention.

Baffles are metal or plastic guards that stand between the feeder and the tree or post, so that climbing animals can't mount a sneak attack on the food. Keep in mind that squirrels are determined creatures, and they may eventually overcome a baffle. They may figure out an alternate approach route and leap directly to the feeder. Or they may learn the acrobatics necessary to keep from sliding off the baffle. At best, a baffle will keep squirrels thwarted all season long; at least, it will slow them down a bit.

If your feeder is mounted on a post, first be sure that squirrels can't reach it by leaping onto it from a tree or roof. Then install a metal cone-shaped or tubular baffle below the feeder. Tubular baffles must be about 14 inches long to deter squirrels and 24 inches long to keep out raccoons. You can make your own baffle from a section of pipe, chosen to fit the diameter of your post, or you can purchase a commercial baffle for easy installation. A section of plastic PVC pipe slipped over the post will deter squirrels for a little while, although they may eventually gnaw through it. Spray-paint the pipe dark green or black to make it less obtrusive in the landscape. Commercial baffles are widely available for both tubular metal posts and thicker wood posts; for a well-made design that will last for years, expect to pay between $15 and $30.

To protect hanging feeders, slip a metal or plastic baffle between the feeder and its hanging hook. These baffles prevent access by tipping as the squirrel climbs

Baffles put a barrier between seed and squirrel, but they may not baffle a determined and agile squirrel forever. A door that slams shut does the trick on this weighted feeder.

onto it, sending the animal sliding off the side or scurrying back where it came from. The slick plastic or metal also prevents the squirrel's feet from getting a secure grip. If you have a choice, go for a metal baffle. Remember that a determined squirrel will gnaw its way through a plastic device. No matter what type of feeder guard you install, keep an eye out—the most persistent of squirrels may eventually figure out a way around even the most well-designed feeder guard.

Some newer models of feeders now come equipped with weight-activated baffles. When a squirrel—or even a large, feeder-hogging pigeon—puts its weight on the perch bar, the pressure pulls down a solid metal wall between the unwanted guest and the food within the feeder. You can even adjust the balance to give only lightweight songbirds access to the seeds. Sturdy steel construction adds heft and cost to these bird-food fortresses, but you can recover the price rather quickly in savings on seeds.

Banding

A TINY ALUMINUM BAND on a bird's leg is an important link to the body of scientific knowledge about birds. The band identifies where the bird was banded and includes instructions on where to send the band if the bird is later found dead. Retrieved bands help researchers fill in the missing pieces of bird ranges and migration routes and dates.

If you're interested in banding, get involved in an existing program. There you will learn techniques and record keeping, and you'll make contacts who will vouch for your abilities should you later decide to apply for your own federal permit. Call your local chapter of the National Audubon Society, or check with nearby nature centers to track down a banding program to join. Or call 1-800-327-BAND (2263) to find out more.

Lightweight leg bands supply scientists with serious information about where birds have been. Find out how you can help through local nature centers.

Beneath the Feeder

BIRDS AT THE FEEDER mean debris beneath it, especially if you're serving up sunflower seed. If you are feeding a large contingent of hungry birds, the fallen seeds and hulls can quickly pile up into a layer several inches deep. You can rake up the hulls, but I prefer to disguise them instead.

Spread a 3-inch layer of wood chips underneath your feeder. Not only will it cover any unsightly accumulation of hulls, it will give a tidy look to your feeder area. The chips also allow ground-feeding birds, such as doves and juncos, to pick through the pile and find edible seeds. Every so often, I drag a garden hoe over the area to turn over a layer of chips on top of newly fallen hulls. The wood chips disguise bird droppings, too.

If you prefer to eliminate debris altogether, offer hulled sunflower seeds, peanut pieces, nutmeats, suet, and other no-mess foods. Niger seed hulls are so small that they rarely become unsightly, so include some niger in your mix to keep the finches happy.

Keep the area around feeders looking neat with a layer of inexpensive wood chips or bark mulch. Refresh the layer by burying seed hulls with a hoe.

Berries

Attract many kinds of birds at various times of the year

BERRIES ARE ONE OF THE BIG REASONS for dramatic declines in bird traffic at feeders in the summertime. Even premium birdseed can't compare to the temptation of ripening blackberries (*Rubus* spp.), blueberries (*Vaccinium* spp.), huckleberries (*Gaylussacia* spp.), mulberries (*Morus* spp.), salmonberries (*Rubus spectabilis*), and dozens of other kinds of wild and cultivated berries.

You'd think that since birds are this attracted to berries, they'd come like magic to a feeder full of these favorites. That's true—sort of. Berries are a big attraction at a feeder, with one big caveat: *if you offer them at times when they aren't available from natural sources.*

Berries at the Feeder

If you find yourself with extra berries of any kind in summer—the last few strawberries in the box, a handful of slightly shriveled blueberries—don't bother putting them in the feeder. You'll probably get no takers when nature's bounty is all around. Instead, pop your leftover spring, summer, and fall berries into a plastic bag or container, and freeze them. In wintertime, the birds will gobble up bruised or battered berry bits as if they were rare treasures (at that time of year, they are!).

Gather berry-laden branches of dogwoods (*Cornus* spp.), hawthorns (*Crataegus* spp.), hollies (*Ilex* spp.), cedars (*Juniperus* spp.), or other bird favorites, and offer them in a tray feeder or on the Berry Branch Feeder on the opposite page. The perch gives robins, thrushes, and other birds easy access to the berries.

Scarlet tanagers stay in the treetops unless there are tasty berries to draw them closer. The purple fruit of a pokeweed plant has strong bird appeal.

Like other thrushes, eastern bluebirds are quick to arrive on the scene when berries ripen. Tempt them to your yard by planting a berry patch for the birds.

Berry Branch Feeder

Here's a simple way to bring berry-loving birds to a spot where you can watch them while they dine.

MATERIALS

Screw eye

Board, approximately 8 × 20 inches

Screws

Sturdy branch

Berried branches of cedar, dogwood, or holly

Flexible wire, such as floral wire

Nails (optional)

Step 1. Screw the screw eye into the middle of the upper third of the board.

Step 2. Using screws, fasten the branch to the lower end of the board, where it will serve as a perch for your visitors.

Step 3. Gather berry-laden branches into a bundle, and wrap wire around the stems to hold them together. Leave enough wire at the end to wrap around the screw eye a few times to hang the bunch securely on the board at bird's-eye level.

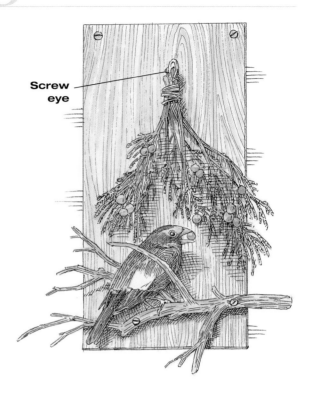

Screw eye

Step 4. Nail or screw the board to a tree, post, or fence, and wait for birds to arrive. Stockpile branches with berries for refilling the feeder.

Berries Bring Them In

If you really want to see the berry-eating birds of summer, growing your own fruit is the way to go. Seasonal fruit on the bush holds much more appeal for a greater variety of birds than the most attractively filled feeder. And you'll see birds that would never venture near your feeders, no matter what you put in them. You may play host to brilliant red tanagers; vivid orange or yellow orioles; soft olive-green vireos, thrashers, and catbirds; and golden-voiced thrushes. Everybody's favorite, bluebirds, are also big fans of berries. When berries ripen, also look for the big and brash great crested flycatcher and flocks of elegantly understated cedar waxwings.

If you never guessed you could enjoy watching such wonderful birds in your own backyard, guess again. If it's loaded with berries, even the smallest yard can attract these birds. Birds are opportunists. When they spot a bush brimming with tasty fruit, they'll move in for the feast, whether that berry bush is in a landscaping strip at the mall, a postage-stamp–size backyard, or a 100-acre estate.

Keep in mind, though, that berry season is sweet but short. From ripening to going, going, gone takes only about 2 weeks, no matter what kind of berry you're growing. You can extend the season by planting different kinds of berries and different cultivars of each berry.

(continued on page 16)

Berries for Birds

INSTEAD OF offering berries at your feeder in the summer, plant berry bushes. It's a guaranteed way to get more birds into your yard when the crop ripens. And what birds they might be! Glorious songbirds that normally will have nothing to do with a feeder will gladly come for berries-on-the-bush. Check out this listing to see what you can plant—and what you may already have—to tempt an array of beautiful birds into your yard.

Berry	Description	Birds Attracted
Strawberries (*Fragaria* spp.)	Clump-forming plants with familiar tasty red fruits; spread into colonies by runners	Catbirds, prairie chickens, crows, grosbeaks, grouse, mockingbirds, pheasants, quails, robins, sparrows, thrashers, thrushes, towhees, wild turkeys
Hollies (*Ilex* spp.)	Evergreen and deciduous shrubs and trees with attractive foliage and red berries	Bluebirds, bobwhites, catbirds, doves, flickers, grouse, jays, mockingbirds, quails, robins, sapsuckers, sparrows, thrashers, thrushes, towhees, wild turkeys, vireos, waxwings, woodpeckers
Cedars, junipers (*Juniperus* spp.)	Evergreen conifers with short gray-green needles, of various habit, from ground-hugging creepers to upright or gnarled trees	Bluebirds, catbirds, Clark's nutcrackers, crossbills, finches, flickers, grosbeaks, jays, mockingbirds, robins, sapsuckers, tree swallows, thrashers, hermit thrushes, yellow-rumped warblers, waxwings
Spicebush (*Lindera benzoin*)	Shrub or small tree, often suckering into small group, with yellow flowers on bare branches in early spring; has glossy red berries; all parts have delightful spicy scent	Bluebirds, bobwhites, catbirds, great crested flycatchers, pheasants, robins, thrushes, vireos
Mulberries (*Morus* spp.)	Deciduous trees with white, red, purple, or black-purple fruits; messy and invasive by seed but tops with birds	Bluebirds, cardinals, catbirds, doves, flickers, flycatchers, grackles, grosbeaks, jays, mockingbirds, orioles, phainopeplas, band-tailed pigeons, robins, house sparrows, tanagers, thrashers, thrushes, titmice, vireos, waxwings, woodpeckers
Virginia creeper (*Parthenocissus quinquefolia*)	Climbing or ground-covering perennial vine with five-part leaves that turn beautiful crimson in fall; has grapelike clusters of deep blue berries	Bluebirds, catbirds, chickadees, flickers, great crested flycatchers, mockingbirds, nuthatches, robins, sapsuckers, tree swallows, thrashers, thrushes, titmice, woodpeckers
Buckthorns (*Rhamnus* spp.)	Many species of shrubs or small trees, both native and introduced, frequently thorny, with small fleshy berries that ripen from red to black; deciduous or evergreen depending on species	Topnotch for pileated woodpeckers; also catbirds, mockingbirds, phainopeplas, band-tailed pigeons, robins, sapsuckers, thrashers, thrushes

SEASON WHEN BERRIES ARE PRESENT   SPRING   SUMMER   FALL   WINTER

Berries for Birds—*Continued*

	Berry	Description	Birds Attracted
■■ ■	**Sumacs** (*Rhus* spp.)	Shrubs or small trees, often spreading into thickets; often brilliant scarlet fall foliage; fuzzy upright clusters of tiny red berries	Bluebirds, bobwhites, cardinals, catbirds, prairie chickens, crows, finches, flickers, evening grosbeaks, grouse, jays, juncos, magpies, mockingbirds, pheasants, band-tailed pigeons, quails, robins, starlings, tanagers, thrashers, thrushes, wild turkey, vireos, pine warblers, woodpeckers, wrens
□	**Blackberries, raspberries, salmonberries, thimbleberries, wineberries** (*Rubus* spp.)	Bramble fruits of various sizes and colors, including red, orange-yellow, purple, and purple-black; most species produce shrubby clusters of arching canes that may be prickly to thorny. Some brambles spread readily from suckers and by rooting where cane tips bend over to the ground to form protective thickets where birds may nest and dine.	Blackbirds, bluebirds, bobwhites, buntings, cardinals, catbirds, chickadees, prairie chickens, crows, grackles, grosbeaks, grouse, jays, mockingbirds, orioles, pheasants, band-tailed pigeons, quails, robins, sparrows, tanagers, thrashers, thrushes, titmice, towhees, wild turkeys, vireos, waxwings, woodpeckers, wrens
□	**Elderberries** (*Sambucus* spp.)	Deciduous multistemmed shrub with attractive white flowers in early summer that develop into clusters of small blue-black fruit	Rusty blackbirds, bluebirds, buntings, cardinals, catbirds, flickers, grosbeaks, grouse, jays, kinglets, magpies, mockingbirds, nuthatches, orioles, phainopeplas, pheasants, band-tailed pigeons, robins, sapsuckers, sparrows, starlings, tanagers, thrushes, titmice, towhees, wild turkeys, vireos, waxwings, woodpeckers, wrens
□■	**Snowberries** (*Symphoricarpos* spp.)	Shrub with nondescript deciduous foliage and pretty round white berries that are held into winter, when branches are bare	Bobwhites, prairie chickens, purple finches, evening grosbeaks, pine grosbeaks, grouse, magpies, pheasants, robins, thrushes, towhees, vireos, wrentits
□■	**Poison ivy and poison oak** (*Toxicodendron radicans; T. toxicarium*)	Deciduous perennial vine or groundcover with shiny three-part leaves and white berries; causes dermatitis in humans but is a favorite of birds	Bluebirds, bobwhites, catbirds, chickadees, finches, flickers, grouse, juncos, mockingbirds, pheasants, quails, sapsuckers, sparrows, starlings, thrashers, thrushes, titmice, towhees, wild turkeys, vireos, waxwings, woodpeckers, wrens
□■	**Mapleleaf viburnum** (*Viburnum acerifolium*)	Deciduous shrub with maplelike leaves that go pink-red in fall and berries that turn from red to black	Cardinals, great crested flycatchers, grouse, pheasants, robins, starlings, thrashers, thrushes, wild turkeys, waxwings, woodpeckers
□■	**Arrowwood** (*Viburnum dentatum*)	Large deciduous shrub with showy white flowers and clusters of blue-black berries	Cardinals, great crested flycatchers, grouse, pheasants, robins, starlings, thrashers, thrushes, wild turkeys, waxwings, woodpeckers
■	**Possumhaw** (*Viburnum nudum*)	Large deciduous shrub with shiny, dark green leaves and bright red berries	Cardinals, great crested flycatchers, grouse, pheasants, robins, starlings, thrashers, thrushes, wild turkeys, waxwings, woodpeckers

SEASON WHEN BERRIES ARE PRESENT ■ SPRING □ SUMMER □ FALL ■ WINTER

Who Are Those Berries for, Anyhow?

When you've planted and nurtured young berry plants for a year or two, you may have a reaction you don't expect when birds arrive to sample the crop. "Hey you! Shoo!" is pretty much normal when you see the first brown thrasher come sailing in to steal your precious few blueberries.

Even lovely bluebirds and waxwings can evoke some strong responses, thanks to their ravenous appetites. It's hard to watch the berry-laden branches of your 'Winter Red' deciduous holly (*Ilex verticillata* 'Winter Red'), for instance, being stripped bare in just minutes. As you watch those pretty red branches being transformed to boring brown sticks, it can be difficult to remember that attracting birds was the reason you planted the holly in the first place.

Growing berries for the birds doesn't mean you have to let them have all the fruit. But keeping some for yourself means taking steps to keep some from the birds. If you have room, separate "your" berries from those intended for birds. As soon as fruits start forming, cover any plants you hope to harvest from with black plastic netting and remove it only when you need to get to the plants to pick.

Birds are gluttons when it comes to berries: They really can't eat just one. When they descend on a berry bush, you can bet it'll be empty of fruit by the time they leave. That flock of robins or tanagers will return day after day until every berry on your dogwood is history. And once the berries are gone, so are the birds.

It may seem a little ungrateful for the birds not to stick around after eating your landscape decorations, but don't take it personally. Just go plant some more berry bushes so that next year your company will stay longer. And remember—your neighbors may still have berries on their hollies. But you're the one who had the pleasure of watching the bluebirds.

> Birds will visit berry-laden bushes and trees until every piece of fruit has been devoured.

Billing and Cooing

"BILLING AND COOING," an old-fashioned expression—popular a half century ago or more—for romantic human behavior, was snitched from the birds. Some species, particularly ground doves, mourning doves, rock doves, and other members of the pigeon family, engage in a seemingly tender display of affection during courtship, which for these "hot-blooded" species can be almost any month of the year. They coo to each other and take turns "billing," a clasping of beaks or reaching into each other's open mouths in an avian "kiss." Some birds, including cedar waxwings, herons, and some water birds, bill but don't coo.

Scientists call this kind of billing by the humanized term "kissing." The male is usually the initiator, although both members of the couple have to cooperate to make it work. When a pair of waxwings are in the mood, for instance, the male bird sidles up close to the female, then tenderly inserts his closed bill into the female's opened beak briefly. Ravens kiss for a longer time, holding each other's bills and sometimes even closing their eyes. Among herons, kissing can be a frightening sight, thanks to those gigantic swordlike beaks. Still, the birds know how to handle the exchange with delicacy so that no harm is inflicted.

Watch for billing and/or cooing in the feeder vicinity. When you spot such behavior, you may notice that other rituals of courtship are also being performed, such as the male pursuing a reluctant female, or the male offering the female a tidbit of food. It's fun to see how various species of birds play the mating game.

> Even ornithologists use the word "kissing" to describe the odd bird behavior of billing.

Binoculars

IMAGINE HAVING A HAWK'S KEEN EYESIGHT: able to see a tiny mouse scurrying through the grass far below as you slowly circle in the sky. People ages ago tried (unsuccessfully, as you can imagine) to improve their eyesight by ingesting the juice of hawk-weeds (*Hieracium* spp.). Today, all you have to do is sling a pair of binoculars around your neck to come as close as human eyes can to a hawk's visual acuity.

All binoculars are not created equal. To find the pair that's right for you, consider four factors:

Magnification power. The first number ("7" in a pair of 7 × 35 binoculars, for example) tells you how many times the image is magnified. In a pair of 7 × 35 binoculars, what you see is seven times larger than with normal unaided vision.

It would be great to be able to see 20 times better, but binoculars of high magnification power have a limitation: They also magnify the slightest movements of the hands that are holding them. Binoculars with 7 or 8 magnification power will give you a clear larger picture, but binoculars of 9 or 10 power are best used only if you have a remarkably steady grip or can brace your elbows on a flat surface. Although you can buy binoculars with lenses of even higher magnification, they will be very difficult to hold still and are best used only when attached to a tripod.

Light-gathering ability. The width of the bottom lens, indicated by the second number in binocular designations (the "35" in 7 × 35), determines how much light can enter the lens during viewing. Common lens sizes are 35—the most popular for all-around use—40, and 50. Ultra-lightweight mini-binoculars sacrifice lens width for portability, using sizes such as 20 for the larger lens. These smaller lenses are fine for bright-light viewing but tricky in dim situations, where you may have difficulty distinguishing a bird from its leafy background. In general, a lens size of 35 or higher designation is well suited to most bird-watching needs, although larger lenses mean larger, heavier binoculars.

Practice is essential for focusing on fast-moving birds like this warbler. When you spot movement in the trees, pinpoint the location, then swing the binoculars to focus on the spot.

Economical 7 × 35 binoculars are powerful enough to give you a good view from a distance, but for magnified detail of head markings or other fine points, try higher power 9× or 10× lenses.

Field of view. How big a picture you see is important because it allows you to find a bird faster by pinpointing it against nearby surroundings—that tree to its left, the branch above its head. The second number is also a clue to the size of field of view: The larger the number, the more you'll see.

Special features. If you tend to be a klutz, look for "armored" binoculars that are covered with a protective rubberized shield to prevent them from getting jarred by knocks and falls. If you'll be spotting birds in places with very bright light, such as on or near water, you'll want coated lenses to reduce glare. A padded strap relieves the tension on your neck from carting around binoculars on long expeditions.

Best All-Around Binoculars

Most birders use 7 × 35 or 8 × 42 binoculars, which offer plenty of magnification, a decent field of view, as well as adequate light for telling one warbler from another. Prices range from $20 at discount stores to more than $1,000 for super high-quality binoculars of this size. A cheap pair is fine for beginners; if you notch the price up to the $100 range, you'll get a fine pair of glasses that will give you years of use. To choose a brand, ask bird-watching friends for their recommendations, look for manufacturers endorsed by national bird-watching societies, and try the binoculars out yourself to make sure they are comfortable for your eyes and are easy to handle.

Practice Makes Perfect

Using binoculars is easy—finding a bird through them and focusing on it before it flies away takes practice. Start by using your binocs on any bird that crosses your path. Track it through your binoculars, following it with the glasses as you would with your eyes. If you lose the bird, drop the binoculars, pinpoint it with your eyes, then raise the glasses for another look. Soon, your binoculars will feel like a part of you, and you'll be following birds with the binocs as naturally as you do with your eyes. Once you are adept at zeroing in on a moving target, practice using the glasses to note smaller features and details such as the shape of the bill, notable markings, and activity that may give you a clue to the bird's identity.

But binoculars are not just an indispensable aid to identification. They also give you a window into bird life, letting you get fascinating, close-up look at nest building, group dynamics, and individual behavior that you would otherwise miss. Focus on a starling stalking your yard, for instance, and you may be gratified to see the bird suddenly stab the ground and yank out a grub. Zero in on a noisy, squabbling bunch of house sparrows in the street, and see if you can pick out what they are quarreling over—a discarded sandwich crust or a strip of plastic, perhaps. Watch a robin on the lawn for a little while, and see if you can begin to guess where its next worm will come from according to how the bird cocks its head.

Spotting Scopes

For watching feeder birds or songbirds in your yard at moderate distances, a magnification power of 7 or 8 is fine. But if you're planning on doing long-distance viewing, such as spotting shorebirds or ducks, you'll want the highest power of magnification you can find, which may mean stepping up from binoculars to a spotting scope mounted on a tripod. The tripod gives the scope stability that your hands just can't provide. Especially with high-magnification binoculars trained on a distant target, even the slightest tremor of your hands affects the view.

Spotting scopes offer incredible powers of magnification—you'll be able to see the scales on a fish being carried off by a flying heron, as well as many other close-up marvels your unaided eyes can't discern. A scope is also a pleasure for viewing backyard birds at the bath or squirrels visiting their feeder. It's a little trickier to locate and focus on a moving target with a scope, but if you set it up in your house, aimed at a water feature or a feeder, you're bound to get a ringside seat at the activity.

Bigger binoculars may not be better if they're too heavy to carry and use comfortably.

Birdbaths

THE OLD-FASHIONED CONCRETE birdbath, a simple basin balanced atop a sturdy pedestal, has been popular for almost 100 years. That kind of longevity can mean only one thing—it works.

Many birds have become accustomed to seeking birdbaths to get a drink of water and have a refreshing splash. Common backyard birds like chickadees, house finches, goldfinches, grackles, robins, and house sparrows will readily use this style of birdbath.

Other birds, generally the shyer types that live in woodlands or large open natural areas, are difficult to tempt to the unfamiliar height and structure of a birdbath. You can increase your bath's appeal by lowering it. Place the basin at ground level to entice the birds that usually drink from puddles and steams.

You can try another tactic and make the landscape around the bath more inviting to shy birds than the typical wide-open expanse of lawn that usually surrounds the birdbath. Groups of shrubs or other corridors of safety will encourage birds to approach without feeling unsafe from exposure.

Water is as big a draw for birds as food, especially in summer when natural H_2O is hard to find. A drip tube lures them with the inviting sound of trickling water.

Advantages of Birdbaths

Over the years, I have added more naturalistic water features in several of my gardens. These features expand the guest list of bathers and attract unusual visitors such as warblers and vireos, but I still keep a pedestal birdbath. It puts birds where I can see them easily—and you will definitely want a view of the antics. Bathing birds are downright comical as they splash and ruffle their feathers. Some are as wary as a toddler about dipping a toe in the water, while others enter the bath with abandon.

My birdbath also functions as a garden accent. It draws the eye, so that I can lengthen a view or focus attention on nearby shrubs or flowers.

Budget Birdbaths

Concrete birdbaths are a real value for the money. Expect to pay about $20 for a fine, classic model that will last for many years. Because the basins may break, you can also buy the top and bottom sections separately. This gives you another good option for providing bathing space for birds. I dot my gardens with just the basins from birdbaths, set directly on the ground or on a low stack of bricks. These low-level birdbaths are just as attractive to my clientele as the one that's parked on a pedestal.

Large, shallow clay saucers, sold for catching drips beneath potted plants, also are ideal for birdbaths. Comparison shop before you buy—a standard birdbath basin may cost less than a clay saucer, and it will hold up to the ravages of weather much longer.

Plastic plant saucers are another option, although they may be too slippery for the birds' comfort. I buy them anyway and rough them up with very coarse sandpaper to give birds something to grip. At a cost of just a couple of dollars each, they're a great way to provide water, and they can withstand freezing and thawing. Keep a few on hand to rotate in the winter—when one freezes up, bring it in to thaw and replace it with a freshly filled saucer.

Seasonal Use

Birdbaths are popular all year because resident birds soon learn to depend on an always-available supply of fresh water. The very presence of birds at the bath may lure stopover migrants, even without the addition of a pump or mister to create water music.

The dry season is prime time for birdbaths. That's when the water source will mostly likely entice unexpected visitors, as natural supplies of the precious liquid dry up and the lack of rain means no roadside puddles.

Winter in cold areas is also a popular time for birdbaths. As freezing temperatures turn natural water sources to solid ice, birds will become loyal visitors at a birdbath with open water. Some birds, including starlings, splash wholeheartedly in water even in winter, but most will content themselves with just a drink. If you live in a cold-winter area, it's well

---

PROJECT

Make an Insulated Birdbath

Boost the power of an immersion heater—and cut your electricity costs—by insulating your heated birdbath for the winter. Even if you don't use an immersion heater, this design will keep a pan of water from freezing as quickly as it would if unprotected from the cold.

MATERIALS

Four 6 × 17¼-inch pieces of 1 × 6 lumber

Nails

Two 18 × 18-inch squares of plywood

Shallow bowl or pan for birdbath

Insulation (Styrofoam peanuts, fiberglass, or foam)

Submersible heater (optional)

Step 1. Nail the four pieces of 1 × 6 into a box frame.

Step 2. Nail one square of plywood to the frame to form the bottom of the box.

Step 3. Fill the box with insulation.

Step 4. Cut a hole in the remaining plywood square to hold the water pan while allowing the edges of the pan to rest atop the plywood.

Step 5. Attach the top to the box. Insert the pan, adjusting the insulation as necessary.

Step 6. Fill the pan with water. Add a submersible heater, if desired.

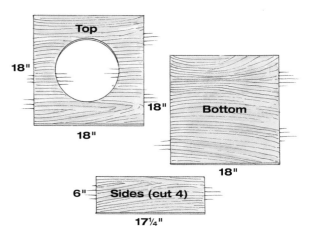

worth investing a few dollars in additional aids to keep your birdbath ice-free.

A submersible electric heater, which retails at about $20 and up, is the top de-icer choice of most backyard birders. In severe cold, don't expect the heater to keep the entire container unfrozen. It may allow only the part of the water very near the heater to stay in a liquid state in frigid weather. Birds will quickly find the open water.

Solar-heated birdbaths are also available. They depend on the warmth of the sun to keep the dark plastic dish ice-free. If your winter weather is mostly overcast as well as icy cold, a solar-heated bath won't be very effective.

Cleaning Birdbaths

Like any pool of stagnant water, a birdbath can harbor a fine crop of algae if you let it go without cleaning for several days. Even worse than the slimy stuff is the fact that a birdbath is the perfect breeding place for mosquito larvae. Those two considerations are more than enough reason to clean the bath frequently.

Any abrasive will get rid of algae. You can use a plastic scouring pad, a scrap of sandpaper, a handful of sand, or a scrub brush. A few stems of horsetail (*Equisetum* spp.), a plant with high silica content, will also work very well. To save steps on cleaning chores, you can keep your scrubbies inside the hollow pedestal of the birdbath. Loop a wire around the top of the pedestal and through the handle of the brush or corner of the scouring pad. When you're ready to clean, tilt the basin to empty it, lift it from the pedestal, and fish out your scrubbing tool. Before refilling the basin with fresh water, drop the tool back into the pedestal.

Landscaping the Bath

Planting around a birdbath to make it safe and enticing requires a careful balance. You need to supply shelter for wet birds but also make sure there is a clear view of approaching danger.

Cats are a real menace around a birdbath. If a stalking kitty is plaguing your birds and you can't exclude the animal from your yard, it's best to keep an open area of at least 10 feet around the bath. That should give birds enough time to become airborne once they spot the stalker. Beyond the bare zone, plant shrubs for birds to dive into for safety.

If cats are infrequent or absent in your yard, plant a shrub close to the bath (or place the bath close to a shrub). Birds like to move from branch to water, then hop back into the shrub to shake and preen their feathers. I plant pussy willows (*Salix discolor*) beside my birdbaths. They appreciate the extra water I dump on their roots every time I fill the bath, and the large bush supplies plenty of room for after-bath primping. Its branches also shelter the bath from overhead attacks by passing hawks.

Added Attractions

Birds won't be your only customers at a birdbath. My fat, lazy fox squirrels are surprisingly adept at leaping onto the rim of my pedestal bath to lap up fresh water. At my low-level basin-only baths, I've also spotted chipmunks, toads, butterflies, and once even a beautiful black snake. Visitors may also show up at night. I suspected my dogs of knocking the basin off my birdbath night after night, until I happened to spy a very large raccoon hanging on to the edge and trying to haul itself up for a drink.

Save steps by hanging a scrub brush from your birdbath's pedestal. Drop the brush into the pedestal if it's hollow, or let the brush hang down the back.

Bird Blinds

THE CLOSER YOU GET to a bird, the more fun it is to watch. You will see details of plumage and anatomy you might have missed from a distance—the position of the toes of a woodpecker compared to those of a sparrow, for instance. You'll spot nuances of body language that give you clues to upcoming bird behavior, such as quick movements of the head that show deference or aggression and that precede the more noticeable behaviors of lowered wings and puffed body feathers.

Watching birds from close quarters also gives you a peep at their private lives. You may hear quiet love songs or lullabies. You can watch the fascinating and intricate process of nest building. You may spot young birds being fed, and with the aid of binoculars, find out what's for dinner. And you may see fledglings practicing their skills before that big first takeoff.

But because birds are naturally wary creatures, you are not likely to get a glimpse of these behaviors as long as the birds are aware of your presence. A portable or semipermanent bird blind that keeps you hidden while you watch is easier to make than you might think, depending on what kind of habitat you want to watch birds in and what kind of materials you have handy. Use your ingenuity.

For watching feeder birds, the windows of your house make the perfect vantage point as long as you avoid drawing attention to your presence with vigorous or sudden movements.

- For the best view, position your feeders as close to the window as you can. Windowsill feeders are a wonderful choice because they bring the birds near enough to let you see every detail.

- Install inexpensive stick-on film that turns the window into a one-way mirror, from which you can see out clearly but the birds outside see only a reflection of themselves.

- A terrific but costlier alternative is to bring the birds "inside" by installing a feeder that replaces the lower part of your window and extends inside the room. (Expect to pay $100 or more for an in-the-window feeder, not including installation.)

For watching water birds, such as ducks, egrets, geese, herons, and roseate spoonbills at refuges or wild places along roadways, your car makes the ideal blind. Stay inside your car and observe through the open window to avoid frightening away the birds.

Your car is also perfect cover for watching hawks as they perch along roadsides watching for prey.

- When you spot a bird of prey on a utility pole or other perch, turn around when you can do so safely and return to a parking place within view of the bird.

- Watch the bird closely as you approach slowly; if it shows signs of nervousness, such as shifting its position or watching your vehicle intently, you will know you have reached the limits of approach. Park safely and sit quietly to observe through the windshield or side window. Remember that hawks have famously sharp eyesight; avoid sudden attention-getting movements.

In your own backyard, try one of these tricks to blend in to the scenery.

- Birds that live or move about in the trees will quickly become accustomed to your presence in a hammock or chaise longue, the most comfortable devices for overhead viewing.

- To cover up a backyard observation post for lower-level bird watching, surround your chair or bench with camouflage netting, sold at hunting-supply stores, draped over the metal poles used to prop up clotheslines.

- Ask at an appliance store for a box from a refrigerator or other large item. Flatten and fold the box for transport. Although the presence of the box blind may alarm birds at first, they will soon become used to its presence. Staple branches, grass, vegetation, or a piece of camouflage netting to the box to make the birds accept it more quickly as just part of the scenery.

Bird Counts

COUNTING BIRDS has been an annual bird-watching ritual for more than a century. Bird counts supply lots of important information, starting with population figures. By counting birds in the same area over a period of years, it's immediately obvious when, for example, numbers of wood thrushes drop to precipitous lows, or that catbirds begin regularly wintering far north of their usual haunts. This alerts scientists who can then look at factors that may have contributed to the change in population or range. Although banding birds offers solid data, too, counting birds supplies more information. Participating in an official or just-for-fun bird count also increases your awareness of just what kinds of birds, and how many of them, are visiting your feeder, backyard, or nearby wild places.

Counting at Home

One of the simplest ways to participate in a bird count is Project Feederwatch, a joint project of several institutions, including Cornell University and the National Audubon Society. From the comfort of home, you can join tens of thousands of participants reporting regularly on their feeder guests. You'll be adding to the bank of important data gleaned from this project, including information on the spread and decline of diseases, population swings of species, and expanding ranges of songbirds. For information on Project Feederwatch, see "Resources" on page 348.

Join a Counting Crew

You don't need to be an expert to join an organized count. Every pair of eyes and ears are important, and even if you are shaky in your identification skills,

Contribute to science by keeping track of your feeder birds on a designated day. Regional and national counts let you see how your bird traffic compares.

you'll still be a help to more experienced birders. If you're shy about joining a count for the first time, as I was, never fear. The folks are invariably friendly and helpful to beginners, and it's just plain fun for adults and kids alike. As you're counting, you'll also enjoy traipsing around, looking at birds, wildflowers, and other great surprises, whether it's a praying mantis or a rare tanager. But beware to the very beginner bird watcher: Although spotting birds is usually done at a snail's pace, without strenuous physical exertion, the intensity of being alert for hours at a stretch can wear you out, and you'll be surprised how tired you are at the end of the day.

To get involved in a count of wild birds in your area, contact the National Audubon Society or a local nature center. Ask about one of my favorite counts, the National Audubon Society/U.S. Fish and Wildlife annual Christmas count, held in the 2 weeks surrounding Christmas. You'll find Web sites, phone numbers, and mailing addresses in "Resources" on page 348.

B
Bird Feeding on a Budget

BIRDS WON'T EAT YOU OUT OF HOUSE and home, but they can put a crimp in your wallet if you're feeding lots of customers. In winter, when feeder traffic is at its peak, it's not unusual for me (actually, my bird visitors) to go through 50 pounds of sunflower seed and about 20 pounds of millet in a week. Add suet and all those high-priced nuts, fruits, and other treats, and it's easy to rack up a $30 bird-food bill every week.

Limit the Menu

To keep costs reasonable, I limit my seed choices to three main foods. I still get plenty of feeder visitors, including all my favorite birds. Here are my recommendations to limit food costs but not avian visitors at your feeders.

- Serve **black oil sunflower** for cardinals, chickadees, jays, titmice, woodpeckers, and other strong-billed seed crackers.

- Offer **millet** for smaller seed eaters, such as finches, juncos, and sparrows.

- Supplement the menu with **cracked corn,** which takes care of visiting blackbirds and starlings.

I also keep one tube feeder filled with niger, and I ration out treats like fruit and nuts in small quantities. And instead of buying those all-too-convenient suet blocks, I stuff my wire suet cages with free (or practically free) fat trimmings from the butcher.

Feeding a multitude? Trim the budget by sticking to millet and sunflower seed, eagerly sought by feeder favorites like this cardinal.

Buy in Bulk

Picking up a plastic bag of birdseed at the supermarket can bring the cost of seed to almost $1 a pound. For bargain prices, buy in bulk. A 50-pound sack of sunflower seeds often costs less than 20 cents per pound. If that seems excessive, arrange to split the cost with a neighbor and fellow bird lover. Once you get the seed home, perhaps your neighbor can also help you unload it.

Peanut butter is one of the best foods for bringing bluebirds to your feeder, but a small jar can come with a hefty price tag. Stock up on economy-size jars of your

---

Skewered Suet

HERE'S AN easy way to provide suet to your bird guests without any cost to you. Save your empty plastic yogurt cups, and fill them halfway with bacon grease or meat drippings. Cover them and put them in the freezer until you're ready to use them. When it's time to feed, remove the lid and trim off the extra part of the cup, leaving only about 1 inch above the level of the frozen suet. Bend a piece of wire into a hanger on one end, and poke it through one side of the cup, twisting it to hold it in place. To provide a stable perch, push the pointed end of a wooden skewer all the way through the fat and the bottom of the cup. These may not be the most beautiful feeders, but when it's 10°F outside, I don't get any complaints from the bluebirds, chickadees, and other customers who come for a bit of high-energy fat.

10 Tricks to Trim the Birdseed Budget

1. Stick to cracked corn. A 50-pound sack costs only about $6 at feed stores. Most birds will readily eat corn if their favorite other seeds aren't available.

2. Offer chick scratch, available at very low cost at rural feed stores. It's welcomed by cardinals, doves, quail, and other birds.

3. Buy birdseed whenever it's on sale and store it in airtight containers for later use.

4. Make your own seed mixes instead of buying packaged products. If you do buy commercial mixes, read the ingredients so you know what you're getting. Fillers like wheat and milo are no bargain.

5. Use small, squirrel-proof feeders to serve more expensive seeds and nuts to favorite songbirds.

6. Install a feeder with a wire cage that prevents larger birds like starlings from entering and gobbling up your seed (see page 100).

7. Ask the produce manager at your supermarket for free, discarded fruit.

8. Grow your own sunflowers, buckwheat, and corn to supplement the feeders. I prefer to let the seedheads stay on the plants, so I can have the fun of watching birds extract the seeds.

9. Collect sprays of seedheads (snip the mature plant at the base) from dock, foxtail grasses, lamb's-quarters, mustards, and other likely weeds. It's interesting to see which birds they appeal to.

10. Plant a patch of amaranths (*Amaranthus* spp.), bachelor's-button (*Centaurea cyanus*), cosmos (*Cosmos* spp.), tickseed sunflower (*Bidens aristosa*), or zinnias (*Zinnia elegans*)—all bird favorites for seeds. You can find seeds for most of these at low prices in spring or at closeout time in fall; the seeds are often sold at 10 packs for $1. Plant the seeds within view of a window, so you can watch the plants sway with birds from fall through winter.

---

local store brand instead. The birds won't be offended that you're not serving them the high-priced gourmet blend: They will eagerly gobble any old brand.

Avoid Impulse Buys

Just as you'll pay more for those last-minute checkout-counter purchases, your birdseed budget can be blown if you forget to plan ahead. Filling in gaps with costly small bags of seed or buying from stores where seed is more expensive than your usual supplier is convenient but pricey. I like to keep an unopened sack of sunflower seed (at least 25 pounds' worth) in reserve, so that I can still satisfy the birds even when I have unforeseen problems with transportation, daily schedules, or bad weather.

A big metal trash can is the perfect storage container for your emergency seed supply. It will hold many pounds of sunflower, millet, or mixed seed and keep out unwanted nibblers, like small rodents or insects. Store a large scoop on top of the seeds, and you'll be all set for those times when your supply runs short. Be sure to replenish your reserve supply whenever you find yourself dipping into it.

Common redpolls, house finches, chickadees, and other small birds quickly adopt a tube feeder. Tube feeders prevent spills and limit the number of guests.

Bird-Friendly Backyard

STAYING ALIVE is the number one concern of all birds. Keep that in mind as you plan your bird-friendly backyard, and your landscape will soon be brimming with birds. Feeders are only the start—birds need more than just food to be safe, healthy, and happy in your yard. You'll also want to include as many plants as possible—to most birds, a big sweep of lawn grass is about as appealing as the Sahara—for food, cover for a quick getaway from predators, nesting sites, and cozy roosting areas. And don't forget water, another important incentive for birds to visit and return to your yard. Safe nesting places, either natural homes in trees and shrubs or bird boxes supplied by you, will boost the population. Supplying nesting materials, grit, and salt are also welcome mats for birds looking for a place to settle down. Provide all this—and discourage predators, too—and your efforts toward encouraging a bird population in your yard will pay off.

Food, water, and sheltering plants make a yard inviting to birds. Shrubs and other plantings allow them to safely navigate across open space under cover.

Food

A feeding station is guaranteed to bring birds to your yard because those active little bodies need almost constant fueling to keep going. You can't go wrong with a general menu of sunflower seed, millet, and suet; adding occasional treats like nuts and fruits makes bird feeding more fun and attracts a wider variety of birds.

Fruit feeders may bring you catbirds, orioles, thrushes, wrens, and other unusual birds. Nectar feeders, for hummingbirds, of course, also appeal to orioles, finches, warblers, and woodpeckers. Mealworms are a treat for bluebirds and even purple martins. Peanut butter, combined with cornmeal to make it stretch a little further, is a big draw for many birds.

Bread and other soft foods may tempt robins and other birds that usually rely on insects.

Speaking of insects, the plants in your yard provide a steady diet of these delectable delicacies to birds. Trees, shrubs, perennials, grasses, and other plants hold a bounty, from bite-sized beetles to juicy caterpillars. Even in winter, birds will scour the plants to find eggs, cocoons, and overwintering insects. In summer, a yard with plenty of plantings is particularly welcome to birds because they need mass quantities of insect food for their young.

Naturally you will want to avoid using any toxic chemicals on your plants, which will kill off the insects and make your yard less appealing to birds, not to mention the possibility of making the birds sick as well. When you notice an outbreak of pests in the garden, you can either wait for birds to clean it up themselves, or, for vegetable plants, you can step in and handpick the offenders. Be careful with applications of "safe" organic pesticides, too. Even though it doesn't harm birds, the commonly used product BTK (*Bacillus thuringiensis* var. *kurstaki*) will kill a wide variety of leaf-eating caterpillars. That's bad news for birds that might make a meal of those caterpillars (and it can cut down on the number of butterflies you enjoy in your yard, too). When you can, let birds handle caterpillar problems in your yard and garden. If caterpillars descend en masse on your plants, be patient: Chances are that catbirds, orioles, and other aficionados of these crawly creatures will soon arrive to snap them up.

Cover

Keeping out of sight is the modus operandi for most birds. Sheltering shrubs and other plants protect them from the gaze and the grasp of cats, hawks, and other hungry bird eaters. Design your yard so that there are only small stretches of open space between plantings, so that birds can move throughout your property safely.

Be sure to consider winter cover, too, when you're selecting plants. You'll want to include evergreens for the valuable shelter their branches offer in the off-season, when deciduous species are bare. Remember to choose first those plants that offer food sources in addition to cover: Hemlocks, pines, and other evergreen conifers will eventually produce a bounty of seed-filled cones as well as insects among their needles. Broad-leaved evergreens, such as bayberries (*Myrica* spp.) and Oregon grape hollies (*Mahonia* spp.), are other good choices.

Nest Sites

When birds feel comfortable and protected in your yard, they are more likely to move in to raise a family. The plants you provide for protective cover will also supply birds with many good sites for nesting. Shrubs with dense branches, especially those with thorns or prickles, are eagerly sought as nest sites because their branches deter predators. An overgrown patch of raspberries or other brambles is ideal. Hawthorns (*Crataegus* spp.), with their spiny branches, and hollies (*Ilex* spp.), with their prickly leaves, are other plants with good nesting potential. A dense tangle of vines, such as autumn clematis (*Clematis terniflora*), may also be used as a nest site.

Robins and phoebes may quickly adopt a horizontal, covered shelf—a simplified, open-walled structure that appeals to these birds—as a nest. Birdhouses themselves are eagerly sought by cavity nesters such as chickadees, woodpeckers, wrens, and even owls, as well as the popular bluebird.

Roosting Places

A densely planted yard also offers birds safe areas to roost at night or in bad weather. Evergreens are especially welcomed for roosting places. If you are lucky enough to already have a large spruce or other evergreen, watch in late afternoon to see what birds fly into its branches. A single 15-foot-tall eastern red cedar (*Juniperus virginiana*) at the corner of my former Pennsylvania home held catbirds, mockingbirds, robins, brown thrashers, and a horde of house sparrows within its dense, prickly branches at night. At my Indiana home, the same kind of tree shelters more than 50 birds every evening in winter: more than a dozen cardinals, plus robins, fox sparrows, white-crowned sparrows, white-throated sparrows, and the ubiquitous house sparrows.

Not all birds seek plants for roosting places. Carolina wrens are apt to wiggle their way into garages, sheds, and other outbuildings. My garage at a former home had a circular opening in one wall where a stovepipe had been removed. In the evening, I watched cardinals, Carolina wrens, chickadees, robins, and titmice enter the hole to roost overnight.

Nest boxes, roosting boxes, and natural cavities in trees are also sought for roosts. On cold winter nights, several birds-of-a-feather may pile into one communal box for warmth.

Water

Adding a water feature to your garden, whether it's a simple birdbath or an elaborate running waterfall, will make your property more inviting to birds, including those that don't visit a feeder. Incorporate the sound of water by adding a recirculating pump, and you will quickly attract migrants and other birds.

Water is a hot item during summer heat and drought, when natural puddles are scarce and birds need a cooling drink and splash. It's also a big draw in winter in cold regions, when creeks and ponds are locked in ice. An electric or solar de-icer is a great investment if you live in a cold-winter area because fresh water in winter is very attractive.

Grit and Salt

A few handfuls of crushed eggshells, fine gravel, and a brick of salt will supply the mineral needs of your birds. Finches, crossbills, and doves welcome a regular source of salt. All birds need grit to provide the necessary abrasion for their grinding digestive processes. While these substances alone won't bring birds flocking to your yard, their presence will make it easy for your feathered friends to fill these supplementary needs while they visit your yard. And that means they will stay longer and return more often.

Predator Control

You can't keep every bird safe from every predator, but you can help to eliminate one major threat—cats. Keep your own feline pets indoors, especially during nesting season, and do your best to discourage strays.

To protect birds from the depredations of hawks, provide them convenient close shelter at feeding areas and water features, so they can dive into dense bushes for a getaway if needed.

Snakes, raccoons, opossums, and owls may also prey on birds, but there's not much you can do to keep these animals out of your yard. Do, however, protect any bird boxes you put up with antipredator baffles on the posts below them. Those sold to keep squirrels or raccoons out of feeders will do the trick for birdhouses as well. Antipredator door guards on nest boxes are also a plus. These plastic or metal tubes extend outward from the entrance hole, making it impossible for a raccoon's paw to reach the eggs inside.

Bird-Friendly Neighborhood

MAKING YOUR YARD ATTRACTIVE to birds is a great start, but if you really want to bring more—and different types of—birds to your yard, inspire your neighbors to join you. If the yards surrounding yours include the same kind of welcoming features as yours does, you'll end up with a bigger bird-friendly space.

Property lines are meaningless to birds—an appealing space is just that. If your appealing bird-safe space flows into a neighbor's, birds will move freely from one place to another. Bigger bird-friendly spaces mean more birds, so both you and your neighbors will benefit. If neighboring yards border a wild area, the extension of plantings may eventually create corridors that birds will use to move back and forth from your backyards to the natural areas. That can result in species that you wouldn't otherwise see visiting your feeder or watering hole, such as bobwhites or bluebirds.

Often, just the appealing sight of a well-planted yard alive with birds is all it takes to make your neighbors want to create their own little sanctuary. A couple of chats over the backyard hedge can also encourage a boomlet of bird-friendly planting in a neighborhood. Talk to your neighbors about the pleasures of watching birds: the fun of seeing a robin splash in its bath, the thrill of your first junco of the season. Invite neighbors for coffee, and let them watch the birds out your kitchen window

Robins often nest close to our homes. Talk to your neighbors about the delights of bird life and your neighborhood may become an impromptu bird sanctuary for other species, too.

or from the patio. Show them the zippy little visitors at your hummingbird feeder or the oriole at the oranges. Tell them about the day last winter when you counted 20 different species of birds visiting the feeders in your yard. Chances are, once your neighbors see how much pleasure you're getting from feeding the birds, they'll want to take part in the fun.

Share the Wealth

DO YOU have neighbors who you suspect are leaning toward bird watching, but you think might need a small push? Help them out with "donations" of bird-friendly plants and other supplies. Purchase larger quantities of plants that attract birds than you need for your yard. (Often, you can save money this way as well.) Then, give the "extras" to the neighbors to plant. Buy feeders at a 2-for-1 sale, then ask your neighbors if they would like one for their yard. Before they realize what's happening, their yard will be full of the overflow birds from yours, and they'll be hooked!

If your neighborhood tends toward lawn competition rather than dense plantings, be sure to tell your neighbors what you're working on as you go about changing the look of your land. Wide, welcoming paths through your garden will do a lot to allay their fears that you may be creating a weedy jungle. Straight paths and fences add a touch of formality to even the wildest garden, showing neighbors that a guiding hand is still in control.

Birding Hot Line

BEING PART OF A CIRCLE OF BIRDERS helps you get reports of unusual sightings quickly, but you can't depend on word of mouth to pass the news when a rare bird rolls into town. By the time a friend remembers to call you, the bird may be already winging its way out of town. And if you're a birder who keeps a life list, you may be willing to travel 100 miles or more to lay eyes on an unusual bird. Once, when a gyrfalcon showed up at a quarry about 50 miles from me, I met birders from 500 miles away who had come to get a look at the highly unusual and beautiful visitor from the Far North. European, Siberian, and far-wandering bird species that turn up in the United States get star treatment, with birders trekking hundreds of miles to lay eyes on them.

Modern technology makes it even easier to track the occasional rare bird and to follow the movements of familiar species. There are numerous birding hot lines (and now Web sites) with recorded telephone messages that birders use to keep up-to-date on visiting birds. You can call in or log on to find out what unusual visitors are nearby. On many, you can also pass along your own observations. Some hot lines and Web sites also include information on migrants: when the first junco was spotted in fall, or the first hummingbird in spring. Hot lines include all bird species, not only songbirds, so you'll also find notices about gulls, shorebirds, herons, birds of prey, and others.

Visit www.americanbirding.org/wgrbaadd.htm, the American Birding Association Web site, to find a state-by-state listing of birding hot lines and Web sites. You can also visit www.birdcast.org, a site sponsored by numerous organizations, including the National Audubon Society and Clemson University.

> To locate a birding hot line in your area, search the Internet or call the National Audubon Society.

Bird Names

A BIRD'S "COMMON" NAME refers to the name we call a bird in conversation. We know spring has arrived when we see a *Turdus migratorius*, but we point and exclaim, "Oh, look! The first robin of spring!" A bird's common name is usually a sensible, descriptive moniker that tells you the type of bird—finch, grosbeak, hummingbird—and supplies a clue to its looks or likes (such as "robin red-breast"). Sometimes the adjectives are uncommon, but don't be discouraged: If you look "pileated" up in a dictionary, you'll discover that a pileated woodpecker is a woodpecker with a crest.

A Bird by Any Other Name

Most birds have more than just one common name, having been tagged simultaneously by locals in various regions. The field sparrow, for instance, was also known at one time and in various places as the bush sparrow, huckleberry sparrow, rush sparrow, wood sparrow, ground bird, and field bunting. Common names in this sense of the word— those invented by common people—are becoming a thing of the past. Most modern birders know birds only by the common name that's listed in their field guide. Whenever I find someone who calls the cedar waxwing "cherry bird," I smile with memories of my mother, who passed to me the names she'd learned from her father. The "official" (guidebook) common names of birds are occasionally changed, which can lead to cries of protest from birders, who rarely bother to memorize the Latin names of even the most familiar feeder birds.

Sometimes, a bird is named in honor of a person, not for attributes of the bird itself. Bachman's sparrow and Bachman's warbler, for instance, are fine tributes to Reverend John Bachman, a John James Audubon crony who supplied his friend with many specimens. But the common names of Bachman's birds don't tell us anything additional about the sparrow or the warbler. If you're interested in the history as well as the attributes of these birds, take your field guide along to the public library, and check the biography section for the scoop on big names in birds.

Old common names are often highly colorful and may reflect old regional dialects or language derivations. In New England, the name "Peabody bird" makes perfect sense for the white-throated sparrow; reflecting their British heritage, they pronounce the word "PEA-biddy." To non-Yankees who say "pea-body" instead and have read a description of the sparrow's song as "old Sam Peabody," there's a language barrier that keeps them from recognizing the true rhythm of the song.

Deciphering Names

Many species of birds have common names that can give you clues about their lives. These include where a bird lives or feeds, what it looks like, how it sounds, and what its habits (usually feeding habits) are. Here are some birds who fit into that category.

Habitat: field sparrow, swamp sparrow, barn swallow, cliff swallow, house wren, marsh wren

Physical attributes: blue jay, red-tailed hawk, horned lark, fox sparrow, golden-crowned sparrow,

"Pileated" simply means "crested," and the pileated woodpecker definitely has an eye-catching one atop its hammering head.

white-crowned sparrow, white-throated sparrow, waxwings, and many wood warblers (orange-crowned, black-throated green, etc.)

Voice: catbird, mockingbird, pewee, phoebe, towhee, veery, vireo

Habits: gnatcatchers, nuthatch, grasshopper sparrow, hermit thrush, worm-eating warbler ("worms" meaning caterpillars, not earthworms), house wren

---

A Bit of Bird Lingo

THERE ARE many terms, some derived from Latin names, that have a specific meaning when they're part of a bird's common name, no matter what type of bird they describe.

Boreal: of the north

Cerulean: blue

Ferruginous: reddish (like rusted iron)

Grosbeak: large beak

Hatch (as in nuthatch): hack, hacker (as in hacking nuts, not computer hacker)

Hepatic: red (liver-colored)

Hoary: whitish

Lazuli: rich blue

Pileated: crested

Rufous: reddish brown

Tit (as in titmouse, bushtit): a small, active bird

Vermilion: vivid red to red-orange

B

Bird Recordings

WHETHER BIRDS use them to greet the dawn, to warn others of danger, or to announce ownership of a tasty treat, birdsongs and calls are hot topics among bird lovers. As evidence, one of the hottest gift items in recent memory is the bird clock, with bird pictures at the numbers on the face and the birdcalls of the 12 species sounding the hours. (A dedicated bird-watcher friend of mine received one as a gift and expected to be irritated by it, but he found he enjoyed it very much—especially when the thing got off-kilter and at the blue jay hour, it honked like a goose.)

Wood warblers are hard to get a good look at as they flit among foliage. Sort them out by song. The ascending trill of the northern parula warbler ends on a loud final note.

Sparrow Sing-Along

While the quality of the calls on bird clocks is nowhere near reality, serious birders can buy recordings of actual bird calls, with a commentator quietly introducing each bird by name before the vocalization. (See "Resources" on page 348.) High-quality tapes and CDs are a great education, and you'll be astounded at the diversity of bird music. Many people find these recordings useful for learning to identify birds by ear. Some bird watchers use specific calls to "lure" birds, not to capture them but to let them know of a food source so that they can enjoy watching them dine and hearing their songs live.

Flushing Out the Finches

Some bird watchers purchase taped alarm calls and owl calls to bring songbirds out of bushes. This is a controversial use for taped songs because the realistic sounds are distressing to birds, who hear "bird in danger," and fly out in fright. I prefer to use these tapes outside sparingly, if at all. Birds have enough panic in their lives without us adding to it.

The western meadowlark is a true songster, while eastern species sing just a few slow notes.

Birdseed

Attracts many kinds of birds at various times of the year

FEEDING THE BIRDS isn't just for the birds. Producing and selling birdseed is a huge industry. The roughly 63 million of us who feed birds spend a whopping *$2 billion* on birdseed every year. That cash outlay has far-reaching effects. It helps support more than just the farmers that raise the sunflowers, millets, sorghum, and other seeds that we pour into our feeders. It helps keep in business the makers of birdseed sacks, the shippers, the distributors, and all the other folks who play a part in getting birdseed from flowering plant to feeding station.

"Birdseed" doesn't describe a single seed. It includes a sampling of many grains and other seeds—from feeder staples like sunflower seed and millet to the wheat, corn, and milo fillers used in inexpensive seed mixes. Safflower and other specialty seeds that we pay dearly for to tempt special birds are also birdseed.

Thanks to the large market for the seed and the increasing savvy of those of us who stock the feeders, birdseed suppliers are adding an ever-growing lineup of seed mixes to the shelves. You can find bags of seed just for finches or bags of heftier seeds designed to bring cardinals and grosbeaks. Armed with some knowledge of which birds prefer what seeds and some information about the seeds themselves, you can become a smarter shopper and spend those big birdseed bucks more wisely.

The Staples

If you stocked your feeder with nothing but **sunflower seeds,** you would be able to satisfy more than 20 different species of feeder birds. All large-beaked seed eaters, including cardinals, grosbeaks, and jays, readily eat sunflower seeds. These birds, who use their big bills to easily crack the shells to free the meaty morsels inside, relish both black oil and gray-striped sunflowers. Chickadees, finches, nuthatches, titmice, and many other smaller-beaked feeder regulars also head for sunflowers as their staple seed of choice.

Birds will eat more—and waste less—of the mix on the lower left, which contains a greater percentage of appealing black oil sunflower and tiny tan millet.

Black oil sunflower seed is the more economical option because the smaller seeds go further than the big, plump gray-striped variety, which has fewer seeds per pound. It also has a higher oil content, so it gives the birds more calories when they eat it. The other advantage to black oil sunflower seed is that smaller birds can crack it readily. That may or may not be a plus, depending on how many house finches you're hosting! When hordes of these smaller-beaked birds descend, you might want them to spend a little longer working for their supper.

Sunflower seeds take care of most fall and winter feeder birds, with some notable exceptions: mainly, the sparrows. Native sparrows will crack sunflowers when they're desperate, but they prefer smaller seeds that they can pick up quickly. They prefer white or proso **millet,** a small, round, tan-colored seed that you probably have noticed in birdseed mixes. Though they will eat red millet, white seems to be more popular.

Not only sparrows siphon up millet. It's favored by bobwhites, buntings, doves, juncos, quail, house sparrows, towhees, and Carolina wrens—the regular cast of characters at most feeding stations. Tanagers also devour millet. Should sunflower seeds be lacking at your feeder, cardinals, purple finches, goldfinches, grosbeaks, jays, and pine siskins will turn to millet.

Millet is a bargain for bird feeding. Because it is so small and lightweight, you will get zillions of seeds in a 50-pound sack, enough to take care of your small feeder birds for weeks.

Budget Alternatives

Cracked corn and **chick scratch**, a crushed feed of corn and other grains, are low-cost replacements for sunflower seeds and millet. If your budget is tight, you can augment the basics with one of these seeds, or you can switch to them entirely. Eliminating sunflowers and millet, however, may cause you to lose the loyalty of purple finches, goldfinches, and some other feeder birds, which may shift to your neighbor's feeder if their favorites are no longer on your menu.

Cracked corn and chick scratch can be a great distraction at the feeding station. Birds that tend to show up in multitudes like starlings, blackbirds, grackles, and house sparrows favor these inexpensive foods. By serving abundant helpings of corn and scratch away from your other feeders, you can segregate the feeding station so that sunflower and millet eaters can dine without feeling pressured by the mobs.

Like coffee, chick scratch varies in the fineness of its grind, as various grades are manufactured to feed baby chicks of different ages. Ask your supplier for a coarse blend. The finely ground, almost powdery type tends to clump up into unpalatable lumps when it absorbs moisture, causing waste and inviting vermin.

Cracked corn, too, may vary in the grind. Most suppliers don't mind if you ask to see a sample. A bag of cornmeal isn't much good for feeding birds for the same reasons that powdery chick scratch is inappropriate. Also, a fine-ground cornmeal doesn't attract larger seed eaters. Coarsely cracked corn will satisfy the most customers.

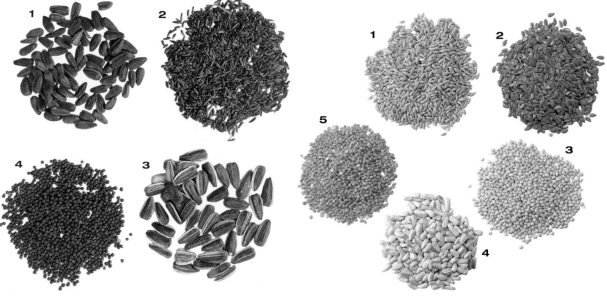

Finch heaven! Black oil sunflower (1), niger (2), striped sunflower (3), and rapeseed (4) will delight all small finches plus siskins, buntings, and larger cardinals and grosbeaks.

Canary seed (1) and flax seed (2) are special treats for finches; white (3) and red (5) millet are sought by all small seed-eating birds; cardinals enjoy safflower seed (4).

Special Seeds

The basic sunflower/millet/cracked corn menu will keep all but the fruit-eating and suet-eating birds at your feeder well fed and coming back for more. Adding special seed treats to the menu, however, will increase the desirability and appeal of your feeding station, and that, after all, is the object of the game. Besides, it's fun to keep an eye on the feeder and observe the visiting birds' individual tastes.

It can be difficult to generalize about the appeal of various specialty seeds because birds vary in their tastes. Midwestern sparrows may eagerly descend on an offering of rapeseed, while eastern sparrows spurn the stuff. Buy specialty seeds in small quantities at first to introduce them at the feeder. When you see which ones have become a hit, you can include them in your daily specials.

Do give birds at least 2 weeks to become accustomed to unfamiliar specialty seeds. It took more than a week for the purple finches at my feeder to sample the flax seeds I offered, but once they tasted them, the flax became their favorite.

Niger. One specialty seed—niger—has almost reached the class of staple, thanks to its guaranteed acceptability. Also called—albeit inaccurately—thistle seed, these tiny black seeds draw goldfinches without fail and also hold great appeal for house finches, purple finches, juncos, and siskins. Doves, house sparrows, native sparrows, and towhees may arrive to enjoy niger seeds, too. You can conduct your own informal inventory of customers by checking which birds are scratching for dropped niger below your tube feeders.

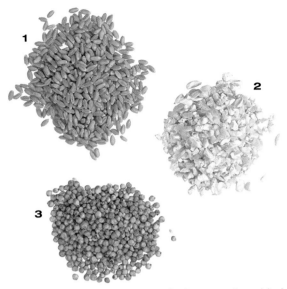

Buyer beware—make sure seed mixes aren't padded with low-cost yet undesirable fillers like wheat (1), cracked corn (2), and milo (3).

Safflower seed. After niger, safflower seed probably ranks next in popularity among the specialty seeds. This hard, white seed appeals to a limited number of species, but it can rapidly become a favorite of those birds. Cardinals are the number-one customer for safflower seed. Doves, purple finches, grosbeaks, jays, and titmice may also partake. As with other unusual seeds, it may take a while to build a client base for safflower. Offer the seed sparingly at first, and be patient.

Other specialty seeds. Other seeds that may convert birds into avid eaters at your feeder include

This Bird Favorite Is a No-No

IN THE more innocent days before the psychedelic '60s, one of the most highly recommended and most eagerly eaten seeds at the feeder was hemp. "Almost all seed-eating birds prefer hemp to any other seeds offered them," explains Thomas McElroy, Jr., in the 1950 *Handbook of Attracting Birds* (Knopf).

Unfortunately, birds aren't the only ones who will show up at your doorstep if you offer hemp seed today. The law would be close behind because the central Asian plant called hemp is also known as *Cannabis sativa*, or marijuana. With efforts now underway to reintroduce hemp as a legal farm crop in this country, perhaps someday our birds can go back to eating this old favorite. In the meantime, stick to millet, niger, and sunflower seed—your feeder will be full of customers, and you'll be home to enjoy watching them.

canary seed, flax, and **rapeseed.** The same birds that peck up millet at the feeder will eat all three. Mixtures that are advertised as "Just for Finches" often include a generous helping of canary seed and flax in the blend.

Seed Mixes

Not all seed mixes are created equal, and you can't judge a bag by its cover. Manufacturers decide what seeds to include, and in what percentages, and the recipe varies widely from one supplier to another. The names of the mixes can be misleading, too: "Seed Mix Deluxe Blend" may be nothing special at all.

To make sure you buy a good product, examine the mix if the bag is transparent or read the label. Laws require manufacturers to state the contents, listed in order of the most used to the least used. The lists usually include content percentages, too. Look for a high percentage of millet and sunflower, the top feeder favorites.

Additions of corn, wheat, and milo or sorghum often fill the balance of the bag. These inexpensive fillers cost much less per pound when you buy them as single-ingredient bags. As part of a mix, they add to the weight and jack up the price. Niger, flax, rapeseed, safflower, and canary grass, if they are included in small amounts, can be a bargain in a mix. But remember, with the exception of niger, your feeder birds may not readily accept these seeds.

Waste-Free Mixes

Bird feeding can be a messy business because hulls will rapidly accumulate beneath your feeders. Most people simply mulch over or scoop up the excess shells. But if you want things tidy, or if you're feeding birds on a balcony, windowsill, or patio, a waste-free mix will keep the feeder area neat and clean.

Naturally the price per pound of these mixes is more than seeds with hulls. But every bit of what you're paying for is edible and the convenience is worth a pretty penny itself.

Waste-free mixes usually include hull-less sunflower seeds (which you can also buy separately), plus bits of peanuts, finely cracked corn, and perhaps some canary seed, millet, or niger, which produce little waste. Compare the price per pound of this mix with

Ingredients are listed on the label beginning with the most plentiful. If fillers like milo top the list, keep shopping unless the bargain bag is your only choice.

the price of individual ingredients like sunflower chips, cracked corn, and chopped peanuts, and you may decide it's more cost-effective to make your own blend. Birds absolutely adore waste-free seed mixes, whether you buy them or stir them up yourself, because they don't have to work to eat the seeds. All large- and small-seed eaters relish the blend. Birds that don't usually eat seeds, such as bluebirds, catbirds, mockingbirds, robins, thrashers, and thrushes, also readily visit a feeder stocked with no-waste mix, where they can find an accessible, nutritious meal.

Treated Seed

To boost the birdseed's food value, manufacturers sometimes treat it with trace minerals or extra nutrients. This is usually unnecessary because birds don't eat only the seeds from your feeder. They also forage for wild foods, insects, and gravel that supply these needs naturally. But these treated seeds won't harm your birds.

Another treatment for birdseed is a great aid if squirrels and other animals are your nemesis. Capsaicin, the burning chemical of hot peppers, is effective at repelling animals from birdseed because it has the same effects on them as it does on us: burning mouth, watering eyes, and an afterburn that makes you yell "Water!" Birds, interestingly enough, are completely unaffected. Treatment methods vary. Some brands are dusted with capsaicin powder while others are soaked in a liquid extract that soaks into the seeds. Researchers at Cornell University tested the effectiveness of the presoaked seed in scientific trials. They found it to be very effective, except during severe winter weather, when squirrels apparently decided that spicy food would be better than no food at all.

Use care when filling feeders with capsaicin-treated seed. Avoid getting the dust into your eyes or breathing it in. Wear rubber gloves to prevent the burning substance from contacting your skin. If you have small children that play in the yard, it may be better to turn to squirrel-proof feeders or other remedies than fool with hot-pepper–treated birdseed. The stuff may hurt your pets, too.

Birdsong

MANY OF US TAKE THE GLORIES of birdsong for granted. When the birds grow quiet in late summer, we realize something is missing from the morning. If you have never spent the dawn hours sitting quietly in your yard, listening to the birds wake up, get up and give it a try. The breeding season, generally April through early July, is the best time to listen to the concert. That's when our migrant songbirds are passing through or have returned to their territories, full of hormones that make them burst into song to proclaim a match, attract a mate, or defend a territory.

You may hear snatches of song practically any time of year, especially if you live in a warm-winter area where nesting of some species continues into winter. Birds sing year-round in places where winter brings snow and cold, too, although there will be fewer performances in December than in June. Still, a melancholy phrase from a white-throated sparrow sounds heavenly in the afternoon dusk of a winter day.

If you pay attention to singing birds during breeding season, you will be able to tell who lives where. Male birds mark the boundaries of their nesting territories by voice, a charming way to tell other males to keep their distance. If you hear a cardinal singing its trademark "What cheer!" couplet, you know there is or soon will be a nest nearby. Late in the summer, listen for the haunting "whisper song" of mockingbirds, tanagers, and other singers, a very quiet, very private performance that takes place from a concealed perch.

Identifying singing birds can be a challenge, but all it takes is a bit of persistence. The best way to do

Common in backyards across America, the well-named song sparrow begins its concerts in late winter and continues serenading for months.

it is by tracking down the singer. Follow your ears and use your binoculars to identify the songster. Some people find recordings helpful, but I find it too difficult to remember the recording after turning off the stereo or remember the birdsong in question when I am back inside with the stereo.

Begin your voice lessons early in the season, when singers are still few and far between. Listen for chickadees and titmice in late winter, bluebirds in late winter to early spring, and then brace yourself for the rush of migrants in midspring. Thrushes are famed for their singing abilities, and one of the best of the family is our common robin. If you have never taken the time to appreciate a robin's song, make it a point to listen this season.

B

Bird Watching

IF YOU'RE A BIRD WATCHER, keeping a bird feeder not only gives you a close look at birds but you also have the pleasure of knowing you're doing them a good turn by feeding them as you enjoy watching their behavior. Birds display many fascinating activities, from sparring to courtship, at or near feeders.

Bird watching is great fun at any age, from toddler on up. Get your kids involved by asking them to help fill or make feeders and by talking about the birds you see and what they're doing as you watch through the window.

You don't "need" any equipment to watch birds, but a field guide and a pair of binoculars will greatly increase your pleasure. Use the field guide to identify the birds you see at home and afield and to identify the type of foods they like best. The binoculars give you a close-up look at details and make it easier to tell who's who in your local bird world.

The feeder window (the window that looks out onto the feeder) will quickly become the most popular seat in the house. If you spend a lot of time inside—by choice or by necessity—you'll find that birds can be good company. The antics and activities of birds at feeders can be calming, cheering, and even therapeutic. Think about places you could put a bird feeder to educate or provide "therapy"—schools, daycare centers, or nursing homes.

The key to being a good bird watcher is to spend time really watching a bird. Observe the bird as long as you can keep it in view, with or without binoculars, and you'll quickly become familiar with typical postures and behavior. As you gain experience and a solid knowledge of the birds you encounter, you'll find it easier to notice birds in the first place and to identify them quickly. A large sparrow scratching vigorously with both feet beneath your shrubs in April could well be a fox sparrow; a large, long-tailed bird singing from your rooftop is likely to be a mockingbird. To attract these birds and keep them coming back, you'll want to plant or put out foods that they particularly enjoy.

Keeping your eye on the birds will also put you in the right place at the right time when more unusual events occur. You may get to see a starling stripping loose bark from your grapevine for nesting material or a house sparrow snapping up Japanese beetles at your roses. Or you could be privy to more intimate moments, such as mating scenes or whisper-song performances. Whenever you watch birds, ask yourself what is the bird doing, and why. You'll learn a lot about behavior as well as about the connections between plants, insects, and birds.

The terms "birding" and "bird watching" generally describe the same activity. In some circles, casual observers may call themselves bird watchers, while birders are considered to be professionals (or dedicated amateurs). To me, when someone says they're birding, the streamlined word may simply be time-saving, or it may be subtle snobbery. I vote for eliminating any distinction between the two. Call yourself a birder or a bird watcher—we're all watching birds.

Simple Feeders for Kids

CHILDREN DELIGHT in the colors, sounds, and lively activity of birds at the feeder. Letting kids watch bird activity from a window overlooking a feeding station is a great way to introduce them to what might become a lifelong passion—without the enforced stillness and quiet of "serious" bird watching. Kids will feel even more enthused if they're involved in filling, maintaining, and even building feeders.

This book contains several simple feeder projects that are great for making with kids inside on a rainy or wintry day. Check out these projects, as well as "Treasures from Trash" on page 299, for fun and easy bird-feeding activities for kids of all ages.

- Roofed feeder (see page 110)
- Soda bottle feeder (see page 257)
- Squirrel feeder (see page 273)
- Tube feeder (see page 306)

Blackbirds

As a rule of thumb, most medium-size, mostly black birds at your feeder are probably blackbirds. But there are exceptions to this rule, and most blackbirds aren't entirely black, so take care when classifying these birds.

Several common black birds may fool you. Adult starlings are black birds, but not blackbirds; they belong to an old-world family that includes myna birds. Big crows and ravens are not blackbirds. The lark bunting, a medium-size black bird found west of the Mississippi, is a large finch, not a blackbird.

Most blackbirds aren't entirely black. The **yellow-headed blackbird** of the West has a striking golden hood; the widespread **red-winged blackbird** has vivid shoulder patches of red and yellow; and the similar **tricolored blackbird** of far western marshes has red and white shoulder decorations. Those elegant, long-tailed strutters known as **grackles** (see Grackles on page 143) have glossy black feathers overlaid with a sheen of bronze, green, or purple. The name of the **brown-headed cowbird** speaks for itself; its relative, the **bronzed cowbird**, glistens with a metallic green-gold iridescence. The **rusty blackbird** and **Brewer's blackbird** come closest to the all-black coloration the name implies, especially at a distance. Upon closer inspection in certain seasons, you will see slight variations on the black dress code. The rusty has a weathered look, but only in fall, when the edges of its feathers show a brownish tinge. The Brewer's has slight purple or green iridescence.

A locally common member of the blackbird family, the black and white male **bobolink** and his brown-streaked mate flock in hay fields. In fall, the male exchanges his bright garb for an outfit similar to the female's, and the birds gather in enormous numbers like their other blackbird kin.

Female blackbirds of all species are much harder to identify than males. Most are brownish, with streaked breasts or bellies. Whenever a female redwing shows up at my feeder (usually in winter), it

Find a front-row seat in spring to watch the courting displays of the male red-winged blackbird. To impress his lady love, he droops his wings and shrugs his gorgeous red shoulders.

A piercing yellow eye stands out against the all-black plumage of the Brewer's blackbird. The shape of the bill is a sure way to identify members of this family.

Cowbirds Don't Linger for Long

WHEN COWBIRDS congregated at my feeders in spring, I used to worry that I was endangering my favorite songbirds by attracting these parasitic birds. Cowbirds lay their eggs in the nests of other species of birds. The unsuspecting foster parents then spend their energy raising the big, loudmouth cowbird nestling like one of their own—and sometimes in place of one of their own. Cowbird piracy increases as we carve our woodlands into pieces, allowing these birds easy access to nests of wood thrushes and other forest dwelling songbirds.

But I needn't have feared for my local songbirds—like other blackbirds, the cowbirds dispersed soon after their hormones began stirring. Once their mating instincts kicked in, the flock dwindled to one or two pairs of cowbirds, as the others returned to their traditional "nesting" territories, far away from my feeder area.

takes a minute before I recognize this unusual, large sparrowlike bird. Immature birds can be difficult to identify as their coloring is similar to a female's. To make things even trickier, the males of most species change their plumage after the breeding season for markings that also resemble the female's rather unremarkable garb.

All blackbirds have fairly long, pointed bills, perfect for their varied diet of seeds, grain, insects, fruit, bread, and just about anything else they encounter. Birds of fields, marshes, and open spaces, they usually walk about on the ground, so a low tray feeder serves them well. Blackbirds also easily adapt to higher feeders.

Blackbird populations at the feeder ebb and swell with the seasons. During nesting time, only a few resident birds generally visit. But during the times of fall and spring migration, and when wintering flocks are in the area, you may be hosting dozens of the birds. A generous handout of inexpensive cracked corn in a low feeder or directly on the ground will keep them busy and away from other feeders that hold pricier foods.

BLACKBIRD FEEDER FOODS

- Apples, blueberries, and other fruit
- Bread and other baked goods
- Chick scratch
- Corn in any form, especially cracked
- Millet
- Milo
- Mixed seeds
- Nuts
- Peanuts
- Raisins
- Suet
- Sunflower seeds

Blackbird Behavior

Listen for the interesting voices of blackbirds at or near your feeder. Many of them include phrases with a gurgling, liquid sound, like water bubbling over rocks, in their repertoire. They also emit ear-piercing screeches and squeals and hoarse squawks.

If you spend time watching the various blackbirds at your feeding station, you will see some interesting "body language." When blackbirds threaten each other, they droop their wings, fluff their feathers, and make harsh noises that make them appear more imposing. A similar behavior takes place during courtship season, with the bird's head generally raised with its beak pointing skyward. Often the male bird will stalk the female, pausing now and then to repeat the display, as if showing off his physique for her to admire.

It's hard to believe somber-colored blackbirds are in the same family as orioles, until you see the yellow-headed blackbird.

Black-Eyed Susans

Attract buntings, finches, sparrows, and other small-seed eaters

BLACK-EYED SUSAN (*Rudbeckia hirta*) is as all-American as a flower can get. One of the few wildflowers that actually hails from this continent, these buttery daisies brighten summer roadsides and gardens from sea to shining sea. That's a good thing as far as birds are concerned because those black "eyes" hold a wealth of nutritious seeds. Related to the ever-popular sunflower, black-eyed Susan seedheads ripen in summer and hold their bounty of bird food into winter—a good reason to let those seedheads remain in your garden at the end of the growing season.

Another related dark-eyed yellow daisy, orange coneflower (*R. fulgida*), is sometimes also called black-eyed Susan. So is *R. triloba*, a more shade-tolerant species. Unfortunately, the highly popular 'Goldsturm' black-eyed Susan (*R. fulgida* 'Goldsturm') holds little attraction for birds. Its seeds lack the meaty centers of the unimproved species type, which is still available and still worth growing. Another cultivated variety, 'Gloriosa' black-eyed Susan (*R. hirta* 'Gloriosa'), offers hearty seeds like those of its wild parent, so it's a good choice for the bird garden. It's pretty, too, with big, beautiful flowers in shades of rust, gold, and bicolors.

Black-eyed Susans reach 2 to 3 feet tall. Their branching stems and dense leaves offer small birds safe shelter where they can forage for insects or seeds. Plant several near your feeding station to encourage buntings, finches, sparrows, and other small birds to linger within view. Black-eyed Susans will attract a flurry of butterflies (bird food on the wing!) to your yard, too, and they're pretty and long-lasting in bouquets. Even after black-eyed Susans lose their golden petals, their dark central "cones" will stand tall atop the stiff stems, holding up their cache of seeds for hungry birds. If you must clean up the faded flowers, gather them into bunches to hang from a feeder or weave them into a wreath of birdseed treats. Easy to grow and drought-tolerant, these plants thrive in USDA Zones 3 through 10.

Stick to "unimproved" black-eyed Susans for attracting birds. Garden favorite 'Goldsturm' does not produce the nutritious seeds birds crave.

Standing stems of black-eyed Susans help shield birds from predators in the winter garden. Common redpolls and other seed lovers will work at the seedheads.

Blueberries

Attract bluebirds, mockingbirds, robins, brown thrashers, woodpeckers, Carolina wrens

BIRDS LOVE blueberries (*Vaccinium* spp.) as much as we do. When the fruits begin to ripen, birds descend on the berry patch and gobble up berry after berry until their bellies are so full they can barely fly. Spy on a catbird in a blueberry bush and you'll see some amazing feats as the bird swallows berries that look way too big to fit down that skinny beak.

Of course, if the berries that catbird is gobbling are the ones you intended for your breakfast bowl of cereal, you may feel a certain conflict of interests. Once a blueberry patch is established and growing for a few years, it produces enough berries for you and the birds to share. But when your bushes are new and small, you may want to throw a sheet of plastic bird netting over the patch to protect your precious crop.

If you've never tried growing blueberries, don't let the "finicky blueberry" reputation scare you off. If you can grow hollies (*Ilex* spp.), azaleas (*Rhododendron* spp.), or rhododendrons (*Rhododendron* spp.), you can grow blueberries. These American natives are well known for liking acid soil, a condition that's usually not hard to meet. Unless you live near a limestone outcrop or in one of the alkaline areas of the West, your soil should be reasonably close to blueberry range. A do-it-yourself soil test will give you the information you need. But if the azaleas in your yard are thriving, you can skip that step and go ahead and plant your berry bushes. An annual mulch of chopped oak leaves, cypress bark, beech leaves, or other acidic material will help keep your soil pH in the range that's just right for blueberries.

Sweet and juicy blueberries are so popular with birds, you'll have to act fast to get a handful for yourself. Plant in groups or as a hedge and put a bench nearby.

Blueberries at the Feeder

Save some blueberries to put in your feeder in fall and winter, times when natural fruit is hard to find. You can freeze or dry fresh berries for later use. To dry blueberries, spread them on a window screen in full summer sun, covered by a layer of gauze or cheesecloth to keep bugs away. Support the screen on blocks so that air can circulate on all sides of the berries.

Unless you're in the blueberry business, your stock will most likely be small. Dole them out a scant handful at a time so that they aren't wasted. Bluebirds, mockingbirds, robins, brown thrashers, woodpeckers, and Carolina wrens may be tempted by the handout. Many of these blueberry-eating birds prefer fruit, mealworms, peanut-butter dough, and other soft goodies to birdseed. To cut down on competition for feeder space, scatter the blueberries in an open tray feeder that you reserve for soft foods.

Bluebirds

BLUEBIRDS ARE THE CROWNING GLORY of any feeding station, and they are relatively easy to attract. Supply their favored foods of peanut butter, mealworms, berries, and other treats, and if they live nearby, they may become regular patrons. Of course, if bluebirds aren't in residence in your neighborhood, the only takers you'll get for your goodies are likely to be mockingbirds, starlings, and other soft-food fans.

Where do bluebirds live? Usually near wide open spaces, with areas of cover: in other words, in the country. Expect to see them in farming areas, in suburban developments bordered by wild space, on golf courses, in cemeteries, near school playing fields, in parks, at the edges of woods, in extensive hedgerows, and along rivers and streams. If you live in the city, where concrete covers most of the open space, don't hold your breath for a bluebird.

East of the Great Plains, the only bluebird you're apt to see is the appropriately named **eastern bluebird.** Like its closely related kin, the **western bluebird,** the male bird wears plumage of a breathtaking rich blue. Thoreau wrote that this exquisite creature "carries spring on its back." Although I think the color is closer to the hue of an October sky than that of

BLUEBIRD FEEDER FOODS
■ Bayberries (*Myrica* spp.)
■ Blackberries (*Rubus allegheniensis*)
■ Blueberries (*Vaccinium* spp.)
■ Bread and other baked goods
■ Dogwood berries (*Cornus* spp.)
■ Juniper berries (*Juniperus* spp.)
■ Mealworms
■ Peanut butter
■ Peanut butter/cornmeal dough
■ Peanuts, chopped
■ Pine nuts
■ Raisins
■ Raspberries (*Rubus occidentalis*)
■ Suet, chopped or block
■ Sumac berries (*Rhus* spp.)

Build it and they will come—but only if your yard is near the wide open spaces where eastern bluebirds prefer to make their homes.

rain-washed April, I won't argue with the romance of Thoreau's feelings. Bluebirds evoke a sense of rhapsody in most of us.

Both eastern and western species sport similar coloration. Look for the blue throat and rusty shoulder patch of the western to distinguish it from the eastern bird. The **mountain bluebird** is blue all over and generally lighter in color—closer to what I think of as a spring sky. It lacks the rusty breast of the eastern and western bluebirds, being paler blue-gray beneath. Although mountain bluebirds live up to their name in nesting season, staying usually above 5,000 feet, in winter they wander to low elevations as food becomes scarce in the mountains. All female bluebirds are brownish blue, with a faded rusty breast in eastern and western species and a grayish brown breast in the mountain species.

Except for some regions in the mountains and plains, where winter cold is brutal, you may see a bluebird at any time of the year. When insects become scarce, the birds supplement their diet with berries and other fruits.

Bluebird Behavior

You can spot an eastern or western bluebird from a distance once you become aware of their typical posture. These birds apparently never practiced walking with a book on their head—they typically sit hunched, with head drawn down into their shoulders. They frequently assume this position when perched atop a fence or other prominent lookout point, where you can identify them by their posture even without seeing their color.

Identify the mountain bluebird by its lack of red on breast or sides. These birds prefer high elevations during nesting season.

Bluebirds often come to a feeder for the first time during bad weather and the availability of appropriate food will keep them coming back. When I know snow, ice, or severe cold is on its way, I mix up a batch of bluebird-tempting food so it's ready for immediate serving at the crack of dawn. Often I'll find a bluebird has already come in and is waiting for its turn at the peanut butter or suet, while its cohorts linger nearby, calling to each other in gentle whistles.

Bluebirds are ideal company at the dinner table. They are reserved and well behaved, never picking a fight with other invited guests. Usually they are quick to depart or at least shift position should a more aggressive bird act threateningly. Provide their food in an open tray so it is easily visible. Once you have their attention, you can switch to a roofed feeder if necessary to protect food from snow or rain. Once they come to a feeder, bluebirds are unusually tame. Approach them slowly and quietly, and they may quickly accept eating from your hand.

Watch the bluebirds in your yard, and you will see that their hunting technique somewhat resembles that

As richly colored as its eastern counterpart, the western bluebird is also a cavity nester. Supplement the supply of holes in trees by mounting nest boxes.

12 Tricks to Tempt Bluebirds

IF YOUR yard is near the kind of open spaces that bluebirds like—farm fields, edges of woods, parks, golf courses, cemeteries—try these tricks to encourage the birds to visit your feeding station.

1. Put up bluebird houses, mounting them about 100 feet apart.

2. Keep a small amount of food to tempt bluebirds in plain view in winter in an unroofed tray feeder.

3. Mount a suet feeder with access for perching birds, such as a tray beneath a wire suet cage. Or mount a wire suet cage horizontally, so that bluebirds can perch on top while they eat.

4. Place a tray feeder stocked with a small supply of mealworms on the side of your property closest to good bluebird habitat.

5. Plant a hedge of sumac (*Rhus* spp.) or blueberries (*Vaccinium* spp.). Blueberries are a favored summer food; sumac will suffice in the dead of winter when other berries are scarce.

6. Learn bluebird calls so that you can tell when they are in your neighborhood.

7. Add a birdbath.

8. Keep a resealable plastic bag of chopped peanuts ready in the freezer in case bluebirds do come to visit your feeders.

9. Allow a plant of pokeweed (*Phytolacca americana*) to grow in your yard. The black-purple berries are a prime wild food for bluebirds.

10. Cover a trellis with Virginia creeper (*Parthenocissus quinquefolia*), another big temptation to bluebirds.

11. Indulge a poison ivy vine (*Taxicodendron radicans*) in a wild corner of your property; the white berries are manna to bluebirds.

12. Plant a group of bayberries (*Myrica* spp.), backed by columnar red cedar (*Juniperus virginiana*), to supply shelter and berries.

of a flycatcher. The birds will perch at a likely spot, then flutter out to nab a passing insect. Bluebirds aren't speedy fliers like flycatchers. They usually pursue the moth or other passing insect to near or at ground level before securing it in their beak. They may devour their catch there on the ground or fly to another perch to dine.

Water is a great draw for bluebirds, which will happily visit birdbaths or low-level water features. A pair that resided in my yard for several years often came to my dogs' outside water dish to drink deeply every morning. More than once when I have been slow about refilling their favorite pedestal birdbath, they turned for water to a bucket holding perennials for transplanting.

Bluebirds are cavity nesters, which means they seek a natural hole or a birdhouse for raising their families. One good way to find out if you have bluebirds living nearby is to put up a bluebird box. If you mount it, they will come: It's really that simple.

Bluebirds can certainly use a helping hand when it comes to real estate. They suffer from stiff competition for nest sites from house sparrows and starlings. Modern orchard management removes dead tree limbs as a matter of course, resulting in fewer natural cavities for these birds. Their natural habitat has declined with fewer woods' edges and hedgerows and with metal fence posts that have replaced wooden ones. Bluebird trails and individual efforts at providing nest boxes have helped bluebirds overcome the odds stacked against them. Populations that had become disturbingly low have rebounded to more comfortable levels, but bluebirds still need all the help they can get. If there's a chance you may have bluebirds in the area, put up a few boxes.

Bluebirds are early birds. They begin nesting as early as February. In northern regions, this is not always a wise move. Severe cold can have fatal effects on the brood and on the food available to parent birds. After deep freezes in the past, bluebird numbers took a nose dive. When not nesting, bluebirds roost together in cold weather in natural cavities or bird boxes—yet another good reason to mount a bluebird box in your yard.

B

Blueberry Bird Granola

Expect visits from bluebirds, mockingbirds, thrashers, woodpeckers, and wrens when you put out this nourishing granola.

INGREDIENTS

1 *cup granola flakes*

1 *cup dried blueberries, chopped*

½ *cup finely chopped peanuts*

½ *cup cornmeal*

½ *cup ground or chopped suet*

½ *cup corn oil or peanut oil*

Combine all ingredients in a large bowl, using your hands to squeeze oil throughout the mixture to bind. Serve in an open tray feeder.

Bluebird Tempter

A taste treat to lure bluebirds for a first-time visit. They'll keep coming back for more.

INGREDIENTS

1 *cup peanut butter, chunky or creamy*

1 *cup suet, chopped*

1 *cup raisins or dried currants, chopped*

1 *cup peanuts, chopped*

   Cornmeal

Combine first two ingredients. Add raisins, peanuts, and cornmeal, mixing by hand until the mixture reaches the consistency of medium-stiff cookie dough. Crumble into an open tray feeder.

Bluebird Winter Berry Mix

A welcome change of pace for eastern and western bluebirds that are already feeder regulars.

INGREDIENTS

1 *cup dried or frozen blueberries*

1 *cup frozen blackberries or raspberries*

1 *cup dried currants*

1 *cup dried cherries, chopped*

1 *cup bayberry, holly, sumac, or juniper berries*

½ *cup figs, chopped*

If the temperature outside is above freezing, thaw the frozen berries, and drain on paper towels to soak up the excess juice. If temperature outside is below freezing, use the frozen fruit as is. Combine all ingredients in a large bowl. Serve in an open tray feeder or scatter on packed-down, snow-covered ground where the mix will be easily visible.

Bread

Attracts blackbirds, grackles, jays, magpies, mockingbirds, robins, house sparrows, native sparrows, starlings, Carolina wrens, and many other species

OUNCE FOR OUNCE, even fortified bread can't compare to the food value of sunflower and other bird seeds, which offer the high-fat, high-protein diet that birds require. But bread is a fine addition to any feeding program—jays, magpies, mockingbirds, robins, native sparrows, Carolina wrens, and many other species will quickly gobble it up. Bread also brings in blackbirds, grackles, house sparrows, and starlings—so if you're trying to discourage these birds, think twice before adding it to the menu. Squirrels, ground squirrels, and chipmunks, as well as raccoons, opossums, and dogs, also eat bread.

I welcome all customers, no matter how unmannerly, at my feeders, but I use bread to keep my clients somewhat separated. Highly visible pieces of white bread seem to be irresistible to house sparrows, jays, and starlings, so I scatter them in trays and on the ground in a separate feeding area, away from the tube feeders and seed trays of sunflower and niger provided for the shyer birds. The ruse works well, and everybody leaves the bird café with a full stomach.

Scatter leftover bread or bread crumbs in feeders. It's best to use a roofed feeder (see page 110) because bread quickly turns moldy if it gets wet. I do feed bread directly on the ground in severe winter weather, when snow or ice makes it impossible for robins, towhees, and other ground-feeding birds to find natural foods. They appreciate a handout they can eat at ground level.

Birds will pretty much eat any kind of bread. As long as you're not feeding your bird guests a bread-only menu, you needn't worry whether it offers great nutrition. A stale slice of refined white bread is just as welcome to hungry birds as a fresh loaf of all-natural multigrain bread. Crumble the bread into small bits to make it easy for doves, sparrows, and other small-beaked birds to eat. Feeding bread as crumbs also keeps birds lingering at your feeder where you can watch them, instead of allowing them to fly off with a big chunk to eat out of your sight. Crumbs also cut down on the inevitable "It's mine!" "No, it's mine!" squabbles that result from offering larger pieces of bread.

Tidbits for Bird Breads

ADD BIRD-FAVORED treats to your favorite yeast bread or quick bread recipe, or try one of the recipes on pages 48 and 49. The following ingredients, in any combination, will help spice up a bread recipe for the birds:

- Acorn nutmeats
- Acorn or winter squash seeds
- Almonds, chopped
- Apples, chopped or coarsely grated
- Beechnut nutmeats
- Blueberries, fresh or dried
- Buckwheat kernels
- Canned whole-kernel corn
- Cantaloupe seeds
- Cherries, fresh or dried
- Currants
- Grapes, chopped
- Hickory nuts
- Hulled sunflower chips
- Millet, whole
- Oatmeal
- Oranges, chopped
- Pasta, leftover cooked, any kind, chopped if large
- Peaches, chopped
- Peanut butter, chunky
- Peanuts, raw or roasted
- Pears, chopped
- Pecans, chopped
- Pine nuts
- Plums, chopped
- Pumpkin seeds
- Raisins
- Strawberries
- Walnuts, chopped
- Watermelon seeds

B

Special Recipes

Baking bread for the birds is a fun weekend project that will fill your freezer with nutritious loaves. I load the dough with lots of extras to make the bread a real treat: dried and fresh fruits chopped into small pieces, nutmeats of any kind, oatmeal, raisins, grated apple, and even leftover pasta that may be lingering in the refrigerator. No matter how lumpy the loaves, the birds quickly flock to the results of my experiments.

Visit a health food store to find nutritious flours, such as millet, amaranth, or whole wheat, to bake into bread for birds. Experiment with bird breads: As long as your offerings are chock-full of nutty or fruity ingredients, birds will relish your efforts. Because the breads will be dense and moist, they may not be as dry in the middle of the loaf as your usual concoctions for human consumption, but the birds won't mind a bit.

`RECIPE`

Oatmeal-Raisin Bluebird Bread

Try this yeast batter bread for attracting bluebirds in winter. Catbirds, jays, mockingbirds, robins, thrushes, and Carolina wrens may also partake.

INGREDIENTS

1½ cups boiling water

¾ cup oatmeal, regular or instant

¾ cup raisins

¼ cup light corn syrup or molasses

3 tablespoons margarine

1 package active dry yeast

¼ cup warm water

4 cups whole wheat flour

Combine first five ingredients. Set aside to cool. Sprinkle yeast over warm water in a large bowl, and stir until dissolved. Stir oatmeal mixture into yeast. Stir in 2 cups flour. Add remaining flour, and blend with a mixer or with hands. Cover and let rise for 30 minutes in a warm place. Grease a 9 × 5 × 3-inch loaf pan. Beat dough 25 strokes with a sturdy spoon, then spread in the pan. Smooth the top with a greased spatula. Cover and let rise until about 1 inch from top of the pan. Bake at 425°F for 45 minutes. Cool; tear into small pieces to serve in an open tray feeder.

`RECIPE`

Delicious Date-Nut Bread for Birds

Finely chopped dates make this quick bread a magnet for fruit lovers like bluebirds, mockingbirds, robins, and thrushes, and the nuts are a bonus for jays and woodpeckers.

INGREDIENTS

2 cups sifted flour

3 teaspoons baking powder

1½ cups finely chopped dates (dip knife in hot water for easier chopping)

1 cup finely chopped walnuts, pecans, or almonds

1 cup milk

¼ cup vegetable oil

1 egg

Stir together flour and baking powder. Add dates and nuts. Mix milk, oil, and egg slightly to combine. Pour into dry ingredients, and stir with fork until moist. Spread in greased 9 × 5 × 3-inch loaf pan. Bake at 400°F for about 20 minutes.

B

Fruitful Feeder Bread

Bluebirds, jays, mockingbirds, robins, wrens, and even orioles may nibble this bread.

INGREDIENTS

2¼ cups sifted flour

½ cup sugar

2 teaspoons baking powder

1 cup blueberries, cranberries, raspberries, or other berries

1 cup finely chopped apple, peel left on

1 cup chopped orange pulp

2 eggs

1 cup milk

¼ cup melted margarine

Stir together flour, sugar, and baking powder. Add fruits. Whisk eggs with milk and melted margarine. Add egg mixture to fruit and flour mixture, stirring quickly with fork until moist. Scrape into greased 9 × 5 × 3-inch loaf pan, and bake about 55 minutes at 350°F. Cool, then slice into thin strips and offer at feeder.

Top-Banana Bread

Sweet, moist banana bread is a special treat for robins in winter. It's also welcomed by jays, mockingbirds, thrushes, and Carolina wrens. Add nuts to entice woodpeckers.

INGREDIENTS

2½ cups sifted flour

3 teaspoons baking powder

1 cup sugar

¼ cup margarine

1 egg, beaten

6 ripe, mashed bananas

¼ cup milk

1 cup chopped nuts

Combine flour and baking powder. In another bowl, beat together sugar, margarine, and egg. Mix in bananas and milk, then add flour mixture, and stir until smooth. Stir in nuts. Pour into a greased 9 × 5 × 3-inch loaf pan, and bake at 350°F for about 65 minutes.

Feeding Bread

To avoid waste, offer bread in small amounts at the feeder, until you can gauge how quickly the birds will eat it. Freeze leftovers for later use. Keep frozen bread, crumbled into resealable plastic bags, on hand for emergencies like snowstorms, when any bluebirds, robins, or other thrushes in the area will be grateful for a handout of this nutritious soft food.

Bread is soft and absorbent, which makes it ideal for soaking up bacon fat, melted suet, beef drippings from a roast or broiler pan, and other oils. Chickadees, jays, titmice, woodpeckers, and many other birds will accept such high-fat offerings eagerly, especially in cold weather. Cut the bread into cubes or crumble it into cool but still liquid fat, and serve in a large, shallow plastic tray to avoid grease stains on wood bird feeders. An old plastic plate or cafeteria tray nailed to the top of a flat post is an ideal feeder for these high-energy treats. Any leftovers will be enjoyed by raccoons, opossums, and cats at night.

Buckwheat

Attracts bobwhite, quail, pheasants, wild turkeys

NOT A WHEAT AT ALL but a relative of the pink-flowered smartweed you pull out of your garden beds, buckwheat (*Fagopyrum esculentum*) is a fast-growing annual with dark green, heart-shaped leaves and fragrant small white flowers. In bloom, it's abuzz with bees, who carry the nectar home to make superb honey. In seed, it's a great temptation to bobwhite, quail, pheasants, and wild turkeys, who relish its small, nutty seeds.

Gardeners and farmers use buckwheat as a summer soil-building crop because it grows quickly, producing lots of green material to till into the soil. Buckwheat is pretty when it flowers, and its small blossoms attract insects, including beneficials that will patrol your gardens for pests. Insect-eating birds will come, too, to dine on the insects visiting the buckwheat blossoms.

Plant buckwheat seeds after all danger of frost has passed in a sunny patch of prepared soil near your feeding area for game birds. It will sprout fast and grow like a weed, creating a solid swath of erect plants that bloom late in summer. In fall and winter, keep an eye on your buckwheat patch, which may at-tract a covey of foraging quail. These shy birds will appreciate the sheltering cover of the dense stems, where they can seek seeds while remaining hidden from predators.

Harvest some of your buckwheat seeds for winter feeding by shaking the seedheads into a large paper sack; you'll hear the seeds falling against the paper. Store the seeds in a tightly closed plastic container in a cool, dry place. During cold weather or snow and ice storms, buckwheat seeds make a good high-energy food that you can scatter directly on the ground for hungry birds.

Other members of the buckwheat family species also produce plenty of bird-attracting seeds, so you may want to think twice before you uproot every bit of smartweed or knotweed (*Polygonum* spp.) in your garden. But don't think about it too long—these weeds can grow quickly out of control! For more about buckwheat's weedy relatives, see Weeds on page 327.

Game birds relish buckwheat's small, nutty seeds and prefer to feed in the shelter of the plants' dense growth.

Bullies

JAYS AND MOCKINGBIRDS are often tyrants at the feeder. It's not because of their glutto-nous habits—they eat no more than any other song-bird at the feeder. It's because of their bad manners and their aggressive "All mine!" attitudes.

These birds are bullies. They flaunt their large size and loud voices to scare other birds away from seed trays and suet feeders. And should these nonviolent approaches not clear the field, the bully birds will re-sort to a more physical approach, threatening with long, sharp beaks and flashing wings.

Jays are more talk than threat, and many smaller birds learn to retreat when the jay comes in, then quickly return once the bigger bird settles down. Mockingbirds, however, are real meanies. When they warn other birds that the feeder area belongs to them, they aren't kidding. They will mercilessly pursue any bird that crosses whatever invisible line the mockingbird defends.

The mockingbird doesn't take much time to eat because the big gray bird spends most of its energy dashing after invaders. If the weather is mild and I know the other birds can resort to foraging for themselves, I often let the mockingbird tire itself out. It usually takes no more than a couple of weeks before the bird wearies of its territorial game.

But if winter weather has settled in and food sources are scarce, I take defensive measures on behalf of my more timid customers. It's easy to add more feeders or move one of the existing ones to another side of the house—out of sight and out of mind for the mockingbird.

One year I discovered that even a flimsy trellis can make an effective barrier. Because I had limited space, I moved a feeder on an iron crook to the other side of a strip of lattice that supported a tangle of bean vines. Although the leaves had long since dropped, the thick, twining stems provided just enough camouflage to allow the birds to eat in peace. I sometimes wondered if the mockingbird could actually see them and was just saving face—not to mention energy.

Small but Mighty

Another notorious bully at feeders and in the garden is the tiny hummingbird. These itty-bitty birds will take on opponents of all sizes once they become obsessed with the notion that a nectar feeder or even a favored plant is their sole territory. Often they limit their attacks to other hummingbirds, but I have also seen feisty hummingbirds zip to the defense against other species. When the silver beech tree near one of my nectar feeders became a magnet for beechnut-eating flickers and blue jays, the male hummingbird who "owned" the feeder single-handedly chased away every last one of them. Its technique was simple: a high-speed approach with rapier bill held straight ahead, aimed at the other bird. No arguing

Just as pugnacious as the notorious bluejays, this red-headed woodpecker is well able to hold its own against their screamed insults.

with that! The other birds wisely retreated, at least for a little while, although the jays made sure everyone within earshot knew how unfair the situation was.

Should a hummingbird become the bully at your feeder, the best solution is to add another nectar feeder, as far away and as much out of the hummer's line of sight as possible. But when the hummingbird claims a plant—fuchsias are a favorite in my yard—there's not much you can do other than enjoy watching the territorial spats.

In recent years, nectar feeders have become battlegrounds for other birds, too. Woodpeckers, house finches, and dozens of other species have learned about this source of food, and the trend is spreading. Often, the very presence of a competitor at the nectar feeder is enough to deter hummingbirds. If a woodpecker or other feeder hog is draining your feeder dry, you may want to shoo the glutton away yourself. Simply approaching the feeder should do the trick.

Buntings

BUNTINGS ARE the size of chipping sparrows, have the same conical seed-eating bill, and belong to the same large finch family. But unlike their generally drab sparrow relatives, male buntings are real beauties. The **painted bunting**, found in Texas and the Southeast, is as vivid as a parrot, decked out in an incredible patchwork of red breast, blue head, and yellow-green back. The **indigo bunting** is common to the eastern half of the country with a range that extends sporadically westward. As brilliant as a sapphire, his color shifts from turquoise through

The intense blue of a male indigo bunting's feathers is a matter of light refraction, which is why this little jewel looks dull black on a cloudy day or in shade.

cobalt blue, depending on how the light hits his iridescent feathers. In the western half of the country, the **lazuli bunting** maintains the colorful reputation of the group; the male wears plumage similar to the eastern bluebird's, with a rich blue head and back, a russet chest, and a snowy belly. The least common species, the **varied bunting**, has purple and blue feathers washed with red. Observers occasionally spot this beautiful bird just above the Mexican border. Female buntings are the complete opposite of their flashy mates—all species are dull brown, with perhaps a faint tinge of color. On the nest the females are practically invisible.

Because of their beauty, we cherish buntings at our feeders. Yet they can be as common as sparrows if your feeding station is close to their natural habitat of brush, hedgerows, or woods' edges. On migration, they can show up just about anywhere. Indigo buntings live in the farm fields outside my small town, but when they pass through in April on their way to breeding grounds, they stop off at my urban feeder for a handout of millet. Once they find a feeder to their liking, whether on migration or as

At first glance, the lazuli bunting looks like a bluebird, thanks to its red, white, and blue coloring. White wing bars are the distinguishing feature to look for.

residents, buntings return day after day, long enough for you to call your friends to come and see these beautiful little birds. Buntings winter south of the United States, so enjoy them during their spring, summer, and fall visits.

Bunting Behavior

Except for the painted bunting, who prefers to vocalize softly, the voice of a bunting seems too big for its body. These birds are tireless singers, persisting in their long, varied choruses even during the heat of a summer afternoon, when other avian singers are silent. They generally choose to sing from a high perch. Listen for a flight song, usually delivered just before dusk from a male bird that flutters high into the sky, then swoops down, singing exultantly.

BUNTING FEEDER FOODS
■ Canary seed
■ Millet
■ Mixed seeds
■ Nuts, chopped
■ Peanuts, chopped
■ Rapeseed
■ Weed seeds

At the feeder, buntings are big fans of small seeds. They eagerly eat ragweed, lamb's-quarters, and other weed seeds, too, which is the excuse I use for letting my lawn and gardens look a little unmanicured. When dandelions go to seed in my yard (and along the roadsides), brilliant indigo buntings will soon arrive. I love to watch them compete with yellow goldfinches and fresh-plumaged white-crowned sparrows for possession of the seed-filled puff. They can be feisty little birds, squabbling with a thrust of an open beak and a harsh warning note, but when food is abundant, as at your well-stocked feeding station, they feed quietly.

Like sparrows, buntings prefer to eat close to the ground. I often find them picking spilled seed from beneath the feeders. Pour their seed into a low tray feeder to pique their interest. They will also eat at higher feeders but are quicker to fly in alarm when perched above the ground.

C

Cake and Cookies

Attract blackbirds, bluebirds, chickadees, crows, jays, mockingbirds, pigeons, robins, house sparrows, native sparrows, starlings, thrushes, titmice, Carolina wrens

IT'S NOT THE SWEETNESS OF CAKE that attracts birds, it's the energy they get from the flour-based food that makes them peck up cake crumbs in the feeder and on the ground. As with bread, white or light-colored cake pieces and crumbs are the easiest to see and attract birds fastest. Carrot, zucchini, and other moist homemade cakes are ideal for birds, especially if you add a heavy helping of nuts or fruit.

All soft-food eaters and many seed eaters dine on cake, including bluebirds, chickadees, jays, mockingbirds, robins, thrushes, titmice, house and native sparrows, and, sorry, blackbirds, crows, and starlings.

Cake absorbs moisture and turns moldy fast in wet weather or when spread on the ground or in a feeder where it's not protected from the elements. Feed sparingly, or stockpile leftover cake in resealable plastic freezer bags for winter feeding, when birds that eat soft foods, such as bluebirds, robins, and Carolina wrens, may visit feeding stations to seek sustenance.

Cookies

Like any grain-based product, cookies appeal to a variety of birds. Birds, such as bluebirds, mockingbirds, robins, thrushes, and Carolina wrens, that eat mostly soft foods may be tempted by an offering of oatmeal-raisin, chunky peanut butter, or other tasty bird-tailored cookies. Of course, keep in mind that blackbirds, crows, pigeons, house sparrows, and starlings also are fond of soft foods, including cookies.

Crush leftover cookies into coarse crumbs for serving to chickadees, titmice, and soft-food eaters at feeders. You can also toss a handful of stale cookies from your pantry shelf onto the ground, where house sparrows and other hardy sorts will quickly peck them into bite-size bits.

> Crumble up stale cookies and leftover cake into beak-size bites for birds that eat soft food.

Canary Seed

Attracts buntings, ducks, house and purple finches, geese, goldfinches, quail, redpolls, native sparrows

CANARY SEED WAS VERY POPULAR with caged-bird owners some 50 years ago, when singing canaries were resident pets in many kitchens and living rooms. As the popularity of these pets faded, the seed made a natural transition to wild birdseed mixes, where it remains popular with all the finch relatives of canaries. Goldfinches, purple finches, and house finches as well as buntings, redpolls, and native sparrows all eat canary seed.

Canary seed is a golden tan, smallish seed that you can buy by the pound or mixed with other choice seeds. The seed comes from a grass called canary grass (*Phalaris canariensis*), which has a notorious relative known as reed canary grass (*P. arundinacea*), a fast-spreading plant that has become a pest in many areas, especially along water. Ducks, geese, quail and other game birds, and songbirds eat canary seed.

Feeder birds can be finicky about canary seed. At feeders in some regions, they take to it readily, while at other feeders, it may join the milo (also known as sorghum) and wheat kicked onto the ground in favor of choicer seeds. Do your own tests to determine whether your birds will take to canary seed by offering a small amount by itself or by checking to see if birds eat the canary seed when it's part of a seed mix.

> Buntings, house finches, purple finches, game birds, goldfinches, and water fowl all eat canary seed.

Cardinal

THE MALE CARDINAL PROVES that a plain red dress is always an attention getter. Add the right accessories—a black face mask and a jaunty crest—and this bird is a welcome presence at any feeder. Yet cardinals are such routine feeder guests that many of us take these birds for granted. If you live in the Midwest, East, or parts of the Southwest where **northern cardinals** live year-round—count your blessings. Those who feed birds in the Northwest, Rockies, and parts of the Southwest never get even a glimpse of this glorious bird.

The female cardinal has paler, browner feathers than the male, but she is a beauty in her own right. Her big, bright orange bill, which you hardly notice in the male bird, stands out in vivid contrast to the subtle coloring of her feathers. It's not an optical illusion, by the way, that males seem to become brighter as spring approaches. Their breeding plumage almost glows with electric color.

Cardinals are beloved for brightening the landscapes of a northern winter. Against snow or the green of conifers, their color brings a welcome flash of life to the scene, like a reminder of summer flowers.

The **pyrrhuloxia,** a close relative of the cardinal, lives in the Southwest. A casual observer may confuse this bird with the cardinal. Both male and female pyrrhuloxia are gray above, with reddish wings and tail, and the male sports a speckled wash of red on the belly. The bill is smaller and more curved than the cardinal's.

Cardinal Behavior

The trademark love song of the cardinal, a loud, whistled "What cheer!" is a welcome antidote to winter doldrums. The birds begin singing in late winter and keep going strong through midsummer. The basic whistle is easy for our human lips to imitate. Try calling back to a singing cardinal and the male may investigate what sounds like a potential rival. A slurred trill is also frequently part of the song. The pyrrhuloxia sounds almost identical.

The male cardinal becomes even brighter as spring approaches and the dull-colored tips of his fall feathers wear away. By the time courtship time nears, the bird will be its most vivid red.

Beautiful in an understated way, the female cardinal wears colors that keep her concealed on the nest. Her strong, triangular bill is a finch-family hallmark.

At the feeder, cardinals may feed singly, in pairs, or as part of a large group. The birds frequently band together in winter, traveling thickets, roadsides, and backyards to search for food. Sunflower seeds are a guaranteed draw, but cardinals consume many other foods as well. Cardinals are one of the few birds that will stand up to a greedy jay at the feeder.

During courtship season, you may witness a tender ritual between the male and female birds. Imitating the posture of a baby bird, the female droops her wings and crouches low with open beak, begging for food. Her mate eagerly obliges her request, depositing a morsel of food into her waiting bill.

Cardinals may seem to be romantic suitors, but strong hormones rule the males during the breeding season. This leads to frequent attacks on other males—or against their own reflection. If a tapping on a window awakens you, you may find a cardinal viciously trying to drive away the phantom bird in the glass. A car mirror may also substitute for a rival. Because cardinals are so single-minded about attacking their adversary, do the bird a favor and cover the offending window or mirror before it batters itself silly. A piece of netting may break up the reflection adequately; if not, use an old sheer window curtain or other covering.

CARDINAL FEEDER FOODS

- Apples
- Bread and other baked goods
- Corn, any type
- Peanuts, chopped or shelled
- Safflower seed
- Suet, ground or chopped
- Sunflower seed, black oil or striped, hulled

Catbird

THAT KITTY MEWING in your bushes may not be a feline but an avian species. The gray catbird, a cousin of the mockingbird and thrasher, bears an appropriate name. Catcalls aren't the limit of this talented mimic's repertoire: The bird may also imitate squeaking gates, other birds, or your mail carrier's whistle.

A shy bird, the catbird ranges across most of the country except for the far West. It keeps to thickets and hedgerows and rarely comes out into the open. Because of its habits, a catbird can be difficult to tempt to the feeder. Your best course is to plant brambles and berried shrubs in a thick corridor, which will provide natural food for this insect- and fruit-eating species, as well as give the bird a route of safety through your yard. The abundant vegetation will also provide a ready supply of the beetles, crickets, grasshoppers, and other insects devoured by the bird.

Catbirds are a gardener's allies in the vegetable garden, which they may visit more readily than a feeder because the plants feel more like home. Dense

Often heard but not so easy to spot, the catbird skulks in shrubbery. Track it down by following the meowing or listen for its melodic song of repeated phrases.

flowerbeds and borders also attract the birds. The persistently pesty Japanese beetle is one of their favorite menu items.

Catbirds usually winter in the far South, coastal Southeast, and southward, though an occasional bird may stay in northern climes. Keep your feeding station stocked with fruit and soft foods year-round, and any catbirds in the area may eventually visit. As with other species, catbirds seem to be learning to associate feeders with a steady food supply. In my first 20 years of bird feeding, I never saw a catbird venture to the tray of food, although local residents did eat heartily of wild grapes and raspberries nearby. In the last decade, I have regularly hosted catbirds, summer and winter, at feeding stations in Indiana and Pennsylvania.

Catbird Behavior

This mimic thrush engages in a special kind of singing, especially in late summer. Listen for its very quiet whisper song, usually sung from dense undergrowth where the singer is well concealed. If you are "lucky" enough to have a tangle of Japanese

CATBIRD FEEDER FOODS
■ Blackberries (*Rubus* spp.)
■ Blueberries (*Vaccinium* spp.)
■ Bread and other baked goods
■ Cereal
■ Crackers
■ Currants (*Ribes* spp.)
■ Grapes (*Vitis* spp.), wild or cultivated
■ Peanuts, shelled; chopped or whole
■ Raisins
■ Raspberries (*Rubus* spp.)

honeysuckle (*Lonicera japonica*) on your property, you may find that vine an ideal location for both a catbird nest and a catbird song.

At the feeder, the catbird is quick to take flight at the first intimation of danger or signs of unrest from other birds. After winter storms, it is one of the first birds to arrive at the feeder and one of the last to leave. At my feeder, one of its favorite summer foods is the tiny champagne grape, a ¼-inch morsel that is similar to the bird's favorite wild grapes in size. Once a rarity in the fresh fruit market, these wine grapes are becoming more available in supermarkets.

Cats

THAT DEAR PET SLEEPING PEACEFULLY on your lap is part of one of the biggest threats birds face. House cats, strays, and other wandering felines account for an unbelievable number of bird fatalities: One estimate suggests more than a million songbirds a year meet their fate at the claws of cats. I've done an informal survey of nesting birds for 2 years in my own small town, where cats claim their territories on every block. According to my records, only one in five nests goes unmolested by cats in the six blocks surrounding my house. And that doesn't include the adult birds that fall prey to predatory felines.

Whatever the actual figure of cat damage, keeping kitties out of your yard should be a prime consideration for any bird lover. Keeping your own pets indoors is a good place to start. They may

protest for a while, but they will eventually become accustomed to house arrest. If you can't bear the thought of confining your pet year-round, at least keep it indoors during the peak breeding season, when birds are at their most vulnerable. A bell on the collar won't do the trick because cats can stalk without a single tinkle.

Because the cats that visited my yard were not my own, I couldn't control their comings and goings. But

> If you care about the well-being of your birds, keep your cat indoors and urge your neighbors to do the same.

I did discourage them from making my yard their private lounge. The old chase-and-yell strategy is highly effective. If you're not the yelling type, drop a handful of pennies into a soda can, tape the opening shut, and shake it as you chase out the intruders. A squirt gun or a blast from the garden hose will also do the trick. Of course, only use the water treatment in warm weather.

No matter how often you chase a cat, it probably will come back because all those birds in one place are just too much to resist. Two other options will give you more permanent results: a fence and/or a dog. After I erected a solid wood-board fence with little room to scramble under, the cat traffic dropped dramatically. The presence of a dog is just as discouraging, although it won't help your birds at night when Fido is asleep on the hearth inside. Combining fence and dog, I've found, works like a charm. After a few close calls when my dog thought he was actually going to catch a cat, the felines apparently passed the word. Now the cats avoid my yard for fear of getting cornered by the dog inside the fence.

Providing protective cover for your birds is a double-edged sword. Sheltering shrubs make it easier for a bird to dash for safety, but they also allow cats to sneak up on unwary birds. If cats are a problem at your feeding station, keep

That single-minded look strikes fear in any bird's heart, and for good reason. Pet and stray cats may kill as many as a million or more birds every year.

cat-hiding vegetation several yards away from feeders and water features. In the end, your observations will help you evaluate the cat-danger situation in your own yard.

Cereal

Attracts common feeder birds plus jays, pheasants, pigeons, quail, starlings

HUNGRY BIRDS IN YOUR BACKYARD will change your whole perspective on stale cereal—instead of seeing that last inch or two at the bottom of the box as a waste of good food, turn it into a popular treat for your feathered friends. You can scatter stale cereal directly on the ground or in a tray feeder, but birds will gobble it up faster if you make it more palatable by adding tasty peanut butter, peanut oil, or meat drippings to the dry flakes. It's easiest to mix peanut butter and other binders with cereal using your bare hands in a large, deep mixing bowl (kids love to help with this hands-on preparation). The result will be a crumbly mixture that the birds can easily pick up and enjoy.

Many of our favorite feeder birds appreciate leftover cereal, but so do pigeons, house sparrows, and starlings. If you're trying to discourage these birds from visiting your feeders, offer the cereal mixtures described on the opposite page in small quantities, scattering about a cup at a time among other seed in the feeders. You can also scatter the cereal mixes beneath a dense shrub or low-branching conifer to tempt jays, quail, pheasants, and native sparrows. Some of the traditionally troublesome birds are more reluctant to feed in those places than at open sites.

I like to collect a wealth of cereal-box leftovers in large resealable plastic bags, stored in the freezer, for winter feeding when blizzards bring crowds of hungry birds to the yard. I scatter the flakes and loops across the open areas of my backyard so that the flocks of birds can easily reach them, and I feel benevolent rather than annoyed as 100 or so starlings chow down.

Choose cereals for birds just as you would for your children or yourself (see "Serving Leftover Cereal" below): Those without sugar coating and marshmallows are healthier. Cereals with dried fruit bits or nuts are a special treat that birds will devour with gusto. They also make a great base for birdfood recipes.

Serving Leftover Cereal

SOME BIRDS will eat almost any kind of cereal, but I've found that some popular brands like Cheerios develop a particular following. Consult the chart below to find out how to prepare cereals or mix them with other foods, what type of feeder to put various cereals in, and what birds these grainy treats will please.

Cereal Type	How to Prepare	How to Serve	Desirable Birds Attracted
Bran flakes	Crush with a rolling pin.	Ground feeder	Doves, juncos, quail, pheasants, native sparrows
Cheerios	Offer whole.	Tray feeder	Blackbirds, chickadees, jays, mockingbirds, titmice
Corn flakes	Crush with a rolling pin.	Ground feeder	Blackbirds, buntings, doves, juncos, pheasants, quail, native sparrows, towhees
	Crush with a rolling pin; mix each cup cereal with ¼ cup peanut butter, peanut oil, bacon drippings, meat drippings, or melted suet to make a crumbly mix.	Tray feeder	Cardinals, chickadees, jays, nuthatches, titmice, woodpeckers, wrens
Crisped rice	Mix each cup cereal with ¼ cup peanut butter, peanut oil, bacon drippings, or meat drippings.	Tray feeder	Cardinals, chickadees, jays, nuthatches, titmice, woodpeckers, wrens
Fruit/nut cereals	Crush lightly with a rolling pin to break up cereal flakes.	Ground feeder	Buntings, robins, thrushes, towhees, native sparrows
		Tray feeder	Bluebirds, chickadees, grackles, grosbeaks, jays, mockingbirds, nuthatches, tanagers, titmice, yellow-rumped warblers, woodpeckers, wrens
Hot cereals (oatmeal, grits, Cream of Wheat)	Mix each cup dry cereal with ¼ cup peanut butter, bacon drippings, or meat drippings.	Tray feeder	Cardinals, chickadees, jays, nuthatches, titmice, woodpeckers, wrens
Puffed rice	—	—	Not appealing to birds
Shredded wheat	Crush with a rolling pin.	Ground feeder	Doves, juncos, pheasants, native sparrows
Sugar-coated cereals	—	—	Not appealing to desirable birds; serve in tray or ground feeder during winter storms only when food is scarce.

C

Chickadees

As CUTE AS A TIN wind-up toy, chickadees are endearing little creatures with jaunty attitudes and spiffy black caps. Their alert bright eyes seem to hold little fear of humans, and indeed these birds are among the easiest species to hand tame. The **black-capped chickadee** is the most widespread species, ranging across the northern half of America. Its "chick-a-dee-dee" call is one of the most widely recognized bird songs. Other chickadee species provide variations on the theme. The **Carolina chickadee** looks almost identical to the black-capped and inhabits the East and Southeast. Listen carefully and you may be able to distinguish its call, which is higher pitched and more rapidly delivered, often with a few extra "dees" tacked to the end of the phrase. In the mountainous West, it's the **mountain chickadee**, naturally enough, that entertains backyard bird feeders. It's distinguished by a black stripe through its eye, which splits the large white cheek patch. Along the Pacific coast, the beautiful **chestnut-backed chickadee** takes over. Its head markings look like the black-capped, but its belly is pure white and its back and sides are a rich russet brown. The **boreal chickadee** dwells in the extreme North, where, like other species, it devours a myriad of insects and frequents conifers to extract seeds from their cones. This species has a brown cap instead of the usual black attire, and a flush of chestnut tinges its sides and back.

Chickadees reside all year in nearly all of their ranges, but in nesting season they may temporarily disappear from your feeding station. Chances are, they will return when the duties of feeding a family are over—often with the young'uns in tow. There are not many things cuter than a row of fuzzy-headed

Black-capped chickadees are just downright cute. Active and unafraid, they are easy to befriend with a handout of their favorite foods. Plant a row of sunflowers for fall and winter snacks-on-the-stem.

The chestnut-backed chickadee flits about in the dim light of moist Pacific Coast forests, from the moss-draped Northwest to the giant redwoods of California.

baby chickadees sitting shoulder to shoulder along a tree limb near the feeder.

Chickadee Behavior

You could spend all your feeder-watching hours observing the antics of chickadees. These birds are active little creatures, always in motion. They flit from tray feeder to tree branches, then to the suet feeder, then to sample a doughnut, then to examine a weed for insects. And that's just in the first 5 minutes of watching! Excellent acrobats, they are adept at hanging upside down or sideways and at contorting their bodies to reach a morsel that is just a bit out of beak range.

CHICKADEE FEEDER FOODS
■ Acorns
■ Bayberries
■ Bread and other baked goods
■ Cornmeal mixtures or baked goods
■ Doughnuts
■ Hamburger, raw
■ Mealworms
■ Nuts
■ Peanut butter
■ Peanut butter mixtures
■ Peanuts, any style
■ Pine nuts
■ Suet
■ Sunflower seeds, black or striped

Chickadees are talkative as well as dynamic. You will hear them calling at any time of year and any time of day. Listen for the whistled two- to four-note songs of chickadees in addition to their traditional calls. This vocalization varies from species to species. To my ears, it's as shrill as one of those supersonic dog whistles—I have an almost uncontrollable impulse to clap my hands over my ears whenever I hear it.

Chickadees readily visit any style of feeder. They are agile enough to handle a tube feeder or homemade coffee can feeder, and they can cling to suet feeders as well as woodpeckers can. Being birds of the trees, they prefer feeders at higher settings than food at ground level, although if you are slow to refill, they will glean seeds from the ground. They welcome nuts, seeds, suet, and soft foods.

In winter, watch for gregarious bands of chickadees mixed with kinglets, nuthatches, titmice, and downy woodpeckers roaming your yard or feeder

A white stripe above the eye, splitting the black cap, is the key to recognizing the mountain chickadee.

area. These mixed-species groups can be heard before they are seen because the birds keep up a constant, reassuring call-and-response conversation.

RECIPE

Chickadee Delight

Mix this recipe for winter feeding, when high-activity chickadees need high-fat foods to keep their small bodies well fueled. Chop the suet finely so that it can be eaten in one bite.

INGREDIENTS

2 cups beef fat trimmings, ground or finely chopped

1 cup hulled sunflowers

1 cup pine nuts

1 cup peanuts, coarsely chopped

1 cup shelled almonds, hazelnuts, pecans, or walnuts, coarsely chopped

Spread the chopped fat on a tray in a single, shallow layer, and freeze until stiff. Break into individual small pieces with hands, and pour into a resealable plastic bag. Return to freezer, and freeze overnight. Dump suet pieces (loosen clumps if necessary) into a large bowl, and stir in other ingredients. Pour into an open tray feeder in a shallow layer.

Chipmunks and Ground Squirrels

CHIPMUNKS AND GROUND SQUIRRELS are hoarders that may spirit away food from your feeding station to store underground. These small, quick, ground-hugging rodents look like downsized, flatter-tailed versions of the larger, usually tree-dwelling squirrels. Most species sport long stripes down their backs.

If you live in the eastern half of the country, you are likely to enjoy the visits of the eastern chipmunk at your feeding station. Smallest of the ground squirrels, this fellow has a body about 9 inches long. In the central plains, Franklin's ground squirrel, an unstriped, solid grayish brown animal, is prevalent. In the West, the 13-lined ground squirrel, also known (albeit incorrectly) as a gopher, fills the same ecological niche. These little rascals can carry surprising quantities of food in their expandable cheeks. They hibernate in the winter and are active from spring through fall.

You can tame most ground squirrels with a bribe of bread or other baked goods. The chipmunk in my former Pennsylvania garden was particularly fond of buttered toast. It would take it daintily from my fingers, then maneuver into its burrow in a stone foundation wall. Chipmunks also munch on nuts and seeds.

These furry visitors can be troublesome, however. They eat young birds and bird eggs, along with tasty morsels from your garden, such as spring bulbs. Their burrows may destroy your favorite plants, too.

The presence of a cat or dog may discourage these rodents from making their home in your yard. You can also try tempting them into live traps for removal to a suitable wild area if they become a problem.

> Chipmunks love baked goods as well as seeds, but they also eat young birds and bird eggs.

Cicadas

Attract buntings, cardinals, chickadees, robins, warblers

THE INFERNAL BUZZING DRONE of cicadas in the summer may not be music to our human ears, but to birds it speaks a welcome message: Food here! Cardinals are adept at catching the buzzing insects in flight, while robins wrestle them to the ground, then stand on the vibrating body to dine. Even tiny buntings, chickadees, and warblers will capture and eat a cicada when they can.

With their loud droning and the large empty shells they leave about the landscape, cicadas tend to attract our attention more than most other insects. When cicada populations are high, you'll notice dead tips on tree branches damaged by egg-laying adults. Immature cicadas live in the soil. When they emerge at maturity and split their brown shells to reveal large, fearsome-looking winged adults, hungry birds will be waiting.

Large, buzzing cicadas may not look like the most delicious item on the menu, but to birds big and small, these summertime insects are a welcome feast.

City Birds

EVEN IN THE HEART of the city, a bird feeder can bustle with activity. You won't attract nearly as many species as you will in less urban areas, but the birds you feed will be just as appreciative of the handout. Birds of any kind are interesting to observe. When you have just a few species to watch, you will enjoy learning their habits even more than if you're trying to keep an eye on a dozen different kinds of birds. With city bird guests, you may even come to recognize individuals, which will give you a more personal pleasure in putting out seed for your "friends."

Love 'em or hate 'em, pigeons are a fact of life in the city. Give them a handout if you don't mind their messy habits.

In any city across America, you can attract house sparrows and starlings. Pigeons in a wonderful array of plumage colors and patterns may also visit. Mourning doves may turn up, too. Depending on just how much of a concrete jungle the neighborhood is, you may not attract any more species. If there are trees nearby, you may entice cardinals, chickadees, jays, and other birds. During migration time, your feeding station may draw passing birds if there are nearby trees or shrubs to shelter them while they rest.

Millet, seed mixes, and cracked corn are excellent choices for satisfying typical city birds—they're economical and eagerly eaten. Keep a small feeder of sunflower seeds for unexpected visitors; true city birds such as sparrows and starlings prefer smaller seeds and soft foods. Bread and cracker crumbs and baked goods are ideal for city birds, which have learned well how to scavenge edibles.

Feed your city birds in feeders that prevent seed from scattering on the ground, such as tube feeders with trays attached beneath them, or other enclosed feeders. Regularly clean up any spilled seed beneath feeders, and feed soft foods in small amounts so that none remains at the end of the day. You do not want to attract city mice and other urban rodents.

City birds greatly appreciate a birdbath as they may have no source of clean, fresh water. They will readily use the standard pedestal type.

Urban Pests

Should you be inundated by pigeons, house sparrows, and starlings and wish to discourage them, a couple of preventive actions will yank the welcome mat out from under their feet. First, switch to tube feeders. These birds have a hard time keeping their grip on the small perches, although they may still visit to vacuum up any seed that spills from the tubes. Weighted feeders that slam closed under the weight of larger birds will also prevent them from gobbling your goodies. You can also try serving only striped sunflower seed, which is difficult for house sparrows to crack. See Nuisance Birds on page 217 for more details on discouraging unwelcome birds.

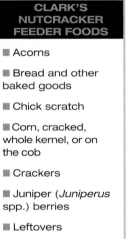

Clark's Nutcracker

IN MOUNTAINOUS REGIONS of the West and Northwest, the Clark's nutcracker may visit your feeding station. This sturdy-looking, jay-size bird has soft gray body feathers and dashing black and white wings and tail. Look for this relative of crows, jays, and magpies near conifers, where it uses its stout bill to pry open the scales and retrieve the seeds of firs and pines.

CLARK'S NUTCRACKER FEEDER FOODS
■ Acorns
■ Bread and other baked goods
■ Chick scratch
■ Corn, cracked, whole kernel, or on the cob
■ Crackers
■ Juniper (*Juniperus* spp.) berries
■ Leftovers
■ Meat scraps
■ Pine nuts
■ Soup bones with marrow
■ Suet
■ Sunflower seeds

I made the acquaintance of this bird while camping near Yellowstone National Park. Like most birds that live near a campground, the nutcracker was unusually tame, snapping up crackers with alacrity from just a few feet away. Later, I saw the birds flying across the mountain valleys, their flashy feathers catching the eye from a distance.

Clark's nutcracker takes the first part of its name from one-half of the famed western exploring team, Lewis and Clark. The nutcracker classification comes from the bird's habit of whacking open cones to get at the "nuts" inside. Pine nuts, the plump kernels of pinyon pines, are a particular favorite.

Friend of the pine forest, the flashy, noisy Clark's nutcracker ensures a crop of young trees, thanks to its habit of burying seeds for winter use.

Watching a nutcracker at the feeder or in the yard, you might think it's related to the woodpeckers. The bird often clings to trees and hammers away with its strong beak to extract hapless grubs. But on the ground, the nutcracker gives away its heritage with its walk, strutting about like a crow, with an occasional hop. Watch for its flycatcher-like feeding behavior, too, when it dashes out to snatch a butterfly in midair.

If you live high in the mountains, you may host a Clark's nutcracker during nesting season, which takes place as early as late winter, when the high-elevation temperatures hover near zero or below. In fall and winter, the birds often shift to lower elevations, where they feast on berries, lupine seeds, carrion, and feeder offerings as well as conifer seeds.

Like jays and squirrels, these nutcrackers are friends of the forest because they "plant" new trees by burying cones and seeds for later use. A Clark's nutcracker can locate its cache even when it's buried under snow. Uneaten seeds start new pine trees.

Clark's Nutcracker Behavior

Like the rest of the crow family, nutcrackers are noisy, and they seem to like causing a commotion. Their voices are mostly unmusical. Squawking is what they do best, often enough to make you cover your ears, especially when the birds arrive in a flock.

Cleaning Feeders

THERE'S NO DENYING that keeping feeders clean can be a chore, but like any other maintenance job—think: weeding—it's a task that's much quicker and easier if you do it routinely rather than wait until the situation gets out of hand.

Clean feeders keep your feeder area looking good, but the benefits go much further than just appearance. Although disease problems seem to be thankfully infrequent at feeder sites, the high concentrations of large numbers of birds in a small feeding area is an unnatural situation that can lead to health problems for the birds. A clean feeder means clean, fresh seed, healthier feeder birds, and less risk of disease. Aspergillosis, for example, a common fungal disease of birds with pneumonia-like symptoms, may spread through moldy seed or infected droppings. Swabbing out feeders regularly with a germ-killing bleach solution helps eliminate potential problems.

Offer Fresh Foods

Given a choice, birds will not eat moldy seed. Like us, they prefer their food fresh. Because it is nearly impossible to keep all seed swept up off the ground, always be sure to have a supply of fresh seed readily available, so that birds are not reduced to picking up bad seed.

At my own feeders and in the wild, I have noticed that birds will peck at or sift through "spoiled" food to find any fresh morsels remaining. Take suet, for example. In summer, my suet feeders begin to look mighty unappetizing, with the fat taking on a covering of black and gray mold. Still, the woodpeckers and other birds work at the chunks of fat, ferreting out fresh white suet from within the blackened shell. I have seen birds do the same at roadkill carcasses. And birds will appreciate withered, bruised, or even fermented fruit that no longer appeals to you. The only danger that birds face from eating spoiled fruit is inebriation: The fermented juices may make them a bit tipsy.

A Clean Scrape

How often you need to clean your feeders depends on how much bird traffic you get and on the weather. I remove spoiled seed and empty hulls whenever they accumulate in the feeders, but I do full-scale disinfecting work only about four times a year.

A good rule of thumb is to swab down your feeders with a 10-percent bleach solution once each season, on approximately the following schedule:

- In late summer, just before migrating goldfinches herald the beginning of increased fall traffic

---

Stock Up on These Supplies

MAKE FEEDER cleaning easier by stocking up on a few useful tools. If you have the right equipment at the ready, you're much more likely to give your feeders an occasional cleaning when it's needed. Unless you have some particularly unusual or elaborate feeders in your collection, this assortment of basic tools will take care of nearly all of your feeder cleaning tasks. I keep my cleaning supplies stored in a single bucket so that they're within easy reach for my monthly cleanup sessions. Here's what I keep handy.

- A sturdy scraper tool, such as a rigid plastic or metal kitchen spatula, for lifting old seed out of tray feeders and scraping off dried droppings

- A brush with short, stiff bristles for removing caked-on seed from other feeders

- A long-handled, elongated brush—sort of like an oversized baby bottle brush—for swabbing out tube feeders

- A water supply, such as a garden hose in summer or a bucket in winter

- Chlorine bleach solution at a ratio of 9 parts water to 1 part bleach

- A scrub brush for applying the bleach solution

- In late fall, when the feeders are filled to capacity daily
- In late winter, when unusual visitors are apt to show up as natural food becomes scarce
- In late spring, when migrants have moved on and feeder traffic hits a lull.

But you'll also need to clean out your feeders much more frequently than this. Seed turns moldy quickly in damp weather and in rainy and snowy seasons, and even covered feeders can't completely protect seed from accumulating moisture. Every time I refill, especially if the weather has been wet, I scrape out any moldy, damp, or bad seed. Instead of pouring good seed in on top of bad, I stick a spatula in my back pocket when I go out in the morning to refill. A quick flip of the wrist and any damp seed is instantly removed from feeders before refilling.

Keeping Seed Dry

Keeping seed dry can be a problem when you have a high-traffic feeder or a particularly wet climate. Here are a few ideas to help you reduce waste and increase customer satisfaction.

- In wet weather, refill your feeders sparingly, so that the seed is consumed before it can absorb moisture. Refilling the feeders more frequently is better than wasting money on wet seed.
- To keep tiny niger seed fresh and dry in tube feeders, use an age-old kitchen trick: Add a few handfuls of uncooked rice to the seed when you fill the feeder. In the 3 years since I started this practice, I have not once needed to scrape out caked, spoiled niger seed from my tube feeders.
- Don't worry about the wet seed that drops and occasionally sprouts under your feeder area. In my experience, birds won't eat wet seed from the ground. But I have seen sparrows nibbling on the fresh green sprouts, especially during winter when tender greenery is scarce.

Cleaning Solutions

A garden hose with a high-pressure adjustable nozzle is my favorite labor-saving aid in the clean-

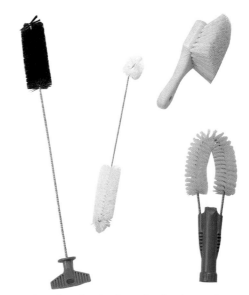

Inexpensive cleaning tools make feeder maintenance quick and easy. Choose scrub brushes that fit your feeders and that make it easy to reach into the corners of trays, hoppers, and tubes.

feeder campaign. I use the hose to spray feeders clean fast, without applying any elbow grease at all. A hose is great for washing out tube feeders, plastic suction-cup window feeders (take them down first), and other feeders with nooks and crannies that are hard to reach with a brush. Allow the feeders to dry thoroughly before you refill them.

When I do my once-a-season disinfecting, I use a bucket of bleach solution (9 parts water to 1 part bleach), a pair of rubber gloves, and a stiff brush. I scrub the surfaces, roofs, and sides of tray feeders and the feeding shelves and perches of other feeders, which are likely spots for germs to accumulate. Then I allow the feeders to dry in the sun, which my mother always told me kills germs, too. Whether that's true or not, I don't know, but it does make my feeders feel fresh and clean.

While the feeders are drying, I turn over the wood chip mulch below the feeder posts, or add a new layer to cover the accumulated droppings and seed hulls. A garden hoe makes this chore a simple operation.

Cleaning Gadgets

Specially designed brushes that have angled tips, long wire handles, or other improvements to make feeder cleaning easier may be worth investing in, especially since most of them cost just a few dollars. Examine each implement before you buy it to determine if you will actually use the tool enough to warrant adding it to your collection. Make sure it is the appropriate size, shape, or length for your particular feeder(s).

Once you begin cleaning your feeders, you'll develop an appreciation for the ones that are easy to clean. Those with decorative nooks and crannies in which seed can get stuck may turn out to be more trouble than they're worth. My favorite feeders are those that are easy for both me and the birds to use. Look for feeders that are sturdily built, simple to fill (don't require two hands to hold open), hold plenty of seed (at least a quart), and are easy to keep clean using basic cleaning tools.

Clematis

Attracts cardinals, catbirds, finches, juncos, sparrows

GIVEN A CHOICE between small-flowered clematis vines like sweet autumn clematis (*Clematis terniflora*) and big, bright-flowered clematis cultivars and hybrids, most gardeners will go for the color and splash of the fancified varieties.

From a bird's-eye view, though, the choice is exactly the opposite. Most large-flowered clematis put their energy into flowers, and the vines themselves are fairly puny things. Small-flowered types, on the other hand, are rampant growers that easily cover a trellis or fence with dense, twiggy growth in a single season. Who cares about flowers when you're seeking shelter on a cold, rainy night or when you need a hidden place to make your nest?

Autumn-flowering clematis (*Clematis terniflora*) makes a sweet bower for nesting birds. Clematis vines also supply nesting materials and attract insects for food.

Bird Benefits Galore

Plant a trellis or fence near your feeders with sweet autumn clematis (*C. terniflora*, also called *C. maximowicziana*) or other small-flowered types such as anemone clematis (*C. montana*), virginsbower (*C.*

virginiana), and your birds will have plenty of reasons to thank you. Here are some:

■ The vigorous, twiggy vines provide excellent shelter from rain or wind for any bird, and the vine is a great place to hide in a hurry should a hawk dive-bomb the feeders.

- The tangle of branches keeps nests of cardinals, catbirds, and sparrows hidden from predators.

- The multitude of tiny flowers are better at attracting insects than those large, colorful hybrid clematis blooms so dear to a gardener's heart. Birds will visit the flowering vines to snap up small flies, wasps, and other insects.

- In fall, when the fuzzy seedheads mature, cardinals, finches, juncos, and sparrows will work busily to tear away the fluff and get at the seeds.

- In spring, sparrows and other songbirds will tug off pieces of bare clematis vine to use in nest building.

Small-flowered clematis are speedy growers that thrive in sun to full shade and are perfect for quick coverage of a fence, wall, or trellis. You may plant these vines for the benefit of birds and find yourself enjoying them, too. What's not to like? These trouble-free vines never need fertilizer and require no additional watering after their first few weeks in the ground.

Just as they make great screens for feeders, they also provide quick and substantial privacy for your deck or patio. And the oodles of small flowers combine to deliver sweet fragrance that's often missing from the larger hybrid blossoms. Look to see what clematis options are available from your local growers, then turn to mail-order outlets, if need be, for an expanded selection. Most clematis grow well in Zones 3 through 8.

Communication

SOME ASPECTS OF BIRD communication are hard to miss. When a jay flies into the feeding station, hollering at the top of its lungs and sending all the other birds scattering for cover, you know that it means "Scram!" Other bird communications are less obvious, and you will need to watch closely to notice them. Learning the language of birds will give you a better understanding of the interactions between them, and that translates into making feeder watching more fun.

Here are some bird communiques to listen for:

- Listen for the shrill cheeping calls of fledglings demanding a meal. Even when they are old enough to get food on their own, the young call for parental assistance, and the parents generally oblige. When you hear a young bird squawking, it's probably perched some distance from the feeder. Locate it by watching to see where the parent carries the food.

- Birds communicate with others of their species using call notes—short, nonmusical chips and twitters. Listen for juncos keeping up a constant chittering as they hop about near the feeders.

During courtship, a female house finch may act like a hungry nestling, crouching with her wings lowered and her beak open for a gift of food from her partner.

During migration time, you may hear call notes filtering from the sky as birds pass overhead.

- Assembly calls gather the flock. Listen for these notes from quail and crows.

- Alarm notes are usually louder than normal bird "conversation," and birds deliver them in a harsh, scolding, attention-getting tone. Should you hear a sudden loud "Chip!" as you stroll about your yard, try to find the bird that's warning you away. A nest may be nearby.

- Danger signals are hard to miss because birds at the feeder will leave in a sudden panic. As you observe your feeding station, see if you can pinpoint the first bird to become alert, stop eating, and then deliver an alarm call. The note varies among species.

- Determining the pecking order makes for constant quarreling among feeder birds, especially if eating space is limited. Watch for birds to make shrill attack notes, usually accompanied by a thrust of the head or a flurry of wings.

Birds frequently use body language in place of verbal chit-chat. They communicate anger with threatening head motions or drooping wings and fluffed-out feathers. Courtship rituals may include the female assuming the posture of a begging nestling, dropping her wings, lowering her body, and begging with open bill.

One of the most fascinating everyday miracles of the natural world is the synchronized flight of flocking birds, such as starlings and blackbirds. As if guided by the same brain, they wheel and dive and change direction in one smooth motion, with no visible sign passed among the members of the group. If you are ever privileged to see a mass flight of dozens of American avocets, you will never forget the breathtaking display. These long-legged, long-beaked birds of coastal and western marshes and shallow lakes are decked out in bold zigzags of black against snowy white wings and backs. In a flock they look like a modern dance troupe in flight, flashing dramatic changes of costume as they shift their postures in midair in near-perfect synchronization.

Competition at the Feeder

IT'S HIGH STAKES FOR A SEAT at a bird feeder, thanks to the tempting spread of food you supply. No matter what you're offering—seed, suet, corn, fruit, nectar, soft foods—you will see birds squabbling over squatting rights. Naturally, the most desirable foods will attract the most competition. Birds will shoulder each other aside at the tube feeder, push and shove or threaten to peck one another at a tray feeder, and defend their perch vigorously at a nectar or suet feeder.

Less aggressive or smaller birds generally yield quickly to backyard bullies, which can leave you with a feeder full of starlings or jays and not much else. Luckily, the solution is simple, with a payoff for both you and the birds: Add more feeders. Increasing the accommodations will decrease the competition and result in more birds to watch.

Large tray feeders are your best choice for feeding a crowd because dozens of birds can pack the edges

Blue jays are not well mannered about sharing feeder space. If they monopolize tray feeders, add tube feeders so other visitors don't go hungry.

to reach the seed. A hopper or tube feeder, on the other hand, usually accommodates only a handful of guests because of limited eating space.

I follow an "All Birds Welcome" policy at my feeding station, but I do take steps to keep gluttons like starlings separated from dainty eaters like chickadees. A large, low tray feeder, homemade from plywood and wire mesh, serves as my all-purpose starling feeder. When the starling traffic increases, I dump my old bread, dog food, apple peelings, whole kernel corn, ground suet, meat scraps, and other starling delights directly on the ground. To birds that often eat out of dumpsters, such accommodations are a natural fit. Jays and the occasional brave crow also forage happily there.

Away from the downscale diner, I keep the usual assortment of trays and tubes, some tailor-made for small birds, some not. As long as I keep the starling arena chock full of goodies, they rarely infiltrate the songbird stations. If the smaller birds have a few feeders just for them, I don't worry about them going hungry should bullies shoulder them aside.

Blackbirds, grackles, or starlings can gather in flocks of thousands in fall and winter, vacuuming off feeders in nothing flat. If you consider these birds your nemesis, you'll want to replace traditional-style feeders with trays, hoppers, and tubes that have wire grids, cage bars, or weight-sensitive devices that deny larger birds access to the food within. Shop in a bird-supply store or catalog such as those listed in "Resources" on page 348 to find just the right model to eliminate most of your feeder competition problems.

Coneflowers

Attract goldfinches, tree and other native sparrows

IF YOU PLANT JUST ONE PERENNIAL to attract birds, make it purple coneflower (*Echinacea purpurea*). One of the longest blooming perennials, this sturdy plant starts putting forth flowers in early summer and keeps going strong right through the first light frosts. And, while it's putting out new flowers, the old ones are maturing into beautiful orange-tinged spiny seedheads, brimming with birdseeds. Snip off some of those seedheads with pruners and let them fall into a large paper sack to dry for fall and winter feeding.

Goldfinches are usually the first birds to take advantage of a ripening coneflower. They perch patiently for as much as half an hour at a time, extracting seeds and nibbling the meat free. During late fall and winter, tree sparrows and other native sparrows gather to take advantage of the bounty, either pulling seeds from the plant or searching out dropped seeds below.

The similar pale coneflower (*E. pallida*) and the coneflowers of the genus *Ratibida*, including

A male goldfinch gives purple coneflower the stamp of approval. The blooms attract insects, the plant itself offers cover, and the seeds are favorites of finches.

prairie coneflower (*R. columnifera*) and gray-headed coneflower (*R. pinnata*), also attract small seed-eating birds in fall and winter. Most of the coneflowers thrive in full sun to light or partial shade in average soil conditions. They're hardy across most of the United States, from Zone 3 in the North to Zones 8 and 9 in the South. Established plants tolerate drought conditions, although you and your bird guests will enjoy more flowers when your plants receive adequate moisture.

Use coneflower seedheads, collected after ripening and dried in shallow cardboard boxes, to decorate wreaths and swags for birds. You can also tie the seedheads into bundles and hook them on a nail in a spot where birds can perch and nibble on these tasty treats.

Butterflies and Other Bugs

All coneflowers attract butterflies and other insects, so when they're in flower they bring in live bird food, too. Small butterflies on their way to and from the plants are likely to be quickly snatched up by flycatchers or English sparrows, and smaller insects become a quick dinner for any wrens in the neighborhood. Because coneflowers attract so many insects, they also attract predatory spiders that often stretch their webs across the branches of the plants. The spiderwebs, in turn, may attract hummingbirds that will flit about, collecting the sticky webs for building their nests.

> Coneflowers mature into beautiful orange-tinged spiny seedheads, brimming with birdseed.

Coreopsis

Attracts doves, quail, white-crowned and white-throated sparrows, towhees

OUR AMERICAN PLAINS WERE ONCE ALIVE with great swaths of wildflowers and grasses and with the multitudes of birds that fed among them. It's fun to use native flowers to re-create even a small bit of that sweeping prairie heritage in a sunny spot near your bird-feeding station.

The prairie flowers of the genus *Coreopsis* include annual and perennial species, all of them loaded with tasty bird-attracting seeds. Other coreopsis hail from desert homes in North and Central America, so no matter where you live, you'll discover rewarding native coreopsis that are appropriate for your garden conditions. Members of the giant aster family, these bright daisies are usually yellow, with the exceptions of calliopsis (*C. tinctoria*), which also blooms in burgundy and bicolors, and pink tickseed (*C. rosea*), a pink-flowered species.

Native sparrows appear most often when coreopsis seeds are on the menu, although other birds also enjoy them. Look for white-crowned and white-throated sparrows among the plants in fall and winter. Towhees may scratch underneath to turn up overlooked bits of seeds, and doves and quail will also forage beneath the plants.

Calliopsis (*C. tinctoria*), a self-sowing annual once used as a dye plant, produces so much seed—thanks to its dozens of blooms—that you can easily harvest the seed for winter feeding. Snip sprays of the seedheads, and weave their thin, wiry stems into wreaths and swags for a decorative bird treat.

All coreopsis are easy to grow in a sunny site in average, well-drained soil. Hardiness varies by species. Two of the easiest and most widely adaptable perennial species are *C. lanceolata* and *C. grandiflora*, dependable performers with bouquets of sunny golden flowers. Start the seeds indoors in late winter for some bloom the same year. Expect to see butterflies at the flowers of any coreopsis you grow.

> Both annual and perennial coreopsis species are loaded with tasty bird-attracting seeds.

Corn

Attracts red-winged blackbirds, buntings, cardinals, grackles, jays, juncos, pheasants, quail, sparrows, towhees, wild turkeys, woodpeckers

IF YOU'RE A budget-minded bird feeder, or if you're playing host to hordes of birds, offering cracked corn is an inexpensive way keep your birds happy. A 50-pound sack can cost as little as $3, depending on the grain market. Corn is near the top of the list for cardinals, jays, and woodpeckers, which eagerly seek out whole ears, whole kernels, or cracked kernels. Red-winged blackbirds and other blackbirds also flock to corn, as do grackles, pheasants, quail, starlings, towhees, and wild turkeys. Smaller seed eaters such as buntings, juncos, and sparrows naturally prefer the cracked variety because of their smaller beaks. And of course, those bushy-tailed squirrels and quick little chipmunks also adore corn.

Dry corn on the cob is cheap entertainment at the feeding station. Here, a red-bellied woodpecker works a neat vertical row.

With all these fans, it makes sense and cents to include corn in your feeder program. Use the whole ears, on spike feeders or suspended from hangers, to keep squirrels and woodpeckers happy. Feed shelled corn—whole kernels separated from the cob—in tray or hopper feeders for cardinals, crows, and jays. Fill low tray feeders with shelled or cracked corn to satisfy blackbirds, doves, game birds, and other ground feeders. Pour cracked corn into feeders, low or high, for buntings, juncos, towhees, and native sparrows. Decoy flocks of blackbirds, house sparrows, and starlings away from other feeders by providing plenty of cracked corn in an area separated from the main feeding station by shrubs or other visual barriers.

Because the hard shell is left intact, cob corn and whole kernel corn keep much longer than cracked corn. Cracked corn may become infested by meal moths and other pests or grow rancid because of its high fat content. Keep only about a month's supply of cracked corn on hand to avoid problems. Store in a tightly lidded can in a cool area. I like to keep a 50-pound sack in the trunk of my car during the winter: The cold storage is ideal, and the extra weight improves traction on slippery roads.

Before you start pouring out cracked corn with abandon, gauge how much your birds can eat at one sitting. Cracked corn can become a real mess if you spread a thick layer and it goes uneaten. It becomes a solid, moldy mass when it absorbs moisture from dew or rain or the soil itself. Cracked corn, however, can be a real lifesaver during severe storms because you can feed great quantities of birds at little cost by simply spreading it over the snow- or ice-covered ground. Should snow cover the corn, rake it into nearby flowerbeds or add it to the compost pile when you find it after the spring cleanup.

Growing Corn

For a fast-growing and attractive hedge that has great bird appeal, you can't beat common corn. Plant a triple row of the kernels, and within weeks, you'll have a knee-high boundary of waving green leaves. By summer's end, ears will be fattening, ready to feed cardinals, jays, woodpeckers, and other birds throughout the fall and winter.

Growing corn is as simple as sticking kernels into the ground with your thumb, about 4 inches apart, in a sunny patch of fertile soil. Mulch around the young stalks to keep weeds away, or interplant with scarlet runner beans, which will twine their way up the stems and attract hummingbirds with their rich red blossoms.

For a dramatic effect, you can plant Indian corn, with foliage that is streaked or tinted in reds and greens. Highly ornamental varieties are now available, with wide leaves swirled in a fantasy of red, white, yellow, and green stripes. And why stick to yellow kernels? Birds like colorful ears, too. Try 'Painted Mountain', the mini-eared 'Wampum' and 'Little Jewels', blue-kerneled 'Shaman's Blue', or burgundy 'Ruby Red'. Birds devour popcorn, too—right from the ear, not fluffed in a popper. Experiment by growing little, plump strawberry popcorn or other varieties. For easy eating, your birds will appreciate

a cultivar called 'Shorty', which tops out at 12 to 18 inches tall, offering its bountiful ears in easy reach of ground-feeding doves, pheasants, wild turkeys, and smaller birds.

Unpopped Only, Please

Stringing chains of popcorn sounds like the perfect approach to decorating an outdoor Christmas tree for the birds. Yet if you try it, you'll quickly find out that your handmade garland goes uneaten. That's because the popping process has exploded the meaty part of the kernel into a fluffy mass that the birds apparently find unappealing.

Instead of decorating for the birds with popped popcorn, hang ears of unpopped mini-corn such as golden 'Tom Thumb', which are just a few inches long, or strawberry-type popcorn ears. You'll find chickadees, jays, titmice, woodpeckers, and, of course, squirrels taking you up on your offering.

> For a fast-growing and attractive hedge that has great bird appeal, you can't beat common corn.

Corn Feeders

SQUIRRELS ADORE IT, woodpeckers welcome it, cardinals crave it—and it's one of the cheapest foods around. All those reasons make corn an ideal menu item at your feeding station. As another plus, a cob of corn offers entertainment value, too. It's great fun to watch squirrels figure out a revolving wheel of corn, and I hate to admit it, but even I smile at the sight of a squirrel sitting at its own little table-and-chair corn feeder, a popular wooden contraption that only looks tacky until you try it.

You can make a corn feeder with nothing more than a scrap of wood, a big nail, a couple of smaller nails, and a hammer. Drive the big nail through the wood, attach the plank to a vertical or horizontal

post with the smaller nails, shove an ear of corn onto the protruding nail, and *voila!* In less than 5 minutes, you have yourself a new corn feeder for both birds and squirrels—and you—to enjoy. (Don't be surprised if it takes even less time for the squirrels to strip the ear of corn down to the cob.)

Whole-Kernel Feeders

A sack of whole kernel corn removed from the cob is excellent, high-fat food for cardinals and woodpeckers. A wire-grid feeder such as those sold for nutmeats and peanuts is also perfect for offering whole-kernel corn. If you want to make your squirrels and chipmunks smile, you can also offer the kernels in a tray feeder.

Squirrel box feeders, which have a flip-top lid that the bushytails open themselves, are fine for feeding shelled corn. (See plans for building a squirrel box feeder on page 273.) Opening the lid will slow them down a bit so that they don't empty the entire feeder in just a few minutes. Plus, the very human look of the animals as they stand and use their paws and nose to wiggle open the lid makes for entertaining action at the feeding station.

Stock Up for Winter

Shop around for the best prices on whole corn and shelled corn. Rural feed stores usually beat bird-supply outlets by a mile. As usual, buying in bulk will bring you the best bargain. You can pay as much as $1 an ear for cob corn, or as little as $10 for 50 pounds—a winter's worth of feeding.

Keep a dozen ears or so in reserve in case of bad weather or increased traffic, but avoid buying much more corn than you can readily use within a few weeks or within a winter, if you live in a cold area. Because of its high oil content, corn is apt to turn rancid in warm weather. In my area, where winter temperatures usually stay below 40°F (sometimes well below!), the corn I stock up on in October is still fresh in February. Store your corn in a mouse-proof, squirrel-proof metal trash can.

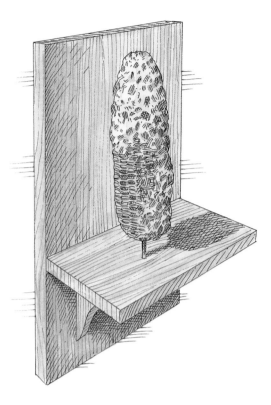

Recycle stripped corn cobs by spreading the cob with suet or peanut butter. Roll in nuts or other treats if you like. Then push the cob back onto its spike and watch for customers to arrive.

Commercial Corn Feeders

IN MY experience, the corn feeders you can buy are more complex, as befits their higher price, but I'm not sure that the birds notice the difference. Here's a rundown on what you'll find.

- One of the simplest is a wire coil into which you drop an ear of corn. Woodpeckers like to peck away at the kernels through the wires around the cob, and squirrels deftly extract the entire

ear and carry it away to their cache in the trees.

- Spike feeders abound in various configurations, from single-ear platforms to holders for multiple ears. It's harder for a squirrel to pull free the cob when it's shoved onto a spike, so they generally eat in place at these feeders instead of doing the old snatch-and-scamper routine.

- The mini table-and-chair setup is deservedly popular (with both squirrels and their human ob-

servers) and sells for $10 to $20 at bird-supply stores and home-town craft shows.

- Rotating feeders, which spin ears of corn like a carnival ride, will keep squirrels busy—and away from your high-priced seeds—for hours, plus they will give you a few good chuckles as you watch the determined varmints try to master the trick. Expect to pay $20 and up for a front-row seat at this squirrel carnival.

Cornmeal

Attracts doves, juncos, native sparrows, towhees, and other ground-feeding birds

HIGH IN FAT AND PROTEIN, cornmeal is the perfect foundation for bird-attracting recipes. It's impractical for feeding alone because it quickly absorbs moisture and becomes rancid if uneaten. You can try sprinkling cornmeal lightly over snow-covered ground for doves, juncos, native sparrows, towhees, and other ground-feeding birds.

Mix cornmeal with peanut butter to extend that expensive spread so that it serves more birds and slides down their gullets more easily. Combine the two at a 1:1 ratio and stuff into holes drilled in a section of 3- to 4-inch-diameter log. Use a heavy duty screw eye in one end of the log to hang it from a branch. This makes an easy feeder that's irresistible to chickadees, nuthatches, titmice, and woodpeckers.

You can also increase the proportion of cornmeal to peanut butter (approximately 2:1), and mix it with your hands until the mixture has the consistency of stiff cookie dough. The resulting "dough" is an ideal bluebird food to stock an open tray feeder. Experiment in your kitchen, combining cornmeal with one or more of the foods listed below in "Mix-and-Match Cornmeal Combos" to create custom-made treats that will appeal to many of your favorite feeder birds.

Mix-and-Match Cornmeal Combos

DEPENDING ON what you have around the house, you can whip up an array of treats by mixing cornmeal with a binding agent—something liquid or sticky—and other special tidbits.

Choose a binding agent from the first list to keep the treats sticking together, then add tidbits from the second list for extra bird appeal. Add enough cornmeal to the mix so that the end product is fairly stiff, like cookie dough, so birds can peck off small bits or pull out special tidbits without getting their head feathers greasy (which can inhibit the feathers' insulation qualities). Start with ¼ cup liquid fat to 2½ cups of cornmeal and 1 cup treats, and add more cornmeal if needed to stiffen the mix.

Binding agents: bacon grease, cool but still liquid; beef drippings; canola (rapeseed) oil; corn oil; peanut butter; peanut oil; suet, melted, cool but still liquid; sunflower oil

Special tidbits: acorn nutmeats, chopped; apples, chopped; bacon, cooked and crumbled; beef, cooked and finely chopped; currants; nuts, any kind, finely chopped; peanuts, chopped; pine nuts; raisins; suet, chopped

Watch your feeder birds' responses to each combination you try, and you'll quickly see which of your experiments finds the most favor with your feathered friends.

Cosmos

Attracts all kinds of seed-eating birds, such as cardinals, doves, goldfinches, sparrows

WE'RE SO USED TO THINKING of cosmos as a garden flower that it's hard to imagine it was once only a wildflower, splashing Mexico and the southern United States with warm orange, yellow, and pink blossoms. In the wild, as in the garden, this aster family member appeals to all kinds of seed-eating birds, from cardinals to doves to sparrows. Plant it in masses in full sun near your feeding station or outside your favorite window, where you can watch the crowds of birds that arrive to dine on its seeds. Look carefully to spot goldfinches, which blend in surprisingly well among the flowers and foliage. A bending stem is sometimes the only telltale clue to their presence.

Like other bird favorites, cosmos can stand all winter long in the garden. Even though this annual is killed off by frost, its ferny stems still provide shelter, and birds will work on its seedheads all through the winter months.

The seeds of both yellow, orange, or red cosmos (*C. sulphureus*) and pink, red, or white cosmos (*C. bipinnatus*) are yummy to birds. These heat-loving annual plants can take a long time to flower, a drawback in short-season areas, where they may just hit their peak when killing frost arrives. To encourage faster bloom, grow them in lean soil with no fertilizer.

Collect cosmos stems after the flowers go to seed and use them in outdoor wreaths for the birds. Some seed eaters will perch on the wreath to dine, while ground-feeding birds such as doves, sparrows, and towhees will congregate beneath the wreath, where they'll quickly clean up any dropped seeds. Birds are bound to miss some that fall to the ground, and those seeds will sprout the following spring to produce a new year's round of flowers and seeds.

A couple of dollars' worth of cosmos seed will yield a big patch of flowers. The seeds are especially popular with goldfinches and other seed-eating birds.

Crackers

Attract blackbirds, chickadees, crows, doves, jays, juncos, nuthatches, pigeons, titmice, sparrows, starlings, woodpeckers

POLLY WANT A CRACKER? Yep, and so do chickadees, doves, jays, juncos, nuthatches, titmice, sparrows, and woodpeckers. Feeder birds, including blackbirds, crows, pigeons, and starlings, quickly devour crumbled crackers.

You can offer commercial crackers of practically any sort at the feeder. Use your hands to break them into small bits that birds can easily nibble. Jays and starlings—and our rodent friends, including squirrels and chipmunks—will also snatch up whole crackers as a real prize. Serve crackers in small amounts because they quickly soak up moisture and become unappealing to all but the hungriest starlings.

For a quick and convenient way to use up bacon grease or beef drippings, crumble saltines into the liquid (but cooled) grease, and stir with a wooden spoon until the coarse cracker crumbs and pieces have soaked up the fat. Woodpeckers are particularly fond of these snacks at my feeders, with jays giving them stiff competition. Small native sparrows and juncos are quick to snatch up any yummy bits that fall to the ground during the larger birds' forays.

Putting out whole saltine crackers is also a good way to grab the attention of birds. When a frigid spell hits in early spring, I toss white saltines onto the ground. Hungry robins are quick to spot them.

> Woodpeckers are particularly fond of saltines crumbled into bacon grease or beef drippings.

Cranberries

Attract mockingbirds, robins, waxwings, Carolina wrens

OUR AVIAN FRIENDS don't appreciate the old-fashioned charm of cranberry garlands on the holiday tree. In my experience, birds rarely prefer these pretty fruits. When I switched from stringing cranberries to stringing grapes and dried cherries, the birds chorused their approval. Mockingbirds, robins, waxwings, and Carolina wrens all became regulars, pecking at the garland decorations until they were bare of fruit.

Fresh cranberries are so appealing to our eyes (and so reasonably priced) that you may want to experiment with the tastes of your own birds.

Birds do eat cranberries in baked goods, and I have discovered that mockingbirds and robins will turn to the dried cranberries at the feeder when no other fruit remains. One year the leftover dried cranberries in my fruit tray feeder enticed a migrating yellow-bellied sapsucker to stick around my area for 2 weeks.

I still scatter cranberries in my tray feeders now and then, especially in winter when natural fruit is scarce. But when it comes to handiwork with needle and thread, I've switched from cranberries to the more appreciated grapes. They are easier to string, too!

> Fresh cranberries are more appealing to our senses than to birds' tastes—they prefer grapes.

Crossbills

CROSSBILLS LOOK LIKE overgrown house finches, but there the similarity ends. These heavy-bodied reddish birds are indeed members of the finch family, but their slow, deliberate behavior is unlike the frantic flutterings of house finches, and their bills are the most bizarre among American songbirds.

A crossbill has a curved beak that looks more like a parrot's than a songbird's. The upper half of the pointed, conical bill crisscrosses the bottom, looking like a pair of misaligned scissors. This odd appendage gives the bird the perfect eating tool for its specialty: the seeds of pines, hemlocks, and other conifers. The bird holds open the scales of a cone with its strong beak, while it extracts the seed with its equally useful tongue.

Unpredictable is the rule when it comes to crossbills. Famed for their irregular jaunts as well as for their oddball bills, crossbills may stray far from their usual domiciles in winter. Although the **white-winged crossbill** usually resides in the pine woods of the North year-round and the **red crossbill** lives

Odd but efficient, the red crossbill's curved, overlapping bill gives these birds the perfect tool for extracting seeds from between the scales of cones.

in the North and West, in an irruption year the birds may wander as far as the Atlantic coast or the Southeast states in winter. (For more on irruptions, see Irruption Year on page 179.) It's an occasion when crossbills arrive at the feeder or in the yard. Their noisy eating habits are a wonder to watch, whether they're snapping sunflower seeds or ferreting seeds from a pinecone. Both species are very similar, with red males and yellow-olive females, but the white-winged crossbills sport a pair of bold white stripes on their black wings. If you ever get the chance to see the males of both species at the same time, you may notice that a red crossbill is a more saturated brick red than the pinker white-winged crossbill.

Crossbill Behavior

Crossbills usually travel in flocks, except during breeding season. They're gregarious birds and given to calling to each other while they fly or feed.

Crossbill acrobatics go along with their oddball eating utensils. Since conifer cones often dangle from the tips of branches, the birds are perfectly at ease maneuvering their bodies in an upside-down position to reach their dinner.

Like other northern finches, crossbills have a hearty appetite for salt. A salt block is a great way to attract their trade if your yard is short on pinecones or if you want to entice them to stay a little longer. Of course, if you have a brick house, you may want to reconsider this strategy because crossbills also relish the mortar between bricks. They seem to have quite a craving for the stuff, especially if it's old and crumbly. During an irruption year, I once watched a flock of 19 crossbills industriously pecking at the 100-year-old mortar of a historical bank building in Mt. Vernon, Indiana. They clung to the brick wall just a few feet from the rush of traffic, oblivious to everything but the task at hand: eating mortar. I wasn't at all surprised to see that corner of the building start to give way the following spring! Luckily, a new bank soon replaced it or who knows what the consequences of the crossbills' appetites might have been.

CROSSBILL FEEDER FOODS
▪ Pine nuts
▪ Salt
▪ Sunflower seeds

Crows and Ravens

EVERYBODY CAN IDENTIFY a crow. Big, black, and loud, crows patrol mall parking lots, feast in downtown restaurant dumpsters, and flock over open fields. Crows and their raven cousins figure largely in human legend as well. Every Native American tribe had its own name for these birds, and their avian intelligence often figured in myths and stories passed down through the ages.

Personality Plus

Crows are intelligent and playful. They tumble, dive, and swoop in the air together apparently for the sheer fun of it. They are also masterful thieves, snatching up any object that appeals to them. Although they are fearless, they are routinely wary and suspicious, and many have learned to stay beyond gun range from humans.

When I lived on the coast of Oregon, I watched ravens routinely steal fish from eagles and ospreys in mid-air or when perching. They would harass the eagle with loud cries and feinting attacks until the raptor dropped its prey, which the wily raven quickly snagged. Once the tables turned when a crow made the mistake of annoying a peregrine falcon that had just landed a duck. Without losing a wing beat, the big falcon turned on its attacker and dispatched him, too, with one lightning-fast strike of its legs and beak.

Big and Black

Biggest of the bunch, the **common raven** can reach an imposing 2 feet from beak to tail, as big as a great horned owl and bigger than a red-tailed hawk. Its strong wings stretch at least 4 feet wide. It's a year-round resident mainly from the Rockies to the Pacific, in the Far North, and much more rarely in the Appalachians. This bird has beautiful, glossy, jet black feathers. Its beak is big and thick, and it has a shaggy, almost swollen look at the throat that distinguishes it from the sleekness of crows. Its cries are low and hoarse. In the Southwest, the smaller **Chihuahuan raven,** which sports a white collar on the back of its neck that is visible when it dips its head, ranges in open farmland areas.

The **American crow** is a common bird over nearly all the country, except for a few arid regions of the Southwest. It is the largest of the crows at 17 inches. The more petite **fish crow** patrols along the eastern seaboard and Gulf, often in the company of American crows. Listen for its more nasal call to tell the two apart. In the Northwest, the appropriately named **northwestern crow** scavenges along the coast.

Feeder Behavior

Crows and ravens find their own food easily. They're omnivorous birds that take advantage of any banquet that presents itself, whether it's roadkill, ripe berries, grubs turned over by a plowing tractor, or stale hamburger buns at a fast food joint.

Usually crows and ravens keep their distance from human dwellings, stalking around the edges of the feeder area until hunger draws them closer. Smaller birds may disappear at first when crows or ravens arrive, but they soon return. The big birds routinely dine on the eggs and young of songbirds, but they pose no threat to adult birds. In fact, they can be a songbird's ally, setting up an alarm at the first sight of any danger.

Some people prefer not to entice these birds to their feeders, but I welcome them. They are fascinating to watch because they interact with each other more like humans than birds. You can almost watch the wheels turning in those bird brains.

Expect to be entertained when you offer new and different foods to a crow. The bird's quick wits are always evident, whether it is maneuvering strands of spaghetti into its beak or peeling a plastic wrapper from scraps scavenged from the neighborhood trash.

CROW AND RAVEN FEEDER FOODS
■ Bones with marrow or meat attached
■ Bread and baked goods
■ Corn, any kind
■ Dog food
■ Eggs, raw in shell, hard-boiled, or scrambled
■ Leftovers
■ Meat scraps
■ Pasta, cooked
■ Suet

Serve food to crows and ravens directly on the ground or in a low open tray feeder. If the birds are reluctant to approach your feeding station, lure them in by spreading eye-catching whole-kernel corn and tempting chunks of beef fat on the ground at the far end of your yard. Gradually move the offerings closer to your feeding area until the big birds are eating within view of your favorite window.

In winter, crows join together in large communal roosting areas that can include hundreds and even thousands of birds. Each morning they head out to forage for the day and return to rest in late afternoon. If the roost is in or near a town or city, the birds can become pests, upsetting trash cans, dirtying cars and sidewalks with droppings, and disturbing the peace with their loud, raucous voices. Some communities seek to dissuade the birds with noisemakers or the more permanent methods of poison or sharpshooting. The songbird laws don't protect these birds, and they often fall prey to target practice or end up as bagged birds during open hunting season.

Deer

Beautiful dark-eyed Bambi can be a real nuisance at the feeding station, causing just as much damage as he and his friends and family do in the garden. Instead of nibbling a mere handful of seeds over the course of the day, deer can vacuum your feeders to bare wood in just one short visit. And because bird-feeder design doesn't accommodate large animals, deer can damage the feeders as well as eat you out of 6 months' supply of birdseed.

If deer are only occasional visitors to your yard or if you enjoy watching them, you may want to set up a feeding station just for them. Of course, there's no way to put up a no-trespassing sign at other feeders. But by offering a bounty of their favorite foods, you may be able to keep them confined to an area apart from more fragile bird feeders. Corn, apples, and other goodies will keep them occupied. You can serve the food directly on the ground or in a sturdily built tray feeder. Deer will also regularly visit a salt block. Should deer run out of eats at their feeding station, they will devour millet, birdseed mix, and just about any other grain-based foods at your other feeders.

Keep in mind that deer are browsers. They nip off the twigs and tips of many garden plants and trees. If

The first deer at your feeders can be a thrill, but Bambi quickly wears out his welcome by devouring pounds of seed at a time. Fencing is the surefire solution.

DEER FEEDER FOODS
■ Acorns
■ American persimmons
■ Apples
■ Beech nuts
■ Bread and other baked goods
■ Cereal
■ Corn
■ Crackers
■ Salt

you invite deer to your yard, they may quickly become a nuisance and injure your treasured plantings. Unless you have a very large property where deer naturally dwell and can supply their food far away from favorite garden areas, it's probably best not to open the door to the potential problems they can cause.

To discourage deer permanently, you'll have to resort to the same methods that gardeners use. The only fail-safe solution is a high fence around your yard. High plastic netting is effective and much less expensive than wire or wood, and its dark color blends in with the background so that you hardly notice it. (See "Resources" on page 348 for sources.) Tie strips of white cloth to the fence at first, so that deer don't blunder into it accidentally. A dog is also a great deterrent to deer. Some folks recommend other home remedies such as scattering bundles of human hair, hanging bars of soap, or spreading dried blood around the property—give them a try if you like.

An interesting low-tech solution to deer at the feeder is to fill your feeders with seed treated with capsaicin, the fiery stuff of hot peppers. Birds don't mind the substance in the least, but mammals are sensitive to the burning effects and will only eat pepper-coated seed as a last resort. The Birdseed (page 33) and Hot Peppers (page 162) entries have more details on capsaicin-treated seed.

Diary

By KEEPING A DIARY of feeder happenings, you'll soon have a record that allows you to compare menu choices and how they are affected by season or weather. You'll also have a better idea of what birds to expect at your feeder as the seasons progress. But apart from the educational data of a diary, keeping a daily or weekly bird-feeding journal is just plain fun.

My diary is a hodgepodge of all kinds of details. Some days, the entry is only a quick note of weather, plus a bare-bones list of which birds were eating breakfast at the feeders. On chattier days, the diary includes notes on behavior ("Tufted titmouse whistling 'Peter' as he approached feeder—spring must be getting closer"). I like to note plumage changes as birds brighten up for breeding season or switch to winter wear, and I often include quick sketches. When I dream up a new recipe, I note it in the diary along with the results! I tape in snapshots and clippings, too. On red-letter days when a fox sparrow or other special bird turns up, I switch to bright marker pens to highlight the occasion.

A bird-feeder diary is almost as good for daydreaming as a seed catalog. In the gray days of winter, I like to re-read my entries from late spring—I can almost hear the buzz of hummingbird wings and smell the oranges the oriole was eating then. And in sultry summer, reading about juncos scratching in the snow serves as a quick reminder of cooler days ahead.

> A bird-feeder diary is almost as good for midwinter daydreaming as a seed catalog!

Dog Food

Attracts blackbirds, crows, jays, mockingbirds, robins, thrashers, thrushes, starlings, Carolina wrens

MOISTENED DRY DOG FOOD is a fine facsimile for the natural soft foods eaten by jays, mockingbirds, robins, thrashers, thrushes, Carolina wrens, and other birds. Inexpensive brands, usually based on corn or other grain products fortified with protein are particularly serviceable. A shallow tray of such food placed at ground level will draw customers, especially in the wintertime when natural substitutes are scarce.

Moistened dog food is also the perfect decoy for luring blackbirds, crows, jays, starlings, and other plentiful, pesky feeder visitors away from more expensive foods for which they compete with less aggressive birds. Dry dog food, unsoftened by water, may also be tempting to chipmunks, squirrels, and other furry visitors.

To serve dog food, fill an old cafeteria tray or serving tray with the kibble, then add warm water—about one-third the volume of the dog food (experiment until you find the right amount of liquid). Aim for soft but not soggy dog food bites, so that birds can easily pick them up in their beaks.

Opossums and raccoons also appreciate dog food, and these nighttime visitors can extend your hours of viewing pleasure at the feeding station. Position a garden light or small spotlight so that you will be able to see the customers in the dark. A motion-sensor light is practical and energy-saving, and your after-hours dog-food diners will soon become accustomed to feeding in the pool of light it casts. (See Opossums on page 221 and Raccoons on page 237 for more about these mammals and their visits to your bird feeders.)

> Inexpensive dry dog food (usually based on corn) makes a fine substitute for birds' usual soft foods.

D

Dogwood

Attracts bluebirds, catbirds, flickers, grosbeaks, mockingbirds, robins, tanagers, thrushes, vireos, waxwings, woodpeckers, and others

IF YOU'RE LUCKY ENOUGH to live near a dogwood-filled forest, you can collect (with permission, of course) one of the best-loved bird foods for fall and winter feeding. Bluebirds, grosbeaks, tanagers, thrushes, vireos, waxwings, woodpeckers, and hosts of other birds adore red, shiny dogwood berries. Once a horde descends on a tree, a few dozen birds can strip it bare in just a few hours.

When you find a tree loaded with berries, gather a few handfuls into a resealable plastic bag and store them in the freezer. Later, string the berries to decorate evergreens or a discarded Christmas tree, or you can offer them in an open tray feeder. In winter, when the berries are long gone from local trees, bluebirds, catbirds, flickers, grosbeaks, mockingbirds, robins, and downy woodpeckers will adore the treat.

Because a dogwood tree tends to attract large flocks of robins, it's a good place to look for albinism, a fairly common occurrence among robins. Watch for birds with white feathers on wings, body, or head. You may even see an entirely white bird. (See Albinism on page 4 for more.)

Flowering Dogwood and Friends

Flowering dogwood (*Cornus florida*) is a superb small tree for a partly shaded site through Zone 5. Other lesser-known dogwoods are just as popular with birds, although they seem to be a well-kept secret among gardeners. Many species are available, including pale dogwood (*C. obliqua*) and redosier dogwood (*C. sericea*), two shrubby dogwoods that make fine windbreaks or cover strips at feeding stations and bear clusters of stemmed fruits that are eagerly stripped by birds. Native dogwoods are often sold at extremely reasonable prices by state departments of natural resources or through county extension offices.

Another good reason to experiment with lesser-known dogwoods is the unfortunate affliction known as "dogwood blight," which is shortening the lives of

Dogwood berries ripen in fall, tempting migrating tanagers and grosbeaks. You may not recognize the birds at first, dressed in their drab winter plumage.

flowering dogwoods in the wild and in the garden. This disease quickly saps the tree's vigor and can kill it within a few years. Flowering dogwoods that are already stressed by other conditions—drought, poor drainage, all-day sun—seem to fall victim more easily than plants in better sites and conditions. Nurseries are doing what they can to stop the spread of the problem from the eastern part of the country by selling uninfected trees that have passed inspection.

Because this dogwood is a beautiful asset to the yard and such a hit with birds, it's worth a try, but plant other species for backup. Settle *C. florida* in a partly shaded site, similiar to the natural open woods where it usually grows, instead of in the middle of your sunny yard. Amend the soil by digging in lots of humus, which you can make yourself from composted fall leaves or buy in bags. Water regularly when rain is scarce for at least the first 2 years after planting. Mulch around it to avoid damaging the bark with a lawn mower, which opens the way to disease.

Dogwoods of Distinction

MANY NATIVE dogwoods (*Cornus* spp.) bear fruit that attracts birds. Most of these North American natives are shrubs with casual growth habits and easily overlooked flowers, although the list also includes a beautiful ground-covering perennial and a western tree similar to the popular and showy flowering dogwood of the eastern states. Try a regionally suited choice from this list, or explore other natives in your area. A field guide to trees and shrubs will help you locate a suitable choice, or you can check with a nearby nature center or native plant specialist to get recommendations for your region.

Dogwood	Description	Range and Hardiness
Pagoda dogwood (*C. alternifolia*)	Deciduous tree, about 20 feet tall, or large shrub; also called green osier. It has a flat-topped, tiered habit like its pagoda namesake and creamy yellow flowers followed by black berries.	Eastern native; hardy to Zone 3
Roughleaf dogwood (*C. asperifolia*)	Large deciduous shrub with beautiful blue berries; a tall variety *C. asperifolia* var. *drummondii* may grow to the size of a small tree and has white berries.	Prairie native with range extending into the Southeast; hardy to Zone 6
California dogwood (*C. californica*)	Deciduous shrub with dark red bark and white berries; considered a hybrid (*C.* × *californica*) of western dogwood (*C. occidentalis*) and redosier dogwood (*C. sericea*) by some taxonomists	Western native; hardy to Zone 8
Bunchberry (*C. canadensis*)	Low-growing groundcover perennial with whorled leaves topped by typical flowering dogwood blossom followed by clusters of red berries	Native to northern North America; hardy to Zone 2
Flowering dogwood (*C. florida*)	Small deciduous tree with large white flowers on graceful branches and red berries in fall; avoid planting in areas where "dogwood blight" is prevalent (check with local cooperative extension office).	Native in the East to Southeast; hardy to Zone 5
Pacific or mountain dogwood (*C. nuttallii*)	Small tree similar to flowering dogwood (*C. florida*) but often has a greenish tinge to the creamy flowers; orange-red berries in fall	Western native; hardy to Zone 7
Pale dogwood (*C. obliqua*)	Deciduous shrub to 12 feet tall, of loose, open habit; great in hedges, mixed with evergreens; has clusters of small white flowers followed by white to pale blue berries	Native to eastern North America; hardy to Zone 4
Western dogwood (*C. occidentalis*)	Deciduous shrub or occasionally small tree; has white berries in summer; western counterpart of redosier dogwood	Western native; hardy to Zone 6
Redosier dogwood (*C. sericea*)	Deciduous, suckering shrub, ideal in a hedgerow or as an informal patch of shelter; good with a background of evergreens to show off the red color of young stems; 'Bailey' is a nonspreading selection. If you cut this back to ground level in early spring to encourage new shoots for good winter color, you'll sacrifice the clusters of small white berries that birds find appealing.	Native to eastern North America; hardy to Zone 2

Doughnuts

Attract chickadees, jays, titmice, and other feeder birds

AH, TO EAT LIKE A BIRD, consuming huge quantities of high-fat foods with never a care for extra calories! The supercharged metabolism of feathered creatures quickly burns a caloric intake that would make couch spuds out of us slower-paced humans. Doughnuts are just one of the fattening foods that birds can safely enjoy. They're favorites of chickadees, jays, titmice and other feeder birds.

Plain doughnuts or doughnut holes, without the coating of powdered sugar that is only an impediment to bird beaks, are the best choice for feeders. Your local bakery or doughnut shop may be willing to reserve any unsold plain doughnuts to sell to you at a reduced price. Ask for dense "cake" doughnuts rather than the yeast-raised glazed type.

Feed doughnuts in a wire suet basket or other container that allows birds to peck at them but prevents chunks from falling to the ground. You can also stick doughnuts on a spike nail, but be prepared for wholesale thievery by jays, squirrels, and starlings. These birds may grasp the treat and fly away with as much of it as they can handle.

> Plain "cake" doughnuts, without a glaze or powdered sugar coating, are the best choices for birds.

Doves

QUIET COOING VOICES and gentle demeanor make doves a welcome sight at the feeder. We often observe these symbols of romance in pairs during the breeding season, which may last all year in warm-winter areas. In cold areas, or when not paired off for nesting, small or large flocks may show up at the feeder to partake of small grain or other feeder foods or to devour berries from backyard plantings.

In every part of the continental United States, you can hear the melancholy cooing of the **mourning dove.** This is the most common native dove, instantly recognizable by its extremely long, tapering tail. The **rock dove,** otherwise known and often scorned as the pigeon, is actually an introduced species that did not exist naturally in America; French explorers brought the bird to these shores almost four centuries ago.

The large **band-tailed pigeon,** which frequents western conifer and oak woods is a lesser-known native dove with a more limited range and a smaller population. When I lived on the coast of Oregon, it was always a surprise to come upon a band of "pigeons" feasting on red elderberry fruits. I thought of

Locally common in western woods, the band-tailed pigeon is big and beautiful. These birds often travel in small groups from one food source to another.

pigeons as city birds, and it took a while to become accustomed to the presence of this woods-loving species. In the Southwest and Texas, the **white-winged dove** is abundant here and there. Its flashy

D

The white-winged dove of the Southwest and Gulf states has a mournful cooing song. In flight, it flashes big white wing patches and white tail corners.

white wing patches make the bird easy to identify. The patches are visible as bars when the bird perches and appear as wide bands when the bird flies.

Two rarities, the **red-billed pigeon** of southern Texas and the **white-crowned pigeon** of the Florida Keys, may occasionally show up at feeders or in gardens in those areas.

Dove Behavior

Doves may look calm and relaxed when feeding, but they can take off like a rocket should they be-come alarmed—which is frequently. The birds seem to be particularly quick to react to any danger, real or imagined. When a group of doves is feeding, watch to see how birds take turns acting as sentry. Without a sound, they pass the duty from one to another, so that the majority of the group can eat greedily while the appointed bird keeps watch.

Doves are ground feeders, though they will visit a raised feeder if seed is not available at lower levels. They do best with a sturdy, open or roofed tray feeder, where their large bodies can find a secure place to stand and peck. Often they will glean dropped seed below high feeders. Offer seed in a low tray feeder or in small quantities directly on the ground. Doves are also quick to patronize a salt block.

If weeding is a garden chore you'd like to do less of—and who wouldn't?—encourage the presence of doves at your feeder and in your backyard. The birds consume massive amounts of weed seeds.

DOVE FEEDER FOODS

- Acorns
- Bread and other soft foods (rock dove)
- Bread crumbs
- Buckwheat
- Cactus fruits and seeds
- Corn, whole or cracked
- Elderberries (*Sambucus* spp.), fresh or dried
- Millet
- Milo
- Nuts
- Peas, dried
- Salt
- Weed seeds
- Wheat

Bygone Birds

HAD YOU lived east of the Mississippi River 200 years ago, you would have witnessed stupendous flights of **passenger pigeons**. They flew from feeding to roosting grounds in flocks numbering millions of birds—so many that they reportedly made the sky turn dark for 3 days on end when passing.

Traveling in such large flocks, these birds were easy targets for hunters who shot and clubbed the birds for their meat.

As careless foresting and hunting to supply local markets took an early toll on the population, the expansion of the railroad brought further disaster to the species. Once the railroad could provide easy transportation east, the hunting of passenger pigeons increased in fervor. Although mass hunting stopped as the species declined in numbers and made the marketing less profitable, the remaining birds did not reproduce sufficiently to resurrect the species. It is not clear why the final birds were unable to survive but the impact humanity had on the species was insurmountable.

Drawing Birds

EVEN IF THEY END UP looking more like Woodstock from the Peanuts cartoon strip than the cardinal in your tree, the pleasure you get out of drawing your feeder guests is the main reason for picking up a pencil in the first place.

There are other good reasons for drawing birds. When you want to identify an unfamiliar bird but don't have your field guide nearby, it takes virtually no artistic skill at all to make a basic bird shape. Then, you can label it with features you want to remember when you get back to a field guide: "about the size of a sparrow," or "two white bars on the wings," or "reddish brown under tail." You'll be surprised at how helpful such notes and sketches are when you try to identify the bird later.

I keep a drawing pad near my feeder window to capture the kinds and behaviors of birds that come to visit the feeder. A few quick lines and I have a record of how a tufted titmouse bends its body to whack open a sunflower seed or of how a robin leans back to pull out a worm. I note the date, and I have a record of who was there when, what they ate, as well as a pleasant visual reminder of their visit. Then I like to page through the notebook after a few months and relive those glimpses of bird life I was privileged to oversee.

The best way I have found to improve at drawing birds is to just do it. You don't need any special equipment: a pencil, eraser, and paper will do just

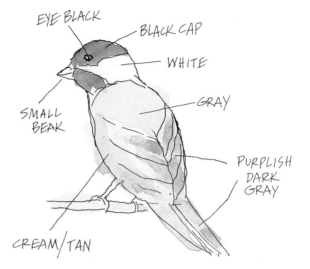

A quick sketch lets you "capture" feeder visitors for later ID, in case the bird doesn't linger. Note all the details you can on your drawing.

fine for starters. The more you draw, the more your sparrows will look like sparrows, and your jays like jays. You'll soon find yourself paying attention to the postures each bird typically assumes and to the way a leg bends or a wing unfolds. Drawing birds not only makes you a better artist, it also makes you a better bird watcher. It's also a soothing activity that leaves you feeling calm and refreshed.

E

Eagles

NEVER DISCOUNT THE POSSIBILITY of any bird at all showing up at a feeding station. Granted, an eagle is not apt to greet you unless you are regularly offering whole fish or ready-to-eat mammals, but unusual visitors do drop in. If you live in eagle country, such as the western states, a spread of unusual "feeder treats" placed far from the house may draw one of the big birds to your property.

If you have a poultry farm in your area, cheap chicken parts may draw the bird of your dreams. A chicken farm I frequently drove past years ago on my way to Hawk Mountain Sanctuary in Kempton, Pennsylvania, spread leftovers from the processing onto their fields. This unusual feeding station attracted dozens of red-tailed hawks, an occasional rough-legged hawk, and, lo and behold, sometimes a bald eagle! Here in southwest Indiana, where bald eagles gather along the Wabash and Ohio Rivers in winter, I came upon a young eagle sitting smack-dab in the middle of a four-lane highway, dining on a white-tailed deer that had met its fate in traffic. When I pulled my car off the road, the eagle glared fiercely at me for several minutes, then returned to his dinner.

Regal and deliberate, the bald eagle is not apt to become your everyday feeder guest—unless you live near water where the bird can find fish.

Eagle ID

Identifying an eagle is fairly easy because no other hawk approaches the size of these gigantic birds, which stand almost 3 feet tall with a wingspan approaching 7 feet. Only the turkey vulture comes close in size, but it tilts its wings in a V when soaring while both the bald and golden eagles hold their wings flat out, often with the feathers spread at the tips like our fingers.

The **bald eagle**, official symbol of the United States, ranges across nearly the whole country in winter, except for the Southwest. This huge bird usually sweeps its way over rivers and lakes and along coastlines or sits perched near a body of water. That's because its main menu item is fish, rounded out with the occasional duck or small mammal (plus roadkill). In winter, bald eagles tend to gather in numbers at good fishing spots.

Golden eagles are less common than bald eagles, except in the West and Southwest, but they may occur anywhere in the country because their diet is more varied. They eat mostly rodents (rabbits, marmots, and prairie dogs) but they will take anything they can kill, including full-size antelope and deer.

When eagles are young, it's hard to tell the species apart. Both are dark brown with blotchy white showing beneath the wings and at the base of the tail. It takes eagles a few years to acquire either a golden sheen or a shining white head and tail.

EAGLE FEEDER FOODS
■ Fish, uncooked
■ Meat scraps, raw
■ Poultry innards
■ Poultry parts
■ Suet, large chunks

Earthworms

Attract robins and other thrushes

ROBINS ARE THE NUMBER-ONE nemesis of these protein-packed wigglers, although other birds, including thrushes, may also dine on earthworms. A subterranean crowd of earthworms will thrive in healthy soil that is high in organic matter. Compost piles are also terrific worm habitat because these superb decomposers dine on decaying vegetable matter. Worms also favor mulched beds, with moist, dark soil protected by layers of chopped leaves, grass clippings, or other organic mulch.

Watch a robin search for worms in your lawn, and you'll gain new respect for the food-finding skills of birds. Experts once believed that the birds could hear the movements of the worms in their earthen burrows, but now it is known that a robin's-eye view is the perfect vantage point for actually seeing worms at work. As the robin cocks its head for a better look, it fixes the point of the worm. One quick beak thrust, a determined drag, and the worm is down the hatch. When you see a robin with a bill full of squirming earthworms, you know a nest is nearby.

Boost your earthworm population by avoiding toxic lawn chemicals and by layering as much organic matter as you can find on garden beds. Anything that is or was once plant material is

The quintessential early birds, robins prize juicy earthworms. Compost, mulch, and organic matter boost the wiggler population and make the hunt a cinch.

fair game, including grass clippings, straw, manure, cardboard boxes, pizza boxes, and newspaper. If your worms are in short supply, you can buy worms at a bait shop or from mail-order sources.

Eggs and Eggshells

Attract chickadees, crows, game birds, grackles, jays, juncos, magpies, purple martins, starlings, house and native sparrows, ravens

IF YOU YEARN FOR PURPLE MARTINS but have had no luck attracting these persnickety birds to your ready-and-waiting martin house, try eggshells. A scattering of crushed white shells on a low tray or directly on open lawn is extremely tempting to these birds and many others, from game birds to native sparrows and

chickadees. Eggshells supply the grit necessary to keep a bird's food-grinding gizzard in fine fettle, and they supply calcium in the diet. To prepare the shells for birds, use a rolling pin to crush the saved, dry shells between two sheets of waxed paper until the particles are moderately fine but not powder.

A parent bird engaging in nest cleaning may drop stray eggshells in your yard, or shell fragments may also tell the story of a less benign event. Some birds, including crows, grackles, jays, and ravens, prey on the young or eggs of other birds, stealing eggs from any nest they can find. They crack the egg to reach the nutritious yolk and white inside. It may seem cannibalistic, but eggs provide nutrients just like other foods do. In fact, many birds will gladly accept cooked eggs as part of the feeder menu. Jays, magpies, house sparrows, and starlings favor leftover scrambled or hard-cooked eggs and juncos or native sparrows may nibble on them as well. Offer the leftovers from your egg dishes in an open tray feeder or directly on the ground.

> Eggs provide nutrients just like other foods do, and eggshells add needed calcium to a bird's diet.

Evergreens

Attract many kinds of birds throughout the year

THE POPULARITY of blue spruces several decades ago was a real boon for birds. If you have one of these giant Christmas trees in your front yard (or smack against the front of your house), keep an eye on it at dusk and in bad weather, and you'll discover that it is a favored roost and nesting site for many birds. The dense branches and prickly needles keep the birds safe from skulking cats and hawks. In fact, it's landscape spruces that get part of the credit for the blanketing of America by the house finch. Using the trees for nesting sites, the birds managed to colonize the Great Plains, a last bastion between the western and eastern populations of the birds.

A chipping sparrow tends its nest within the dense, prickly branches of a needled evergreen. Broad-leaved evergreens also provide places to nest and roost.

Make an evergreen, or two or three, your first choice when adding plants to make your yard more bird-friendly. All evergreens provide shelter for birds, and most are also good food plants. Unlike deciduous plants, they offer birds year-round protection. They are perfect as windbreaks, which protect your feeding area from chilling gusts and blowing snow and rain. A hedge of evergreens offers exactly the kind of cover birds seek when moving from one place to another, as well as a gathering spot where they can hang out when not foraging.

Think Native

No need to look to Siberia or Japan for rare specimens: The best candidates for bird-attracting evergreens are right in your backyard. Native birds have evolved along with native plants that offer them food when they need it and appropriate shelter that stands up to local foul-weather conditions. From a gardener's point of view, native plants are also ideal.

You won't need to fuss with soil improvements, fertilizer, extra watering, or winter protection because the plants will thrive naturally in your climate.

Topping a long list of good evergreens is the pine, a genus that includes plants for almost every part of the country. Only in the treeless prairies and some deserts are native pines absent. Along with oaks, pines

(*continued on page 92*)

Native Evergreens for Birds

ALL EVERGREENS provide good bird shelter, and many are tops for food, too. Satisfy your landscaping needs and the food and shelter needs of local birds at the same time with some smart choices from among the many native evergreen species that are available.

Evergreen	Food for
Firs (*Abies* spp.)	Chickadees, Clark's nutcrackers, crossbills, grouse, magpies, nuthatches, sapsuckers
Manzanitas (*Arctostaphylos* spp.)	Evening grosbeaks, grouse, jays, mockingbirds, fox sparrows
Salal (*Gaultheria shallon*)	Blue grouse, spruce grouse, band-tailed pigeons, wrentits
Huckleberries (*Gaylussicia* spp.)	Bobwhites, catbirds, crossbills, pine grosbeaks, grouse, jays, orioles, quail, tanagers, towhees, wild turkeys
Hollies (*Ilex* spp.)	Bluebirds, catbirds, mourning doves, flickers, grouse, jays, mockingbirds, phoebes, quail, robins, sapsuckers, white-throated sparrows, thrashers, thrushes, towhees, wild turkeys, vireos, waxwings
Junipers (*Juniperus* spp.)	Bluebirds, catbirds, Clark's nutcrackers, crossbills, purple finches, flickers, grosbeaks, jays, mockingbirds, band-tailed pigeons, quail, robins, sapsuckers, Townsend's solitaires, starlings, thrashers, thrushes, wild turkeys, yellow-rumped warblers, cedar waxwings
Magnolias (*Magnolia* spp.)	Sapsuckers, towhees, vireos, woodpeckers
Bayberries, wax myrtles (*Myrica* spp.)	Bluebirds, bobwhites, bushtits, catbirds, chickadees, crows, flickers, boat-tailed grackles, grouse, meadowlarks, mockingbirds, phoebes, starlings, tree swallows, scarlet tanagers, brown thrashers, hermit thrushes, titmice, towhees, wild turkeys, vireos, yellow-rumped warblers, red-bellied woodpeckers, red-cockaded woodpeckers, Carolina wrens
Spruces (*Picea* spp.)	Chickadees, crossbills, pine grosbeaks, grouse, red-breasted nuthatches, pine siskins, cedar waxwings
Pines (*Pinus* spp.)	Bobwhites, chickadees, Clark's nutcrackers, brown creepers, crossbills, mourning doves, ground doves, house finches, purple finches, flickers, goldfinches, blue grouse, spruce grouse, grosbeaks, jays, juncos, magpies, nuthatches, band-tailed pigeons, pine siskins, yellow-bellied sapsuckers, brown thrashers, titmice, towhees, wild turkeys, myrtle warblers, pine warblers, red-bellied woodpeckers, Carolina wrens
Rhododendrons (*Rhododendron* spp.)	Grouse, hummingbirds (nectar)

GARDEN DESIGN

An Evergreen Combo for the Birds and You

Think of an evergreen, and the first plant that comes to mind is likely to be a "Christmas tree"—a pine (Pinus *spp.*), spruce (Picea *spp.*), fir (Abies *spp.*), balsam (Abies balsimea), or other conifer. These trees and their relatives have needlelike leaves, which may be short and prickly, like firs, or long and graceful, like pines. With few exceptions—including larch (Larix *spp.*) and dawn redwood (Metasequoia glyptostroboides)—all conifers are evergreen.

But not all evergreens are conifers. The magnificent live oaks (Quercus virginiana) of the South and the West, the rhododendrons (Rhododendron *spp.*) around your front door, and many other fabulous bird plants hold their leaves all year, making them invaluable for shelter from the storm. Their overlapping leaves work like roof shingles to keep rain from reaching the birds perched beneath the foliage.

A mixed planting of conifers and broad-leaved evergreens makes your yard look more interesting than a group of either kind alone. Combining the textures, shapes, and colors of these plants can be such a pleasure that you may find yourself with a new hobby as an evergreen connoisseur—or at least with a new garden bed for your collection. Keep in mind that, as with other shrubs and trees, an isolated specimen is less useful than a group of plants, both to birds and for garden appeal, although a mature pine or other evergreen will definitely attract birds by its sheer size and the bounty of food it produces. The plants listed for this garden will grow to fill a 30 × 40-foot space, so plan accordingly, or choose fewer plants (or more) to suit your space requirements.

PLANT LIST

1. Hemlocks (*Tsuga* spp.)
2. Oregon grape holly (*Mahonia aquifolium*)
3. Bayberries (*Myrica* spp.)
4. Bearberry (*Arctostaphylos uva-ursi*)

are favored as food by more birds and animals than practically any other plant. A long list of songbirds and game birds seek out the seeds from species such as pitch pine (*Pinus rigida*) and white pine (*P. strobus*) in the Northeast; slash pine (*P. elliottii*), longleaf pine (*P. palustris*), loblolly pine (*P. taeda*), and scrub pine (*P. virginiana*) in the Southeast; and lodgepole pine (*P. contorta*) and Ponderosa pine (*P. ponderosa*) in the West—and that's just a sampling from among 30-plus native species.

The evergreens at your local garden center may or may not include natives, but since local plants typically go unappreciated in their own backyard, it's more likely that the evergreens for sale will include rhododendrons, Chinese hollies (*Ilex cornuta*), and yews (*Taxus* spp.)—mostly nonnatives. It may take a bit of work to ferret out native plants for your area, but the extra effort is worth it. A privately owned nursery or garden center is usually happy to order plants for you. Or you can go to mail-order sources. Check also with the

Many birds seek out pines for their seed-laden cones. Some birds' beaks are specially adapted for extracting pine nuts from the cones.

cooperative extension office in your area: Many state offices sell native plants raised in their nurseries at bargain prices. Stick with natives that are adapted to your climate and your native birds, and you can't go wrong. Consult a reference book or local nature center for plant recommendations for your area.

Falcons

WHEN YOU ENTICE many smaller birds to your yard, you may be inadvertently issuing an invitation to birds of prey, which will gladly come to the party. Falcons are one of the types of raptors that may arrive to dine. Swift fliers, they are skilled at following the desperate twisting, turning flight of their avian prey, usually nabbing the bird in midair with a hard strike that snaps its neck.

Smallest of the falcons, and most likely to frequent a bird-feeder area, is the **American kestrel.** This elegant species has a streamlined body, long pointed wings, and snazzy black sideburns. Females are rich chestnut brown marked with subtle mottling. Males have blue-gray wings that set off the warm tones. About the size of mourning doves, these birds often perch on roadside wires and posts, where they keep a keen eye on the ground below for stirrings of grasshoppers, rodents, or small birds.

Falcon Behavior

The American kestrel's nickname is "sparrow hawk," which gives you a good idea of the size prey this bird will seek near your feeders. Juncos and other ground-feeding species are frequent targets, but any bird that lags behind its brethren when the hawk attacks may fall to its clutches. Although watching the food chain in action can be disturbing, take comfort in knowing that the force of the falcon's strike usually dispatches its prey instantly. The kestrel usually carries off its prey to pluck and eat elsewhere, generally on a high perch.

The dramatically large **peregrine falcon** was once

Its sideburns identify the elegant American kestrel, a small falcon. In summer, the kestrel eats grasshoppers and rodents; in winter, it targets small birds.

FALCON FOODS

- Chickadees
- Goldfinches
- Juncos
- Mice
- Mourning doves
- Pigeons
- Quail
- Siskins
- House sparrows
- Native sparrows
- Starlings
- Voles

so rare that it was unthinkable to consider it a possible threat to feeder birds. But now that reintroduction programs have brought peregrines back to the scene, the bird may occasionally dart through a backyard in the city or countryside to grab a feathered bite of fast food. While the kestrel seeks out small birds, the much larger peregrine goes for the big prey. In the wild, it's famed as the "duck hawk," but should it choose to focus on your feeder, it will seek pigeons, doves, and starlings for its main course—although it dines on smaller birds, too. The peregrine may devour its dinner on the ground, protecting its catch by drooping its wings to form a cloak or "mantle."

Interestingly, bird feeders in cities have the advantage for peregrine visits. Originally cliff dwellers in wild places, these big falcons have adapted to the "cliffs" of skyscrapers and other edifices in our American cities. As the peregrine population improves, city pigeons may become less of a nuisance.

Fall Feeding

FALL USHERS in the prime season at backyard feeding stations. Migrating birds arrive from points north, stopping to spend a day—or three— restocking their bodies with the calories they burned on the long flight. Goldfinches and grosbeaks are among the early crowd. The yellow "wild canaries" are a sure bet to pack the perches of tube feeders filled with niger seed, while the grosbeaks are a distinct possibility for lunch-time customers at the sunflower tray. You'll want to make sure you have plenty of high-fat foods on hand for these hungry travelers.

Feeder visitors vary with the seasons. In fall, you are likely to be treated to visits from family groups or small flocks of blue jays and other species.

As birds that overwinter in your area move in, they'll spend a while foraging in fields and wild areas to feast on seeds before they settle into winter territories and become regulars at your feeding station again. When you spot the first tree sparrow at a feeder, it's a sure sign that the rest of the crowd won't be far behind.

What to Watch For

You may not recognize some of the birds at your feeders in the fall—at least, not at first. Many male birds change clothes after the spring/summer breeding season, taking on colors that are similar to the female's and a far cry from their bright breeding plumage. Leaf through your field guide to familiarize yourself with the fall dress of blackbirds, bobolinks, orioles, tanagers, and other birds. Also study the pictures of immature birds, which may be making an appearance at the feeders as well.

Many birds will visit your feeders in groups of the same species, instead of singly or in pairs, as is more typical in breeding seasons. As the weeks go by, you'll see the numbers of each kind of bird rise and fall as the migrants arrive and then depart.

As the weather turns cold, the traffic at suet feeders is likely to become a waiting line. Because suet feeders are so small and don't result in much litter, I put up as many as I can squeeze in.

Be sure to keep an eye on your garden as well as on your feeders in fall. Those gone-to-seed flowers and weeds you left standing are a prime target for migrating birds, as are shrubs and trees that sport bright berries. Ground-feeding migratory birds, such as blackbirds and sparrows, may sift through leaves and mulch in your garden in search of fallen seed.

One of my favorite fall activities is to listen to birds flying overhead at night. Many songbirds migrate under the protection of darkness to avoid hawks, which fly by day. If you listen carefully, you can hear their quiet calls and chip notes filtering from the sky overhead. When I hear many birds passing over during the night, I make it a point to be outside at the crack of dawn, even before the sun rises. That's when birds drop from the sky to find food and resting places for the day. One morning, my son and I watched dozens of Baltimore orioles

10 To-Dos for Fall

1. Thoroughly clean all your feeders. Repair any loose perches, weak corners, and other structural points; rickety feeders that may have held up to light summer traffic need to be in tip-top shape for the busy season.

2. Invest in new feeders: You can never have too many! Try buying a suet feeder, nut feeder, or another specialty type that you don't already have.

3. If you live in an area where freezing weather doesn't arrive until late fall, set up an oriole feeder for nectar-drinking woodpeckers and other larger birds.

4. Clean out your birdseed storage bins. Inspect remaining stored seed. If you find seed that's infested with insects, discard it on the compost pile. Stock storage containers with fresh seed, usually available at bargain prices after the farm harvest season.

5. Replace old suet with fresh blocks or chunks.

6. Freshen the mulch beneath your feeders. Spread a 2-inch thick layer of wood chips or bark mulch over the area where seeds and hulls usually fall.

7. Plant new shrubs and trees. Find spots for them near your feeder area. Check the regional lists of bird-friendly trees and shrubs in Landscaping on page 184 to see which plants are recommended for your area.

8. Collect ripe berries of holly (*Ilex* spp.), sumac (*Rhus* spp.), and other shrubs, as well as weed seeds, flower seeds, and nuts and acorns for the feeders. It's fun to use these treats to bring birds such as waxwings out of the bushes for easier viewing when they visit your feeders.

9. Remove fallen leaves from birdbaths daily.

10. Set up a salt block to attract finches, siskins, and other birds.

---

and scarlet tanagers dropping like falling leaves into the shade trees of our small town. Within an hour, the berry-covered pokeweeds and dogwoods in my garden were filled with breakfasting birds.

Millet and Nectar for Fall Stragglers

The changing leaves of fall are the signal for me to make sure I have plenty of millet on hand. This is the season when native sparrows are moving through in droves on their way to southern wintering grounds. At first the heavy sparrow traffic is made up mostly of transients, but there are always a handful of birds that stay behind to spend the winter months in my neck of the woods. The related juncos arrive soon after the sparrows, reminding me that winter will soon be here. Both sparrows and juncos prefer the tiny golden seeds of proso millet, and with 100 birds or more clustering in open tray feeders and hopping about on the ground beneath, they go through a lot of seeds. Though a sack of millet goes a long way because of the small seed size, I lay in an extra 50 pounds to make sure I'm not caught short in fall feeding season.

Hummingbirds' tiny bodies need ample fuel for the grueling trip south and to keep them warm on chilly nights. Early fall often brings many pairs of humming wings to the nectar feeders that I keep filled to the brim. Even at Thanksgiving time, a laggard may make an appearance.

Autumn marks the switch for birds from insects to seeds. Many male birds also change from bright breeding plumage to duller colors as fall arrives.

Fast Foods for Birds

Attract many kinds of birds

IT HAPPENS TO THE BEST OF US—it's the height of feeder season, the yard is filled with customers, and you realize the birdseed can is empty. I learned my solution at my mother's knee—ransack the kitchen for anything remotely edible! Stale bread, withered fruit, and peanut butter are all fine fill-in-the-gap foods.

Keep the food preferences of your feeder birds in mind as you scan the shelves. Human foods based on grains, meat, or fruits will also appeal to your bird friends. Look, too, for anything that has nuts in it. The last slice of lunchmeat, diced into small pieces, makes a treat for jays, Carolina wrens, and other insect-eating birds that will appreciate the protein.

I usually stoop to raiding the dog food supplies, too. You can soak dry dog food in warm water to moisten it, or crush it into crumbs. Sparrows and juncos are among the first takers of this offering.

Combine various ingredients in ways that make sense to the birds: Dry foods for seed eaters, soft foods for the birds that prefer a softer diet. Proportions don't have to be exact to be a hit. Use the recipes below as a starting point for your own creativity. Such impromptu stop-gap measures will keep your birds well fed until you can get out for supplies.

Like this pigeon, most birds must rely on you to visit the drive-through for them—or to provide another source of "fast food" to satisfy their nutritional needs.

RECIPE

Blenderized Breakfast

Make this nut meal to keep chickadees, nuthatches, titmice, and woodpeckers content.

INGREDIENTS

A variety of nuts

Bacon, crumbled (optional)

Pour almonds, peanuts, pecans, walnuts, or other nuts, or a combination of nuts, into a blender or food processor. Process briefly until nuts are finely ground but not liquefied into nut butter. Stir in crumbled bacon if available. Pour into open tray feeder.

RECIPE

PB&J for the Birds

Fruit eaters and peanut butter lovers alike enjoy these quick and easy mini-sandwiches. They may tempt bluebirds, chickadees, jays, mockingbirds, orioles, robins, woodpeckers, and Carolina wrens.

INGREDIENTS

Peanut butter, creamy or chunky

2 slices bread

Grape jelly

Cornmeal

Spread peanut butter thickly on one slice of bread. Coat a second slice of bread with grape jelly. Sprinkle cornmeal thinly onto the jelly and thickly onto the peanut butter. Press slices together to make a sandwich. Using a sharp knife, slice into ½-inch chunks. Spread in tray feeder.

RECIPE

RECIPE
Stuffing-Mix Stop Gap

This multipurpose blend will fill the bellies of blue-birds, chickadees, jays, mockingbirds, nuthatches, titmice, woodpeckers, and Carolina wrens.

INGREDIENTS

Stuffing mix or bread crumbs

Hamburger, fresh or thawed

Vegetable oil, such as canola, corn, peanut, safflower, or sunflower

Check your shelves and breadbox for stuffing mix or bread crumbs, either packaged or made from fresh bread. Pour into large bowl. Add as much thawed hamburger as you can spare. Add a liberal amount of vegetable oil, and mix with a gentle lifting motion to combine. Allow 10 minutes for the bread to soak up the oil. Serve in tray feeder.

RECIPE
Spaghetti Supreme

Instant breakfast for crows, jays, robins, or starlings.

INGREDIENTS

Spaghetti, dry or leftover cooked pasta

Vegetable oil, such as corn, peanut, or sunflower

Raisins, currants, or chopped dried fruit

Cook spaghetti per package directions, or use leftover cooked pasta. Pour in a liberal amount of oil. Toss to coat well. Stir in raisins, currants, or chopped dried fruit. Or drain canned fruit, chop, and add to pasta. Serve in low feeder or directly on ground.

Feathers

IF YOU HAVE EVER SNUGGLED under a down quilt, you already know one of the major benefits of feathers. These specialized structures preserve body heat, a vital factor for a creature whose temperature runs about 10°F hotter than our own. Snug in their personal down jackets, birds can tolerate extremes of cold that would have an unprotected body turning blue. Take a look at the chickadees or other birds at your feeder on a chilly winter day, and you will notice that they look like butterballs, with feathers fluffed. Trapping air between the feathers increases their insulation against outside temperatures. On hot days, birds can also raise and ruffle their feathers to release excess heat.

Even a quick glance at a bird will show you that feathers vary in shape and structure. Feathers closest to the body are soft and fluffy like bits of thistle-down, while the outer body feathers have a definite shape and give the bird its contour and color. The long, stiff feathers of wings and tail serve as steering devices and provide the sturdy support needed for flight. In some birds, the tail feathers are adapted for special needs, such as the rigid, pointed tail feathers of woodpeckers, which work as props to keep the bird secure against a tree trunk.

Watch your feeder birds after a bath or following a rain shower, and you will see they don't look wet for long. Aided by applications of oil that the bird applies from the preen (or uropygial) gland near its tail, the feathers shed droplets of water like a yellow rain slicker, quickly returning to a sleek or fluffy state.

To truly appreciate the marvel of a feather, take a close look with a magnifying glass when you find a dropped feather. You will see an intricate system of interlocking hooks, or barbs (and smaller barbules), that keep every bit of the feather in place. When you see a bird drawing a feather through its bill, it is realigning these barbs to restore its structural integrity.

> In winter weather, birds fluff up their feathers to trap an insulating layer of air against the cold.

Feeder Birds

CERTAIN BIRDS ARE so well adapted to taking advantage of bird feeders and so widespread in their range that you can expect to see them just about anywhere. Friendly chickadees, finches, loudmouth jays, and juncos crop up at feeders from California to Maine. Learning the names of the regulars is the easiest way to start bird watching. You will have the luxury of looking at a bird long enough to find it in a field guide, and you will have the pleasure of getting to know the personalities and behavior of different species.

The arrival of uncommon visitors is what makes feeding birds so much fun. At migration time in spring, unusual birds may stop over for a bite of fast food before they take to the skies again, or they may visit to restore their energy before settling down nearby. In southern Indiana, I can count on a few rose-breasted grosbeaks to stop for a share of sunflowers every spring, but I know they won't stick around to nest. About the same time, brilliant indigo buntings also arrive and siphon up tiny millet seeds for a few weeks before they disperse to nearby nesting grounds.

Fall arrivals are more predictable and provide just as much pleasure. In fall, the regular feeder guests grow by several species, as northern birds take up residence for the winter. When I spot the first white-throated sparrow or junco, I know it's time to check the weather stripping and get the house in shape for winter.

Winter storms can bring unexpected customers. During one blizzard, a great blue heron sailed into my feeding station, astonishing me and panicking the songbirds. A few years ago, my sister in Pennsylvania found a juvenile night heron perched like a big brown chicken at her tray feeder. A red-shafted flicker I found after a major snowstorm—some thousand miles off course—now resides in the specimen collection of the Museum of Natural History in New York. In inclement weather when natural pickings are unreliable or nonexistent, horned larks or snow buntings may come in from the farm fields, bluebirds may travel long distances from their usual sheltering hedgerows, and birds of prey may patrol or even sample some suet.

Cardinals, jays, sparrows, and others flock together at a winter feeder. In exchange for a meal, birds will give you hours of entertainment on a snowy day.

A bobbing head feather adds to the California quail's comical charm. They are frequent winter feeder guests throughout their western haunts.

The birds you can expect to host at your feeder will depend on your geographical location and what your wild surroundings are like. If your property adjoins or is near grasslands, you may get regular visits from dicksissels, meadowlarks, quail, or vesper sparrows. In forested areas of the Northwest, the varied thrush, towhee, and fox sparrow will be regulars. In forested areas of the Midwest, you will never see a varied thrush but the spectacular scarlet tanager may honor you with its presence.

Seed eaters are the best customers at feeders because the menu is tailored to their natural preferences. Their numbers include scores of interesting species, from grosbeaks to goldfinches to the curious crossbills. Sparrows alone can become an obsession: Trying to figure out which is which can easily use up several Saturday mornings! Woodpeckers are fond of feeders, too.

Many insect-eating birds, including flycatchers, robins, wood warblers, wrens, and others, also enjoy berries and soft foods such as suet, which may lure them to your feeding station, especially when hunger is strong and natural food is scarce. Don't expect to see strictly insectivorous birds at your feeder, however: Swallows and swifts, for instance, will not be interested in your offerings. No matter how delectable, feeder food just can't compete with insects on the wing.

Most Common Feeder Birds

With a few regional variations, the following birds are most likely to visit your feeders:

- Cardinals
- Chickadees
- Doves
- Finches, such as goldfinches, house finches, and others
- Jays
- Juncos
- Nuthatches
- House sparrows
- Native sparrows, such as song sparrow, tree sparrow, white-throated sparrow, and others
- Starlings
- Titmice
- Woodpeckers

Feeder Covers

AN OPEN, UNCOVERED FEEDER gives you a great view of the birds that come to visit. That's the good news. The bad news is that an uncovered feeder also gives soaring hawks a fine look at the smorgasbord of bird life below. And it exposes the seed—and the birds—to rain, snow, and wind. Uncovered feeders also give squirrels and other seed-hogs easy access to the seed you put out for your preferred feeder visitors.

Despite these drawbacks, open feeders are still my favorites, and they are highly popular with my feeder birds. But when rainy weather settles in come the fall, I add covers to some of the tray feeders so that birds can have a choice of dining *al fresco* or beneath an awning.

Blame It on the Wind

My feeder "roofs" are functional rather than beautiful, reflecting my limited carpentry skills. But they do the job. The simplest arrangement employs a slanted roof to block prevailing winds and weather. The angle of the roof also ensures that water and snow will run or blow off. I make it from a piece of plywood that I screw to the rear corners of the tray with easy-to-remove wing nuts. My most elaborate cover design stands above the feeder on stubby wooden legs of two different lengths, providing a slanted roof that shields the entire seed tray.

In times of desperation, when winter snows blow in and birds are frantic for food, I have resorted to stapling branches of spruce and hemlock to the edge

(continued on page 101)

PROJECT

A Pest-Preventing Wire Cover

Here's how to make a wire cover that will keep out both squirrels and large birds. A feeder that's covered in this way is a good place to offer dried fruit, chopped suet, nutmeats, peanuts, and other treats that would be quickly gobbled at open-access feeders.

MATERIALS

Enamel-coated wire mesh

Wire cutters

Heavy-duty work gloves

6-inch-wide scrap board for bending wire

Twist-ties (optional)

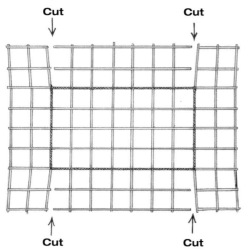

Step 1. Measure the inside dimensions of your open platform tray feeder. Buy a piece of stiff, enamel-coated wire mesh with a 1½-inch-square grid, such as that sold for garden fencing, that is 12 inches wider in both dimensions than your feeder measurements. For example, if your feeder is 12 inches × 24 inches, buy a piece of wire that measures 24 inches × 36 inches. Ask to have the wire cut to size at the store where you buy it; this timesaving step is usually free or less than a dollar.

Step 2. Using a pair of wire cutters, make two 6-inch-deep cuts, 6 inches from the left and right edges, on one long side of the piece of wire mesh.

Step 3. Repeat on the other long side.

Step 4. Don heavy-duty work gloves to protect yourself from scratches, and bend the wire to form a box shape, folding 6 inches along each edge toward the center. A 6-inch-wide board makes a good measuring tool and a useful edge to form the fold.

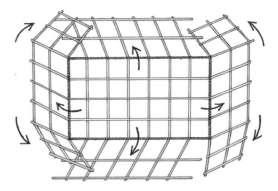

Fold to make an open-bottomed box.

Step 5. Using pliers, bend in the outer "flaps" to form the corners of your box. Lap the flaps over the corners to overlap the long edges.

Step 6. Fasten the corner flaps with twist-ties, or if the wire mesh has loose edges, by bending these wires around the grids.

Step 7. Push snugly into place inside the walls of your tray feeder.

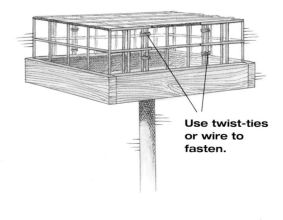

Use twist-ties or wire to fasten.

of the tray feeders on the side that faces the wind. The densely needled boughs cut the wind-driven snow much like an old-style roadside snow fence so that the feeder tray stays mostly clear of the white stuff.

No-Pest Covers

Another reason for covering feeders is to limit the kind—or size—of the visitors dining from it. A recent innovation in pest-preventing feeder design is deceptively simple—and highly effective. Wire-grid feeder covers snap into place over tray feeders, keeping out pest birds or pest animals, such as our favorite squirrels. Two styles are widely available. One includes a rigid grid that rests just above the surface of the seeds. It allows birds of all sizes to eat freely because their beaks can fit between the wires of the grid. The birds also appreciate the grid wires, which make ideal perches for feeding on the seeds below. But it's highly frustrating to squirrels.

The other style is also a wire grid, but this one is tall, raised several inches above the surface of an open tray feeder, with larger holes in the wire. Small birds easily fit between the wires to reach the feeder tray, where they can dine in peace. Larger birds, such as jays and starlings, are simply too big to squeeze in, so they are excluded. Squirrels, too, are denied entrance by the wire mesh. Both these feeder covers are fairly easy to fashion yourself.

Feeder Maintenance

THE WEAR AND TEAR OF BIRDS, squirrels, and weather takes its toll on feeders. Hooks may pull free, side boards may split, corners may come unglued. And accidents do happen—such as when your cold fingers drop the glass pane of a hopper feeder. Luckily, a little timely repair will usually save the day and give your feeder more years of useful life.

If you possess excellent carpentry skills and have a workshop full of craftsman's tools, go to it! Even if you're not a natural-born handyperson, you can still manage a number of basic feeder repairs. Here are my tools of the trade, useful even for a klutz like me for making quick feeder fixes:

Can of wood putty. This is great for filling cracks and holes where a hook has pulled free.

Putty knife. This tool's flat metal blade is useful for digging putty out of the can and applying it where holes and cracks need filling.

Screw-eye hooks. The screw-in bottoms of these handy gadgets require no tools at all to install, just a steady hand and a bit of pressure. I use them when a feeder will no longer hang from its original hook, usually because the wood has rotted around the old screw. A couple of eye hooks and a length of wire, and the feeder is ready to go again.

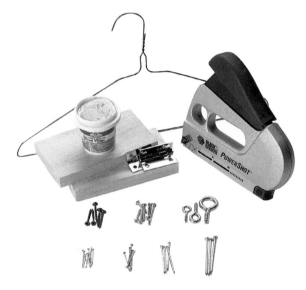

A few dollars' worth of repair tools and supplies will help you keep your feeders in working condition. These items are all handy to have on hand.

Wire coat hangers. A great source of new hooks and hanger material, coat hanger wire is flexible enough to bend into shape, yet strong enough to support a filled feeder. Double the wire for extra strength.

L-shaped metal hinges. I use these to reinforce corners that have pulled apart on feeders. Buy the largest size that will fit your edges, and screw them on with rust-proof screws.

Assorted screws and nails. It always helps to have some ready hardware when you need to do quick repairs. You can buy a prepackaged assortment, or assemble your own at a hardware store that sells loose nails and screws by weight. I prefer the latter, just because it's more fun to pick them out myself. Make sure you get weatherproof hardware that won't rust during wet weather.

A heavy-duty staple gun. You can do a lot with staples, and fast! I use my staple gun to rejoin corners that have pulled apart, attach a new side ledge, or hang a mesh bag of fat from a post. Staples are not a permanent fix for feeder repairs, although thanks to my procrastinating, they sometimes seem to be. Eventually it's best to replace these fasteners with screws or nails.

The friendly folks at my local lumberyard. When a feeder breaks, I remove the damaged side, top, or bottom, and take it to the experts, who are very willing to cut me a suitable replacement of the exact size I need. The cost is low, and the banter is always fun.

Replacing Glass

A broken hopper isn't the end of the line for a feeder as long as the rest of it is still in decent shape. Carefully remove the broken glass, and measure it exactly. Then check the Yellow Pages of your telephone book to find a business that cuts glass to size. Check whether the glass slides within a channel; if it does, take a piece of the original glass along when you go to order the glass so that they can match the thickness. Consider replacing the glass of a hopper feeder with clear, heavy-duty rigid plastic, which won't pose the danger of broken glass in case of another fumble-fingers accident.

Feeder Mounts

BIRD LOVERS EVERYWHERE cheered the introduction of black metal "shepherd's crook" poles for mounting feeders. Instead of digging a hole in the ground to sink a wooden post, or climbing into a tree to affix a dangling chain to a branch, we now need only step on the anchoring foot of a sturdy metal pole to sink it securely into the ground. And a shepherd's crook is not only easy to install, it is a good-looking addition to the garden as well.

Shepherd's crooks come in many varieties to suit your yard, your feeders, and your bird population. You can find single-armed models to hold a lone nectar feeder, tube feeder, or seed feeder. Double-armed designs will easily secure a pair of feeders. There are even crooks with multiple arms at the top to attach several feeders. If that's not enough, you can also buy add-on arms that secure onto the shaft of the pole for hanging additional feeders at various heights. Thanks to the popularity of these appealing

hangers, manufacturers have designed shepherd's crook feeders for more urban sites as well: There are short crooks that mount on deck railings, as well as hooks with heavy, flat, umbrella-stand bases for the patio.

Although I use metal hangers in my setup, I rely on wood posts to carry most of the weight—literally. Many of my feeders receive a lot of traffic, and the shepherd's crook, while strong, can sometimes tip with the weight of its customers. A wood post's solid heft supports tray feeders securely, and its brawn is well matched to the proportions of most seed feeders, looking solid and sturdy instead of puny beneath its burden. Wood posts also have a natural look that blends in with plantings and gives the feeding station a permanent feel. Because I like both looks for feeder stands, though, I do both, using some feeders on crooks and some on posts, and I even combine the two by mounting a hook on the side of a post.

Aim for Eye Appeal

Feeders are a focal point in the garden, drawing your eye as much as any carefully chosen garden ornament. Before you begin adding bird feeders willy-nilly, consider the overall look of your installations. Select the design of feeder mountings just as you would do with a piece of statuary. For tasteful good looks, keep it simple, and keep the following design concepts in mind.

Match proportions. Large feeders hanging from skinny poles or chains jar the eye because of disproportion. Match your feeders to their mounts according to their size and visual weight: A hefty horizontal feeder looks best securely mounted atop a good-size post; a see-through plastic dome or tube feeder is fine on a narrower pole.

Employ repetition. Use similar mounts, or those with complementary features, rather than mixing and matching different styles. Keep colors similar, too: Avoid mixing white and black poles, for instance. If you prefer a more formal effect than weathered wood, paint all posts black or green-black.

Think straight and solid. For the most unobtrusive arrangement, choose hangers and stands with straight lines and solid shafts, such as metal poles, long steel hooks, or wooden posts. A dozen feeders dangling from chains can make your backyard look junky.

Practice simplicity. It's easy to purchase and install shepherd's crook iron hangers, but a forest of black stands can have the same effect as a gathering of pink flamingos. I find that three black hangers is the limit for my midsize feeding area.

Mount in multiples. Think vertically as you design your feeder setup to avoid feeding station clutter. A single tall, solid wood post can support half a dozen suet, corn, or fruit feeders along its sides.

Go easy on the curves. Curved lines call for attention. Keep them to a minimum, or arrange them in a coherent way so that the eye travels naturally from one to the other rather than jumping about. Three curving iron hooks look better stacked in a vertical arrangement on

> Choose hooks and hangers to support the weight of seeds and squirrels as well as feather-light birds.

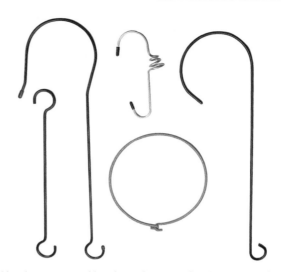

Use hangers and hooks to improve feeder access for you and birds. The small, coiled hook (*top, center*) lets you lift a feeder to a branch on a broom handle—no step-stool needed. Large hooks fit over thick branches, and the circular hanger keeps squirrels from knocking down a feeder.

the same side of a tall post than they do staggered at varying heights and positions around the post.

Hangers and Hooks

Most feeders are sold with a handle or hook on top for hanging. Examine this attachment before you buy to make sure it is sturdy and strongly attached with screws or bolts rather than staples. If a wood feeder is cracked at the point of attachment, pass it up. Look for one with a handle or hook that will hold up to heavy wear.

Also determine whether the feeder hanger will get in the way of refilling. If you have to jiggle the lid of the feeder to open it because of an intrusive handle, refilling will be a chore. Look for tube feeders with lids that slide up the bail of the handle, instead of those that have to be completely removed and replaced after filling; if you're prone to forgetting the gas cap on your car, you're likely to do the same with these feeders. I've pressed more than one mayonnaise-jar lid into service as a temporary replacement for the misplaced cap of a tube feeder.

You'll find a multitude of hooks and chains in hardware and discount stores, garden centers, bird supply shops, and other outlets. Keep stability in mind as you make your selections. Birds may be featherweights, but seed adds pounds to the weight of a feeder, and visiting squirrels can drop with force from nearby trees. Choose sturdy S-hooks that will support the weight of the birds, chain, feeder, and seed.

When purchasing your hanging equipment, go easy on the chain—swinging feeders waste seed. Niger, nectar, and small seeds can spill out easily with every sway of the feeder. Choose hooks and hangers that will keep your feeders as stable as possible. The longer the chain or the series of hooks, the more wildly the feeder will swing in strong winds or under the weight of arriving and departing customers.

Spilled food is not a problem for suet feeders, corn cob feeders, and fruit feeders, which hold food securely on spikes, in bags, or in wire cages. If you have a spot that requires lowering the feeder substantially so you can enjoy the view as your feathered friends feast, these are the feeders to suspend from wire, chain, or linked hooks.

No matter what arrangement you use for hanging your feeders, be sure they are within easy reach for cleaning and refilling. It's no fun to stretch for a feeder and have seed—or worse, sticky nectar—spill down your arm or neck.

A couple of mechanical devices that are simple to attach, widely available, and best of all, low-cost will prevent frustration with hanging feeders. Instead of unhooking your hanging feeders to refill them, or tipping them sideways to pour in seed, just attach them to a small pulley. The device will allow you to raise and lower feeders or retrieve them from a distance without stretching on tiptoes. If you use a chain or other long hanger with your feeders, invest a couple of dollars in a swivel hook to attach feeder to hanger. As the feeder turns in the wind or under the weight of birds, the swivel will prevent the chain from getting all wound up. If you can't find these labor savers in the bird feeder aisle, ask at a hardware store.

Creative Shopping

Arts and crafts shows are a great place to pick up interesting feeder mounts. Blacksmithing seems to be enjoying a comeback, and metalworkers are turning out lots of lovely styles of hooks and poles. There's a gamut of selections, from poles topped with a simple leaf shape or two to fanciful work-of-art designs with birds, hearts, and flowers—whatever suits your fancy.

Antiques shops, architectural salvage stores, and plain old junkyards are always fun to treasure-hunt in, too, if you want a bird feeder mount that functions as a garden ornament.

Feeder Placement

PUTTING OUT a spread for the birds isn't a purely altruistic gesture on our part: The payoff for us is the pleasure of watching the birds go at it. The life and color birds bring to the view outside the window is well worth the small investment in sunflower seed and other goodies. That's why the best place for your feeders is where you can easily see them. There's no point placing feeders far away from the house, unless they are supplementary stations meant to attract shyer birds that prefer to stay back, or unless you need more than one feeding station in order to accommodate an overflow crowd or a bunch of hungry squirrels or other feeder gluttons.

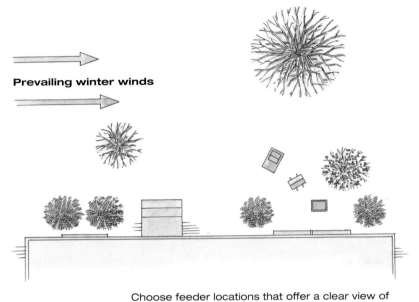

Prevailing winter winds

Choose feeder locations that offer a clear view of visiting birds and easy access for refilling. Enhance bird appeal with nearby plants for shelter.

Location, Location, Location

Deciding where you place your feeder may not be the simple decision you expect it to be. Here are some feeder placement matters for you to consider when you're choosing a location.

- Your view of the feeders
- Window dangers
- Sheltering plants for quick cover
- Height of feeders
- Prevailing winds
- Ease of filling

A Room with a View

Watching birds—and other feeder guests, such as squirrels and chipmunks—has a soothing effect on human observers. It's a great stress reliever, no matter what birds are part of the view. Whether you're watching house sparrows and city pigeons from an urban apartment, or chickadees and cardinals in the backyard of your suburban house, feeling calm and optimistic seems to be a very common "side effect" of watching birds.

When you place your feeders near a window in your house, you'll have a fine view of bird activity with or without binoculars. It's hard to get interested in feeder activity when the clients are just moving specks. But when the birds are near enough to see well, it won't take long before you and the other family members get into the habit of checking the feeder every time you walk by. You'll want to show each other unusual or interesting sightings, too, so be sure to allow plenty of room for friends and family to gather nearby.

Even family members who profess to be completely disinterested in watching birds are likely to undergo a change of heart, though it may take them some time to admit it. When my sister put up a feeder, her husband at first wanted nothing to do with it. He'd barely glance up as he walked by on his way to the living room. But within just a few short weeks, watching the birds had become a regular part of starting their day together.

Plan the position for your feeders according to how you spend your time in the house. If you wash dishes by hand, a feeder outside the window over the sink is in a perfect place. If your family gathers around the kitchen table for bagels and coffee, outside a window near the table is another excellent site. A multifeeder setup outside a family room window is another possibility. Just make sure there is clear visibility to the feeders from a sitting position and that there are comfortable chairs for viewing.

Plants in the Feeder Area

It takes much longer to lure birds to a feeder in the middle of a wide, bare lawn than to a feeder that is in a well-shrubbed area. Birds feel safer if there is cover near the feeder into which they can quickly retreat, should danger threaten. Visiting a feeder in the middle of a lawn is asking for trouble, from a bird's point of view.

A group of shrubs or a single conifer can provide enough shelter to make birds feel more comfortable. Flowerbeds, shade trees, vegetable gardens, ornamental grasses, and berry patches all contribute to a bird's sense of safety.

Be sure to keep an alert eye out for predators in this Eden, especially the ubiquitous house cat. Keep your own cats indoors, and chase away visitors or strays. (See Cats on page 57 for more ideas for pulling the welcome mat out from under a prowling kitty.)

High or Low

Birds such as chickadees and woodpeckers that spend most of their time in the trees are accustomed to eating at higher levels than birds such as towhees and sparrows that usually skulk about at ground level. That's why you will want to place your feeders accordingly.

Birds will adapt to feeders at unaccustomed heights if they are hungry enough. But your aim is to attract birds not only during winter blizzards, when the snow covers everything in sight. You also want to tempt birds to your feeders even when natural food—or the neighbor's feeder—is competing for their attention. Putting up both high and low feeders is an important way to make birds feel more at home.

Of course, seed will soon be kicked out of high feeders by foraging birds, so ground feeders like mourning doves and white-throated sparrows will still be able to find food at the level they prefer. But suet, corn, and other foods usually served in high feeders are often inaccessible to birds that stay near the ground or that lack the ability to cling to these feeders. A low tray near ground level is ideal for offering these foods to juncos, robins, and other low-level eaters.

Know Which Way the Wind Blows

Keeping warm and dry is a primary concern of birds because calories burned to stay cozy mean less energy to fuel other body functions. You'll want to put your feeder in a place protected from chilling fall and winter winds, and out of the line of driving rain and snow. Seasonal wind direction varies in different parts of the country, but in general, cold air tends to move from the north or northwest.

Block the path of prevailing winds with existing shrubs and trees or with newly planted windbreaks. Evergreens are best for the job because their dense foliage is effective in winter. You can also erect trellises of vines to cut the wind.

Keeping feeders clear of blowing snow can be frustrating. Feeder traffic is high during bad weather, and the hungry birds may be quickly reduced to pecking at a few small open areas of seed. The morning after a storm, birds will most likely be out and about before you are, and if deep or crusted snow covers their seed, they'll have a hungry wait until you help them out. In emergencies, you can erect temporary windbreaks of plywood or an old Christmas tree, which will break the force of blowing snow so that at least a small area on the leeward side stays relatively bare of snow and gives birds access to the seeds within.

Easy Filling

Another reason to place feeders near the house is so that you don't have far to go to refill—which can be every morning during peak season. Keep in mind where the door of the house and the seed storage area are when you choose a feeder location. A short walk in summer may be an arctic trek come December.

If you live in an area of particularly bad winters, or if you know you will have difficulty leaping the drifts, consider a convenient windowsill-mounted feeder. One of the first types of bird feeders, these simple trays allow you to refill from inside the house by simply sliding open the sash and pouring in a fresh scoop of seed.

Feeder Problems

PESTS ARE THE MAIN PROBLEM at a feeder. Birds and animals can easily become nuisances, thanks to the abundance of delicious food there for the taking. Changing the menu to foods they find less appealing or changing the feeders to models that they cannot use are the best alternatives.

Feathered pests fall into two categories: bullies and hordes. Crows, jays, mockingbirds, and ravens are the bullies. They can wreak havoc with the gentle daily life of a feeding station. Apparently these birds missed their kindergarten lessons on learning to share because when they arrive at the feeder, all they see is "Mine, mine, mine!" They chase away less aggressive birds with raucous calls or threatening dashes. Mockingbirds can be especially irritating because unlike the other bullies, they don't leave the feeder when they're through eating. They stick around the feeder area, making life miserable for any other bird that dares to approach. The solution to bully birds is to add more feeders, especially models that prevent them from patronizing the feeder. In the case of a territorial mockingbird, you can empty the feeders altogether until the bird moves on, or you can set up other feeders at a location separated by a large visual barrier, such as a high fence or your house.

Bird pests that arrive in hordes are troublesome because they use up most of the feeder space as well as gobble much of the food. One starling at a time is not a problem. But when a dozen of them descend on your suet feeders, there's no room for a wren or nuthatch to get a bite. Blackbirds, which flock in fall and winter, can also arrive in multitudes. House finches, too, are well known for swarming a feeding station, although in recent years their numbers seem to be taking a slight downturn. Feeders with protective wire grids or cages, or with weighted perches, are highly effective at keeping at least some of your feeders free for the use of smaller birds. My solution to the hordes keeps everybody happy: I add more feeders or offer cracked corn, an excellent decoy food for blackbirds, well away from other feeders.

In the cute-but-furry department, we have the notorious squirrels, plus various pests ranging from

Neighbor Relations

A WELL-USED feeding station can strain relations between neighbors if the birds are many or the feeder is near a property line. Try these tricks to keep your neighbors smiling at you and the birds.

- If you suspect that flocks of blackbirds or other birds are becoming a neighborhood nuisance, alter your feeder offerings to discourage their presence. Large gray-striped sunflower seed is usually less appealing to flocking birds.

- If starlings or blackbirds have become a burgeoning presence, switch to tube feeders, or feeders that allow entrance only to small birds.

- Limit highly visible foods such as bread, baked goods, and larger fruits to contained feeders, instead of scattering it on the ground where from a distance it may look like debris.

- If neighbors have a clear view of your feeders, keep the area looking tidy by frequently freshening the mulch beneath the feeders and removing the hulls if needed.

tiny mice through hundred-pound deer. Dogs are highly effective deterrents for most furry pests. Squirrel-proof feeders will slow those varmints down or encourage them to stick to their own feeders. Better sanitation will discourage mice and other small rodents. Fencing helps keep out larger pest animals and is the only permanent solution for deer. Or, if you can't beat 'em, you might choose to enjoy them. Apples, corn, and other offerings served at a distance from the bird area are eagerly welcomed. Once the pests aren't raiding your feeders, you may enjoy watching them as much as you do the birds.

Feeders

FEEDER DESIGN HAS NOT CHANGED drastically since I began feeding birds some 30 years ago. There's a very good reason: The styles that worked well years ago still work today. The only major innovation I have seen in those years was the introduction of the tube feeder, an instant classic thanks to its sensible design, ease of use, and popularity with the birds.

Most seed feeders are simple constructions of wood, metal, or plastic that are built to last for years. Those with hoppers that dole out seed automatically are designed to hold a good quantity, so that you don't have to refill frequently. Other types of feeders are tailor-made for offering birds special treats other than the staple seeds.

Choosing a feeder is a matter of satisfying your needs and those of the birds you hope to attract. The birds that come to your yard will determine the types of food you offer, and the food, in turn, will determine which feeder(s) you use. You may need to exclude squirrels or even some pest bird species.

Baker's Dozen for the Birds

The selection of feeder types includes designs for serving just about any bird-attracting food you can imagine. Try some of these styles in your yard.

- Tray (platform) feeder
- Hopper feeder
- Suet feeder
- Tube feeder
- Stick-on window feeder
- Squirrel-proof feeder
- Caged feeder to exclude large birds
- Hanging plastic sphere feeder
- Nut feeder
- Corn feeder
- Fruit feeder
- Doughnut feeder
- Peanut butter feeder

Shopping Tips

Feeder prices vary dramatically from one supplier to another. Homemade feeders are usually the least costly, whether you make them yourself or buy them at nearby nature centers or other outlets for local craftspeople. Feeders of unusual, complicated design—such as gazebos—or those made to look like antique ornaments are the Cadillacs of the feeder business. In between, you'll find dozens of models priced affordably.

Shoddy feeders are no bargain. They'll fall apart when it's least convenient—usually just after you've filled them with the last of your seed supply. And squirrels will take advantage of lightweight and poorly constructed feeders by chewing through them with amazing speed or by dropping them to the ground to spill out the contents. Expect to pay $20 and up for a moderate-size, well-constructed feeder made of solid wood. Examine the feeder before you buy, and look for signs of good quality, such as these:

- Solid wood, not plywood

- Nails or screws at joints, not staples

- Sturdy screened bottoms in tray feeders (for drainage in wet weather and improved air circulation to prevent mold formation)

- Strong attachments for hangers

- Metal reinforcing around feeder holes to keep squirrels from chewing their way to the seed inside

Also be sure that the feeder you like is easy to open and fill. Remember that it won't be sitting on a convenient shelf when you refill—it will probably be swinging from a hanger or atop a post, and you'll be opening the feeder with one hand while you hold the container of fresh seed in the other. If you can do the imaginary filling job without frustration, take the feeder home with you. If it's tricky to handle in the store, it will likely be even more frustrating in

Simple, sturdy feeders generally are easier to fill and maintain than fussy styles. This quartet holds niger, nuts, suet, and loose seeds, satisfying all feeder birds.

your backyard on a cold, snowy day when you're wearing a pair of heavy gloves or mittens.

Size of Feeders

At least one of your feeders should be a large one that holds plenty of seed and plenty of birds. Otherwise, you will be spending an inordinate amount of time trekking to the feeder to refill.

A large, homemade tray feeder is the foundation of my feeding station. The big open tray provides abundant space for dozens of birds. They perch on the sides and scratch and peck in the tray itself. This feeder attracts both small seed eaters, such as finches and chickadees, as well as larger birds, including cardinals, jays, and grosbeaks.

Small-size feeders, such as the clear plastic kind that are attached to windows with suction cups, hold very little seed. I don't mind including small feeders in my feeding station because I enjoy the variety of shapes and sizes, and I like to watch which birds prefer the different models. Small feeders are fine for supplemental treats, but a flock of small feeders is not a suitable replacement for a large-capacity mainstay feeder.

(continued on page 112)

A Simple Roofed Feeder

With the aid of a few basic tools, you can turn out sturdy, long-lasting feeders of simple design at very reasonable cost, usually $10 or less. You'll need a solid work surface and a few tools. A jigsaw works best for cutting the curved sides of this feeder but, if cutting curves is beyond your carpentry skill level, you can make the sides straight instead.

Many nature centers offer feeder-making workshops, at which the process is taught step-by-step. Materials may already be cut to size, a nice advantage for the beginner carpenter. You can find plenty of plans for feeders in books at your library and in birding magazines. Or, if you're a more experienced handyperson, you may be able to reproduce a commercially made design in your own workshop by drawing some preliminary sketches and plans.

MATERIALS

½-inch plywood or other scrap lumber

Nails and screws, as needed

Caulk

Step 1. Cut (or have cut) the wood into pieces with the dimensions shown in the illustration. Be sure to cut two side pieces.

Step 2. Drill a hole in the center of the back piece, near the top, for hanging the finished feeder.

Step 3. Use nails or screws to attach the sides to the outside edge of the floor. Nailing the pieces together will speed assembly, but using screws will make a sturdier feeder. Predrill holes for screws, if needed.

Step 4. Fasten the front piece onto the exposed edges of the sides and floor.

Step 5. Attach the back piece to the exposed edges of the sides and floor.

Step 6. Put the roof on last, attaching along the top edges of the two sides and placing it as flush to the back piece as possible. Run a bead of caulk along the joint between the roof and the back to keep out water.

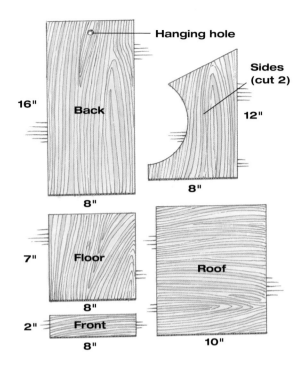

Step 7. Use the hanging hole in the back to mount your feeder on a likely post or wall where you can enjoy watching birds dining from it. No paint is necessary; in fact, unpainted, weathered wood is easier for the birds to grip.

A Touch of Elegance

Why not create a truly handsome feeder that includes a decorative and functional copper-clad roof? Applying sheet copper to a feeder or birdhouse roof is not as difficult as it might seem; even a first-time craftsperson can achieve good results. You can make a homemade feeder fancy with the warm glow of copper, or you can gussy up a plain-Jane commercial bird feeder by covering its wooden roof with copper for a custom touch.

MATERIALS

Sheet copper, 28 gauge

Straightedge

Sturdy nail

Heavy-duty gloves

Pliers

Copper screws (optional)

Fine-grade steel wool

Polyurethane lacquer (optional)

Step 1. Measure the existing roof. Add 4 inches to the length to allow for bending copper around edges. *Note:* If the sides of the feeder extend to the roof, cut enough copper to cover only the top and edges of the roof, without bending around to the underside. To secure this type of roof, drill holes along top sides and insert short screws.

Step 2. Cut (or have cut) 28-gauge sheet copper to correct dimensions.

Step 3. To cover a flat roof, mark the dimensions of the actual roof area on the copper, using a straightedge to measure and a nail to scribe the marks on the metal.

Step 4. Position the copper along the edge of a worktable or straight-edged counter. Wearing gloves, bend the copper along the inscribed line. Repeat at inner line.

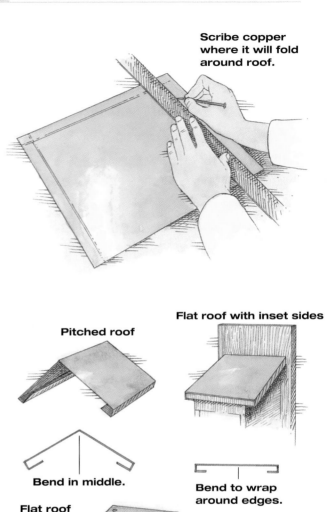

Scribe copper where it will fold around roof.

Pitched roof

Bend in middle.

Flat roof with inset sides

Bend to wrap around edges.

Flat roof with flush sides

Holes for screws

Bend to cover edges.

Step 5. For a pitched roof, bend the copper in the middle.

Step 6. Repeat Step 4 on other side of the copper sheet.

(continued on page 112)

Step 7. Slide the copper onto the roof. Tighten the copper around the roof's edges by squeezing with pliers, as necessary.

Step 8. Copper weathers when it's exposed to the elements, acquiring a soft green patina. If you want to keep its burnished metal color, you'll need to cover your finished copper creation with three coats of durable, gloss polyurethane lacquer. Before applying the polyurethane, sand the top side of the metal roof with very fine-grade steel wool to remove fingerprints and other blemishes; handle only at the edges of the metal after sanding. If you prefer a natural patina, leave the copper untreated.

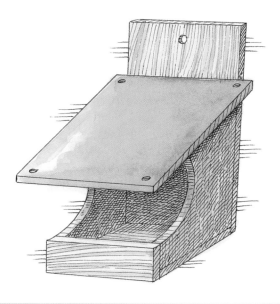

(continued from page 109)

Feederless Feeders

One of the more interesting developments in the bird-feeding business isn't a feeder at all, in the usual sense of the word: It's a compressed block of food that makes its own feeder. At about 8 inches square, the blocks are a bit smaller than a salt block, and as an added benefit, they last a long time.

You can buy seed blocks made from sunflower, millet, and other favored seeds, or from a combination of corn, sunflower, and peanuts. Both mixtures appeal to birds as well as to squirrels, chipmunks, and other feeder visitors. Simply set the block on the ground, and it's ready to eat.

Compressed cornmeal, formed into a hard-packed cylinder for gnawing or pecking, is also available. The cylinder pushes onto a metal rod in a similar fashion to a corncob feeder. Although they cost more than corncobs, the cylinders are waste-free because all parts of it are edible, and longer-lasting, so you won't have to refill as often. They are also more difficult for squirrels to remove from the spike than a corncob, which means they won't disappear after a day or two. They're good for offering on decks or balconies.

The oldest type of feederless feeder has been around at least as long as I've been feeding birds—four decades now and counting. Though the price has gone up from the early days, "seed bells" are still a long-lasting bargain. They are made of birdseed mix or sometimes all sunflower seeds, packed tight into a molded bell shape. The bell accommodates only a single customer or perhaps two and is accessible to any clinging bird—chickadees, finches, nuthatches, titmice, and woodpeckers are the usual customers. Once the bell begins to acquire an irregular shape after weeks of nibbling, it may also be visited by less agile birds such as jays, mockingbirds, and starlings.

In the wintertime, I like to decorate the bare branches of the walnut tree in my side yard with seed bells. I vary the heights of the bells hanging from the branches, using heavy twine to attach them. To attach some bells to higher branches, I tie a generous length of twine to the bell, then knot the twine around a good-sized stone. I pitch the stone over the higher branches, retrieve the end of the string, remove the stone, and fasten the loose end of the twine to the bell.

Feeding Myths

FOLKLORE IS RAMPANT in the bird-feeding world, with myths being passed along over the backyard fence as well as through publications. When someone tells me that they've "always heard" that some bird "fact" is true, I don't believe it until I check into it myself. Thanks to the Internet, finding science-based information is a simple matter. I look for sites of reputable research institutions, such as the Audubon Society, Nature Conservancy, or university laboratories of ornithology. If you don't have access to a computer, a phone call to your local chapter of the Audubon Society or to a naturalist at a nearby nature center or state park can often yield the information you seek.

Red-dyed sugar water won't hurt your hummingbirds, but it won't help attract them either—the touches of red plastic on the feeder are enough for that.

Here are some of the most popular myths that regularly make the rounds or are accepted as fact.

Adding red dye to hummingbird nectar will make the birds sick. FALSE. Some of us of a certain age may remember the red dye scare of a couple of decades ago, when a popular food additive was found to have carcinogenic effects in humans and was eliminated from processed foods and supermarket shelves. Perhaps that's where the hummingbird red dye myth originated. The truth is that there are no scientific studies that indicate a negative effect on hummingbirds from red dye. However, the rest of the truth is that colored nectar doesn't attract any more hummingbirds than clear nectar, as long as there's a bit of red plastic near the feeding ports. So why waste your time adding it to nectar? On the other hand, if you prefer the convenience of instant-mix commercial nectar products (which often include red coloring), there's no need to worry about killing off hummingbirds with red nectar.

Red pepper keeps squirrels from eating birdseed. TRUE. Birds aren't affected like mammals by the irritating capsaicin in hot peppers. Spraying your seed with pepper extract or buying treated seed will discourage squirrels strongly. In winter, when food is scarce, give squirrels their own feeder of untreated seeds, corn, and nuts, or they may overcome their aversion and eat the hot stuff anyway.

Clean feeders prevent disease. TRUE AND FALSE. Most instances of birds acquiring diseases at feeders are based on experiences of captive game birds or pets, which can't seek alternate food sources. I've noticed that my feeder birds don't bother with moldy seed; they simply fly off elsewhere to seek fresh food. An effort at good housekeeping is easy insurance. But the situation at feeders can also spread disease simply because of the unnatural gathering of large numbers of birds in a small place.

Should you spot a sick bird, take it as the cue to tidy up. Rake or cover hulls, and scrub feeders with a 10 percent bleach solution (10 parts water to 1 part bleach). If a few birds are showing signs of illness, empty your feeders so that the birds disperse and there is less chance of contagion. Take this opportunity to do your general housekeeping, covering the hulls and washing the feeders with a bleach solution to prevent the problem from spreading. After 1 or 2 weeks, restart your feeding program.

House finches are dying out because of eye disease. PARTLY TRUE. Those hungry hordes of house finches probably won't disappear anytime soon. House finch populations have dropped in many areas because of the spread of mycoplasmal conjunctivitis, a condition that effectively blinds the birds, after which they meet their fate from accidents, predation, or starvation. The disease is a bacterial respiratory infection that may occur in other species besides house finches. Although the disease spread dramatically at first, it appears to have tapered off, with perhaps up to 10 percent of house finches affected at any one time.

If I keep my nectar feeders up, hummingbirds won't migrate. FALSE. Birds migrate according to an internal timetable set to the hours of daylight, not because your food is too good to leave behind. Keep your nectar feeder up: After the bulk of hummingbirds depart, it can be a lifesaver for stragglers.

Don't throw rice at weddings or serve it at feeders— it will swell up in the birds' stomachs and kill them. FALSE. Rice is a big part of the diet of bobolinks, which regularly scour rice fields in the South. At the feeder, it's usually ignored in favor of other seeds. But if birds do eat it, there'll be no ill effects.

Hummingbirds migrate south by perching on the backs of flying geese. FALSE. I thought this old chestnut was dead and buried, but it seems to have come back to haunt us again. Although it may seem impossible, tiny hummers really do reach Central and South America under their own steam.

If I stop feeding the birds, they'll starve. FALSE, EXCEPT IN WINTER. But they may have a hard time for a while, until they locate other food sources. Do keep your feeders stocked in winter if you live in a cold area and if you don't have nearby neighbors that also feed birds. Low temperatures and a scarcity of natural food during a hard winter take a toll on birds, and a full feeder can mean the difference between life and death. If you're planning a winter getaway to the snowbelt, add extra suet feeders and top off the tube and hopper feeders before you go, or enlist the aid of a friend or neighbor to make sure your birds don't find the cupboard bare.

Feeding birds can change their natural habits. NO DEFINITIVE ANSWER YET. Feeders will never replace natural foods from a bird's point of view. I guess insects and wild seeds just taste better.

I am concerned, though, about the fast-increasing usage of nectar feeders by birds other than hummingbirds. After watching a downy woodpecker eschew suet and sunflowers day after day in favor of draining the sugar water dry, I couldn't help but wonder about the lack of balance in the bird's diet. Scientific research is just beginning on this question. If you worry about your birds' seeming addiction to sugar water, use nectar feeders without perches to limit access.

On the other hand, seed and suet feeders do make a difference in winter survival rates, and that is probably part of the reason why some birds are expanding their ranges. Evening grosbeaks, which used to move from the frozen Far North only in times of dire need, are much more common winter feeder visitors than they were even 20 years ago. Carolina wrens have moved in the other direction, spending winters several states northward of where they once drew the line. Several species of hummingbirds have shifted their wintering ranges, with some individuals of the species no longer trekking to Central and South America, but instead lingering in the South, where nectar feeders are abundant. The evidence could be circumstantial: Flowers have always bloomed year-round in the extreme south of this country. It's uncertain yet how big a part backyard feeders play in the expanding and changing ranges of American birds because other factors such as habitat loss, climate changes, and temporary weather conditions also play a part.

By the way, that story about swallows hibernating in the mud in swamps is a myth, too.

Feeding Stations

BIRD FEEDERS ARE like potato chips—one is just not enough. I guarantee that after you mount your first feeder, you'll soon be shopping for more. Additional feeders mean more birds, and a variety of feeders means a variety of birds. When you combine a cluster of diverse feeders, you create what is known as a feeding station: a place that birds of all kinds can come to satisfy their need for food.

The Basics

Seed feeders and suet feeders are the must-haves for any feeding station. They will supply the needs of nearly all birds that commonly visit backyards, from chickadees to jays.

Tray feeders are ideal for feeding a crowd. If you prefer to keep your seed protected and not in a help-yourself buffet, you can create more feeding room by adding more hopper-style or other enclosed feeders. Tube feeders are another good choice.

Suet feeders are always busy in winter, when this nutritious high-fat food provides ready calories to keep birds warm. Because suet feeders are small, you can provide several at your feeding station to accommodate more customers.

Special-Needs Feeders

To attract birds that don't depend mainly on seeds, you may decide to include other specialized feeders at your station. Fruit feeders and soft-food feeders that can hold doughnuts and other delights are a good place to start. Supplement these with nut feeders and corn feeders, and your feeding station will be ready to cater to just about any bird on the block.

Include several feeding devices on which to offer mockingbirds, orioles, and other fruit eaters their favorite treats. A simple nail spike feeder is perfect for skewering half an apple or orange. Small open trays are good places to pour a few handfuls of dried or fresh berries and grapes. And a plastic plant saucer makes a fine impromptu fruit feeder, since it won't absorb the juice.

Salt block

A mix of cover and open space creates ideal surroundings for a feeding station. Combine various feeders and ever-ready water—and make sure you have a good view.

To cater to bluebirds, provide a place in your feeding station to offer mealworms. You'll want a separate feeder for these bluebird favorites, where the shyer birds can dine in peace on their favorite treat. Position the bluebird mealworm feeder several yards from feeders frequented by aggressive guests, with an intervening shrub or trellis if possible. Or just let your bluebirds learn to share with other mealworm lovers, such as Carolina wrens.

Other Attractions

For a complete feeding station, make provisions for the other needs of birds. Grit, salt, and water will make your feeding station a one-stop shop for any bird. Clear an area for a salt block, protecting the soil beneath it and any nearby plants from leaching by lining the area with heavy-duty plastic. The shallow lid from a large plastic storage container is a good solution; cover it with a thin layer of wood chips to make it look better. Scatter grit or eggshells on open lawn, over bare soil, or in a low tray feeder.

Watching birds sip and splash in the bath is just as entertaining as watching them dine. Adding a birdbath or other water source near your feeders will accommodate birds and give you a great place to watch them bathe and drink. Keep the water far enough away from feeders to keep shells and other debris from falling in the bath. If your space is limited, a good solution is to hang a shallow basin from a hook or tree branch near a low, ground-level feeder.

Plants also add to the appeal of a feeding station, making it look more attractive to both you and the birds. Berry bushes, such as blueberries and sumac, along with other plantings that offer fruit, seeds, or insects, will satisfy the needs of birds for natural food that they can enjoy in every season.

A deck feeding station puts feeders nearby for easy filling in inclement weather. Use hull-less sunflower seed and tube feeders to reduce debris.

Field Guides

A FIELD GUIDE ILLUSTRATED WITH DRAWINGS, not photographs, is your best bet as a beginner. The classic Peterson's field guide, with separate volumes for eastern and western birds, is a great place to start. Clear drawings with arrows pointing out identification clues, such as wing bars or a notched tail, make it easy to separate one species from another. Birds are arranged by family, a great aid to learning the anatomical differences, such as shape of bill or wings. This will help you quickly peg any bird you see as a finch, say, or a blackbird—the first step to narrowing down an identification.

Although I learned many of my birds with the help of Peterson's, my favorite field guide is Golden Press' *A Guide to Field Identification of Birds of North America*, a book that covers all species found on this continent. The birds are shown in lifelike poses against a scrap of typical background: a yellow warbler on a willow branch, for instance—one of its favored haunts. The book's wide coverage was an eye-opener to me after my first few years with Peterson's narrower view. I knew the tufted titmouse from the Peterson's field guide *A Field Guide to Eastern Birds*, for example, but until I paged through the Golden guide, I had no idea that my little gray bird had such interesting western relatives. Another plus is that range maps are on the same page with the bird, unlike Peterson's guide, which sends you to an appendix of maps at the back of the book. I also like the informative text, which like all Golden guides, packs tons of interesting facts into very small spaces.

The Audubon series of field guides, illustrated with photos instead of drawings, is a book to add to your shelf for the pleasure of looking at its pictures and reading its well-researched text. But I find the photos, in which parts of a bird may be obscured by shade or vegetation, much more difficult than clear drawings to use for initial identification.

Choosing a field guide is a matter of personal taste and practical consideration. Consider these factors when you visit the bookstore.

How easy is the book to use? Pretend you have just seen a starling or robin for the first time. Try to find it in the field guide. If you fumble around or end up leafing through the book one page at a time, try another book.

How is it organized? If you're a visual person, choose a guide that has illustrations of each bird. If you prefer descriptions, focus on whether it clearly describes the birds' features.

How big and how heavy is the book? I like to carry my field guide in my pocket so I can whip it out whenever I hear or see an unfamiliar species. If the book is a convenient size to take along, you will identify birds more easily than if you have to wait until you're home to consult your bird book.

What does the book include? If you live on the water, choose a guide that will help you identify waterfowl. If you live in an area that gets extremely cold and your purpose is to provide foods for the birds you identify, make sure that information is supplied in the guide you choose.

What kind of binding does the book have? Look for a book that is stitched together at the spine, instead of only glued. Your field guide is going to get a lot of wear and tear. Select one that will last.

The Advanced Class

Once you've mastered the basics, you may want to graduate to the advanced field guides, which offer great help for figuring out the identification of shorebirds, wood warblers, and other frustrating species.

Familiarity with the birds themselves is just as vital as an advanced field guide in your backpack. The more time you spend watching birds, the more familiar you'll become with their behavior and their voices. I find that once I know the difference between the ways similar species sound and act, I'm not likely to be confused by variations in plumage. Referring to advanced field guides is a shortcut to spending hours in the field because they include notes on behavior that can help you tell similar species apart.

F

Finches

THE FINCH FAMILY is a large one that includes birds commonly called finches as well as buntings, cardinals, grosbeaks, siskins, sparrows, and others. Goldfinches also belong to the big finch family, but because they are one of the most common and widespread feeder birds, they warrant their own entry in this book. Except for the goldfinch, the birds that share the common name "finch"—the house finch, purple finch, Cassin's finch, and three western rosy finch species—have one obvious thing in common: The adult males all are blushing with beautiful rosy color.

Look for the perky cap and deep raspberry color to distinguish the purple finch from its reddish relations. Females have a distinct white eye stripe.

The ubiquitous **house finch** is the most common of the four species. Once a California bird known as the linnet, its now coast-to-coast range is yet another example of humans interfering with nature. Traders sold it illegally as a cage bird during the heyday of canaries and other avian pets some 50 years ago. When federal authorities began closing in on East Coast pet shops, owners released the captives illegally. The species readily adapted to life on the opposite side of the continent, and the quickly expanding population met the West Coast birds that were simultaneously spreading eastward. The popularity of blue spruces in the home landscape made the once-treeless Plains bridgeable, encouraging the house finch's expansion. Be alert for color variations in the male house finches that visit your feeder. Some birds are orange or golden instead of reddish purple.

House finches can build to huge numbers at feeding stations. In recent years, the house finch population has decreased somewhat due to a wave of infectious eye disease called mycoplasmal

It takes a sharp eye—or a careful ear—to separate the Cassin's finch of western conifer forests from its similar relatives. Its unique song offers positive ID.

F

conjunctivitis, which spreads quickly through the inbred eastern house finches.

Less invasive and often more welcome at feeders are two other similarly colored finches. In the West, **Cassin's finch** is fairly common, although it forages mainly in the wild and in backyard conifers rather than at feeders. The **purple finch**, most intensely colored of the three, breeds far in the North but winters south to the Gulf Coast and California. It is often confused with the house finch, although when the birds are side by side, it's easy to see that the purple finch is more brightly colored, with a distinctive eye stripe.

Females of these three species are streaky brown. The female purple finch sports a bold white eye stripe.

In the West, three species of rosy finches join the group. The **gray-crowned rosy finch** is most widespread. These birds are tinted with rosy pink over their brown bodies, and they wear a noticeable light gray cap with a black patch above the beak. The **black rosy finch**, an uncommon bird of western mountains, is dramatically dark in color with rose-colored wings and a gray cap. The **brown-capped rosy finch**, found in a very limited range especially in Colorado, is similar to the gray-capped but has a brown head. All three races live high in the mountains, nesting above timberline, although they come to lower elevations in winter. They are uncommon at feeders.

Finch Behavior

The red finches have lovely, warbling voices and sing loudly and often. Even the female house finch is renowned as a singer; she sometimes holds forth even when sitting on the nest. That beautiful song issuing from the tree canopy could very well be coming from a singing finch.

Often misidentified as a "purple finch," the house finch is so populous in some areas that it has become too much of a good thing.

When finches visit your feeder in quantity, they can forget their manners in a fight for the food. Keep squabbles to a minimum by providing plenty of feeding space where they can reach their favorite seeds.

Finches are big fans of salt. Provide a salt block to satisfy their craving for the mineral. Cassin's finches may not come for seeds at your feeder, but they are likely to visit a salt station. Gravel and grit also attract them.

In late winter, watch for finches sipping sap from broken twigs on maples, box elders, and other trees. House finches seem particularly fond of this treat. Addicted to nectar feeders, these birds may hog the perches at a hummingbird feeder for hours at a time.

FINCH FEEDER FOODS
■ Bread crumbs
■ Crushed eggshells
■ Fruit (house finches)
■ Millet
■ Nectar (house finches)
■ Niger
■ Salt
■ Sunflower seeds, any kind

Finches   119

Flax

Attracts buntings, goldfinches, purple and other finches

IF YOU'VE EVER POURED a premium finch seed mix into your feeder, you may have noticed a lovely volunteer plant growing nearby a few months later. Extremely delicate, with small needlelike leaves on a fine stem topped by a cluster of silky, sky blue flowers, flax is a beautiful garden flower as well as a favorite of finches. It also produces the fiber used to make linen fabric.

Flax seed is ultra-high in oil. Use the back of your thumbnail to press one of the flat, shiny brown seeds against a piece of paper and you'll see a greasy smear. That's great news for buntings, goldfinches, purple finches, and other small, high-energy birds, who seek out the high-calorie seeds to keep their active bodies stoked with fuel.

Most birdseed dealers sell flax seed only as part of a high-priced mix. Check with your closest feed mill or farm-supply store to see if you can buy the seed at bulk prices, which will save you a bundle when you make your own custom birdseed blends.

You could build a whole cottage industry around annual flax (*Linum usitatissimum*), which is simple to grow in a sunny spot. Besides fabric and birdseed, flax is also used to make thin paper—for Bibles, cigarette rolling papers, and old-fashioned onionskin writing paper. The seeds are pressed commercially to yield linseed oil and animal feed additives. But if you want to limit your plantation to birdseed, simply scatter the seeds thickly over prepared soil, press into the soil with a lawn roller, and wait for a field of blue flowers to appear. Let it stand in bloom, and as the flowers fade, it will attract birds for months.

The mission in life of an annual flower is to reproduce itself, and that means lots of seeds, since its roots won't survive a second season. But perennial flax species are also attractive to birds, even though their seeds aren't as abundant as those of most annual species. The plant most commonly known as perennial flax, *Linum perenne*, is a popular garden flower because of its graceful appearance and pretty

Silken blue flowers make flax a beautiful addition to the bird-friendly garden, but it's the shiny brown seeds that birds love. They're a goldfinch magnet.

sky blue flowers. Its clumps of wiry stems are clothed in delicate needle-like foliage. Like annual flax, its blossoms open in the morning and close by afternoon, except on cloudy days. The lookalike prairie flax (*Linum perenne* subsp. *lewisii*) of western North America has a slightly more robust look, as does the species *L. narbonense*, which is gaining popularity in perennial gardens.

If blue doesn't fit your color scheme, how about yellow flax, red flax, or white flax? With more than 200 species in the big *Linum* genus, there's a color to suit every garden. I adore the silky rose-red flowers of *L. grandiflorum*, another super-easy annual to grow in a sunny spot, and the finches and siskins adore its seeds. Golden flax (*L. flavum*) glows with warm color, but this perennial is tough when it comes to winter cold—I've seen it flourishing in Zone 4 gardens. Whatever flax you choose, be assured that the birds will approve.

Flickers

Is it the call or the flashy white rump patch that gives flickers their name? Before you decide, consider a third possibility: that these big, brown woodpeckers were nicknamed for the glimpse of bright color beneath their wings that shows only in flight.

Flickers may hold the record for bird nicknames. According to the definitive collection made by Frank L. Burns and published in the *Wilson Bulletin of Ornithology* in April 1900, there were once 126 names for the bird, including yellowhammer, goldenwings, partridge woodpecker, pigeon woodpecker, high-hole, harry-wicket, wake-up, and, my favorite, yawker bird.

A bird with that many names obviously was conspicuous in 1900, and it remains hard to overlook. Its loud, ringing "Wicka-wicka-wicka" call can be heard resounding through woods, across small town streets, and over country fields and golf courses. Besides their loud voice, these big, beautiful woodpeckers boast a white rump patch visible in flight that tells the world who they are from a distance.

The species known as the common flicker includes three races, or subspecies, which together provide a

Unlike most woodpeckers, flickers wear brown feathers instead of black and white. They're named for the white rump patch that "flickers" when they fly.

flicker for almost every corner of the country. All races have brightly colored undersides of wings and tail feathers that help distinguish them. In the eastern two-thirds, the **yellow-shafted flicker** flashes shining golden feathers with every wing stroke. Like the others, this race has a barred brown back, with a wildly spotted white breast and belly and a dashing slash of black across its throat. In the Southwest, the **gilded flicker**, also a yellow-winged race, rules the roost. In the West, it's the striking **red-shafted flicker** that prevails. Just to make things confusing, the ranges of the races overlap, and these closely related birds frequently hybridize. It's not unusual to see a flicker with the head markings of a yellow-shafted but the wing color of the red-shafted race, or any other combination you can think of. Red-shafted birds occasionally stray far eastward of their normal range.

Flicker Behavior

Unlike most woodpeckers, flickers don't stick to the trees. You will frequently see these birds on the ground, where they gobble beetle grubs or nip up ants. Lawns are attractive to them. A flicker or two or six often join the mixed flocks of starlings, robins, and other birds that settle on lawns in late summer and fall.

In breeding season, flickers can be a pain in the ears. Not only do they vocalize loudly, they also drum on resonant surfaces to mark their territories or to impress a mate. Flickers favor tin roofs and wood-sided houses as percussion instruments.

FLICKER FEEDER FOODS

- Amelanchier (*Amelanchier* spp.) berries
- Blueberries (*Vaccinium* spp.)
- Bread and other baked goods
- Grass seeds
- Peanut butter
- Peanut butter and cornmeal recipes
- Suet
- Sumac (*Rhus* spp.) berries
- Watermelon

Flicker courtship is amorous indeed. If you see a female bird perched on a tree or pole, with two or more males below her, you can bet they are dueling for her attention. Taking turns, first one male will hitch up the tree toward the female, contorting his body and finally flashing his wings in an attempt to blind her with his suitability as a mate. Then the next bird gets his turn to impress. I have sometimes watched as many as five male flickers wooing a single female.

Starlings often take a liking to flicker nest cavities, sitting back while the woodpeckers do the excavating work and then attempting a hostile takeover when the nest hole is ready. If you hear flickers making a commotion, it may be the beginning of a fierce anti-starling defense of their home.

Flickers are a great reason to treasure the anthills in your yard or the trails of ants walking up and down tree trunks or to your nectar feeder. The big woodpeckers eat these insects like candy. Of course, when they finish chowing down on the ants at your nectar feeder, they may settle on the container for a long bout of sugar-water sipping.

Flickers are agile clinging birds that can use high-level feeders, low trays, suet cages, and nectar feeders (which tend to swing violently initially under their weight). In the parched Southwest, try putting out a half of a watermelon or chunks of the sweet fruit on a tray feeder to tempt the gilded flicker to visit your feeding station.

Eastern flickers boast golden yellow underwings, but salmon red identifies this western bird. Both subspecies may wander, so watch flying flickers closely.

In colder regions, flickers may stick around in winter instead of migrating southward if the weather is milder than usual. A hand-cranked meat grinder, which you can buy from catalogs or at country stores, especially in Amish or Mennonite areas, is the perfect accessory for winter flicker feeding. Use it to grind suet into hamburger-like consistency and spread in an open tray feeder to delight every lingering flicker in the neighborhood.

Male or Female?

LOOK CLOSELY at the heads of flickers with binoculars to learn to tell male from female and one race from another. All races and both sexes have a black throat swash.

Flicker Race	Sex	Head Cap	Red Nape	Mustache	Face	Underwing Color
Yellow-shafted	M	Gray	Yes	Black	Tan	Golden
Yellow-shafted	F	Gray	Yes	None	Tan	Golden
Red-shafted	M	Brown	No	Red	Gray	Salmon-red
Red-shafted	F	Brown	No	None	Gray	Salmon-red
Gilded	M	Brown	No	Red	Gray	Golden
Gilded	F	Brown	No	None	Gray	Golden

Flowers for Birds

Attract many birds at various times of the year

FOR THE MOST PART, gardeners choose the flowers they grow based on color and/or fragrance. But birds have an entirely different agenda when it comes to their floral favorites. If you want to use your flower garden to tempt birds into visiting your yard, look for flowering plants that provide edible seeds, useful nesting materials, or shelter for safety and nesting. Except for nectar-sipping orioles and hummingbirds, birds are uninterested in the blossoms themselves unless they attract small insects, another mainstay on the bird menu.

More is better when it comes to bird gardens. A single potted plant won't attract much, if any, avian attention. But a wide bed with a variety of plants is bound to be a popular spot, thanks to the insects that live among the leaves, branches, and flowers. Those aphids you despise are a delicious appetizer to chickadees; your plump tomato hornworms are as desirable as prime rib to a brown thrasher. Even the Japanese beetles devouring your roses are appealing to foraging birds.

Flowers for Food

Keep in mind that a yard filled with flowers attracts zillions of insects, which are manna to birds. Even if you're growing flowers that don't yield seeds or fruits for bird dining, they'll still add something for hungry birds to munch on. Daisies (*Chrysanthemum* spp.), oregano (*Origanum vulgare*), yarrows (*Achillea* spp.), and other flowering plants that produce clusters of many tiny nectar-rich flowers are best for attracting the small insects that bring in the birds!

Foraging birds move fast, unless they're shelling seeds or sipping nectar, so you may not even notice

Flowering plants tempt birds with cover as well as seeds and nectar. Branching plants benefit birds seeking shelter. Insects add even more bird appeal.

the many songbird visits to your flower garden. Place a comfy bench or small tea table and chair near your flower garden and notice who comes to call, especially in early summer when nesting is at a peak and parent birds have hungry mouths to feed. You may spot bluebirds, catbirds, orioles, thrushes, towhees—in fact, any nearby resident birds—flitting from plant to plant for munchies on the move.

If you hope to grow seeds for your flock along with your flowers, start with the plants listed in "Annual Flowers for Birds" on page 126. Annuals are prolific seed producers and, therefore, a best bet where birds are concerned. Perennial flowers tend to be stingier with their seeds, but some are worthwhile from a bird's point of view. Take a look at "Perennial Flowers for Birds" on page 127 to see which "seedy" perennials to include in your birdseed flowerbed.

Flowering weeds are also great for the bird garden: common chicory, goldenrod, the dandelion-like hawkweed, and the tiny pink-flowered plants called knotweeds are just a few of the weeds that help feed the birds. (For more on weeds attractive to birds, see Weeds on page 327.)

Flowers for Nesting Material

Plant fibers and twigs are two top components of many bird nests. If you let your garden plants stand over winter, their stems will be weathered just right for birds to strip long lengths of fiber from them at spring nesting time.

Any perennial or annual flower with stiff, slim twiggy branches is a prime candidate for nesting material. If you can bring yourself to delay spring cleanup, you can watch birds collecting sticks or stringy leaves from many garden flowers, including bearded iris (*Iris* bearded hybrids), Siberian iris (*Iris siberica*), mallows (*Hibiscus* and *Malva* spp.), liriopes (*Liriope* spp.), and many others. If you prefer a tidy garden, collect the stalks of fibrous plants and pile them beside your compost pile or in view of a favorite window for orioles to harvest at nesting time.

Flowers for Shelter and Nesting Sites

A densely planted flower garden that features tall, branching plants as well as clumps of plants closer to the ground provides useful shelter to birds in your backyard. Lush flower gardens give birds a place to wait out rain and wind. If the flowers are near your feeders, birds can use the flowerbed as an escape route in case of predators or panic. Be aware that prowling cats may also use flowers near feeders as cover for sneaking up on birds. If cats are a problem in your yard, keep the flowers at least 6 feet from the feeders.

Birds that spend most of their lives on or near the ground may even become residents of your flower garden. Buntings, native sparrows, and common yellowthroats are the birds most likely to turn up because they aren't as shy as others when it comes to human interference. In relatively undisturbed corners, you may also find thrushes and towhees making themselves at home.

Ground-nesting birds like to snuggle their woven cups against a dense clump of grass or among thick

Composite flowers like this zinnia are made up of many small flowers, each of which produces a seed. A single zinnia seedhead can keep a goldfinch busy for an hour, as it cracks its way through the nutritious banquet, one seed at a time.

plant stems, where they're hidden from view. Flowers that grow into shrub-size plants or those that form thick colonies are ideal nesting sites for indigo buntings and the common yellowthroat. Song sparrows often nest among daylilies (*Hemerocallis* spp.) and in groundcovers, while white-crowned sparrows favor lupines (*Lupinus* spp.).

Designing Flower Gardens for Birds

Time to think like a bird again: When it comes to designing a garden, you'll want to provide protective cover and food first because these two work hand in hand to tempt birds into lingering in your yard. Begin by considering where birds spend their time in the wild and where they hunt for food naturally. Then apply those insights to your flower garden plan, keeping in mind what birds you want to attract:

- Robins and a few other birds, like grackles and starlings, appreciate a sparsely planted garden, with neatly weeded space between the plants because that gives them easy access to open soil for pulling worms and finding bugs.

- Grosbeaks, orioles, tanagers, vireos, warblers, and other birds that spend most of their time in the trees are lured to lower levels by abundant fruit or insects—their favorite foods. They prefer to stick close to cover, so make sure your flowerbeds form a corridor that leads to and from the safety of trees.

- Buntings and native sparrows are low on the food chain, so they spend most of their time in thick vegetation. In the wild, they stay in the brushy edges of fields and roadsides. In your flower garden, they'll appreciate plenty of taller, branching plants that mimic the shrubs in their wild habitat.

- Cardinals, catbirds, mockingbirds, and wrens aren't as shy as other songbirds because they're accustomed to living around people. But densely planted flowers of varying heights will keep them safe while they search for food in your garden.

GARDEN DESIGN

Birdseed Flower Garden

Seed-eating birds are, of course, accustomed to getting their seeds from plants as well as from bird feeders. This garden lets you cut out the steps of buying seed and putting it into feeders. Instead, grow a lush garden filled with these seed-producing flowers and enjoy the view: pretty flowers for you and plenty of seeds for your bird buddies. You can grow all of these annuals from seed started indoors in late winter or sown directly where you want your garden to grow.

PLANT LIST

1. 'Lemon Queen' sunflowers (*Helianthus* spp.)
2. 'Rosa' cosmos (*Cosmos bipinnatus* 'Rosa')
3. Bachelor's buttons (*Centaurea cyanus*)
4. Love-lies-bleeding (*Amaranthus caudatus*)
5. 'Vanilla Ice' sunflowers (*Helianthus* spp.)
6. Garden balsam (*Impatiens balsamina*)

F

Annual Flowers for Birds

ANNUAL FLOWERS are terrific bird plants because they produce ample amounts of snackable seeds. Think how many seeds are in a double-flowered zinnia—one seed per petal—and multiply by the dozens of blossoms a plant produces to get an idea of the bounty an annual garden brings for birds. Plant self-sowing annuals where their free-seeding ways won't turn them into perennial garden pests.

Flower	Description	Birds Attracted	Comments
Tickseed sunflower (*Bidens aristosa*)	Billowy, ferny-leaved plant to 4 feet tall and wide, with masses of fragrant yellow daisies that attract butterflies	Bobwhites, buntings, cardinals, chickadees, goldfinches, house finches, purple finches, other finches, pheasants, redpolls, siskins, sparrows, titmice	Self-sows abundantly; nice to fill a sunny hillside. Buntings and sparrows may nest at the base of a cluster of plants. Flowers attract many insects that bring in flycatchers, orioles, vireos, warblers, and other insect eaters.
Cosmos (*Cosmos bipinnatus, C. sulphureus*)	Tall, graceful plants with ferny foliage and flowers in shades of pink, white, or red-purple (*C. bipinnatus*) or yellow and orange (*C. sulphureus*)	Buntings, goldfinches, house finches, redpolls, siskins	Seeds ripen while other flowers are still blooming; look closely to see feeding birds. Self-sows.
Annual sunflowers (*Helianthus annuus, H. debilis*)	Tall, usually single-stemmed plants with cream, yellow, rust, or bi-colored flowers atop and along stem; *H. debilis* types are multibranching.	Cardinals, chickadees, finches, jays, titmice, woodpeckers	Plant at 2-week intervals for a steady seed supply. Cut some heads to save for fall and winter feeding. Self-sows.
Garden balsam (*Impatiens balsamina*)	Short, bushy plant with hummingbird-attracting flowers in pastel pink, lavender, and white	Cardinals, grosbeaks, hummingbirds, towhees	Self-sows. Watch for towhees scavenging fallen seeds beneath the plants.
Impatiens (*Impatiens wallerana*)	Familiar bedding and container plant with bright or pastel hummingbird-attracting flowers in all colors but blue	Cardinals, grosbeaks, hummingbirds	Perennial in mild climates
Marigolds (*Tagetes* spp.)	Ruffled, multipetaled or single flowers in shades of gold, rust, maroon, and yellow; ferny, aromatic foliage	Juncos, siskins, native sparrows	Not as popular as other annuals, but birds will visit them in winter when other seeds are scarce if you let the plants stand.
Mexican sunflower (*Tithonia rotundifolia*)	Eye-catching plant to 6 feet tall with zingy orange-red daisies that attract multitudes of butterflies and hummingbirds	Buntings, cardinals, doves, finches, hummingbirds, jays, sparrows, titmice, towhees	Look for birds both on the seed-heads and at the base of the plants. Buntings and sparrows may nest beneath these bushy plants in an undisturbed garden area.
Zinnias (*Zinnia* spp.)	Fast-blooming favorites in sizes from dwarf to tall, with single or multipetaled flowers in rich, saturated hues and delicate pastels; all colors but blue	Buntings, cardinals, chickadees, goldfinches and other finches, redpolls, siskins, sparrows, titmice	Plant shorter varieties in front of tall types to hide ragged bottom foliage.

Perennial Flowers for Birds

PERENNIALS ARE rarely as generous as annuals with their seeds, although exceptions exist among members of the daisy family, which often produce a bumper crop. Some perennials make up for their sparse seed production by yielding bird-attracting fruits. When its spikes of black berries are ripe, the common groundcover liriope attracts bluebirds faster than a tray of mealworms.

Flower	Description	Birds Attracted	Comments
Jack-in-the-pulpit (*Arisaema trifolium*)	Three-part leaves grow below an unusual hooded flower that matures to a tight-packed cluster of glossy red berries; shade lover	Pheasants, gray-cheeked thrushes, wood thrushes, wild turkeys	Chipmunks will also nibble seeds. Pluck a few seeds to start in pots to expand your planting.
Purple coneflower (*Echinacea purpurea*)	Clump-forming plant produces many lavender-purple daisies with attractive raised golden centers	Buntings, finches, juncos, siskins, sparrows, towhees	Attracts butterflies and other insects, which may lure flycatchers and orioles to your garden. Self-sows moderately.
Perennial sunflowers (*Helianthus* spp.)	Tall, branching golden daisies that usually spread to the point of invasiveness by underground roots	Buntings, finches, juncos, sparrows, towhees	Plant in a natural meadow or wilder part of the garden where their aggressiveness won't swamp neighboring plants. Good with native grasses.
Liriopes (*Liriope* spp.)	Short, grassy clumps of foliage with spikes of purple or white flowers followed by black berries	Bluebirds, mockingbirds	Edge a bed or fill a shady nook with liriope to attract bluebirds from a distance.
Lupines (*Lupinus* spp.)	Dense spikes of pea-blossom–shaped flowers arise from clumping or sprawling plants; with nearly 200 native North American species, size, habit, and color vary widely.	Bobwhites, Clark's nutcrackers, quail, native sparrows, wild turkeys	All legumes, lupines included, are good food sources for game birds and some ground-feeding songbirds.
Buttercups (*Ranunculus* spp.)	Buttery yellow 5-petaled flowers spark clumps of deep green leaves; often spreading	Bobwhites, buntings, grouse, pheasants, quail, redpolls, sparrows, wild turkeys	Good for the natural garden or around the garden pool. Some species can be invasive; *R. constantinopolitanus*, *R. glacialis*, and *R. rhomboideus* are not overly aggressive.
Gloriosa daisy (*Rudbeckia hirta* 'Gloriosa')	Clump-forming biennial to perennial plant with tall stems of large daisies in buttery yellows and rich rusty browns; some bicolors	Buntings, cardinals, finches, juncos, siskins, sparrows, towhees	Self-sows moderately. Don't confuse with *Rudbeckia* 'Goldsturm', a sterile cultivar that rarely sets edible seeds and thus holds no interest for birds.
Goldenrods (*Solidago* spp.)	Plumes of golden flowers atop plants ranging from knee-high to shoulder height, depending on species	Prairie chickens, goldfinches, grouse, juncos, pine siskins, swamp sparrows, tree sparrows	Especially handsome combined with blue or purple late-blooming asters
Violets (*Viola* spp.)	Ground-hugging plants with usually heart-shaped leaves and dainty blue, purple, or white flowers	Bobwhites, doves, grouse, juncos, quail, native sparrows, wild turkeys	Wild turkeys scratch out and eat the tuberous roots of violets, while other species favor the seeds.

Flying Squirrels

IF YOUR BIRDSEED is disappearing overnight, the leading suspect may be a creature that flies in from the treetops. No, this isn't some unusual seed-eating owl that's emptying your feeders—it's a flying squirrel.

Nocturnal cousin of the chipmunk and ubiquitous squirrels, the flying squirrel is a gentle little creature with huge dark eyes—the better to see in the dark with, my dear. It is soft brown with a pale belly and an odd, flattened tail that looks as if it was pressed between the pages of a book. Folds of furred skin along the side of its body stretch open when the animal spreads its front and back legs wide, catching the air like a parasail as it glides downward from the trees.

Recent research indicates that flying squirrels may be even more numerous than our familiar daytime squirrels. Because they are rarely seen, they were once thought to be a rarity. But scientists have taken to the trees to find them and are still collecting data on flying squirrel populations.

The first flying squirrel I ever saw was rustling like a mouse in a box of peanut brittle on my kitchen counter. The rustling alerted my cat and me at the same time, but I investigated first. Instead of the mouse I expected, I met a fearless little animal—cute is the only word to describe it. It sat up on its hind legs and looked at me with bright button eyes. It didn't seem at all scared and was easily tempted to nibble daintily on some black walnuts I offered.

Once I knew I had flying squirrels in my neighborhood, I began looking for them at the feeder. Every night at about 11 P.M., two to five squirrels would arrive one by one, sailing in from the oaks (*Quercus* spp.) and tulip poplars (*Liriodendron tulipfera*). They'd sit in the open tray feeder of sunflower seeds and feast for an hour or so, then depart to look for acorns beneath the oak.

Look for flying squirrels at dusk, when they become active, often sailing across roads or from one

A nocturnal charmer, the flying squirrel is less of a glutton than its daytime kin. These tame mammals probably visit feeders more often than we realize.

large shade tree to another. The smaller type occurs from Maine to Minnesota, south to Texas and Florida; a larger subspecies ranges across the North; and a third type populates mountains from Canada south to California, Utah, and Tennessee. Flying squirrels make their homes in rotted-out knotholes or other cavities high in the treetops, or they may nest in dead snags and even bird boxes.

These squirrels are actually excellent gliders, since they are unable to achieve lift and thus don't actually fly. Observers have measured single glides of more than 150 feet starting from a perch 60 feet high. On the ground, flying squirrels are speedy runners. Although their habits are not fully known, they probably dine on bird eggs and perhaps nestlings as well as their favored acorns and nuts. The flying squirrels at my feeder also enjoy peanut butter, suet, raisins, grapes, and an occasional slice of apple.

Freezer Treats

Attract many kinds of birds

IT'S EASY TO STORE plenty of birdseed year-round, but soft foods such as bread and leftovers can pile up quickly, especially in summer, when the feeder traffic slacks off but the family keeps eating. I solve the storage problem by using my freezer. In winter, I'm always glad I did because I can pull out ready-to-feed freezer treats whenever the birds need extra food or a change of pace.

Resealable plastic bags in large and small sizes are my main storage containers. They let me see at a glance what's available, unlike rigid plastic containers that don't show the inventory.

Here's what's usually in my freezer:

- Cottage-cheese cups filled with suet or bacon fat
- Bags of chopped suet
- Bags of nuts, bought on sale
- A large bag of mixed crackers, stale bread, and other baked goods
- Bags of leftover fruit, or meat and egg scraps for making treats
- A stockpile of bird-appealing, hand-molded logs, balls, and cups of frozen food (see below)

Collecting Ingredients

Every day, I add bread crusts, cornbread crumbs, bagel remains, and any other grain-based products to a plastic freezer bag that I keep on the counter. When I wipe breakfast toast crumbs or the flour from rolling out pastry from my table or counters, I swipe the crumbs directly into the mixed bag.

I use another plastic bag when I'm cooking or serving fruit. Stray grapes, squishy blueberries, past-their-prime bananas, and apple cores all go in the bag. Meats, eggs, and fatty foods, like leftover meatballs, chicken skin, trimmed fat from roasts, bacon crumbles, and other goodies go in another bag when it's cleanup time. Nuts and peanuts, which are always precious because they're so popular and

An old-fashioned meat grinder is the best tool for reducing chunks of suet to bite-size pieces for birds. Grind a big batch to stock your freezer for winter.

expensive compared to other foods, go in another bag. The last bag—for leftovers—comes in handy after the meal or when I periodically clean out the refrigerator. It feels great to toss that half-cup of cooked spaghetti or applesauce into a bag for the birds instead of watching it grow green mold in a hidden corner of the fridge.

The last big plastic bag in my freezer is a conglomeration of leftovers that I didn't bother sorting: stale cereal, sandwich crusts, pizza slices, meat drippings, old lunchmeat—whatever stray foods look like they might have bird potential. Anything based on grains, nuts, fruits, or meats is fair game. Don't overlook that last spoonful of soup or stew—chances are, it has something bird-edible in it.

Cookbooks usually have advice about what to freeze and what not to. In my experience, the reason for not freezing some foods is that the texture may change for the worse by human standards.

Birds aren't nearly so fussy. Unless you serve them something they don't eat at all—cooked green beans, for example—they'll gobble it up whether it's mushy or not.

The quick and easy way to serve this stuff is to merely dump it into an accommodating feeder, but that invites a few too many starlings, even for my tolerance level. If I'm trying to distract pesky birds away from the main feeding area, the dump-it method is appropriate. But usually I hoard my leftovers to make recipes that will attract the birds I treasure most: jays, woodpeckers, wrens, and the other smaller feeder customers. By combining ingredients to appeal to fruit, nut, or meat eaters, I can better target the beneficiaries of my kitchen cleanups.

Preparing Freezer Treats

In my house, bread and other baked products outnumber other leftovers by a huge margin. That should probably make me ashamed of wasting so much food, but instead it makes me feel as rich as Midas. As I watch the resealable bags pile up, I count my wealth in bread crusts instead of gold.

Because so many of my feeder friends welcome bread crumbs, I use my blender to whirl the frozen baked goods into coarse or fine crumbs. Chickadees, juncos, robins, sparrows, towhees, and their chums don't mind a bit that they're consuming crumbs of uncertain parentage. Was it a frozen waffle or an onion bagel? The birds don't care!

I invented my freezer treat recipes by watching what the birds at my feeders prefer to eat. So far, the only things that my birds usually spurn are raw or cooked vegetables, white rice, cheese, and other dairy products (although a friend swears that her mockingbird downs sour cream). Experiment with your own combinations. It's fun to get to know which blue-plate specials your regulars order most often.

Experimenting also comes into play when you're figuring out how much of a binding material, such as oil or peanut butter, you'll need to make your treats. Start with small amounts. You can always add more oil as you need it, but if you pour in too

much, you may have to sacrifice that loaf of crusty fresh bread to the mix.

Don't worry about mixing the ingredients thoroughly. Frozen foods clump together, and it's not necessary to have uniform-size small pieces. Just crumble any large lumps so that your mixture holds together better. If your treasure bags have frozen into a solid mass that you can't break up, partially thaw before using at room temperature or on the defrost setting in your microwave.

Serving Freezer Treats

I reserve my homemade treats for winter feeding, when low temperatures slow spoilage and feeder visitors are abundant. If you live in a mild-winter area, or if you want to serve your treats at other seasons, offer them in a tray feeder, where birds can snack on any bits that fall away.

In cold-winter areas, you can stick your treats onto spike-type feeders, such as you use for corncobs or orange halves. Densely packed loaves, logs, and balls will hold together as birds nibble or whack at them.

One of the big benefits of a freezer is that it makes serving fat-based foods much less messy. In summer, suet blocks and peanut butter can melt in the heat, wasting good food and staining your post or porch with grease. I've gotten in the habit of storing extra commercial suet blocks as well as homemade fat-based treats in the freezer for a few days before serving. Even in winter, the birds that eat them can still peck off bites of food no matter how hard it's frozen. And in summer, it lengthens the life span of these treasured treats.

You can fill plastic cottage-cheese or similar containers from any of your bags or a combination of frozen food scraps. Store in the freezer to serve anytime. Poke the containers onto big nails hammered through a board backing, so they remain securely in place while birds work at the contents.

> Turn leftovers from your freezer into a smorgasbord of bird-tempting custom blends.

Woodpecker Favorite

This treat is tempting to chickadees, jays, nuthatches, titmice, and woodpeckers.

INGREDIENTS

2 *parts from the bread bag*

1 *part from the meat bag*

1 *part chopped suet*

½ *part from the nut bag*

   Vegetable oil (optional)

Pour into large bowl. Break apart chunks as necessary. Work ingredients with your hands until they are reasonably blended, and the mixture clings together. The suet will melt as you work, providing the binding agent. If mixture seems dry and crumbles instead of sticking together, add some peanut, walnut, or corn oil. Mold into balls or corncob-size logs. Serve on a spike feeder, or put in a mesh bag and hang from a tree branch.

Best for Bluebirds

High in fat and calories, this fruity mixture is tailor-made for bluebirds. It's a welcome meal for mockingbirds, thrashers, thrushes, and Carolina wrens, too.

INGREDIENTS

2 *parts from the fruit bag*

2 *parts chopped suet*

1 *part from the bread bag*

1 *part from the meat bag*

½ *part cornmeal (optional)*

Combine all ingredients. Spread on cookie sheet lined with wax paper. Refreeze until hard. Pour into large resealable plastic bags. Serve in an open tray feeder, especially after winter storms. *Note:* If fruits are particularly juicy, add ½ part cornmeal to mix.

Mockingbird Manna

Also favored by bluebirds, robins, thrashers, and Carolina wrens.

INGREDIENTS

2 *parts from the fruit bag*

2 *parts from the bread bag*

1 *part chopped suet*

½ *part from the meat bag*

½ *part from the leftovers bag*

   Corn oil or peanut butter (optional)

Combine all ingredients until partially mixed, using hands to break up any large clumps. Squeeze a handful; if it falls apart, pour in ½ cup of corn oil or peanut butter and mix again. Increase oil if necessary. Shape into low loaf shape, about 2 inches high, and serve in a tray feeder or on a horizontal spike feeder.

Starling Pleaser

Win the loyalty of crows, jays, magpies, and starlings with this treat. Mix in large quantity to make a big, long-lasting block that will keep these birds busy and away from your seed feeders.

INGREDIENTS

4 *parts from the bread bag*

2 *parts chopped suet*

2 *parts from the meat bag*

2 *parts from the leftovers bag*

1 *part from the fruit bag*

   Corn or peanut oil (optional)

Mix ingredients in a large bowl. Mold into a block or loaf, adding corn or peanut oil if necessary for binding. Serve directly on the ground, away from songbird feeders.

F

Fruit

Attracts many kinds of birds at various times of the year

A TASTE FOR FRUIT has made many birds less than welcome with commercial orchardists and backyard fruit growers. These folks must constantly protect their crops of apples, cherries, peaches, and other juicy fruits from the ravages of house finches, orioles, robins, and other fruit fanciers. "Ravages" is the correct word, too. Although birds eat small fruits such as cherries and grapes whole, they usually damage large fruits rather than consume them. The birds that descend on a tree use their sharp bills to stab the fruit and nip the flesh or sip the juice, leaving the rest to rot while they move on to another piece of fruit.

Fruits that taste good to us humans seem to be real bird pleasers, too. Juicy blackberries are plucked quickly by all fruit-eating birds.

This fondness for fruit gives backyard bird feeders another good way to tempt birds to feeding stations and the surrounding yard. Fruit on the tree will attract birds first because they naturally seek food in there. But in the off-season or when lured to the area by fruit trees, fruit-eating birds may soon move to the feeders.

Fruit at the Feeder

When fresh fruits are ripening in gardens and orchards, you won't have much luck getting birds to visit your feeders. They can pick sumptuous fruits at the height of ripeness in the shade of their leafy restaurant. I reserve most of my fruit offerings for midfall through winter, when the real thing is scarce. I do serve fresh oranges during spring, summer, and early fall in my oriole feeders, and I provide a year-round supply of apples, which feed squirrels as well as feeder birds.

You can feed fresh, dried, and even frozen fruits to birds. Take advantage of low prices at harvest time to lay in a supply for winter, when blueberries and many other fruits are worth their weight in gold at the supermarket. Resealable plastic bags make freezing a

---

Freebie Fruit

GET TO know the manager of your supermarket's produce department, and you'll tap into a great source for unusual feeder foods at little or no cost. Produce that is too far past its prime to go to food bank programs still has plenty of life left as bird food. Find out what days fruit is removed from the counters, then be sure to visit to collect grapes, oranges, grapefruit, apples, and other goodies for just pennies a pound—or even better, for free!

Ask at local farmers' markets to find out how the vendors dispose of their faded goods, too. The end of the last day of market is often a time when less-than-perfect fruit goes for rock-bottom prices. And, if you're lucky enough to gather more bargain fruit than you can use right away, store it in the fridge or freeze it in resealable plastic bags for future feeder filling.

Birds That Favor Fruit

PLANT A fruit tree in your yard, and you'll attract a bounty of birds when the crop ripens. It's not unusual to see dozens of species feasting on a fruit tree at the same time. Sling a hammock or settle a chaise longue near the tree for comfortable viewing. Many of these same fruit-fancying birds will also visit a feeder that offers fruit regularly.

- Blackbirds
- Cardinals
- Catbirds
- Chickadees
- Crows
- House finches
- Purple finches
- Flickers
- Great crested flycatchers
- Grackles
- Grosbeaks
- Black-headed grosbeaks
- Jays
- Kingbirds
- Magpies
- Mockingbirds
- Orioles
- Phainopeplas
- Phoebes
- Band-tailed pigeons
- Robins
- Sapsuckers
- House sparrows
- Starlings
- Tanagers
- Thrashers
- Thrushes
- Titmice
- Vireos
- Waxwings
- Woodpeckers
- Wrens

cinch. I freeze small fruits and cut pieces of larger fruits on wax-paper–lined cookie sheets first, then slide them into the plastic bags. That way, they stay separated instead of freezing into a solid lump that even a woodpecker would have a hard time hacking apart.

Apples, fresh, chopped, or dried, are one of the most widely popular fruits with birds. I like to put a few whole fresh apples on the ground beneath the feeders and watch how birds attack the problem of getting to the fruit. Usually it's a jay or starling that first punctures the tough skin. When the bigger birds move away from the prize, chickadees, juncos, and other small birds move in to get a bite of sweet flesh. You can easily dry apples in a warm oven or the microwave. Slice them into rings before drying. No need to remove the core or peel the fruit first. Children enjoy threading the slices into garlands for draping a fence, decorating a cast-off Christmas tree, or hanging down a post.

Serve large fruits on the ground, in tray feeders, or impaled on the spikes of fruit feeders. Scatter chopped fruits, dried fruit pieces, or small fruits in open tray feeders or directly on the ground once you have established a clientele.

Best Fruits for Birds

Any fruit, from apples to figs, cherries to cactus, will have its takers at the feeder or in the garden. Apples, cherries, figs, and plums appeal to the largest variety of birds, but any fruit good enough for human consumption is good enough for the birds.

Birds also treasure wild fruits. Amelanchiers, hackberries, mulberries, sassafras, sour gum, and other trees that produce fleshy or juicy fruits are a guaranteed draw with many birds. As with other bird-attracting plants, regional natives will bring you plenty of customers because they are familiar to the birds. But both native and introduced species of mulberry are so popular with birds that even a single tree will bring great crested flycatchers, thrushes, vireos, and other unusual species winging from far away to feast on the fruits.

Growing Fruit for Birds

If you want to grow fruit yourself, choose varieties that thrive in your area and crops you will enjoy sharing if the birds let you.

Birds are much less fussy than we are. A few wormholes or brown spots are no drawback at all, and smaller fruits are just as welcome as giant specimens. That means you won't have to bother with thinning fruits so they attain the largest possible size, and you can dispense with sprayers and sticky traps to control pests. You don't even need to
(continued on page 135)

GARDEN DESIGN

A Fruit Garden for Birds

Dwarf trees make it simple to add fresh fruit to your yard, even if it's a small offering. Most plants have pretty, fragrant flowers that look good in the garden, so you can integrate the fruit trees into your landscape plans just as you would any ornamental flowering tree. They provide clouds of bloom in spring—that attract insect-eating orioles and warblers—and later are absolute bird magnets when the crop ripens.

One fruit to beware of is the crab apple. Many hybrids have fruit that is apparently unpalatable. However, birds may feed on the fruit of some older cultivars and unimproved species varieties of these trees, available from native plant nurseries. Look around your neighborhood in winter, and you'll see crab apple trees bare of birds, weighted down by their burden of fruit. If you decide to add a crab apple to your garden, visit the nursery yourself—in winter—and tag the trees that attract bird traffic.

If you're planting a whole area in fruit for the birds, fill in around fruiting trees with a few different types of berry bushes and a grapevine to attract the greatest variety of birds. Otherwise, mix fruit-bearing trees and shrubs into your landscape plantings to give them added bird appeal.

PLANT LIST

1. Serviceberry (*Amelanchier* hybrid)

2. Blueberries (*Vaccinium* spp.)

3. Concord grape (*Vitis* spp.)

4. Crab apple (*Malus* spp.)

prune—when your customers have wings, branches that are out of reach of an arm or a ladder are no problem at all. An elderly peach tree that I inherited along with my Indiana house attracts hordes of house finches, orioles, downy woodpeckers, and the occasional yellow-bellied sapsucker. The birds don't seem to mind a bit that the peaches are borne only at the very top of the tree and are usually so pocked with insect holes that each fruit is studded with oozing sap.

Dried Fruit

Store-bought dried fruit is too costly to make up a lavish part of your feeder menu, but birds treasure it as an occasional treat. Bluebirds, chickadees, mockingbirds, thrushes, titmice, and waxwings are all fond of fruit, whether it's fresh or dried. In winter, when wild or garden fruit is hard to find, such dried fruit offerings may draw birds that usually don't visit a feeder, such as catbirds, thrashers, and yellow-rumped warblers.

Serve dried fruit sparingly until you can gauge how rapidly your feeder birds devour it. Sprinkle a scant handful on a higher tray feeder for blue-birds, jays, and mockingbirds, or directly on the ground for robins and other low-level feeders. Nut feeders made of large-grid wire may be perfect for feeding fruit: Chop the pieces into a size that will fit between the holes of the wire. If you have time and patience, it's fun to fashion small life-like clusters of dried fruit to hang from shrubs or tree branches.

Dried fruit is a real bonus to have on hand when you concoct bird-attracting recipes, such as breads and muffins. (See Bread on page 47 for some easy fruit bread recipes for birds.) Chop the fruit into small bits and add to the batter before baking. You can also use chopped dried fruit in uncooked cereal or cornmeal mixtures. It is best not to add dried fruit to suet mixtures you cook up yourself. While it is true that many of the same birds that like suet also eat fruit, the fat is enough of a draw without squandering dried fruit. Also, the presence of the fruit within the fat may encourage birds to dig in deeply to reach the favored bits, greasing their feathers and decreasing the insulating properties that protect them from the cold.

Small Fruit for a Big Yard

IF YOU want to see every fruit-eating bird within, oh, ½ mile of your property, plant a mulberry tree. Birds can't resist the bite-size fruits, which grow in such abundance that they usually cover the ground beneath the tree in a purple blanket. That's one way to spot a roadside mulberry: The dark stain from squashed berries stains the road surface for a stretch of 20 feet or so.

The **red mulberry** (*Morus rubra*) and the **Texas mulberry** (*M. microphylla*) are the native species in America, but the introduced **white mulberry** (*M. alba*), brought to feed a fledgling silkworm industry, is also a common escapee along roadsides and woods' edges. **Black mulberry** (*M. nigra*), another introduced species, shows up wild here and there. Birds appreciate the fruit of all mulberries, and they will descend on the tree in huge numbers even before the fruit is completely ripe.

Birds are responsible for the spread of mulberries because they "drop" the undigested seeds wherever they get the urge. This method of plant distribution makes mulberries less popular with humans—thanks to the purple juice of the berries, the deposits leave very noticeable splotches wherever they land.

Mulberry trees may reach 80 feet tall. They were common door-yard trees in years past, when people welcomed the fruits for fresh eating and used them in jams, pies, and wine. The delicious fruit was well worth the occasional purple-splattered laundry on the line.

If you have a large property, a mulberry is the best bird fruit tree you can plant. The bird watching is excellent, as bluebirds, orioles, tanagers, vireos, and scores of other species arrive to dine. If you have a smaller yard or nearby neighbors, you should stick to a more well-behaved cherry tree.

Fruity Mix for Winter Birds

Make a batch of this dried-fruit and nut mix to tempt bluebirds, catbirds, purple finches, black-headed and rose-breasted grosbeaks, mockingbirds, robins, thrashers, and Carolina wrens into becoming regulars at your feeders. Dedicate a separate feeder to the food, so that the intended recipients feast upon it and it doesn't get kicked to the ground by nonfruit-eating sparrows.

INGREDIENTS

2 *cups raisins, golden or regular*

2 *cups dried cherries*

2 *cups chopped dried apples*

2 *cups chopped almonds, pecans, walnuts, or other nuts*

1 *cup chopped prunes*

1 *cup chopped peanuts*

1 *cup dried squash or melon seeds*

Recycle a window screen into an outdoor fruit dryer for a sunny summer day. Cut thin slices of apples or other fruits so they dry quickly; prop the screen so air circulates underneath.

To chop dried fruit more easily into beak-size bites, use a sharp knife, and dip it in cornmeal when fruit begins to stick to it. Pour all ingredients into a bucket or large bowl, and stir to combine. Store leftover mix in a brown paper sack in a cool, dry place until it's time to refill your fruit feeder.

Dry Your Own Fruit

DRYING YOUR own fruit is an easy project. Harness the power of the sun, the oven, or the microwave to turn fresh berries and thin-sliced apples, bananas, and other fruits into delectable bird treats. In an oven, a low setting—200°F or less—works best. The time it takes to dry sliced fruits varies, depending on the thickness of the slices and the juiciness of the fruits. Start with 30 minutes, then check the tray of fruit for dryness. This method may take several hours, during which you need to check the fruit often.

Because microwave ovens vary in power, you'll have to experiment to find the right timing. Try 2 minutes at low power to start; gradually add time in 1-minute increments, as needed. In summer, an old window screen makes an ideal fruit dryer. Arrange the fruit in a single layer, and cover it with a layer of cheesecloth to deter insects. If you are lucky enough to have a wood-burning stove, check country auctions or country stores, especially in Amish regions, for a "bean dryer." This large metal box holds water and provides a flat surface for drying fruit (or beans). Load the dryer with fruit and set on top of a burning wood stove for drying in the winter months.

G

Game Birds

"GAME BIRD" IS a common nickname referring to birds that come to dinner—on a platter, with a side of savory stuffing. Plump-breasted quail, pheasants, grouse, and other meaty species face the brunt of hunting pressure nowadays, although in years past, hunters included robins and other songbirds in their list of quarry.

Modern game birds belong to the order Galliformes and are called gallinaceous birds. The word is from the Latin for "domestic fowl," quite appropriate as these birds resemble chickens. Their similarities to barnyard fowl include both appearance and behavior. Their rather long legs, with familiar chicken-type feet are adapted for fast running. A game bird can rocket away from a crouched hiding position in a heart-stopping burst of flight when necessary. Add the famous springtime courtship displays of strutting and crowing, and you can see how these birds are related to the good old chicken.

In forest and open areas scattered across North America, the **wild turkey,** largest of the game birds, presides. Ben Franklin nominated this native bird for the symbol of America but the bald eagle won the vote, and the turkey continued to be a popular bird on the dinner table. The wild bird is unlike its ranch-raised relatives, butterballs on the hoof, so to speak. This is a wily and wary bird, seldom seen, thanks to its habit of skulking away from intruders. Only during breeding season, when the woods reverberate with its gobbling love calls, is it a likely target for hunters. In the wild, turkeys seek out acorns, fruit, and seeds, gathering in flocks to roost in trees after feasting all day. Like other game birds, it enjoys corn and other grains at the feeder.

Another game bird of the woods is the grouse, represented across the country by five species that range mostly in the North and Northwest. These short-tailed, chickenlike birds roam about at ground level, picking up seeds and berries and nipping tender bits of vegetation. If you live near conifer forests, you may host the **blue grouse** and **spruce grouse** at your feeder year-round and the **ruffed grouse** in winter. In

You'll hear a bobwhite long before you see one, thanks to its name-saying call. Try mimicking the easy two-note whistle and you may start a "conversation."

summer, ruffed grouse, which also occur in the eastern mountains, move to clearings to forage. The well-named **sharp-tailed grouse** and **sage grouse** live in more open areas rather than forests. Look for sharp-tailed grouse in prairies and brushy areas of the northern half of the country. The sage grouse moseys through sagebrush regions of the West.

In the grasslands of the Midwest, **greater** and **lesser prairie chickens** once abounded. Their populations declined due to intense hunting—their tasty meat made them popular while their tame manners made them easy prey for hunters. The added pressure of habitat loss has made it difficult for the birds to reestablish themselves and today they are uncommon to rare. You probably won't see one at your feeder, but you can visit them on special reserves. Ptarmigans also won't partake of your feeder banquet, although they may come to nibble tender willow leaves if you live in the Far North or in the High Sierra, where the introduced and well-established **white-tailed ptarmigan** resides.

Far more common and widespread are quail, which wander about most areas of the West, and their relative, the **northern bobwhite,** a bird that ranges in the eastern two-thirds of the country. Quail look like cute Walt Disney birds, with a silly curled feather bobbing over their heads and a fat, cuddly-looking body. **California quail** and **Gambel's quail** have adapted well to living with humans and are frequent feeder guests. In the mountainous West, the **mountain quail** strolls in woodlands and chaparral and in backyards nearby. **Scaled quail** and **Montezuma quail,** which lack the head plume, are the common quail species in the Southwest.

In various areas of the country, near open fields and hedgerows, you may find the **ring-necked pheasant,** an exotic bird with a ridiculously long tail, introduced from Asia. Pheasant populations wax and wane because the birds don't build up their numbers naturally in North America and are augmented by captive-bred birds released for hunting. Perhaps remembering the easy life on the game farm, pheasants are often quick to move into feeding stations near their natural haunts during the winter months.

Several kinds of quail visit western feeders. Although they look similar, their ranges and habitats are usually distinct. These California quail travel in flocks.

Game Bird Behavior

Watch game birds as they respond to danger, and you'll see they prefer to run away through camouflaging grass or brush rather than fly. But these birds can fly when necessary. If you ever make the mistake of stepping too near a well-camouflaged game bird in hiding, it will make your heart pound with a sudden blast of wings as it flies rapidly to freedom. Some game birds are unusually tame, showing little fear of your comings and goings around their feeding area.

GAME BIRD FEEDER FOODS			
■ Acorns	■ Blueberries (*Vaccinium* spp.)	■ Greenbrier (*Smilax* spp.) berries	■ Salal (*Gaultheria shallon*) berries
■ American persimmons (*Diospyros virginiana*)	■ Buckwheat	■ Milo (sorghum)	■ Strawberries
■ Apples	■ Corn, on the cob, whole kernel, or cracked	■ Peanuts	■ Sumac (*Rhus* spp.) berries
■ Bayberry (*Myrica pensylvanica*)	■ Dogwood (*Cornus* spp.) berries	■ Pecans	■ Weed seeds, including dandelion, goldenrod, ragweed, and smartweed
■ Bearberries (*Arctostaphylos* spp.)	■ Dried peas and beans	■ Pine seeds	
■ Blackberries (*Rubus* spp.)	■ Grapes (*Vitus* spp.)	■ Raspberries (*Rubus* spp.)	■ Wheat
	■ Grass seeds	■ Rose hips	

Game birds are ground feeders. Scatter cracked corn or other foods directly on the ground for pheasants and turkeys. Quail will also dine from a low tray feeder. Planting a patch of buckwheat, milo, or corn is a good way to attract game birds, which will forage at ease among the sheltering stems. Most species, especially quail, also appreciate a low source of water. Conifers are a major attraction for grouse, which eat the needles and roost in them.

Game birds spend a good deal of time browsing on leaves and buds. What they eat depends on where they live. The grouse of northern forests dine on conifers and willows. The sage grouse fills almost 75 percent of its nutritional needs with leaves and flowers of sagebrushes (*Artemisia* spp.). If your property features regionally native shrubs, trees, and other plants, you have provided for grazing game birds. It's fascinating to watch the birds stroll through your yard, nipping off a leaf here, a bud there.

The habits of game birds differ from those of songbirds, although their needs for food and shelter are the same. Turkeys may visit singly or in family groups of a male, his assorted wives, and their collective offspring. Grouse are usually loners. Quail travel in groups called coveys and appoint a lookout to remain watchful while the rest of the group feeds.

Some game birds are famed as musicians and show-offs. Blue grouse, sage grouse, prairie chickens, and ptarmigans engage in booming contests, producing the sound by releasing air in a sudden huff through inflated sacs in their necks. Ruffed grouse also are percussionists deluxe—they fan the air with their stiffened wings, beating a fast rhythm and deep sound that reverberates like far-off timpani through the forest.

Although at first glance many gallinaceous birds appear to be mostly brown, the males have fabulously barred and striped tails that they strut as proudly as any peacock. Neck and head feathers also add to the display as the birds raise and lower them.

Springtime heralds the onset of courtship rituals, which look bizarre because of the male bird's exaggerated postures. Watch for displays and territorial battles between males. Listen for hooting, booming, crowing, and gobbling, too.

Ring-necked pheasant populations may rise and fall with the fortunes of the hunting season. Farm-raised game birds released for sport may visit at your feeder.

Wild turkeys are increasing dramatically in many areas. By day, the birds forage in woods and fields and may visit feeding stations. At night, they roost high in trees.

G

Goldfinches

THE POPULAR **AMERICAN GOLDFINCH** is one of the most common birds at the feeder, thanks to its continent-wide range and ability to adapt to varied habitats. Familiarity in this case breeds fondness, not contempt, perhaps because of the beauty of this perky yellow-and-black bird or because of its mannerly feeder habits. Give a goldfinch a tray of sunflower seeds or a tube of niger, and he and his cronies will contentedly crack seeds, with only an occasional flash of wings to betray a small squabble.

In the West and Southwest, the buttercup-yellow American goldfinch shares its habitat with the **lesser goldfinch,** who wears its yellow on the breast and belly, with a green or black back. **Lawrence's goldfinch,** a gray bird with small splashes of yellow and black, is another possible feeder visitor in dry areas of the Southwest and coastal Pacific.

Identifying female and immature goldfinches is a good test of birding skills, especially if more than one species ranges in your area. They are all generally olive green, washed with yellow, with faint wing bars. In winter, the males also lose their bright plumage, fading to drab greenish yellow. Around the time pussy willows bloom in my area, the males begin to regain

Easy to attract, sunny yellow American goldfinches may gather by the dozens at feeders in spring. They punctuate their flight with bursts of song.

their dapper black caps, bold black wings, and buttery yellow body feathers, although they definitely have a blotchy look for several weeks.

Sunflower and niger are the mainstays of a goldfinch's menu at the feeder, but they also enjoy other small seeds, such as millet. Weed seeds are a big attraction, which is a good thing to remember the next time you're muttering at your dandelions or burdock, two of their favorites. They will eagerly devour the seeds of many garden flowers, eating from standing plants or from stems you have cut and laid in a feeder tray.

Goldfinch Behavior

All goldfinches are gregarious types that travel in small flocks most of the year, except during nesting season. In areas where the species overlap, all three may intermingle. In the southern third of the country, goldfinches are mainly winter birds. In all other regions, except for the Far North, they are

---

GOLDFINCH FEEDER FOODS

- Aster (*Aster* spp.) seed
- Bachelor's-button (*Centaurea cyanus*) seed
- Canary seed
- Coneflower (*Echinacea* spp.) seed
- Coreopsis (*Coreopsis* spp.) seed
- Cosmos (*Cosmos* spp.) seed
- Flaxseed
- Goldenrod (*Solidago* spp.) seed
- Grass seeds
- Lettuce (*Lactua sativa*) seed
- Millet
- Niger
- Rapeseed
- Sunflower seed, especially black oil
- Tickseed sunflower (*Bidens* spp.) seed
- Zinnia (*Zinnia* spp.) seed

common year-round. During migration, your feeder population of these finches may swell into the dozens or even hundreds, filling nearby trees with their tinkling, musical voices.

If cleanliness is next to godliness, then goldfinches must be saints. Goldfinches are inordinately fond of birdbaths and other water features. Whenever it rains at my house, I can count on goldfinches showing up within minutes after the storm to splash and frolic in the puddled rainwater. They are daily visitors at the birdbath and even at my dogs' outside water dish. Unlike most of my bathing birds, goldfinches don't take long to abandon themselves to the joy of a bath. They remind me of 4-year-old kids in the tub, splashing and ducking their heads and throwing water everywhere.

The frequent chattering "conversation" of goldfinches is one of the reasons they are such a delight. They keep up a long stream of sweet, varied notes, occasionally punctuated by a querying "Sweeee?" that sounds exactly like the note my mother's pet canary used. Indeed, German immigrants who were familiar with the Old World songbirds quickly dubbed the bright American goldfinch the "wild canary."

Salt is another big lure for all three species of goldfinch. If they're not at the feeder gobbling seed, or splashing up a storm in the bath, they're apt to gather in a talkative group around your salt block. Supplying nesting materials such as unspun wool, cotton puffs, and down-lined milkweed pods is another good way to attract goldfinches.

Goldfinches can get feisty with each other, spreading their wings or making darting head gestures in a fit of pique over feeding rights. But they usually behave well with other species around their size, such as sparrows, and are quickly intimidated by larger birds, such as jays.

Gourds

IF YOU ARE LUCKY ENOUGH to have a long, hot growing season that lasts at least 90 days, invest a dollar or two in a packet of birdhouse gourd seeds. The fast-growing vines make an excellent quick cover to hide a chain-link fence or scramble up a trellis, and the night-blooming flowers, which unfurl their pristine white petals at dusk, attract interesting hummingbird-like sphinx moths.

At the feeding station, birdhouse gourds can be fashioned into utilitarian scoops and even impromptu feeders. Slice away until the gourd is shaped to suit your need. By the way, save the seeds you remove from the gourd: Put some aside to plant a new crop next year, and serve the rest to your feeder birds.

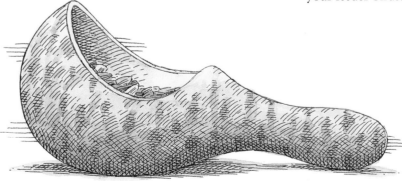

Birdhouse gourd vines produce enough gourds in a single season to supply a new home to a dozen birds. You can also turn them into sturdy birdseed scoops and feeders.

PROJECT

A Basic Gourd Bird Feeder

Birdhouse gourds got their name from their useful-ness as, of course, birdhouses. But they also make serviceable feeders. After the gourds mature (let the vines die back before you pick them), you can pick and dry them overwinter. Lay them in a warm, dry place and turn them weekly. If mold appears on the gourds, rub it off with a dry cloth. By spring the gourds should be dry (they'll feel much lighter) and are ready to become birdhouses and other handy items. Cut an opening, clean out the seeds, and hang a gourd as a feeder for several kinds of small-seed eating birds. Here's how to make your own home-grown bird feeder for your local bird friends.

MATERIALS

Dried birdhouse gourd

Wire for hanging

Feeder treats, such as nuts or sunflower seeds

A single gourd makes a fine freehanging house for wrens and chickadees, although it is not as quickly accepted as a nest box is. Purple martins, however, adore group gourd housing.

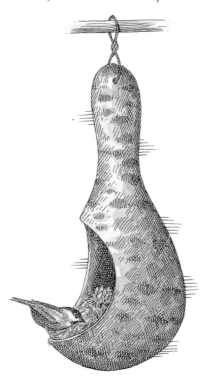

Step 1. Give the gourd a firm whack on the palm of your hand to loosen the seeds.

Step 2. Measure and mark the size of the opening with an indelible felt-tip pen.

Step 3. Carefully cut out the opening with a very sharp utility knife.

Step 4. Shake the gourd, opening side down, until most of the seeds have dropped out.

Step 5. Drill a hole through the neck of the gourd just below the stem, and insert a wire for hanging the feeder from a handy branch.

Step 6. Fill the feeder with nuts, sunflower seeds, or other treats. Birds will soon learn to seek its contents.

Grackles

GRACKLES COULD take first prize in an avian beauty contest, thanks to their sleek, svelte bodies, elegant all-black dress, and long, streamlined tails. But the harsh, squeaky vocalizings of grackles will make you want to run for the can of WD-40.

Like most other blackbirds, grackles fit in well with the changes humans have wrought to the natural landscape. They're opportunistic feeders, swallowing insects, seeds, and fast-food leftovers with equal delight. The **common grackle** is a universal presence in farmland, cities, and suburbia everywhere east of the Rockies. Like other grackles, this species wears a patina of iridescence on its glossy black feathers; variations in the flash of color determine whether the bird you're hosting is the purple or the bronzed. The common grackle has a keel-shaped tail—the feathers form a distinct V-shape, like the bottom of a boat. The **boat-tailed grackle,** a common species in Florida and along the Gulf and Atlantic coasts also has a keel-shaped tail. Longer than the common grackle by 4 to 6 inches, this is a big bird that can reach 16 inches from the tip of pointy beak to the end of the last tail feather. Another extra-large species is the **great-tailed grackle,** which stalks

The male common grackle's bright yellow eye shines against his black plumage like an 18K gold brooch. Grackles are among the bravest birds and will quickly come to the rescue when other birds need help.

GRACKLE FEEDER FOODS

- Acorns
- Apples
- Bayberries (*Myrica pensylvanica*)
- Beech nuts
- Bread and other baked goods
- Corn, whole kernel or cracked
- Grapes (*Vitus* spp.)
- Leftovers
- Meat scraps
- Millet
- Milo
- Pasta, cooked
- Suet, chopped
- Wheat

about in the Southwest, sweeping its incredible tail like the train of a bridal gown. Both the boat-tailed and great-tailed show clear differences between the sexes. While the males gleam with purple iridescence over dramatic dark feathers, the females are soft brown to gray-brown. Most adult male grackles sport bright yellow eyes.

Grackle Behavior

Grackles don't always visit feeders because they fend for themselves extremely well. They prefer to eat at ground level, so you will often spot them beneath feeders. On the ground, they are a delight to watch, thanks to their strutting walk, extravagant tails, and often exaggerated body language.

Watch the grackles in your yard, and you'll see how varied a diet they enjoy. Practically anything edible goes down the hatch: caterpillars, grubs, snails, crayfish, beetles, mice, seeds, and other treats. Should you be visited by a large group of grackles at the feeder, offer cracked corn to keep these big birds busy and conserve your more expensive seed.

Grapefruit

Attracts chickadees, house finches, mockingbirds, robins, starlings, and other birds

RUBY RED OR PALE GOLDEN, grapefruits are great additions to the bird-feeder banquet. Filled with their own luscious, juicy pulp, they may attract the attentions of chickadees, house finches, mockingbirds, robins, and other birds. Orioles may sample the flesh, though sweet oranges tempt these birds more easily. Emptied of their contents—by you or the birds—grapefruit rind halves make sturdy, simple minifeeders for filling with bacon fat, melted suet, or other offerings.

Grapefruit is also a suitable distraction for starlings, which may forsake the main feeder area for an offering of grapefruit halves in easy reach. You can put the halved fruit into wire baskets (a suet feeder usually fits), or impale a half grapefruit on a sturdy nail, either horizontally, for perchers such as starlings and mockingbirds, or vertically, for clinging birds such as chickadees.

Make feeder baskets from empty grapefruit halves by sticking a wire through the rind at three equidistant points, about ¼ inch from the top. Twist the wires together and suspend from a branch or shepherd's crook. Chopped apples, raisins, currants, sunflower seeds, or peanuts are good in grapefruit baskets. The edge of the rind makes a serviceable perch for lightweight birds such as chickadees.

> Impale a grapefruit half on a large nail for a juicy treat. Empty rinds make simple holders for suet, seeds, or other foods.

Grapes

Attract bluebirds, cardinals, catbirds, great crested flycatchers, grosbeaks, mockingbirds, tanagers, thrashers, thrushes, woodpeckers, wrens

GRAPEVINES ARE GREAT VINES, as far as birds are concerned. Like other rampant-growing vines, grapes offer good cover, shelter from the elements, and protected nesting spots. Their fruit is a favorite of cardinals, catbirds, great crested flycatchers, grosbeaks, mockingbirds, tanagers, thrashers, thrushes, woodpeckers, wrens . . . the list goes on and on. Their sweet-smelling flowers attract a myriad of tiny bugs—more fodder for foraging birds. And the peeling bark of their vines is easy for birds to strip and use for nest weaving.

If you didn't inherit Grandma's grape arbor, start your own on a strong trellis by planting a fast-growing, easy-care 'Concord' vine if you live in the North (Zones 5 to 8) or a muscadine if you are a southern gardener (Zones 7 to 9). In 2 years, you'll have a decent crop. Don't fret about pruning;

Wild grapes have bite-size fruit beloved by cardinals and other birds. Grapevines are likely to sprout from bird-deposited seeds around your feeding area.

just give the vine a haircut now and then to keep it in bounds. It'll bear fruit regardless of your pruning skill.

In the meantime, while your vine grows, get your grapes from other sources. Salvage any strays from your refrigerator fruit bin; birds don't mind bruised or withered fruit. Place single grapes in an open tray feeder for easy visibility, preferably in the soft-foods feeder so that grape lovers don't have to compete with seed eaters for feeder space.

Like other fruits, grapes attract the most attention from birds in fall and winter when natural fruit is scarce. But if you have fruit eaters such as bluebirds, catbirds, mockingbirds, or Carolina wrens nesting in or near your yard, you may enjoy a steady stream of customers to your fruit feeders through the summer, especially if there's no natural fruit nearby.

Since birds are creatures of habit, it's a good idea to put grapes in the same spot if you offer them regularly. Hook clusters of grapes on hooks or nails, or fasten them on branches of shrubs or trees. To prevent these watery, thin-skinned fruits from freezing fast to snow or frozen soil, freeze a supply of individual grapes in resealable plastic bags for winter use. After winter snow or ice storms, chop grapes coarsely (whole frozen grapes are too big to swallow), and scatter them on the ground for robins and other birds to scoop up.

> Add a cup hook to the end of your wooden feeder and hang clusters of grapes from it for fruit-loving birds.

Grasses for Birds

Attract many kinds of birds at various times of the year

It's FUN TO SEE where birdseed comes from, which is why I always let a few of the volunteer plants beneath my feeders grow to maturity. Many will turn out to be sunflowers, but the rest are sure to be grasses—planted by birds that dropped the seeds.

Without grasses, you and I and our bird friends would be mighty hungry. That bowl of cornflakes we crunch for breakfast, the bread that makes our lunch-time sandwich, and the millet that we pour in our feeders for the finches all come from grasses.

Of all the plants in the giant Gramineae, or grass family, grains like corn and wheat are the most useful to us humans, but birds and other wildlife appreciate almost every one of the hundreds of grass species. Next time you're yanking up a clump of crabgrass (*Digitaria* spp.), think of chipping sparrows and song sparrows, which adore the tiny, tasty seeds of your quick-crawling weedy enemy. (For more on weedy grasses that attract birds, see Weeds on page 327.)

Grass is golden where birds are concerned. Native species like this switchgrass produce abundant seeds and supply nesting material and good cover.

Grasses for Birds   145

Volunteer grasses spring up from birds scratching in feeders or from tube feeders tilting in the wind. Millet (*Panicum miliaceum* and other species) is my top crop, thanks to messy eaters who kick the little tan seeds out of their feeders. You may get other grass volunteers sprouting around your feeders since some seeds eaten in the wild may survive the trip through a bird's digestive tract intact.

Plant a Grassy Garden

Young grasses all look alike at first—like a lawn that needs a haircut. But if you let them grow, they'll turn into a garden of birdseed: millets, canary grass (*Phalaris canariensis*), foxtails (*Setaria* spp.), milo (*Sorghum bicolor*), and wheat (*Triticum* spp.). If the look of a few stragglers under the feeders is less than appealing to you, plant a patch of grasses just for the birds as a complementary feeding station.

Choose a site in full sun, in average soil. Prepare the site as you would for a bed of annual flowers, by digging or tilling to a depth of about 6 inches. There's no need to add fertilizer: Grasses grow well on a lean to average diet of soil nutrients.

To keep your neighbors from turning you in to the weed police, make the area square or rectangular, which gives it a controlled look, and mark the planting with a metal plant label. Include a few clumps or a back row of native perennial grasses, such as switch grass (*Panicum virgatum*), to give the bed year-round substance. Sow separate swaths of the seeds of these annual grasses: millet, annual canary grass, and milo. If you have space, annual ryegrass (*Lolium multiflorum*), a common lawn-grass seed, is also appreciated by seed-eating birds. Keep the planting well watered while you're waiting for the seeds to come up. Don't worry about weed grasses that invade your plot: Chances are, their seeds will be just as eagerly sought as the ones you planted.

Grasses are fast-growing. By mid- to late summer, some of your plants will be pushing up seedheads loaded with grain. Let the plants ripen naturally to attract birds where they stand. Buntings, quail, siskins, sparrows, and other small-seed eaters will scratch about for dropped seeds or pull down seedheads all through fall and winter. Before the birds get all the bounty, cut a few handfuls of plants to save for winter bird feeding. Their long stems are easy to work into outdoor arrangements for the birds, or you can simply lay them in a feeder or on the ground.

A garden of grasses also attracts birds because the dense stems and clumps provide good cover. Use corridors of grasses, annual or perennial, to help birds move through your yard undetected by predators. Let your bird grasses stand over winter to continue serving as shelter. Robins, sparrows, and other birds will use the dried foliage for next spring's nest building.

Natives Work Best

Don't shy away from searching a bit to track down native perennial grasses for your garden: The payoff

---

A Trio for Shade

ALTHOUGH MOST grasses crave sun, several bird-attracting species thrive in shady places. If your yard features shade-casting trees where birds nest and feed, add a few of these grasses in the shady spots beneath them for bird food and interesting landscape texture.

In lighter shade, **hairgrasses** (*Deschampsia* spp.) create clouds of delicate seedheads, valued by birds in the cool mountain areas where the species originated.

Bottlebrush grass (*Hystrix patula*) is a great addition along shady paths, as a treat for songbirds and human visitors. Birds love the plump seeds of this easy-to-grow native grass, and kids of all ages enjoy stroking the whiskery seedheads, which look just like their namesake. When the seedheads are fully ripe, they shatter under the touch, which just makes things easier for the small songbirds that seek the seeds on the woodsy floor.

For pheasants, quail, and other game birds, **deer-tongue grass** (*Panicum clandestinum*) is just the ticket. This handsome plant has pointed, 1-inch-wide leaves that jut at angles from furry stems tipped by airy panicles of fat little seeds. All of these shade-tolerant grasses are native American plants.

---

for paging through those catalogs is more birds in your yard. Birds are accustomed to finding food from the grass species in their native range, so they'll soon seek out your planting. Blue grammagrass (*Bouteloua gracilis*), switchgrass (*Panicum virgatum*), little bluestem (*Schizachyrium scoparium*), and many other native grasses are chock-full of good birdseed.

Keep in mind that many birds travel over a wide range of country during their migrations, so unless you're trying to re-create a natural ecosystem, you don't have to limit yourself to a narrow region when you're choosing native grasses. The red-winged blackbird that seeks out the prairie grasses in your midwestern garden in fall, for example, may be gleaning seeds from subtropical species in his winter home in the South.

Although natives are tops with birds, weedy grasses that originally hailed from lands across the ocean have plenty of takers, too. There's no need to learn what every grass in your yard is—just watch whether birds eat it. I let grasses of any kind grow among the shrubs of a hedge or in a corner of the yard, or wherever I can sneak in a discreet weed patch without alarming the neighbors. Native sparrows and juncos especially appreciate a grassy patch gone wild, where they can forage all winter among the standing stems. Disguise your weed patch, if you must, by bordering it with a double row of zinnias—tall ones in the back, dwarfs in the front—for a tidier look and extra seeds.

> Ornamental or weedy, grasses offer seeds, shelter, and nest-building materials for many kinds of birds.

See "Resources" on page 348 for nurseries that feature native plants. You may also find native grasses at well-stocked local nurseries (ask if they will order them for you) or via Internet sources.

Grit

Attracts all birds

TEST YOUR TEETH on a kernel of dried corn, and you'll see why grit is a necessity for birds, which lack the dental structure needed to break down hard foods. Birds depend on a muscular organ called the gizzard where small stones and grit provide the abrasion necessary to break down their food into a digestible state. Birds frequently gather in flocks along roadsides to pick up the tiny stones and gravel they need to replenish their gizzards.

You can supply the much-needed grit near your feeders for your feathered friends. Washed, natural aquarium gravel is an ideal source of larger grit. Builder's sand, the coarse tan variety that you can find at any home-supply store, will serve their need for finer grade gravel. Crushed eggshells or crushed clam and oyster shells can also provide grit for birds.

Making grit is a great way to recycle those seashells you lugged home from the ocean—the ones that now reside in the drawer or on the back porch, unloved and out of sight. That 2-ton tool in your driveway is a quick way to smash seashells: Just drive back and forth over them a few times, then sweep them up and put at the feeding station. Or you can give last summer's souvenirs a few good whacks with a hammer. I slip my clamshells into a thick, stretchy sock or wrap them in an old hand towel before hammering away, to prevent sharp bits from flying into my eyes.

Offer grit on a flat, vegetation-free area of your yard or on top of a large flat rock, near the feeders where birds can easily find it. Choose a raised area so that rain puddles don't submerge the grit. Keep the supply replenished year-round.

> Birds fill their gizzards with grit and small stones to make up for their lack of teeth.

Grosbeaks

GROSBEAKS GET their name from their big, conical bills. Among the largest members of the finch family, these birds have beaks that rival the cardinal's in size and seed-cracking power.

Two mostly northern species and three more southerly and westerly species give us a full spectrum of grosbeaks. In the North and the West, the yellow, olive, and black **evening grosbeak** patrols conifer forests, moving southward irregularly to land at feeding stations. The rosy red **pine grosbeak** joins its yellow counterpart in spruce and fir forests and also sweeps southward, though more rarely than the evening grosbeak. In the eastern half of the country, particularly in the northern quadrant and in mountains southward, it's the striking **rose-breasted grosbeak,** with his brilliant crimson throat, snowy belly, and black-as-coal upper parts, that fills the niche. Across the southern half of the country, look for the beautiful **blue grosbeak.** This cobalt-colored bird, with touches of rust on its wings, dwells in hedgerows and other brushy areas and farming country. In the West, the vivid golden orange **black-headed grosbeak** patrols open woodlands. Females of all species wear dowdy dress of varying shades of olive- or grayish green or brown.

A male rose-breasted grosbeak in spring finery is one of the most beautiful birds in America. His relatives are just as colorful in other hues. Tempt them down from the treetops with sunflower seeds.

Except for the blue species, grosbeaks are birds of the canopy, spending much of their time over our heads. It's a real occasion when these large and beautiful birds move into feeding stations or stop at a birdbath or other water feature.

Grosbeak Behavior

At first glance, an evening grosbeak may remind you of a big goldfinch, but that's where the similarity ends. Unlike flighty, fast-moving goldfinches, which

GROSBEAK FEEDER FOODS			
■ Acorns	■ Corn, whole kernels or cracked	■ Elderberries (*Sambucus* spp.)	■ Virginia creeper (*Parthenocissus quinquefolia*) berries
■ Blackberries (*Rubus* spp.)	■ Crackers	■ Figs (*Ficus carica*)	■ Wheat
■ Cherries, fresh or dried	■ Dogwood (*Cornus* spp.) berries	■ Sumac (*Rhus* spp.)	■ Wild grapes
■ Common ragweed		■ Sunflower seeds	

panic at every opportunity, grosbeaks are slow-moving birds, as deliberate in their motions as parrots, and often almost tame. Big and bold-colored, they are a real treat at the feeder, although their appetites match their body size. When a flock of these birds descends on your sunflower seeds, they can make short work of what seemed like an abundant stash of seeds. They eat wherever they find food: at a high feeder, low feeder, or tube feeder, or on the ground. They generally don't seek other feeder foods if you supply plenty of sunflower seeds. They are also fond of salt.

Grosbeaks are adept at acrobatic maneuvers. You may spot them hanging upside down like parrots while they dine on the seeds of catalpa trees or the buds of maples and other trees. One of the best tricks I've seen grosbeaks do was to capture the seeds of jewelweed (*Impatiens capensis*) from the plant without exploding the hair-triggered seeds.

Listen for the pretty, warbling songs of grosbeaks in your yard. Their call notes—the "Pink!" of the rose-breasted, the chirp of the evening—are another clue that grosbeaks are in the area. If you are lucky enough to host grosbeaks at your feeder, watch for the eye-catching splashes of white in most species' wings as they arrive or leave. The birds are unusually "confiding," as birders say, showing little fear of humans. In fact, an evening grosbeak was the first bird

The black-headed grosbeak resembles an oriole, thanks to its vivid coloring. But the big conical bill reveals its true identity.

I hand-tamed: It readily accepted a palm full of sunflower seeds when I very slowly approached it at the feeder. Pine grosbeaks, like other birds of the Far North, are the most unafraid of all their kin. It's easy to snap close-range pictures of them as they feed on seeds in a tray or berries in your yard.

Groundcovers

Attract fox sparrows, thrushes, towhees, and other ground-dwelling forest birds

IF YOU HAVE A LOVELY SWEEP of green lawn beneath your feeders, either you're not much of a success at bird feeding, or you're stocking your feeders with waste-free seeds. With all the traffic at a feeding station, the surrounding area will soon look less than perfect, thanks to all those little bird feet scratching among the seeds and shells that they drop.

Many feeder keepers don't mind the accumulation of debris beneath the feeder, but if you prefer a neater look, there's an easy solution: Cover the ground directly beneath the feeders, in about a 3-foot-diameter circle, with wood chips or other coarse mulch. (See Mulch on page 211 for details.) To make birds feel at home as they approach and exit the feeders and to cut down on maintenance, I plant an oasis of groundcovers extending from the mulch to the shrubs and other plants that border my feeding station. I've noticed that fox sparrows, thrushes, towhees, and other ground-dwelling forest birds seem much more comfortable about approaching the feeder when they can move from clump to clump of vegetation rather than travel over barren lawn grass.

It helps to think like a bird when choosing groundcovers for around your feeding area. The criteria for bird-appealing groundcovers are a little different from the usual things that we people look for in a groundcover:

- Instead of a continuous, dense, low-growing effect—the typical groundcover look—aim for plants separated by a few inches of open space. Or try a continuous sweep of plants that have room for birds to move beneath their branches.

- Choose plants for food value as well as appearance, to get more use out of the planting.

- Deciduous groundcovers are often preferable to evergreen, unless you live in a mild-winter area. By the time the plants make their reappearance in spring, you'll welcome the fresh greenery to hide the winter debris.

Choose groundcovers that do double duty as both cover and food. Bearberry forms mats of evergreen leaves decorated with bird-appealing berries.

Room to Move

Birds have a hard time moving through the thickly tangled stems that groundcovers such as periwinkle (*Vinca minor*) produce. They prefer plants like Allegheny pachysandra (*Pachysandra procumbens*) that are tall enough and erect enough to allow passage between their stems. My birds also avoid ground-hugging cotoneasters (*Cotoneaster* spp.) and junipers (*Juniperus* spp.); the birds tend to travel around the plants rather than through them. But birds welcome those groundcovers with higher branches and a few inches of open space beneath them and soon establish favorite routes under the sheltering branches.

Great Groundcovers

Many low-growing plants bear excellent crops of bird food on their stems and branches. Low-growing blackberries (*Rubus* spp.), blueberries (*Vaccinium* spp.), and other ground-hugging fruits draw in birds

that rarely visit a feeder, including tanagers and thrushes. I'm not a big fan of liriope (*Liriope spicata*), but when I found an armload of the plants on the local yard waste dump, I planted them in my shady front garden near the feeder. I was happy to find out that the black liriope berries that ripen in late summer are a magnet for bluebirds, which visit for a week or more to pluck the fruit.

A top-notch berry for bird appeal and groundcover use is one so common, it's probably already growing in your vegetable garden or, if you're lucky, in nearby wild places: the common strawberry (*Fragaria* spp.). Plant any variety you like, including native wild strawberries, and birds will be sure to brighten your yard.

In a sunny spot, ornamental grasses can cover the ground with a natural meadow look. Since ornamental grasses can be costly to buy, I like to experiment with native grasses and grasslike sedges that I import from other places in my yard or from the property of friends and family. Many species that aren't well mannered enough or well known enough for the nursery trade are perfect for birds. Three of my favorite finds are purple love grass (*Eragrostis spectabilis*), a delicate beauty with

Groundcovers for Birds

THESE PLANTS are easy for birds to navigate through. Many have tempting fruits or seeds for birds, too, and some can be used as nesting material.

Groundcover	Bird Use
Bearberry (*Arctostaphylos uva-ursi*)	Travel corridor, berries
Bunchberry (*Cornus canadensis*)	Travel corridor, berries
Strawberries (*Fragaria* spp.)	Travel corridor, nest site, fruit
Wintergreen (*Gaultheria procumbens*)	Travel corridor, berries
Huckleberries (*Gaylussacia* spp.)	Travel corridor, fruit, nest site
Junipers with branches at least 4 inches off the ground (*Juniperus* spp.)	Travel corridor, berries, nest site
Liriope (*Liriope spicata*)	Travel corridor, berries
Partridgeberry (*Mitchella repens*)	Travel corridor, berries
Allegheny spurge (*Pachysandra procumbens*)	Travel corridor, nest site
Mayapple (*Podophyllum peltatum*)	Travel corridor
Smartweeds (*Polygonum* spp.)	Travel corridor, seed
Chickweed (*Stellaria media*)	Travel corridor, seed, edible leaves
Blueberries dwarf or low-growing (*Vaccinum* spp.)	Travel corridor, fruit, nest site
Violets (*Viola* spp.)	Travel corridor, nest site
Clump-forming grasses such as fescues (*Festuca* spp.), switchgrasses (*Panicum* spp.), prairie dropseed (*Sporobolus heterolepsis*)	Travel corridor, seed, nesting material
Ferns such as maidenhair fern (*Adiantum pedatum*), cinnamon fern (*Osmunda cinnamomea*), interrupted fern (*O. claytonia*), polypody ferns (*Polypodium* spp.), and Christmas fern (*Polystichum acrostichoides*)	Travel corridor, nest site

clouds of airy flowers in fall; deer-tongue grass (*Dichanthelium clandestinum*), a shade lover with leaves that remind me of bamboo; and wood sedge (*Carex sylvatica*), a liriopelike evergreen species in my area.

It's amazing how fast your opinion of weeds will change once you consider their potential as bird-attracting groundcover plants. If you can bear the thought, you may find you get as much delight as I do in the ultracommon dandelion (*Taxacum officinale*). I actually removed the lawn grass and sowed a solid patch of dandelion around my feeding station in the sunny backyard. This perennial stays green most of the winter, then brightens March with its flowers. I don't mow it down when the flowers are done because it draws indigo buntings, goldfinches, white-crowned sparrows, and other great birds to its charming—yes, really!—puffs of seed.

I also pamper any plants of henbit (*Lamium amplexicaule*), purple dead nettle (*Lamium purpureum*), and common chickweed (*Stellaria media*) near the sunny-site feeders. Like most annual weeds, these rarely stay in one place for long, but every few years I'm rewarded by a big, beautiful patch of purple by the feeders. Sparrows and other birds nibble the fresh leaves and also eat the seeds.

Before you go out to buy groundcover plants, look around your yard and think creatively. An ideal groundcover may be right under your nose—or foot.

Groundcovers   151

Ground Feeding

IF THE DOVES, juncos, quail, sparrows, and towhees at your feeders had their druthers, they would want their food as close to the ground as possible. These birds are ground feeders that in the wild typically scratch seeds from the soil or pick insects from leaf litter. Although they will adapt to using bird feeders at the usual waist-high setting, they will eagerly accept food offered closer to or directly on the ground.

Commercial feeder manufacturers have accommodated these birds by adding low-level tray feeders to their product lineup. You can find them at bird-supply stores or in catalogs such as those listed in "Resources" on page 348. You can also make your own short-legged tray feeder. Four equal lengths of 2 × 4, each about 6 to 12 inches long, will make a stable set of legs for a low-level feeder. Nail a leg onto each corner of an existing tray feeder, driving the nails down through the tray and into the top of the 2 × 4. For the sake of appearance, orient all four legs in the same direction.

A large rock with a concave surface also makes an ideal bird feeder for ground-feeding birds. Quail, in my experience, take to such a setup immediately. You can also rest a plastic plant saucer or an old platter on a stack of bricks.

Pouring seed or other food directly on the ground can lead to problems for birds because the food may quickly turn moldy in wet weather. Although wild birds I have watched will not bother with moldy seed, it can cause problems if any do ingest it. They may suffer health problems such as aspergillosis, a

When you're hosting a large flock, it's simple to scatter seed on the ground. If seed gets wet and moldy, birds will avoid it unless there's no alternative.

serious fungal infection that can quickly spread through birds feeding at spoiled grain. Spreading seed directly on the ground can also encourage the visits of mice and other rodents, who will creep out to take their share of the feast.

Keeping these caveats in mind, you can still feed birds on the ground if you follow two basic guidelines: Feed small amounts at a time, so that seed does not accumulate and spoil or attract vermin, and remove any seed that gets wet. During winter snows, when feeder visitors increase dramatically, I often handle the overflow by pouring seed onto an area of packed snow protected by a windbreak of evergreen boughs or by a piece of slanted plywood. I also put out bread and other baked goods on the ground so the small birds and robins can get their share without fighting the competition at the feeder.

Hand Feeding

TAMING WILD BIRDS to take food from your hand or your hat brim is easier than it looks. The only tool you need is patience. Bad weather helps, too, because hunger is a big incentive for birds to get over their natural fear of humans. Winter is the best season to tame birds. The morning after a snowstorm or ice storm, you can have birds eating out of your hand—the only "feeder" available—in as little as half an hour. In summer, when birds can turn their backs on the sunflower seed and snitch caterpillars from your garden, it takes much longer to entice them to eat out of your hand.

Once birds are regulars at your feeder, they will probably be waiting for your arrival in the morning to refill their dishes, especially if you stock feeders at about the same time each day. Should a brave chickadee or other bird come close, offer it a handful of seed before you fill the feeders. It may surprise you by accepting it immediately or after just a few minutes of standing patiently and quietly.

I have found walnut kernels a real temptation for taming birds: Chickadees, jays, nuthatches, titmice, and woodpeckers have eagerly eaten them from my hand. To hand-tame cardinals, goldfinches, purple

Nothing compares to the thrill of hand-feeding a wild bird. With a week or so, you can coax one of the fearless species, like this chickadee, onto your fingers.

finches, evening grosbeaks, and pine siskins, I use sunflower seeds. I find crossbills, red-breasted nuthatches, and redpolls, which visit infrequently from the Far North, almost fearless; these birds will often immediately take a seed from my fingers if I approach them slowly at the feeder. For bluebirds and mockingbirds, a handful of enticing crumbled peanut butter and cornmeal dough is the key.

Have 'Em Eating out of Your Hand!

YOU CAN train feeder birds to eat out of your hand by becoming a regular presence there yourself, a process that takes about a week. Time your visits for early morning, when birds are hungriest after a night without food.

Start by emptying all feeders but one—a basic open tray model. Fill that feeder, then pull up a lawn chair near the feeder, about 3 feet away. Dress appropriately for the weather and sit still. Your guests, which probably headed for the hills when you arrived, should return in less than half an hour. Remain sitting quietly while they feed for another half hour.

Repeat the procedure the next day, but this time position the chair directly beside the feeder. Again, sit and wait while activity returns to normal and the birds accept your presence.

The third day, rest your hand in the feeder, with a tempting handful of nuts or sunflower seeds in the palm. Don't worry if birds eat the seeds around your hand but not those in it; just stay still and non-threatening.

The fourth day, empty the feeder and repeat the offering on your palm. You should get at least one taker—generally a chickadee or titmouse. Nuthatches can also be among the first to approach.

Continue the sitting posture for another day or two, until birds freely visit your hand. Then dispense with the chair, and try standing at the feeder. Once a few friendly birds accept you as a new walking feeder, they may alight on your shoulder to ask for food as you stroll the yard. Be sure to carry some of their favorite seeds or nuts in your pocket.

Harvesting Seed

BEATING THE BIRDS to the best seeds in your garden can be a challenge because they're monitoring the ripeness of the maturing seedheads even more often than you are. Thus, the presence of seed eaters such as goldfinches at your sunflowers, zinnias, or other seed-bearing plants is a sign for you to start collecting if you intend to put aside any ripe seeds for later feeder use.

Harvesting seeds before they are completely ripe helps you beat the birds. Many seeds continue to ripen even if harvested from the plant when green. In general, look for seedheads that have filled out with plump green seeds that are beginning to turn to yellow. These seeds usually will dry to a ripe golden or brown color even if removed from the plant.

If you intend to use seedheads in wreaths, swags, or bundles, allow long stems when picking. Otherwise, you can snip individual clusters into a large brown paper sack. To separate the seeds, tightly close the sack and shake briskly, causing the ripe seeds to fall free from the seedhead. Pour off the seeds into containers for later use.

If you are picking seeds that are not fully ripe, spread the seedheads in shallow cardboard trays in a dry place protected from birds and rodents. Cardboard trays for shipping soda cans are available at convenience stores or supermarkets and will do the trick. An unheated garage is perfect. Check the seeds daily, and when they are ripe, transfer the seedheads and any fallen-out bits to paper bags to shake off the seeds as described above.

Many flowers and weeds lend themselves to seed collecting. It's fun to observe which birds prefer

When sunflower heads start to droop, harvest quickly if you want to save the seeds for future bird feeding. Once the seeds are dry, store them in a rodent-proof container.

which seeds when you offer them later at the feeder. Here are some easy ones to get you started:

- Amaranths
- Ragweed (if you're not allergic to it!)
- Safflower (*Carthamus tinctorius*)
- Lamb's-quarters
- Chicory
- Cosmos (*Cosmos sulphureus, C. bipinnatus*)
- Purple coneflower (*Echinacea purpurea*)
- Sunflower, annual
- Garden balsam (*Impatiens balsamina*)
- Lettuce
- Marigolds
- Dandelions
- Zinnias

Hawks

WITH EYESIGHT sharper than any other bird, hawks are supremely well adapted for their job of feathered predator. They can catch motion and discern a grasshopper from a 30-foot utility pole or zero in on a junco while soaring high overhead. If you have a feeding station patronized by daily crowds of birds, it is likely to catch the attention of a hawk in the area. Hawks usually seek out feeding stations in winter because the pickings are a lot easier at this literal bird buffet than in the wild.

First, consider it a compliment if a hawk comes to visit. Its presence means your yard is teeming with birds. Then admire the cool beauty of these creatures. Whether your visitor is a large, heavy-bodied red-tailed hawk of the *Buteo* genus; a streamlined, sharp-shinned hawk representing the *Accipiter* clan; or a small, slim American kestrel, a widespread member of the genus *Falco*, your meat-eating guest has its hunting skills honed to a fine art. No member of the hawk family wastes energy getting a meal, though methods of catching prey differ. Buteos include the nationwide **red-tailed hawk;** the **red-shouldered** and **broad-winged hawks** of the eastern half of the country; and the southwestern **zone-tailed hawk.** They usually hunt from a perch, spying on surroundings until they spot a rodent, insect, reptile, or bird. Accipiters are swift and agile fliers. The **sharp-shinned** and **Cooper's**

A soaring Cooper's hawk makes smaller birds dive for cover—and for good reason. Birds top the menu for this agile flier and its lookalike cousin, the sharp-shinned hawk.

HAWK FOODS

- Suet, large chunks
- Meat scraps, raw
- Poultry scraps, raw
- Mice
- Voles
- Squirrels
- Pigeons
- Game birds
- Songbirds
- Starlings

hawks, found across the continent, and their larger brother of the north, the **northern goshawk,** generally drop from the sky to snatch a bird, a habit that once earned them the nickname "blue death." The once-rare **peregrine** and **prairie falcons,** and their smaller falcon kin, the **American kestrel** and the **merlin,** are the fastest fliers in the hawk family and loath to let a bird escape once they have spotted it. They may fly through a feeder area to see what they can scare up.

Hawk ID

Figuring out what hawk is terrorizing your bird feeder isn't as easy as it may seem. Hawks vary widely in their plumage as they mature; males and females also may have different coloring. Mottled coloring rather than the clearly defined areas of solid brown or other hues shown in your field guide are the hint that you're looking at a youngster.

It helps to learn the flight patterns and general sizes of the hawks in your area. The big buteos—red-tails, red-shoulders, and a few others—are extra large size birds; they may flap or soar. Accipiters like sharpshins and Cooper's hawks are slim, trim birds with longer tails and narrower wings, but the real clue is their flight—it's a distinctive pattern of a few flaps followed by a spread-winged glide. Falcons are fairly easy to recognize, thanks to their pointed wings, as sharp as a Russian scimitar. Keep your binoculars handy if a hawk becomes a regular. Over the winter feeding season, you're sure to get a fix on it.

Protecting Feeder Birds

You may want to discourage a hawk from returning once you witness his first meal at your feeder. Even if you find the food chain in action a fascinating sight, you may wrestle with the question of whether it is ethical to lure potential prey to your yard. You can usually give the hawk the hint by withholding seed for a week. By that time, smaller birds will have stopped flocking to the area and will have dispersed to wilder haunts, and the hawk may move on to look for another concentrated gathering of birds.

Of course, if the hawk arrives in the middle of severe cold or snow, you'll be sending your dependents out to face a food shortage if you withhold seed. That may be as fatal as a hawk strike. If this is the case, serve songbirds their meals beneath a sheltering tree or shrub, where they can instantly find cover and protection. In winter, I surround my feeders with discarded Christmas trees for quick and portable cover.

Hawks are not always hunting for birds at your feeder. Most species also relish mice, rats, and other rodents. Tell your squirrels—or not!

Hawk Behavior

If a hawk drops in, pull out the binoculars and take a close look. The strong beak, built for tearing flesh, and the tightly gripping talons are marvels of form-fits-function. Hawk plumage is also beautiful through binoculars, exhibiting subtle bars and streaks. Take a look, too, at the color of the eye; some species have a piercing yellow orb, while others gleam blood red.

In winter, a red-tailed hawk may claim a feeder as its private diner, preying on daily guests. If your feeders seem suddenly birdless, look for a perched hawk.

If you are feeding large hunks of suet or meat scraps to your feeder birds, you may find hungry hawks tearing at the meal during cold weather or storms, when their natural food is in hiding or locked in ice. Should the hawk make a kill at your feeder, watch to see where it goes so you can observe how it devours its prey. The plucking process is fascinating, and so is the most favored first bite—often the head. If you feel squeamish at the thought, take comfort in the knowledge that these birds of prey usually kill their intended meals instantly.

It's not cruelty that causes hawks to prey on birds—it's just a natural step in the food chain. The only unnatural part is what we do—encourage smaller birds to gather in concentrated numbers at a feeding station. The hawk is just doing its job.

Hedges and Hedgerows

Attract many kinds of birds at various times of the year

BACK IN THE DAYS before monster combines and tractors the size of a small house, farmers kept hedgerows along the edges of their fields to provide homes for game birds, rabbits, and other wildlife. As farming became big business and clean fields the norm, hedgerows disappeared, eliminating precious habitat and prime nesting sites.

Recreate those farm hedgerows on your own property, and the numbers of birds that visit and reside at your place will increase dramatically. The same mix of plants that worked in the old days—basically whatever came up and survived in the strip of land next to the fence—is ideal today, but it fits best into a more relaxed landscape.

I think of a hedge as a row of a single type of plant—flowering shrubs or berry bushes, for instance—and a hedgerow as a multilevel mix of both planned and unexpected delights. More formal or better-planned hedges with fewer types of plants will also supply shelter, but they aren't nearly as appealing to birds as a hedgerow's casual, jumbled mix of young trees, shrubs, vines, weeds, and grasses.

Diversity Makes the Difference

Diversity brings in the birds. In a mixed hedgerow, seeds and fruits ripen at different times, providing months of tasty food. Various insects are attracted to different plants, so that those birds that seek aphids can find beetles, too, and those that prefer caterpillars can eat their fill. An assortment of plants also supplies a variety of nesting sites, so that your hedgerow can host shrub-dwelling catbirds, branch-building robins, and ground-nesting sparrows all at once.

A little laissez-faire also helps a hedgerow appeal to birds. Keeping a hands-off approach lessens the intrusions of your disturbing presence into possible nesting territory. No self-respecting bird will build a nest where the gardener is always fussing around with hedge clippers or string trimmers. Declaring a moratorium on weeding or string trimming around the woody plants also creates a dense undergrowth of weeds and grasses—plants that are perfect from a bird's eye view because of their bounty of seeds.

Although it can be difficult at first to change your standards from manicured garden to dirty-fingernails natural, you'll find a big payoff, not only in birds but also in the amount of interest the hedgerow holds. You can watch as wildflowers take hold and retreat, as blackberries or roses move in, as tree seedlings sprout and grow—the whole story of succession in one small strip of plants. You'll also find a whole world of fascinating creatures besides birds, from beetles and praying mantises to tree frogs and deer mice.

Include a Few Evergreens

For year-round use and unbeatable shelter in rainy weather, be sure to include a few evergreen shrubs and trees in your hedge. Look for those that supply berries or cones, including Oregon grape hollies (*Mahonia* spp.), hollies (*Ilex* spp.), and conifers, or suit your own sensibilities and plant whatever evergreens you like. Rhododendrons and azaleas (*Rhododendron* spp.), camellias (*Camellia* spp.), magnolias (*Magnolia* spp.), and other broadleaved types are as useful as needled evergreens for nesting and shelter.

For instant usefulness to birds, invest in a few good-size evergreens that already sport the dense branches that appeal to birds. From the time they're waist-high, hemlocks (*Tsuga* spp.), upright junipers (*Juniperus* spp.), and spruces (*Picea* spp.) are highly appealing to shelter-seeking birds, and they are usually available at a reasonable price. Evergreens that grow more slowly are usually priced accordingly: Plants that fit a limited budget are apt to be small in stature. In addition to instant-utility plants, you may want to include pines (*Pinus* spp.) and other evergreens that have open branches when young and gradually fill out with age.

Starting a Hedgerow

Experimenting with the combinations for a hedgerow makes an entertaining game. The best part is that there is no wrong way. I like to include a few basic types of plants in the row, and then let nature take over and fill in or weed out the rest. Native plants that can tough it out among the competition are best for a hedgerow. To start this great bird area, begin with a selection of excellent bird plants, arranged in any order you like. That's all you need. The bare spaces will soon be filled in, as birds drop seeds of vines and creepers; squirrels bury nuts and acorns; and weeds, grasses, and wildflowers sprout from the soil. Consider using these plants:

- A few nut trees, like pecan (*Carya illinoinensis*), shagbark hickory (*C. ovata*), and butternut (*Juglans cinerea*)
- Native fruit trees, such as wild plum and wild cherries (*Prunus* spp.)
- Hazelnuts (filberts) (*Corylus* spp.)

Creating Hedges

Hedges are useful as windbreaks around the feeder area, and they provide corridors of safety for birds as they travel about your yard or to neighboring properties. Annual sunflowers and several other good bird plants make almost-instant hedges that can tower 6 feet or taller in a single season. Other hedges are a long-term proposition, starting small and gradually filling in over a period of years. Whether you plant one or both types, choose plants for the hedge that will supply birds with food as well as shelter, if possible. Exercise your creativity by combining plants in a sort of linear garden, or plant a row of all the same kind.

ONE-SEASON HEDGE PLANTS

Love-lies-bleeding (*Amaranthus caudatus*)

Tall amaranth (*Amaranthus* spp. and cvs.)

Tickseed (*Bidens aristosa*)

Sunflowers (*Helianthus annuus, H. debilis*)

Mexican sunflower (*Tithonia rotundifolia*)

Indian corn (*Zea mays* var. *indurata*)

Popcorn (*Z. mays* var. *praecox*)

Corn (*Z. mays* var. *rugosa*)

Tall zinnias (*Zinnia elegans* cvs.)

A hedge of annual plants such as corn (1), Mexican sunflowers (2), amaranth (3), and branching sunflowers (4) provides plenty of seeds for birds to eat and creates a quick and colorful privacy screen for your yard.

Watch your hummingbirds when they leave the feeder, and you'll see they typically move to a perch to sit for a spell. These birds have the highest metabolism of any North American animal, except perhaps the shrew. That means they have to eat almost constantly during daylight hours. They intersperse periods of filling their bellies with brief resting periods from sunup to sundown.

Hummingbirds visit nectar feeders from the time of spring migration—which can be as early as February, depending on your location—through departure in fall, as late as November. Here in southern Indiana, I associate hummingbirds with federal income taxes: They both are due on April 15. Like other birds, hummingbird arrivals and leave-takings cleave to a schedule that usually varies by only a few days. Unlike seed eaters, hummingbirds are more at the mercy of the weather, which can retard the blossoming of the plants they depend upon for food along the migration route. If it's a late spring and nectar flower buds open late, hummingbirds may arrive up to a week after I expect them.

I get my feeders out early and leave them hanging until cold weather threatens to freeze the sugar water. Straggler birds are not unheard of, and a feeder that's still filled can be a literal lifesaver. In the several years I've lived in the Midwest, I have twice hosted hummingbirds in December. They stayed for a week, restoring their depleted energy reserves; then they bravely headed south.

At the feeder, hummingbirds can be hogs. These birds are among the most combative of any feathered species. They often claim a food source and defend it viciously against all comers. Don't be surprised if only one bird at a time visits your nectar feeder. Others may want to partake but the territorial first arrival may prevent them. I fill my yard with a half-dozen nectar feeders to accommodate more birds—for their nourishment and my pleasure.

Flowers for Food

The reason sugar-water feeders are so popular is that the solution tastes like flower nectar. Before bird feeders, hummingbirds depended on the nectar held

The male Costa's hummingbird sports a bib of violet purple with feathers that extend beyond its head. This little beauty roams around southwestern desert areas.

within blossoms to fuel their fast little bodies. Even with hummingbird feeders on every block, they still rely on flowers for food.

Flowers attract plenty of hummingbird traffic, especially if they're red. Red-orange and some shades of pink also get their attention. Once a hummingbird is in your garden, though, it will sip nectar from any suitable blossom, no matter what color the flowers. You'll want to place your nectar feeders in or near a flowerbed, so that you can enjoy longer hummingbird visits and watch the birds feed and behave naturally.

Color is foremost in grabbing the initial attention of a hummingbird. Once you've attracted one, choose flowers that are tubular in shape, with petals flaring from a long throat, such as honeysuckle, salvia, and bee balm, to keep the bird visiting. Flowers that really tempt hummingbirds also offer plenty of elbow, er, wing room. They often hold flowers arranged in spikes or clusters at the tips of stems. The spike of a salvia, for instance, holds the individual flowers arranged around the stem, with leaves below, so that hummingbirds can circle the blossom and sip from every flower without working in crowded quarters.

GARDEN DESIGN

A Patio-Side Hummingbird Garden

The list of good hummingbird flowers is a very long one, with lots of possibilities no matter where you live. Be sure to include some native plants, which offer their nectar-rich blossoms at the times hummingbirds most need them. Wild columbines (Aquilegia canadensis, A. formosa) bloom in time to greet spring migrants, and Texas sage (Salvia coccinea) feeds fall migrants. Create a colorful drift of these hummingbird staples next to your patio or deck, and you'll enjoy hummingbird activity all summer long.

PLANT LIST

1. Butterfly bush (*Buddleia davidii*)

2. 'Enchantment' lily (*Lilium* 'Enchantment')

3. Blue or white annual or perennial salvias, such as *S.* × *superba* 'May Night' or *S. farinacea*

4. 'Lady in Red' Texas sage (*Salvia coccinea* 'Lady in Red')

5. 'Casablanca' lilies or other similar-size white cultivar (*Lilium* 'Casablanca')

I like to mount nectar feeders on my porch and stick them on the window at my desk, and I also use potted plants to bring the birds in close. Red-orange impatiens and fuchsias flourish on my shady front porch and ensure that I'll see a hummingbird almost every time I glance out the window while working.

Some friends have strung thin wire between the posts of their porch near their hummingbird feeders. It encourages the birds to perch in a colorful row, right by the feeder, as they rest between drinks.

If your feeders run dry, the birds may remind you by hovering outside a window or near the feeder when you go outside. You can easily train hungry hummingbirds to drink nectar from a small bottle such as test tube you hold in your hand. They will also fearlessly sip from a flower you hold out to them. Once they learn to accept food from you, you can get them to sip nectar from the palm of your hand. Be forewarned—it tickles!

Neat Nesting

At nesting season, you may see hummingbirds gathering spiderwebs in their bills, for use in gluing their nest together. They also collect tiny bits of lichen for camouflaging the outside of the nest, which looks exactly like a natural knot as it hugs a tree branch. Hummingbirds are not poster birds for a committed relationship. Males will mate with any female that allows it. Females seek males only to fertilize their forthcoming eggs, then live a life as single parents, building the nest and raising the young alone. Should you discover a hummingbird nest, you'll love the way a mother bird sits with only her belly in the cup and her long bill extending over the side. When the young fill the nest, they will often sit with their beaks pointing skyward, perhaps so they don't stab each other.

Hummingbirds do sit still—more often than you think. This lucifer hummingbird has dined and now perches before feeding again, a habit it will repeat all day.

Migration-Time Multitudes

Depending on where you live, you may notice that the number of hummingbirds at your feeders and in your garden increases as summer turns to fall. That's a sure sign that migration is hitting its stride. If you live near the middle or at the southern end of a migration route, you will likely be blessed with dozens or even hundreds of hummers. These visitors will create a constant hum in your yard as they single-mindedly fuel up for the next leg of the trip.

Lucky-13 Hummingbird Flowers

YOU WILL attract hummingbirds if you plant these attention getters around your nectar feeder or in containers on a porch or balcony to bring hummingbirds near where you can observe them. Hummingbirds can't resist them!

- Wild columbines (*Aquilegia canadensis, A. formosa*)
- Butterfly bush (*Buddleia davidii*)
- Trumpetvine (*Campsis radicans*)
- Delphiniums (*Delphinium* spp.)
- Impatiens, red-orange–flowered cultivar (*Impatiens wallerana*)
- Cypress vine (*Ipomoea quamoclit*)
- Gilia (*Ipomopsis* spp.)
- Cardinal flower (*Lobelia cardinalis*)
- Bee balm (*Monarda didyma*)
- Penstemons (*Penstemon* spp.)
- Red-flowering currant (*Ribes sanguineum*)
- Red-flowered salvias, such as pineapple sage (*Salvia elegans*); red salvia (*S. splendens*, any cultivar); and Texas sage (*S. coccinea*)
- Mexican sunflower (*Tithonia rotundifolia*)

Whether flowers or plastic, red and red-orange colors grab a hummingbird's attention. This beauty is the magnificent hummingbird, also known as Rivoli's.

The holes on nectar feeders are positioned for easy access by this hovering ruby-throated hummingbird, the only one commonly seen east of the Mississippi.

Multiples of hummingbirds do gather around a single good food source in nonmigration times. Flowering trees are famous for attracting dozens of hummingbirds, but unless you look up, it's easy to miss them. Check out the next red-flowering buckeye, horsechestnut, or mimosa you come across—it may be swarming with hummingbirds.

During fall migration, hummingbird populations can build to astounding numbers. In southeastern states, where ruby-throated hummingbirds gather strength before jumping across the Gulf of Mexico, it is a common and wonderful sight to see hordes of hummingbirds at any likely food source. I have seen them zooming up and down city streets in Pensacola, Florida, sampling every window box and flower garden and even investigating red bathing suits on the beach. I once counted 85 hummingbirds in one city block, and the birds went almost entirely unnoticed by the tourists on the street! One burly fellow walking across an oceanfront parking lot had a red bandanna hanging from his back pocket, and a hummingbird was following close behind like a friendly dog panting at his heel.

Hummingbirds can feed without perching, but they'll perch if they can. A plastic antibee guard covers the feeding hole beside this rufous hummingbird.

I

Icicles

FINDING WATER CAN BE a tricky proposition in cold winters, when all natural sources have long frozen over and ice-free birdbaths are few and far between. Yet birds still manage to satisfy their thirst. Icicles are one way to sip a bit of liquid. A tufted titmouse that was a regular client of my feeding station for years (he was identifiable by a white wing feather) also routinely visited the long icicles that spiked the eaves of my log house. Thanks to the warm sun of the southern exposure, the icicles began dripping at their tips by 11 A.M. and continued until the sun sank in late afternoon. The titmouse would perch beneath the longest icicle, which was just a few inches from a porch post, and stretch his neck to sip droplets from the end of the icicle. I've watched house sparrows do the same trick, and I'm sure other birds have perfected this technique.

In late winter, when sap is rising in the trees but the nights are still cold, icicles quickly form when passing street traffic or storms break a branch tip. On sugar maples, box elders, and other trees in the maple family, these "sapcicles" have a faintly sweet flavor, which may be what makes them appealing to the birds that gather nearby when the icicles begin to melt. I've watched blue jays, house finches, and even a yellow-bellied sapsucker help themselves to the natural sweet treat on a February or March morning.

When natural sources of water are frozen over, sipping from icicles is a way for birds to get needed liquid.

You can't do much to encourage the formation of icicles, but you can keep an eye out for birds that may be getting a drink from these winter decorations.

Identifying Birds

GETTING TO KNOW THE NAMES of your guests is vital so that you can brag about your feeder to other enthusiasts! Of course, identifying your birds also makes it easier to learn about them from reference books or other birders and to keep records and participate in data-gathering feeder counts sponsored by research organizations. Knowing the names of your diners even makes you a smarter shopper: Many birdseed mixes are labeled according to the birds they are intended to attract.

To figure out who's who, you can compare live birds to a field guide, using the shape of the bill and the color of the plumage to key the bird to its picture. Or make a quick sketch (no ability required!), writing notes on colors or other features that may help you find the bird in a field guide (see Field Guides on page 117 or "Recommended Reading" on page 352)—a useful technique if the bird isn't lingering at a feeder, or if it's an unusual one you haven't seen before.

Curved beaks Straight beaks Seed beaks

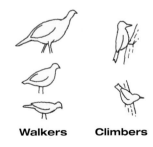

Walkers   Climbers

Use your field guide to familiarize yourself with the bills and body shapes of various bird families, so it's easier to narrow down the choices at identification time.

Insects

Attract many kinds of birds at various times of the year

PRACTICALLY EVERY BIRD EATS INSECTS—if it weren't for birds nabbing insects out of the air, off the ground, and from the bushes, insect populations would skyrocket in no time. Some birds eat more insects than other birds. The purple martin, which loops through the air, bill agape, scoops up thousands of flying insects, from dragonflies to mosquitoes, every day. One observer measured a full quart of cucumber beetle wing covers in a single nesting compartment of a martin box!

Even birds that depend mostly on seeds, such as native sparrows, also consume huge quantities of insects. You may even begin to appreciate starlings when you realize that they enthusiastically devour ants, millipedes, spiders, and wasps—and countless Japanese beetle grubs.

Because of their appetite for insects and arachnids, such as spiders and ticks, attracting birds to your yard means better health for your plants. Birds work tirelessly all year to glean insect eggs, young, adults, and cocoons from their hiding places among foliage, in bark crevices, or under leaf litter on the ground. Watch any bird, as it moves about your yard, and its insect-searching behavior will be evident.

An Insect for Every Taste

As with feeder foods, birds also have their preferences when it comes to insects. We owe this knowledge to the painstaking work of tireless researchers who have spent years counting, one by one, the individual insects contained in bird stomachs (now there's an interesting occupation to consider).

Other observers keep count by watching the process in action. A brown thrasher feeding young carried 247 grasshoppers, 425 mayflies, 237 moths, and 103 cutworms, plus smaller numbers of many other insects, to its brood in a single day.

It's fascinating to try to figure out who's eating what in your own backyard. You can learn a lot just

Nature's balancing plan works superbly: When the insect tide swells in early summer, even seed eaters like this field sparrow switch to an insect diet.

by watching birds at work. If a bird lingers at a plant and is obviously picking off insects, go find out what it's eating. You may discover that the bark is teeming with ants, or that tiny green caterpillars are looping their way through the leaves. When I saw a vivid blue indigo bunting making repeated forays into a clump of ornamental grass, I investigated and discovered scores of young grasshopper nymphs walking up the leaf blades. I quickly retreated so the bunting could finish its work.

Of course, birds make no distinction between so-called good bugs and bad bugs. They don't care if a sphinx moth caterpillar is chomping your precious tomato foliage or a wild catalpa tree: To a bird, that caterpillar is just a nice big bite of protein. Still, if you are an absolute arachnophobe, it's nice to know that hummingbirds, native sparrows, and wrens are on your side, nipping spiders out of their webs and hiding places with dexterity. Of course, those same spiders are important predators of insects in the garden, including many pests.

Don't bother trying to figure out what birds to attract to get rid of specific insects. While you will surely appreciate the efforts of grosbeaks in eating potato bugs, all bird efforts are vital in the grand scheme of things. Natural life is a balance, and birds help keep it that way.

Prime Time for Insects

In summer many birds use insects as a main staple of their diet. There are caterpillars and other delectable tidbits everywhere you look, and birds take full advantage of such easy pickings. Later, when seeds ripen and insects become scarce, finches and other seed eaters return to a seed-based diet.

Early to midsummer when nesting is at its peak, many insects are reaching their highest populations. That dovetails nicely from a bird's-eye perspective because there is abundant protein-packed food available just when nestlings need it most. Nestling birds aren't capable of cracking seeds or eating tough-skinned fruits with their tender bills, so parents seek bite-size bugs to stuff in their hungry mouths. By the time the young birds have left the nest and are

Here an ant, there an ant: Like other birds, this female Bullock's oriole is pest control on the wing, keeping insects from taking over your yard.

learning to hunt on their own, insects fill every nook and cranny of the yard and in wild places.

Birds quickly arrive on the scene when insect populations reach enormous cyclical highs. When

Each One Seeks One

EACH BIRD species has its particular way of searching out this favored food. Here are a few ways birds have evolved to seek this important protein-packed item of their diet:

- Nuthatches hitch their stubby-tailed bodies from the crown of a tree down its trunk, keeping a sharp eye and a sharper beak at the ready in case they spy any choice morsels under flaps or in the cracks of the bark.
- Brown creepers spiral up trees from the base to the branches, affording a view of any insects overlooked by nuthatches on their way down.
- Woodpeckers drill into trees, probing with their long tongues to extract larvae or adult insects from the wood.
- Robins patrol the lawn, heads cocked alertly as they look for earthworms to betray their presence.
- Kinglets and warblers are in constant motion about tree tops, fluttering through the foliage in a supercharged game of find-the-insect.
- Bluebirds, flycatchers, and kingbirds find a comfy perch to survey their domain, poised for instant flight after passing prey. Hawks often behave similarly.
- Grackles and thrashers use their bills to whip aside leaf litter and other debris on the ground to find the six-legged treasures hidden there.
- Native sparrows do a two-legged, hop-front–scratch-back movement that loosens the surface of the soil so they can find insects (as well as seeds).

Who Eats What—Birds and the Bugs They Love

BIRDS ARE opportunists that eat the insects found in their native habitat: Birds of the grassland eat grasshoppers; birds of the treetops dine on caterpillars; birds of the air eat whatever happens to fly by. Here are a few of the top insect and arachnid menu items of some common birds.

Bird	Favored Insect Food*
Red-winged blackbird	Beetles, caddis flies, cankerworms, gypsy moth and tent caterpillars, grasshoppers, grubs, mayflies, moths, spiders
Yellow-headed blackbird	Alfalfa weevils, beetles, caterpillars, grasshoppers
Eastern bluebird	Beetles, crickets, grasshoppers, katydids
Mountain bluebird	Beetles, weevils
Western bluebird	Beetles, crickets, grasshoppers
Indigo bunting	Aphids, beetles, cankerworms, cicadas, grasshoppers, mosquitoes, weevils
Painted bunting	Cankerworms, caterpillars, crickets, flies, grasshoppers, spiders, wasps, boll weevils
Cardinal	Aphids, beetles, caterpillars, cicadas, crickets, grasshoppers, leafhoppers, codling moths, scale insects, spiders, termites
Black-capped chickadee	Caterpillars, codling moths, codling moth caterpillars, insect eggs, spiders
Flickers, all races	Ants
Common grackle	Ants, beetles—Japanese, June, and others—sphinx moth caterpillars, cicadas, earthworms, flies, grubs, grasshoppers, boll weevils
Black-headed grosbeak	Bees, beetles, cankerworms, codling moth caterpillars, flies, grasshoppers, scale insects, spiders, wasps
Evening grosbeak	Beetles, spruce budworm, cankerworms
Rose-breasted grosbeak	Colorado potato beetle and other beetles, cankerworms, tent caterpillars, gypsy moth caterpillars, grasshoppers

gypsy moth caterpillars marched their armies into the woods at my house in Pennsylvania some years ago, their archenemies were close behind. Although I had never before hosted a nesting pair of cuckoos, these large, long-tailed birds (both yellow-billed and black-billed species) moved in within a week. Aided by orioles and blue jays, they devoured countless fuzzy caterpillars. Even an outbreak of aphids can mean a bonanza for neighborhood birds. The Carolina chickadees in my southern Indiana yard regularly patrol for these soft-bodied plant pests, and I've even seen ruby-throated hummingbirds taking aphids from infested stems. Of course, sometimes there simply are too many insects for the birds to control, as with serious gypsy moth

outbreaks. But for day-to-day suppression of insects, birds provide efficient, effective control.

Insects Affect Travel Plans

Migrant songbirds that retreat from cold areas for the winter months are often birds that depend mainly on insects. Swallows, martins, and swifts, which catch insects on the wing, are among the earliest to move southward. They can't take any chances of a sudden cold front wiping out their sole food supply.

Unfortunately, spring weather is full of surprises, and purple martins are sometimes caught by a late-season cold snap after they have already started nesting. Your local bait shop can be the key to their

Who Eats What—Birds and the Bugs They Love—*Continued*	
Bird	**Favored Insect Food***
Blue jay	May beetles and other beetles, tent caterpillars, gypsy moth caterpillars, grasshoppers, spiders
Junco	Ants, beetles, caterpillars, spiders, wasps, weevils
Black-billed magpie	Flies, grasshoppers, maggots, ticks
Yellow-billed magpie	Ants, bees, beetles, grasshoppers, wasps
Northern oriole	Caterpillars, especially hairy ones such as gypsy moths and tent caterpillars
Orchard oriole	Ants, aphids, beetles, cankerworms, caterpillars, crickets, grasshoppers, mayflies
Robin	Earthworms; also beetles, cicadas, grasshoppers, termites, many others
Chipping sparrow	Ants, leaf beetles, caterpillars, grasshoppers, leafhoppers, spiders, weevils
Song sparrow	Ants, army worms, beetles, cutworms, grasshoppers, ichneumon flies, wasps, many others
White-crowned sparrow	Beetles, caterpillars, flies, mosquitoes, spiders
White-throated sparrow	Ants, beetles, flies
Plain titmouse	Aphids, true bugs, leafhoppers, scale insects, many others
Tufted titmouse	Mainly caterpillars
Downy woodpecker	Carpenter ants, click beetles, spruce beetles, wood borers, tent caterpillars, cicadas, moths, nut weevils, pine weevils, many others
Hairy woodpecker	Mostly larvae of wood borers, plus others, including large stag beetle
Pileated woodpecker	Carpenter ants, wood-boring beetles
*Includes earthworms and arachnids, such as spiders, which are not insects	

survival: $5 worth of mealworms, offered in an open tray feeder, fills a lot of martin bellies.

Most flycatchers, orioles, tanagers, vireos, and warblers migrate early, too, long before frost creeps in to still the insect life. These birds can supplement their diet with berries, fruit, and sometimes seeds, so a few hardy souls may linger into winter. These stragglers are one reason why soft food can be so valuable at your feeding station. When a sudden snowstorm surprises a lingering catbird or flock of robins and they can't find their usual fare, they welcome a handout. Ground suet, bread, special recipes, or other soft foods can mean the difference between life and death.

Seed-eating birds such as finches and juncos make less dramatic long-distance flights in fall because their natural food is available in nearby climates that may be only a few hundred miles south. Crows, jays, and woodpeckers may not move on at all, being able to find food in any weather.

No Special Sauce, Please

Birds are our best allies in restoring the balance of insects in yard and garden. When grasshoppers begin to peak in late summer or when caterpillars hatch in hordes on my young oaks, I don't fret because I know the insect-eating birds won't be far behind. In 40 years of gardening, I have never lost a plant to insect pests, thanks to my feathered helpers. (I do occasionally handpick pests that can threaten food crops like squash or tomatoes seemingly overnight.)

Pesticides disrupt the natural equilibrium of your yard. Although your goal is to get rid of a particular pest when you reach for a bottle of pesticide, you are probably also killing off populations of other insects.

Loss of these insects makes it harder for your backyard birds to find the insects they need. Chemicals may also have adverse effects on birds directly; DDT was rightfully notorious for causing thin eggshells that wouldn't support the weight of parent birds, as well as other dangers. Chemicals such as diazinon—only a few years ago a common ingredient of "green lawn" treatments and still in use on golf courses and other places—may also have serious repercussions for bird health, as well as for humans and pets.

Keep your yard free of pesticides, and let the bird crew do the work of keeping insects in balance. After all, they've had a few million years of practice.

A catbird eats hundreds of insects a day and stuffs even more bugs into the beaks of its demanding nestlings. Pesticide use can spell slim pickings for insect-eating birds and their young.

Internet Resources

THE INTERNET MAKES being a bird watcher easy and fun. Shopping for anything bird-related is simple, whether you're buying a field guide, a sack of seed, or a squirrel-proof feeder. You can also shop for bird-related travel needs, from a cruise to the Amazon to bed-and-breakfast accommodations in prime Arizona hummingbird territory.

But even better than armchair shopping are the human-based resources you'll find on the Internet. Chat rooms and Web sites will put you in touch with other folks who've experienced the same problems you have. Whether you want to learn more tricks for deterring squirrels or just enjoy the comfort of commiserating with other birders besieged by the charming varmints, you will find likely sites to visit and people to "talk" to. You can also hook up with bird watchers in your area and farther afield to share sightings or plan trips.

Serious research sites are also available on the Internet, with the latest information about such topics as species of special concern, hummingbird feeding how-tos, and just about anything else you can think of.

Because Internet addresses change frequently, it's best that you do your own exploring to avoid the frustration of visiting a recommended site and finding it no longer in service. Use the search feature of your Net browser to type in the subjects that interest you most. Then just follow your instincts or Web-site links to get connected. "Audubon Society" is a good place to begin your search.

You can contact bird watchers in your area and farther afield to share bird sightings or plan trips.

Irruption Year

DEDICATED BIRD WATCHERS and backyard bird feeders get mighty excited when they hear reports of boreal chickadees, crossbills, purple finches, pine and evening grosbeaks, red-breasted nuthatches, redpolls, pine siskins, and Bohemian waxwings filtering in from other bird-feeding friends. The presence of large numbers of these birds, which make their homes in the cold stretches of the Far North, is a cause for celebration in more southerly climes, where they are rare.

Although a few of these birds may turn up each year at feeders, a true irruption year involves a massive relocation of these species, making them common guests at feeders far south of their normal range. Irruptions are thought to occur when the natural foods—mainly tree seeds, including those of pines, spruces, birches, and maples—fail to yield a good crop. Rather than face starvation, the birds fly south, where they find a true feast awaiting at feeders stocked with a constant supply of sunflower seeds.

It may be the popularity and abundance of backyard feeders that have influenced the movements of some northern birds, particularly evening grosbeaks. Once a rare sighting, these big golden birds have now become a much more common sight at winter feeders.

Another northern bird, the magnificent and huge snowy owl, also flies south irregularly when its rodent prey is unusually scarce. Like its northern relatives, this bird may show up in unlikely places far removed from its usual isolated haunts. I have seen snowies perched on utility poles in city neighborhoods, on split-rail fences in suburban lots, and in the wide-open spaces of airports, which are some-

Evening grosbeaks are an unexpected pleasure at the feeder. Once straying from their far northern homes only during irregular irruption years, they now make more frequent feeder visits.

what similar to their tundra habitat. With their beautiful white plumage and large, unblinking golden eyes, they are a memorable sight. Like the smaller birds of the Far North, the giant owls are unusually trusting of humans, much less apt to flap away than our typical owl residents.

Other northern birds of prey, including great gray owls, rough-legged hawks, goshawks, and northern shrikes, may also move south in an irruption year caused by rodent scarcity. They seem to adapt quite well to whatever rodents or other prey are available, instead of their usual diet of lemmings and voles.

Jays

JAYS ARE SMART and loud, two traits that they put to good use to clear the decks at a feeding station. With a raucous scream, they announce their approach, sending other birds scattering in alarm. Once settled on the feeder, they are usually not aggressive toward the other birds that quickly return to the feeders. For three winters, I hosted a junco that apparently figured out that the jay was all bark and no bite and so refused to budge from the feeder tray. Unfortunately, when the jay swept through one day crying "Thief! Thief!" in earnest because of an approaching hawk, the junco kept cracking seeds calmly. A few seconds later, all that was left were a few gray feathers floating to the ground.

Don't let that sweet look fool you—blue jays are loud, aggressive, and practically fearless. Watching them at the feeder is like having a front-row seat at the circus.

The only eastern representative of the clan is the **blue jay,** a crested bird with beautifully barred wings and tail and a white belly. In the Rockies and westward, **Steller's jay** takes over. This bird is darker than the blue jay, shading from bright blue to almost black, and lacks its white accents. Three crestless jays also roam the West: the **scrub jay,** a blue, white, and gray bird that skulks in thickets; the **gray-breasted jay,** blue on the back, which travels a small area of the Southwest; and the **pinyon jay,** a stubby-tailed blue-gray bird of the West that looks more like a starling at first glance. In the North and the Rockies, the soft-colored **gray jay,** or camp robber, is a familiar sight.

Jay Behavior

Members of the crow family, jays rank as geniuses among the birds. Instead of keeping beak to the grindstone like most other species, these bright birds make time for play. Jays are fond of shiny objects, which they may snatch and hide or use to play can't-catch-me. Teasing is a big part of their games. They pester crows, hawks, and owls, and they can be unmerciful with pets.

Once I watched a blue jay spend the better part of a morning playing "chase" with my dog, who was lounging near the feeders. The bird would alight near Blackie, and when the dog ran in pursuit, the bird took off with a flash of wings and a loud cry. Over and over, the jay repeated the maneuver, until the dog finally gave up and sulked.

Beautiful as well as impudent, jays are fascinating to watch at the feeder. If you host a crested species, take note of how that feathered cap predicts the jay's behavior. When it's stiffly erect, the bird is on the alert and when it's lowered, peace reigns. They pal around in groups when not raising a family, and feeder forays are often dash-in, dash-out affairs.

The cops of the bird world, jays instantly sound the alarm when they perceive danger. They will harass birds of prey, snakes, cats, and other predators.

They stay just a fraction out of harm's way with perfectly timed daring dives. It's always worth investigating when you hear jays making a fuss. The same songbirds that rely on jays to sound an alarm may also occasionally be victims of jays themselves. Jays are fond of eating bird eggs and nestlings. When you spot a robin or other typically docile bird pursuing a jay, you can be sure the jay has been out a-hunting.

Jays indulge in detective work, investigating any unusual objects, which means they will be one of the first birds to sample new foods at the feeder. These big birds also cache food, including nuts and acorns, which they often bury under leaf litter, contributing unwittingly to the growth of young trees that sprout from the seeds they "plant." The sunflowers that sprout in odd places around your yard may well be the work of jays, who typically fill their beaks with seeds, then fly off to crack them one by one or hide them for a rainy day.

During nesting season, other birds may chase a Steller's jay, thanks to its habit of raiding nests for eggs or young. Notice its large, expressive crest.

JAY FEEDER FOODS

- ■ Acorns
- ■ Amelanchier (*Amelanchier* spp.) fruits
- ■ Bread and other baked goods
- ■ Corn, any kind
- ■ Crackers
- ■ Eggs, hard-boiled or scrambled
- ■ Fruit, fresh or dried
- ■ Grapes
- ■ Mealworms
- ■ Meat scraps
- ■ Nuts
- ■ Peanut butter
- ■ Peanuts
- ■ Suet
- ■ Sunflower seed, any kind

Although most jays are boisterous birds, all species become extremely secretive in nesting season. Their mating rituals are quiet, bobbing dances and soft love songs, and they approach and exit the nest site with great stealth.

Jays use their perfectly designed bill for whacking open hard shells. They can chisel open nuts by splitting them along the seam or peck into an acorn to get to the meat. At the feeder tray, you will often see them cracking sunflower seeds gripped in their feet. Corn of any kind and sunflowers are top staples on the feeder menu with jays, but they also are quick to sample many other treats.

A gray back and thin white "eyebrows" distinguish the scrub jay, a crestless western species, from the gray-breasted jay with no stripe and a denim-colored back.

Juncos

SOFT-COLORED, SOFT-VOICED JUNCOS are mostly winter visitors at feeders, arriving in early fall and lingering until spring. Many of us know them as "snowbirds," partly because their arrival makes us think of winter and partly because of their coloring, which combines the gray of a cloudy sky with a snowy white belly. We separate juncos into two species, the **dark-eyed**, which has several sub-species or races, and the **yellow-eyed**, a rusty-backed bird of forests of the Southwest. The **slate-colored junco,** one of the dark-eyed variants, ranges across most of the country in winter when it leaves its breeding grounds in the Far North. This is the classic gray-above and white-below bird. In the western mountains, the **gray-headed junco** joins the slate-colored subspecies. This dark-eyed race has a splash of rusty red on its back, like the similar yellow-

Mirroring wintry sky above and snowy ground below, the slate-colored junco is one of the most widespread winter feeder birds. It seeks seeds such as millet.

eyed. The **Oregon junco,** which shows up across the western half of the country in winter, also breeds in some western mountain areas. This is a beauty among the quiet-colored juncos, with a showy black hood, chestnut back and sides, and snow-white belly. Another variation, the **pink-sided junco,** wears a gray hood. Several other races may appear in limited ranges, such as the **white-winged junco** of the Black Hills and southern Rockies. Female juncos of both species look much like their mates, but they may be paler and brownish with occasional streaking on their back, breast, and head.

JUNCO FEEDER FOODS

- Bachelor's-button (*Centaurea cyanus*) seeds
- Birdseed mix
- Bread crumbs
- Cosmos (*Cosmos* spp.) seed
- Cracker crumbs
- Grass seeds
- Millet
- Peanut butter, offered at a low height
- Pine nuts
- Suet, chopped, offered in a tray feeder
- Weed seeds
- Zinnia (*Zinnia* spp.) seed

Junco Behavior

In most areas, the juncos at our feeders are on vacation. They flock together in small or large groups, rarely visiting one at a time. Their short, conical beaks mark these birds as members of the finch family. Like their relatives, the sparrows, they prefer to feed on the ground, although they will visit higher feeders. Offer small seeds, particularly millet in a low tray, directly on the ground, or in higher feeders to please these winter visitors.

Listen for the twittering sounds of juncos, which they use for companionable conversation. They also sound distinctive chips when alarmed or as a scolding when they are feeling crowded at the feeder.

Most of us who host juncos at our feeders tend to take them for granted until one day we wake up to find that they have moved on. I keep a weekly feeder count on my wall calendar so that weeks don't slip by before I realize that the juncos have gone. Just as the arrival of my snowbirds portends winter, their departure means frost is a thing of the past.

K

Kinglets

HYPERACTIVITY IS the hallmark of tiny green kinglets, which rarely sit still. These quick, jerky birds flit nervously among tree branches or at feeder hangouts. Both species are olive green, and it can be difficult to distinguish between the two. If a bold dark stripe over the eye decorates the bird's head, you're watching a **golden-crowned kinglet,** who wears a pretty yellow patch on the top of its head. A wide-eyed look characterizes the **ruby-crowned kinglet,** which has a white-rimmed eye and no stripes on the head. You'll have to look closely to see the colorful patch of head feathers that gives this bird its name. Both kinglets range across the United States, with the ruby-crowned nesting farther southward than the golden-crowned. In breeding season, they stay in the northern third to half of the country and in western mountains. In winter, the golden-crowned ranges across most of the country, while the ruby-crowned stays in the southern third and in the warmer west. Females lack the red patch on their heads, although the female golden-crowned kinglet does wear the yellow cap.

It's tough to glimpse the spot of head color on a ruby-crowned kinglet—these tiny birds rarely sit still. Move in for a closer look: Kinglets are unafraid of humans.

Kinglet Behavior

The tiny dark bills of these birds indicate that they eat mainly small insects and their eggs and larvae, which they seek in their endless forays through the trees. They also sip sap and eat some small berries. In winter, kinglets hang out with mixed flocks of other gregarious birds, including chickadees, brown creepers, nuthatches, and titmice. When such a company visits your feeder area, the kinglets may nibble some soft food or small berries, but their favorite feeder food seems to be sugar water. They have become common fall-through-spring visitors at my "hummingbird" nectar feeders.

Kinglets don't seem to fear people, so get close for a good look when these birds stop by. Watch for the frequent wing-flicking movements of the ruby-crowned, which will soon allow you to identify this dynamic kinglet at a distance.

Although kinglets are similar in appearance and habits, their voices are very dissimilar. The golden-crowned's fuzzy, high-pitched call is pitched just below those inaudible dog whistles. They also sing a louder song at times. The ruby-crowned species is a virtuoso singer, with a lovely melody that rings so loudly, you can't believe it's coming from such a tiny body. Both belong to the old-world warbler family, which also includes the hyperkinetic gnatcatchers.

KINGLET FEEDER FOODS
■ Elderberries (*Sambucus* spp.), fresh or dried
■ Nectar
■ Persimmons (*Diospyrus virginiana*)
■ Raw hamburger bits
■ Suet, finely chopped
■ Sumac (*Rhus* spp.) berries

L

Landscaping

BIRDS DON'T CARE HOW GOOD your landscape design skills are. As long as your yard supplies them with food, water, shelter, and a safe way to move about, they'll happily spend hours there. But a yard with bird appeal should also look good to our eyes.

The hardest part about landscaping is remembering that plants come last. If you can control your buying and planting urges, you'll wind up with a garden that beckons to you and to birds.

Whether you like the straight edges, right angles, and controlled plantings of a formal style, or the casual plantings and curving lines of an informal or naturalistic garden, you can take steps to build in bird appeal. Remember that birds are more likely to take up residence in an area that is relatively undisturbed. If you can keep at least part of your yard undisturbed, or nearly so, with low maintenance or naturalistic plantings, birds will soon build nests in the hedges, shrubs, and trees. Beds of groundcovers and shrubs, meadow gardens, and woodland gardens all supply welcoming bird habitat.

Lawn areas are useless to most birds, except for robins, grackles, and a few other species, so you'll want to minimize the grass and focus on the plantings. Choose plants that offer food or year-round shelter as well as beauty to your yard. Instead of a traditional yew (*Taxus* spp.), for example, try a hemlock (*Tsuga* spp.), which will soon be bearing nutritious cones. You don't need to obsess over this point, though, because birds will find plenty of insects on whatever plants you fill your yard with.

Avoid using pesticides. The insects they kill might have been dinner for a bird, and their effects on bird health may be detrimental. Pest outbreaks are usually minimal in a garden that's filled with birds. It's their job, after all, and they're very good at it. If you need to help out, do so by hand-picking or using barriers like floating row covers to protect your crops.

No matter what style of garden suits you, plan your bird-friendly landscape step by step:

10 Landscaping Tips

1. Vary the topography of a flat yard by adding berms, walls, or sunken areas. The changes in surface height will make your yard more interesting, and it will seem bigger, too. Also vary height by including trellised vines and arbors, which will supply more bird plants in a small amount of space.

2. Plant shrubs and young trees in groups. Three dogwoods or hollies planted together are more visually appealing—and more bird appealing—than isolated specimens.

3. Include broad-leaved and needled evergreens for textural contrast and four-season greenery (and bird shelter).

4. Experiment with native plants to supply food, nesting materials, and shelter that birds are familiar with.

5. Install birdhouses, with entrance holes custom-sized for your favorite birds. Natural wood boxes will soon mellow to gray, blending in with the background instead of standing out like sore thumbs.

6. Place the feeding station in the most accessible site. It's no fun lugging birdseed through winter snowdrifts.

7. Add the sound of running water to your yard, and give yourself a nearby sitting spot to enjoy the water music and the sight of birds at the bath.

8. Plant a shady garden in layers as in a natural woodland: tall trees, smaller trees or large shrubs, small shrubs, ferns and wildflowers, groundcovers, leaf mulch. It will offer a more appealing habitat.

9. Tie garden areas together with sheltering shrubs or beds so that birds can move safely through your yard.

10. Untidiness is a virtue in bird gardens. Let some weeds stand to entice small-seed eaters. Delay cutting back garden plants until late winter, so birds can shelter among their stems.

Step 1. First, decide on the best area for a permanent feeding station, a site where you will have a clear, close-up view from a favorite room of the house. Install the feeders, so you can have the pleasure of watching birds while you work on the landscaping.

Step 2. Next, plan for permanent features: water garden, fence, patio, play space, paths. Sketch their locations on paper. Install these "hardscape" features as time and money allow, but be sure to reserve the spaces you allotted for them. The space that's left is what's available for planting.

Step 3. Invest in trees and shrubs before you go whole hog on the flowers you're dying to plant. Woody plants take longer to grow than perennials and annuals, so every extra month in the ground is important. They also anchor the landscape design.

Step 4. Plant tall-growing ornamental grasses and hostas next. They also carry a lot of visual weight in the landscape and are permanent garden partners that need a few years to reach their potential. Add groundcovers around shrubs and tree groupings to make them look more cohesive as well as to cut down on maintenance and avoid unnecessary disturbance to resident birds.

Step 5. Finally, the moment you've been waiting for. After all the permanent foundation plants and features are in place, add the beauty of flowers. Plant perennials, then fill in with annuals, if desired. (If you hunger for color long before this step, fill containers with colorful annuals and use them as accents in the developing garden.) Mulch the beds and feeder area to cut down on bird-disturbing maintenance chores like weeding and dragging around a watering hose.

A Wild Corner for Birds

When it comes to landscapes, birds prefer things on the casual side. In fact, the less tended an area is, the better, where birds are concerned. Naturalistic plantings provide the features that bring birds winging in for a visit and invite them to stay awhile. The plants in this garden offer food, shelter, and nesting sites and will make an especially pretty picture in the fall when the asters and goldenrod bloom and the sumac turns bright red. Watch for cedar waxwings dining on rose hips; these handsome fruit lovers don't often visit feeders but will come to your yard if there's fruit on-the-branch.

PLANT LIST

1. Staghorn sumac (*Rhus typhina*)

2. Wild rose (for example, *Rosa setigera*)

3. Canada goldenrod (*Solidago canadensis*)

4. Big bluestem grass (*Andropogon gerardii*)

5. New England asters (*Aster novae-angliae*)

6. Fescue (*Festuca* spp.)

7. Foxtail grass (*Setaria* spp.)

Native Woody Plants for Birds and Gardens

SELECTING NATIVE woody plants for the foundation of your garden will make your area's native birds feel right at home: They are already familiar with the shelter and food such plants supply. Inventories of birds' eating habits point to native plants as a prime source of year-round food. The suggestions on this list combine prime bird appeal with good looks in the garden. All will slip into a naturalistic or informal landscape with ease; most of them can also be used in a more controlled garden, except for the free-spirited colony-forming plants. Use these native trees, shrubs, and vines to create a garden that will welcome birds year-round with food, shelter, and nesting sites. In addition to the uses listed below, remember that birds will seek insects from any of these plants year-round, so that even when your plants are young, they will attract birds.

EAST

Include some of these plants in your garden if you live anywhere from New England to Wisconsin and south to Virginia.

Plant	Description	Nonfood Uses
Spicebush (Lindera benzoin)	Graceful large shrub to small tree with yellow flowers studding bare branches in early spring, golden fall foliage and red berries in fall; host plant for spicebush swallowtail butterfly	Nest sites
Northern bayberry (Myrica pensylvanica)	Suckering shrub with deciduous to semi-evergreen foliage and whitish berries	Nest sites; shelter
Virginia creeper (Parthenocissus quinquefolia)	Fast-growing vine with 5-part leaves that turn crimson in fall; clusters of dark blue berries	Nest sites
Pines (Pinus resinosus, P. rigida, P. strobus)	Evergreen conifer trees, fast-growing when young; develop craggy character with age	Nest sites; shelter; nest material (needles)
Wild cherries (Prunus pensylvanica, P. serotina, P. virginiana)	Super fast-growing small to large trees with small fruits that may be bitter, tart, or sweet, depending on species	—
Oaks (Quercus alba, Q. coccinea, Q. palustris, Q. rubra, other species)	Stately deciduous shade trees of several species; classified generally as "white oaks," with rounded-lobe leaves, or "red oaks," with leaves whose lobes end in points	Nest sites
Sumacs (Rhus copallina, R. typhina)	Colony-forming shrubs or small trees bearing pinnate foliage with beautiful red color in fall and dense clusters of fuzzy berries	—
Elderberries (Sambucus canadensis, S. pubens)	Large multistemmed shrubs bend under a heavy load of deep purple-black or bright red berries	Nest sites
Eastern hemlock (Tsuga canadensis)	Densely branched needled evergreen, valuable even when young as shelter; bears diminutive cones	Shelter; nest sites; nest material
Wild grapes (Vitis aestivalis, V. vulpina, V. labrusca, V. riparia)	Fast-growing vines that clamber up trees or over fences	Nest material (bark); nest sites

SEASON FRUIT IS AVAILABLE   SPRING   SUMMER   FALL   WINTER

Native Woody Plants for Birds and Gardens—*Continued*

SOUTHEAST
Landscape your southeastern or southern garden with these plants.

Plant	Description	Nonfood Uses
Hackberries (*Celtis laevigata, C. occidentalis*)	Large trees with curious warty gray bark and a bounty of small fruits	Nest sites
Dogwood (*Cornus florida*)	Graceful deciduous tree with white flowers followed by red berries	Nest sites
Persimmon (*Diospyros virginiana*)	Small tree with open branches, often slightly drooping, with unusual brown flowers and astringent fruits that turn sweet after frost	—
Southern wax myrtle (*Myrica cerifera*)	Suckering shrub with evergreen foliage and whitish berries	Nest sites; shelter
Black gum (*Nyssa sylvatica*)	Tree with brilliant glossy red fall foliage that hides small deep blue fruits	Nest sites
Oaks (*Quercus laurifolia, Q. marilandica, Q. nigra, Q. virginiana, other species*)	Stately deciduous shade trees of several species; many evergreen in this region	Nest sites
Pines (*Pinus echinata, P. palustris, P. rigida, P. strobus, P. taeda*)	Evergreen conifer trees with long or short needles	Nest sites; shelter; nest material (needles)
Wild grapes (*Vitis aestivalis, V. rotundifolia, V. vulpina*)	Fast-growing vines that clamber up trees or over fences	Nest material (bark); nest sites

MIDWEST
Try these plants from east of the Rockies through Illinois.

Plant	Description	Nonfood Uses
Hackberries (*Celtis laevigata, C. occidentalis*)	Large trees with curious warty gray bark and a bounty of small fruits	Nest sites
Hollies (*Ilex decidua, I. glabra, I. verticillata*)	Evergreen and deciduous shrubs and trees with attractive form and bird-magnet berries	Nest sites; shelter
Cedars (*Juniperus scopulorum, J. virginiana*)	Evergreen-needled conifer trees with abundant pale blue berries on female plants; be sure to plant at least 1 male tree with your females if wild cedars are scarce in your immediate area.	Shelter; nest sites; nest material (bark)
Wild cherries (*Prunus pensylvanica, P. serotina, P. virginiana*)	Super fast-growing small to large trees with small fruits that may be bitter, tart, or sweet, depending on species	—
Oaks (*Quercus imbricaria, Q. macrocarpa, Q. marilandica, Q. stellata, other species*)	Stately deciduous shade trees of several species; most deciduous; some evergreen	Nest sites
Riverbank grape (*Vitis riparia*)	Fast-growing vine that clambers up trees or over fences	Nest material (bark); nest sites

SEASON FRUIT IS AVAILABLE   ■ SPRING   □ SUMMER   □ FALL   ■ WINTER

Native Woody Plants for Birds and Gardens—*Continued*		
WESTERN MOUNTAINS AND DESERT Plants on this list suit gardens from the Rockies to the Cascades and into the Southwest.		
Plant	**Description**	**Nonfood Uses**
Serviceberries (*Amelanchier alnifolia, A. utahensis,* other species)	Usually suckering or colony-forming shrubs or small trees with a cloud of white spring flowers and deep blue fruits in summer	Nest sites
Arizona madrone (*Arbutus arizonica*)	Small to medium-height tree with white to pink nectar flowers followed by small orange-red fruit	Shelter
Manzanitas (*Arctostaphylos glauca, A. patula, A. pungens*)	Shrubs or small trees with beautiful smooth red bark, evergreen foliage, and small fruits	Shelter; nest sites
Cedars (*Juniperus occidentalis, J. scopulorum, J. utahensis*)	Evergreen-needled conifer trees with abundant pale blue berries on female plants; be sure to plant at least 1 male tree with your females if wild cedars are scarce in your immediate area.	Shelter; nest sites; nest material (bark)
Prickly pears (*Opuntia* spp.)	Cacti with flat oval pads linked together into jointed "branches"; showy, waxy flowers followed by red and yellow fruits	—
Spruces (*Picea engelmanni, P. glauca, P. pungens*)	Short-needled evergreen trees with dense branches	Shelter; nest sites
Pines (*Pinus cembroides, P. flexilis, P. contorta var. latifolia, P. ponderosa*)	Evergreen-needled conifer trees	Shelter; nest sites; nest material (needles)
Quaking aspen (*Populus tremuloides*)	Small- to medium-height tree with glossy leaves that tremble in the breeze; tasty winter buds and catkins in spring	Shelter
Mesquite (*Prosopis juliflora*)	Medium-height tree with fragrant yellow flowers from spring to late summer, highly attractive to bees; seeds in summer and fall	Shelter
Oaks (*Quercus chrysolepis, Q. emoryi, Q. gambeli, Q. utahensis,* other species)	Stately deciduous shade trees of several species; many evergreen in this region	Shelter; nest sites
Buckthorn or redberry (*Rhamnus crocea*)	Medium to large shrub with dense branches, spiny foliage, and red fruits	Shelter; nest sites
Wild grapes (*Vitis arizonica, V. californica,* other species)	Fast-growing vines that clamber up trees or over fences	Nest material (bark); nest sites

SEASON FRUIT IS AVAILABLE: SPRING, SUMMER, FALL, WINTER

Native Woody Plants for Birds and Gardens—*Continued*

PACIFIC NORTHWEST

Gardeners in coastal Oregon, Washington, and northern California can have fun experimenting with these plants.

Plant	Description	Nonfood Uses
Firs (*Abies concolor, A. magnifica, A. nobilis, other species*)	Short-needled evergreen conifer trees with dense branches	Shelter; nest sites; nest material (needles)
Red alder (*Alnus rubra*)	Quickly spreads into dense thicket of small trees; avoid planting where roots can invade neighbor's yard. Good for a naturalistic wet site. Bird-tempting buds, catkins, and seeds	Shelter; nest sites
Alders (*Alnus sinuata, A. rhombifolia, and other spp.*)	Pretty, colony-forming small trees but invasive in limited-size residential yards; check if neighbors are agreeable before planting.	Nest sites
Manzanitas (*Arctostaphylos glauca, A. patula, A. pungens*)	Shrubs or small trees with beautiful smooth red bark, evergreen foliage, and small fruits	Shelter; nest sites
Dogwoods (*Cornus californica, C. nuttalli, C. occidentalis*)	Small trees or shrubs with white spring flowers followed by delectable fruits	Nest sites
Salal (*Gaultheria shallon*)	Shiny-leaved evergreen shrub to small tree spreads by roots into dense colonies; good as groundcover; waxy flowers followed by black fruits	Shelter; nest sites
Pines (*Pinus contorta, P. jeffreyi, P. monticola, P. ponderosa, other species*)	Short- or long-needled evergreen conifer trees	Shelter; nest sites; nest material (needles)
Douglas fir (*Pseudotsuga menziesii*)	Tall needled evergreen conifer excellent for cover even when young; cones contain small, winged seeds	Shelter; nest sites
Oaks (*Quercus agrifolia, Q. chrysolepis, Q. douglasi, Q. garryana, other species*)	Stately deciduous shade trees of several species; many evergreen in this region	Shelter; nest sites
Elderberries (*Sambucus caerulea, S. callicarpa, S. melanocarpa*)	Large multistemmed shrubs bend under a heavy load of black, blue, or bright red berries	Nest sites
Blueberries (*Vaccinium spp.*)	Small to large deciduous shrubs, good understory plants for shady garden; sweet dark blue to blue-black fruit	Shelter

SEASON FRUIT IS AVAILABLE   ▢ SPRING   ▢ SUMMER   ▢ FALL   ▢ WINTER

L

Larks

IF YOU LIVE NEAR the wide open fields that larks inhabit, you may find the birds showing up at your feeding station, particularly after winter storms. The North American birds called larks belong to two separate families. The **eastern** and **western meadowlarks,** two nearly identical-looking species, are not truly larks but are classified in the blackbird family. Both have a chubby, short-tailed look, very similar to a starling in silhouette. They wear vivid deep yellow from throat to belly, slashed with a broad black band across the upper breast. Their backs are mottled and streaked brown and white, the better to blend in with grassy fields where they dwell. Fine points of plumage, such as a yellower cheek, distinguish the two species, but I depend on their songs to tell them apart. The eastern bird gives forth in melancholy, downward-slurring whistled phrases, while the western has a loud and beautiful fluting song.

The **horned lark** is the only native North American member of the true lark family (the Eurasian skylark has been introduced in British Columbia). This slender bird is brown above, white below, with a finely detailed head pattern of black sideburns and breast swash and a yellow face that is striking through binoculars. Tiny feather tufts form the decorative "ears." Their delicate tinkling voices often

The horned lark spends nearly all its time earthbound in open fields and grasslands. But at courtship time, it soars into the sky with ethereal song.

trill over fields across America in all seasons, although the birds themselves are hard to see except when in motion.

Lark Behavior

It's hard to tell whether a lark lives up to its "happy" reputation, but you will undoubtedly be smiling should one of these birds show up at your feeder. An unusual visitor is always a delight to get to know. In the wild, these species are practically invisible thanks to their camouflage, but at the feeder they are standouts. All feed on the ground, so offer grain and seed in low feeders or directly on the ground.

LARK FEEDER FOODS			
■ Bayberry (*Myrica pensylvanica*)	■ Millet	■ Suet, chopped, served at ground level	■ Weed seeds, such as pigweed, common ragweed, and common lamb's-quarters
■ Canary seed	■ Milo		
■ Corn, all types	■ Native grass seeds	■ Sunflower seed, black oil	
■ Lawn-grass seeds	■ Oats		■ Wheat

Lawns

Attract blackbirds, flickers, grackles, robins, starlings

YOUR LAWN IS a great place for backyard parties and outdoor games, but do wild birds like lawns? My answer is: They're not prime bird habitat, so don't go to the trouble of maintaining a lawn just for the birds' sake. But if you have a lawn in your yard, chances are, you'll spot several kinds of birds foraging there.

Flickers appreciate a lawn where they can scour the area for ants. Worms, grubs, beetles, and other lawn delectables also appeal to some bird species.

Lawn Birds to Watch For

Robins are the number-one bird visitor to lawn areas. The open space gives them plenty of room to hop about and the close-cropped grass gives them a good view of the worms they seek.

Flickers are another common lawn bird. These big brown woodpeckers hunker down on the grass near anthills, picking off the inhabitants by the beakful. When ants swarm in a dense mound, or when the winged adults leave the ground in search of mates, don't reach for the ant spray: Flickers and other ant-eating birds are likely to show up for the feast.

You may not appreciate starlings chowing down at your feeders, but you'll love the way they gobble white grubs, which are the larval stage of Japanese beetles and other pests. Starlings stalk about lawns in search of grubs, stabbing their long pointed beaks deep into the soil to extract the delectable morsels. (Blackbirds and robins also grab grubs.)

While flickers, robins, and starlings are the most common birds you'll spot on or around your lawn, there are others to watch for as well.

■ Killdeers and roadrunners, which chase after their insect prey, appreciate the open space of lawn as a happy hunting ground. They'll scoot after grasshoppers, lizards, beetles, and other bites of living bird food.

■ Grackles spend much of their time stalking about open areas looking for insects or eating seeds. When they're at work on your lawn, you can get a good look at the iridescent sheen on their elegant black plumage. You may also spy red-winged or yellow-headed blackbirds, rusty blackbirds, or other blackbirds hard at work on your lawn.

■ Horned larks or meadowlarks may visit your lawn if your yard adjoins open wild country. These birds prefer a more unkempt grassy area than the typical lawn, but they may deign to go slumming in your clipped grass if the insect pickings are abundant.

■ Bluebirds and flycatchers that live in or near your yard may flutter over your grass as they hunt down butterflies, moths, and other flying insects. Border your lawn with flowerbeds to attract these types of food-on-the-wing, and supply a few wooden posts to serve as perches for the insect-hunting birds.

- Swallows and swifts, which won't visit a feeder, skim over open areas of lawn to collect flying insects. It's fun to lie back in a hammock and watch them swooping overhead.
- Even hummingbirds find something to like about a lawn: They use the unobstructed space to indulge in show-off courtship stunts, where they swing and swoop and dive through the air like buzzing mini-airplanes.

Lawn Care for Bird Watchers

Dousing your lawn with pesticides or herbicides may give you picture-perfect grass, but using these chemicals will also decrease the bird life in your backyard. Birds won't come hunting if all the bugs are belly-up after a drenching with chemicals! So instead of spraying, let the birds keep the pest population in balance. Part of the reason that insects reach pest proportions in a lawn area is because it's an unnatural environment. Single-species plantings of lawn grass don't occur spontaneously in nature. If your lawn is plagued with ants, Japanese beetles (*Popillis japonica*), June beetles (*Phyllophaga* spp.), and other lawn pests, it may be time to downsize that grassy expanse.

As for lawn weeds, keep in mind that many weeds may host caterpillars that birds view as delectable treats. During nesting season, catbirds, orioles, robins, and other songbirds may scour your less-than-perfect lawn, looking for fritillary caterpillars on the violets that have infiltrated your grass, or picking off buckeye caterpillars (*Junonia coenia*) from plantain (*Plantago major*) leaves. Should your lawn be blessed with a crop of dandelions (*Taraxacum officinale*), you'll find the puffy seedheads are a favorite treat of indigo buntings, white-crowned sparrows, and other native sparrows.

Less Lawn Means More Birds

Robins and other lawn-appreciating birds don't need an acre of mown grass to feel at home. A smaller patch suits them just fine. If you want a greater diversity of birds to visit, plan on reducing the size of your lawn. The birds will be happy, and you will be, too, because you'll spend less of your precious time on monotonous lawn care.

If you make a large lawn drastically smaller, any killdeers in residence will probably desert you for bigger open spaces. But blackbirds, flickers, grackles, robins, and (sorry!) starlings will still come visiting. The insects they seek are plentiful in plantings of flowers and groundcovers, too.

A Balanced View

OPEN AREAS of lawn are a double-edged sword for always-vulnerable birds: They give birds a clear view of your neighbor's stalking kitty, but they also make songbirds sitting ducks for predatory hawks dropping from the sky or for fast cats who've mastered the rushing attack.

The only way to solve this dilemma is to take a hint from the birds themselves. Spend a few hours watching the birds on your lawn, and take note of their behavior. You can expect to see your lawn birds pause frequently to look and listen. (Sometimes groups of birds seem to appoint a lookout who watches for danger on behalf of the group.) But if the birds seem restless and edgy, ready to startle into panicked flight at any instant, that's a sign that the birds feel unsafe and need more cover nearby. A few shrub groupings, a hedge, or a wild corner can make your yard come alive with bird life.

Watch for predators that visit your yard, too, when you're deciding how much lawn to leave. If the neighbor's kitty frequently comes calling, help your birds avoid her clutches by siting birdbaths and feeding areas in open areas of lawn. Kitty will have a much harder time catching birds if he has to cross 20 feet of clipped lawn grass to reach them. If your problem is hawks, not cats, give your birds as much cover as possible. Speedy hawks win easily in life-or-death pursuits with songbirds when they can zoom across large, wide-open lawn areas.

As the plant diversity of your yard increases, so will the bird population. You may not have as clear a view of your robins as you once did, but instead, you'll hear song sparrows and catbirds singing in the hedges and goldfinches calling among the flowers.

You'll probably want to set aside enough lawn to play ball with the kids, toss a frisbee for the dog, or entertain your summer party guests. The rest of the turf can go! Here are some ways to painlessly reduce the size of your lawn:

- Plant a hedge along the perimeters. As always, choose plants that offer good sheltering places and food: shrubs with berries, evergreens, and even statuesque annual flowers all do the trick. A 3-foot-wide strip of sunflowers down the edge of your yard will save you at least two swipes of the mower while supplying plenty of birdseed-on-the-stalk.

- Break up large areas of lawn by planting a group of shrubs, a bed of groundcovers, or a corridor of flowers of varying heights.

- Add another bird-feeding station to your yard and cover the area beneath it with wood chip mulch.

- Replace an area of lawn grass with a prairie or meadow garden. Plant it with native grasses that thrive in your region and sturdy wildflowers, such as bee balm (*Monarda* spp.) and perennial sunflowers (*Helianthus* spp.), that have spreading roots and can hold their own without coddling. Sow seeds of annual flowers for added color.

- Create a new water feature, whether it's a simple clay-saucer birdbath balanced on a rock or a triple-tier waterfall. Once you add water to your yard, you'll find that you can't help but create a garden around it. A few clumps of rushes, some spiky red cardinal flowers—before you know it, you've got another garden beckoning to the birds.

> If you want a greater diversity of birds to visit your yard, reduce the size of your lawn.

Lean-Tos

IN A DISCREET AREA OF MY YARD, beside the foundation of my house, I keep a motley assortment of emergency supplies for winter feeding: sections of plywood of various sizes, lengths of 2 × 4s, stacks of bricks, and even a few concrete blocks. At Christmastime, salvaged evergreen boughs also get added to the pile. This is my lean-to construction collection.

When winter snows blow in, I erect emergency lean-tos to protect feeding areas from the brunt of wind and blowing snow. Lean-to feeding areas are much appreciated by ground-feeding birds, including doves, pheasants, quail, towhees, and sparrows. In my area, cardinals also make good use of them. In areas with hot summers, lean-tos also create welcome shade and break the force of dry summer winds.

Construction is simple: Just lean a piece of plywood at about a 45-degree angle, tilted so that prevailing winds sweep up and over its surface. The specific angle of your lean-to is less important than the comfort of your intended guests: If birds feel penned in under a shelter, they'll avoid it. Use bricks and blocks to help hold the plywood in place, and prop up the contraption with sections of 2 × 4s so that the shelter doesn't collapse and conk birds on their heads.

If you live in an area of frequent snows, you don't need to disguise your lean-to because the white stuff will take care of that. But if the snow won't cooperate, try my trick of stapling evergreen boughs to the plywood. Arrange branches so that their tips drape over the top edge of the board, which gives it a more natural look. Pines, spruce, hemlock, magnolia, bayberry, and other evergreens work well.

> In a pinch, you can even use a pizza box held in place with a brick to make a temporary wind block.

Leftovers

Attract blackbirds, chickadees, jays, mockingbirds, robins, thrashers, wrens, and many others

THAT PLASTIC CONTAINER in the back corner of the refrigerator may hold the makings of a fine meal for your feeder birds. Many "human" foods are chock-full of the fat and carbohydrates that birds crave. Like other unfamiliar foods, leftovers may linger for a few hours until birds are brave enough to sample them. Seasoned scavengers such as crows, jays, magpies, pigeons, house sparrows, and starlings are usually the first clients. Thus food scraps are an excellent food for distracting these birds from other feeder areas. Bluebirds, robins, mockingbirds, woodpeckers, and other birds may also welcome leftovers depending on whether the offerings are animal-, fruit-, or grain-based. If the birds don't eat your leftovers, squirrels or nighttime opossums and raccoons may enjoy them.

Too stale? Too much? Pass leftovers along to chickadees and others, which will peck off the good parts. A tray feeder lets the cleanup crew work freely.

Leftovers for Lunch

IF YOUR family's not into leftovers, try feeding them to the birds—the leftovers, not the family! Here are some "people" foods that may find favor with your feathered friends.

Food	Where to Serve	Birds Attracted
Cooked corn, on the cob or kernels	Drain any liquid and spread on low tray feeder.	Blackbirds, crows, jays, mockingbirds, starlings, woodpeckers
Fruit pies or fruit pastries	Empty suet feeder	Bluebirds, chickadees, mockingbirds, orioles, starlings, titmice
Fruit salad or canned fruit	Drain any liquid and spread on raised tray feeder.	House finches, mockingbirds, orioles, starlings, thrashers, Carolina wrens
Green salad	—	Not appealing to most birds; house sparrows may nibble a small amount.
Lasagna and other pasta dishes with sauce	Directly on ground or on shallow plastic tray low to ground	Crows, jays, magpies, starlings
Meat scraps, any kind	Empty suet feeder	Chickadees, crows, jays, magpies, starlings, titmice, woodpeckers, Carolina wrens
Quiche	Directly on ground	Chickadees, crows, jays, magpies, starlings, titmice
Sandwiches	Tray feeder or directly on ground	Chickadees, crows, jays, magpies, mockingbirds, robins, starlings, titmice
Withered or bruised apples and other fruit	Raised tray or spike feeder	House finches, mockingbirds, orioles, starlings, thrashers, Carolina wrens

Lettuce

Attracts purple finches, goldfinches, pine siskins, native sparrows

GOLDFINCHES ARE SO FOND of lettuce seeds that they used to go by the name "lettuce birds." In your bird-friendly backyard, you can plant lettuce to attract not only goldfinches, but also purple finches, pine siskins, and native sparrows.

Living Lettuce-Seed Feeders

Lettuce (*Lactuca sativa*) is a prolific seed producer. This simple-to-grow salad plant zooms to the flowering stage and produces seed stalks as soon as the weather warms up. Plant successive crops in a sunny spot, and you'll have a ready-made goldfinch feeder right through frost. Lettuce seeds are reluctant to sprout when temperatures climb over 80°F; to overcome this problem during the heat of summer, put the seeds in the fridge for a week before you plant them.

Although finches will eventually find even a single isolated lettuce plant, you'll have better luck if you plant a block of lettuce, either near other goldfinch-attracting plants (such as cosmos) or near your regular finch feeder area. Any variety will do the trick, but leaf lettuce matures much faster than head lettuce. Be sure to plant your lettuce where you'll have a good view of the birds as they come to feast upon it.

Wild lettuces are worth considering, too. Be forewarned that they often have slightly prickly leaves and the flowerstalks may reach 7 feet tall, with open clusters of tiny daisies at the top. The most common, *Lactuca scariola*, is a widespread weed from Europe and is probably already trying to colonize some bit of open space in your yard. Another worthy wild lettuce is telegraph lettuce (*L. floridana*), a 3- to 6-foot-tall species crowned with small dusky blue flowers in summer to fall. Check a wildflower field guide to find out what grows in your area and get to know the plants so you can encourage a few in your yard. No matter what species your lettuce is, seed-seeking goldfinches will love it.

Let your lettuce bloom, and you'll see its floral resemblance to other members of the vast composite family, which includes asters, sunflowers, and other daisies whose seeds birds love.

Buying and Saving Lettuce Seed

Purchased lettuce seeds are generally too pricey to pour into the bird feeder as a regular meal. For an occasional treat, buy untreated seed at bulk prices from local hardware stores, farm and garden supply stores, or mail-order seed catalogs, and fill a niger tube feeder with the tiny, lightweight seeds.

It's much cheaper to save seed from your own lettuce patch. Just clip the seed stalks into a brown paper sack, and store them in a dry place until you're ready to serve them to the birds. Lettuce seeds are surrounded by fluff, but there's no need for you to clean the seeds if you feed your homegrown seeds in a tray (not tube) feeder. Birds are adept at sorting out seed from fluff, and any seeds that manage to drift from their grasp will yield a nice crop of volunteer lettuce plants to produce seeds for next season.

Liriope

Attracts bluebirds, mockingbirds

I USED TO SCORN LIRIOPE (lilyturf) as too boring for my garden. The only reason I tried it was that I found a truckload of the grasslike groundcover pitched on a pile at the county waste dump. The indestructible perennials were still alive and growing, even though most of them were upside down.

Anything that determined deserved a home, I figured, and I had just the spot: a strip of dry shade beneath sugar maples where even hostas sulked. I carted the thick mats of liriope home, ripped them into smaller pieces, and used them to fill in along my sidewalk. Grateful for the reprieve, they rewarded me with fresh growth and a beautiful burst of lavender-blue flowers a few weeks later.

When the liriope flowers ripened into black berry-like fruits, I found out what a prize my rescued plants really were. A pair of eastern bluebirds, which usually strayed no farther than the hedgerow bordering the farm fields near my house, braved the town traffic to settle on the spikes of black berrylike liriope fruits. In fact, the only thing in my garden that bluebirds like better than liriope is the berries of deciduous hollies.

A No-Care Groundcover

Liriope muscari is tough as nails and thrives in sun or shade through Zone 6. Its thin, strappy, dark green leaves look like lush grass and reach about 1 foot tall. The spikes of lilac-blue flowers appear

Liriope is a tough groundcover, and when its berries ripen in late summer, bluebirds can't resist flying in to feast on them.

above the foliage in late summer. Liriope is a plant-it-and-forget-it groundcover or edging plant that shrugs off drought, disease, humidity, and pests. If your yard is within a ¼ mile of bluebird habitat, don't turn up your nose at this commoner. Liriope may be just what you need to lure those beautiful birds right to your doorstep.

Magpies

ONCE YOU SEE A MAGPIE, you'll never forget it. This striking crow-size bird resembles a harlequin in sharply contrasting patches of black and white. If you're close enough and the light is right, you'll catch a beautiful iridescent sheen of blue, purple, and green on the bird's magnificently long tail, which streams out behind it in flight like the tails of scarlet macaws of the Amazon rain forest.

But pretty is as pretty does, and magpies, despite their beauty, are tough customers. They are bullies and, like crows and ravens, have a strong taste for meat, whether it's carrion, rodents, or songbirds and their nestlings. Years ago, ranchers killed thousands of these western birds because of their unsavory habit of picking at still living but defenseless livestock, either newborn, sick, or just branded.

Magpies have unpleasant voices as well as uncouth eating habits. Their loud, harsh cries echo wherever these big birds dwell.

The **black-billed magpie** is by far the most widespread species; it ranges winter and summer across the West, venturing barely into the Southwest. In a small strip of the far West, the **yellow-billed magpie** joins its relative.

Magpie Behavior

Magpies aren't all bad. Most of their diet consists of insects, and they eat zillions of grasshoppers every season. They are intelligent birds and are as

Bold patches of black and white adorn the magpies of the West. This one is the black-billed species, which builds humongous, highly visible nests.

MAGPIE FEEDER FOODS
■ Amelanchier (*Amelanchier* spp.) berries
■ Apples
■ Blueberries and other small fruits
■ Bones
■ Bread and other baked goods
■ Cereal
■ Corn
■ Figs
■ Grapes
■ Leftovers
■ Meat scraps
■ Suet
■ Wheat

fond as crows are of playing with shiny objects or with each other.

Keep magpies occupied at the feeder with any leftovers you can scrounge up: old ham bones, cold pasta, meat loaf, bread—they'll eat practically anything. Be sure to serve the magpies' food far from the seed feeders, so that your smaller birds can eat undisturbed. These bright birds quickly learn the feeder-stocking routine and may be waiting when you come on your morning rounds. They are also rewarding to hand tame. Great at pest control, magpies will gobble up any mouse that dares show its whiskery face.

If magpies are a feeder nuisance you'd rather do without, switch to feeding seed in weight-operated feeders that deny them access, or in tube feeders. See the Nuisance Birds entry on page 217 for other ways to discourage them.

Mealworms

Attract bluebirds, purple martins, robins, yellow-rumped warblers, woodpeckers, Carolina wrens

THE SIGHT OF SQUIRMING, segmented whitish tan larvae may make you squeamish but mealworms are a four-star meal as far as bluebirds are concerned. A simple open tray feeder stocked with a single layer of these wiggly critters can make bluebirds a regular presence in your yard.

What's so appealing about these undeniably homely creatures? They're packed with protein! Birds that eat caterpillars, grubs, and earthworms include mealworms in their diet. Woodpeckers of all sorts, purple martins, Carolina wrens, and yellow-rumped warblers may also dive into the feeding frenzy at a mealworm buffet. Robins, too, enjoy a generous helping of the nutritious larvae.

I make sure that I keep a few containers of mealworms on hand in late winter and early spring, when the capricious weather may clamp down on migrant martins or bluebirds that are already nesting. The larvae give them a ready source of critical food when no natural insects are on the wing because of chilly or rainy weather.

Mealworms are the larvae of meal beetles (also called darkling beetles) that are pests in granaries and other grain storage places. You can buy mealworms at reasonable prices at a local bait shop or through mail-order sources such as those listed in "Resources" on page 348. Start small with your mealworm ranch, making the initial offering to your birds and keeping any extras in the refrigerator in a securely closed container.

If you find you're feeding every bluebird within a mile, you can buy in quantity or grow your own. A plastic 5-gallon bucket with a secure lid makes a great home for mealworms. Fill it with a few inches of cornmeal for the larvae to eat, add an initial small container of mealworms from a bait shop, and you're in business. Put a damp paper towel on top to supply moisture. The insect larvae will mature in the container and reproduce, giving you an expanding colony for feeder fodder. Your crop will do better if

If you long to see bluebirds at the feeder, lure them with mealworms. Keep the mealworm feeder filled and enjoy the bluebirds that fly in to dine.

you toss in a piece of lettuce every few days to keep their environment slightly moist.

If you don't fancy a mealworm farm in your home, ask a bait shop owner if he or she will raise the critters in quantity for you. If you assure them of your patronage, the shop owner may agree.

Other grubs may also appeal to your bluebirds and other larvae-eating birds. In southern Indiana, late spring and early summer are marked by the appearance of two big beetles. May beetles emerge from the soil in May, followed a few weeks later by iridescent green June beetles. Both spend their formative months as unappealing whitish grubs in the soil.

One year, I dropped some grubs into a lidless box. I intended to raise them indoors so I could watch them transform into beetles, but the bluebirds who'd been watching had other ideas. As soon as I moved to the far end of the row, the pair swooped from their birdhouse and gobbled up the hapless grubs.

Melons

Attract cardinals, doves, grackles, jays, nuthatches, sparrows, titmice, woodpeckers

SPITTING WATERMELON SEEDS across the yard at family picnics is about the most any of us do with melon seeds. Usually we scrape them out into the compost bucket without a second thought (until a cantaloupe vine comes sprawling out of the compost next summer).

It wasn't until a friend visited me from Kuwait, bearing gifts of crunchy toasted cantaloupe and watermelon seeds, that I realized I was throwing away a healthy snack every time I scraped out a melon. That's when I started saving my melon seeds by scooping them into a colander, rinsing with a strong spray from the hose, and pouring them onto my patio table to dry in the sun.

One morning I scared up a pair of cardinals from the table, and when I went to investigate, I found a pile of cantaloupe-seed hulls, each with the meat neatly removed. That's right—birds like melon seeds, too. Cardinals, doves, grackles, jays, nuthatches, sparrows, titmice, and woodpeckers eagerly devour the dried seeds of any melon: cantaloupe, honeydew, watermelon, or fancy French 'Charantais'.

If you want to add melons to your feeder menu, you'll find that the seeds dry fast and easily on old window screens supported on lawn chairs. Wash seeds in a colander before spreading them out on a screen, and crumble clumps occasionally as they dry to keep them from sticking together. If you want to save the seeds for fall and winter feeding, cover them with a single thickness of cheesecloth to keep birds out while the seeds dry. Pour the dried seeds into brown paper bags and store them in metal containers.

If you buy a melon in winter, wash the pulp off the seeds in a colander, shake off excess water, then spread the seeds on a section of newspaper, and dry on top of the refrigerator or another warm place. Turn the seeds daily to prevent mold. Or you can save time and just scrape the fresh seeds into the feeder for birds to sort out themselves.

> Little more than annoyances to us, melon seeds make a welcome treat for seed-eating birds.

Mesh Bag Feeders

MESH BAGS ARE ONE OF THE EASIEST and most convenient feeders, both for you to make and hang, and for birds to visit and feed from. When fishnet stockings went out of style along with go-go boots, I grieved slightly, but I'm glad to see that they're making a comeback in some areas—not because of the style involved, but because their flexible mesh makes great bird feeders. If you have some old ones lying around the house, cut them into large sections, tie one end, and voilà! mesh bag feeder, ready to be filled. If you happen not to have a pair handy, substitute the plastic mesh bags used to hold onions, potatoes, and other products that you buy at the supermarket.

Mesh bags make great impromptu feeders when the need arises. You can fill them with suet, nutmeats, peanuts, sunflower seed, raisins, or anything else that won't fall out between the holes in the mesh. And it's easy for birds to slip their beaks between the strands and pick out the delicacies you serve them.

No-Mess Mesh

Making a mesh bag feeder couldn't be easier: Just stuff the bag with food, tie off the top, and hang it by a string. Don't be afraid to fill the bag to bulging; the plastic net is tough and resists tears, and the suet or nut pieces peeking out between the cracks will quickly alert the birds to a new food source. As an added bonus, they cost virtually nothing when you use a recycled bag (or, of course, those old stockings). Still, commercial dealers have gotten into the act by offering already filled mesh bags. You may choose to buy some for the convenience they offer— no filling, no tying, just hang on a nail or hook and they're ready for customers. I have invested in thistle mesh bags just so I could have the empty bags to re-fill later. Their mesh is finer than the bags I find at grocery stores, so I can fill them with a wider variety of smaller feed items; although they are sold as disposables, I reuse them several times.

Unfortunately, mesh bag feeders are popular with squirrels, cats, and raccoons as well as birds. Without much effort, larger animals can tear open the mesh to get at the food inside. To counteract this somewhat, I tie long strings to the bags for hanging, which does slow down the thieves a bit. The string adds to the entertainment value, too: One night I watched a determined coon pull a bag up by reeling in the string hand over hand. I figured he deserved his prize of suet after that ingenuity.

Cheap and effective, a feeder made from a plastic mesh bag filled with fat will delight your suet customers. Recycle an onion bag to make this feeder.

Mice and Rats

AMONG THE MANY FURRY RODENTS that visit your bird-feeding station, mice and rats may show up for their share of the handouts, particularly if you allow seed and other food to lie on the ground. When these undesirable guests begin to arrive, it's a clear signal to improve your feeder housekeeping.

Traps are the quickest and most reliable way to eliminate a rodent problem. Forget the old-fashioned whack-'em traps; they'll get rid of your mice and rats, but they can also snag a bird or flying squirrel. Use only live box traps that allow the animals to enter but not leave. You can find plastic or metal models at discount stores, hardware stores, bird-supply shops, and home-supply outlets, or you can order them from catalogs, such as those listed in "Resources" on page 348.

I depend on multimouse traps, which can accumulate a night's worth of small rodents in a single large box, instead of the one-at-a-time traps that require resetting night after night. I take my mice to a wild area far from my home to release them. Rats are larger and smarter and may be harder to catch than mice. Wear heavy leather gloves when releasing rodents from the traps to avoid rat bites and protect yourself from disease. Keep the traps away from your face to avoid breathing in any contaminants—scientists believe the deadly Hanta virus spreads through the air. Wash your hands thoroughly with antibacterial soap after handling the traps, and avoid touching your face before you clean up.

To prevent rodent problems before they start—and once started, they multiply fast—practice good sanitation around the feeder area. Avoid feeding birds on the ground, and shovel up spilled seed regularly. Letting your cat prowl at night is an excellent preventive (but keep Kitty indoors during nesting season). Opossums, raccoons, foxes, and coyotes may also catch and eat mice.

Though you want to control your mouse and rat populations quickly, you may soon attract owls while the pests are in residence. Screech owls, which live even in cities, are better mousers than any cat you've ever had. Larger owls, such as the great horned owl and the barn owl, make quick work of rats in both towns and rural areas.

Little dramas play out at the feeding station when small animals creep out to dine on spilled seed. Silent and swift, owls are fond of a midnight snack of mice.

Migration

THE FIRST TIME I LOOKED DOWN from an airplane window, I suddenly understood how it must feel to be a migrating bird. After a long night of flying, navigating by starlight or magnetic instinct or with rivers and mountains as guides, the breaking dawn would illuminate for the birds the very same oases I was seeing far below my soaring jet. Islands of trees announce loud and clear that here is safety, food, and shelter.

From the air, the shade trees in an old neighborhood look just as appealing as a natural forest. Understanding this made me realize why migrants drop out of the sky in large numbers in spring and fall to seek sustenance, even in city neighborhoods.

It's only a short flutter of the wings to reach a hospitable feeding station or berry-filled backyard once the migrating birds are in your neighborhood. Whether they've alighted in a nearby natural area or

Rose-breasted grosbeaks at the feeder are one of the grand surprises migration may bring. As birds stream north in spring, they may refuel far from their homes.

just down the block, migrants will soon show up at your well-stocked feeder, since eating is the number-one order of business on these long trips.

Birds migrate north in spring, once insects and other foods are available on their breeding grounds. In fall, they reverse the process, heading south when short days signal the onset of winter cold and the forthcoming lack of food.

Migration Patterns

Nearly all birds that depend mainly on insects and nectar—the hummingbirds, orioles, thrushes, vireos, and warblers—commit to the long haul. These long-distance flyers travel 1,000 miles or more to reach a region where their favored foods will be abundant.

Goldfinches, jays, and other birds that depend on more varied or more easily available foods may go for just a short jaunt. They travel a few hundred miles to what must seem like greener pastures, so to speak. The birds they replace may similarly travel a short distance southward. Unless you live in the northern extreme limit of these birds' range, you will have what seems like all-year residents of these species. In fact the birds you host in winter may be different individuals from those that dine at your feeders in the summer months.

Not all birds migrate. Some stick around all year, showing up at the feeder with their families in summer and stopping by singly in wintertime. Most titmice and woodpeckers follow this pattern.

Migration Means New Birds

After months of feeding the same old reliable cardinals, chickadees, jays, and woodpeckers, it's a real treat to host somebody new and different. That's why bird watchers get so excited by the arrival of migrants at the feeder.

In spring, a grosbeak, an oriole, or a tanager passing through may grace your feeder. In fall, you can welcome back the native sparrows and juncos that bring life to winter bird feeding. Of course, the birds you see during and after migration will depend on where you live. If you're near the northern end of the route, you will get most of your unusual visitors in spring, when northern-nesting birds return. If you're at the southern terminus, orioles, robins, and other long-distance travelers may swamp your feeders in winter. If you live somewhere in the middle of the migration route, you'll get to welcome great birds both coming and going.

Tailor your feeder menu to the needs of the migrants you expect to see, or add new foods quickly once they arrive. Fruit, suet, peanut butter, bread crumbs, and mealworms are popular with orioles, tanagers, thrushes, and other travelers that eat mostly insects. These delicacies may entice them to linger a little longer at your feeding station. They will also come to drink and bathe in fresh water, especially if you add a drip device so the birds can hear the water from a distance.

Red-Letter Days

KEEP TRACK of the arrivals of new birds at your feeder, so that you can anticipate them next year. And try—although it's harder than you might think—to jot down the date, or a close approximation, when birds leave your area.

Migration schedules are almost like clockwork: In 35 years of keeping notes, my records show deviations of usually only a day or two in arrival dates. Barn swallows in southern Indiana, for instance, always show up on or close to my birthday, April 25.

I keep a bird calendar a year in advance, so I can mark the expected arrival dates of birds. When I turn the page to the new month of April, for example, last year's arrival of indigo buntings, rose-breasted grosbeaks, and scarlet tanagers will be clearly marked. I love anticipation!

Many local chapters of the National Audubon Society ask members for their observations of migration comings and goings. If you don't already belong, join the club and ask if they have a list of past records. That way, you'll know when to expect the first junco or say goodbye to the last oriole.

Feeder Observations

You certainly will notice the absence or appearance of migratory birds at your feeder. But if your area is host to the same species summer and winter, it's often hard to tell whether you're looking at the same birds or their seasonal replacements, since all birds of a feather tend to look pretty much alike. That's why it helps to pay attention to the small details of the birds at your feeder. If you notice an individual with a distinctive call or unusual albinistic coloring, for example, you will easily be able to distinguish it from the rest of its kin and thus gauge its seasonal movements.

Much of migration is still a mystery. But bird-banding efforts and other observations add more details to the picture every season. Your contribution of data, through local bird counts and Project Feederwatch, are a big aid to the science of bird travel. See Banding on page 11 and Bird Counts on page 23 for more details on how you can help.

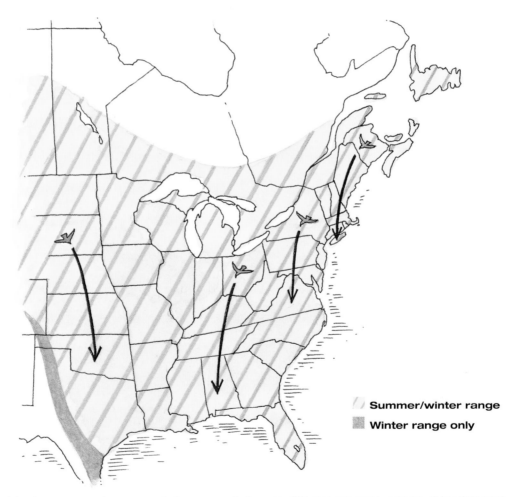

Summer/winter range

Winter range only

The blue jays you see in your yard all year may belong to different migratory groups. A jay that nests in Canada may spend its winter break in New York, while the New York jay takes off for Virginia. The migration paths shown here are from actual bird banding records.

M

Millet

Attracts buntings, doves, finches, juncos, pheasants, quail, siskins, native sparrows, towhees, varied thrushes, Carolina wrens

MILLET IS A BEST BUY in birdseed. Although 50 pounds of millet costs about 50 percent more than 50 pounds of sunflower seed, a sack of tiny, dense millet seed holds millions more seeds than a sack of bulky sunflower. That means you can feed a lot more birds with a sack of millet than you can with a sack of sunflower.

Any Millet Will Fill the Bill

Several species of grass yield the grain commonly called millet. Most belong to the genus *Setaria*, while one "millet" hails from the *Panicum* genus—*P. miliaceum*, better known as broom corn. German millet (*Setaria italica*), also called foxtail millet, Italian millet, or Japanese millet, is the most widely available. This annual grass shoots up like a rocket, reaching 5 feet in height, with stout seedheads that may stretch almost 1 foot long! You don't need to become a millet expert to make your birds happy: They will eagerly eat any millet, no matter what botanical name the parent plant goes by.

By the way, millet is good food for people, too. It's a dietary staple in countries such as India, Korea, and China.

A Real Crowd Pleaser

Pour some millet in a tray feeder or even right on the ground, and it will quickly attract buntings, doves, finches, juncos, pheasants, quail, native sparrows, towhees, siskins, and Carolina wrens. In the Pacific Northwest, the gorgeous orange-and-blue varied thrush is another big fan of millet.

Millet is a good choice for year-round feeding. When winter snow or ice storms make it hard for birds to find food, even bluebirds and robins will readily eat millet. During spring migration, another time when fast fuel is at a premium, scarlet tanagers may stop at your feeder for a few quick mouthfuls of millet.

Millet is a common ingredient in birdseed mixes, but you can also buy the seed plain, by the pound or in bulk, in case you'd rather make your own custom blends or if you want to feed birds at a bargain rate.

Millet seeds are small and round and may be golden tan or reddish brown, depending on which plant species the seeds came from. Birds eat both colors of seed with alacrity, but the white proso millet will bring them to a new feeder faster because it's easier for the birds to see.

A Millet Garden for Birds

MILLET IS an annual grass that's simple to grow in any sunny spot. In fact, it's probably growing beneath your feeder already! (See Grasses for Birds on page 145 for more on volunteer millet.) Grow a garden of millet, and your birds will thank you by gracing the seedheads of the grasses all through fall and winter. Any seeds that drop will be welcome fodder for doves, juncos, quail, native sparrows, towhees, and other ground-feeding birds.

The easiest way to grow a millet garden is to simply sow some birdseed. Or you can plant a sampler of varieties from specialty catalogs. I like to sow millet seed purchased from bird-supply stores because it's fun to see what kind of millet it will turn out to be. My favorite surprise was the crop I got from planting sprays of long, arching millet seedheads that I found at a cage-bird supply store. This pendant variety of Japanese millet (*Setaria italica*) turned out to be the most ornamental grass in my entire garden!

A crop of millet will mature 6 to 10 weeks after planting, so you can plant it anytime in spring or summer. Prepare the soil as you would for a bed of annual flowers, removing existing vegetation and loosening the top 4 to 6 inches of soil. Scatter the seed thickly, cover lightly with soil, and water with a sprinkler or hose sprayer. Keep the soil moist until the millet is up and growing well, usually a matter of a week or two.

Milo

Attracts doves and some game birds

MILO IS THE SEED OF LAST RESORT for most feeder birds. If you've ever found an uneaten collection of hard, round, reddish seeds among the hulls of sunflower and other seeds at your feeders, it's milo. When other seeds are there for the taking, birds will kick milo out of the feeder or leave it untouched in the tray. Only doves and some game birds seem to favor milo seeds.

Why do seed mixes contain milo if birds won't eat it? Because it's cheap and relatively big, so it's a popular filler in low-priced mixes. If you want to feed milo to game birds like pheasants or wild turkeys, buy it separately from a feed store. Save your birdseed budget for a good-quality seed mix that contains seeds songbirds *like* to eat, such as millet and sunflower.

Milo is also called sorghum (the plant's botanical name is *Sorghum bicolor*); commercial farmers raise sorghum for syrup production. Milo is an annual grass that's easy to grow in your own backyard, where it may attract doves, pheasants, quail, wild turkeys, and other birds that forage among the stout, cornlike stalks. The seed has a hard coat so it lasts through winter. Plant milo in the spring, as you would corn, after the soil has warmed. Prepare the soil as for any annual and scatter the seed thickly—

Milo, or sorghum, seems to be more attractive to red-winged blackbirds and other birds when it's on the stem. At the feeder, the seeds usually go uneaten.

or plant in rows if you prefer. Cover lightly with soil, and wait for the flush of vigorous green shoots. Don't worry if weeds crop up: The milo can hold its own, and birds will enjoy the weed seeds, too.

Mimicry

AS A SENSITIVE TEENAGER, I was appalled to hear a distinct "wolf whistle" issuing from an apartment window every afternoon when I walked home from school. I ignored it for several days until I couldn't stand it anymore. Looking up toward the open window and cupping my hands, I shouted "Stop it!" at the top of my lungs. To my surprise, a friendly woman pulled aside the curtain and invited me to come up and meet my harasser.

The flirt turned out to be her pet myna bird. The bird was pleased to have an audience and immediately ran through a repertoire that included sailor-worthy expletives as well as assorted whistles and a maniacal laugh.

The myna, an old-world species, is close cousin to our introduced common starling, one of the most gifted mimics in the North American bird world. The only other birds that have a real knack for copycat sounds are the well-named "mimic thrushes"—the catbird, the mockingbird, and thrashers (particularly the brown and California)—and several members of the crow family.

Like the starling, skilled mimic thrushes can imitate dozens of other bird species, from bobwhites to blue jays, along with dog barks, gate squeaks, coyote howls, hawk screams, and frog croaks. They also have their own songs, which can be beautifully intricate and sweet. Don't be surprised to hear them switch from song to raucous mimicry in an instant.

Crows and their relatives, including jays, magpies, and ravens, readily adopt other sounds as part of their vocal repertoire. Birds of these species that were kept as pets learned to mimic human words, as well as the usual laundry list of bird calls, animal noises, whistles, and mechanical sounds.

Why some birds have a knack for imitation is unknown. Other than humans, they are the only animals that imitate sounds not part of their natural language. (By the way, it is an old wives' tale that splitting the tongue makes a bird "talk" better.) Some individuals are much more gifted than others. Members of the crow family are the Mensa club of the bird world. Some are intelligent enough to perform well at human tasks, such as counting and memory games. It's fun to try to teach wild birds of these species to imitate a distinctive whistle of your own. If you frequently whistle for your dog, you may have already served as inspiration!

> Starlings, catbirds, mockingbirds, and crows are gifted mimics that can copy a wide variety of sounds.

Mockingbird

AMONG SONGBIRDS, mockingbirds are the bullies on the playground. Like a 6-year-old who hasn't learned to share, this big gray bird flies in to a feeder proclaiming it "Mine! Mine! All mine!" and causing milder-mannered birds to scoot out of the way and head for cover.

Despite their hoggish habits at feeders, mockingbirds are a valuable ally to other birds. These seemingly fearless birds will charge after any threat to their families, whether it's a cat, hawk, squirrel, or snake. If another bird sounds an alarm call, the mockingbird is first on the scene to investigate and pitch in. Their long sharp beaks, which they don't hesitate to use, are excellent weapons for driving off climbing snakes. Augmented by flashing white wing patches and a harsh, loud voice, a mockingbird in battle mode is fearsome enough to drive even a trespassing human away.

Although they also have their own original music, mockingbirds get their name from their remarkable

Mockingbirds sing sweetly on summer nights, but they defend their home and food aggressively. They often perch conspicuously overlooking "their" territory.

ability to imitate other birds' songs. That's why a mockingbird from the eastern United States sounds very unlike a western mockingbird cousin.

Listen to a mocker in Arizona, and you'll hear songs of local birds like Scott's oriole, scrub jay, and plain titmouse. In Pennsylvania your mocker is likely to imitate a Baltimore oriole, blue jay, and tufted titmouse.

It's not just birdsong that mockingbirds mimic. If your garden gate has a nice loud squeak, or if your neighbor whistles for his dogs daily, you may hear those variations worked into a mockingbird's theme song. This talent makes it easy to recognize your own neighborhood mockingbird.

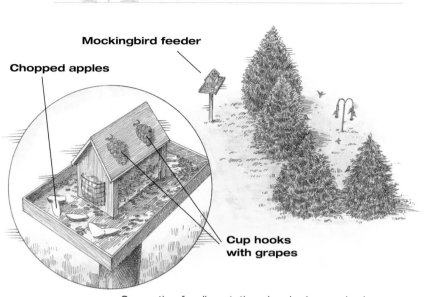

Mockingbird feeder

Chopped apples

Cup hooks with grapes

Separating feeding stations by shrubs or a hedge or placing separate feeders on opposite sides of the house is the only way to deter a mockingbird from driving all other birds away from your feeders.

Mockingbird Behavior

Mockingbirds have high-voltage personalities, which makes them fun to observe. Look for threatening displays of drooped, outspread wings and tail, which the birds use to scare insects out of hiding or to chase snakes away. Listen for them singing on summer nights, often from a rooftop or antenna. Their "whisper song" is a tender, quiet warbling from a hidden perch that's audible only for a short distance.

Since mockingbirds eat just about anything, you can't just switch the food in your feeders to discourage a territorial bird. When a mocker claims your feeder, the best thing to do is put up another feeder on the other side of a hedge, fence, or the building. The obstacle may prevent the mockingbird from claiming that one, too.

If a territorial mockingbird patrols your yard, you might try teaching it some tricks since you will be spending plenty of time together (you filling the feeder, the mockingbird watching you). When I began whistling a jaunty three-note phrase every time I set out its favorite foods, only a few weeks passed before the bird began imitating my "soup's on" call. When nesting season began and the bird left my yard, I still occasionally heard that whistle when I took a walk.

MOCKINGBIRD FEEDER FOODS			
■ Bread and other baked goods	■ Crackers	■ Hamburger, raw	■ Mealworms
■ Cereal	■ Dogwood (*Cornus* spp.) berries	■ Hawthorn (*Crataegus* spp.) berries	■ Meat scraps
■ Chopped suet	■ Fruit, fresh or dried	■ Holly (*Ilex* spp.) berries	■ Millet
■ Corn, all types	■ Grapes	■ Leftovers	■ Oranges

Mold

MOLDY SEED IS A FACT OF LIFE. When dry seed absorbs moisture from dew, rain, snow, or errant sprinklers, mold can quickly set in because of the lack of air circulation at most feeders. In my experience, birds do not eat bad seed, but keep in mind that moldy conditions can, at worst, set the stage for bird illnesses or, at least, ruin a perfectly good tray, hopper, or tube of seed.

To prevent mold, keep seed dry. During the rainy season, use feeders such as tube feeders with enclosed seed storage or roofs. Or feed sparingly, filling open feeders with only as much seed as the birds will down that day. Birds eat wet seed readily, so even if it rains during feeding hours, they will still devour the offering. Before refilling your feeders, scoop out any leftover wet seed or wet hulls to keep fresh seed dry longer, and serve seed in a very shallow layer. Also, look into using tray feeders with wire bottoms to help seed stay fresh. These feeders drain away excess water and allow air to circulate around the bottom of the seed.

If accumulated seed on the ground begins to mold, rake mulch over it to bury it. I find that in extended periods of wet weather, dropped seeds will sprout before they get moldy, giving me a pleasing fresh green carpet beneath the feeders.

> Tray feeders with wire bottoms drain away water, let air circulate, and help seed stay fresh.

Moles

MOLES ARE GRUB EATERS and earthworm eaters. They are not interested in your birdseed, but your feeder area may attract them if the moisture-holding layer of sunflower shells and other debris attracts the prey they seek. Other than occasionally pushing a plant out of the ground as they burrow along, they are harmless.

Moles are fantastic diggers, thanks to their huge scooping paws, which look like the business end of a steam shovel. They are so proficient at their digging that you may think your yard is hosting a horde of moles, when in fact it's only a single animal. Flatten the tunnels by walking on them.

Voles, which are more closely related to mice than to moles, also burrow, but their tunnels are smaller and usually not raised. These animals can be highly destructive to fruit trees and ornamentals because, like mice, they eat bark. Vole populations can build to enormous numbers during cyclical population swings, during which years the hawk and owl population also rises—voles are a staple food for birds of prey.

Shovel-like front feet and tiny eyes mark the mole, a tunneler extraordinaire. Moles may tunnel near the feeder, where worms are beneath the seed hulls.

Morning Glories

Attract hummingbirds

MORNING GLORY fans will be pleased to learn that the vines are also great for providing quick covers for birds near a feeding station. The vines grow thick and fast, making a tangle where birds can easily take refuge. A trellis of morning glories is just the thing to shelter your feeders from hot summer winds and to give feeder birds a quick hideaway when danger threatens.

A trellis of morning glory vines is terrific next to a birdbath, too, because the trellis gives wet-feathered birds a safe place to preen. Hummingbirds like morning glory flowers, too, so I like to hang a hummingbird feeder from a trellis covered with morning glories.

Morning Glory Choices

Fast-growing annual morning glory (*Ipomoea tricolor*) can brighten a garden just about anywhere. Choose a sunny garden spot for your trellis, and plant the seeds next to it in spring after danger of frost is past. If summers are short in your area, start the seeds indoors about 3 weeks before the last spring frost date. Otherwise, the vines may not have time to produce flowers before fall frost kills them. Morning glories grow well in containers, too, so you can let them wrap around an upper deck railing or twine along a window frame.

Hardy morning glories are even better than annual morning glories for providing cover for birds. Weird but wonderful "man-of-the-earth" (*I. pandurata*) thrives through Zone 6. Its white flowers are splashed with red-purple middles and look like any pretty morning glory; but below the earth, this perennial vine grows enormous tubers that once were used as food by Native Americans.

Large morning glory flowers may tempt a passing hummingbird, but for continual hummer traffic, plant one of the small-flowered red species. Cypress vine (*I. quamoclit*) is a delicate climber with soft, feathery leaves that look like the foliage of cypress or

Morning glories greet each day with fresh new faces and climb quickly to cloak a trellis or fence. The tubular flowers are practically magnetic to hummingbirds.

dawn redwood. Let it ramble about the perennials in your beds, or grow it on a trellis. Red star morning glory (*I. coccinea*), with thick, heart-shaped foliage, is a more vigorous plant that grows best on a trellis or fence. Both will buzz with hummingbirds all summer long. Cardinal climber (*I. × multifida*), a hybrid of these two species, is just as irresistible to them.

All of the red morning glories flourish in containers. I sometimes plant cypress vine seeds in windowboxes and give the plants string to climb so they can frame my windows with flowers that lure hummingbirds right to eye level.

M

Mosquitoes

Attract many species of insect-eating birds

THE WHINE OF A MOSQUITO may send you searching for the swatter, but to birds it sounds like the dinner bell. Buntings, martins, native sparrows, swallows, and swifts include these prolific, widespread, and generally slow-moving insect pests in their diets. Many other bird species will also snap up a passing bloodsucker.

People have long considered purple martins excellent mosquito controllers, but there is some disagreement about this reputation. Mosquitoes tend to be most active in the dim hours before sunrise and after sundown, when most martins are snug in their high-rise houses. Martins are probably not prone to seeking out mosquitoes, but any of these insects in the air naturally get swallowed along with beetles, flies, and other flying food when the birds are flying.

It's the smaller insect-eating birds, not purple martins, that shine as chief mosquito catchers. When I walk the trails at a nearby bald-cypress slough in southern Indiana, a crowd of excited blue-gray gnat-catchers gathers in the branches overhead. In constant motion, they zip after the mosquitoes that accompany me through the wetlands. Native sparrows, thrushes, and wood warblers are also quick to grab a passing mosquito. In the marshes and other wet areas where mosquitoes breed en masse, mallard ducks, phalaropes, and many kinds of sandpipers feed on these pests.

You certainly don't want to breed mosquitoes to attract birds. Exercise common sense in mosquito control by emptying stray water-filled containers (such as old tires or forgotten buckets) that may serve as breeding sites. Don't overlook the rain gutters, as clogged gutters can support large numbers of larvae. The birds in your yard will do their best to keep up with the natural mosquito population and keep your outdoor experiences itch-free.

> Purple martins may not deserve their reputation as mosquito eaters. The birds are abed when mosquitoes are active.

Moths

Attract many species of insect-eating birds

SHHH, DON'T TELL THE MOTHS, but these winged insects and their eggs, caterpillars, and cocoons make superb bird food. Bluebirds, flycatchers, orioles, phoebes, robins, and dozens of other species make moths a staple in their diets. In winter, the tough fibrous cocoons of many moth species, from the giant cecropia to the common woolly bear, are targets for chickadees and titmice, which work industriously to tear open the tough silk and get at the meaty morsel within. Eggs and egg masses of moths are a big hit with nuthatches, woodpeckers, and other guardians of the trees. Moths on the wing make a quick snack for any bird near enough to grab a bite. Even screech owls seek out moths, particularly the large, fat-bodied giant silkworm moths, such as the cecropia.

A garden free of pesticides will support a wide variety of moths. With 10,000 species fluttering around North America, your yard is apt to include more moths than you can count. The moth world is incredibly varied. Species range from pesky tent caterpillars and codling moths to the throngs of nondescript tan and gray moth species that feast on lawns, shrubs, trees, and other plants. The translucent jade-green luna moths and beautiful underwing moths, which hide vivid red or yellow, black-striped hindwings under camouflaged forewings, contribute to the diversity. Because nearly all moths are night fliers, you won't actually see many of them, but your bird friends will find them, hiding during daylight hours on tree bark, beneath leaves, or in other concealed places.

Adding native plants—trees, shrubs, vines, grasses, flowers—to your yard is the best thing you can do to boost your moth population. Not only will the extra vegetation give moths more places to seek shelter, the plants will also serve as suitable hosts for the caterpillars, which have evolved along with our native plants and are often finicky in their tastes. Naturally you will want to avoid the use of pesticides, including BT (*Bacillus thuringiensis*), which kills leaf-eating caterpillars—which is most caterpillars! Also avoid planting genetically engineered corn or other crops that include BT in their genes.

Should you see a caterpillar inching along, wish it luck. In a yard full of birds, many moths are destined to wind up as someone's dinner.

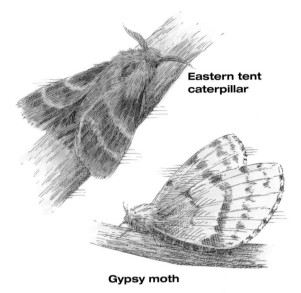

Eastern tent caterpillar

Gypsy moth

Hungry beaks snatch moths up at all stages, from egg to caterpillar to cocoon. Even night-flying winged adults aren't safe—owls also eat moths.

Mulch

WITH ALL THE BIRD TRAFFIC at a feeder area, it can be tricky to keep the ground below feeders looking good. I cover the area with wood chips, which I get free from the utility company or from tree trimmers, who are happy to have a place to conveniently dump a truckload. If you don't have storage space for large quantities, you can buy bags of wood chips at the garden center. Chips are long-lasting, and their color and texture provide excellent camouflage for dropped seeds, hulls, and bird droppings. When the layer of mulch begins to look shabby, turn it over with a hoe and expose fresh stuff, or spread another inch or two over the top.

If you choose to plant under your feeders instead, avoid flowers, which soon look bedraggled, thanks to birds perching on their stems or scratching among their roots. Instead, go with a hardy groundcover such as Virginia creeper (*Parthenocissus quinquefolia*) or bearberry (*Arc-*

tostaphylos uva-ursi). These groundcovers are generally tougher than flowers and hold up better to high traffic—from both boots and bird feet.

Beware of Sunflowers

All those sunflower seeds your birds are cracking their way through will soon give you inches of hulls beneath your feeder. It looks like it would make good mulch, but don't spread it around treasured plants. Like the black walnut tree, sunflowers are allelopathic—their hulls contain chemicals that inhibit the growth of plant competitors. I even avoid adding sunflower hulls to my slow-burning compost pile, for fear of aftereffects in the garden. Instead, I rake them onto a ground sheet and drag the pile to a discreet corner, where I pile the hulls until the worms and other natural decomposers turn them back into earth. You can also leave the hulls in place beneath your feeders, if you like their appearance.

N

Nectar

Attracts hummingbirds, orioles, and dozens of other species

MIX NECTAR FOR ALL SUGAR-WATER drinkers at a ratio of 4 parts water to 1 part sugar. Boil the water so that it melts the sugar when you mix the two together, or try my trick of using superfine sugar, an instantly dissolving sugar available at supermarkets and restaurant supply stores. The superfine sugar dissolves instantly in cold water with just a quick stir. I mix my nectar in 2-cup batches to fill my most-used feeder perfectly. I pour ½ cup of sugar into a 2-cup liquid measuring cup, then add water while stirring until it is a shade over the 2-cup marking to allow for the displacement of the dissolved sugar.

Prepackaged nectar mixes are fine for feeding hummingbirds and orioles, but much more expensive than mixing it yourself. If you want to eliminate the inconvenience of boiling water to melt granulated sugar, switch to superfine as I do.

You can use a slightly weaker homemade solution of sugar water, but avoid making it stronger. Too high a concentration of sugar may taste delicious, but it is not necessary to attract birds, and some ornithologists believe it may have negative effects on the birds' health if continued long term.

Adding red dye to attract hummingbirds is probably harmless, but totally unnecessary. They birds will suck up the sweet stuff just fine once they locate the feeder—and they won't forget where

Nectar is a favorite of orioles as well as hummingbirds. Add a feeder designed to accommodate these perching birds, so that it's easier for them to get a sip.

they found it. Hummingbirds are loyal feeder visitors, returning every few minutes or at least every day to the same food sources. If the feeder isn't emptied within a week, clean it and refill with fresh solution. Once hummers become regular visitors, you may find you need to refill feeders every day or even more often!

Other Nectar Sippers

MORE THAN 60 species of birds—besides hummingbirds!—have been seen snitching a sip of sugar water from nectar feeders. Check your feeders frequently to see who's visiting yours. The most common non-hummingbird guests are orioles and house finches, with woodpeckers close behind. Also look for these bird species:

- Cardinals
- Chickadees
- House finches
- Purple finches
- Goldfinches
- Black-headed grosbeaks
- Rose-breasted grosbeaks
- Jays
- Orioles
- Tanagers
- Titmice
- Warblers (13 species and counting)
- Downy woodpeckers
- Hairy woodpeckers
- Red-bellied woodpeckers
- Red-headed woodpeckers

Nectar Feeders

HUMMINGBIRDS ARE THE number-one customer of nectar feeders and the number-one reason that we put them up. Getting these incredible birds into the yard is as easy as filling the feeder and hanging it in the garden. Because hummingbirds cover nearly all of America (they're scarce in the North, however), you're sure to attract customers within a week, if not almost instantly. As soon as a passing hummingbird spots your feeder, it'll be over to investigate.

Orioles are also famed for their attraction to sugar water. With the proliferation of backyard feeders, the behavior is becoming more common among orioles than it once was, and the birds seem to be quicker to accept a nectar feeder as a food source.

House finches, warblers, woodpeckers, and a laundry list of scores of other species are also making increasing use of nectar feeders. No specialized feeders are on the market yet, but the birds are agile at accessing even a model without perches. To prevent wasting your nectar solution, hang an extra feeder with perches for these birds to prevent it from tipping and spilling the liquid when the heavier birds fly in for a landing. Because I worry about my non-hummingbird guests getting a balanced diet (some of them will hog the feeder for hours at a time until it is drained dry), I keep a large feeder with perches for these nectar drinkers, and alter the nectar mix by replacing 1 part of the water with 1 part unsalted beef

Nectar feeders include two basic designs: the vertical bottle and the horizontal "flying saucer." Clear is best; it's hard to tell when opaque feeders are empty.

broth, to supply protein that the birds would be ingesting in a normal diet.

Choosing a Nectar Feeder

Easy cleaning is the main priority when you shop for a feeder. Sugar water can mold quickly, so you'll need to swab out the feeder before every refill. Make

Keeping Nectar Feeders Clean

THE BEST way to save time cleaning a nectar feeder is to buy a well-designed feeder in the first place. Since you'll most likely be cleaning and refilling the feeder every few days for months on end, you'll save yourself a lot of frustration by choosing a product that is fast and simple to disassemble, with unobstructed access to all parts of the feeder.

Check the accessories aisle of a local bird-supply store or a specialty catalog like those listed in "Resources" on page 348 for brushes that will make cleaning your feeder easier. At a cost of only a few dollars, these small, flexible brushes are a bargain because they'll save you hours of time over the nectar season. Regular bottle brushes, available in any discount store and many supermarkets, work well for cleaning the main reservoir of nectar feeders. Pipe cleaners are also handy for snaking grime out of the feeding holes of nectar feeders. If you use plastic snap-on devices to deter bees at the feeder holes, use an old toothbrush for a quick cleanup across their grids.

sure the feeder model you like comes apart easily and allows you to get into all those nooks and crannies without using sleight of hand.

Horizontally oriented feeders, with the drinking holes above the solution, are available in very easy-to-clean models that separate into halves that are as simple to wash as a salad plate. Vertically oriented feeders, the most commonly available, are more difficult to clean because only the cap comes off. Buy yourself a bottle brush to make the job quick and easy.

Make sure the feeder is not opaque. Artsy ceramic feeders may be pretty, but you won't be able to tell when the sugar water is getting low. Of course, if hummingbirds zip in, then immediately leave, you'll get the hint.

If this is your first nectar feeder, choose one with lots of red plastic to grab the attention of passing hummingbirds. Install all first-time feeders in an open area, where birds can easily see them. Once you have regulars at the feeder, you can move it to another part of the garden. You can then also replace the tacky, big red feeder with one that just has a discreet dab of red to mark the spot.

A jumbo nectar feeder reduces refills if you're hosting thirsty orioles or hummingbirds. They're handy in late summer, when migrating hummers arrive in droves.

Niger

Attracts house finches, purple finches, goldfinches, pine siskins

GOLDFINCHES ARE the big customers for niger seed—it's their absolute favorite at the feeder. The birds seem to spot a new tube feeder as soon as it's hung, and they'll quickly investigate to see if it's filled with niger. House finches, purple finches, and pine siskins also adore niger.

Niger also goes by the name "thistle seed," but how it got the name is a mystery because the seed comes from a daisylike plant that's native to Africa. It's not a thistle at all. Perhaps the name came about because goldfinches love niger and they also adore real thistle seed. Whatever the reason, it's caused lots of bird lovers unnecessary worry that

they might be spreading a plague of pest plants while feeding their birds. Rest easy! Whether you call it niger or thistle seed, niger is perfectly safe to feed to birds, and it won't create a weed problem in your yard.

Making the Most of Niger

Niger is costlier by the pound than most other birdseed, but a little goes a long way unless you're hosting hordes of finches (which can happen during migration, when hundreds of goldfinches settle at a well-stocked feeding area). Serve niger in a tube feeder for the least amount of

waste. Invest in a feeder with heavy metal trimmings to add weight, so that it doesn't swing crazily at every breeze and dump your expensive seed all over the ground.

House finches can become feeder hogs when you feed niger. You can buy feeders with perches above the seed holes to discourage them. Acrobatic goldfinches just reach upside down to eat from these feeders, but the less acrobatic house finches can't reach the seed. In many areas of the country, though, house finches have become just as adept at handling upside-down perches as goldfinches are. Until a truly house-finch-proof feeder comes along, you may as well fill a regular tube feeder with niger for the house finches and hope they take the easy route and leave the other feeder to the goldfinches. If not, at least you're boosting the odds of having an available perch when a hungry goldfinch comes a-calling.

A Goldfinch Bonanza

You can put niger in hopper and tray feeders, but you'll inevitably lose some of the seed. Wind sends the tiny seed sailing, but at certain times of the year, I think the results are worth some lost seed. During the goldfinch migration season in March and April, I spread a thin layer of niger in my open tray feeders. At first, the seed will attract a handful of goldfinches. The next day, 20 birds will show up, and within a couple of weeks, I'm feeding 200 or 300 goldfinches every

Offer niger in small amounts or in a tube feeder to avoid wasting this pricey seed. Most small birds, like this common redpoll, eat niger, but goldfinches love it.

day! If I only put out tube feeders, they'd quickly desert me. I don't mind going over budget on niger for a few weeks: The payoff in goldfinches is worth a million bucks at least. And when I wake up one morning to find the whole kit and caboodle has moved on, I know the resident house finches will quickly clean up any leftovers from my extravagance.

The Source of Niger

NIGER SEED comes from a yellow daisy named *Guizotia abyssinica.* The last part of that mouthful of a name, *abyssinica,* tells us that the niger plant hails from the ancient land of Abyssinia, which we know today as Ethiopia.

Niger seed is heat-treated to prevent germination because, although it's not a thistle, it does spread like a weed, sowing itself by the zillions. An occasional niger seed may remain fertile, so if you find an unfamiliar branching plant bearing a bouquet of yellow daisies near your feeder, you may find yourself

the proud owner of a genuine specimen of guizotia.

In hot, dry areas like California where farmers grow the plants to produce seed for the birdseed industry, niger may escape cultivation and sprout along roadways and in other empty ground, making the western finches mighty happy.

Night Singers

OWLS, OF COURSE, ARE OUT and about at night, and herons may squawk nocturnally. You will often hear killdeer shrilling their "Kill-eeee!" calls as they fly in the dark. But when it comes to songbirds, nearly all of them limit their performances to daylight hours, with a few exceptions. The mockingbird is the most well-known exception to this rule. Fond of singing night or day, the mockingbird's virtuoso performances often take place from a chimney, rooftop ridge, or roof-mounted satellite dish.

Now that most people sleep with closed windows and air conditioners humming, mockingbirds have a much smaller audience than they did on lazy summer nights when a screen was all that stood between the singer and the listener. If a mocker is residing in your neighborhood, it's worth throwing up the sash on a June night to revel in the romantic concert. Of course, if you have to listen to a mockingbird whistle night after night, holding forth in the wee hours of the morning, you may be less than enchanted by the bird.

Other members of the mockingbird family, including the catbird and thrashers, may occasionally sing at night. But most other birds are sound asleep once darkness falls. If you happen to hear a quick, short burst of song from a cardinal, robin, sparrow, or other bird, the bird was most likely disturbed on its nest or at its roost. Oddly enough, birds sometimes break into a line of melodic song when they are roused unexpectedly from sleep, instead of the alarm or distress call you'd expect.

Modern lighting "improvements" have had a huge effect on night-singing birds. In my small town, birds once slept soundly through the nighttime hours, even with white-bulb streetlights dotting the streets and backyards. But once the white lights were replaced with yellowish ones that cast a much greater light, the birds no longer slept soundly until natural break of day. Now robins begin singing at 2:00 A.M., and cardinals, wrens, and others aren't far behind. In cities, starlings may twitter all night long, even though they're perched for rest in communal roosts.

There's something romantic about a songbird on a warm summer night. Throw open your window in June or July to hear a mockingbird's moonlight serenade.

You may also hear bird voices at night during spring and fall migration. Listen closely on a quiet night for soft cheeps and twitters overhead, beginning a few hours after sunset and continuing into the early hours of the morning. As I listen to the conversations overhead, I like to imagine the determined wings flying through the night and wonder where they've been and where they're going. Once in a while, I'll recognize a call note of a thrush or warbler, but usually the voices aren't recognizable. March through early May and August through September are the best times to hear long-distance travelers on the wing at night.

In the East, the Baltimore oriole represents the species known as the northern oriole. It eats mainly insects, often gleaned from flowering trees.

The Bullock's race of the northern oriole ranges across the western states. The white wing patch is a sure way to identify this flashy bird.

Oriole Behavior

Color is the first thing you'll notice when an oriole visits your feeder. Its plumage is bright enough to spot from afar as the bird makes its way to your buffet. But you probably will have to look up to see an incoming oriole. These are arboreal birds, which means they stay mostly in the trees. If shade trees dot your yard, you can watch the birds use them for stopping points as they fly from one place to another. As they move about at feeders or in foliage, orioles often adopt a slinky posture, with head and body lowered, moving sinuously.

Once they reach your offering of oranges or suet, two top favorites, orioles may spend many minutes enjoying the food. They also welcome birdbaths and other water features. If you are camping in the Southwest in summer, set a shallow skillet of water at your campsite and you may lure a Scott's oriole as your guest.

Orioles aren't as fast to find a nectar feeder as hummingbirds, but be patient. If you live in a mild-winter area, plant agaves and aloes around the nectar feeder to help catch the attention of these birds, which also occasionally visit flowers for the sweet stuff.

ORIOLE FEEDER FOODS			
■ Amelanchier (*Amelanchier* spp.) berries ■ Apples ■ Berries, especially mulberries (*Morus* spp.), blackberries (*Rubus* spp.),	blueberries (*Vaccinium corymbosum* and *V. angustifolium*), and huckleberries (*V. ovatum*) ■ Corn, cracked or whole-kernel	■ Elderberries (*Sambucus* spp.) ■ Figs (*Ficus carica*) ■ Nectar (use a feeder with perches) ■ Oranges, halved	■ Peaches ■ Pears ■ Peas, fresh, dried, or frozen ■ Suet, chopped

Quick and Easy Oriole Feeder

Orioles are birds with sweet, um, beaks. This easy-to-assemble feeder is sure to bring them in to satisfy their taste for sugary foods. Mount the feeder on a post where the ants it may also attract won't become a problem. Place it near a water source, so you can hose off any grape jelly residue from time to time.

MATERIALS

Quart jar lids

12- to 18-inch length of 1 × 6 lumber

Small nails

Several large nails

Grape jelly

Orange halves

Step 1: Nail a few lids to the top side of the board, using small nails that don't protrude to the other side.

Step 2: Drive a few big nails through the bottom side of the board so they protrude between the jar lids.

Step 3: Lay the board flat atop a fence post, and nail it in place with the lids and nail points on top.

Step 4: Fill the lids with grape jelly and impale halved oranges on the protruding nails.

Step 5: Find a spot for viewing your feeder as the orioles fly in for a treat.

Ornithology

ORNITHOLOGY, THE SCIENTIFIC STUDY of birds, takes its name from *ornis*, the Greek word for "bird." Ornithologists work in various areas. Some work with the physical understanding of this feathered animal. Others are dedicated to the science of classification, or taxonomy, which examines the genetic and evolutionary heritage of birds, from the first fossil records in stone to the present day, in order to arrange them by genus and species. Much work is being done today in ornithological studies of ethology, or bird behavior; ecology and distribution; and applied ornithology, the science of birds' relationships with humans, of which conservation is a major concern.

Because birds are such a vital part of the web of life, some bird scientists work to develop ways that we average folks can help out our native species. Studies are conducted and research is carried out on all aspects of bird life, and this information translates into practical advice and products for the everyday bird watcher. You'll find birdhouse designs, feeder plans, and even the contents of seed mixes that trace their roots to scientific studies that determined their attractiveness to birds.

Much of what is known about which bird eats what is thanks to ornithologists, who spent hours dissecting birds and inventorying the contents of their stomachs. I can't imagine having the patience to count—let alone identify—parts and pieces of grasshoppers, mosquitoes, worms, weed seeds, or other food items, so I'm very grateful to the scientists who did.

Reading about old-time ornithologists is always interesting. Often, their research is fascinating and has practical implications as well. Even John James Audubon himself was an experimenter of sorts; once he played with a least bittern, the smallest species of heron, only robin-sized, to see how narrow a gap the bird could fit between. A space of 1½ inches between upright books in his library was adequate for the bird to pass through, he noted in his journals, although he omitted telling us just which books formed the gateposts. Today, when constructing nest boxes for birds, this information is good to have at hand so we know what size openings are appropriate for each species.

Modern ornithologists work on any questions that still need answers and investigate new problems that crop up. When the unusual disease called West Nile encephalitis showed up for the first time in America, ornithologists became involved because the disease is carried by birds, then transmitted by mosquitoes to humans.

Most research takes place today at universities and other institutions, although amateur observations are still solicited, such as the data collected during regular bird counts or through Project Feederwatch (see page 23). If you are interested in a career in ornithology, check with a local college or university or browse the Internet or your public library for more information on getting an education or career path opportunities in this field.

> Much of the information about which bird eats what is known thanks to ornithologists.

Owls

IT'S NOT THE OFFERINGS YOU PROVIDE in your feeders that will bring owls to your yard—it's the rodents that scurry around at night, picking up dropped seed. Owls are the number-one enemy of mice, rats, voles, and other small furry creatures. Their huge eyes are very keen even in the dimmest light. Their unbelievably sensitive hearing, almost as good as sonar, can pick up the sound of sneaky little paws from far away. As if that's not enough to stack the deck, owls also fly on silent wings, thanks to special feather adaptations that eliminate the noise of the air stream passing over them.

The songbirds, squirrels, rabbits, chipmunks, and other denizens of your yard will not thank you for attracting owls. Both larger species, such as the **barred owl, great horned owl,** and **spotted owl,** and small owls, such as the **burrowing owl, screech owl,** and even the tiny **saw-whet owl,** are just as satisfied to snatch a sleeping or nesting bird as they are a rodent. Almost any bird you can think of is on the owl menu, from diminutive hummingbirds to hefty Canada geese. The avian guardians of the bird

Large but hidden ear openings and extra-large eyes give owls a hunting edge. This northern saw-whet owl, just 7 inches tall, is one of the smallest and tamest.

kingdom—crows, jays, and ravens—are quick to make a commotion when they happen across a roosting owl. What they're really saying with those loud alarm calls is "Murderer!"

Owl Behavior

Owls can see perfectly well in daylight, but most species only come out at night. Some species are crepuscular, preferring the twilight at dusk and dawn, while others are nocturnal, hunting only after dark. The short-eared, barred, pygmy, snowy, and hawk owls often hunt by day.

When they're not on the wing, owls roost in trees, often in conifers, well hidden from the harassments of crows and jays. Because of their mottled brown plumage, owls are almost impossible for our weak human eyes to spot casually. If you follow a group of cawing crows or screaming jays, you may find an owl is the object of the hubbub being raised.

Because owls fly on silent wings and dispatch their prey without a squawk, you can't depend on the sound of the hunt to alert you to their presence. But there are a couple of sure ways to find out if you have owls in the neighborhood. First, sit outside at night and listen for owl calls. When you hear a far-off hooting or whinnying, imitate the call; the bird will often come closer to investigate its supposed compatriot. Or try playing a recording of owl calls at night in nesting season. For owls, that begins much earlier than songbirds—sometimes in January.

OWL FOODS
■ Bats
■ Chipmunks
■ Flying squirrels
■ Game birds
■ Mice
■ Moths
■ Rabbits
■ Skunks
■ Songbirds
■ Voles

Late January to early March is a good time to try getting a response to recorded calls. Carry a portable tape or CD player outside and play a single species' call, starting with a common owl such as the screech, barred, or great horned. Click the recording off and wait a few minutes, then repeat the call. If nobody answers your recording after half an hour, try the voice of another common species.

Chances are, you may never know that you have an owl regularly patrolling your yard. One giveaway, however, is the presence of owl "pellets," the compressed bundles of feathers, bones, and other inedible parts that owls cough up after they eat. If you can set aside your squeamishness and pull apart a pellet with tweezers, you will find a fascinating record of the owl's last meal.

P

Peanut Butter

Attracts bluebirds, chickadees, jays, nuthatches, starlings, titmice, woodpeckers, Carolina wrens

IF YOU POLLED THE BLUEBIRDS, chickadees, jays, nuthatches, titmice, woodpeckers, Carolina wrens—and let's not forget the starlings!—at your feeder, they would tell you that peanut butter is a perfect food: It's ultrahigh in fat and full of protein, which makes it a super food for cold weather feeding, when birds need extra calories, and a real treat any time of the year.

There are two drawbacks to feeding peanut butter: Because it's so popular, it can get expensive as a regular menu item, and it can be messy, leaving grease stains on wood posts or trees or even melting in bright sun.

It's easy to overcome these challenges. Birds aren't fussy about brands, so buy the cheapest peanut butter you can find. I like to use chunky style rather than creamy because picking out the nuggets of peanuts slows the consumption—while one bird pauses to swallow the peanut, another can grab a quick bite. Besides, I know from my own long history with peanut butter that it can be difficult to get down the hatch, although I've never noticed birds having difficulty with either creamy or chunky peanut butter.

To stretch your peanut butter, mix it with cornmeal, a low-cost product that's readily eaten by the same birds that enjoy peanut butter. Start with a mixture that's heavy on the peanut butter side, and over a period of days, work more cornmeal into the offering until you find a ratio that the birds seem to enjoy.

It's best to offer peanut butter or peanut butter mixtures in small amounts to prevent your treasured treat from being devoured before your eyes by starlings and squirrels and other rodents. Put out only what the birds will eat in an hour or so. You can always renew the feeding later.

Making your own peanut butter (or any true nut butter—almond, filbert, or walnut) is a fun project, especially with kids, who will get a whole new perspective on their favorite spread. Simply pour roasted peanuts, which you can buy in bulk in the generic-foods aisle of some supermarkets or at health-food stores, into a blender or food processor and grind until the peanuts turn into, well, peanut butter. Stop when the mix is still coarse, for chunky blend, or pulverize until it's creamy smooth. If you have long, hot summers, you can grow peanuts yourself from seed. It's fascinating to see the plant "peg" its stems to the ground and fun to dig the harvest from the soil later.

Peanut Butter Feeders

My simple homemade peanut butter feeder consists of a scrap of bark-on lumber that I picked up from a local sawmill. I nailed the wood to a porch post for a permanent feeder. All I do is smear the peanut butter directly onto the bark with a small spatula (or butter knife). The crevices and rough texture hold it in place and provide a good grip to woodpeckers and other customers. When I noticed that juncos, sparrows, and other small birds gathered beneath the feeder to pick up any dropped bits, I decided to cater to them, too. I made a similar feeder and hammered it horizontally to the bottom of my wood feeder post, so the peanut butter is just a couple of inches above the ground.

For neat peanut butter feeding, use a section of log drilled with cavities for holding the stuff. This is the perfect vehicle for birds that feed at relatively high feeders, such as chickadees, titmice, and woodpeckers. It also prevents those mobs of starlings that may attack if you serve peanut butter in an open tray. Birds that stay low to the ground also enjoy the nutty treat. Serve them in a low, wire-bottom tray feeder tucked under conifers or shrubs, where it is less visible to starlings. If starlings or jays do become pesky, put your peanut butter in a tray feeder protected by a wire cage that allows small birds access but blocks larger species and squirrels (see Feeder Covers on page 99).

> Birds aren't fussy about brands, so buy the cheapest peanut butter your store offers.

Peanuts

Attract chickadees, jays, juncos, nuthatches, sparrows, titmice, woodpeckers

PLUMP, MEATY PEANUTS MAKE a nutritious mouthful for many of your regular feeder birds. Chickadees, jays, nuthatches, titmice, and woodpeckers are all peanut appreciators. Other visitors, such as juncos and sparrows, may nibble smaller peanut pieces, but their beaks are generally too small to get a grip on a large kernel.

Grow 'Em or Buy 'Em

Peanuts (*Arachis hypogaea*) are not true nuts; they're the underground tubers of the peanut plant. You can actually grow peanuts in your garden, although if you live in the northern half of the country, you'll need to choose fast-maturing varieties. You plant peanuts in the spring and harvest in the fall when the plants' leaves turn yellow.

Of course, you can also buy peanuts to feed to your birds, and that's what most people do. Check the bulk-food bins at supermarkets or health-food stores for bargain-priced peanuts—they may cost less than those sold especially for bird feeding. Unsalted peanuts, either in or out of the shell, are the best choice for birds, although birds will also gobble the salted variety. That extra heavy dose of sodium won't harm your birds, but be sure water is freely available to slake their thirst. Roasted and raw peanuts seem to be equally popular.

Whichever type of peanuts you feed, be sure to buy fresh stock. Old peanuts may be rancid and unpalatable. Examine peanut pieces sold for bird food carefully before you buy: They may contain a high proportion of a bitter-flavored part of the peanut that is discarded by peanut-butter manufacturers. Look for very small elongated pieces: the bit of the peanut that lies between the two meaty halves and forms the tip of the kernel. These bits may be chopped up in the processing and hard to recognize. When in doubt, try a taste yourself. If the peanuts taste good and nutty to you, your birds will devour them like kids at a ballpark.

A male red-bellied woodpecker extracts peanuts from a wire mesh feeder filled with this highly favored food. Most feeder regulars eagerly eat peanuts year-round.

Foil Peanut Thieves

One way to outsmart squirrels and chipmunks (who also love peanuts) is to be stingy: Dole out a handful of peanuts at a time on fall and winter mornings, when the feeders are hopping with birds. Your presence should send squirrels scurrying, which is just enough time for the birds to swoop in and grab a nutty snack. By the time the squirrels return, all that's left of the peanuts will be a tantalizing aroma.

You can make your own squirrel-resistant peanut feeder by covering a shallow tray feeder with a piece of strong ½-inch wire mesh. Squirrels may still spend hours trying to wrest the wire from the wood, and their presence will discourage birds. If that is the case, invest in a sturdy "large seed" feeder made of metal, with a heavy-duty wire cage surrounding a central tube feeder. The wire allows birds easy access to the peanuts but blocks squirrels from reaching the tasty treats.

Pears

Attract bluebirds, catbirds, house finches, mockingbirds, orioles, robins, thrashers, thrushes, wrens

CATBIRDS, HOUSE FINCHES, MOCKINGBIRDS, orioles, robins, thrashers, wrens, and other fruit-eating birds have a definite sweet tooth. Even though many of these birds may not be regular visitors to your feeders, you can use sweet, soft pears to entice them to a feeding station. Homegrown or store-bought will do, as long as they're ripe.

Place pears directly on the ground for robins. For other birds, offer pears on a platform mounted on a post or in a tray feeder, about 3 feet high. Place the feeder near sheltering shrubs or a hedge so that these somewhat shy birds can feel safe while they eat. Slice the pear in half and offer it cut side up.

Fall migration time and winter in areas where these birds live year-round are the best times to offer pears. Natural fruits are abundant at other seasons, and unless the birds are already regulars at your feeder, they probably won't be interested. If a major snow or ice storm blankets your area, pears can be a lifesaver for birds that can't get to their natural foods. At times like these, you can even offer canned pears. Chop the fruit into small pieces so the birds can eat even if it freezes.

Plant a 'Bradford' Callery Pear for Birds

'Bradford' pear trees (*Pyrus calleryana*) are beautiful in bloom, striking in red to purple fall color, and tempting to bluebirds, thrushes, and other songbirds when their tiny fruits ripen. On the downside,

A 'Bradford' pear's fragrant flowers attract small insects that invite bug-eating birds to dine. Robins, thrashers, and others enjoy the fruit that comes later.

'Bradford' pear trees tend to have problems after about 10 years: They drop limbs, crack down the middle, or keel over in storms. 'Chanticleer' is considered a sturdier, longer-lived callery pear.

You may find a callery pear for $25 or less at discount garden centers in early spring, a small price for 10 years' worth of better backyard bird watching.

Bird Watching at a Callery Pear

ALMOST AS common as forsythia, callery pear trees are favorites for backyard birds. Here's why.

- Dense, leafy growth makes the trees a favorite roosting spot, at night or during rainy weather.

- When the trees are in bloom, the cloud of white blossoms attracts swarms of tiny insects, great fodder for orioles, tanagers, vireos, wood warblers, and other bug-eating birds, which makes a callery pear in the backyard a hot spot for at-home bird watching.

- Fall brings ripening fruit, which look more like tiny, hard cherries than pears. Great news again for backyard bird watchers: The fruit ripens just as flocks of bluebirds, robins, thrushes, and waxwings are passing through in search of sustenance.

Peas

Attract blackbirds, cardinals, crows, doves, grackles, grosbeaks, grouse, jays, quail, pheasants, English sparrows

FRESH PEAS ARE ONE of the delights of a home vegetable garden, and dried peas are a favored food for doves, grouse, quail, pheasants, and large songbirds, including cardinals and grosbeaks.

Raising Peas for Birds

If you live near game-bird habitat, you can grow peas for fall and winter food right in place. A planting of peas will provide long-lasting food for foraging quail and other game birds, but growing peas for birds is a slightly schizophrenic process. In order to provide a bountiful harvest for birds when the peas mature, you'll have to discourage other birds from eating the seeds at planting time. Blackbirds, crows, grackles, jays, and English sparrows have an uncanny knack for finding a newly planted pea patch (I think they must hide and watch). To prevent them from robbing the seeds, cover the planting with floating row covers or straw.

If you have the space to plant a truly large area—a quarter-acre or more—of peas or other wild bird food, get in touch with your local cooperative extension office. They can supply the details you need to grow a successful crop. Unless you have plenty of free time and determination and lots of muscle, you'll need farm equipment such as a plow or tractor to do the planting and tending of such a quantity.

For a "large" backyard planting of, say, a 5-foot-wide 100-foot row, or for a smaller patch, prepare the soil as for any annual plant: Remove vegetation, turn the soil, and rake to a moderately fine texture. Scatter pea seeds thickly over the bed, and cover with enough soil so that the tempting, light-colored seeds don't grab the attention of blackbirds, which will be happy to devour them before they sprout.

Rural feed stores sell pea seed in bulk at prices reasonable enough to plant a large area—1,000 square feet will take around 10 pounds of seed. Combine the pea seed with corn seed at a ratio of 1 pound peas to 5 pounds corn, and you'll provide more food plus a built-in trellis of cornstalks for the peas to climb. In a smaller yard, try covering a fence or planting a hedge of fast-climbing pea vines, and let them dry and ripen in place. The birds will find the seeds without any further effort from you.

Feeder Peas

Many suppliers treat pea seeds with chemicals, so be sure to ask for untreated seed when you purchase your peas. You'll have to look a little harder for untreated bulk seeds, but they are available. Check mail-order sources such as those listed in "Resources" on page 348, or ask at local seed suppliers, especially Mom & Pop hardware stores in rural areas or at farm supply stores. Or you can try planting a plastic bag of dried soup peas from the supermarket! (Be sure to use whole peas, not split peas, which won't germinate.)

At the feeder, birds often overlook dry peas in favor of the ever-popular sunflower seeds and other

---

Legumes for the Birds

PEAS AND beans belong to the plant group called legumes, which also includes perennial flowers and even some shrubs and trees. Nearly all game birds like to eat a variety of legume seeds. Partridge pea (*Cassia fasciculata*, also known as *Chamaecrista fasciculata*), a pretty yellow-flowered perennial legume, is a particular favorite of quail. It's easy to add to this perennial to your wildflower meadow or prairie garden, where it will add late-season color and winter-long food. Partridge pea is hardy to Zone 5. It may bloom the first year from an early sowing, but it usually requires two full seasons to perform; if you live in Zone 3 or 4, you can take your chances and try it anyway, mulching deeply with fall leaves to help it live through the winter deep freeze.

offerings. If you scatter a handful of dry peas among a tray of black sunflower seeds, the eye-catching white seeds may draw the attention of woodpeckers.

Another way to encourage wild birds to shift to eating a new food like dried peas or small dried beans is to wait until the feeders are almost empty and then put out about a cupful of the peas in place of the sunflower seeds that would normally fill the feeder. Once the birds get a taste for the new food, usually within a day, you can return to the regular food and mix the dried legumes among them.

You also can place dry peas in a low tray feeder or directly on the ground for doves, pheasants, and other ground feeders or in open tray feeders for cardinals and grosbeaks.

Garden "Peas" for Birds

Other plants in the same family as peas—the legumes—produce pea-like seeds that birds also find appealing. The pretty pink blossoms of redbud trees, for instance, are distinctly pea-flower-shaped, and you may see chickadees and titmice working at the overwintering seedpods. The seed heads of clover and vetches are favored by game birds, native sparrows, and doves. Lupines, both native species and splashy garden cultivars, are just tasty peas in showy disguise. Though eating lupines can cause problems in livestock (the infamous locoweed is a lupine), golden-crowned sparrows and other birds eat the seeds of these pretty ornamentals with impunity.

Photographing Birds

YOUR FEEDING STATION is the perfect setup for taking pictures of birds. The birds are accustomed to visiting the spot, so you know you will always have subjects handy. Although you can snap your shots through a window, you'll get clearer pictures outdoors.

Either set up a blind (see page 22) from which to photograph, or get the birds used to your presence by using a good dose of patience. If you sit quietly near the feeder, the birds will eventually accept you—with luck, in less than an hour—and return to feeding as usual.

Getting a Good Photo

Most beginners' bird photos look the same: a lot of sky, a lot of plants, and a tiny speck of bird. You need to get very close to a bird to get a good shot—either by actually being very near to the bird yourself, or by using a powerful lens. Combining the two will get you incredible close-up bird shots.

Read the fine print on those extreme close-up shots we drool over in magazines, and you'll see they were usually shot with a 400mm lens or larger. Big lenses like this are expensive. If you aren't ready to invest hundreds of dollars (or thousands) in a close-up lens, finagle yourself into the nearest position to

Getting top-quality bird photos takes time and money. High-power lenses and other gear add up. But snapshots can be worth it, if you get close to your subject.

your subjects you can find to make up for your lack of equipment. You may find that if you are reasonably close, you can get perfectly satisfying shots from an automatic point-and-shoot 35mm camera with a zoom lens. Ever-improving digital photography lets you adjust elements of a less-than-perfect photo.

Photogenic Tricks

Birds are high-energy creatures, and you will need to be quick to capture them on film. Start by aiming your camera at feeder birds, which usually stay put in the same general area long enough to focus on.

It's fun to document the birds that come to your feeder, but you don't want every shot to look the same: Cardinal at the feeder, goldfinch at the feeder, junco at the feeder gets boring in a hurry. For more interesting shots, it helps a lot to vary the settings and to aim for the most natural-looking background you can find.

Turning the area around your feeding station into a naturalistic landscape will help get you some great bird pictures. Instead of a bevy of quail eating from a tray feeder, you can catch them sidling through grasses or perching on a rock. A towhee or fox sparrow looks much better scratching among leaf litter than rooting around in 2 inches of old sunflower hulls.

An easy trick for getting natural-looking photos is to hide the bird food. Smear peanut butter on the back of a dead branch "planted" at the feeding station, and snap the titmouse or chickadee as the bird alights. Sprinkle millet at the base of a rock or among clumps of grass to get pictures of feeding doves, juncos, and sparrows.

Natural-looking water features also lend themselves to appealing bird photos. Chiseled-out or naturally concave rocks, waterfalls, or the shallow edges of garden pools are pretty places to shoot bathing or drinking birds. If you do photograph a bird in a pedestal-type birdbath, aim for an extreme close-up that catches the bird and the splashing water but cuts out as much concrete as possible.

Locating a nest on your property can also bring you some fine bird photos. Do not get so close that your presence alarms the birds; if you hear warning "Chip!" notes, back off a bit until the parent bird calms down. With luck, you can catch the parents bringing food or fledglings leaving the nest.

Patience Is Key

Bird photography takes time and patience. The longer you spend with camera at the ready, the more likely you are to find something worthy to shoot. Keep in mind that birds take the "early bird" adage to heart: They're out and about early in the morning, with peak activity at the feeder going strong until about 10 A.M. Bird activity dwindles during midday (unless the weather is cold or a storm is coming in) and picks up again in late afternoon, a couple of hours before sunset. Take advantage of these times of increased activity, and be ready with the camera.

> Turn the area around your feeding station into a naturalistic landscape for better bird photos.

Pinecones

Attract many kinds of birds at various times of the year

ONE OF THE sloppiest bird-treat projects is also the most successful: Smear a pinecone with peanut butter, and you're guaranteed to draw in hungry birds from chickadees to woodpeckers. Even without the peanut butter, pinecones attract birds because they hide a multitude of tasty seeds.

You're probably familiar with pignolia or pine nuts, the plump, pale yellow-to-tan seed of the pinyon pine (*Pinus cembroides*), used in pesto and other recipes. Birds love these uncommonly large pine nuts (they're expensive, though), but the tiny, lightweight seeds of many other pinecones—as well as cones from other types of evergreens—are also popular with foraging birds (and squirrels). Tiny cones, like those of the hemlock, attract little birds like chickadees and titmice. Bigger cones draw in crossbills, grosbeaks, and larger jays. Crossbills depend so heavily on pinecones that their beaks have evolved as custom-made tools for quickly scissoring seeds out of cones.

Plant a "Pinecone Tree"

Spruces, hemlocks, firs, balsams, and other conifers all bear cones, and we commonly refer to all of them as "pinecones." Winged seeds flutter from the cones when mature, but birds will often descend on these trees and extract the seeds before they fall. Native conifers are an excellent choice for your landscape because they're well adapted to the climate and local birds are accustomed to feeding on the cones.

Plant conifers from spring through early fall so that they have time to settle in a bit and grow new roots before the ground freezes. These trees can be pricey, especially larger specimens. To help protect your investment, plant in late spring to early summer. Most conifers stay green and healthy-looking in cold weather, regardless of their condition. Once the weather warms, it can take several weeks for a tree that failed over winter to show signs of decline, so it could be late spring before you see browning needles. If your nursery's 1-year guarantee runs from June to June, you'll know by then if you need a replacement.

In addition to their popular seeds, conifers provide a safe haven for roosting and nesting birds.

Any conifer will attract birds to its sheltering branches. Hemlocks are one of the fastest to bear cones. A single mature conifer has great bird appeal, but a group planting is even better because of the greater cover it provides.

Predators

LIFE IS TOUGH when you are a feathered package of prey. With hungry cats creeping through the bushes and high-flying hawks patrolling overhead, it's no wonder birds are so jumpy and alert. Danger can come from any direction when they least expect it. Crows, jays, owls, raccoons, and snakes are also a threat to nestlings and parents at the nest.

Making your feeding area safe from predators is a matter of life and death for birds. If cats prowl your yard, discourage them. Keep your own felines indoors; they will soon become accustomed to it. If stray cats or neighbors' cats are a problem, chase them away whenever you see them. Clapping your hands, running toward the cat, or squirting it with water (warm weather only, please) may solve the immediate problem, but the attraction of birds is so great that the cats may return when you're not watching.

A fence may deter cats, especially if they are trapped within it and can't get out quickly when you are chasing them away. But a dog is your best defense against cats. Dogs rarely chase birds because they are usually unsuccessful at catching them; dogs are also easier to train to stay away from the feeding station.

To give your feeder birds a fighting chance against hawk attacks, provide dense cover near the feeding area. A hedgerow, bramble patch, or group of shrubs provide safe places to hide. You will also want to supply safe access routes to and from your feeders and about your property. Plant a hedgerow-like corridor of trees, shrubs, grasses, or other vegetation to keep birds hidden from sight as they move through your garden. Be sure to include a few evergreens in the mix, so that birds can seek shelter year-round and safe nesting sites in spring.

Preferred Foods

SUNFLOWER SEEDS, MILLET, and other feeder staples are the meat and potatoes of most birds' diets. They'll eat them day in and day out, just like your dog downs its bowl of dry kibble, because the offerings are abundant and readily available. But birds also have their preferences—the foods they seek out first, at the feeder or in the wild.

When acorns and beechnuts ripen, for instance, birds will desert the feeder in favor of these natural foods. The juicy fruits of a mulberry tree (*Morus* spp.) will also divert the attention of feeder birds that may have come to your place to pick up raisins or other fruity offerings. Ragweed (*Ambrosia artemisifolia*), lamb's-quarters (*Chenopodium album*), dock (*Rumex crispus*), and dandelion (*Taraxacum officinale*) seeds as well as holly (*Ilex* spp.) berries all have their fans. Watch the action in your yard, and you'll see that your gone-to-seed zinnias or the fuzzy thistles you overlooked in the garden draw a bigger crowd of finches than even the most expensive tube feeder of niger.

Your birds aren't being disloyal by spurning your offerings and turning to wild foods. They're only doing what comes naturally. Each species has its preferences, learned through ages of evolution. They seek the seeds, nuts, nectar, or fruits of plants that best supply the nourishment they need in the natural world.

Spring and summer insects are probably the biggest magnet for birds of all types. These high-protein niblets are everywhere during warm weather, and birds take advantage of the bounty. Soft-bodied insects are also the ideal food for nestlings, which can't crack the seeds in your feeders. When insect life is at its peak, feeder traffic drops off dramatically. Birds don't need to travel to seek sustenance, as they do in wintertime when insects are few and finding wild seeds requires effort. Don't feel discouraged when feeder traffic slackens in late spring. Just bide your time and the birds will return. Meanwhile, keep the feeders filled with a small amount of seed and other foods and the birdbath brimming with fresh water. Your friends haven't deserted you—it's just that after a winter of dry food, a succulent caterpillar is too tantalizing to ignore.

Individual Preferences

Many species preferences are easy to determine—goldfinches prefer niger and sunflower seed over other feeder foods, and woodpeckers seek suet with a side order of sunflower seed. Birds usually go first to feeder foods that most closely resemble their natural diet. But birds also display regional and individual preferences. The cardinals at your feeder may adore safflower seed, while a few hundred miles away the red birds are reaching for cracked corn.

It's fun to experiment with new foods at the feeder. Keep track of how quickly your birds take to the new foods and which birds eat what. One red-bellied woodpecker that visits my feeders scolds me if I forget to have his ear of corn ready, while his compatriots ignore the corn in favor of feeders filled with suet and sunflower seeds.

You can even do a semiscientific test of bird tastes by adding dividers of wood lath to an open tray feeder. After partitioning the feeder, serve only one kind of seed in each section. I depend on the eyeball method to tell me which foods are most popular. It's easy to see at a glance that sunflower disappears fastest and that milo is the last on the list. For the sake of fairness, I set up both a high tray feeder and a low tray feeder for this test because often the birds that feed on or near the ground prefer a different menu than those that eat at higher feeders.

> Use preferred foods to increase the odds that a particular bird species will visit your feeders.

Think of lists of preferred foods, like the one on the opposite page, as the standard menu of your bird café. Then add daily specials and watch the takers.

Bird Preferences at the Feeder

EXPECT YOUR feeder birds to head first for the preferred foods on this list. But birds enjoy occasional variety in their diet, too, and will eagerly eat other foods. They also nibble other edibles when their favorites are lacking, or when a jay or other disruptive bird is keeping them away from their favored foods. Bird "tastes" may also vary from one individual to the next, with one of your titmice heading for the suet while the other visits the sunflower seeds. Check the specific bird entries in this book for suggestions of other foods to offer your favorite guests.

Bird	Most Preferred Foods	Also Highly Enjoyed
Bluebirds	Mealworms, peanut butter	Suet, berries, bread and baked goods, raisins, fruit
Cardinals	Sunflower seed	Safflower seed, fruit, millet, bread and baked goods, fruit
Chickadees	Peanuts, nutmeats, peanut butter, suet	Sunflower seed, bread and baked goods
Doves, pigeons	Millet	Cracked corn
Finches	Niger, sunflower seed	Millet, pine nuts, peanuts, birdseed mix, suet
Goldfinches	Niger, sunflower seed	Millet, flax, canary seed, suet, chopped peanuts, birdseed mix, grass seed
Grosbeaks	Sunflower seed	Fruit, suet, millet, safflower, bread and baked goods
Jays	Nutmeats, peanuts	Sunflower seed, suet, corn, bread and baked goods
Juncos	Millet	Sunflower seed, cracked corn, bread and baked goods, nutmeats, chopped peanuts
Kinglets	Suet	Bread and baked goods
Mockingbirds	Fruit	Bread and baked goods, suet, sunflower seed, millet, birdseed mix
Nuthatches	Nutmeats, suet, peanut butter	Sunflower seed, corn
Orioles	Nectar, oranges	Grape jelly, fruit, suet, softened raisins
Pheasants	Cracked corn	Millet
Quail	Cracked corn	Millet
Roadrunners	Meat scraps	Suet, leftovers
Robins	Mealworms, berries, fruit	Suet, bread and baked goods, raisins
Native sparrows	Millet	Suet, bread and baked goods, sunflower seed, canary seed, grass seed
Tanagers	Fruit, suet	Millet, mealworms, bread and baked goods
Thrashers	Fruit	Birdseed mix, millet, sunflower seed, suet
Titmice	Peanuts, peanut butter, nutmeats	Sunflower seed, suet, bread and baked goods
Towhees	Millet	Sunflower seed, cracked corn, bread and baked goods
Woodpeckers	Suet	Sunflower seed, nectar, fruit
Wrens	Peanut butter, suet	Bread and baked goods, fruit

Pumpkins and Squash

Attract cardinals, jays, nuthatches, titmice, woodpeckers

THE NUTTY INNARDS OF PUMPKINS and squash are delectable to many seed-eating birds, including cardinals, jays, nuthatches, titmice, and woodpeckers. These vegetables usually produce a generous quantity of seeds, providing a ready source of free bird food to add to your feeder offerings.

Pumpkins and squash are fall and winter crops, which is perfect timing because that's when feeders are at their busiest. Preparing the seeds is easy, as long as you don't mind a little mess. It's best to work outdoors, so you won't have to worry about picking up slippery seeds from the kitchen floor, and you can easily dump the scooped-out flesh onto your compost pile after you separate it from the seeds.

Processing Pumpkin Seeds

Use a large, sturdy, sharp-edged spoon to scrape out the seedy part of the pumpkin or squash into a colander. Run the colander under a strong spray of water to help dislodge clinging bits of squash fibers. Then spread the seeds, separating them as much as possible, on an old window screen to dry in the sun. You can also spread them out on a sheet of wax paper on your picnic table.

If you are working indoors, you can dry the seeds in your oven set at a very low temperature of 175° to 200°F and check for dryness every 5 or 10 minutes. With apologies to my feathered friends for an insensitive choice of cliché, I usually kill two birds with one stone by drying squash and pumpkin seeds at the same time I'm baking dinner or dessert. I spread the wet seeds on a metal cookie sheet or pizza pan, and set it on top of the rear burner of my electric stove–where the heat from the oven escapes. Long before the oven dish is done baking, the seeds have been turned, dried, and poured into storage bags.

Don't waste those pumpkin seeds! Toast some for yourself and dry the rest for birds in the fall and winter feeder. Squirrels and chipmunks enjoy them, too.

Turn the seeds with a spatula occasionally to speed the drying process. When the seeds are dry, store them in a paper grocery bag in a cool, dry place. If you have a big hoard of seeds, put the bag or bags into a closed metal container, such as a pretzel tin, to keep rodents from raiding the stash.

Like other unusual foods, the seeds may sit unnoticed in your feeder for a few days before birds begin to sample them. Scatter a few of the light-colored seeds in an open tray of black sunflower seeds to help the birds spot them more easily.

Chipmunks, squirrels, and other furry feeder visitors also delight in eating pumpkin and squash seeds. If you have separate feeders for squirrels and other wildlife, add these seeds to the menu. You'll enjoy watching how they pick up the seeds one by one in their small paws to nibble away the shells.

Raccoons

THE NIGHTLIFE at your feeding station can be just as entertaining as the daytime activity, especially if you are hosting raccoons. These common and intelligent animals thrive in residential areas as well as rural surroundings.

At the feeder, raccoons aren't particular. They adore a feast of corn but also eat sunflower seeds, fruit, and soft foods. Dog food, cat food, and leftovers are welcome treats. Raccoons relish suet and a visiting 'coon may open your wire suet feeder with its dexterous black paws and make off with an entire block.

A water source will give the raccoons in your neighborhood another incentive to visit your yard. They are quick at catching fish and frogs, and they may also carry food from your bird feeders to the water to "wash" it before eating it.

These carnivorous animals also catch mice at the feeder area. They may nab nestlings or eggs from wild birds' nests as well. Protect your nest boxes by using metal predator guards on the posts beneath them. In most areas, raccoons hibernate in the dead of winter and breed when they wake up from their seasonal sleep.

Like many feeder visitors, raccoons are often regular in their habits, visiting the feeding station at about the same time each night. Put out a fresh supply of whole-kernel or cob corn before dark, and check hourly to see if you have visitors. In my yard, they usually show up from around 9 to 10 P.M.

Unfortunately, raccoons are susceptible to rabies, which can quickly spread through wild populations. The disease is particularly prevalent in the East but can crop up anywhere. To play it safe, avoid getting too close to the animals, no matter how cute they are. Hand feeding can lead to a nip from an overly enthusiastic eater, and that's a risk you don't want to take. Because raccoons are nocturnal, spotting one in broad daylight is a signal that the animal is likely to be sick. Keep away from such an animal or from a raccoon that

A raccoon performs a highwire act while trying to get his paws on the seeds in a tube feeder. Enjoy the antics of these cute-but-wild critters from a distance.

is walking unsteadily or stiffly, walking in circles, or falling down.

Raccoons are strong and determined animals, and if they visit your feeding station only to find no accessible food, they'll do their best to make it accessible by tearing apart feeders with their dexterous paws and sharp teeth. I don't argue with them: I provide easy-access corn, apples, and pizza crusts to keep them content and to give me the pleasure of watching them—from a safe distance. I do like to play with my raccoons by challenging their agility. Once I hooked a toy ladder to a hanging feeder stocked with highly aromatic canned cat food. You should have seen those bandits stretch to grab the dangling ladder, then climb to their reward.

R

Rain

A LITTLE RAIN DOESN'T BOTHER BIRDS. During a rain shower, you'll see birds at your feeders, cracking seeds and nibbling suet, giving an occasional shake to flick water from their feathers.

When rain intensifies, or if there are gusty winds or lightning, birds wait out the storm in the shelter of densely branched trees and shrubs. To make sure birds will feel at home in your yard no matter what the weather, be sure they have a spot to take shelter from heavy rain. If your yard is very open, try planting a couple of bushy junipers (*Juniperus* spp.) or camellias, hollies, rhododendrons, or other broad-leaved evergreens to provide some quick shelter.

Bathing in the Rain

Rain is a vital source of water for birds. They'll gather at puddles of rainwater to drink and bathe. Smaller birds, including warblers and hummingbirds, may even splash in a thin film of water trapped on a leaf. If hummingbirds frequent your garden, watch their behavior when it starts raining—you may see them drinking from or splashing on a leaf.

Keeping the Kids Dry

To birds on the nest, rain is a danger to eggs and young ones because water can quickly chill them. The parent bird uses its body to offer protection from the raindrops, spreading its wings to cover the nest by a tent of feathers. I once saw a pair of robins protecting their young during an extra-heavy downpour. The female was sitting in the nest, and the male was perched on the rim with outspread wings, as if chivalrously holding an umbrella for her. Not all birds are as ingenious, and you may find dead nestlings in your yard after a heavy rain—the force of the downpour can dislodge them from the nest. Nests themselves may also fall out of the tree or other site, especially if wind accompanies the rainstorm.

Checking for Wet Seed

At the feeder, especially tray feeders and hopper feeders, rain means wet seed. Check your feeders after the weather clears, and remove any wet seed so that it doesn't turn moldy or ruin new seed that you add. Suet and whole corn cobs can stand up to rain; they will dry out without damage. If the wet weather is prolonged, however, even cob corn may rot, and tube feeders may accumulate moisture inside that causes seed to clump up and decay. You may need to compost the spoiled food and replace it with fresh.

Surviving Little or No Rain

In the arid Southwest, and in other places, such as the Northwest, where rain is scarce or nonexistent for months at a time, birds have evolved to take advantage of water wherever they can find it. Morning dew is a treasured source of water, but like puddles and streams, dew also disappears when rain fails to fall and air and soil become parched. But the biggest sources of liquid refreshment for desert birds are succulent plant parts and living food. Fruits are eagerly sought, for their thirst-satisfying juice as well as their food value. Prickly pear, cholla, and barrel cactuses are good places to bird-watch when their colorful fruits ripen and lure quail and other birds to the feast. Other plant parts also contain water. California and Gambel's quail seek out the juicy leaves of chickweed and the western weed called filaree, while the Montezuma quail uses its feet to scratch out bulbs of nut grass. Insects, snails, lizards, and other invertebrates add more water to the diet.

Where rain is scarce or during a drought, a regular source of water is even more attractive to birds than the most carefully selected banquet at the feeder. Birdbaths and water features will have a steady stream of customers. To ensure room for all, place shallow clay saucers or other impromptu bird-baths at ground level throughout the yard, so your birds can quench their thirst or freshen their feathers.

> If birds begin to avoid feeders that still contain food, check to see if the seed is wet or spoiled.

Raisins

Attract bluebirds, catbirds, mockingbirds, robins, woodpeckers, Carolina wrens, and other fruit eaters

RAISINS ARE AN INEXPENSIVE fruit choice for feeder birds, but it may take a while before birds readily accept these dried grapes. Instead of sprinkling them in a feeder, start by incorporating them in a mix of other soft foods that bluebirds, catbirds, mockingbirds, robins, woodpeckers, Carolina wrens, and other fruit eaters enjoy. I like to keep a small open tray feeder just for these customers, where I can experiment with various foods and recipes to see which one gets the most takers. The birds, too, become accustomed to visiting this feeder for their treats, which means they're quick to sample anything I put there.

Birds seem to accept golden raisins, which are made from white (green) grapes, more rapidly as a new feeder food, perhaps because they are more visible than the dark kind. To lure birds to a raisin handout, I combine either light or dark raisins with chopped suet, or add the fruit to a mix of peanut butter and cornmeal. Raisins are also easy to add to any bird-bread recipe. I sometimes chop dried cherries and raisins and fill empty grapefruit halves for a treat that delights waxwings. In winter snows, I scatter dark raisins on the ground, where robins and the occasional brown thrasher or catbird eagerly snap them up. It's fun to keep track of who samples your raisins: Kinglets, rose-breasted grosbeaks, or yellow-rumped warblers may enjoy the fruit alongside the usual clients.

For the best bargain, look for raisins in bulk bins at the grocery store or at health food stores, where they usually cost much less per pound than commercial-brand boxes. Store extras in your refrigerator.

> Birds seem to go for golden raisins (made from white grapes) more rapidly than the dark kind.

Rapeseed

Attracts buntings, doves, finches, sparrows, towhees, and others

RAPESEED IS A POPULAR INGREDIENT in seed mixes for both pet birds and wild birds. It's the tiny round seed of a European mustard (*Brassica napus*), and it's also called canola—it's the source of the canola oil sold for cooking. In the Midwest and Canada, you can spot fields of rapeseed from great distances—acres of yellow blossoms that glow like pure sunshine.

Rapeseed is very easy to grow. It sprouts vigorously in just about any soil and needs hardly any care. It also self-sows sparingly to generously (depending on how many seeds the birds overlook). A dense patch of rape will delight buntings, doves, finches, sparrows, and other birds that seek small seeds. I like to scatter some rapeseed in my flowerbeds, where its yellow blossoms add a cheerful touch and attract butterflies as a bonus. In fall and winter, foraging fox sparrows, towhees, and other birds diligently scratch beneath the plants to gather dropped seeds.

Rapeseed is very high in oil content, which makes it an ideal seed for cold weather feeding when extra calories are exactly what's needed. You can buy the seed, for bird feeding or for planting, from rural feed stores as well as some mail-order catalogs. Offer rapeseed in tube feeders, trays, or hopper feeders, or use it as an ingredient in your own custom birdseed mixes. Combined with millet and canary seed, it adds to an appealing menu for goldfinches, purple finches, and other small birds.

> Rapeseed gets its name from the Latin *rapa*, meaning "turnip."

Rapeseed 239

Rare Birds

NEVER DOUBT YOUR EYES when you see a bird that "shouldn't" be dining at your feeder. The most unusual visitors will drop by now and then at a feeding station. Stray birds that typically range hundreds of miles from your home may show up. A red-shafted flicker arrived one winter at my Pennsylvania feeder, many miles from its Midwest haunts. Species that you'd never dream that you'd host may also turn up, perhaps drawn by the presence of other birds. I've had a great blue heron at my feeding station during a March snowstorm. The giant bird stood before my high tray feeder, scything its beak through the millet while sparrows and juncos pecked around near its long-toed feet.

It's always fun to alert a birding hot line when an unusual visitor shows up at your feeder (see Birding Hot Line on page 30). Of course, be prepared for slow-moving vehicles near your house as other birders try to get a glimpse of your rare bird. You can also call a local nature center and your local chapter of the National Audubon Society to report your finding, which may turn out to be significant. When a least bittern, a tiny heron the size of a robin, showed up at a small pond just down the road from my Pennsylvania house, it turned out to be only one of a scant handful of sightings in the county—ever.

Rare birds can arrive anytime, but I've noticed that most of my more unusual guests show up after winter storms. When a deep blizzard struck in early spring one year, a dickcissel, a meadow lark, two horned larks, and a blue grosbeak joined my regular feeder clients. These birds would never typically visit a small town bird feeder but empty bellies had driven them in from outlying farm fields.

If you spot a bird at your feeder that you can't find in a field guide, take a photo if possible. Also jot down careful notes about plumage, size, eating habits, and behavior, and make as detailed a sketch as possible. When an oddball sparrow I simply could not identify showed up at my feeder, I spent hours trying to convince experts I had something rare, but no one could

It looks like a fairytale, but a great blue heron landed at my feeder in winter and gobbled millet with the juncos. Keep a camera ready for your unusual guests!

identify the bird until I showed them a snapshot. Then they informed me my bird was a hybrid between a slate-colored junco and a white-throated sparrow. Keep in mind the possibility of albinism, too, when you consider a bird. One fellow I knew thought he had a brand new blackbird species at his feeder: all black he said, with a pure white head. One look at the bird in real life showed me that it was a cowbird in all ways except for its albinistic white head. Still, it was definitely a bird you don't see every day.

That's the pleasure of rare birds: No matter how you define it, a bird of a different color makes feeder watching more exciting—even after it leaves!

R

Raspberries and Blackberries

Attract many kinds of birds when berries are ripening

AS A HEDGEROW OR SPOT PLANTING in your bird-friendly yard, raspberries and blackberries can't be beat. You can use bramble bushes like these to create an inviting area of cover near feeders, or you can plant them in a sunny corner of your yard, where the arching canes can recline against a fence. When you plant bramble bushes to attract birds, there's no need to worry about trellising or pruning—birds don't care what the plants look like! In fact, an overgrown berry bush is doubly inviting to birds because of the extra protection they find among the dense, prickly branches.

Untidiness pays off with bramble bushes, which birds visit most often when they are grown into a jungle rather than when the bushes are neatly pruned for maximum fruit. The larger size of the unshorn bush and the dense tangle of branches give the birds the protection they desperately need when roosting, nesting, or taking shelter from the storm. I limit pruning to the minimum: I cut out dead canes so that new ones have room to grow.

There are many blackberry and raspberry cultivars to choose from, so you can find plants that will thrive in your yard no matter where you live. In many regions, the bushes thrive as part of the wild landscape, especially in old fields that are slowly returning to woods. Be sure to choose a thorny cultivar, not a thornless variety, when planting for the birds, so that your bushes can do triple duty: food source, nesting site, and safe place to hide from predators.

Spotting Birds Among the Berries

Morning is the best time to watch birds feeding at berry bushes. A hedge studded with ripe red raspberries or other brambles will attract many species of delightful birds, including some, like the great crested flycatcher and larger vireos, that don't like to visit bird feeders.

I like to settle on a comfy bench or chair about 20 feet from my patch long before the berries ripen, and make it a habit to sit quietly there for a little while as often as possible so that the birds become accustomed to my presence. By the time June brings ripe berries, I have a prime seat for viewing the feast. Do pay attention to bird voices in and around the bushes, though. If you hear the sharp "Chip!" note that indicates alarm, the cause for concern may be you. Mature bushes make highly desirable nest sites, and you may be too close to a nest. If you think a bird is telling you to back off, move your seat or yourself back several yards, until life in the bush returns to normal.

A Berry Special Feeder Treat

RASPBERRIES AND blackberries cost a mint at the market. You may find them sold for less by local growers, but even so, these small, sweet fruits are too expensive to buy for your birds except as an occasional treat. But birds can help ease the pain you feel when berries you've purchased or picked go past their prime before you get to eat them. Toss those faded fruits into a freezer bag, and store them for a time when fresh fruits aren't around, then take pleasure in watching the birds enjoy the berries you missed out on.

It's difficult to tempt fruit-eating birds to a feeder during summer, when raspberries and blackberries ripen in the wild. With woods, fields, and roadsides brimming with natural fruit, birds generally prefer to seek out berries on the bush rather than berries in a tray. The best time to use berries as a feeder treat is from late fall through very early spring, when fresh fruit is just a fond memory to wild birds. Scatter blackberries or raspberries in an open tray feeder that has sheltering shrubs nearby, and you may lure catbirds, mockingbirds, robins, thrashers, wrens, and even cedar waxwings to feed.

Redbud

Attracts chickadees, hummingbirds, orioles, titmice, vireos, warblers

REDBUD IS THE perfect small tree for a small-scale yard. Redbud delights our hearts with its early bloom, partnering elegant dogwoods and spring flowers with a splash of deep pink color. The trees also delight chickadees, titmice, and other small seed eaters, which seek out the seedpods in winter. The small flowers hum with nectar-seeking insects, which in turn attract hungry orioles, vireos, and warblers. Hummingbirds may also visit for the nectar.

Redbuds belong to the plant family called legumes, which also includes garden peas and beans. Take a close look at redbud blossoms, and you'll see that the shape of the flowers is just like that of the garden pea flowers in your vegetable patch or the sweet peas climbing your picket fence. Another hint of this tree's heritage are the flat pods that decorate the branches after the flowers mature to seed. The small "pea pods" ripen to brown or red and dangle thickly from the branches all winter long.

The leaves have a pretty heart shape and are great for flattening in a heavy book to use in notecards or other crafts. Redbuds are precocious trees that grow fast and bloom early. In my yard, where seedlings sprout from native trees in the surrounding woods, it takes as little as 4 years to reach blooming size. Once you have flowers, you'll have pods. The number of pods varies from year to year; my guess is that cold or rainy weather that inhibits pollinator activity in early spring affects the pod production.

In late winter, when I'm starved for flowers, I clip a few branches of redbud and stick them in a jar of water. When the pink blooms open on the

Pretty redbuds attract seed eaters, insect eaters, and nectar eaters alike.

branches bare of leaves, they have a stylish oriental line that adds elegance even in my cluttered kitchen. I let them linger after the blossoms fade because of the beauty of the brand-new leaves, which unfold into small, shining, tender green hearts.

Redbuds are fine small trees for large or small yards. Native redbuds thrive across most of the United States. Eastern redbud (*Cercis canadensis*) is hardy in Zones 4 to 9. The Texas redbud (*C. canadensis* var. *texensis*) is hardy only to Zone 7, while the Mexican variety (*C. canadensis* var. *mexicanis*) is hardy only to Zone 8. All flourish in full sun to part or light shade. In the West, the native western redbud (*C. occidentalis*), hardy in Zones 9 and 10, and its varieties—*arizonicus*, from Arizona, and *orbiculata*, from Utah—are the trees of choice for a sunny site. White-flowered cultivars and red-foliaged selections are available, too. They vary in mature size, depending on the variety and the characteristics of the individual plant.

Safflower

Attracts cardinals

Golden orange safflower is an asset in the flower garden and at the feeder. The shaggy blossoms yield plump, hard white seeds, which you can also buy.

VIVID ORANGE SAFFLOWER (*Carthamus tinctorius*) blossoms are definite attention getters in a garden of birdseed plants. This annual is easy to grow from seed sown directly in sunny soil, and birds will come flocking once its flower heads mature into small, plump white seeds.

At the feeder, cardinals are the main customer for safflower seeds. It may take the red birds a while to discover the seeds, but once they do, they'll be regulars at the feeder. Packaged cardinal seed mix is often nothing more than black sunflower seeds mixed with white safflower—a fine combination tailor-made for cardinal tastes but usually much less expensive to blend yourself from seed bought in bulk.

If your cardinals aren't used to eating safflower, start with just a scant handful of the seeds sprinkled atop a tray of black oil sunflower seeds. Once you can see that the birds have started eating the safflower seeds, you can increase the serving. Safflower seed is a good choice if you prefer not to host jays at your feeder because they're generally not interested in it. With any luck, they'll depart for better vittles at another bird café when you switch to feeding mainly safflower. Squirrels don't care for safflower seed either and will bypass a feeder filled with it to seek their food elsewhere.

Salt

Attracts house finches plus buntings, doves, purple finches, goldfinches, jays, pigeons, pine siskins, house sparrows, and others

JUST LIKE PEOPLE, birds have different preferences when it comes to adding salt to their diet. Some like to eat it straight, while others can get along fine without even a sprinkling. The easiest way to feed salt is with a long-lasting salt block, available at feed stores for just a few dollars. House finches will be your best customer for salt, but buntings, doves, purple finches, goldfinches, jays, pigeons, pine siskins, house sparrows, and other birds also partake of the mineral.

Rain melts salt, causing it to soak into surrounding soil, endangering plants. To avoid tainting your ground and ending up with a large circle of salted "dead zone," settle your salt block on a sturdy waterproof platform with a lip. An upside-down, concave trash can lid, large plastic plant saucer, concrete birdbath bowl, shallow dishpan, or litter tray will work. For a more attractive presentation, place the salt block on a heavy-duty plastic liner that's held in place with gravel and hidden by a layer of wood chips.

Salt has always been popular with birds and animals. In the eastern half of the country, where an unbroken hardwood forest once stretched, giant shaggy bison and mobs of now-extinct passenger pigeons sought out salt licks and salt springs. Nowadays your neighborhood deer population may cause you to think twice before adding another incentive for them to visit your yard. If deer are a problem, keep the salt block far from any feeders that they can quickly empty. Rabbits, mice, and other animals may also visit a salt block. Nonbird visitors usually visit under the cover of darkness. Shine a strong flashlight on the area or set up a motion-activated light to see who's nibbling on your salt block—or check for teeth marks in daytime.

In days gone by, salt licks were well-trodden gathering places for American bison and immense flocks of passenger pigeons. They're still popular with birds, such as these evening grosbeaks.

Sand

JUST IMAGINE TRYING to survive on a diet of hard, dry corn kernels, acorns, and sunflower seeds—without teeth! That's the dilemma for our bird friends, who can crack open shells with their bills but can't chew the tasty pieces they find inside. They depend on a muscular organ—their gizzard—to grind their food, with the aid of small, abrasive stones, or grit, which the bird must constantly replenish.

Birds find grit in the wild anywhere they can. In regions where slippery roads are a common occurrence in winter, many highway departments spread sand to improve traction. As the snow melts to expose the edges of the road, keep an eye on the birds that gather there. You will frequently see cardinals, doves, and other birds picking up grains of sand from the roadside. The sides of roads that have been sanded for traction in wintertime are popular gathering places.

Coarse sand is an ideal source of grit for birds, which is why you'll want to include it among the offerings in your backyard. Buy the sand at a building supply store, not in the children's play area. Soft, white sandbox sand may be great to play in, but it is too fine for birds. River sand is ideal because of its large-grain size. If you have a gravel or river-rock operation nearby, ask if you can buy a few scoops. In my experience, they'll laugh and say, "Take all you want, it's free!" A bucketful will probably last a year.

Spread sand on the bare ground and let birds help themselves. It's a good idea to keep the supply in the same place year after year, so that your birds get accustomed to a reliable source.

> Sand at the feeder is like forks and spoons at a picnic—you're providing utensils so your guests can eat the meal.

Sap

Attracts house finches, hummingbirds, orioles, sapsuckers, and woodpeckers

TREE SAP IS NATURE'S VERSION of sugar water, although if you sample it, your human taste buds will discern only a very faint sweetness. The well-named yellow-bellied sapsucker as well as its relatives the red-naped and red-bellied sapsuckers are famed for drilling into trees to create sap runs. The birds return to the sap runs over and over to sip the sweet stuff and pick off the insects drawn to it. In summer, the acorn woodpecker of the West bores into branches of oaks to collect tree sap. House finches, orioles, and other woodpeckers may also visit trees that are oozing sap.

Sapsucker borings are easy to recognize. Look for a closely spaced series of holes in a nice, neat horizontal line. People once believed that such drillings caused serious tree damage, and orchardists killed sapsuckers to defend their trees. The true verdict is still unclear, with some researchers suggesting that the bore holes may not be as harmful as once believed. Diseases and pests that attack trees are also responsible for creating sap flows on the bark of a tree limb or trunk.

As well as enjoying the birds that visit sap, you can also discover many intriguing insects arriving for a sip of sap. In daylight hours, monarchs, red admirals, and anglewing butterflies, to name just a few, come to drink up. I like to take a flashlight out at night to look for large underwing moths (whose top wings look like a fragment of mottled bark, but whose bottom wings are startlingly colored) and big beetles, along with other interesting critters. Occasionally I even come upon a flying squirrel having a bit of dessert after dark.

Hummingbirds get at sap the natural way, hovering before the tree just as they would at a nectar feeder. Birds that never visit a feeder, such as flycatchers and vireos, as well as feeder birds like cardinals and titmice, will come by a sappy tree to pick off butterflies and insects during the day. And owls may come for the flying squirrels at night.

> Sapsuckers and some woodpeckers drill into trees for sap. Once it's flowing, hummingbirds may fly in for a sip.

Scouring Rush

UNCHANGED SINCE PREHISTORIC DAYS, the peculiar, primitive plant known as scouring rush is a species of horsetail (*Equisetum* spp.). As you might suspect from the name, scouring rush makes a great pot scrubber. It also does a superlative job of cutting through the algae in birdbaths, leaving a clean bowl behind after just a few swipes. The odd, jointed stems are so rough with grains of silica that you can feel the grittiness when you stroke the stem with your fingers.

Horsetails thrive in wet soil, but they also tolerate even extremely dry soil. They do so well in containers that they're commonly used in accent planters in commercial and residential landscaping in southern California. These tough perennial plants can put up with just about any conditions. Established plants spread by underground runners to form thick, solid colonies. Although it may take years for a garden planting to reach that stage, be prepared to pull up the extras to control the spread if necessary, or grow the plants in containers to avoid invasive problems.

I like to have horsetails near my water gardens, but the clump I couldn't do without grows at the base of my pedestal-style birdbath. If I had to trek to the house for scrubbing tools every time my birdbath needed a cleaning, I'm afraid to guess what its condition would deteriorate to. But when I can simply stoop, snap off a handful of scouring rush, wad it up, and swish it around the bowl, keeping the birdbath clean becomes more fun than work. The birds appreciate it, too.

Horsetails come in two very different-looking types. Some, such as common horsetail (*E. arvense*), look like little Christmas trees, with branches growing in whorls around the stem; other species have only unbranched, spare, straight green stems about as thick as pencils, marked with contrasting bands of color at the joints. *Equisetum hyemale*, the horsetail I grow, is one of these minimalists. Although horsetails can be aggressive spreaders, I've found this species takes a few years to settle in; if it does spread out of bounds, a quick yank on the unwanted explorers is all it takes to keep it under control.

An architectural ornament in the garden, horsetails also are practical. Their stems are loaded with silica, which makes a handful great for scouring birdbaths.

Seed Hoarding

PUTTING ASIDE SOME SEEDS for a rainy day is such a habit for a few species of birds that they will cache sunflower seed, corn, nuts, and other tidbits even when you offer a fresh supply every day. The nuthatches at your feeder will snatch up a morsel, fly off to a likely hiding spot, and hammer it tightly into place to retrieve later. For every sunflower seed my white-breasted nuthatch splits and eats at the feeder, he stuffs another dozen into cracks in my porch posts and in nearby tree crevices. One fall a red-breasted nuthatch chose a food storage area no other bird had thought of: the crack between the window gasket and door frame of my parked pickup truck. Every time I opened the door, a shower of sunflower seeds fell on my head.

Clark's nutcracker, crows, jays, nuthatches, titmice, and some woodpeckers are all hoarders at heart. Unfortunately, all this careful work often comes to naught when another bird discovers the cache. In winter, when my feeders are hopping, a white-breasted nuthatch often busies itself stuffing bits of my peanut butter and cornmeal dough into the bark of the maple trees. Frequently a brown creeper arrives within minutes to scour the tree and make short work of the unexpected treats. Hoarded nuts and seeds forgotten by jays often sprout into trees to replenish our forests.

The acorn woodpecker of the West turns trees and poles into vertical "Chinese checkers" boards with its hoarding habits. The bird drills shallow holes into trees, then crams an acorn into each hole. Although most storage trees hold dozens of acorns, in 1923 a pine tree was reportedly studded with 50,000 acorns!

> Jays' forgotten hoards of nuts and seeds often sprout into trees to replenish our forests.

Shrikes

LUCKILY FOR ALL of our small songbird friends, shrikes are not common birds. The two American species bear the unsavory nickname of "butcher bird," which speaks for itself. They prey on birds, small animals, and insects, which they impale on stout thorns or barbed wire to eat later.

Both shrikes look much the same: like big-headed, short-necked mockingbirds. Unlike the mockingbird, they sport black wings and tail and a sinister black mask. You may see the **loggerhead shrike** anywhere across the country except for a small strip of the Appalachians and New England, and in most places, at any season of the year. The **northern shrike** nests only in the extreme Far North. Like other birds of this region, it sometimes wanders irregularly southward in winter. Immature birds seem to be particularly prone to wanderlust. Unlike their gray parents, these young birds are dull brown rather than silvery gray.

Shrike Behavior

Take a closer look the next time you spot what appears to be a mockingbird perched on a conspicuous pole, post, or tree top. If it holds its tail nearly horizontally and hunkers its body down, you may be watching a shrike. Like hawks, these energy-efficient hunters spend much of their time perched, waiting for prey to pass. Double-check any "shrike" you see to make sure it's not a mockingbird. The gray-and-white mocker resembles the shrike and may further fool you by chasing other birds (although not for prey).

When a shrike took up residence near my feeding station in Pennsylvania, it chose a wild multiflora rose bush for its habitual perch. The rose thorns provided a convenient place to store

Close to robin-size, the loggerhead shrike is an uncommon predator that impales its feathered prey. Shrikes are classified in their own family.

SHRIKE FEEDER FOODS
■ Bread
■ Eggs, hard-boiled or scrambled
■ Hamburger, raw
■ Meat of any kind, raw
■ Poultry, raw
■ Soup bones with marrow and meat
■ Suet

the accumulating wealth of the shrike's daily kills. The hillside where the bush grew gave the bird a great vantage point to oversee the brush below—and my bird feeders beyond.

Like many other birds of the North, shrikes seem unusually tame and unafraid around humans. None of my usual tactics—mainly running and hollering—had any permanent effect on the shrike. He obediently flew off when I attacked, only to return when I went back inside.

I consoled myself with the thought that the shrike's forays, like those of hawks, were eliminating the weakest birds—those that were most unwary or slowest in reaction time or flight. Still, I found survival-of-the-fittest cold comfort for the loss of my trusting chickadees and gentle juncos.

Shrikes also hang their prey from the crotches of trees as well as stick them on thorns, and like squirrels, they go back to their cache with an unerring memory. Their hunting habits vary, depending on the prey. They may drop from the air or hop about on the ground to drive small birds out of the bushes.

When I encountered a shrike in the date-growing region of California, near Indio, my first reaction was to toss the bird a piece of the honey-sweet fruit that we were eating. It immediately pounced on the date, perhaps attracted by the motion, then took it to a nearby tree to pluck it into pieces and gulp down. At the feeder, shrikes will be very appreciative of a handout of mice, whether you "serve" them scurrying about beneath the feeder or offer contributions from your mouse-traps. For a less squeamish entree, try raw hamburger or other soft food offerings.

Inviting a shrike to dinner won't endear you to the other guests. But providing food for the butcher bird may make it less prone to look for prey. At any rate, keep the "shrike feeder" far, far away from the feeding station, and increase the protective cover you offer your songbirds. They'll need all the help they can get.

The adult northern shrike is paler gray on top than the loggerhead shrike. Immature birds are light brown, with black markings like the adult's.

Pine Siskin

IF YOU LIVE IN THE WEST, pine siskins are most likely frequent guests at your feeder, snacking on niger and sunflower seed like their close relatives, the goldfinches. In the eastern two-thirds of the country, however, siskins are an occasional winter sight and not always a sure thing. Their winter migrations tend to be irregular, sometimes bringing large flocks from the Far North where they nest, and sometimes delivering only a stray bird or two to join the other small birds at your seed feeders.

Both male and female siskins look alike, resembling a streaky brown goldfinch. They have yellow bars on their wings, which expand into noticeable patches of color when the birds fly, and a bit of yellow under their sharply notched tail.

Despite their woodsy-sounding name, pine siskins eat mostly weed seeds, although they do

At first glance, the pine siskin looks like a streaky brown goldfinch. Look closely to see the wingbars that create the flash of yellow when the bird flies.

consume large quantities of pine and alder seeds as well. In the West, the seeds of a nonnative annual flower called filaree (*Erodium* spp.) is the food of choice. Common ragweed is another favorite seed source in all areas where siskins range, a bonus for allergy sufferers.

SISKIN FEEDER FOODS

- Bachelor's-button (*Centaurea cyanus*) seed
- Birdseed mix
- Canary seed
- Cosmos (*Cosmos* spp.) seeds
- Millet
- Nectar
- Niger
- Sunflower seeds, especially black oil or hulled
- Zinnia (*Zinnia* spp.) seeds

Siskin Behavior

Siskins nibble daintily at feeders and perform acrobatics to collect seeds as their goldfinch relatives do. Siskins are tamer than goldfinches, and they are fairly easy to coax into eating sunflower seeds right out of your hand.

In temperament, they tend to be crabby little guys, often quarreling noisily with their companions at the feeder.

Siskins are very fond of sap and have learned to use nectar feeders. A salt block is a certain enticement to siskins. Like their goldfinch relatives, they enjoy splashing, so a birdbath or other water source is another big draw.

Siskins may show up at your feeders alone or en masse. If only one or a few birds arrive, you may not even notice their presence at first. Their unremarkable streaky brown color blends right in with the female house finches, and in silhouette, their sharply notched tails make them look just like a goldfinch. I find it's a good idea to check the customers, especially at the tube feeders, every morning, scanning with binoculars to get a better view of who's visiting. If you spot a bird that you think may be a pine siskin, keep watching until it flies, when the yellow patches on its wings are more noticeable.

Sleeping

As YOU STRETCH YOUR LEGS in your comfy bed tonight, consider the fact that songbirds sleep standing up. Their extraordinary legs and feet lock into place around a perch, keeping them upright while they snooze. Most birds do snuggle down to sleep, fluffing out breast feathers to cover their legs and tucking their heads under a wing. Listen closely as dusk falls in your yard, and you may hear bird "lullabies": the quiet twitters of sparrows, juncos, and other sleepyheads turning in for the night. Birds usually band together at night, positioning themselves on a comfortable perch in a shared bush or evergreen. Birds favor cedars (*Juniperus* spp.), spruces (*Picea* spp.), and other dense conifers as roosting spots.

In extremely cold weather, cavity-nesting birds such as bluebirds, chickadees, titmice, and wrens seek holes in trees, branches, or wooden fence posts or retreat to bird boxes to help preserve heat. They may crowd together in groups of a dozen or more of the same species. If you spy a bird at your feeder with an oddly curved tail, it may have spent the night in tight quarters. If you're an early bird yourself, you may spot birds leaving a nest-box roosting site. Tap on the box just after daybreak, before birds are flocking to the feeder, and be prepared for a possible rush of wings as occupants leave in a hurry.

I like to sit on my porch near dusk to watch the birds retire for the night into my neighbor's big, dense blue spruce. It's amazing how many birds that tree can hold—60, at the highest count! Native sparrows, house sparrows, juncos, finches, robins, jays, doves, and cardinals all find a place within its sheltering arms.

> Dense conifers, such as cedars or spruces, offer birds a protected place to perch for a good night's sleep.

S

Snow and Ice Storms

WHEN WINTER STORMS hit your area, it's hard times for birds. Because the ground is covered with snow or ice, birds have to scratch vigorously to reach seeds that may—or may not—be underneath the white stuff. Tree buds, berries, nuts, and even the last withered crab apples may be encased in ice or frozen to impenetrable hardness. Weed stems are bent and bowed under a layer of snow. What's a hungry bird to do?

Why, come to the feeder, of course, where the food is plentiful even when snow keeps falling. Snowflakes and sleet are your signals to bring out the stuff you've been hoarding. Reach for the freezer and pull out the suet balls, the muffins, and the scraps of sandwiches, and offer them with a free hand. Don't hold back on seed or other foods now because your handouts can literally keep birds alive.

Getting caught short when birds are depending on you is a hard way to learn to keep emergency food supplies. If you can't get out, birds will go hungry.

Winter Fuel for Birds

You can't serve hot cocoa to your birds, but you can do the next best thing: Give them high-fat, high-carbohydrate foods that will quickly refuel their calorie-burning bodies and supply the store of energy they need to survive through long, cold nights. Add bacon grease, doughnuts, nuts, and peanut-butter recipes to the menu of standard seeds and suet.

Be an Early Bird

Birds are out early the morning after a storm, and you should be, too. Keeping your guests waiting while you brew coffee and find your galoshes is not just rude right now, it's dangerous to their well-being.

At least make sure the covered feeders are fully stocked before you turn in for the night. Your mission is to keep food available as long as birds need it.

Falling snow or freezing rain and ice can cover feeders fast, so erect lean-tos and other temporary shelters over and around your feeders to divert falling or drifting snow.

Lots of items will do the trick as a temporary lean-to. I keep a few scraps of plywood and a prized section of corrugated metal siding on my porch, ready to grab in case the need arises. I've even pressed empty pizza boxes into service during unexpected snowstorms. Any piece of stiff, flat material will work. Use two or three sturdy sticks or 2 × 4s to prop up the protective shelter. I save the broken handles of garden tools for props, too. Make sure the supports are strong and evenly spaced, so that the weight of snow doesn't cause a collapse of your impromptu shelter.

If you have a multitude of customers, you can serve seed and other foods directly on the ground. Clear the loose snow, scatter the food, and before you get back in the house, the birds will be eating. If snow keeps falling, sweep aside the new snow as often as you have time and patience to do so.

Soda Bottles

BEFORE YOU HAUL those plastic soda pop bottles out to the curb for recycling, set a few aside to transform into bird feeders. Large, 2-liter bottles can be easily adapted into feeders with the aid of commercially made screw-on devices that attach to the former cap end. Smaller 20-ounce plastic soda bottles also make fine additions to your nectar feeder collection. And, as an added bonus, they are also a handy item in your first-aid kit for baby birds: Use them as hot water bottles to keep nestlings cozy until you can deliver the birds to a rehabilitator.

For more free feeding devices, slice the bottom from a large soda bottle, using a sharp-bladed kitchen knife. Nail two or three of these plastic cups to a board. Fill with raisins, chopped apples, ground suet, and other treats.

You can even make a tube feeder from a small bottle. Here's how to do it:

PROJECT

Simple Soda Bottle Bird Feeder

Turning a plastic soda bottle into a bird feeder is about as easy as projects get—this is a great activity for kids, or just for your own satisfaction. The paper towels in the bottom of the bottle are meant to prevent a layer of wasted seed that birds can't reach—be sure to use them or some other barrier in your feeder. Don't expect to be overrun with compliments on the beauty and style of your soda bottle bird feeder, but you can congratulate yourself for creating an extremely functional feeder out of an object that, at best, was destined for recycling of some sort. In fact, one of the great things about this homemade feeder is that you can recycle it when its useful life as a feeder has ended.

MATERIALS

20-ounce plastic soda bottle, empty and dry, with cap

Dry paper towels

2 wooden skewers

Wire for hanging

Step 1. Stuff a dry paper towel into the bottom of the bottle, using the handle of a wooden spoon. Repeat if necessary until the bottom ½ inch of the bottle is filled with paper towels.

Step 2. Insert a pointed wooden kitchen skewer for a perch, about ½ inch from the bottom of the bottle, just above the paper towel. Push the skewer in one side, through the bottle, and out the other side.

Step 3. Repeat, inserting a second skewer a couple of inches above and perpendicular to the first one. Trim so that only 2 inches of each perch extends outside the bottle.

Step 4. Insert more paper towels, filling the bottle to a total height of about 1½ inches with paper. This will prevent unreachable seed from being wasted in the bottom of the bottle.

Step 5. Use a utility knife to cut a narrow slit, about ⅛ inch wide, about 1½ inches above each perch.

Step 6. Use a funnel to fill the bottle with niger seed, and replace the cap.

Step 7. Loop a piece of wire around the neck, twist to tighten, and hang the bottle feeder from a handy branch or hook.

Soft Foods

Attract bluebirds, catbirds, mockingbirds, robins, thrashers, thrushes

BREAD, FRUIT, SUET, day-old doughnuts, and leftover pizza and pasta all fit into the category of soft foods. Soft foods include anything a bird can swallow straight down the hatch, without first cracking through a hard shell. Both seed eaters and nonseed eaters enjoy soft foods. Bluebirds, catbirds, robins, thrashers, and thrushes are difficult to attract to feeders that offer only seeds and suet because that menu is foreign to these insect and fruit eaters. Only in times of scarcity will these birds come to rely on the handouts you offer. The rest of the time, they can find their own favored foods easily enough, thank you. All of these species, plus other more common feeder visitors such as mockingbirds and Carolina wrens, are likely to be drawn to a feeding station that offers soft foods, which are similar in beak appeal to the natural foods these birds eat. Like fruits and insects, they are swallowed gulp by gulp, with no pecking necessary except to extricate a bite-size morsel.

Soft foods can be a real lifesaver in the cold months, especially after storms that make natural food hard to come by. I go through dozens of loaves of bread after a snowstorm, when the many robins that winter in my area are desperate for a bite to eat. It's a good idea to stock your freezer with soft foods so you have plenty on hand in case of a weather emergency. I keep a shelf reserved for resealable plastic bags filled with meat scraps, leftover spaghetti, pizza crusts, sandwich scraps, and other goodies. When it's time to feed, I thaw the delicacies in the microwave and spread them in a feeder. The mix may not appear palatable to me, but the birds seem to enjoy picking through the smorgasbord. It's fun to see what they go for first.

In times of need, the very presence of feeding birds of any kind will attract the attention of other species, even if they are not usually inclined to sit shoulder to shoulder with sparrows. I serve soft foods directly on the ground or in open tray feeders, where the birds that aren't accustomed to the feeding station can easily spot them. Avoid going overboard with this approach, though, because starlings are also big fans of soft foods. If starlings become a problem, save these foods for desperate times, unless you don't mind accommodating a horde of starlings in exchange for the occasional sighting of a brown thrasher. Or unless, like me, you also enjoy feeding starlings.

Soft Foods to Avoid

These soft foods do not usually attract desirable birds, but crows and starlings may find them interesting.

- Cheese
- Potatoes, any type (mashed, baked, boiled)
- Salad greens
- Tomatoes
- Vegetables, except corn

Soft Foods to Keep in Stock

OFFER THESE foods in a tray feeder, or place them in a weighted feeder that prevents large birds like crows and starlings from gaining access to the treats.

- Bacon
- Bread
- Cake
- Canned corn
- Cereal
- Cookies
- Dog food
- Doughnuts
- Eggs
- Fruit, dried or fresh
- Lunch meat
- Meat scraps
- Muffins
- Pancakes and waffles
- Pasta, cooked
- Peanut butter
- Pizza
- Raisins
- Sandwich scraps
- Suet
- Toast

Sparrows

FIGURING OUT the grosbeaks, jays, and other large birds at your feeder is the easy part of bird identification. You'll know you've graduated from the novice stage when you start to sort out sparrows. More than 32 different species of native sparrows fill just about every niche in the country, flocking in companionable groups that usually include more than one species.

To preserve the reputation of our native sparrows, it's important to know that house sparrows (or English sparrows) are neither sparrows nor native birds. The sparrows we're discussing in this section are all-American birds that belong to the several genera of the finch family that ornithologists consider sparrows.

All sparrows have small, conical beaks, typical for birds that eat mostly seeds. These little birds devour millions of seeds of weeds-to-be including ragweed (*Ambrosia artemisifolia*), curly dock (*Rumex*

The chipping sparrow is a dapper backyard resident that often nests in a foundation shrub or tree. Listen for its distinctive song, a series of rapid chips.

crispus), and dozens of other plants. They also eat insects, and many of them enjoy fruits and berries.

All sparrows have brown backs, except for a few species that live in sagebrush country in the West. Of these western birds, the **black-chinned sparrow** is deep

---

SPARROW FEEDER FOODS

- Baked goods
- Birdseed mix
- Blackberries (*Rubus* spp.)
- Blueberries (*Vaccinium* spp.)
- Bread crumbs
- Cereal
- Cherries
- Chick scratch
- Corn, cracked or ground
- Crackers, crumbled
- Elderberries (*Sambucus* spp.)
- Evening primrose (*Oenothera* spp.) seeds
- Foxtail grass (*Setaria* spp.) seeds
- Grapes
- Grass seed
- Millet (*Panicum* and other genera)
- Milo (*Sorghum bicolor*)
- Oats (*Avena sativa*)
- Rapeseed (*Brassica napus*)
- Seeds of garden flowers, including cockscomb (*Celosia cristata*), bachelor's buttons (*Centaurea cyanus*), sweet alyssum (*Lobularia maritima*), and marigolds (*Tagetes* spp.)
- Suet, chopped
- Weed seeds, including pigweed, common ragweed, smartweed, dandelion, and many others

charcoal with brown shoulders, the **sage sparrow** is lovely gray with a white belly, and the **black-throated sparrow** is a soft gray-brown. The **lark bunting** is another sparrow that doesn't dress in brown. This midwestern species is black with snazzy white wing patches. Juncos are sparrows, too; check the Juncos entry on page 182 for more information on them.

A sparrowlike bird of grainfields and farm country, the **dickcissel** bears a silly-sounding name that echoes its call of "Dick, dick, dick, sissel!" The dickcissel looks like a cross between a sparrow and a meadowlark, with a streaky brown back and a bright golden breast boldly marked by a black bib. In summer, it rarely visits feeders, but on its wintering grounds along the Gulf and Atlantic coasts, it may turn up with the sparrows at your feeder.

Sparrows at the Feeder

Although America holds dozens of sparrow species, only a handful regularly partake of the fare at feeding stations. Expect to enjoy regular visits from the **song sparrow** in all seasons and the **white-throated** and **white-crowned sparrows** especially in winter. In the far West, look for the **golden-crowned sparrow** in winter. The golden-crowned closely resembles the smaller white-crowned species, and members of the two species often flock together.

You may also play host to the **chipping sparrow** in spring and summer and the **American tree sparrow** in winter. The **field sparrow** may visit in any season. One of the largest sparrow species, the beautiful rich-colored **fox sparrow** may come to call in various seasons depending on where you live.

Many native sparrows, even widespread species such as the **grasshopper sparrow, lark sparrow, savannah sparrow, and vesper sparrow,** do not usually frequent feeders. These birds stick to their natural haunts in prairies and meadows, fending for themselves without needing extra assistance. Other sparrows of more limited range, including the marsh-loving **LeConte's sparrow, Nelson's sharp-tailed sparrow,** and **seaside sparrow,** also tend to ignore even the most inviting feeder setup in favor of natural food. But don't be surprised to see any

The wide-eyed look of a white eye ring identifies the field sparrow, a bird that frequently forsakes wild places for the abundance at a winter feeding station.

The fox sparrow is one of the easiest to identify and one of the largest. In the West, these feeder birds are dark umber; in the East, they're ruddy chestnut.

sparrow in this book turn up at your spread of tempting seeds, especially in times of severe weather or during migration.

Millet and other small seeds are the primary feeder food of all sparrows. These birds will visit higher feeders, but they are more at home closer to ground level. Supply a low tray feeder for them, or feed directly on the ground. Sparrows often feed under feeders, where they scratch to turn up fresh seeds dropped by other feeder guests.

Identifying Sparrows

No, all sparrows don't look alike—it only seems that way sometimes, which is what leads many bird watchers to lump them together as "LBBs"—little brown birds, or "LBJs"—little brown jobs. These small members of the finch family are a challenge to identify because their differences are subtle, and their behaviors are often similar.

Naming sparrows at the feeder is only a matter of patience because you can compare the visitor to the pictures of the field guide while the bird eats its fill. But when a sparrow is in the yard or in the wild, giving you only a quick, tantalizing glimpse, identification is a different story. Is it a swamp sparrow or a tree sparrow scolding you from the hedge? By the time you pull out your field guide—usually after the bird has flown—you may forget many of the fine points, if you noticed them in the first place.

Sparrows' distinguishing differences are noticeable if you have an eye for details. Look for the dark "stickpin" on a song sparrow's streaky breast.

When I spot an unfamiliar sparrow, I first make a quick sketch of its head, noting stripes, if any, and colors. Sometimes that's as far as I get before the sparrow skedaddles. If I have the luxury of a longer look, I run down a quick checklist of other features that could help me identify the bird, such as wing bars or a dark "stickpin" mark on the breast. Look specifically at head markings and tail shape when

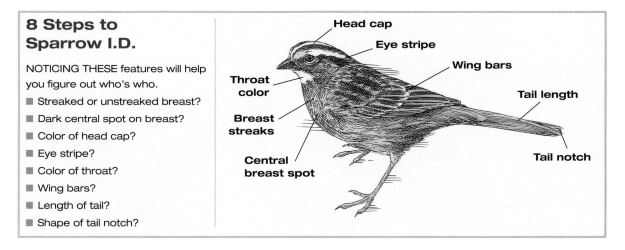

8 Steps to Sparrow I.D.

NOTICING THESE features will help you figure out who's who.

- Streaked or unstreaked breast?
- Dark central spot on breast?
- Color of head cap?
- Eye stripe?
- Color of throat?
- Wing bars?
- Length of tail?
- Shape of tail notch?

Head cap
Eye stripe
Wing bars
Throat color
Tail length
Breast streaks
Central breast spot
Tail notch

you're trying to sort out sparrows; these characteristics are often enough to make a final classification.

I also note the habitat in which I saw the sparrow. This is a big help in nesting season, but less so during migration and in winter, when sparrows range far afield of their usual haunts. I make quick notes of any behavior I notice, too, which help me remember the bird the next time. If the sparrow is feeding, I jot down what and how: "scratching for seeds beneath dock," for instance, or "perched on goldenrod stem, fluffy stuff flying." You don't have to be scientific with these field notes; just record information that you will understand when you read it later.

A winter feeder visitor, the tree sparrow sports an interesting two-toned bill. Disregard the name—this bird usually hops about in fields, gardens, and brush.

Sparrow Behavior

Native sparrows are the perfect teachers for a course in weed appreciation. If you keep a less-than-perfect lawn, you get extra points with these spritely brown birds. In winter, song sparrows keep me company as I hoe off clumps of chickweed and toss the clumps out of the patch for them to enjoy the seeds at leisure. In late spring, when my lawn is dotted with puffs of dandelions gone to seed, migrating white-crowned and white-throated sparrows squabble over the parachute seeds. In fall, when the crabgrass that kept the yard green in summer has stretched out into seedheads, the same species come to visit again on their trip southward, drawn to the banquet of weed seeds that my slightly shaggy yard offers them.

In addition to eating weed seeds, sparrows also scour asters (*Aster* spp. and other genera), goldenrod (*Solidago* spp.), and garden flowers such as tickseed sunflower (*Bidens aristosa*), cosmos (*Cosmos* spp.),

---

Weed Eaters Deluxe

SPARROWS DEVOUR zillions of weed seeds every year. The list of their favored edibles sounds like a gardener's worst nightmare. Here are some of the plants you'll see less of, thanks to sparrows:

- Pigweeds (*Amaranthus* spp.)
- Common ragweed (*Ambrosia artemisifolia*)

- Common lamb's-quarters (*Chenopodium album*)
- Tarweed (*Cuphea petiolata*)
- Crabgrasses (*Digiaria* spp.)
- Filarees (*Erodium* spp.)
- Yellow wood sorrel (*Oxalis stricta*)
- Pennsylvania smartweed (*Polygonum pensylvanicum*)

- Knotweeds (*Polygonum* spp.)
- Common purslane (*Portulaca oleracea*)
- Sheep sorrel (*Rumex acetosella*)
- Docks (*Rumex* spp.)
- Foxtail grasses (*Setaria* spp.)
- Nightshades (*Solanum* spp.)
- Common chickweed (*Stellaria media*)

and marigolds (*Tagetes* spp.). Visiting sparrows are the main reason I let my garden plants stand through winter. The stems provide a sheltered place where these small birds, very conscious of their low rung on the food ladder, can forage for seeds without fear of hawks or other predators.

Watch as sparrows move across a stretch of open space, and you will see how they have perfected flight patterns to avoid being picked off by predators. Some skulk from one clump of low vegetation to another, while others make a mad dash, zigzagging evasively across the dangerous open ground.

Sparrows usually behave well at the feeding station, even when they visit in flocks. They peck busily at the seeds with quick motions, always ready to take flight in an instant. Many sparrows scratch as they feed. Some use a one-legged technique, while others hop front, then back, to turn over the debris.

If you live in an area of winter snows, you may see a song sparrow working industriously beneath your

The white-crowned sparrow looks highly alert, thanks to the eye-catching bright white stripes atop its head. Juvenile birds wear duller colors.

feeder after a fresh snowfall. I have seen song and fox sparrows feeding in 6-inch-deep pits shortly after daybreak, when hunger urged them to try to reach the seed buried beneath the deep white blanket.

Sparrows appreciate fresh water, and several species, including the chipping sparrow, are fans of

A Weed to Plant

HOLDING THE number-one place in the stomachs of many sparrow species are smartweeds (*Polygonum* spp.), a genus that includes many common and widespread plants. You probably have smartweeds (or the similar knotweeds) growing in your yard right now, or in nearby wild places. All have spikes of close-packed tiny flowers, usually pink but also white, depending on the species.

Once you pay attention to smartweeds, you'll notice that many species have definite garden potential. Taller, shade-loving species are appealing with ferns and hostas; low growers are best en masse. Experiment with those that grow well in your own area; you will encounter some smartweeds with fine garden potential. Many bloom for weeks, providing an understated ruff of color with perennials or other plants.

I encourage a ground-hugging variety (*Polygonum persicaria*) that has vibrant, deep pink flowers to cover the spaces among my native ornamental grasses. This smart-

weed is a very late bloomer that comes into its own when the purple top grass (*Tridens flavus*) is standing tall and somber in bloom, and the panic grass (*Panicum virgatum*) is mellowing into tawny fall color, making a beautiful combination of color and texture. The finishing touch is another sparrow-beloved weed, purple love grass (*Eragrostis spectabilis*), which produces soft, low clouds of pale pinkish purple seedheads. After I enjoy the show of grasses and smartweed, my many winter-resident sparrows work at the seeds for months.

salt. In spring, some sparrows, such as the golden-crowned, like to nip off the petals and buds of garden flowers. Tender green sprouts of weeds and veggies tempt others—I've learned to cover my peas until after the white-crowned sparrows have left in spring. Small fruits are also a staple in their diets.

There are so many sparrows in America and they eat so many insects that the USDA issued a publication 80 years ago (before pesticides were commonly used) ranking sparrows by their usefulness to farmers. Their yen for beetles, cutworms, grasshoppers, weevils, and other garden menaces make sparrows a presence to be encouraged in your backyard.

The white-throated sparrow has a beautiful but melancholy song. You may hear it at the feeder as spring nears. It prefers dense plantings and shrubs.

Spring Feeding

TRAFFIC REMAINS HIGH at backyard feeders in early spring. Mating season hasn't begun or is just starting for most species. Migration is getting under way, bringing temporary bird visitors as well as the resident birds of summer into your area. Snowstorms and other severe weather can still sweep through, causing a rush on the feeding station. Keep your supplies well stocked just in case. I usually add an extra jar of peanut butter and a few more suet blocks to the larder, just in case. Should cold weather hit hard, these will help the birds through the tough time. Purple martins and bluebirds are particularly susceptible to cold weather, which keeps insects out of sight. During a cold snap, invest a few dollars in mealworms and offer them with a free hand at an open tray feeder for these birds—it can mean the difference between life and death. Spring also brings hummingbirds to nearly every part of the country, so make sure your nectar feeders are ready and waiting.

What to Watch For

Although you won't notice much of a change in the number of birds at your feeders early in the season, you will see a change in behavior. Instead of congregating in congenial groups, many species are now beginning courtship maneuvers and forming pair bonds. Sparring over females is common, and territorial jousting can occur between males of the same species.

Feeder birds sound different in spring, too. Their hormone levels are changing, triggering them to begin singing their love songs. Blackbirds, bluebirds, chickadees, meadowlarks, nuthatches, song sparrows, starlings, and titmice are among the first to start singing. Watch them to see whether they're trying to impress a mate or stake out a territory.

Arriving spring migrants are cause for big excitement at the feeders because now is the time when some of the most colorful, most unusual birds may show up. Insects are still scarce, and the need to refuel quickly is paramount, which means that tanagers may choose an hour of feasting at your feeder over an afternoon of foraging for themselves.

If your feeders offer generous helpings of favored foods, you may find an ever-increasing number of birds as migrants come into the area and stop for a few days. Goldfinches, particularly, can build into enormous flocks at a well-stocked feeder. In spring, my usual number of 6 goldfinches swells to 200. They fill the trees over the feeders and make the air come alive with their musical twitterings. Even my dozen feeders aren't enough to accommodate them, so for a couple of weeks, I resort to pouring black sunflower seed directly on the ground. When the sunny horde descends on the seeds, it looks as though a big patch of dandelions has come into bloom overnight.

Watch for the birds that passed through on their way south to stop again on their way north. Often, I'm convinced, it's the self-same bird. I remember a fox sparrow that lingered for 3 or 4 days on both legs of its migratory voyage. I had moved my feeding station between fall and spring, but this sparrow returned to where the feeder used to be.

Migration is usually gradual. Not every bird species has a departure ticket for the same day. I like to keep a head count once a week to stay on top of the changes; otherwise, one day I look out the window and notice that there's not a single junco in sight. As winter residents leave for more northerly

Rose-breasted grosbeaks may stop at your feeder on their spring trip northward. The feeder scene changes as winter residents move on and summer birds return.

breeding grounds, you won't need to fill your feeders as often.

As spring progresses and the birds move to nesting territories, their visits to your feeder will likely become fewer and farther between. By late spring, nesting season is in full swing, migration is over, and feeder traffic usually drops off dramatically. Don't worry, though: Some of the faithfuls will stay regular customers right through summer.

10 To-Dos for Spring Feeding

1. Increase the amount of millet in your feeders to satisfy the many small seed eaters that may be stopping in, such as indigo buntings, finches, siskins, and native sparrows.

2. Add another tube feeder if needed to accommodate the burgeoning numbers of goldfinches.

3. Pull out the special treats to keep birds loyal to your feeder: nuts, peanuts, fruits, peanut-butter delicacies.

4. Put out hummingbird feeders.

5. Serve mealworms, a real treat for migrating tanagers, thrushes, and other insect eaters.

6. Offer crushed eggshells to replenish minerals.

7. Keep a ready supply of fresh water available to the birds.

8. Watch for plumage changes in male goldfinches, as they switch from winter olive drab to dandelion yellow spring dress.

9. Learn bird songs as you begin to hear them from courting couples.

10. Note the arrival dates of spring migrants this year on a calendar page for the same day the coming year; it's fun to know when to expect them next year.

Sprinklers, Drippers, and Misters

ANY DEVICE THAT makes water audible is a prized addition to a bird-attracting yard. Recirculating pumps fill the bill, as do fountains in garden pools. Keep in mind that you don't need to create a torrent to attract birds. Their hearing is acute, and they can pick up just a ripple or a drip. In the days before water meters and water-table awareness, I often let my garden hose run on the ground. (I still do sometimes when I forget to turn it off after watering.) That very low-tech approach attracted a multitude of birds to the yard, including thrushes and towhees from the nearby woods.

A lawn sprinkler delights birds as well as kids. Keep watch to see who's frolicking in the water. Hummingbirds, like this Anna's, are fond of a bath on the wing.

Sprinklers

A good old lawn sprinkler makes a low-tech, low-cost approach to creating water music. Robins and flickers are particularly fond of this bath; they will linger beneath the spray for a long time, fluttering their wings as they luxuriate in the gentle water. Birds prefer a sprinkler that waters the same area for a long time rather than an oscillating sprinkler that swings from one place to another.

If hummingbirds visit your yard, the spray of a sprinkler may serve as a hummingbird shower—an event that is a delight to watch. Instead of alighting like other birds, hummers swing back and forth through the spray, then retire to a nearby perch to freshen their feathers. These endearing little birds may even bathe in the spray from a handheld hose nozzle.

Drippers

On a smaller, more sensible scale, a gentle drip-drip-drip is also highly effective. You can create your own dripper, albeit a funny-looking one, by suspending a leaky bucket over the birdbath. Poke a nail into the bucket from the inside to make a single hole in the center. Fill with water and let 'er drip. If you want a splashier sound, poke two or three holes, but be aware you'll have to refill the bucket more often.

Commercial dripper devices are widely available for attachment to your garden hose. They are a simple piece of copper or other tubing, bent into a curve at the top like the handle of a cane, with a connection for attachment at the other end. These accessories are perfect for a ground-level birdbath or garden pool.

Misters

Misting devices, which break up spray into superfine droplets, are a real treat for birds. They exult in the fine spray regularly once they discover it. A mist head that attaches to your hose is a real bargain at about $20. The attachment may tempt bright-colored orioles and tanagers, as well as robins, sparrows, and a host of other songbirds to the delights of the bath. Hummingbirds will also soon be regulars. You can attach the mist head to a branch, post, or other support. Point the spray toward a place where birds can alight to enjoy it. Hummingbirds, of course, need no perch for the pleasure of their bath; an upward-pointing mister is ideal for a hummingbirds-only bathing area.

Hoses

No matter how good I try to be, invariably at least once a season I forget to turn off the garden hose. The running water is a big attraction for robins, towhees, and other birds, which sip and splash until I remember my lapse and the water dries up.

A pair of inexpensive misters offers water for songbirds, hummingbirds, and butterflies. In summer, birds may find water more tempting than food.

Y-connector

Squirrels

NOBODY IS NEUTRAL ABOUT SQUIRRELS. When it comes to these bushy-tailed rapscallions, we either laugh at their comedy routines and put up with their raids on the birdseed, or we declare a vendetta and do everything we can to bar the door.

Unfortunately, squirrels are darn smart. They can figure out how to raid almost any feeder, including those sold as squirrel-proof. Combine that native intelligence with an agile body and dexterous front paws, plus the leaping ability of Superman, and it's no wonder that the Great Squirrel Wars have been going on almost as long as folks have been scattering bread crumbs.

Tales from the Front

Everyone who keeps a feeding station has their own tales of battle, and some of them are downright incredible. Even I have a hard time believing some of the squirrel antics I've witnessed, and I was there!

One early winter morning after a fresh snow, I watched two squirrels cooperate to drag away an entire plastic bag of corn on the cob—10 pounds'

Cunning squirrels will put their wits to work to outsmart your antisquirrel tactics. A tube feeder with metal guards will at least slow their seed consumption.

worth. Each squirrel had a corner of the bag in its teeth, and they dragged it between them as if pulling a sled over snow. How they split up the spoils, I don't know, but I did find the empty sack in the woods, far behind the house and up a steep hill.

I have watched squirrels vacuum up a tray feeder of sunflower seeds in less than half an hour—and as far as I could tell, there were only four of them working at it. I have watched squirrels leap outward a distance of 12 feet (I measured), attempting to reach a peanut feeder. They completed the jump by wriggling violently in midair to throw their bodies upward at the end of the arc. I have seen squirrels launch an aerial attack on a feeder, misjudge a landing, fall from a branch 20 feet off the ground, and scamper off, none the worse for wear.

My favorite squirrel feat stars one determined creature who inched his way *upside down* along 30 feet of skinny-wire wash line to reach a feeder hanging in the center of it. Naturally I had no camera to record that acrobatic stunt and no binoculars handy to see how he managed to grip the wire while supporting his body weight beneath it. Sometimes it still seems unbelievable.

Such tales fill the annals of bird feeding, which is one reason why many of us choose to live with squirrels rather than without them. They're too much fun to watch to give it up over the cost of a few extra bags of birdseed.

Like other species, the fox squirrel may spend an hour or more dining. Birds shy away from a squirrel-occupied feeder; offer them alternative feeding sites.

Nasty Habits

Squirrels do have a dark side. Those strong rodent teeth just love to chew through plastic tube feeders to get at the seeds inside. Along with chewing feeders to smithereens, they may also enlarge the entrance holes of birdhouses to turn them into cozy squirrel shelters for the long winter nights. (A metal entrance guard will keep them out.)

Squirrels can consume enormous amounts of birdseed and other feeder treats. Although they are often willing to eat peaceably beside birds, the presence of the animal in the feeder is enough to keep away most of the regulars. Once a squirrel arrives, it's often there for the long haul. It sits quietly in the feeder, snacking through seeds for an hour or more

---

Chip off the Block

FOR AN easy way to feed squirrels, chipmunks, and other close-to-the-ground animals, try a block of birdseed. These all-in-one feasts come in a hefty size that holds several pounds of seed and nuts in a large, tightly compressed block. It's fun to watch the animals nibble at their favorite morsels in the block, and it slows consumption and saves bird feeders from squirrel visits. Cardinals, jays, and other birds may also visit the feeder-in-a-block when squirrels are taking a temporary break.

S

Friend of the Forest

THE ACTIVITIES of squirrels play a huge role in the health of our forests. These animals believe in saving for a rainy day, so to speak, so they bury their nuts and seeds in the soil to retrieve later, when stores are running low. Often they overlook a hickory nut, an acorn, or other seed, which sprouts the next season into a seedling tree. Along with jays, which also bury food, squirrels are the chief natural reforesters of our native woodlands.

If you host squirrels in your yard, you will often discover many squirrel-planted trees springing up after winter cold subsides. I let these seedlings grow if they fit well in my landscaping scheme. They mature faster than transplanted nursery-grown trees, with oaks reaching 4 feet tall in just 3 years or so and nut trees growing even faster. Although it will take years for the young trees to bear a crop, the trees provide valuable cover for birds and often host a bounty of insects for bird food. Native tree species, including sweetgum (*Liquidambar styraciflua*), walnuts (*Juglans* spp.), and wild cherries (*Prunus* spp.) even when young, also provide vital home sites for the caterpillars of giant moths, such as the gorgeous luna and the huge cecropia.

before it's had enough and moves on—only to make way for the next squirrel in line.

Squirrels live in cavities or in leafy nests. But once in a while, an intrepid individual may take up residence in your house or use your attic as personal storage space for its winter cache of nuts and seeds. One autumn, I thought for sure I had ghosts in my attic—and they apparently had a bowling league going in full swing. My ghosts turned out to be squirrels rolling black walnuts across the attic floor. Of course, the furry fellows couldn't stay; the bowling was bad enough, but squirrels also may gnaw on the insulation of electric wires, a little habit that can start a house fire. I evicted mine with the aid of a live trap baited with peanut butter and then took measures to screen or otherwise seal up any openings that might grant them readmission to my attic.

Far worse than their gluttony at the feeder is their appetite for birds. Tree-dwelling squirrels are notorious for the havoc they wreak on nesting birds, devouring eggs and nestlings at will, and parent birds when they can grab them. One study estimated that a single red squirrel may eat 200 birds a year. Before you start casting an evil glare toward your local squirrels, remember that these creatures are part of nature's checks and balances. They're just doing what comes naturally.

It is we humans, with our destruction and alteration of wild habitat, that have pushed songbirds to the danger point. With fewer numbers of birds around, the destruction wrought by squirrels takes on a more ominous weight. We can't eliminate all the dangers birds face. But we can do our part to provide nesting habitat on

SQUIRREL FEEDER FOODS

- Acorns
- Amelanchier (*Amelanchier* spp.) berries
- Apples
- Blackberries, raspberries, and other small fruits
- Bread and other baked goods
- Buckeyes (*Aesculus* spp.)
- Cereal
- Chestnuts (*Castanea* spp.)
- Corn, any kind
- Crackers
- Dried peas and beans
- Eggs, hard-boiled or scrambled
- Holly (*Ilex* spp.) berries
- Leftovers
- Leftover "trail mix" snacks
- Meat scraps
- Nuts, any kind
- Peanut butter
- Peanuts
- Pine nuts (*Pinus cembroides*)
- Suet
- Sunflower seeds

our property and keep birds thriving with nutritious foods.

Squirrels themselves face fatal encounters with other menaces of civilization: cars and cats. Hawks and owls also help keep them in check, as does hunting in wild places. In backyards, there's not much you can do to get rid of squirrels. Live trapping works, but moving the squirrel to an unfamiliar territory only passes along the predator and confuses the squirrel that you dump in an unfamiliar area. We can only hope that squirrels and birds manage to regain a balance that keeps both kinds of animals thriving for generations to come.

If You Can't Beat 'Em . . .

I gave up on trying to keep squirrels away from my feeders a long time ago. Once I learned that all I had to do was give them their own setup stocked with corn and the occasional sunflower seed handout, I called a truce. Where else can you get so much entertainment for such a small investment?

Of course, now and then a greedier—or smarter—individual comes along, who refuses to stay where he belongs and moves into the bird feeders instead. I usually put up with the thievery for a while, then make a concerted effort to shoo Mr. Squirrel away from the no-trespassing area. If my madwoman dashes, accompanied by clapping hands and loud shouts, don't do the trick, I move the bird feeders within the fence that holds my dogs. Squirrels don't dare tread there.

To reach your bird feeders, squirrels will undertake feats that a ringmaster might describe as "death-defying." Grab a window seat and enjoy the show!

See Ya, Squirrels

A dog is your best weapon against squirrels, unless the bushy-tails learn that Rover can't reach them. If that happens, they seem to take pleasure in taunting the poor pet as he lunges below them, barking frantically. But the presence of a dog will definitely make squirrels think twice about treating your yard as their own private nature preserve.

Many manufacturers sell squirrel-proof feeders. Some designs attempt to exclude the animals by

---

Don't Kill Them with Kindness

IN MY small town, where almost every block holds at least one squirrel corn feeder, the squirrels often battle the bulge. They put on weight quickly once we stock our feeders in the fall, at first looking lovely and sleek as they fill out from their usual skinny selves. But soon their overindulgence shows.

The extra weight eventually hinders their movements, and they aren't nearly as nimble as they were when lean and rangy.

This is bad news for the squirrels, and in winter the population drops dramatically once hawks and cats discover the easy pickings. Many of the unathletic individuals also fall victim to cars, whose drivers expect them to scamper out of the way with the

same speed they exhibited in their summer prime.

If the squirrels were wild woods dwellers instead of tame town squirrels, they would probably burn the extra calories in their daily forays around the forest. But here, it seems, their only activity is getting from nest to feeder and back again. Perhaps what we need now is a low-fat corn cultivar, just for feeding sedentary city squirrels.

dropping a lid when a heavy visitor lands on the feeder. My squirrels outwitted one model of this type by reaching from above for the seeds. I have switched to all-metal tube feeders, after one too many plastic models yielded to squirrel teeth. Tube feeders with metal guards at the seed slots may also deter them from gnawing their way in.

Conical or dome-shaped baffles also slow squirrels down. At first, your squirrels will look as if they're at an amusement park, as they slip and slide over the baffle, trying to reach the feeder it protects. I use baffles to discourage squirrels from most of my hanging and post-mounted feeders. While it may not stop them completely, it makes them work for their food and they return more readily to the squirrel-feeding area, leaving the birds alone.

The newest development in the antisquirrel battle is seed treated with hot-pepper extract. The great news is that it works. The bad news is that it costs more than untreated seed, although prices will probably drop as more suppliers get into the game. I've experimented recently with a homemade version of the commercial products (see "Chemical Warfare" on this page), and it also seems to be effective.

Meet the Squirrels

Growing up in eastern Pennsylvania, I thought the gray squirrels in our woods and backyards were the only squirrels that existed. Then I discovered that the **gray squirrel** is just one of the arboreal, or tree-dwelling species. The feisty **red squirrel** of the Northeast and Great Lakes areas is another arboreal species, as are the **Fremont's squirrel** of the Rockies and the wonderfully named **Douglas' chickaree**, a rusty red fellow of Pacific conifer forests. Even the gray squirrel has western relatives: the **western gray squirrel**, which has a broader tail than the eastern species, and the perky long-eared **Abert's squirrel** and its subspecies, the **Kaibab squirrel**. Some color variations keep gray squirrels interesting. In isolated regions, the squirrels may be so dark we call them black squirrels, or they may veer to the other extreme and become albino white squirrels.

Moving down from the trees, you'll find animals that spend much of their time at ground level,

---

Chemical Warfare

THE SUBSTANCE in hot peppers that makes your skin burn, your mouth breathe fire, and your eyes water furiously should you get it near them is capsaicin. Hot peppers vary in their levels of this naturally occurring compound, with the degree of heat being measured in Scoville Heat Units (SHUs). A fairly mild jalapeño pepper checks in at about 5,000 SHUs; a hotter-than-heck habanero leaps off the chart at 500,000 SHUs!

Since I had a bumper crop of hot-hot habaneros last year, I decided to experiment with treated feeder foods. I didn't bother with birdseed, which I don't mind sharing with the squirrels. But I did want to protect my stockpile of nutmeats and whole peanuts, which birds treasure, because I feed them in small amounts that squirrels quickly wipe out.

My experiment was very simple. Wearing rubber gloves to protect my hands, I tossed about a dozen ripe peppers into a gallon of water and let it sit for two days. Then I poured some of the firewater into a recycled pump-spray bottle. Out of curiosity, I made the mistake of dipping my finger in and taking a lick, just to see how hot it was. Whoo-ee!

Now that I knew I had bottled fire, I spread 5 pounds of walnut meats on a window screen and spritzed them with the pepper solution. I was very careful not to touch my hands to my eyes or risk any other exposure to my skin because these babies burn. The nuts dried quickly in the sun. I turned them with a spatula and sprayed the other side. When the nuts were thoroughly dry, I scooped them into plastic resealable bags for storage (still wearing gloves). The bags make it easy to pour out the nuts without touching them.

At feeding time, the nuts entice the squirrels but the confused critters soon retreat, rubbing their faces and shaking their heads. The birds don't seem to notice any difference.

The red squirrel is a smaller species with a bad temper. Fights erupt frequently among red squirrels; gray squirrels that trespass are swiftly driven away.

A cob of dry corn on a spike pleases this gray squirrel and keeps it out of the bird feeder. Woodpeckers and jays may share the corn when the squirrel is away.

although they also climb trees. In western campgrounds, I met the friendly **rock squirrels,** which are chubbier and slower moving than tree squirrels. **Ground squirrels** are similar to chipmunks, and some have similarly striped backs. Here in southern Indiana, the most abundant squirrel is the **fox squirrel,** a beauty with a tawny golden belly and tail. Nonarboreal squirrels seem to be tamer than those that roam the treetops, or maybe they simply spend less time in the frenetic activity of scurrying and leaping. **Flying squirrels** (see that entry on page 128) are the nocturnal replacement for the daytime tribe.

All squirrels are nut and seed eaters. Their diet varies, depending on what's available where they live. Those that reside in conifer forests fill their bellies with the seeds of cones from pines, Douglas fir, hemlocks, and other evergreens. In deciduous woodlands or mixed forests, acorns, beechnuts, hickories, and other meaty nuts are also mainstays on the menu. Farm fields and game plots provide some squirrels with a big part of their food, including corn and wheat.

Squirrels also eat fruit, particularly wild species like blackberry, mulberry (*Morus* spp.), wild grapes, and amelanchiers (*Amelanchier* spp.), and the berries of dogwood (*Cornus* spp.), black gum (*Nyssa sylvatica*), and other trees and shrubs.

At the feeder, squirrels will devour just about anything you serve them, though they will dine on their natural foods first. Put out corn and peanuts, and you'll have squirrel friends forever.

Squirrel Behavior

Squirrels are easy to observe. They are large, active creatures, and they quickly become semi-tame around the feeder. Enjoy their antics as they attempt to reach off-limit feeders or snack at the squirrel station. Because squirrels often sport *(continued on page 274)*

A Box for Munchies

This hinged box lets you serve squirrels their favorite treats in a hopper protected from the elements. When the squirrel wants a snack, it uses its hands or head to lift the lid and take a sample. Stock the munch box with whole peanuts, acorns, nuts in the shell, or other treats.

MATERIALS

1 × 6 lumber, cut to the dimensions shown

Plexiglas, cut to the dimensions shown

Nails

2 hinges

Step 1. Cut ⅛-inch grooves 1 inch from the short end of the sides to serve as channels for the Plexiglas.

Step 2. With the grooves vertical at what will be the front of the box and facing inward, nail the floor to the sides.

Step 3. Nail the back to the sides and floor. Nail the second back to the first one.

Step 4. Attach the lid at the rear by the hinges.

Step 5. Slide the Plexiglas into the grooves in the sides.

Step 6. Nail the finished box to a tree or post.

Step 7. Fill with peanuts and other squirrel treats.

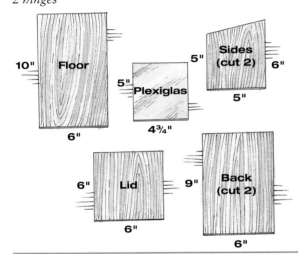

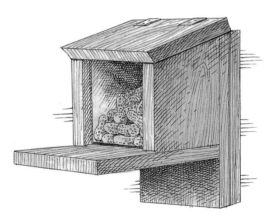

Squirrel-Friendly Mix

Serve up this crunchy mix in a squirrel-operated munch box or in an open tray feeder and it might keep the squirrels so busy that they leave your bird feeders to the birds! Of course, when squirrels aren't around, birds will drop in to nibble on the sunflower seeds and shelled nuts.

INGREDIENTS

4 parts whole-kernel dried corn

2 parts peanuts in the shell

2 parts striped or black sunflower seeds

2 parts walnuts, in shell

1 part shelled peanuts

1 part small dry beans, such as navy beans

1 part walnut, almond, or pecan pieces

Measure ingredients into metal pretzel can or large metal popcorn tin. Stir to combine. Replace lid tightly after filling your squirrel-friendly feeders.

distinguishing characteristics—a ratty tail, a fat belly, a white forehead star—you may soon be able to identify some of the troupe. Recognizing individuals will give you a more personal connection to the varmints.

I like to keep sketches of squirrel "tail language." Squirrels use these fluffy appendages to signal all kinds of communications, from danger to aggression to playfulness. Squirrels are great game players, often indulging in an apparent game of tag with as much abandon as a bunch of 7-year-old kids. They chase each other up and down trees, across the ground, and in and out of rock and brush piles. Plenty of trash talk accompanies such games. Listen for "chirrs," rattles, and barking cries.

During courtship and mating season, usually in fall to late winter, squirrel games take on a new seriousness. The promiscuous males attempt to run down any female they see, and battles between suitors are intense.

The list of favored feeder offerings is a long one for squirrels; most will try anything you serve. Inexpensive whole corn is a staple, as are sunflower seeds. They are fond of fresh water, too. A low-level pool or dish is easiest for them to reach, but they will also visit a pedestal birdbath.

Starling

STARLINGS ARE CERTAINLY A NUISANCE. They're noisy, they gobble up feeder food like gluttons, they travel in crowds, their bathroom habits are none too delicate, and they aren't even pretty. Worse yet, they outcompete cavity-nesting flickers and other native birds for prime real estate in dead trees and bird boxes.

That's the bad news.

The good news is that starlings are extremely useful at controlling another imported pest, the Japanese beetle, which makes lacework out of your grapevines and devours your rosebuds before they open. They eat both adults and larvae, stabbing into the soil with their dagger beaks to extract the plump grubs. The starling's destruction of weevils, cutworms, and other beetles and their larvae also helps polish the starling reputation.

Starlings are clever and interesting, once you begin observing them with a more tolerant eye. And, though they do engage in shrieking contests, they also have a pretty, gurgling love song. Although often dismissed as plain or even ugly, starlings have an understated beauty, with their plumage decorated with a delicate pattern of creamy white "stars" in winter and an iridescent sheen in spring. Starlings can help predict when spring is coming or winter nears, as their beak changes color with the seasons.

Imported from overseas 100 years ago, starlings are here to stay. Although messy and loud, they're not all bad, as they consume their fair share of insect pests.

Welcome to America

Starlings are not American natives, and they are not "blackbirds." They belong to the myna or starling family and originally hail from Eurasia, where they have been just as pestiferous and just as useful as they are in America. In the late 1800s, starlings saved the day when they descended in enormous numbers to contain a potentially disastrous outbreak of the spruce moth in Bavaria. A couple of decades later, they descended like "black clouds" on Swiss vineyards, stripping the vines bare of fruit.

Eugene Scheifflin performed the first successful introduction of starlings from 1890 to 1891 in Central Park, New York. Like the alien house sparrow, starlings quickly found their niche in this country, settling into cities and countryside, usually living close to humans.

Bluebirds, flickers, great crested flycatchers, purple martins, house wrens, and other woodpeckers have all suffered loss of nest sites thanks to starlings. The house-hunting starling stands by while the other birds do the work of carving out a home, then make a determined move to oust the original dwellers. Thanks to birdhouses with custom-size holes that exclude the larger starlings, we can help provide suitable homes for nearly all of the starling-displaced birds. Flickers, larger woodpeckers, and the great crested flycatcher, however, must still battle the interlopers. Because of their size, these bigger birds are often successful in ejecting the starling squatters. However, it's often an ongoing battle, with another starling ready to slide in when the nest defender discourages the first.

In winter, the starling shows why it bears that name. Each feather is tipped with a tiny chevron of pale yellow, which gives the body a star-spangled look.

Starling Behavior

These rowdy, ungainly looking birds lack the svelteness and delicacy of many songbirds, and even a few starlings make quite an impact on your food supply as they scarf down seeds and monopolize suet feeders and soft foods. Basically, the birds are gluttons. (See the Nuisance Birds entry on page 217 for tips on discouraging them from interfering with your feeding station.)

Starlings usually forage on the ground for their natural food, but I serve them in higher tray feeders so the leftovers don't attract vermin. At night, they gather in huge communal roosting

STARLING FEEDER FOODS			
■ Apple peelings	■ Cereal	■ Holly (*Ilex* spp.) berries	■ Milo (*Sorghum bicolor*)
■ Birdseed mix	■ Corn, cracked	■ Leftovers	■ Pasta, cooked
■ Bones, to clean off bits of meat or marrow	■ Crackers	■ Meat scraps	■ Raisins
	■ Dog food	■ Millets (*Panicum* spp. and other genera)	■ Suet
■ Bread and other baked goods	■ Fruit		■ Wheats (*Triticum* spp.)

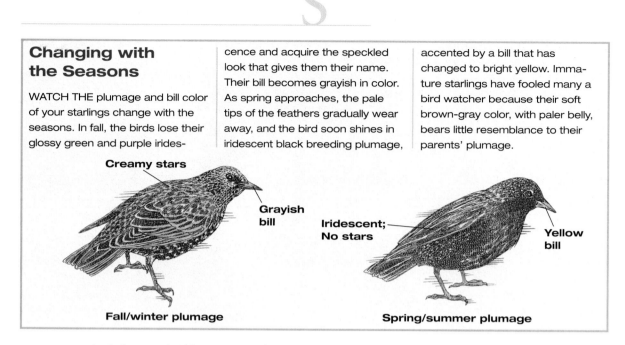

Changing with the Seasons

WATCH THE plumage and bill color of your starlings change with the seasons. In fall, the birds lose their glossy green and purple irides- cence and acquire the speckled look that gives them their name. Their bill becomes grayish in color. As spring approaches, the pale tips of the feathers gradually wear away, and the bird soon shines in iridescent black breeding plumage, accented by a bill that has changed to bright yellow. Imma- ture starlings have fooled many a bird watcher because their soft brown-gray color, with paler belly, bears little resemblance to their parents' plumage.

Creamy stars

Grayish bill

Fall/winter plumage

Iridescent; No stars

Yellow bill

Spring/summer plumage

groups to seek shelters on buildings, in conifers, or other protected sites.

Listen for the warbling courtship songs of star- lings, which usually start up in late winter. Some birds may also mimic barking dogs, crows, and other birds as well as inanimate objects like a squeaking door.

To their credit, starlings also protect themselves and other birds from foraging raptors. Should a hawk appear at your feeding station, starlings will rush to the attack. They form a tight group around the flying bird, mobbing it with a mass escort that is apparently so annoying that the hawk soon flies elsewhere.

Storing Seed

PUT SOME THOUGHT INTO WHERE you will store your seed supplies because you'll be visiting them frequently—probably every morning during the busy fall and winter feeding seasons. When choosing a storage location, look for a site that meets these criteria:

- **Close to feeders and close to house.** Every step counts when it's cold or raining.

- **Easy to clean.** Spills are a frequent occurrence; keep a dustpan and broom handy.

- **Out of reach of deer, raccoons, and squirrels.** You don't want your seed devoured before you get it to the feeders.

- **Away from human food.** Keep possible grain pests, such as meal moths, from infiltrating your pantry.

- **As cool as possible.** Oils in seed can turn rancid in hot weather; metal containers heat up fast if placed in direct sun.

- **Dry.** Moldy seed is a waste of money.

An unheated garage is an ideal spot for seed storage. It's under cover, convenient to feeders and your house, and protected from larger animals.

Storage Containers

A metal can with a tight-fitting lid is the best con- tainer for storing birdseed, corn, and other dry feeder items. The metal provides an impenetrable barrier to the hungry teeth of mice and other rodents, and the lid keeps out insects and animals bent on pilfering from your supply.

If you keep only small amounts of seed on hand, a pretzel or popcorn tin will work well. For storing seed in bulk, a metal trash can is ideal. I usually keep my big bags of seed in the larger can, and I use the smaller can for keeping 1 or 2 days' supply of birdseed at the ready. My birdseed "pantry" actually holds a few smaller cans, in which I keep my own custom seed mixes for restocking various feeders. One holds a mix of black oil sunflower and safflower—my "cardinal blend"; another holds millet, grass seed, canary seed, and niger—my "finch magnet" mix. A third can stores peanuts in the shell, plus whole kernel corn, nuts in their shells collected from the wild, and acorns—that's the "squirrel treat" can. A fourth can keeps auxiliary bird supplies at the ready: a giant jar of peanut butter, a sack of cornmeal, bags of raisins and stale bread, and, in winter, a few extra suet balls ready to hang. I also keep a large plastic mixing bowl and a supply of disposable wooden paint stirrers in the can for stirring up concoctions with these ingredients, a job that's swift and less messy outdoors than at the kitchen table.

Protect your precious seed supplies from insects, mice, other unmentionable rodents, and moisture by storing them in a metal container with a tight-fitting lid.

I label the cans with waterproof black marker on a strip of masking tape across the lid, so that I don't waste time fumbling to see what's what at morning refill time. Just to make sure I don't confuse my seed mixes, I also stick a label across the can itself in case I mix up the lids.

Strawberries

Attract catbirds, mockingbirds, robins, thrashers

IT'S HARD TO KEEP BIRDS AWAY from strawberries in the garden. Those juicy red fruits peeking from beneath the leaves are just too tempting. So use that appeal to lure fruit-eating birds such as catbirds, mockingbirds, robins, and thrashers by planting strawberries (*Fragaria* spp.) wherever you can squeeze them in: Use them as an edging along a driveway or walkway, as groundcover around a birdbath, or as a border at the front of your flowerbeds or birdseed gardens.

Birds aren't particular about what variety of strawberry you plant. Their sharp beaks can easily nip a slice out of even the biggest strawberry, while small wild (*F. vesca*) or alpine strawberries (*F. montana fraga*) go down the hatch whole. Select a variety that thrives in your area and is disease-resistant. Or locate native wild strawberries at a specialty nursery. Order your strawberry plants early from a catalog for the best selection of your favorite varieties. Plant the bareroot plants as soon as they arrive in spring, following the directions included in the package. Or buy plants in early spring at local nurseries; they are usually sold in bareroot bundles. Plant so that the growing tip of the plant, from which the leaves will emerge, is above ground. After the ground freezes in the fall, cover your strawberry bed with several inches of hay or straw mulch for winter protection. Remove the mulch in the spring before the plants begin to grow. Strawberry plants send out runners from the parent plant in subsequent seasons. Expand your planting by slicing off the plantlets at the ends of the runners and transplanting them.

You can save strawberries for later bird feeding by drying them. (If you don't grow your own, buy berries in bulk at the height of the season when prices are low.) Slice the berries and dry them on cookie sheets in the sun, turning the slices occasionally. Cover the drying fruits with a layer of cheesecloth or a piece of window screen to keep the birds from enjoying their treat early. Store dried berries in a jar or in resealable bags in a cool, dry place. In fall and winter, when your feeders are hopping with hungry birds, you can add the dried berries to birdseed mixes or other recipes for a real treat for fruit-loving birds.

Birds like strawberries as much as we do—maybe more. Squeeze in a few plants wherever you can find room—along a sidewalk, as a groundcover, or in a container on the patio.

Quick and Easy Strawberry Pancakes for Birds

Blackbirds, bluebirds, doves, grackles, jays, mockingbirds, robins, starlings, and others may arrive for this special breakfast treat.

INGREDIENTS

1 cup dried strawberries, chopped into small pieces*

Pancake mix to make 10–12 pancakes, prepared as directed on package

Stir dried strawberry pieces into pancake batter. Pour into hot, lightly oiled skillet until bottom of pan is almost completely covered. Cook over medium heat until bubbles appear. Flip pancakes; cook other side until lightly browned. Remove to plate; cool. Repeat until all batter is used.

Using a sharp knife, slice across each pancake at about 1-inch intervals. Rotate plate one-half turn and repeat, so that you end up with small, 1-inch-wide sections of cooked pancake. Serve pancake sections and any crumbs in an open tray feeder or directly on the ground.

*Fresh or thawed frozen strawberries will also work just fine in this recipe. They're a lot juicier than dried berries, which means you'll need to reduce the amount of water you add to the batter by one-third or so. An interesting side effect: Strawberry juice makes pink pancakes!

Suet and Fat

Attract many kinds of birds

ADDING A SUET FEEDER to your bird-supply station is one of the best investments you will make. The ready-made wire baskets sold in bird-supply stores, discount chains, and hardware stores cost only $5 or so, and the suet to fill them adds only another dollar to the cost. A constant stream of chickadees, jays, nuthatches, titmice, and woodpeckers jockeying for a bite of their favorite food will reward you. You may also get unexpected visitors, including bluebirds, catbirds, kinglets, mockingbirds, and yellow-rumped warblers. Resurrect Grandma's meat grinder to turn chunks of suet or beef fat into the hamburger-like "worms" that these birds adore, maybe because they look like the grubs and caterpillars on their natural menu. Cardinals, juncos, native sparrows, and other birds will eagerly consume any bits that fall to the ground. To make it easier for low-level eaters, I drill a 2-inch-diameter, ½-inch-deep cavity just above ground level in my wood feeder posts to accommodate a few dabs of the prized fat.

Birds favor all types of fat including greasy drippings in your roasting pan, trimmings from the supermarket, and prepackaged blocks of suet that slide neatly into a feeder. You may even spy woodpeckers and other birds working away at the carcasses of deer and other roadkill, although that option is one you won't want to include at the feeder.

Preventing Pests

The major drawback to suet is that it is also one of the favorite foods of starlings, crows, raccoons, and cats. If you prefer not to feed every suet

"Suet" is used to include other animal fat, which birds like just as well. Beef fat trimmings cost less than pure kidney-fat suet and are available at any meat counter.

eater in the neighborhood, the solution is simple, though a little more costly. Pest-proof feeders that allow access only to desirable birds are widely available through catalogs such as those listed in "Resources" on page 348 or on the shelves at bird-supply stores.

Because I like to feed any hungry bird or animal that comes along, I supply suet and fat in abundance. Wire feeders are at many locations in my yard, and in winter my shrubs and trees take on a festive air, thanks to my collection of homemade red mesh-covered suet balls hanging from their branches. A few hanging, horizontal sections of log, drilled with holes underneath to stuff suet into round out my suet stations. These log feeders are easily accessible to acrobatic woodpeckers, nuthatches, and brown creepers, but not to starlings, which leave them alone in favor of suet offerings that are easier for them to reach.

PROJECT

Bark Slab Sandwich Feeder

Recently, an interesting new pest-proof feeder has come on the market. Although it is synthetic, it looks very much like two slabs of natural bark with a narrow slit between, which you can fill with fat, peanut butter, or other treats. Woodpeckers, with their long bills and longer tongues, have no trouble clinging to the feeder and reaching into the crevice for the fat.

You can duplicate this feeder easily by visiting a sawmill and buying a couple of slices of bark backed by a thin layer of wood. Screw the slabs together at top and bottom corners and add a wire handle for hanging. To prevent the suet from falling out at the bottom, stuff the bottom of the crack with a wood shim.

MATERIALS

2 trimmed bark slabs, about 6 × 12 inches

4 long bolts and nuts to fit them

Plastic tubing to fit over bolts

Wood shim

Wire for hanging

Step 1. Drill a hole in each corner of both bark slabs.

Step 2. Insert bolts through holes in one slab; slip a ½-inch piece of plastic tubing over each to hold space between the slabs.

Step 3. Run the bolts through the holes in the other slab and secure with nuts.

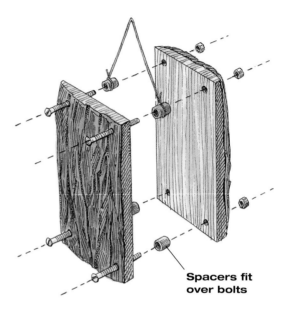

Spacers fit over bolts

Step 4. Wrap wire around the two bolts/spacers on one end to create a hanger.

Step 5. Push the shim into the opposite end between the slabs to keep the suet from falling out the bottom.

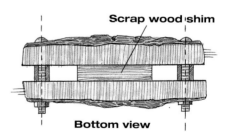

Scrap wood shim

Bottom view

Step 6. Stuff the spaces between the slabs on the sides with suet or peanut butter.

Step 7. Hang the finished feeder.

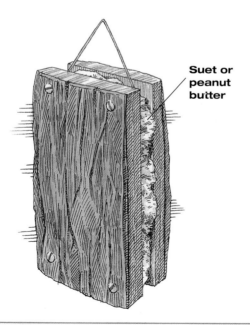

Suet or peanut butter

How to Buy Suet

Prepackaged slabs, wrapped in plastic and purified so they stay fresh for a long time are the most convenient form of suet. At about a dollar or two apiece, they are a great buy, lasting for several weeks in the feeder, depending on the traffic.

Because I feed lots of fat to my birds, I buy beef trimmings from the supermarket, too, stockpiling them in the freezer so that I always have a good supply on hand. Ask at your local meat counter for beef trimmings, and you may get the precious fat for free or quite cheaply. Some butchers will grind the fat for you if you ask, which makes it easier to include in recipes or offer to birds that have a hard time clinging to wire feeders, such as bluebirds and native sparrows.

You may also be able to buy pure suet, which is the layer of fat that covers an animal's kidneys, from the butcher. Since this is more expensive than just plain old fat, I usually don't bother with it, although birds welcome it.

You can also pour bacon grease, beef drippings, or other melted fat into washed cat food or tuna cans for quick fat feeding. I save my cooking fats in a large coffee can in the refrigerator so that I can prepare feeders when I have a convenient amount of grease. It stays soft enough to scoop out with a spoon.

How to Feed Suet and Fat

There's no need to melt the suet or fat before offering it to birds. If you're working with true suet or beef trimmings, just slice off chunks or strips with a

> Use a meat grinder to turn suet chunks or beef fat into "worms" that birds gobble up just like live worms.

stout chef's knife and fill your containers. I save the plastic mesh bags from onions for instant suet feeders: Just fill the empty mesh bag with fat, tie the top closed, and hang from a branch, hook, or nail.

Most suet feeders hang near our eye level, but many ground-feeding birds also like some fat in their diets. To accommodate these guests, I feed ground or chopped suet in a tray feeder near ground level.

Small, shallow cans left over from cat food or tuna are time-honored bases for suet feeders. Punch a hole in the can with a nail and attach a wire for hanging, then fill with melted suet, let it solidify, and hang.

To keep my throngs of wintertime starlings occupied, I also feed the largest chunks of fat I can find. I put these hunks of fat in a feeder away from the main feeder area, but in a place where I can watch the action. It's fun to watch them peck and pull at the offering. When hunger and the presence of other birds drive crows to investigate my feeders, they also like the big chunks of fat at the starling area.

Added Ingredients

Some of the products marketed for birds have more appeal to those that feed them than to the birds themselves. You'll find suet blocks with fruit, suet with nuts, and suet with seed offered for sale. Sounds

---

Greasy Bird Stuff

FEED SOFTER fats, such as meat drippings and bacon grease that you have accumulated, by spreading the stuff onto a rough piece of bark. Don't try this trick on porch posts or living trees: The grease creates an unsightly stain. A local sawmill can supply a thin piece of wood with bark still on, or you can use a rough-cut wood shingle called a shake. Even a rough-cut piece of 2 × 6 board will do the trick. If the surface of the wood is too slick for the fat to adhere to, collect fallen pieces of bark from your trees and staple them into place for a more textured surface. You can also spread soft suet into a corner of a wooden tray feeder, if you don't mind grease stains. Smear some fat low on the wood post near ground level for juncos and sparrows. If you'd prefer something other than this sort of "smear" campaign, use the grease to moisten leftover cereal, crushed crackers, or small bits of bread. See the Cereal entry on page 58 for tips on which types of cereal work well for this feeding method. Offer the resulting food mix in a tray feeder.

tempting, especially when it's marked with a label like "Suet for Bluebirds" or "Suet for Orioles." Feel free to experiment with such specialties, but be aware that suet alone is enough of a draw to attract all kinds of birds without other enticements. Once a bluebird discovers your suet feeder, it will return again and again whether or not peanuts or other tidbits enhance the fat. The presence of the additives won't make birds come to the feeder any sooner than they would otherwise.

Steer clear of suet that includes birdseed mix, such as millet and other small seeds. The main customers for fat do not eat these seeds, and the ground-feeding birds that do eat the seeds don't visit suet cages. Also, birds can get their feathers greasy if they try to reach in for the seeds, which may affect the vital insulation properties of their plumage.

I prefer to save my special treats for use in recipes with ground or chopped suet, not melted fat. In an impromptu test I tried, I filled a wire suet feeder in a new location with a block of suet sold specifically to entice bluebirds. Then I filled a new tray feeder next to it with a fast mix of chopped suet, raisins, and chopped peanuts that I squeezed with my hands into a loose loaf. The bluebirds ignored the "bluebird block" and flocked to my homemade mixture along with a catbird, robins, and Carolina wrens. After 2 weeks of regular forays, the bluebirds still hadn't tried the suet cage, perhaps because of the frequent visits of chickadees, nuthatches, titmice, and woodpeckers, who apparently didn't know they were feasting on fat for bluebirds.

Benefits of Feeding Fat

The reason suet is so popular as a bird food is that it is pure fat, and that means lots of calories to fuel the high-speed metabolism of your feathered guests. Suet and fat are ideal foods for winter feeding when high-calorie foods are vital to keep birds cozy through the long, cold nights. The smaller the bird, the faster its body burns calories. The time a bird spends at a suet feeder provides an excellent ratio of energy expended to calories consumed. Compared to the expense in energy of foraging in

A mesh bag filled with fat chunks makes a fine feeder as far as these pygmy nuthatches are concerned. If raccoons are a problem, serve fat in pest-resistant metal cages.

the wild and flitting from tree to tree or from field to hedgerow, sitting at a suet feeder is as close to being a couch potato as it gets in the bird world.

Summer Suet Feeding

The peak of customers occurs in winter, but suet and fat are popular all year. In spring and autumn, they attract migrants such as flickers and yellow-bellied sapsuckers as well as resident birds. In summer, parent birds often select these soft foods for their nestlings and fledglings. Keep a suet feeder up in summer, and you're apt to receive a visit by a family of fuzzy-headed chickadees, nuthatches, or titmice. If you see a bird take a beakful of fat and fly away instead of swallowing it on the spot, watch to see where it goes. You may discover a nest, or even better, a lineup of adorable juveniles on a nearby branch.

Suet and fat can melt quickly in the heat of summer. This is the time when feeding purified blocks makes sense. Commercial suet blocks are very slow to melt or turn rancid in warm weather. If you're feeding your own collection of fats, keep the offerings small, so that the stuff stays palatable. Move feeders to the shade or keep them out of direct sun to slow the melting. For a more solid, slower-melting product, heat fat and suet over low heat on the stove, discard the bottom layer of particles in the pan, and use only the top layer to fill feeders.

Beef trimmings can look pretty disgusting after they sit for a while in warm weather: They turn gray or black and may shrivel. Despite the unappealing appearance, birds will continue to visit as long as they can uncover a bit of fresh white fat. When the offering is no more than an empty shell, pitch it and replace with fresh fat.

RECIPE

Better'n Bug Eggs

This combination provides plenty of protein and fat. It also offers a dollop of carbohydrates. If you can get ant eggs or mealworms, add them to the mix. All suet-eating birds will gobble it up. Serve in a tray feeder for best visibility.

INGREDIENTS

5 cups unseasoned bread crumbs

5 cups hulled sunflower seed pieces

1½ cups fine-chopped or ground suet

1½ cups hamburger (high fat, not lean, is best!)

1½ cups raisins, dried berries, dried cherries, dried figs, or dried apples, chopped (a mix is fine)

Mix with hands (wear rubber kitchen gloves if desired) until all ingredients are well combined. Spread a small amount in tray feeder. Call birds for dinner.

Suet Feeders

SUET IS A REASONABLE FACSIMILE of natural insect food, which is why it's such a favorite of chickadees, nuthatches, titmice, woodpeckers, wrens, and other bug-eating birds. When you add suet feeders to your yard, you'll soon notice that these wire cages and mesh-covered bags are almost constantly in demand.

It's interesting to note the various suet-eating styles of different birds: While high-energy chickadees and other small birds tend to dart in, snatch a beakful, and dart out, woodpeckers are much more slow and deliberate in their undertaking. A single red-bellied woodpecker, for instance, may spend more than an hour quietly pecking away at the soft white fat.

Suet Strategies

Simple wire cages are an excellent way to serve suet. You can either slide in a preformed commercial

Wire cages for suet blocks are so convenient: Slip a block in the feeder and suet's on! Feeders with drilled holes take longer to refill but birds like them, too.

block, or stuff the cage yourself with chunks of fat from the butcher. The sturdy grid of wire protects the suet from being carried off whole by other feeder visitors, especially nocturnal prowlers like cats and coons. Suet cages are so inexpensive to buy (about $5) that you will save little money by attempting to duplicate them yourself. If, however, you come across an old-fashioned coated-wire soap dish at a yard sale, snap it up: Its design is very similar, and when nailed to a board or post, it will do a fine job of holding fat.

Some feeder designs incorporate a suet feeder at the side of the seed tray or hopper. I steer clear of combination feeders so that the suet eaters can have their favorite food all to themselves, without the interruptions of arriving and departing seed eaters.

If the traffic is heavy at your suet feeder, you may want to add more than one outpost for the food, or invest in a large-capacity suet feeder, which holds two or three preformed blocks, rather than just one.

Mesh Suet Feeders

Because suet is so popular, I save my mesh onion and potato bags year-round so that I can hang lots of minisuet feeders during the months of peak demand. You can stuff these strong plastic mesh bags with as much or as little suet or beef fat scraps as you like.

When I have some time to spare, I fill the bags with fat and fasten them tightly with a long twist-tie. I store the bags in my freezer, where they look like an arsenal of red snowballs, and pull them out whenever I want to give the birds a treat. Sometimes I hook these bags onto a nail or other hanger, and sometimes I hang them from a length of string attached to the branches of shrubs or trees.

I save one 5-pound mesh potato sack to make a giant-size suet bag to keep the starlings happy. It lasts for weeks. Given their own easy-access supply, the big birds stay away from other suet feeders where they have a harder time keeping their balance while eating. I hang the bag from a length of strong fishing line to prevent raccoons from demolishing it wholesale.

Suet Cups and Cans

I also serve suet and other fats in a collection of cat food and tuna cans. Once they're washed and their labels are removed, they make surprisingly attractive containers for the soft stuff. I nail the filled cans to a vertical board or wood post, pounding in a large nail partway so it can double as a perch. When the cans are empty, it takes just a minute to pull out the nail with a claw hammer, replace the empty can with a full one, and reset the nail.

Containers from yogurt, cottage cheese, sour cream, and other products also can be easily recycled into fat feeders. Melt suet or collect bacon grease or other meat drippings, cool, and pour into the containers. It will solidify into a delectable bird treat. Because these fats are softer than suet, they are best served in cold weather to prevent them from oozing out of containers mounted with the open side down to discourage starlings. Or you can mount the containers with open end up. I keep a board handy with nails driven through it as spikes, on which I can impale the fat-filled cups. This "feeder" doubles for fruit when my collection of meat grease is low.

One of my favorite impromptu suet containers is a jar lid. These shallow containers are perfect for two reasons: (1) You can fill them quickly with just a few tablespoons of melted fat, and (2) birds empty them quickly, so they're ideal for summer feeding when the fat disappears before it begins to drip. I raid my local recycling center for lids as well as saving my own from jars of coffee, peanut butter, and other staples. To turn a lid collection into a suet feeder, just nail the lids to a board in whatever configuration you like. Metal lids are getting harder to find, but plastic is just as utilitarian. I made a simple, 5-minute horizontal deck-rail suet feeder from a scrap of 2 × 4 and three snazzy red plastic lids nailed in a row. A heat-proof glass measuring cup makes it easy to pour the warm but not hot melted fat into the lids when it's time to refill.

Jar lids, tuna or cat food cans, yogurt cups, and other containers work well for serving up suet and bacon fat.

Anti-Starling Suet Feeder

Starlings are notorious suet lovers. If they begin hogging your feeders so that woodpeckers can't enjoy their favorite food, treat your less aggressive birds to a feeder designed to keep starlings at bay. The trick is simple: Instead of suet being held within easy reach for a perched bird, the fat is hidden on the underside of the feeder. Only birds with acrobatic skills need apply—and that means no starlings!

MATERIALS

Wire suet cage feeder

½-inch plywood

2-inch-wide furring strips

Staple gun and staples

Screw eye

Chain

Step 1. Measure a standard wire suet cage feeder. Make a sketch, marking the dimensions of the four sides and the bottom.

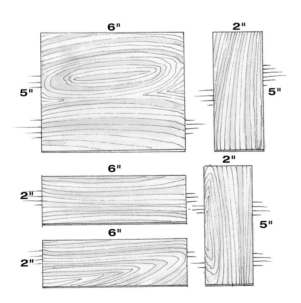

Step 2. Cut a piece of ½-inch plywood to the length and width of the suet cage bottom.

Step 3. Cut strips of 2-inch-wide wood furring strips to the length of the four sides.

Step 4. Staple the furring strips at the corners into an open box shape.

Step 5. Staple the plywood bottom to the firring strip frame.

Step 6. Insert the wire cage into the wooden box, making sure that the side that opens faces outward from the box.

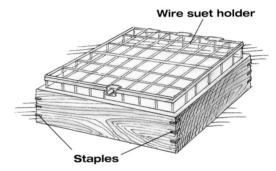

Step 7. Staple the cage to the walls of the frame. Staple the cage to the plywood bottom.

Step 8. Screw in a screw eye for hanging to the center of the plywood back. Attach the chain to the hook.

Step 9. Open the cage and insert the suet.

Step 10. Hang from the chain.

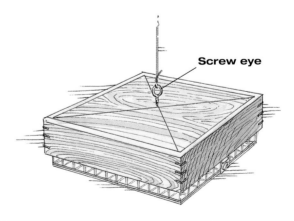

Sumac

Attracts more than 20 kinds of birds, from bluebirds to wrens to game birds

SUMACS (*RHUS SPP.*) GET SHORT SHRIFT in most home landscapes, probably because they're such common wild plants across the country that they become part of the background scenery, hardly drawing a second glance. Only in autumn, when sumac leaves become burnished crimson or orange, and in winter, when their branches stand bare and stark with a candelabra of deep red fruits, can sumacs be considered eye-catching. This doesn't mean these shrubs and small trees are unappealing plants. On the contrary, their compound, sometimes glossy leaves and graceful form make them good additions to a casual or natural garden.

In spring and summer, birds search sumac foliage for insects, just as they do any other plant. The panicles of whitish green, pink, or yellow flowers attract many small insects, a veritable feast for vireos, warblers, and other bug snatchers. But it's in winter that sumac becomes a standout with birds. Those spires of fuzzy fruits provide long-term food in the leanest months of the year. Sumacs flourish from Zone 2 through 10, depending on the species, and in an assortment of conditions. Most grow best in full sun to light shade and are very drought-tolerant.

Sumac Appreciators

Name a bird that dwells in your region in winter, and it's a sure bet that it samples sumac fruits at some time from late fall to very early spring. Only sparrows seem to disdain sumac for reasons they haven't yet told me. Although sumac isn't a preferred food, like acorns or nuts, it is very much appreciated by birds as a food of last resort. More than 50 species of birds, plus an assortment of rabbits and chipmunks, flock to sumac.

Some of my best winter bird watching has been done from the bench that overlooked a sumac thicket I planted. I'll never forget one cold, brilliantly clear winter day, when a flock of 26 eastern bluebirds settled onto the bushes to feed. It was a beautifully color-coordinated scene, with the birds' breasts echoing the

A male purple finch echoes the color of sumac berries. Sumacs attract all kinds of takers in winter, when other foods are scarce or snow-covered.

red of the berries, their backs mirroring the sky, and their white bellies as soft as the snow underfoot.

When snowstorms move in with a vengeance, sumac is a natural for birds. The berries rarely go ignored in bad weather because their shape and position shrugs off most of the snow, so that birds can reach life-giving food. After one overnight snowstorm, which left the feeders piled high with the white stuff, I stepped outside to find golden evening grosbeaks sharing sumac with robins and a brown thrasher who was probably wondering why he hadn't flown south, while beneath the bushes, a busy flock of juncos picked up leftovers as they dropped.

When I go afield in winter looking for birds, I never pass a copse of sumac without waiting awhile to see what turns up.

Summer Feeding

THE SUMMER SCENE at the feeding station is sparse compared to the overflow crowds of fall and winter. With insects abundant and wild fruits ripening, birds don't need to depend on your generosity to satisfy their needs. Many species are nesting, too, which means they'll be spending most of their days in a frantic search for insects rather than leisurely kibitzing among themselves at your backyard feeders.

Still, you'll find that some loyal customers remain regulars at your feeders throughout the dog days. Cardinals, chickadees, finches, grackles, jays, and other birds will drop in to grab a snack daily. And, for better or worse, house sparrows and starlings will never desert you!

The summer feeding season is the time to enjoy the fruits of your landscaping labors. Now the payoff of all that planting is at hand, as birds flock to your yard to find food in your shrubs, trees, and garden beds. They'll be looking for fruit and berries, but they'll also be patrolling for creeping, crawling food like caterpillars and beetles. This is a great time to watch birds acting naturally in your yard, as they gather food for nestlings and a bit later bring the young'uns to your sanctuary.

Many feeder keepers take a break from stocking seed in summer. With gardening in full swing, many of us are no longer lingering over coffee with the

Add a plastic bottle full of sugar water to a screw-on feeder, and you're ready for hummers. Instead of cleaning the bottle, simply rinse, recycle, and replace it with another one.

chickadees but are instead strolling the yard before work or other daily routines to see what's sprouting or blooming. Birds won't suffer if you stop feeding them in summer as they would in winter, but I still like to keep a few feeders stocked with fresh seed, for

10 To-Dos for Summer Feeding

1. Cut back on your servings so that seed doesn't go to waste in feeders or attract undesirables.

2. Monitor seed supplies for webbing, larvae, or other signs of insect infestation.

3. Clean up hulls beneath feeders and replace mulch.

4. Move suet feeders to the shade to slow melting.

5. Replace beef-fat trimmings with processed suet blocks, which resist melting.

6. Add an oriole nectar feeder for sweet-toothed songbirds.

7. Give nectar feeders a weekly cleaning, especially around feeding holes, and refill anti-ant moats or renew petroleum-jelly ant barriers as needed.

8. In early summer, plant a hedge or windbreak of sunflowers or corn; birds will devour the seeds for weeks.

9. Freeze blueberries and other small fruits for winter feeding when the birds will really appreciate a sweet treat.

10. Keep birdbaths scrubbed free of algae. Install a misting sprinkler for irresistible bird bathing.

my own enjoyment as much as theirs. A tube feeder of niger and one or two hopper or tray feeders accommodate the summer seed-eating guests, while a suet feeder or two and the popular nectar feeders satisfy the other birds. I don't bother with fruit feeders in summer, since my offerings can't compete with natural fruit and berries, but I do keep up the regular handout of mealworms for the bluebirds and wrens.

The slowdown at the feeders may or may not dovetail with your seed supply. If you have only a few pounds of seed at the end of the spring season, that's great—you can replenish it by buying small amounts as you need it over the summer. I usually end up with most of a big sack or two of sunflower or other seeds. In my steamy southern Indiana summer, insects quickly infest the seed in storage, making it much less appealing to birds. Cracked corn not only suffers infestation by meal moth larvae and other pests, it also turns rancid in heat. To prevent waste, when feeder traffic slows to a

handful of birds, I dump out most of the seed directly on the ground, where it attracts hordes of house sparrows and grackles, which quickly polish off most of it. Suet acquires an unappealing black mold in summer and melts in the sun. Move your suet feeder to a shady spot; your loyal woodpecker customers will soon find it.

Summer is the ideal time to thoroughly clean and repair feeders and to rake hulls and freshen mulch beneath feeders. Remove and store any unused feeders for tidiness' sake.

If you've been hankering for a garden pool, this is the season to install one. Summer heat and drought will bring glorious orioles, tanagers, and other bright-colored beauties to water. And the sound of water in your yard will make your place a favorite hangout for doves, finches, robins, sparrows, and other backyard regulars. Be sure to include a place where you can put your feet up and watch the birds near the water!

Sunflowers

Attract cardinals, chickadees, finches, grosbeaks, jays, nuthatches, titmice, woodpeckers

SUNFLOWER SEEDS ARE SO IRRESISTIBLE to birds that you could make them the only foods you ever offer at your bird feeders and *still* please the crowd. Both gray-striped and black oil sunflower seeds are high-fat, high-protein, and apparently delectable foods that give birds maximum food value for minimum effort. Grow sunflowers in your garden, and you'll have birds snitching the seeds before you even realize they're ripe. Serve sunflower seeds in a feeder, and you'll have all the customers you can handle as soon as the word gets around.

Sunflower Eaters

Who eats sunflower seeds? Cardinals, chickadees, finches, grosbeaks, jays, nuthatches, titmice, woodpeckers, and other birds with stout beaks will crack the hulls of sunflowers seeds to reach the

The birds that eat sunflowers at a feeder will also pick them from the plant. Here a tufted titmouse extracts a seed. Act fast if you plan to harvest some yourself.

meat inside. Blackbirds, juncos, sparrows, and towhees don't have large enough beaks to crack sunflower shells, but they'll search through the feeder or on the ground below to garner bits left behind by larger-billed birds. Tanagers and buntings may also show up to dine occasionally on sunflower seeds.

Squirrels, chipmunks, and ground squirrels also can't resist a banquet of sunflower seeds. These eating machines can empty a feeder faster than a horde of evening grosbeaks—and those big yellow-and-black birds go through the seeds so fast it makes a crackling noise that sounds like the feeder is on fire! Rodents will also use your sunflower feeders to stock their larders for a later snack. They can stash their cheek pouches full and transport sunflower seeds back to their cozy dens.

To deter squirrels and other gluttons, you'll need armored feeders that keep them from reaching the seeds. No feeder is entirely squirrel-proof because these intelligent and determined animals can figure out how to outwit just about any trick, from counterbalanced perches to slippery baffles. (For more on discouraging squirrels, see the Squirrels entry on page 267.)

This male goldfinch will happily pick out seeds from sunflowers with small, large, or gigantic blossoms, so grow the varieties with the flowers you like best.

Annual Sunflowers

Sunflowers are happy-face flowers. We've rediscovered the joys of growing these all-American flowers, and plant breeders have responded by releasing a flurry of new varieties to cash in on the craze. You can still find the classic tall, single-headed sunflower on seed racks and in catalogs, but you'll also see a fantastic range of new sunflowers, all selected from the parent species, *Helianthus annuus*, the common sunflower.

Growing Annual Sunflowers

A FENCE or wall is the perfect backdrop for a planting of tall annual sunflowers. It will shelter them from summer wind storms that could topple unprotected plants. Branching sunflowers, which bear a multitude of small flowers, are less prone to toppling than the big monsters that may suddenly keel over from top-heavy seedheads.

Tall sunflowers make a great hedge for attracting birds and creating privacy, at least for the summer. Use them to enclose a sitting area or patio or to create visual boundary lines in your yard. Shorter varieties are easy to work into flowerbeds. All sunflowers add appeal to a vegetable garden, but be sure to plant them where they won't block the sun from lower-growing plants.

Plant these agreeable annuals in full sun and in average to lean soil to encourage flowering rather than leafy growth. Learn to recognize sunflower seedlings—once your yard is busy with birds, you'll find volunteer seedlings popping up here and there, wherever a bird dropped a seed. These work-free seedlings will grow into a fine feast for birds.

You can grow sunflowers in dramatic autumnal shades of rust and copper; in pint-size versions with full-size blooms on knee-high plants; with fluffy, double flowers that look more like a cactus-flowered zinnia than a sunflower; and in varieties that are pollen-free, so that cut flowers don't dust your end table with a golden shower. You can even grow ancient varieties that were bred by native Americans, with seeds of burnished chestnut, deep charcoal-blue, or creamy white.

As far as birds are concerned, tasty seeds are the main reason for growing sunflowers. So choose the varieties that appeal to your personal taste, as long as they bear a bountiful crop. How can you tell? The birds will let you know. If cardinals, chickadees, goldfinches, titmice, or other sunflower eaters aren't perched on the seedheads after the petals wither, you've planted a dud.

Plants that sprout from dropped birdseed also produce excellent seeds for birds, but the plants won't look like their parents. Instead, they'll have stout, single stems, and the flower heads may be much less flashy-looking. These volunteer plants are the same type of sunflower (*Helianthus annuus*)

that decorates roadsides from Missouri to the Rockies each summer in a wide swath of shining yellow. If you're experimenting with new varieties, do your birds a favor and find a spot where you can plant some plain old birdseed sunflowers for insurance, just in case your prettified plants don't produce good seeds.

Perennial Sunflowers

North America, the home of sunflowers, boasts dozens of species of native perennial sunflowers. The flower heads are much smaller than those of the annual sunflower, but they're still crammed with small, bird-attracting seeds. All have sunny yellow daisy flowers on plants of varying height, form, and foliage. Maximilian sunflower (*H. maximilianii*), for instance, is a regal plant, stretching 8 feet or taller, with flowers borne thickly along the top 2 feet of each stem. Soft sunflower (*H. mollis*), on the other hand, tends to flop or recline against neighboring plants. Its velvet-soft gray foliage and clusters of furred buds are as pretty as its buttery yellow flowers, which usually appear about 2 feet from ground level.

Growing Perennial Sunflowers

PERENNIAL SUNFLOWERS are used to fighting for space among the tall grasses and stout flowers of the American prairie, so they can be pushy. Most species spread like lightning from underground roots. Be forewarned: It can be very frustrating to try to pull out all those roots if you decide you don't want a sunflower plantation in one particular location. Jerusalem artichoke (*H. tuberosus*) is the worst offender because its brittle roots snap easily when you attempt to dig or pull them up, and each piece of

left-behind root sprouts a vigorous new plant.

Plant perennial sunflowers in average soil in a sunny to partly shady location, depending on the species. They laugh at drought, bloom their heads off in high heat and humidity, and come through bitter cold without a qualm.

Combine perennial sunflowers with equally tough plants, such as prairie grasses (*Andropogon gerardii, Panicum virgatum, Sorghastrum nutans,* and others), goldenrods (*Solidago* spp.), and ironweeds (*Vernonia* spp.), and you'll have an instant, self-maintaining garden that's super appealing to many birds.

Luckily, climate and growing conditions are often effective at limiting a sunflower's spread. But before you invite perennial sunflowers into your treasured beds and borders, give them a trial run in an isolated part of your yard. Because they're so determined, perennial sunflowers are ideal plants to use in a naturalized area or meadow or prairie planting.

Most perennial sunflower species bloom late in the season and continue blooming even after light frost. Birds are fond of their small seeds and begin eating them as soon as the first flower head matures.

Thrashers

THRASHERS ARE large, slim birds with long bills and tail feathers. In some species, such as the **California thrasher** and its western cohorts, the **curve-billed, LeConte's,** and **crissal thrashers,** the beak is extravagantly long, with a decided down curve. The birds are easy to recognize as thrashers but difficult to tell apart because most are equally plain with soft gray-brown feathers. The **brown thrasher, long-billed thrasher,** and **sage thrasher** are much more distinctive, thanks to their streaked white breasts. The brown thrasher is the only repre-

Big and beautiful in its cinnamon garb, the brown thrasher may come to a feeder for suet, a food attractive to insect eaters. Thrashers also like fruit.

sentative east of the Rockies. The other species roam in the Southwest, with the California thrasher making its home in far western California.

A thrasher's businesslike bill comes in handy as it feeds on the ground beneath bushes and trees. The habit of threshing or thrashing through litter in brushy thickets to dislodge insects earned the bird its common name.

Thrashers fill their bellies with insects, fruits, and occasionally seeds in the wild. The most common thrashers at the feeder are the brown thrasher and the California thrasher, although the crissal and others may occasionally stop in for a bite. Fruit and soft foods are the big temptations for thrashers. Occasionally, a bird will linger north of its usual winter

range, and those hardy souls often become feeder regulars until insects are once again plentiful.

Use a low tray feeder to lure thrashers to the feast. Once they are accustomed to visiting your feeding station, they may join other birds at higher feeders. Thrashers often visit birdbaths and other water features, especially in the dry West and Southwest.

Thrasher Behavior

Members of the mockingbird family, thrashers are talented singers with sweet, melodious songs. They engage in extended songfests, usually from

THRASHER FEEDER FOODS			
■ Amelanchier (*Amelanchier* spp.) fruits	■ Cactus fruits	■ Holly (*Ilex* spp.) berries	■ Suet, chopped or ground
■ Apples, halved or chopped	■ Cooked pasta	■ Leftovers	■ Sunflower seeds, hulled
	■ Cracked corn	■ Meat scraps	
■ Bread and other baked goods	■ Grapes and other small fruits	■ Nuts	

a perch atop a shrub or tree. The brown thrasher and California thrasher carry on the family tradition of mimicry, inserting imitations of hawks, other birds, and inanimate objects into their extended songs.

In the feeder area or in your yard, you will notice that thrashers tend to go on foot or use short flights to make their way from one patch of cover to the next. They are agile runners, too. The California thrasher is the speedster of the group pointing its tail up when it darts across open spaces. Thrashers fly low, a behavior that causes many collisions with cars when the birds are moving from bushes on one side of the road to the other.

Western thrashers, including the sage and the curve-billed, may seem almost tame once they begin visiting your yard. But all thrashers are fierce defenders of the nest, particularly when it comes to snakes. That long, sharp bill is a good deterrent to most slithering predators, but the thrasher adds to the attack with flashing wings and fanned tail.

The California thrasher's beak looks lethal, but the bird uses it mainly to scythe through leaves in search of insects or to pluck fruits from spiny cactuses.

Thrushes

IT'S A RED-LETTER DAY when a thrush shows up at the feeder. These quiet, docile birds usually forage for themselves in the woodsy areas where they make their homes. But one of the members of the family may visit your feeder during fall and spring migration or at other times if your property is near thrush habitat.

Thrushes are famed for their singing, not their looks, but the western **varied thrush** is a beauty as well as a vocalist. Dressed in glowing orange and deep blue, this bird's haunting melody of drawn-out single notes is common in the mossy woods of the Northwest. More typical of the thrush clan are several species with brown backs and dark-spotted white bellies. The **wood thrush,** once a common nesting bird of eastern woods and suburbs, and the **veery,** a wider-spread species with a few spots on its white underside, are endangered by the parasitic

The hermit thrush's habit of raising and lowering its tail makes it easy to distinguish from its similar relatives. Listen for its clear, bell-like tones at dusk and dawn.

Tree Seeds and Buds

Attract many kinds of birds at various times of the year

YOU CAN SEE why trees that bear large, meaty seeds, like acorns and nuts, and those with fleshy or juicy fruits, like crab apples, attract birds. Dining on these seeds and fruits fills a bird's belly fast. But smaller tree seeds and even tender buds are also relished by some birds, particularly crossbills, finches, game birds, and grosbeaks.

One winter day I was strolling around my yard when I noticed a flurry of tuliptree seeds drifting to the ground around me. This was odd because there was no wind to stir the tree, and at first I thought perhaps it was just the time for the conelike seedheads to shatter. Then I looked up into the top of the 100-foot tree and discovered a flock of about a dozen evening grosbeaks, quietly and industriously working at the cones to pull free individual seeds.

The strong, conical bills of grosbeaks are as efficient as a pair of pruners at nipping off buds of maples, ashes, and other trees, and even conifers aren't safe from their nibbling. I was pleased to host pine grosbeaks one year until I noticed that they were devouring the tender growing tips of my young pear tree.

Although dedicated scientists have done painstaking inventories of birds' stomach contents for decades, it can still be a surprise to see what your birds are dining on. When an irruption year brought common redpolls to my yard in Pennsylvania, I discovered that the birds enjoyed the plump buds of my lilac bushes as much as they liked the sunflower seeds at the feeder.

Look to the Trees

It's easy to forget about looking up as you wander your backyard, but if you do, you'll discover that birds are often above you. If they're not actively flitting after insects or combing the bark and branches, they may well be dining on the seeds still held on the tree or nipping off fat buds. Look down to find

The tender buds or tasty seeds of trees are favored foods of many birds, especially finches. Fluffy down from cottonwoods is often used as nest material.

evidence of birds at trees, too: Nipped branch tips on the willows at the garden pool may be the clue to grouse or turkeys. Doves, juncos, towhees, and other ground-feeding birds often pay close attention to the ground beneath trees, where seeds may have dropped from the branches above.

Keep a Record

I keep an informal diary to help me remember when to look for certain birds in my trees: In early spring, for example, I check my elms for pine siskins; in winter, I look for them in tulip trees. The data I collect from my own sightings of birds dining in my neighborhood trees also helps me select bird-attracting plants to add to the garden.

Tree Seeds and Buds for Birds

KEEP AN eye on the trees in your backyard and in your neighborhood, and you may spot birds munching on their seeds or buds. Double-check with your binoculars when you see a bird apparently feeding in a tree—it's fascinating to watch how various birds approach the task of freeing the seeds or reaching for buds. You may see other birds besides those listed here at trees; the wild foods that birds eat is an area that needs more study, and your own anecdotal notes are important. (Trees that bear acorns, nuts, cones, and fruits or berries are not included here.)

TREE SEEDS

Tree	Seed Eaters
Acacias (*Acacia* spp.)	Doves, quail
Maples and boxelders (*Acer* spp.)	Chickadees, prairie chickens, finches, grosbeaks, grouse, nuthatches, quail, wild turkeys
Alders (*Alnus* spp.)	Goldfinches, grouse, pine siskins, redpolls, woodcocks
Birches (*Betula* spp.)	Chickadees, crossbills, purple finches, common redpolls, pine siskins, fox sparrows, tree sparrows
Hornbeam (*Carpinus caroliniana*)	Bobwhites, grouse, pheasants, myrtle warblers
Catalpas (*Catalpa* spp.)	Cardinals, finches, grosbeaks
Ashes (*Fraxinus* spp.)	Cardinals, finches, grosbeaks, quail, wild turkeys
Sweetgum (*Liquidambar styraciflua*)	Bobwhites, chickadees, purple finches, goldfinches, white-throated sparrows, towhees, Carolina wrens
Tuliptree (*Liriodendron tulipifera*)	Redwing blackbirds, cardinals, chickadees, purple finches, goldfinches, evening grosbeaks
Magnolias (*Magnolia* spp.)	Towhees, red-eyed vireos, woodpeckers
Ironwood, hophornbeam (*Ostrya virginiana*)	Purple finches, rose-breasted grosbeaks, downy woodpeckers
Sycamores (*Platanus* spp.)	Finches
Aspens, poplars, cottonwoods (*Populus* spp.)	Crossbills, finches, quail
Mesquites (*Prosopis* spp.)	Doves, quail, ravens
Black locust (*Robinia pseudoacacia*)	Quail
Elms (*Ulmus* spp.)	Chickadees, purple finches, goldfinches, rose-breasted grosbeaks, grouse, pheasants, wild turkeys

Tree Seeds and Buds for Birds—*Continued*

TREE BUDS

Tree	Bud Eaters
Conifers (many species of *Abies, Picea,* and *Pinus*)	Crossbills, finches, grosbeaks
Maples (*Acer* spp.)	Cassin's finches, purple finches, goldfinches, grosbeaks
Birches (*Betula* spp.)	Prairie chickens, grouse
American hornbeam (*Carpinus caroliniana*)	Bobwhites, grouse, pheasants
Ashes (*Fraxinus* spp.)	Finches, grosbeaks
Aspens and poplars (*Populus* spp.)	Prairie chickens, purple finches, grouse, quail, Abert towhees
Cottonwoods (*Populus* spp.)	Pyrrhuloxia
Willows (*Salix* spp.)	Grosbeaks, grouse, redpolls
Elms (*Ulmus* spp.)	Cardinals, finches, grosbeaks, pine siskins

Trellises and Arbors

WHETHER YOU HAVE a large garden or a small one, adding height with trellises and arbors will make it look more interesting. These structures also supply more growing room because plants tend to go up, not out. Around the feeder area, trellises and arbors supply shade, serve as windbreaks, and block the force of winter rains and snow so that feeder birds can eat in a sheltered nook. The vines on these vertical supports give birds quick shelter, too, should danger threaten.

Another advantage to using trellises around your feeders is that they provide a visual barrier to territorial birds. Should an aggressive mockingbird decide to lay claim to its favorite feeder, you can install another feeder on the far side of the trellis or arbor barrier where other birds can eat in peace.

The more plants in your yard for food and shelter, the better for birds. Multiply your plantings by growing upward. Here American bittersweet climbs a trellis.

Best Plants for Bird Trellises

CHOOSE PLANTS to cover arbors and trellises using the same criteria as you would for other plantings in your bird-friendly yard. Select those that do double duty, offering a food source as well as shelter.

Native vines are an excellent choice for bird arbors because they have evolved along with the birds that use them. Their fruits ripen when birds need them most, and the tasty treats they provide stay edible into winter. Here are my four top picks for fast-growing, fruitful native vines:

American bittersweet (*Celastrus scandens*): A tough, twining vine hardy to Zone 2. The bright orange-and-red fruits are eaten by bluebirds, grouse, pheasants, quail, robins, and wild turkeys. Plant both a male and a female vine to assure fruiting.

Virginia creeper (*Parthenocissus quinquefolia*): A relative of Boston ivy, Virginia creeper is hardy to Zone 3 and has five-part leaves that glow translucent crimson in fall. Its clusters of deep blue berries on bright red stems are eagerly sought by many birds, including bluebirds, chickadees, flickers, great-crested flycatchers, nuthatches, robins, sapsuckers and other woodpeckers, sparrows, thrushes, thrashers, titmice, and vireos.

Greenbriers (*Smilax* spp.): An interesting and unusual choice. Native mostly to the eastern two-thirds of the country, these glossy-leaved, woody vines bear fleshy fruits that are favored by cardinals, catbirds, flickers, grouse, mockingbirds, pheasants, robins, sparrows, thrushes, wild turkeys, waxwings, pileated woodpeckers, and, in Florida, fish crows. Both thorny and smooth species are available for Zones 4 through 10. Some species are evergreen.

Wild grapes (*Vitis* spp.): Native to almost all parts of the country, except for the northern mountains. Wild grapes are vigorous, fast growers, and their usually tiny fruits are devoured with relish even when old and dried in winter. If you can't find a native wild grape, any cultivated variety will also attract birds. Grape lovers include bluebirds, cardinals, catbirds, purple finches, grackles, grosbeaks, jays, juncos, kingbirds, orioles, robins, sparrows, thrushes, woodpeckers—you get the idea. There are few birds that won't be tempted by grapes. All game birds, including doves, pheasants, quail, and turkeys also eat them readily.

Tube Feeders

ONE OF THE MORE RECENT INNOVATIONS in bird feeder technology, tube feeders were an instant hit when introduced a few decades ago and have remained popular ever since.

Why such universal acceptance? First, tube feeders are ideal for the frugal. They save you money because they conserve seed. Because birds pull out just a seed or two at a time, little is wasted to spills or messy eaters.

Tube feeders are easy to use, too. Slide up the lid, pour in the seed, and the feeder is stocked for as long as a few weeks, depending on the size of your feeder and the traffic it gets. With limited seating area, the seed lasts a long time.

Tube feeders are also the only practical way to offer niger seed, an extremely small and lightweight seed that gets lost in most seed mixes and is easily blown out of other feeders. Goldfinches, house finches, purple finches, redpolls, and pine siskins are regular customers at feeders filled with niger seed.

Another factor in the popularity of tube feeders may be that they are used only by small birds, including finches, redpolls, and pine siskins. Starlings and other larger perching birds can't get a grip on the short perches, and they're at least a slight deterrent to seed-seeking squirrels.

Seeds for Tube Feeders

The first tube feeders were fit for only niger seed, but today's models have adapted the design to accommodate larger seeds, such as seed mixes, sunflower seed, and even nuts.

Choose your tube feeders according to the kind of seed you want to serve in them. Of course, you can always include a variety of tube feeders at your feeding station! Multitube models can serve a mixed banquet all at once, with one tube holding niger, another millet or mixed seed, and a third sunflower seed.

Holding capacity isn't as important to keep in mind when you choose a commercial tube feeder because the seed is doled out slowly to a limited number of consumers. Still, bigger is better if you want to save yourself frequent refilling trips or if you plan to be away during the peak bird-feeding season from fall to early spring.

Tube Feeder Construction

Tube feeders are usually made with a plastic tube and metal lid, bottom stopper, and metal perches, although the materials may vary depending on the quality of the feeder. Feeders with metal guards around the seed openings help prevent the holes from becoming enlarged through use over time. Metal parts also add weight to the feeder, which helps keep it stable in winds that can rock and tilt the feeder and cause seed to spill.

Niger seed is one of the costlier bird foods, and I'm a real penny pincher, so I'm always on the lookout for ways to avoid waste. I've discovered that the longer the chain or hook attached to my tube feeder, the greater the arc the feeder will sway in when the wind blows—and that means a greater possibility of spilled seed. Instead of dangling my tube feeder on a chain, I prefer to hook the metal feeder handle directly to a stationary support, such as a bracket arm attached to a porch post, so that there is as little free play as possible. You can also mount some models atop a wood or metal post. If

A tube feeder with ports below the perches helps slow niger consumption by less-agile house finches. Goldfinches don't seem to mind dining upside down.

Goldfinches, pine siskins, and house finches feed in harmony at a tube feeder. Metal reinforcements prevent squirrels from enlarging the feeding holes.

you see your post-mounted feeder swaying, either you have giant moles at work or you'd better grab the earthquake preparedness kit.

Outwitting the Squirrels

If the squirrels in your neighborhood are particularly determined (or if my squirrels have been e-mailing them about tricks of the trade), they may try to gnaw their way into a tube feeder. A feeder that contains niger is of little interest to squirrels, but one that's chock-full of nuts, corn, peanuts, or other favored foods will certainly get their attention. Thin plastic walls are not much of a barrier to the incisors of a hungry squirrel, which can mean a new feeder for you and a full belly for your furry friend. If you suspect that squirrel attacks may be likely, try an all-metal tube feeder or add a baffle above the feeder to deter them—at least for a while.

PROJECT

Make a Wire Tube Feeder

You can make your own tube feeder from a cylinder of wire hardware cloth, sized to serve larger seeds such as sunflowers, peanuts, and corn. With this type of feeder, you don't need to include perches because chickadees, nuthatches, titmice, woodpeckers, and other birds can cling to the wire itself. I like to supply a perch near the bottom of the feeder, though, so that less athletic birds, such as cardinals, can get a bite to eat, too.

MATERIALS

½-inch mesh hardware cloth

2 jar lids of the same size

Wooden dowel

Wire for hanging

Duct tape

Step 1. Measure and cut a piece of ½-inch-grid hardware cloth to 14 inches high and 8 inches wide. Cut one end of the 14-inch side through the grids, so that loose ends are left on the cross wires.

Step 2. Roll the wire so that the ends overlap to form a tube just slightly smaller in diameter than your jar lids. Bend the loose ends of the cross wires around the grids of the mesh where they meet. A needlenose pliers makes short work of this job. Wear gloves so you don't get poked by sharp wire ends.

Step 3. Insert a wooden dowel through the feeder, about 2 inches from the bottom of the feeder. Trim to 3-inch-long perches on either side of the wire feeder.

Step 4. Insert a strong wire through the sides of the feeder near the top; this serves as a handle for hanging.

Step 5. Cap the bottom of the feeder with a jar lid or other close-fitting cover. Tape to the wire with duct tape to hold it in place.

Step 6. Use another lid to serve as the feeder cap; this one need not be as close-fitting as the bottom cap. Fill the feeder with seed, close the feeder cap, and hang.

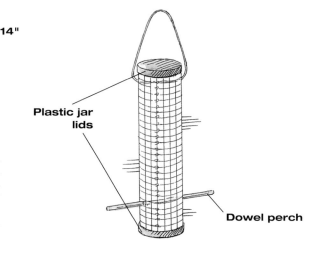

Plastic jar lids

Dowel perch

14"

8"

V

Vegetable Gardens and Birds

Attract many kinds of birds at various times of the year

ALTHOUGH BIRDS can be friends or foes in your vegetable garden, most of the time they're your good friends. When you notice a bird bustling through your garden, don't assume it's there to grab a strawberry or a kernel of corn—it's probably searching beneath the leaves for insects to feed to its hungry babies.

When veggie gardens are reaching their peak in early to midsummer, bird life is at its busiest, with many a shrub and tree holding a nest of baby birds. This is perfect timing for us gardeners because parent birds with a nest near the garden will quickly adopt our patch as part of their regular food-finding beat.

Nestlings need soft foods such as fat caterpillars, beetles, ants, and aphids. Every 10 minutes or so, there's another baby bird in the brood waiting to be fed, so parent birds are almost constantly on food patrol. Catbirds, song sparrows, and wrens are just three of the many species that frequent vegetable gardens in search of insects, and practically any bird in your neighborhood may turn up in your garden. I've even seen purple martins, which spend nearly all their time nabbing insects from the air, plucking squash bugs from my pumpkin vines without ever alighting.

Bring On the Birds

Because birds do such a good job of controlling pests in vegetable gardens, you'll want to do everything you can to encourage them to visit yours. The vegetation alone will attract birds because they know there are bound to be bugs there. Even though you may do a fine job of hand-picking beetles and other

Provide housing for birds, and they'll gladly patrol your garden for pests. Some birds may also nibble tender sprouts; be ready to discourage them if necessary.

pests, you're bound to overlook some creepy-crawlies, and those are the ones birds will zero in on.

Put shrubs on the side. A vegetable garden is typically set in an isolated sunny spot, surrounded by lawn grass. To make your veggie garden more bird-friendly, try planting a corridor of shrubs (raspberries and blackberries, perhaps) nearby, so that birds can move to and from the garden in safety.

Set up a nearby feeder. A feeder near the garden is a good idea, too, especially in fall and winter. That's when birds will move from the feeder to the garden itself to pick over the soil for any weed seeds or slumbering insects. Ground-feeding birds are what you want to attract to this area, so make the feeder a low-level tray and fill it with millet, flax, and other seeds favored by doves, juncos, native sparrows, and towhees.

Plant a nest box in your garden. House wrens, which are remarkably unafraid of humans, may quickly adopt a nesting box mounted on a post right in your garden—which gives them easy access to creeping, crawling food. The wrens that lived in the birdhouse in my garden were particularly adept at keeping the cabbage loopers from devouring my broccoli and cabbage.

Install the birdhouse in an area of the garden that has at least 4 feet of private space around it, so you won't disturb the birds at their nest. This is a great place to sprinkle a "surprise garden" packet of mixed annuals that won't require much tending from you. Wrens are vocal birds and quick to voice their displeasure, so if you find your wrens scolding you with "Chirrs" and rattling sounds, back off quickly. If your garden is small, place the nest box nearby instead of in the middle of it to make the real estate more appealing to potential tenants.

Add water. A nearby birdbath will also draw helpful birds to your garden. The old-fashioned pedestal-type bath makes an appealing centerpiece, and nearby garden plants will appreciate the extra water you splash on them when refilling the bath.

Keep an eye out for interesting and unusual visitors in your garden. If you live near woods, you may spot fox sparrows, thrushes, or towhees ferreting out insect food on the ground beneath your plants. Even grosbeaks, orioles, and bright-colored tanagers may visit a vegetable garden to glean what they can. In times of drought, when insects are especially drawn to your succulent, well-watered veggies, birds will soon follow because the pickings are much better there than on the parched vegetation in the wild.

Keep Out! This Means You!

Occasionally, birds will enjoy raiding your garden for seeds or plants; for example, birds may forget their good manners if you're growing sweet corn. Newly planted seeds and some sprouts, such as those of peas and lettuce, may also bring in birds to feast on your prized plantings. If you plant strawberries in your vegetable patch, you may come out to pick your morning bowl of berries and find the berries marred by beak marks or, worse, completely consumed by your bird buddies.

The best way to protect your garden from losses is to use barriers to deter marauders. Netting, floating row covers, and wire cages (for berry bushes) will absolutely keep birds from getting even a nibble. Less drastic measures, such as making a scarecrow, hanging cat's head cutouts, or distributing rubber snakes among your crops may discourage birds for a while, but when the devices prove harmless, the birds will move in again. Flashy strips of silver Mylar or Grandma's trick of hanging aluminum pie pans to dangle in the sun may also prove effective, at least for a while.

Appreciating House Sparrows

THE VEGETABLE garden is one place where I appreciate hosting house sparrows. When the lean-to shed near my vegetable garden had a thriving colony of these community nesters, I was sure they were planning some kind of raid on the patch, though I couldn't imagine what. I just couldn't imagine that house sparrows would be beneficial birds, but that's exactly what they proved themselves to be. When cucumber beetles reached dangerous numbers, they spent a couple of days snapping up every beetle they could find. Same thing when Colorado potato beetles moved in.

In Boston, Massachusetts, I saw more evidence of helpful house sparrows in a thriving urban garden. Every square inch of the backyard was crammed with crops, from oregano to heirloom tomatoes to grapes and figs. The gardeners kept a small patio bare of everything except a couple of chairs and a scattering of bread crumbs. "Why the bread?" I asked. "Sit down and see," they invited. As I watched, house sparrows approached from neighboring rooftops, drawn to the bread. After the birds squabbled over the last crumbs, they moved into the garden and gobbled up invisible insects like a flock of animated vacuum cleaners. Then they were off, back to another busy day among the Boston rooftops.

V

Viburnums

Attract cardinals, catbirds, robins, sparrows, thrashers, waxwings

BERRIES ARE THE BIGGEST bird draw that a viburnum offers—but they're not the only bird-friendly feature of these plants. The berries come in red, blue, and orange, and robins, thrashers, waxwings, and other berry-eating birds love them. Viburnums are a diverse group of shrubs and small trees—there are more than 150 different kinds. They bear plentiful blooms and some have fall foliage that's as brilliant as a sugar maple.

Viburnum foliage is dense, making the shrubs a protected location where birds can search for insects or hide nests. Cardinals, catbirds, and sparrows all like to nest in viburnums. These shrubs are fast-growing, too, so they're a fine choice for a hedge or shrub grouping to provide the cover that makes your yard more appealing to birds in general. A mixed group of viburnums staggers the berry-ripening schedule, so birds don't clean off all the bushes in one fell swoop.

Plant breeders have developed dozens of garden-worthy viburnum cultivars, but in some cases, changes due to breeding have caused the berries to lose their appeal to birds. If you want surefire berries for birds, stick to the native species that grow in your region. Don't discount the cultivars altogether, though. Even if birds don't eat the berries, the clusters of small flowers will attract a myriad of nectar-seeking insects. Those insects will draw insect-eating birds such as vireos and warblers to the shrubs.

Six Bird-Friendly Native Viburnums

IT'S UNFORTUNATE, but true, that native viburnums are not as widely available in nurseries and garden centers as introduced species. And the introduced species very often are not attractive to our native birds. To get you started on your search for homegrown viburnums that birds will come flocking to, here are six fine viburnums to seek out:

Mapleleaf viburnum (*V. acerifolium*): An ideal cover or hedge plant, this 4- to 6-foot-tall, multi-stemmed shrub often spreads by suckers to form a small colony. Pretty maplelike leaves are beautiful in fall, when they turn crimson and purple. Many small clusters of white, mildly fragrant flowers ripen into red fruits that gradually turn black. Hardy to Zone 3.

Arrowwood (*V. dentatum*): One of two viburnums commonly called arrowwood (the other is *V. rafinesquianum*), this large, fast-growing shrub reaches its mature height of 8 to 15 feet in as little as 3 years. Its new branches are remarkably straight and were long ago used as arrow shafts. Like most viburnums, its shape is undistinguished—this one has an upright form widening at the top. Fuzzy, white, slightly fragrant flowers bloom in spring, followed by deep blue berry clusters held above reddish foliage in fall. Hardy to Zone 2.

Nannyberry (*V. lentago*): Tall shrub or small tree grows to 25 feet tall and has creamy, fragrant flowers followed by clusters of red fruits that turn black when fully ripe. Beautiful red fall color. Hardy to Zone 2.

Black haw (*V. prunifolium*): Branching, tall shrub or small tree grows to 25 feet tall, with rounded oval leaves that flash red and yellow in fall. Deep blue, nearly black fruits in autumn. Hardy to Zone 3.

Southern blackhaw (*V. rufidulum*): A tall species that may eventually grow into a small tree to 30 feet tall. Lovely shiny, rounded leaves and checkered bark on older trees. Large clusters of sweet-scented white flowers, followed by clusters of dark blue fruits. Fall color varies; may show red and yellow. Hardy to Zone 5.

American cranberrybush (*V. trilobum*): An eye-catcher in fall, when heavy crops of red fruit glow on this upright, 9-foot-tall shrub. White spring flowers may have some fragrance; fall color can be striking or muted, in shades of yellow to red. Hardy to Zone 2.

Viburnums differ greatly in hardiness, although most can adapt to a range of soil, moisture, and light conditions. Some species, such as the blue-black fruited American natives nannyberry viburnum (*Viburnum lentago*) and *V. rafinesquianum* flourish as far north as Zone 2; others, including many of the Chinese species and cultivars, are far more tender, surviving only to Zone 9. In general, most species are hardy to at least Zone 6. Check the catalogs and nurseries of native plants specialists to find viburnums that are adapted to the climate, conditions, and bird life of your area. (See "Resources" on page 348 for mail-order possibilities.)

Viburnums' flowers attract birds indirectly by attracting insects. The twiggy branches also make good cover for birds like this white-crowned sparrow.

Vines

Attract many kinds of birds at various times of the year

FOOD AND COVER ARE THE NAME of the game when it comes to attracting birds, and flowering vines can provide both. Planting annual and perennial vines is also a great way to add an interesting new feature to your garden or yard. You can plant a vine in a flowerbed to add a tall accent or to create the impression of a "wall" between one area of your yard and another. A trellised vine can also serve as a windbreak or as shade to protect your feeding area from the glare of summer sun and the brunt of blustery winter winds.

Annual Vines

Annual vines grow as fast as Jack's beanstalk, always a plus if you like almost-instant gratification from a garden. Here are some ideas for adding bird-attracting annual vines to your yard. It's best to start from seeds sown in place because many annual vines grow a deep taproot that doesn't transplant well. For faster germination, soak the seeds overnight in a saucer of water to soften their seed coat and keep the planting area moist until they sprout. A sunny spot of average, well-drained soil is all you need for success with annual vines. Avoid fertilizing, which encourages leafy growth and can delay flowering.

■ Easy-to-grow climbing beans are a terrific vine for birds. Plenty of insects like to feed on their foliage, and the birds will feast on those juicy morsels and feed them to their nestlings, too. The flowers of scarlet runner bean (*Phaseolus coccineus*) will bring hordes of hummingbirds to your yard.

■ Purple-flowered hyacinth bean (*Lablab purpurea*) is great for covering a wall of your house or a masonry retaining wall; its dense, high-climbing vines are so sturdy that birds may be tempted to nest there as well as seek shelter in them.

■ The flowers of morning glories (*Ipomoea* spp.) and cardinal creeper (*I.* × *multifida*) attract hummingbirds, and Carolina wrens and other small birds may nest among the thicket of stems. Use these vines to cover chain-link fences or other spots that could use some camouflaging greenery. In just a few weeks, you'll transform ho-hum features into corners of bird-attracting beauty.

■ Climbing roses, while not truly vines, provide similar benefits for birds: a safe place to perch, plus insects on flowers and foliage, and tasty rosehips in the fall and winter. Climbing 'New Dawn' is one of the best because of its disease resistance and long, arching stems.

■ Birdhouse gourds, pumpkins, and squash cover fences and trellises with superfast greenery, and they offer a bonus at harvest time. You can make gourds into seed scoops, feeders, or birdhouses, while pumpkins and squash yield seeds for winter bird feeding.

If your yard is short on shrubs and other permanent cover, install trellises of annual vines near your feeding station so that birds can make a quick getaway when danger threatens. Bathing birds will also appreciate a simple lattice trellis of annual vines near the birdbath, where they can find secure perching places among the vines to preen their feathers after bathing. Hummingbirds and mockingbirds like to perch on trellises, regardless of what vine is growing there because they can get the high vantage point that these feisty, territorial birds desire.

Perennial Vines

Annual vines die away each fall, but when you plant perennial vines, they grow bigger and better every year, as well as heavier. Weight is something to keep in mind when you're deciding what vines to grow and what kind of support structure to use.

> A trellised vine creates a beautiful backdrop for a birdbath and gives wet birds a safe place to dry off and preen.

Dress up a fence with handsome Virginia creeper. In fall, the dark blue berries with their pretty red stems attract wonderful surprises like this hermit thrush.

Plant them in spring, starting with potted plants to get a head start. Although it is possible to grow perennial vines from seed, results are two to three years swifter and much easier if you begin with potted plants. Choose your perennial vines according to the conditions of your yard: Some thrive in shade, while others flourish in full sun. All will grow well in average, well-drained soil. Most of the plant's energy will go into producing roots the first year, so don't be disappointed to see little new growth aboveground. By the second growing season, your perennial vine should be settled in and ready to push out new growth in earnest. A wisteria vine or trumpetvine (*Campsis radicans*) may look puny when you put it in the ground, but in a few years, it may be threatening to swamp your yard like some tropical nightmare. Of course, most birds would like nothing better!

Most perennial vines are vigorous growers, but they are easy to keep in bounds with a haircut every now and then. Pruning perennial vines is easiest in winter, after the vine has dropped its leaves and you can easily see the branch structure. But you can keep established plants in bounds by snipping them back with pruners at any time of year if they stray from their supporting trellis. Don't be shy about cutting back a perennial vine; these hardy specimens will quickly recover from even a drastic pruning session. Usually, nipping back side branches is all the pruning you'll need to do. But you can even cut a mature vine to the ground and expect vigorous regrowth.

Exploring perennial vines pays off for both gardeners and birds. As with an annual vine, a trellised perennial vine adds height to your garden. The dense growth makes it a good choice for creating a shady nook to shelter a garden bench or to protect a bird feeder. The tangled stems deter predators, making it a sought-after site for nesting and roosting birds. Catbirds, for instance, often seek a vine to hold their cupped nest.

Vining Vegetables

Because it's cover and insects that attract birds to vines (plus any edible fruit), some of the plants you relegate to the vegetable garden are worth considering in other areas. My favorite veggie vine is the birdhouse gourd, not because of the gourds it yields for musical shakers or bird dwellings, but because it has delicate white flowers, as beautiful as any

> Even dead or dormant vines benefit birds: They provide shelter, roosting spots, and nesting material.

poppy, that open in the evening. Vining squash, melons, and pumpkins also make a good, quick fence cover—and you can serve the seeds to birds and squirrels later. You can even grow cherry tomatoes as a vine—just keep tying the stems to a fence or trellis as they grow. The plump tomato hornworms that occasionally plague the plants are a fine snack for catbirds, wrens, and other garden friends.

One year, a particularly energetic gourd vine I grew outstretched its trellis, crawled across the roof of the house, and clambered high into the branches of a maple overhead. Amazed at its prowess, I let it ramble. In fall, when all that was left was a tangle of bare stems, the vine became an access route to my feeders. Chickadees, jays, and downy woodpeckers, among others, used the ladder of dead, twisted stems to move from the sheltering treetop to the deck feeder.

Off-Season Vine Care

Birds still find vines useful even after the stems are dead or the leaves have dropped because they pro-

Vines to Try

PLAYING WITH perennial vines holds interesting possibilities for the bird-friendly yard. Try these ideas when you're deciding what to plant.

■ Native perennial vines are often overlooked, but there are many good choices among them. Passionflowers (*Passiflora* spp.), for instance, support butterflies as well as birds. Natives are easier to care for and weather extremes of climate better than

most imported plants. Another big advantage to choosing regionally native vines—or native shrubs, trees, and perennials—is that you'll avoid introducing or contributing to ecological disasters. Japanese honeysuckle (*Lonicera japonica*), anyone? Or maybe a nice little sprout of kudzu (*Pueraria lobata*)? Birds find both these introduced species very useful, but these rogues have become a bane to gardeners and wildflower enthusiasts.

■ Think like a bird when choosing vines for your yard, and you'll find many good selections that will suit your own taste, too. The perennial morning glory known as blue dawn flower (*Ipomoea indica*), a tender perennial hardy only to Zone 9, is perfect for covering an arbor and attracting birds to its sheltering tangle of stems. Its ethereal blue flowers will lift any gardener's heart. Grapevines (*Vitis* spp.) and some clematis species (*Clematis* spp.) are also ideal bird plants.

vide shelter and places to perch. A chain-link fence covered in morning glories, for instance, has value even in winter, when the vines have dried to tan, twisting stems. Sparrows and other birds often use the remains of annual vines as a place to gather on fall and winter days, and the branches of honeysuckle or other perennial vines may host a congregation of birds and even shelter them at night. Another advantage to letting annual vines stand is that they will drop their seeds, giving you a fresh crop of volunteers next season without spending a penny! Of course, if you prefer a tidier look to your yard, you can cut back your annual vines at the end of the growing season and replant them next year.

For the most benefit to birds, let perennial vines stand all winter as a roosting haven and windbreak. Prune them back into shape if desired in very early spring. Nearly all perennial vines bloom on "new wood," that is, stems that sprout from older branches in spring, so you won't have to worry about snipping off next season's flowers when you prune. Consider how severely grapevines in vineyards are routinely pruned—allowing only a few short branches on the main stem of the vine—and you'll see that vines are forgiving plants. Even if you should sacrifice flowers, the vines will still attract birds with their abundant insect-hiding foliage and sheltering stems.

Reduce maintenance chores for trellises and arbors by using supports made of wood that can weather naturally or weather-resistant metal or PVC. Plastic trellises and arbors continue to improve from the early days when they looked flimsy and fake. Many of today's plastic structures are almost indistinguishable from classic painted wood, and they come in plain or fancy styles and price ranges. Avoid painted supports for perennial vines because you'll discover it's tricky work to touch up the paint when there's a vine wrapped around the posts. Check your trellises and arbors in early spring to make sure they are still firmly seated in the ground; repair any weak parts if necessary by replacing or bracing damaged sections.

W

Walnuts

Attract chickadees, jays, nuthatches, titmice, woodpeckers

WANT TO HAND-TAME A CHICKADEE? Invest in a pound of walnuts. Before you reach the bottom of the bag, you'll have a little bird nibbling nuts right out of the palm of your hand.

Walnuts are a welcome treat for many birds, including jays, nuthatches, titmice, and woodpeckers as well as chickadees. Of course, your bushy-tailed "friends" also adore them, and that means you'll want to dole them out a bit at a time to prevent squirrels or chipmunks from skedaddling with bulging cheeks, leaving a suspiciously empty feeder in their wake.

Serving Up Walnuts

Birds will quickly snatch up big walnut pieces, but they will fly away from the feeder to a tree limb or other protected spot where they can eat the meat bit by bit. If you want the birds to linger, use a rolling pin to break the nuts into smaller chunks before you put them in your feeders. If you'd rather sharpen your skills at bird watching away from the feeder, put out larger pieces and follow the birds with your eyes or binoculars as they fly off to a tree, and then watch them break the nut down to size.

Shelled nuts are best at the feeder, but birds also appreciate broken pieces of walnuts still in the shell.

It's fun to watch how skillfully they extricate the nutmeats from the shell, especially black walnuts (*Juglans nigra*), which don't yield their tasty morsels easily. If you've ever tried to clean a bucket of black walnuts, you'll appreciate the finesse and sometimes frustration with which birds attack the nut.

Birds like both English (*J. regia*) and black walnuts. If you're lucky enough to have your own tree, collect some nuts (quickly, before the squirrels do!), and store them away for winter bird feeding. Black walnut is a native American tree, and the nuts are often available free for the asking along country roadsides (do be sure to ask permission). Whack the nuts with a hammer to break them for the bird feeder. Wear rubber gloves if you're handling black walnuts; the husks and shells will stain unprotected fingers deep brown. If you've managed to collect a large amount of black walnuts, you can crack them quickly by driving over them. Don't try this if an unblemished driveway is important to you—the nuts will stain concrete, gravel, and any other material.

Shelled walnuts are widely available, but you'll generally find the best prices at supermarket bulk-food bins or through co-ops or health-food stores. During prime baking season from Thanksgiving to

Strategy for Survival

WALNUTS AND other members of the *Juglans* genus have evolved a highly effective way of making sure their species survives: Their roots exude a toxin called juglone that stunts or kills many other plants that dare to trespass near the tree. Although walnuts, especially the black walnut, are notorious for this "allelopathic" defense system, other plants use the same trick,

with chemical toxins that differ according to the plant. Sunflowers, for instance, will inhibit the growth of many other plant neighbors; even the seed hulls can have a negative effect on other plants.

In most cases, the reaction is mild enough to go unnoticed by us gardeners. But black walnut is a real thug when it comes to claiming its space. The chemical lingers in the soil for years after a tree has been cut down. Even its leaves and nuts are toxic to other

plants to a lesser degree, which is a good reason to be tidy and clean up the shells after the birds are done with them. Wood chips from a black walnut tree can also have a negative effect on other plants.

Before planting a black walnut, think about where its roots will reach. Keep the tree well away from prized flowerbeds and other ornamentals, and forget about planting your nut grove near the veggie garden: Tomatoes are highly sensitive to the black walnut's warfare.

Christmas, stores often sell walnuts at discounted prices. Store extras in your refrigerator to prevent the oil from turning rancid at room temperature.

Nocturnal Nut Nibblers

A nighttime offering of walnuts, spread in the feeder after dark, especially in fall and winter, may bring you the enchanting surprise of a flying squirrel in your feeder. These gentle, dark-eyed creatures are unusually fearless around humans, and if you approach quietly, they will let you watch close up while they eat. They're particularly fond of walnuts.

Start a Shady Grove

If you have been offering whole walnuts in your feeders or if you have walnut trees in the neighborhood, you may already have a start of a backyard walnut grove, thanks to the efforts of your friends, the squirrels. Both English and black walnuts will sprout from whole nuts, a neat trick to try yourself, especially if you let the kids help: Just poke a few whole walnuts, still intact in their shells, 3 inches deep into the soil, spacing them several feet apart. To keep squirrels from digging up your nuts, lay a piece of wire mesh hardware cloth over the site.

You can also buy walnut trees from catalogs and garden centers. English walnuts grow into large, graceful shade trees with wide-spreading branches, while black walnuts are more upright in shape. Birds also favor the related Japanese walnut, or heartnut (*Juglans ailanthifolia*). Several cultivars are available that yield nuts with thinner shells or larger meats than the usual unimproved variety. Choose a cultivar that is hardy in your climate (English walnuts thrive through Zone 5; black walnuts into Zone 4), and plant it in a sunny spot where it will have room to spread its limbs.

PROJECT

Bird Treat Balls

Birds—and other feeder visitors—adore these tasty balls shaped from walnut pieces and chopped peanuts. To make the treat extra special for mockingbirds, cedar waxwings, and Carolina wrens, mix in dried cherries along with the nuts. Unflavored gelatin holds the treats together, and a sprig of holly berries adds a festive touch. Treats such as this one are best offered only in cold weather, when you can rely on the gelatin to hold the goodies together.

MATERIALS

Packet unflavored gelatin

1 quart walnut pieces

1 quart chopped peanuts

1 to 2 cups dried cherries (optional)

Wire for hanging

Sprig of holly berries (optional)

Step 1. Mix the packet of unflavored gelatin according to the label. In another bowl, combine walnut pieces, chopped peanuts, and dried cherries (if desired).

Step 2. Spread the nut mixture onto a cookie sheet.

Step 3. Fill a squirt bottle with the liquid gelatin, and spritz the nut mix liberally. Stir the mixture with your hands, and mold into 3-inch-diameter balls.

Step 4. Push a length of wire through each ball, bending at the bottom to prevent slippage and making a loop at the top for hanging. Top the ball with a sprig of holly berries.

Step 5. Place the balls in the freezer to solidify them; store in cool conditions until use.

W

Yellow-Rumped Warbler

WARBLERS ARE TINY BIRDS, chickadee-size but slimmer, that live almost entirely on a diet of insects. Dozens of species roam the country from spring through early fall, but most of us rarely see them because the birds pursue their daily bugs far above our heads, in the treetops. Learning the warblers is a challenge because the little birds are perpetual-motion machines, flitting from one branch to another before you can get your binoculars glued on them. This would be okay if each species was a bird of a different color: a red one, a blue one, a yellow one. But the rest of the bad news is that many warblers look alike, being yellowish green with only tiny details—an eye ring here, a wing band there—to tell them apart. Worse yet, in fall, the males lose their distinguishing bright colors and become the notorious "confusing fall warblers."

Sorting out warblers is an intriguing challenge, but you won't have to worry about it at the feeder. Of the 40 or so wood warblers, only 3 or 4 species eat anything other than insects, which means you can eliminate most of them right off the bat. To make matters even simpler, only one species is more than a rare visitor to feeders: the yellow-rumped warbler.

The myrtle and the Audubon's races of the yellow-rumped warbler are almost identical, but the myrtle has a white throat and the Audubon's throat is yellow. Named for its fondness for wax myrtle and the related bayberries (*Myrica* spp.), the myrtle warbler ranges across the country but is most abundant near the coasts. The Audubon's breeds across the West, retreating westward and southward in winter. Poison ivy berries are another favorite of these birds. Whenever I

Once known as the myrtle warbler, the yellow-rumped warbler frequents the coasts in winter, where it feasts on myrtle berries. Suet may attract it to the feeder.

WARBLER FEEDER FOODS

- American persimmon (*Diospyros virginiana*) fruits
- Bayberries (*Myrica* spp.)
- Figs
- Red cedar (*Juniperus virginiana*) berries
- Suet
- Sumac (*Rhus* spp.) berries

---

spot one of these plants with ripe fruit, I pause for a few minutes, keeping my ears alert for the distinctive call note, a low-pitched "Chuck."

Warbler Behavior

Look for the flash of white in the tail and wings and the eye-catching yellow rump, easily visible as the well-named bird flits among branches or hovers briefly to probe a likely spot or snatch a berry. In winter, when bands of chickadees, creepers, and kinglets roam the woodlands and backyards, a myrtle warbler or two may accompany them.

I never see yellow-rumped warblers at the feeders until fall, no doubt because insect food is so abundant in other seasons. At the feeder, insect eaters love suet, and yellow-rumped warblers are no exception. I spread chopped bits of suet in an open tray to tempt them and Carolina wrens, although they will also peck the fat from a suet holder.

Water Features

You may have noticed that the species that come to dine at your feeders are just a fraction of the birds that live in or pass through your area. Many birds ignore feeding stations, preferring to forage for natural food on their own. So while you can realistically hope for every woodpecker under the sun to visit your feeder, waiting for wood warblers to drop in from the sky is unrealistic. Like other nonfeeder birds, warblers feed almost entirely on insects, and no matter what delicacies you offer, you can't compete with the largesse of Mother Nature. Flycatchers, tanagers, and vireos will largely be no-shows, too.

The sound of trickling, dripping, or gently flowing water is music to birds' ears. Song sparrows and many other bird bathers will regularly visit shallow, moving water.

The best way to entice these hard-to-get birds to your yard is with water. All birds need H_2O for drinking, and nearly all birds enjoy a splashing bath in fresh water. Birds are quick to visit natural ponds, streams, and other areas, as well as backyard water features, but they are also adept at making do with even a temporary source of water. After a rain, or when snow melts, they will flock to a shallow puddle. Even a melting icicle may slake their thirst. Watch your garden after a rain, and you may be lucky enough to spot a chickadee, hummingbird, or other small feathered creature sipping or even splashing in the thin layer of water held by a cupped leaf. Dew supplies many birds with necessary liquid, too.

Guaranteed to Please

Water is so irresistible that the sound of it dripping or burbling or splashing is a guaranteed draw, no matter where you live. Not only will it bring regular customers to the bath day after day, but it will also tempt migrants in spring and fall and unusual backyard visitors any time of year.

One summer, during a drought, visiting birds overwhelmed a small bubbling "spring" I created at ground level. Bobwhites jockeyed for space with mourning doves, wood thrushes shyly waited until the bluebirds finished drinking, and goldfinches were a noisy, constant presence. Cedar waxwings perched on nearby shrubs, awaiting the unspoken agreement of the flock to descend en masse. At daybreak, it wasn't unusual to see a plain-red summer tanager sipping beside a red-and-black scarlet tanager—both species among the earliest visitors. Phoebes and flycatchers visited late in the afternoon, and in the heat of the day, bank swallows and barn swallows traveled from their colony a quarter-mile away to quench their thirst.

My traditional pedestal-type birdbath was not nearly so successful as the water feature that attracted birds with the quiet murmur of running water. The birdbath still attracted plenty of catbirds, doves, finches, and robins, but the naturalistic water feature got the lion's share.

Keep It Shallow

It feels great to us to sink into hot water up to the chin, but birds don't feel safe in anything but shallow water. Knee-deep is perfect; belly-deep is scary. If a bird loses its footing in deep water, it can quickly become helpless and thus vulnerable to attack or to drowning. No wonder shallow water with secure footing is so important!

Here's yet another place to take a lesson from the way birds behave in the wild. Keep your eyes open for bathing birds, and you'll soon see that shallow places attract them. Lakes hold no appeal, except around the very edges, and then usually for drinking, not bathing. Isolated puddles are the top temptation for birds—an idea you can mimic in your own yard very successfully. Like people who have a fear of the vastness of the ocean, birds seem to feel safer when their bathing spot is finite. At creeks, you will see them splashing in the small stretches of quiet, shallow water sheltered by surrounding rocks—not in the wide open areas.

Bath Mat for Birds

Think rough when designing a water feature or selecting a birdbath. A nonslippery surface gives birds a feeling of security just as a rubber bath mat provides that for you in your bathtub.

The most beautiful birdbath in the world will stand unused if the surface beneath the water or on the rim is slick metal or glazed pottery. If birds can't get a grip when they land on the edge, they are unlikely to risk stepping down into the bath. I learned this lesson the hard way after buying a beautiful birdbath glazed cobalt blue—my favorite color. It made a pretty yard ornament, but birds wouldn't stop to sip until I covered the blue interior with a layer of rough sandstone that let them feel safe.

Concrete, sandstone and other rough-surfaced rock, and synthetic materials topped with a grainy surface are ideal for birdbaths. Vinyl pond liners,

Songbirds like this blue grosbeak prefer the safety of shallow water and a nonslip surface for bathing. Create water features that slope gradually at edges.

smooth metal or ceramic saucers, and slippery plastic containers are trouble, from a bird's perspective. Although they may visit a water feature with these surfaces, it will only be when they can't find water elsewhere.

Keep It Low

You won't find natural water at waist height unless it's dropping over a cliff. Water pools near the ground, and that's the first place birds look for it.

Anything you can do to recreate natural circumstances will increase the numbers and kinds of birds that visit your water features. Setting up a bath at ground level is an easy first step. See the Birdbaths entry on page 19 for more details on creating a simple low-level bathing area.

Best Water Features for Birds

Once you're ready to graduate from a simple pedestal or hanging birdbath, your next thought is likely to be of a garden pool. Now that even discount stores are stocking preformed garden pools, the hobby of water gardening is available to anyone who can invest a weekend's work and around $100. That's all it takes to add the pleasure of a permanent water feature to your yard. A single free-form or more formal pool, a suitable pump, a few hours of digging, and the basics are in place.

Before you leap for the shovel, though, consider the benefits of a garden pool to birds. Remember what's important to them—shallow water and a good drip—and you'll see that a garden pool is actually not very effective as a bathing place for your feathered visitors. The water is too deep. Worse yet, instead of a gently sloping approach, it drops almost instantly from the rim to a depth that birds will avoid.

You can alter a garden pool to serve birds better, but it's probably easier to turn your sights to a different kind of water feature. Create a bath just for birds that imitates the shallow, protected wild places they seek.

Design Considerations

Seeing things from a bird's point of view is vital when you're choosing a water feature to add to your yard, but don't forget to factor in your own sense of style, too. Birds won't notice if you arrange the rocks around the water casually or symmetrically in a formal style—but *you* will. A rippling "stream" or naturalistic waterfall is perfect for an informal garden or country look. But if your tastes run to straight-edged beds and a more controlled appearance, an informal water feature would stick out like

A water-lily pond is too deep for bird bathing. But it will attract nonfeeder birds like this prothonotary warbler that come to dine on insects found around the water.

Old Faithful. In a more formal garden, a rectangular pool with a gentle bubbler would be more at home.

When you shop for ready-made water features, you'll find products that run the gamut from unabashed tackiness to elegant simplicity, and every stop in between. Before the plastic revolution, which has put good taste (and bad taste) in the hands of the masses, choices were much more limited. "The shell

---

Improving a Pool for the Birds

INCREASE THE accessibility of your garden pool by making these improvements to a standard pre-formed installation. All will provide bird visitors with a secure place to perch while drinking or access to shallow water for bathing.

- Lay rocks into one end of the pool, so that their surfaces are just below water level, with part of the rock above the water. This will give birds a place to stand for drinking and perhaps a place to splash.

- Leave spaces between some of the rocks around the rim of the pool to provide a sheltered nook where birds can get a drink or wet a feather.

- Place potted aquatic plants close to the edge of the pool, in the water, so that the surface of their containers extends to or very near the rim of the pool.

Birds may use the pots' edges as perches.

- Pile a wide plastic container, such as a dishpan or kitty-litter tray, with rough stones or gravel, mounding it higher in the center. Settle the container onto bricks or an overturned pot beneath the water, so that the heaped stones in the center of the container are above water level, while those at the edges are just under water.

of the giant clam (*Tridacna gigas*) makes a most attractive birdbath," suggests one older book on my shelf, noting that garden-supply shops can supply specimens. The run on giant clams may have contributed to today's scarcity. They are now an endangered species, and apparently those old birdbaths didn't last because I can't remember ever seeing one of these natural wonders outside a museum.

Buy It or Build It

Thanks to the buying power of backyard bird watchers, all sorts of great water features are on the market, with more added every year. Some are for connoisseurs, such as estate-quality cast iron constructions that cost about the same as college tuition. Others are designed for everyone, with lightweight plastics that will give several years of good use.

If you like working with your hands, you may prefer the creativity of making your own water features instead of the convenience of buying ready-made ones. Working with concrete or PVC liner material to make a permanent puddle is as messy as making mud pies, and just as much fun. Once you give it a try, you may decide to graduate to making a recycling stream or even a waterfall—both entirely possible projects for even a rank novice. I can testify to this: I started with common sense and a memory of favorite wild places. Armed with several feet of ½-inch tubing and a small recirculating pump, I lugged four big, flat rocks into place and made a very satisfying waterfall that spilled into a sunken plastic tub.

Whichever route you choose, keep the "Big Three" criteria in mind:

- Shallow water for safety
- Rough surface for sure footing
- The tempting sound of running water to lure birds from a distance

Adding a naturalistic water feature to your yard will bring wonderful surprises. Even the ungainly-looking beak of the red crossbill can sip from shallow water.

Commercial Products

Manufacturers have made it easy for us bird lovers. Just make a trip to the garden center, home-supply store, or discount center, and you can carry home a self-contained kit that includes everything you need to attract birds with water. Best of all, it takes no installation—just choose a spot, fill the container with water, and plug in the pump.

Availability of the products may vary with regional markets and suppliers. Keep the "Big Three" desired features in mind when you go shopping, and you'll have no trouble satisfying your sense of aesthetics and making the birds happy, too.

One of the most appealing commercial products I've seen had two tiers of basins, a large bottom one and a smaller top one, made of molded plastic that looked just like stone. A small pump kept water spilling over the top ledge into the lower basin. The surface felt like sandstone, rough and grainy the way birds like it. At a little over $100, the water feature was an investment that would pay off fast with increased bird traffic. I saw it in a country greenhouse,

(*continued on page 324*)

Simple Pool for Bird Bathing

Working with concrete was the only choice for making birdbaths just a few decades ago. Today heavy-duty plastic liners make it much easier for the average klutz to create a water feature. The liner material prevents water from seeping into the soil. All you need to do is scoop out a depression, lay the liner in place, decorate the edges, and fill with water. You can cut the liner material with a utility knife to tailor it to the size of your excavation.

MATERIALS

Pond liner

Mix of medium and large rocks for rim

Sand

Gravel

Landscaping materials: shrubs, grasses, perennials, and/or groundcovers

Small recirculating pump

Step 1. Dig a shallow, sloping hole, about 3 feet across, 6 inches deep in the center. The hole can be circular, oval, free-form, or even rectangular if yours is a formal garden. Slope the sides gradually from the edges.

Step 2. Lay a piece of pond liner in the hole. The size of your pond liner will need to be the length and width plus the depth. The liner for this pool should be about 4 feet × 4 feet. Trim off excess material around the edges, allowing a 6-inch overlap onto surrounding soil.

Step 3. Anchor the liner with rocks around the edges.

Step 4. Cover the liner with 2 inches of coarse sand or river rock or other smooth stones or gravel. If you use rough gravel, cover the liner with a layer of sand first to prevent cuts from the sharp edges on the gravel.

Step 5. Landscape around the pool.

Step 6. Install a small recirculating pump to attract birds. Fill with water, plug in the pump, and watch for your first customers.

A typical garden pool drops off sharply at the edges. Re-dig this one so that the sides make a very slight transition in steepness, and you won't have to fiddle with laying in rocks or bricks so that birds can walk into the water.

where an open door allowed some of the accumulated heat to escape. The greenhouse was alive with hummingbirds and butterflies, and several of them were drinking at the trickling fountain.

Concrete is still a good option for making water features. It's inexpensive and fun to do with kids. And it gives you the pride of saying "I did it myself," even if the result is less slick than a purchased model. A sack of quick-setting concrete makes the job fast and simple. I mix it in an old metal wheelbarrow, using a garden hoe for stirring and a wide mason's trowel for spreading it. Plan your water feature, collect any materials, and do the digging before you mix the concrete—it hardens remarkably fast.

Unless you're an expert, stick with a simple design. I made a serviceable pool for my birds by digging a sloping, shallow hole and spreading a 2- to 3-inch layer of concrete in the depression. I don't like the stark look of whitish concrete, so I used a commercial dye to tint the mix to a deep charcoal gray. Before the concrete hardened, I stuck a few rocks into place in the pool and at the edges to give it a natural look and to provide perching opportunities. Two coats of waterproofing compound after the concrete dried gave me added insurance against leaks. I was a little worried about the pool being damaged in my Zone 6 winters, but it lasted for almost a decade before finally cracking—and then I simply patched the crack.

Almost-Natural Waterfall

If you have a slightly sloping area in your yard, you can build a natural-looking waterfall in just a couple of weekends. Enlist a helper to lessen the load and make it easier to lay out the liner. Sketch your design on paper and collect your materials before you dig the first scoop of soil, so you can easily follow the steps. Collect some long, flat rocks if you want a curtain effect for the waterfall, or, if you prefer a wild tumble, use irregular rocks to make the spillway. It's fun to play with water and easier than it looks to do this project. If needed, break it up into steps that you can accomplish gradually.

MATERIALS

Sandbags, as needed

Sand

Pool liner

A mix of rocks for the rim and waterfall

Solvent

Small recirculating pump

Flexible tubing

Landscaping materials: shrubs, grasses, perennials, and/or groundcovers

Step 1. Excavate a channel and pool. Keep the channel shallow, about 8 inches deep, and use the removed soil to create a berm along each side to contain the water. Gradually slope the pool to as deep as you wish in the center.

Step 2. Pile removed soil as a foundation for the head of the waterfall. Add sandbags for extra fill.

Step 3. Level the pool hole, and pour in a layer of sand. Moisten it and smooth it, so that it follows the contours of the pool.

Step 4. Measure and cut the liner for the pool, allowing extra for overhang at the edges. To figure the liner size, measure the width of the pool, add the depth of the two sides, and add another 12 inches for overhang. Do the same calculations for the length of the pool.

Step 5. Lay the liner over the hole (easier with a helper). Smooth out wrinkles as much as possible.

Step 6. Lay rocks around edges to hold the liner in place. Trim off excess liner.

Step 7. Measure and cut liner for waterfall/stream channel, allowing 1 foot overlap onto pool liner. Use solvent (available at home-supply stores and garden centers) to weld the overlap to the pool liner.

Works of Art

Don't we all want a stream in our yards? How about a waterfall? Thanks to the wonders of flexible pond liners, we can have it all. The technique is simple. Basically, you dig a sloping channel, line it with sand, lay in PVC liner, edge with rocks, and install pump and tubing that continuously returns water to the headwaters of your creek.

These ambitious water features may take a couple of weekends to get just right, but they will give you years of pleasure. Running water is just as delightful to our eyes, ears, and psyches as it is appealing to birds. The stream or waterfall you install will be a major attraction in your yard for as long as you live there. It will become such a part of your place that you may find yourself forgetting that once you had nothing but lawn.

Use some thought when deciding where to place your stream. The first criterion is to locate it in a place where you can watch the activity from a favorite window inside the house, or from a garden bench or other sitting area outside. Make sure it won't be an obstacle to foot traffic—wading across stepping stones is a charming thought, but a lot less fun if you have to do it every time you pick up the mail. You will also need to select a sloping area to build the watercourse—water flows downhill. It's the job of the pump to return it to its starting point. Also be sure you have

Step 8. Set large rocks in place along the channel and at the waterfall to anchor the liner. Experiment with the placement until you find it pleasing, lifting and lowering rocks carefully so as not to rip the liner.

Step 9. Install a recirculating pump in the pool and run flexible tubing back to the waterfall, disguising it among the rocks.

Step 10. Slowly fill the pool, until you are satisfied with the volume of water flowing through the stream.

Step 11. Add additional rocks in the streambed and at the waterfall to create bathing and drinking pools for birds. Mark off a few shallow areas of the pool by placing rocks between them and the deeper water, so birds can feel safe in shallow water.

Step 12. Landscape the area with shrubs for preening after bathing and perennials and ornamental grasses to give it a natural appeal.

Once your garden pond and waterfall are installed, plant around it to create a more natural setting. Branching and fruit-bearing shrubs near the water will provide damp birds with safe places to sit and preen.

a convenient outdoor electrical outlet to power the pump.

You can use preformed garden pool sections to create the stream and waterfall, or use an earthen bed topped with sand and a pond liner. Good-sized rocks are another necessity. They disguise the edges in a natural way and help anchor the construction. If you don't have a handy supply of fieldstone around your property, you can find dealers in stone and rock who will deliver the material or let you pick it up yourself. Be sure to select rock that fits your area, so that it doesn't look incongruous in your landscape.

Faux rocks are another possibility. They've come a long way from the first "that's a fake" effect. Now plastic boulders and stones look so natural that you can't tell even by touching. Their slight weight is a welcome improvement over real stone, which always seems heavier than it looks.

See Your Stonemason

Stone fountains and other stone water features usually carry exorbitantly high prices because of the limited market, the shipping weight of the material, and the amount of design and labor that goes into them. If you yearn for one of these beautiful objects and won't settle for plastic, you can cut costs—often dramatically—by finding a stonecutter to do the work for you.

Thankfully, cutting stone is an art that's still alive, and you can find its practitioners in your Yellow Pages. Your nearest supplier of cemetery headstones may also have the equipment and skills necessary to transform a block of sandstone, granite, or limestone into a work of art. As with any custom job, be sure you and the craftsperson agree on what work is being done, what the schedule is, and how much it will cost.

Put your birdbaths and other water features where you can see them so that you don't miss the fun. Here a chipping sparrow indulges in a morning splash.

Think from a bird's point of view as you arrange rocks to make your water features. This white-throated sparrow and other birds seek out shallow places with easy access.

Weather Predictors

IS A BIG SNOW COMING? Just take a look at the feeders. If they are jam-packed with birds, and if the birds linger until past their usual last-call time, you can bet bad weather is on the way. Birds are sensitive to atmospheric pressure, and the lows that precede a storm are a signal to stock up while the getting is good.

Here in the tornado belt of the Midwest, I take my severe-weather cues from the birds as well as the Weather Channel. If the birds fall silent during daylight hours, I know something big is coming, and I head for cover. Long before the meteorologists issue the all-clear, the birds let me know that the danger is past. That first chirping robin or trilling song sparrow sounds glorious after a bad storm.

Yellow-billed and black-billed cuckoos, which rarely visit feeders, are known as "rain crows" in some areas because of their habit of calling before a thunderstorm. On heavy summer afternoons, when humidity is thick, their mournful "Coo-coo-coo" is a common sound in the woods and hedgerows they frequent.

Birds have a knack for knowing a winter storm is approaching. You can count on a mob before a blizzard as birds keep the feeders hopping.

Weeds

Attract many kinds of birds at various times of the year

STOP MOWING YOUR GRASS, put away the dandelion digger, and by the end of summer you'll have every bird for blocks hanging out in your yard. Of course, you might also encounter the zoning officer at your door reminding you of the need to conform to neighborhood standards. The fact is, birds love weeds, but you (and your neighbors) might not.

To birds, weeds mean just one thing: food, and lots of it. Find a stand of giant ragweed in winter, and you're sure to find a horde of cardinals, finches, and native sparrows, which come to feast on the abundant seeds until the spiky seedheads are picked clean. Same thing with lamb's-quarters: A thicket of the 4-foot-tall plants will attract scores of buntings, chickadees, finches, siskins, sparrows,

and others. Even a single plant doesn't escape notice. I've watched white-crowned sparrows desert the easy pickings at my feeder in favor of a single stem of lamb's-quarters growing nearby, which they fought over as if it were candy. Lamb's-quarter seeds must definitely be delicious to attract as many birds as they do, but to my uneducated palate, the tiny seeds don't taste like much. I'd take sunflower seeds any day.

The Best Weed for Birds

The number-one weed for birds is the pretty annual grass known as foxtail, or bristlegrass. You've probably seen the fuzzy spikes of this common weed along roadsides and fields nearby or even sprouting in your own flowerbeds. The bristly seedheads may be arching or they may stand erect, depending on species, but birds gobble them no matter what position they're in. Practically every seed-eating bird in America seeks out foxtail grass, a close cousin of the millet so popular at the feeder. Doves, ducks, grouse, quail, and other game birds are huge fans. Among the songbird clan, everyone from cardinals and grosbeaks to sparrows and thrashers—at least 46 species—relish the small, crunchy seeds. This is one of the most abundant American weeds and one of the easiest to collect for later offerings at the feeder. In fall, I pick a lavish bouquet of tan, ripe foxtail grass seedheads for the fat brown crock on my kitchen table. When I get tired of my dried arrangement indoors, I just tie the stems together and hang it below the feeder.

Weedy Gardens Are Great for Birds

If you can tolerate a few weeds in your yard—or better yet, if you have a discreet corner that you can let "go wild" with weeds—you'll increase your bird life by a bushel. Plus you'll get to observe the interesting ways birds devour different seeds. You may see an indigo bunting neatly pulling one tuft after another from a dandelion puff or perhaps a tree sparrow hopping off the ground to pull down a seedhead of curly dock so it can stand on the stem while it eats. Acrobatic goldfinches and siskins are amusing to watch as they go after every remaining seed in a stem of wild mustard that bends beneath their weight.

If you can't bear the thought of encouraging "plain old weeds," at least consider some of the weeds that have been civilized for garden use: The ornamental amaranths are almost as seedy as their pigweed cousins. And chicory bears garden-worthy blue flowers; just plant it behind something low and bushy to hide its ratty foliage.

Weeds are so attractive to birds that (shhh! don't tell) I sometimes resort to subterfuge and hide a weed plantation behind a fool-the-neighbors strip of annual flowers. Tall, branching sunflowers on the out-

Pretty flowers help people accept weeds like chicory; goldfinches and others like their seeds. A diverse, weedy corner will welcome many hungry birds.

side, lamb's-quarters, pigweed, and whatever else wants to come up on the inside—it's a fine arrangement that doesn't distress the neighbors, and it gives me months of good bird watching on the "weedy" side of the garden.

I also let the occasional weed grow in my more traditional flower gardens, and I haven't had a sudden bumper crop of weeds after tolerating their presence. I credit the birds with that—they clean up the seeds so thoroughly that few get added to the reservoir of weed seeds already in the soil.

The moral of this story? If you want more birds to visit your yard and to linger longer, invite a few weeds to stay. You may find yourself beginning to look on common weeds with a brand new perspective. From there, it's just a small step to actually cultivating these scorned plants.

Winter Food Plants

STOCKING YOUR yard with plants that hold their seeds, berries, or cones into the winter months is a great way to draw foraging thrushes, cedar waxwings, and other birds that may be reluctant to visit a feeding station. Natural foods also provide a welcome change of pace for your feeder regulars. All conifers (pines, spruces, hemlocks, firs, and others) are a good source of winter food, but consider rounding out the menu with a few other possibilities, such as the following:

Long-Lasting Seedheads

Amaranths (*Amaranthus* spp.): Annual weeds or decorative garden plants, this genus holds seed-packed fuzzy spikes relished throughout the cold months by buntings, doves, finches, goldfinches, juncos, horned larks, pheasants, quail, redpolls, native sparrows, and towhees.

Ragweeds (*Ambrosia* spp.): Common annual weeds, ranging from knee-high to head height, depending on species, produce abundant small, oily seeds sought by cardinals, doves, finches, pine siskin, native sparrows, waxwings, and many other birds.

Big bluestem (*Andropogon gerardii*): Very tall native perennial prairie grass, to 6 feet, with interesting "turkey foot"–shaped seedheads that eventually keel over in late winter, providing food for juncos, native sparrows, towhees, and other ground-feeding birds.

Broomsedge (*A. virginicus*): Perennial grass almost identical to little bluestem (*Schizachyrium scoparium*), with more of a "whisk-broom" look near the tops of the stems; acquires rich orangeish color in fall and winter. Small seeds sought by rosy finches, juncos, native sparrows, and game birds.

Little bluestem (*Schizachyrium scoparium*): Clump-forming native perennial prairie grass that grows to 3 feet tall and turns beautiful warm orange in fall and winter. Fuzzy seed clusters along stems furnish food for finches, game birds, juncos, and native sparrows as well as small mammals.

Winter Berries or Fruit

Manzanitas (*Arctostaphlyos* spp.): Striking smooth, red bark characterizes many of the shrubby species of this western and southwestern genus, which also includes ground-hugging bearberry (*A. uva-ursi*). Red or brown berries are prime food for grouse, grosbeaks, jays, mockingbird, and fox sparrow as well as for small mammals—skunks particularly like them!

Hackberries (*Celtis laevigata, C. occidentalis,* and other spp.): Lovely shade trees with interesting warty gray bark and a multitude of small fruits that ripen in late fall to early winter. Source of food for catbirds, flickers, jays, mockingbirds, orioles, robins, sapsuckers, starlings, thrashers, thrushes, titmice, woodpeckers, and wrens, which devour the bounty while still on the tree. Towhees, fox sparrows, and other native sparrows join in the feast when the fruit drops.

Persimmons (*Diospyros virginiana, D. texana*): Native trees with alligator-hide–checkered bark, large, simple leaves, and astringent orange to orange-red fleshy fruit that softens and sweetens when ripe. Beloved by bluebirds, catbirds, mockingbirds, robins, sapsuckers, starlings, wild turkeys, yellow-rumped warblers, and waxwings. Also a favorite of the raccoon and its close relative, the unusual ring-tailed cat of Texas, the Southwest, and West.

Cedars (*Juniperus* spp.): Deep green or gray-green conifers with often prickly foliage and lovely blue berries, much sought by bluebirds, catbirds, crossbills, doves, finches, flickers, grosbeaks, jays, mockingbirds, robins, sapsuckers, thrashers, thrushes, yellow-rumped warbler, and waxwings as well as game birds.

Sumacs (*Rhus* spp.): Native shrubs or small trees with foliage that turns brilliant red to orange in fall and dense, pointed clusters of red (white in some species) fuzzy berries held upright. A food of last resort, the berries are eaten in winter by crows, ruffed grouse, pigeons, quail, wild turkeys, and many songbirds, including bluebirds, cardinals, catbirds, purple finches, flickers, jays, magpies, mockingbirds, starlings, thrushes, woodpeckers, and wrens.

Greenbriers (*Smilax* spp.): Evergreen or deciduous native climbers, some thorny-stemmed, absent in parts of the West and abundant in the Southeast. Berries may be yellow, black, blue, or green and are devoured eagerly by many birds: Bluebirds, catbirds, fish crows, flickers, mockingbirds, robins, fox sparrows, white-throated sparrows, thrushes, cedar waxwings and pileated woodpeckers are among the prime customers.

yard increases because of flocking patterns. Blackbirds and house finches may arrive in large flocks, and cardinals, finches, grosbeaks, sparrows, and other birds now pal around in groups instead of living the solitary life.

The cast of characters at your feeder remains fairly stable in winter, except that the numbers will swell temporarily when bad weather moves in. Occasional rare birds, either unusual for your region or unusual for your feeder, also appear at feeders in the winter, driven by hunger. For example, from spring through fall, I never see a crow anywhere near my small town yard. But I can count on several big black birds stalking the feeding area during the winter season, particularly when snow (even a light dusting) covers the ground. Often they join the starlings at the dog-food pan or turkey carcass.

If you live in the Deep South or southern California, the scene at your winter feeders may be quite different than the view in cold, snowy areas. Rufous and black-chinned hummingbirds are in winter residence along the Gulf coast, busily visiting nectar feeders. Red-breasted nuthatches, a southern rarity in spring and summer except during migration, now settle in across the southern half of the country for a sunny winter vacation, as do chipping sparrows and fox sparrows. In the West, the beautiful varied thrush moves in, giving winter feeder keepers all the way to Baja some color to enjoy. Western and mountain

This is the scene that warms a feeder host's heart: birds filling their bellies at the feeding station when natural food is scarce.

bluebirds move into the southern regions of the West. In the Deep South and along the southern Atlantic coast, house wrens may visit for mealworms; catbirds, robins, and brown thrashers may turn up at the chopped suet or fruit feeder; and Bullock's and Baltimore orioles may grace the nectar feeder. As the days gradually start to lengthen at the end of winter, you'll notice that the birds at your feeders are beginning

10 To-Dos for Winter Feeding

1. Stock up! Lay in a week's supply of your most popular seeds in reserve.

2. Be sure you have plenty of suet on hand; extra fat in the freezer is easy to pull out when needed.

3. Keep feeders free of ice and snow. Erect lean-tos or add roofs so that at least some feeders are covered.

4. If you're blessed with deep snow or frequent treacherous ice, temporarily move a few feeders very close to the house, so that you can refill them easily without risking your neck.

5. Try hand taming: It's easy in cold weather, when birds are motivated to take the food.

6. Keep a calendar of daily visitors, or a weekly census. It's fun to know exactly whom you're feeding.

7. Save leftover soft foods, such as bread and pancakes, for catbirds, robins, wrens, and other soft-food eaters. If you run out of kitchen leftovers, serve these birds moistened dog food.

8. Watch for hawks patrolling from above or perched to wait for your feeder birds.

9. Recycle your Christmas tree into a windbreak alongside a low-level tray feeder.

10. Make homemade treats for the bird, such as the ever-popular peanut-butter–smeared pinecones. Kids love to help, and it gives them an early sense of connection to the birds outside their window.

to behave differently. Male cardinals, juncos, native sparrows, and other males of the same species that formerly ate companionably side by side now become short-tempered, turning to each other with flashing wings and threatening opened beaks. It's only natural—longer daylight hours kick the reproductive hormones into gear, and battles over elbow room and mates become a more frequent occurrence. Doves, owls, and woodpeckers are among the earliest to actually start a family, often in late winter.

Plan Ahead

The most important rule of winter feeding is: Be prepared. Storms can move in quickly, making that little jaunt to the birdseed store a nightmare or just plain impossible. Besides, your own family's needs will no doubt take precedence over feeder birds. That's why you'll want to keep an extra sack or two of birdseed on hand for emergencies. I keep at least a week's worth in reserve during winter, which for my feeders means a 50-pound bag of sunflower seed, a 50-pound sack of cracked corn, and 20 pounds of millet, plus about 10 ears of whole corn for my squirrels.

You'll appreciate your freezer and pantry in the winter months, too, if you have stockpiled them with bird treats such as the following:

- Chopped suet and raw hamburger are prized foods at the winter feeder, as are meat scraps and leftovers.
- Nuts of any kind offer excellent nourishment and are so popular that they may be the cause of bird disputes.
- Grain-based foods from the kitchen, such as cereal recipes, bread crumbs, and baked goods, are a hit with many kinds of birds.
- Frozen or dried fruits and berries come in handy for bluebirds, catbirds, robins, thrashers, wrens, and other birds that usually eschew seeds.
- An extra jar of peanut butter, economy-size, is a treasure in winter, when severe weather is likely to bring any bluebirds in the area to your feeders.
- Mealworms are snatched up fast at the winter feeder.

Feeder birds don't mind sharing space at the table when a snowstorm sends everyone fluttering to find food. Here a Carolina wren dines with a cardinal.

If you've included a salt block at your feeding area, you'll see it's as popular in winter as at other times of the year. Winter brings winter finches sweeping down irregularly from the North, and salt is a big hit with these unusual birds. Keep an eye open for crossbills, redpolls, and siskins at your salt block along with the usual doves and house finches. Focus your binoculars on the odd scissors bill of crossbills at the salt lick, and you will see that they make this food live up to its name: they actually lick up the salt with their tongues.

Birds still search for water in winter, too. Since most natural sources of water are frozen, a birdbath or other water feature free of ice will make your yard a magnet for birds. They splash about in fresh water even when the temperature is frigid, as long as they find a sunny perch afterward where they can dry their feathers. You can set out a shallow basin of warm water daily or invest in an electric heater for the birdbath that will keep at least part of the water ice-free. The Birdbaths entry on page 19 has more helpful hints for ensuring a steady supply of precious water.

Woodpeckers

IF MY ONLY FEEDER VISITOR was a woodpecker, I could be quite content (at least for a while!). Even when they're motionless, these highly specialized birds are wonderful to watch. They are beautiful birds with complex feather patterns, variations of head markings between species and sexes, and an intriguing structure and use of the tail. In action the birds are fascinating as they use their heavy beaks to pry, chisel, chop, whack, and delicately probe. They also have fascinating feet that help them cling to tree trunks.

Eighteen different American woodpeckers (not counting the flickers, which you can learn about in their own entry on page 121) ensure that no matter where you feed birds, a woodpecker will accept your hospitality. Supply suet, supplemented with seeds and other treats, and you'll have feeder friends for life. Year after year, woodpeckers return to feeding stations where they have learned to find food.

Most Common Feeder Visitors

Several woodpeckers are frequent feeders across the country. These common species are among the most adaptable of the family, often leaving their traditional forest homelands for new dwelling places in suburbia and towns. Not only will they visit your feeders regularly, they are also likely to quickly adopt a nest box or a dead branch in your yard for raising their family.

The downy woodpecker is a regular at feeders across most of the country. A nonmigrating species, the downy will visit daily in all seasons.

Every feeder host has a soft spot for the little **downy woodpecker,** the smallest of the tribe, and a reliable year-round guest at the suet and seed tray. This black-and-white bird occurs across nearly the entire country, except for a few areas of the Southwest. Its larger look-alike cousin, the **hairy woodpecker,** is less common but just as widespread. If a

---

WOODPECKER FEEDER FOODS

- Acorns (*Quercus* spp.)
- Almonds
- Amelanchier (*Amelanchier* spp.) berries
- Cherries, fresh or dried
- Corn, on cob, whole, or cracked
- Dogwood (*Cornus* spp.) berries
- Elderberries (*Sambucus* spp.)
- Figs
- Grapes
- Hazelnuts (*Corylus* spp.)
- Hickory (*Carya ovata*) nuts
- Holly (*Ilex* spp.) berries
- Mealworms
- Meat scraps
- Mulberries (*Morus* spp.)
- Nectar
- Peanut butter
- Pecans (*Carya illinoiensis*)
- Pine (*Pinus cembroides*) nuts
- Suet
- Sunflower seeds
- Walnuts (*Juglans* spp.)

bird shows up at the feeder looking like a downy on steroids, it's probably a hairy. The hairy's body is bigger and its beak is heavier than the petite downy's.

In the eastern half of the country, another likely feeder guest is the **red-bellied woodpecker,** a bird that's big enough to give even a jay a hard time. The first thing you'll notice about this deceptively named woodpecker isn't its belly—it's the head splashed with vivid red from bill to nape (crown to nape in the female). One of the "ladderbacked" group of woodpeckers, this bird has finely barred black and white feathers on its back that look like rungs on a ladder. Bird watchers in bygone years called it the "zebra bird." If you can get a glimpse of the bird's belly, you may see the flush of reddish feathers that gives it its common name. But since woodpeckers typically cling against a support to eat, the red patch is hard to spot. Like other ladderbacks, this nonmigratory bird doesn't budge when the seasons change; the red-belly eating suet in December is the same bird you see in July.

The **yellow-bellied sapsucker** is a common bird, but not so commonly seen. While most woodpeckers are noisy and outgoing, this species is an introvert. It's so shy that it will hitch its body around to the other side of the tree if it notices you watching it. One sapsucker I spotted was shy but not too savvy. Like a 2-year-old playing peekaboo, the bird hid only its head under a branch, as if positive I could no longer see it. Western sapsuckers include the **red-breasted sapsucker** and **Williamson's sapsucker.** Sapsuckers have other behaviors peculiar to their kind—they don't drum on resonant dead branches or other percussion "instruments" like other woodpeckers, and they drill for sap. Their work produces rows of small holes, spaced closely together, in the bark of trees. The birds sip the sap as it flows from

The red-bellied woodpecker gets my vote for most poorly named bird. I'd call it red-naped—that red on the back of its neck is the first thing you see.

the tree. A wonderful array of butterflies, hummingbirds, gorgeous underwing moths, large beetles, and other interesting visitors also enjoy the sap.

Locally Common Woodpeckers

The presence of some woodpeckers is a matter of luck. These "locally common" birds are thick in some areas and rare just a short distance away. Why this occurs is a mystery as suitable habitat doesn't seem to matter. If you're lucky, the **red-headed woodpecker** may visit you. Shining black on the back, with a snow white breast, this bird wears a hood of rich crimson that covers its head and neck. Large white wing patches meld with its white rump when the bird flies, creating a tricolor picture of red, black, and pure white. It ranges across the eastern two-thirds of the country, but this bird is a now-you-see-it, now-you-don't species. If you have a red-headed woodpecker at your feeder, count yourself a privileged person.

Lewis's woodpecker, named for one-half of the intrepid exploring team of Lewis and Clark, is another of those tantalizing "locally common" species. It's a possibility across most of the West. This bird looks like a smudged facsimile of the red-headed species, with greenish black back, red face, pink belly, and mottled grayish breast. Sticking to a narrower western range is another teaser, the locally common and vividly distinct **white-headed woodpecker.** This striking bird is solid black except for a bright white head and throat, a white wing patch, and a dash of red at the nape.

Even more limited in range is the **black-backed woodpecker,** which ranges through some Northwest and Far North conifer forests. It peels slabs and flakes of bark from dead trees to get at insects. Along with a black back, this bird has a bright yellow crown, like the **three-toed woodpecker,** another locally common western and northern bird. You may have a hard time counting his toes, but the three-toed woodpecker has a bright yellow crown that's visible from quite a distance.

A Woodpecker for Every Tree

With so many kinds of woodpeckers guarding our forests and shade trees from insects, you're sure to have some interesting individuals in or near your backyard. One you won't miss, should it deign to visit, is the giant-size pileated woodpecker. Almost as big as a crow, this super bird sticks mainly to fallen logs and stumps, although, it may also visit feeders for suet, seeds, peanut butter, and other offerings.

Western feeding stations may host the **acorn woodpecker,** which has a quizzical look, thanks to its white head markings, and a nifty habit of stashing acorns in any handy hiding place. Often it bores its own larder, hollowing out a honeycomb of holes in a dead snag, perfectly sized to hold a single acorn apiece. In saguaro country of the Southwest, the harsh cries of the **gila woodpecker** ring out. If you live in the Southeast, keep your eyes peeled for the rare **red-cockaded woodpecker** and maybe the last surviving **ivory-billed woodpecker,** a species that may already be extinct. Both these species have suffered from loss of their natural piney woods habitat.

Woodpeckers at the Feeder

Several species of woodpeckers are common, everyday feeder visitors. But even those that stick

Count yourself lucky if you host a red-headed woodpecker at your feeders. Although they're not all that rare, these birds keep to extremely local ranges.

mostly to wild places may come to sample your goodies. As with all insect-eating birds, suet is a big attraction, whether it's served in a solid block or chopped in a tray. Many woodpeckers welcome sunflower seeds, corn, and nuts, too.

Any kind of suet feeder will serve woodpeckers, unless it's routinely overrun with starlings. They prefer higher feeders for other offerings.

A recent development in feeder preferences is spreading fast as an apparently learned behavior. Nectar feeders are irresistible to many woodpeckers. Once a woodpecker homes in on one, the bird may sit for hours sipping the sweet stuff and fending off any hummingbirds that venture near. It's quite a sight to see a large, heavy-bodied, red-bellied woodpecker or other species clinging to the feeder—the whole contraption tilts madly when the bird lands on it, scrambling for a foothold. In addition to your hummingbird feeders, provide a large-capacity feeder with sturdy perches to accommodate any woodpeckers that drop in. Those sold for orioles are serviceable, but it may not be long before we see woodpecker nectar feeders on the market.

PROJECT

Woodpecker Feeder Tree

This special "tree" of woodpecker treats gives these striking-looking birds a place of their own where they can enjoy their favorite foods and you can enjoy watching their fascinating behavior. If you have a wooden fence post already standing on your property, it's easy to modify it to make this feeder and you can leave it right where it is.

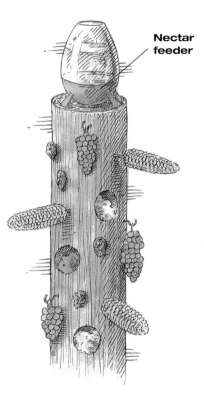

Nectar feeder

MATERIALS

Wood 4 × 4 fence post or length of log

Several large nails

Cup hooks

Smaller nails

Nectar feeder

Suet and/or peanut butter

Whole ears of dried corn

Bunches of grapes

Figs

Step 1. Drill 1½-inch-deep, 2-inch-diameter holes in a fence post to hold suet or peanut butter.

Step 2. Use large nails to nail a few ears of corn to the sides of the post.

Step 3. Screw in cup hooks between holes and ears of corn for holding bunches of grapes.

Step 4. Use smaller nails to fasten some figs to the post.

Step 5. Nail, wire, or otherwise fasten the nectar feeder to the top of the post.

Step 6. Mount or hang the feeder vertically (if not a standing fence post).

Step 7. Fill the nectar feeder and suet/peanut butter holes. Replenish corn, grapes, and figs, as needed, and as these treats are available.

Woodpecker Behavior

Woodpeckers are single-minded at the feeder: They arrive, quickly locate a favored food, then usually sit tight until they have eaten their fill. Watch for their viciously threatening head gestures, especially among the larger species, should another bird dare to come near while the woodpecker is eating. Woodpeckers will even take on a much larger squirrel, should it dare to come near the cob of corn or other delicacy that the bird is dining at. If the animal doesn't get the hint, the woodpecker may rout the squirrel with a swoop straight at it. Starlings are another story. Perhaps it's because starlings usually travel in a gang, or maybe they're just more persistent, but the woodpeckers I've watched, so fierce with squirrels, turn to sissies around starlings.

At any season but especially during breeding time, you will hear a whole litany of weird rattles, "Chirrs," squawks, and other vocalizing from the woodpeckers in the area. Their voices carry quite a distance—I can tell when my neighbor two blocks away is hosting a red-headed woodpecker by listening to its "Yowps" as it arrives. Woodpeckers are great percussionists, too, pounding in staccato rhythms on a favored hollow tree or other noisemaker. When I lived in a tin-roofed Pennsylvania farmhouse, an ear-splitting drum roll was my reveille at the crack of dawn every morning for weeks—a red-bellied wood-pecker found the corner of the roof above my bed-room exactly to its liking. Just about the time I was ready to take drastic measures, the bird switched to an empty metal barrel by the barn.

Be sure to pull out your binoculars when a wood-pecker arrives at the feeder. First look at the way the tail feathers prop up that big body perfectly. They're stiff, strong, and sharply pointed (as well as intricately patterned or polka-dotted in many species). Then check out the bird's feet. Unless you're looking at a three-toed woodpecker, you'll see the short legs and long toes that make it possible for the birds to cling close to tree trunks. Notice, too, how the bird holds two toes facing forward, two toes pointing back, in-stead of the three-and-one arrangement typical of songbirds. This helps the bird maintain a firm grip.

Chisel Beaks and Spear Tongues

I'd often watched woodpeckers rip through dead wood to snack on grubs, but it wasn't until I dumped a handful of whole black walnuts into a feeder that I found out just how powerful the muscles are that drive that chisel beak. Black walnuts are notoriously hard to crack—I resort to a hammer instead of a nut-cracker—but the red-bellied woodpecker at my feeder calmly assessed the nut, drew back his head, and with two solid whacks had the thing split open. That dead-eye aim and strength are just part of the amazing de-sign of woodpeckers. Some behind-the-scenes details can give you a new appreciation for these birds.

Ever blow a coiled-paper New Year's Eve party whistle? That's a reasonable facsimile of the way a woodpecker tongue works. Until the bird is ready to snatch its prey, the extraordinarily long tongue lies coiled around a special pair of bones in the skull.

You can't have too many acorns, says the acorn woodpecker, a bird of extreme single-mindedness. It stows its hoard in holes drilled just for that purpose.

Then it zips forward when the bird zaps an ant or delves for a deep grub.

Even with the aid of binoculars, you probably won't be able to see the other niceties that make woodpeckers so successful at their jobs. But if you watch closely when a woodpecker eats, you will see the effects of these adaptations. All species, except for sapsuckers, have a sharp spear-tipped tongue and backward-pointing barbs that make sure the grub or other morsel stays impaled despite its squirmings. Sticky saliva coats the tongue, too, snagging ants and other insects like a piece of sticky tape sucks up lint. Sapsuckers have unique tongues, too, with small hairs at the tip that work like the bristles of a paint brush to soak up sap.

Wreaths and Swags

A WREATH ON YOUR FRONT GATE says welcome to family and friends, and if you make it from the right materials, birds will also drop by to get a close-up view of your decorating skills. In late summer to fall, when the yard is brimming with ripening berries and seeds, I collect anything that looks as if it has bird potential. I watch for vines of wild grapes and bittersweet, for privet berries on the hedge, for sunflowers going to seed in the garden, and even for likely candidates among the weeds. A smattering of fuzzy foxtail grass and a sprawl of the common pink-flowered smartweed appear as weeds in the garden, but when I work the seedheads into a lush arrangement for the front-door lamppost, the "weed bouquet" gives my house a country touch and supplies the birds with weeks of good eating.

You'll need a surprisingly large amount of plant material to make a wreath or other decoration. I stockpile my treasures in shallow cardboard boxes (recycled pizza boxes work great) in a dry, sheltered area until I have a big stash. Then, on a bright fall day when it's a pleasure to work outdoors, I sort and separate the plants at the picnic table.

(continued on page 343)

Eat-It-Up Winter Wreath

Sticky gelatin holds seeds to a cardboard base for a wreath that birds can peck away at for weeks. Save this project for winter: Unless temperatures are below or close to freezing, the gelatin may slide off the base. This is a good, messy project that kids will enjoy. If your winter temps hover in the fifties or below, you can substitute peanut butter for the gelatin to make a reasonable facsimile. Cover your kitchen table with a plastic tablecloth and dig in!

MATERIALS

Piece of corrugated cardboard

Packet clear gelatin

2 quarts mixed seeds and nuts

Length of wire

Bow or cluster of California pepperberries (optional)

Step 1. Cut a circle of corrugated cardboard to a diameter of 10 inches.

Step 2. Mix packet of clear gelatin, according to the package directions.

Step 3. Pour 2 quarts of seeds and nuts into the gelatin.

Step 4. Stir to coat the seed mixture. If the mixture is too loose and doesn't hold together when you squeeze a handful, add more seed.

Step 5. Mold by hand onto the cardboard form.

Step 6. Attach loop of wire for hanging. Attach a bow or cluster of California pepperberries for decoration, if desired.

PROJECT

A Fruitful Della Robbia Wreath

Fruit-loving birds will enjoy this colorful circle of fruit. Depending on the time of year when you hang it, you may see catbirds, house finches, purple finches, flickers, grosbeaks, magpies, orioles, robins, tanagers, thrushes, waxwings, and woodpeckers flying in for a treat. You can vary the fruit on the wreath according to what you have available.

MATERIALS

Greenery (fir, pine, boxwood, bayberry)

Heavy-duty wire wreath form

Floral picks or wire

A variety of fruit, including orange halves, figs, persimmons, small apples, crab apples, pepperberries, grapes

Step 1. Wire greenery to the form.

Step 2. Use floral picks or wire to secure large fruits to the form.

Step 3. Fill in between the large fruits with figs, crab apples, persmimmons, and grapes or other small fruits.

PROJECT

Swag for Cedar Waxwings

Berry-laden juniper branches are a magnet for handsome cedar waxwings. Use a decorative swag of evergreen boughs and juniper branches to bring these attractive birds to your yard for a visit.

MATERIALS

Length of wire

Evergreen boughs (fir, pine, boxwood, bayberry)

Rope, cut to desired swag length

Juniper branches with berries, 4 to 6 inches long

Holly berries or California pepperberries (optional)

Step 1. Wire overlapping bunches of greenery to rope.

Step 2. Wire on juniper branches amid greenery.

Step 3. Accent with holly berries or pepperberries and hang.

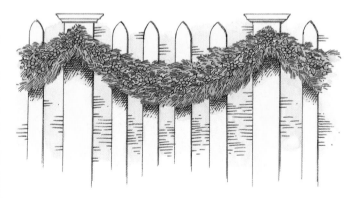

Garland of Grains

Recycle the seedheads of grasses and grains from craft shops or your own yard to make a swag brimming with nutritious seeds. As cardinals, finches, and other birds work at the seedheads, their spills will be quickly cleaned up by juncos, towhees, doves, and other ground-feeding birds not acrobatic enough to cling to the garland. I like to make this swag when I put up my fall decorations—it adds a homemade harvest touch to my fence. Use whatever grass and grain seedheads you can find— they're natural foods that birds eagerly eat.

MATERIALS

Lightweight floral wire

*Any grasses or sedges with seeds still in seedheads (examine to be sure), such as little bluestem (*Schizachyrium scoparium*), big bluestem (*Andropogon gerardii*), Indian grass (*Sorghastrum nutans*), crabgrass, yellow nut sedge, fescue (*Festuca spp.*), bluegrass (*Poa pratensis*), purpletop (*Tridens flavus*), northern sea oats (*Chasmanthium latifolium*), foxtails*

Any grains with seeds, such as milo (sorghum), oats, wheat, rye, barley

Heavyweight wire

Wire cutters

Step 1. Use lightweight floral wire to tie grasses into bunches. Keep seedheads in a bouquet, and snip off extra lengths of stems so that they are even and about 6 inches long.

Step 2. Using heavier wire, wrap bunches into a continuous garland, overlapping as for a wreath. Wire seedheads of the second bunch over the stems of the first, so that the heads of both bunches are snugly side by side. Continue in this fashion. The length of heavier wire holding the bunches together will form the support for the swag.

Step 3. Hang and wait for birds to discover your tasty decoration.

A Simple Spray

Got 5 minutes? That's all it takes to make a lush, beautiful, and bird-attracting "weed bouquet." Just gather a thick double handful of plant material together and wrap the stems tightly with floral wire to make a bouquet. Top with a bunch of corn cobs wired together or a few sunflower seedheads, and your country feast is ready to hang

You can use any combination of handy plant material. I aim for a variety of textures, including twining vines, stiff seedpods, and soft grass seedheads. It's fun to see who arrives to dine on what.

Among the most popular-with-birds combinations I've tried are:

- Bright orange bittersweet, tiny black-purple wild grapes, and clouds of tickle grass (*Panicum* spp.), all common weeds in my area—robins loved it until a mockingbird claimed it.

- Deep brown rose mallow seedpods (*Hibiscus* spp.), masses of foxtail grass seedheads, and catalpa tree (*Catalpa* spp.) beans attracted evening grosbeaks and purple finches.

- Sprays of pale tan ash-tree seedpods (*Fraxinus* spp.), spiky tuliptree cones (*Liriodendron tulipifera*), and zinnia seedheads were a favorite of goldfinches and siskins.

- Oak tree branches with acorns attached, sunflower seedheads, and miniature corn ears—chickadees, jays, titmice, and woodpeckers adored it.

A Circle of Seeds

Fashioning a wreath is a bigger project than making a spray, but it's such fun that you won't want to stop at just one. I purchase a wire form for only a dollar or two to use as the base for my bird wreaths. I can reuse the forms over and over. You can also use straw or grapevine circlets as the base. A roll of floral wire, wire cutters, and a pair of pruners are my only other aids. You can also use long twist-ties to fasten plants to the wreath. A large wreath makes a fine focal point on the front door or gate, but birds enjoy small, quick-to-make, 4- to 6-inch wreaths just as much.

To make your wreath, take a handful of plant material, clip the stems to about 5 inches, and wire securely to the form. Take another bunch of material, snip off extra stem length, and overlap the seed heads onto the stems of the first bunch, so that the "seedy" parts of your material fit snugly together. Wire in place. Repeat until you fill the entire wreath. To hide the bare stems of the last bunch, poke some plants, a sunflower seed

Fasten bird food wherever there's space, keeping in mind the way birds eat. Dining from overhanging seedheads is a natural for the birds that will enjoy this.

head, or a few ears of miniature corn through the stems and wire them into place on the back of the wreath.

Fruit is a great addition to a bird wreath. I keep small apples fresh for months in the fruit bin of my refrigerator to use for wreath making. You can also use orange slices and grapes wired into place. Dried fruit is easy to add to wreaths, too.

Beautiful and Useful

FOLLOW THESE tips to create a pretty country-style wreath with plenty of bird appeal.

- Select a variety of colors and textures when choosing your materials, so that your bird-food wreath looks good to your eyes, too.

- Hang the wreath where birds can visit freely, without being disturbed by activity within the house.

- Debris beneath the wreath is a sign that it's a success! Hulls and bits of broken plants will naturally accumulate there as may bird droppings. A fence or feeder post may be a better location than your front door.

- Fasten materials securely, so that birds can perch on plants and tug at seeds without fear of falling.

- Hang the wreath as solidly as possible so that it doesn't swing under the weight of birds. Unexpected movement when they alight may cause them to avoid it.

- Don't forget ground-feeding birds! Supply wreaths or hang a spray of seedheads at low levels, too.

Drape a Swag

A swag is an elongated spray, or a wreath without the circular backbone of a rigid form. A spool of versatile floral wire does the trick here, too, holding the overlapping bundles of plant material into one continuous rope. In fact, if you are making a thick swag or using heavy plants such as evergreens, a real rope can come in handy. I use a piece of wire-reinforced plastic clothesline as the supporting player for my swag, wiring the branches all along its strong, flexible length.

I save my swag making for Christmastime, when I drape ropes of greenery and berries across the fence and around the entrance, but you can also use fall-themed plants to create a harvest-home decorative swag. As with other crafty decorations, think like a bird when you choose plants to put together. Items that are popular with birds in the garden or at your feeder are fine candidates for a swag.

At my house many birds enjoy a swag of hemlock branches with the cones attached and dotted with sprigs of bright holly berries. Bluebirds, chickadees, visiting crossbills, nuthatches, berry-eating robins, and the troublesome "It's mine, all mine" mockingbirds visit repeatedly. One year, I delighted my squirrels and cardinals by wiring ears of yellow field corn together end to end. The simple golden chain looked lovely draped across a latticework trellis—at least at first! When the corn swag began to look moth-eaten as kernels disappeared, I wrapped it around a tall feeder post for further squirrel and bird forays.

Sometimes it's easy to forget that the reason you're making these decorations is to feed the birds. Don't expect your bird food wreaths and swags to stay in their original state for long. Celebrate the lively birds they bring to the garden, and accepting the eventual fate of your creations will be easier.

Wrens

WHEN AUTUMN feeder traffic swings into gear, the juncos and white-throated sparrows crowd the trays and goldfinches swing on the tube feeders. I get so caught up in the excitement that I forget all about one of my favorite feeder birds: the **Carolina wren.** I'll be filling the feeders on a crisp October morning when I hear an almost mechanical chirring sound that halts me in my tracks for the split second it takes me to place it. Then a jaunty, toasty brown bird swings into view, and I remember the pleasure of wrens at the feeder. Carolina wrens have expanded their range northward, so that now anyone with a feeder in the eastern half of the country might spot them summer or winter. If you live in the Southwest, watch for the thrush-size **cactus wren,** a giant among this family. It's a frequent visitor to feeders.

Most familiar among backyard bird watchers with its almost nationwide range, the small brown

A white eye stripe and warm buffy breast identify a Carolina wren, as does its repertoire of loud, clear whistled phrases and odd whirrs and chirrs.

house wren is much less common at feeders. This insect-loving bird retreats to the deep southern edge of the country and southward once cold weather arrives. **Bewick's wren,** common in the West and ranging into the Southeast and Midwest, is as unafraid of humans as the house wren and often takes up residence around houses and farms. Other wrens, including the tiny **winter wren** of the far West and East, the wetland-loving **marsh wren,** and the rock-dwelling **canyon wren** and **rock wren** of the West, are usually not feeder regulars. But as with any bird, individuals may show up when natural food is scarce or if your yard is part of their territory.

Win a house wren's heart with mealworms, suet, and peanut butter. This tiny but talented singer practically spills over with burbling song in spring and summer.

WREN FEEDER FOODS
■ Apple, halved or chopped
■ Bread and other baked goods
■ Bread crumbs
■ Elderberries (*Sambucus* spp.)
■ Leftovers
■ Mealworms
■ Meat scraps
■ Peanut butter
■ Suet

Wren Behavior

You'll hear wrens long before you see them because these little birds can't seem to help sounding off. They have beautiful singing voices that ring out with liquid notes, performing long, complicated songs in some species or short carols in others. A grab bag of scolding rattles, harsh chirrs, and general jabbering comes along with the virtuoso performances. If you hear a repeated unmusical birdcall from your yard, it's probably a wren.

Wrens eat mostly insects, so they are great little pals to have in the garden. At the feeder, they like suet, bread crumbs, and other soft foods. Active and acrobatic, they can easily reach any type of feeder. Wrens are feisty toward other birds at the feeder but never are pests because they usually show up singly or in pairs.

Most wrens nest in cavities, which may explain why the birds have a propensity for exploring nooks and crannies. Or they may just be curious. Leave a garage door open, even a crack, and you may find a Carolina wren exploring when you return. Several types of wrens nest and roost in sheds, garages, and other outbuildings or in dense vines against a porch.

Zinnias

Attract buntings, cardinals, doves, goldfinches, hummingbirds, native sparrows, titmice, towhees

ZINNIAS (*ZINNIA* SPP.) are one of the easiest annual flowers to grow—and that's good news for bird lovers. Zinnias have bright, daisylike flowers that attract a bounty of butterflies when they're in full bloom, but that's only the beginning. Red- and orange-flowered zinnias also lure hummingbirds to their nectar. And when the flower heads begin to go to seed, goldfinches are first on the scene. If you leave your zinnia patch standing through fall and into winter, you'll spot buntings, doves, native sparrows, and towhees, busily scratching for seeds around the plants.

Colorful and foolproof, zinnias will attract butterflies and hummingbirds all summer long. Let the plants stand in fall and winter to feed songbirds.

Zinnias take only 10 to 12 weeks to burst into bloom, counting from the time you plant the seeds. They flourish in full sun, in rich or lean soil, and in clay or sandy places. Traditional cactus-flowered or double-flowered zinnias (Z. *elegans*) are excellent for songbirds, hummingbirds, and butterflies; for smaller seed-eating species, the lower-growing zinnia cultivars 'Bonita Red' and 'Bonita Yellow' or old-fashioned Persian carpet (Z. *haageana*) are tops.

Zinnias are prone to powdery mildew, which causes a whitish dusting on their foliage. The effect is cosmetic: It's not fatal to the plants, and flowers are usually unaffected. Because mildew is most noticeable when the plant is a tall one, I add mid-height and dwarf zinnia cultivars in front of my giants to hide their foliage, just in case it becomes disfigured. Or you can stick to planting mildew-resistant cultivars.

If you plant a large sweep of zinnias, you can easily snip off seedheads and offer them in feeders later in the season, or work them into a wreath for birds. Try cutting the ripe seedheads with long stems attached, tie them together with twine, and attach them to a lamppost, fence post, or door—they'll attract cardinals, titmice, and other birds. Save some of the seeds for planting next year. If you save seed of named cultivars, you may find the next generation doesn't look very much like its parents. If your garden color scheme is important, sow the saved seeds in an out-of-the-way spot, where a sudden unexpected jolt of fuchsia or scarlet won't disrupt your soft pastels. I like the surprises of color and flower form I get from saved seed, but if reliable results are what you want, stick to packaged seeds.

Zinnias are great flowers for first-time gardeners: They sprout in just a few days, the seedlings are big and hearty, and they grow fast and bloom quickly. If you want to give a child a love of gardening, pass along a packet of zinnia seeds. They're as close to foolproof as gardening gets.

Resources

Bird-Feeding Supplies

The ever-growing popularity of bird feeding means that sources of feeders, food, and other bird-related items abound. Your best source of supplies may be your local garden center or wild-bird specialty shop, but you'll also find bird feeders and birdhouses at most discount stores and hardware stores. Feed mills are a great source of low-cost birdseed and grains if you buy in large quantity. Fast-dissolving superfine sugar, which melts instantly even in cold water and is great for making nectar, is available at some supermarkets or from restaurant- and bar-supply shops.

Many cottage-industry bird box and feeder makers have entered the market. Check the back pages of any bird or wildlife magazine (see "Recommended Reading" on page 352 for listings) for advertisements and places to send for catalogs. You may also want to shop for supplies from the mail-order firms listed here.

The Audubon Workshop
5100 Schenley Place
Lawrenceburg, IN 47025
Phone: (812) 537-3583

Down to Earth
4 Highland Circle
Lucas, TX 75002
Phone: (800) 865-1996
Fax: (972) 442-2816
E-mail: sales@downtoearth.com
Web site: www.downtoearth.com
Makes simple cypress-wood houses and wonderful see-through bird feeders and birdhouses that you can attach to windows.

Droll Yankees, Inc.
27 Mill Road
Foster, RI 02825
Phone: (800) 352-9164
Fax: (401) 647-7620
E-mail: custserv@drollyankees.com
Web site: www.drollyankees.com

Duncraft, Inc.
102 Fisherville Road
Concord, NH 03303-2086
Phone: (800) 593-5656
Fax: (603) 226-3735
E-mail: info@duncraft.com
Web site: www.duncraft.com

Plow & Hearth
P.O. Box 5000
Madison, VA 22727-1500
Phone: (800) 627-1712
Fax: (800) 843-2509
Web site: www.plowhearth.com

Wellscroft Farm Fence Systems
167 Sunset Hill-Chesham
Harrisville, NH 03450
Phone: (603) 827-3464
Fax: (603) 827-3666

Wild Bird Centers of America, Inc.
Phone: (800) 945-3247 (to locate a store near you)
Web site: www.wildbirdcenter.com

Wild Birds Unlimited
Phone: (800) 326-4928 (to locate a store near you)
Fax: (317) 571-7110
Web site: www.wbu.com

Wild Wings Organic Wild Bird Foods
220 Congress Park Drive #232
Delray Beach, FL 33445
Phone: (800) 346-0269
Fax: (800) 279-5984
Web site: www.wildwings organic.com
Certified organic bird foods

Organizations and Programs

American Bird Conservancy

P.O. Box 249
The Plains, VA 20198-0249
E-mail: abc@abcbirds.org
Web site: www.abcbirds.org

A nonprofit organization that builds coalitions of conservation groups, scientists, and the public in order to identify and protect important sites for bird conservation. Annual membership fee includes ABC's quarterly magazine about bird conservation and a newsletter on policy issues affecting birds.

Backyard Wildlife Habitat Program

National Wildlife Federation
11100 Wildlife Center Drive
Reston, VA 20190-5361
Phone: (800) 822-9919
Web site: www.nwf.org

Free information on developing a bird-friendly backyard; provide a certificate if you follow through.

National Audubon Society

700 Broadway
New York, NY 10003
Phone: (212) 979-3000
Fax: (212) 979-3188
Web site: www.audubon.org

Founded in 1905, this is one of the biggest nonprofit conservation organizations and is active worldwide in all kinds of conservation issues as well as birds. Join a local branch to meet other birders, participate in bird counts, and enjoy other bird-related activities.

National Bird-Feeding Society

P.O. Box 23
Northbrook, IL 60065-0023
Phone: (847) 272-0135
Fax: (773) 404-0923
Web site: www.birdfeeding.org

Organization devoted to bird feeding. Annual fee includes bimonthly newsletter and other information on bird feeding.

North American Bird Banding Program

Learn how to create your own banding research program or volunteer with other banders.

For U.S. residents, contact:

Bird Banding Laboratory

U.S. Geological Survey—
  Biological Resources Division
Patuxent Wildlife Research Center
12100 Beech Forest Road, Suite
  4037
Laurel, MD 20708-4037
Phone: (301) 497-5790
Fax: (301) 497-5784
E-mail: BBL@mail.fws.gov
Web site: www.mbr-
  pwrc.usgs.gov/bbl/bbl.htm

For Canadian residents, contact:

Bird Banding Office

National Wildlife Research Centre
Canadian Wildlife Service
Hull, Quebec, Canada K1A 0H3
Phone: (819) 994-6176
Fax: (819) 953-6612

North American Rare Bird Alert (NARBA)

P.O. Box 6599
Colorado Springs, CO 80934
Phone: (719) 578-9703
Web site: www.americanbirding.org
  (go to the Rare Bird Alert link)

Project FeederWatch

Winter counts of feeder birds are conducted by "regular people" all across North America. The data collected contribute to scientific understanding of changes in bird populations and distribution. Annual fee covers project newsletter and participation.

For U.S. residents, contact:

Project Feeder Watch

Cornell Laboratory of
  Ornithology
159 Sapsucker Woods Road
Ithaca, NY 14850-1923
Phone: (800) 843-BIRD
E-mail: feederwatch@cornell.edu
Web site: birds.cornell.edu/pfw

For Canadian residents, contact:

Project Feeder Watch

Bird Studies Canada
P.O. Box 160
Port Rowan, Ontario N0E 1M0
Phone: (888) 448-BIRD;
  (519) 586-3531
Fax: (519) 586-3532
E-mail: pfw@bsc-eoc.org

Songbird Foundation

5215 Ballard Avenue NW
Seattle, WA 98107
Phone: (206) 374-3674
Fax: (206) 374-3675
E-mail: info@songbird.org
Web site: www.songbird.org

Nonprofit group working to raise awareness about the negative impact of sun-grown coffee production on songbird habitat. Funds projects that promote shade-grown/organic coffee growing.

Sources of Seeds and Plants

When you shop for plants, visit local nurseries that grow their own plants or buy from mail-order firms. Plants from discount stores often haven't been cared for properly and may not establish themselves as well in your garden. Some mail-order companies charge a small fee for their catalogs; you'll often get a credit on your first order.

The following is just a small selection of mail-order nurseries. Ask gardening friends what companies they recommend, too.

Native Plants

Boothe Hill Wildflowers
921 Boothe Hill
Chapel Hill, NC 27514
Phone: (919) 967-4091
Specializes in seeds and plants of native and naturalized wildflowers for the Southeast and throughout the United States

Busse Gardens
17160 245th Avenue
Big Lake, MN 55309
Phone: (800) 544-3192
Fax: (763) 263-1473
Web site: www.bussegardens.com
Reliable and beautiful perennial plants that can take cold but also thrive in milder gardens

Edible Landscaping
P.O. Box 77
Afton, VA 22920-0077
Phone: (434) 361-9134
Fax: (434) 361-1916
Web site: www.eat-it.com
Plants for you and the birds (and other wildlife); lots of fruit-bearing trees and shrubs

Finch Blueberry Nursery
P.O. Box 699
Bailey, NC 27807
Phone: (252) 235-4664
Web site: www.danfinch.com
Wide selection of blueberries for your bird garden

Forestfarm
990 Tetherow Road
Williams, OR 97544-9599
Phone: (541) 846-7269
Fax: (541) 846-6963
Web site: www.forestfarm.com
More than 2,000 plants, including wildflowers, perennials, and an outstanding variety of trees and shrubs

Kurt Bluemel, Inc.
2740 Greene Lane
Baldwin, MD 21013-9523
Phone: (800) 498-1560
Fax: (410) 557-9785
Web site: www.kurtbluemel.com
Specializes in ornamental grasses

Louisiana Nursery
5853 Highway 182
Opelousas, LA 70570
Phone: (337) 948-3696
Fax: (337) 942-6404
Web site: www.durionursery.com
Vines for hummingbirds; many trees, shrubs, and perennials

**Meadowbrook Nursery–
We-Du Natives**
2055 Polly Spout Road
Marion, NC 28752
Phone: (828) 738-8300
Fax: (828) 287-9348
Web site: www.we-du.com
Impressive selection of wildflowers and perennials, including lots of woodland plants

Niche Gardens
1111 Dawson Road
Chapel Hill, NC 27516
Phone: (919) 967-0078
Fax: (919) 967-4026
Web site: www.nichegdn.com
Generous-size plants of grasses, nursery-propagated wildflowers, perennials, and herbs

Plant Delights Nusery
9241 Sauls Road
Raleigh, NC 27603
Phone: (919) 772-4794
Fax: (919) 662-0370
Web site: www.plantdelights.com
A broad and eclectic selection of new and unusual perennials, along with many old favorites; many natives

Prairie Moon Nursery
Route 3, Box 163
Winona, MN 55987-9515
Phone: (507) 452-1362
Fax: (507) 454-5238
Web site: www.prairiemoon
  nursery.com
An outstanding variety of native prairie grasses and wildflowers; also lots of seeds

Prairie Nursery, Inc.
P.O. Box 306
Westfield, WI 53964
Phone: (800) 476-9453
Fax: (608) 296-2741
Web site: www.prairienursery.com
An excellent source of native wildflowers and grasses, many of them ideal for bird gardens

Raintree Nursery
391 Butts Road
Morton, WA 98356
Phone: (360) 496-6400
Fax: (888) 770-8358
Web site: www.raintreenursery.com
A wide selection of fruit trees and shrubs

Shooting Star Nursery
444 Bates Road
Frankfort, KY 40601
Phone: (502) 223-1679
Fax: (502) 227-5700
Web site:
   www.shootingstarnursery.com
Diverse assortment of plants and seeds native to the forests, prairies, and wetlands of Kentucky and other eastern states

Sunlight Gardens, Inc.
174 Golden Lane
Andersonville, TN 37705
Phone: (800) 272-7396
Fax: (865) 494-7086
Web site:
   www.sunlightgardens.com
Terrific selection of wildflowers, all nursery propagated, of southeastern and northeastern North America

Tripple Brook Farm
37 Middle Road
Southampton, MA 01073
Phone: (413) 527-4626
Fax: (413) 527-9853
Web site:
   www.tripplebrookfarm.com
Lively catalog of wildflowers and other northeastern native plants, plus fruits and shrubs

Wildlife Nurseries
P.O. Box 2724
Oshkosh, WI 54903-2724
Phone: (920) 231-3780
Fax: (920) 231-3554
Excellent, informative listing of plants and seeds of native grasses, annuals, and perennials that attract birds and other wildlife; also water garden plants and supplies

Woodlanders, Inc.
1128 Colleton Avenue
Aiken, SC 29801
Phone/fax: (803) 648-7522
Web site: www.woodlanders.net
A fantastic collection of native trees, shrubs, ferns, vines, and perennials, plus other good garden plants. It's a list only, no pictures or descriptions, so if you're a newcomer to plants, pull out a plant encyclopedia to consult as you go.

Native Roses

Forestfarm
990 Tetherow Road
Williams, OR 97544-9599
Phone: (541) 846-7269
Fax: (541) 846-6963
Web site: www.forestfarm.com

Hortico, Inc.
723 Robson Road, R.R. #1
Waterdown, Ontario, Canada
   L0R 2H1
Phone: (905) 689-6984;
   (905) 689-3002
Fax: (905) 689-6566
Web site: www.hortico.com

The Roseraie at Granite Ridge
3202 Friendship Road
P.O. Box R
Waldoboro, ME 04572-0919
Phone: (207) 832-6330
Fax: (800) 933-4508
Web site: www.roseraie.com

Water Garden Plants and Supplies

Lilypons Water Gardens
6800 Lilypons Road
P.O. Box 10
Buckeystown, MD 21717-0010
Phone: (800) 999-5459
Fax: (800) 879-5459
Web site: www.lilypons.com

Van Ness Water Gardens
2460 North Euclid Avenue
Upland, CA 91784-1199
Phone: (800) 205-2425
Fax: (909) 949-7217
Web site: www.vnwg.com

Recommended Reading

Books

Adams, George. *Birdscaping Your Garden.* Emmaus, PA: Rodale, 1998.

Barnes, Thomas G. *Gardening for the Birds.* Lexington, KY: University Press of Kentucky, 1999.

Burton, Robert. *National Audubon Society's North American Birdfeeder Handbook.* Rev. ed. New York: DK Publishing, 1995.

Ellis, Barbara. *Attracting Birds & Butterflies: How to Plan and Plant a Backyard Habitat. Taylor's Weekend Gardening Guides.* New York: Houghton Mifflin, 1997.

Harrison, George H. *Garden Birds of America: A Gallery of Garden Birds & How to Attract Them.* Minocqua, WI: Willow Creek Press, 1996.

Kress, Stephen W. *National Audubon Society: The Bird Garden.* New York: DK Publishing, 1995.

National Audubon Society. *The Audubon Society Handbook for Birders.* New York: Charles Scribner's Sons, 1981.

Proctor, Noble. *Garden Birds: How to Attract Birds to Your Garden.* Emmaus, PA: Rodale, 1996.

Ricciuti, Edward R. *Backyards Are for the Birds: Creating a Bird-Friendly Environment Outside Your Window.* New York: Avon Books, 1998.

Roth, Sally. *Attracting Birds to Your Backyard: 536 Ways to Turn Your Yard and Garden into a Haven for Your Favorite Birds.* Emmaus, PA: Rodale, 1998.

Roth, Sally. *Natural Landscaping.* Emmaus, PA: Rodale, 1997.

Sunset Staff. *An Illustrated Guide to Attracting Birds.* Menlo Park, CA: Sunset Publishing Corporation, 1990.

Terres, John K. *Songbirds in Your Garden.* Chapel Hill, NC: Algonquin Books of Chapel Hill, 1994.

Terres, John K. *The Audubon Society's Encyclopedia of North American Birds.* New York: Random House Value Publishing, 1995.

Thompson III, Bill. *Bird Watching for Dummies.* Foster City, CA: IDG Books Worldwide, Inc., 1997.

Tufts, Craig, and Peter Loewer. *The National Wildlife Federation's Guide to Gardening for Wildlife.* Emmaus, PA.: Rodale, 1995.

For a unique series of books about American birds, chock-full of anecdotes and lively, informative reading, check at your local library or secondhand book store for the *Life Histories of North American Birds* series by Arthur Cleveland Bent, first published in the early decades of the twentieth century, and reprinted in paperback by Dover Press. A few titles in the series are:

Life Histories of North American Marsh Birds (1927)

Life Histories of North American Gallinaceous Birds (1980)

Life Histories of North American Flycatchers, Larks, Swallows, and Their Allies (1989)

Life Histories of North American Woodpeckers (1992)

Magazines

Audubon
700 Broadway
New York, NY 10003
Phone: (800) 274-4201
Web site: magazine.audubon.org

Birder's World
21027 Crossroads Circle
P.O. Box 1612
Waukesha, WI 53187-1612
Phone: (800) 533-6644
Web site: www2.birdersworld.com

Birds and Blooms
5400 South 60th Street
Greendale, WI 53129
Phone: (800) 344-6913

Bird Watcher's Digest
P.O. Box 110
Marietta, OH 45750
Phone: (800) 879-2473
Web site:
   www.birdwatchersdigest.com

Living Bird
c/o Cornell Laboratory of
   Ornithology
159 Sapsucker Woods Road
Ithaca, NY 14850-1923
Phone: (800) 843-BIRD
Web site: www.birds.cornell.edu

Organic Gardening
Rodale
33 East Minor Street
Emmaus, PA 18098
Phone: (800) 666-2206
   (subscriptions)
Web site:
   www.organicgardening.com

Wild Bird
P.O. Box 52898
Boulder, CO 80322-2898
Phone: (800) 365-4421

Bird Field Guides and Recordings

The beauty of a field guide lies in its portable nature: These compact books fit easily into a daypack or glove compartment, so you can always have one handy when there's a bird you want to identify. They're also nice to keep near your favorite feeder-watching window, so you can look up any unusual guests. Their small size doesn't mean that field guides lack information—on the contrary, they're packed with useful identification tips and may also tell you what foods each bird eats and a little about its nesting habits. Here are a few good ones.

A Guide to Field Identification: Birds of North America by Chandler S. Robbins, Bertel Bruun, and Herbert S. Zim (New York: Golden Press, 1983) Birds are illustrated in lifelike poses and on a plant where you're likely to see them. Range maps are inserted at each bird's entry, so you don't have to flip to a separate section in the back of the book as you do with Peterson's. The book includes all birds of North America, which will give you a wider perspective.

The Peterson Field Guide series (Boston: Houghton Mifflin Co., 1998) is also excellent, but they're regional guides and birds are drawn in flatter, less lifelike poses than in the Golden field guide, without any hint of habitat in most pictures. Peterson uses arrows to point out field marks to look for, for definitive identification. Also look for the audio series *Birding by Ear,* which includes *Birding by Ear: Eastern/ Central,* edited by Richard K. Walton (Houghton Mifflin Audio, 1999); it includes three CDs or audiotapes.

The Audubon Society Field Guide series (New York: Alfred A. Knopf, 1987), another regional set of guides, uses photos instead of illustrations, which are not as accurate for identifying field marks. The guides also include a lot of interesting information about each bird.

Stokes Field Guide to Birds: Eastern Region and *Stokes Field Guide to Birds: Western Region* (Boston: Little, Brown and Co., 1996) are two photographic field guides that also offer information on feeding and nesting habits and other behavior. There is also a *Stokes Field Guide to Bird Songs: Eastern Region* (or western region) that is by Lang Elliot (Time Warner Audio Books, 1997) and includes three CDs or audiotapes and a booklet.

Photo Credits

Em Ahart 132
Animals Animals/C. C. Lockwood 221
Frederick Atwood 182
Ron Austing 32 (top), 152, 327, 334
Bill Beatty 31, 174
Lance Beeny 98 (bottom), 220
Cliff Beittel vi (right), xi (right), 32 (bottom), 40, 44 (top), 223 (right), 294, 319, 345
Gay Bumgarner viii (middle), 142, 237, 309
David Cavagnaro vii (right), 76, 82, 145, 196, 352 (middle), 305, 354 (middle)
Carolyn Chatterton viii (right), x (right), xiii, 140, 148, 180, 286, 354 (right), back cover (right)
Bruce Coleman, Inc./Michele Beck 96
Bruce Coleman, Inc./J. C. Carlton 120, 208, 348 (middle)
Bruce Coleman, Inc./Robert P. Carr vii (middle), 24
Bruce Coleman, Inc./Steve Solum 58, 150
Colephoto/Mary Clay 61
Colephoto/Arthur Morris, Birds as Art vi (left), 44 (bottom), 52 (top), 56, 155
Kent and Donna Dannen 113, 179, 282
Daybreak Imagery/Richard Day xvi, 8, 23, 26, 29, 43, 51, 64, 69, 70, 89, 123, 178, 198, 200, 201, 212, 214, 228, 253, 256, 259, 265, 268, 289, 297, 312, 336, 338, 307 (bottom)
Dembinsky Photo Association/Rob Plank 62
Chris DeGray 227
Ed Eller 270, 307 (top)
Tim Fitzharris xii (left), 68, 168, 197, 225, 244
Michael H. Francis 254 (top)
Frosty Dog/Kay McElrath Johnson 87
Geo Imagery/Judi L. Baker 93, 156
Geo Imagery/Charles Sleicher viii (left), 122, back cover (left)
Gnass Photo Images/Frank Cleland 137, 318

Larry Higgins 254 (bottom)
Cathy and Gordon Illg 55 (top), 85, 175, 245
The Image Finder/Mark and Sue Werner 262
Stephen Ingram 138, 248
Jay Ireland and Georgienne E. Bradley 163, 217
Bill Johnson 6 (top)
Byron Jorjorian 139 (bottom)
KAC Productions/Kathy Adams Clark 292 (bottom)
KAC Productions/Larry Ditto 205
Dwight R. Kuhn 88, 154, 195
Tom and Pat Leeson 4
Mitch Mandel 1, 9, 11 (top), 33, 34, 35, 66, 101, 103, 109, 129, 136, 162, 213, 236, 279, 283, 287, 332
Bill Marchel ix (middle), ix (right), 42, 60 (top), 118 (top), 161, 190, 233, 243, 291
Rick Mark inside back flap
Brian K. Miller 39 (top)
Northwind Pictures xii (middle), 330
William Palmer 218, 337
Photophile/Anthony Mercieca 166
Rick Poley Photo/R. J. and Virginia Small xii (right), 320, 321
Positive Images/Margaret Hensel 67
Positive Images/Jerry Howard 278
Positive Images/Ben Phillips x (middle), 252, 347, back cover (middle)
Marie Read 25, 41 (bottom), 79, 194, 288
Leonard Lee Rhue III 10, 55 (bottom), 299
Jeffrey Rich Nature Photography xi (left), 77, 292 (top), 322, 354 (left)
George Robbins Photography 80, 119
Jim Roetzel 231
Bob Schillere 149, 172 (bottom right)
Johann Schumacker 12 (top), 143, 348 (left)
Rob and Ann Simpson x (left), 128, 183, 215, 219, 260 (bottom), 352 (right)
Richard Hamilton Smith 272 (left)

John Sorensen 39 (bottom), 84, 52 (bottom), 118 (bottom), 181, 261 (bottom), 263, 264, 340, 346, 348 (right)
Scot Stewart 94
Gerald D. Tang 37, 328
Connie Toops 12 (top), 266, 335
Waverly Traylor 272 (right)
Mark Turner vi (middle), 6 (bottom), 41 (top), 153, 209, 267, 352 (left)
Unicorn Stock/Tom Edwards 275
Unicorn Stock/Dede Gilman ix (left), 222
Unicorn Stock/MacDonald Photography 206
Unicorn Stock/Martha McBride 242
Unicorn Stock/Ted Rose 223 (left), 296
Visuals Unlimited/R. Calentine 303
Visuals Unlimited/Gary W. Carter 19, 326 (bottom)
Visuals Unlimited/John D. Cunningham 216
Visuals Unlimited/Derrick Ditchburn 60 (bottom)
Visuals Unlimited/Wally Eberhart vii (left), xi (middle), 2, 92
Visuals Unlimited/Tom Edwards 139 (top)
Visuals Unlimited/Carlyn Galati 171
Visuals Unlimited/William Grenfell 165, 169
Visuals Unlimited/Dick Kean 229
Visuals Unlimited/S. Malowski ii, 98 (top), 121, 144, 313
Visuals Unlimited/Joe McDonald 172 (top left and top right)
Visuals Unlimited/William S. Ormerod Jr. 63
Visuals Unlimited/Inga Spence 11 (top), 249
Visuals Unlimited/David Stuckel 72
Visuals Unlimited/Jan L. Wassink 191, 274, 326 (top)
Visuals Unlimited/William J. Weber 250
Mark F. Wallner 260 (top)
Rick Wetherbee 95

Index

Note: Page references in **boldface** indicate illustrations. Page references in *italics* indicate photographs.

USDA Plant Hardiness Zone Map

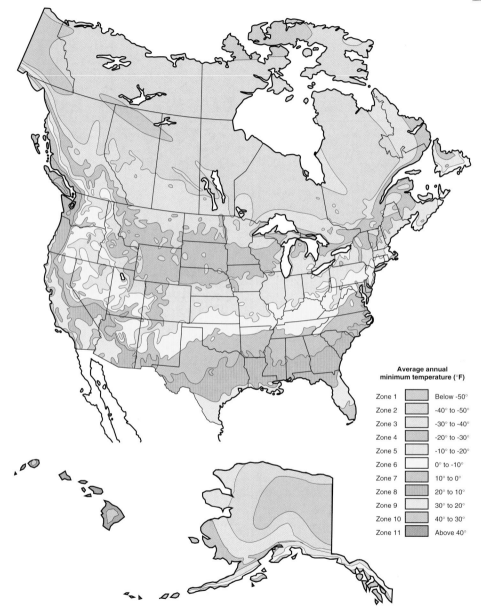

Average annual minimum temperature (°F)

Zone 1		Below -50°
Zone 2		-40° to -50°
Zone 3		-30° to -40°
Zone 4		-20° to -30°
Zone 5		-10° to -20°
Zone 6		0° to -10°
Zone 7		10° to 0°
Zone 8		20° to 10°
Zone 9		30° to 20°
Zone 10		40° to 30°
Zone 11		Above 40°

This map was revised in 1990 and is recognized as the best indicator of minimum temperatures available. Look at the map to find your area, then match its pattern to the key above. When you've found your color, the key will tell you what hardiness zone you live in. Remember that the map is a general guide; your particular conditions may vary.

The Backyard Bird Lover's

FIELD GUIDE

Secrets to Attracting, Identifying, and Enjoying Birds of Your Region

SALLY ROTH

RODALE

Rodale books may be purchased for business or promotional use or for special sales. For information, please write to:
Special Markets Department, Rodale Inc., 733 Third Avenue, New York, NY 10017

Printed in the United States of America
Rodale Inc. makes every effort to use acid-free ♾, recycled paper ♻.

Book design by Christina Gaugler
Illustrations by Neil Gower

Library of Congress Cataloging-in-Publication Data

Roth, Sally.
    The backyard bird lover's field guide : secrets to attracting, identifying, and enjoying birds of your region / Sally Roth.
       p.   cm.
    Includes bibliographical references and index.
    ISBN-13 978-1-59486-603-6 hardcover
    ISBN-10 1-59486-603-1 hardcover
    ISBN-13 978-1-59486-602-9 paperback
    ISBN-10 1-59486-602-3 paperback
    1. Birds—United States—Identification.   I. Title.
  QL682.R68 2007
  598.07′23473—dc22
                                        2007015222

Distributed to the trade by Holtzbrinck Publishers

2 4 6 8 10 9 7 5 3 1 hardcover
2 4 6 8 10 9 7 5 3 1 paperback

RODALE
LIVE YOUR WHOLE LIFE™

We inspire and enable people to improve their lives and the world around them
For more of our products visit **rodalestore.com** or call 800-848-4735

For Gretel and David, with love

CONTENTS

ACKNOWLEDGMENTS

Writing a book reminds me of growing a garden. Without the sun and rain, without the wiggly earthworms and the wrens, without the seeds and the nurturing, a garden wouldn't look like much.

Thanks to senior editor Karen Bolesta for guiding this book from the first sprout of an idea to the full-flowering result you now hold in your hands. Just as important, Karen, thanks for always being ready to lend a supportive ear, whether I was whining about work or about the eddies of my personal life.

Weeding and arranging makes a garden look its best, and an editor does the same for a book. Anne Halpin White, a birder herself, is the kind of astute and good-natured editor that writers usually only dream of. She edited my words with grace and good humor, even when the schedule was at its tightest—right at Christmastime! Thanks, Anne, for keeping me laughing. A whole sackful from Santa Claus can't compare with the gift of your work on this book.

As any gardener knows, watching for pests is part of the process. On a book, copyeditors are the last line of defense. They notice every little spot where a missing comma or misplaced phrase might give a reader pause. Senior project editor Nancy Bailey and copy editor Claire McCrea did a great job of polishing the details and alerting me to places where my typing fingers raced too far ahead of my brain, where readers might be left scratching their heads and wondering, "What does she mean?"

Have you ever noticed how a summer shower refreshes the garden? Kris Kennedy, the best naturalist I've ever met, kept me inspired by sharing the joy of nature both afield and in conversation. He generously contributed his own knowledge of western birds, and he tirelessly researched the latest science to make sure my observations were in keeping with the experts. Sometimes that wasn't the case, which led to spirited discussions about discrepancies between what real live bird-watchers see for themselves and the historical "facts" in literature that sometime turn out to be only repeated lore. In those cases, I relied on my own observations instead of those of the experts. I may not have a string of initials following my name, but after a lifetime of watching birds, I trust my own eyes.

Beauty is one of the big reasons we love our gardens, and it's just as important in a book. A big thank you to associate art director Christina Gaugler, who prettied up these pages with an eye toward the aesthetic. That's quite a trick, when you consider that the pages also have to be readable and inviting. Thanks, Chris, for your artistic design—any chance you can work on my wardrobe next? Photo editor Robin Hepler added more beauty to these pages with her careful selection of photos. For the bird profiles, she managed to find photos that show each bird in detail, but also give a glimpse into their personalities. Thanks to layout designer Faith Hague, who grappled with the tough task of finding room for all of my observations, anecdotes, and fun facts on each bird profile page. And finally, thanks to artist Neil Gower for his beautiful map illustrations.

Of course, without somebody to share the thrill of those first ripe tomatoes or sweet-scented roses, a garden isn't nearly as much fun. My most heartfelt thanks goes to you, the backyard bird lover. Writing with you in mind makes me feel like we're looking at birds together, telling stories and sharing observations. I hope you feel that way, too.

INTRODUCTION

Iwas exploring the Cascade Mountains with a naturalist friend one fine fall day when we stopped to better admire the fantastic draperies of old-man's beard lichen decorating the firs. The gray lichen hung down 3 feet or more, backlit by the sun low in the sky and swaying with the slightest breath of wind.

The lichen was beautiful but was instantly upstaged as soon as my friend asked, "What's that bird?"

It's unusual for us not to announce a bird by name: Usually we say "Junco," or "Pileated," or "Varied thrush," not "What's that bird?" So I hurriedly focused my binoculars on the small bird perched quietly on a bare branch in the treetop.

"Owl!" I exclaimed, recognizing the bigger than usual head and neckless look. "Saw-whet? Pygmy?" I'm not nearly as good at identifying owls as I am at identifying songbirds in the Northwest region where I live. All I was sure of was that this was one of the small owl species.

"Not a saw-whet," my friend said with surety. "Pygmy. Look at that tail."

Meanwhile, I was scrabbling through my Sibley field guide, flipping through pages as fast as I could while trying to keep one eye on the bird.

"Northern pygmy owl," I confirmed, finding the match for our small, long-tailed bird.

We went back to looking, quietly commenting on the details—the speckled back, the boldly striped breast, the white-freckled face. Even with the sun behind it, we could make out enough markings to be certain of the ID.

The 7-inch owl stayed put, occasionally turning its head to look at us. I pulled out the book again. "Largely diurnal," I read, and right then, the bird took off. Leaving his treetop perch, he sailed downward across the dirt road, swooping upward at the end to a new perch just a few feet from the ground, exactly like a varied thrush, a common bird in these forested hills, might do.

"Wow, he looked just like a thrush flying," I said. "Wonder how many times I've seen one and thought 'thrush'?"

We never got another look at the owl, which stayed hidden among the dense branches. But ever since, I've looked longer and harder at any bird I've seen, just in case it's a 7-inch owl instead of a songbird.

It was Jim Brett, curator emeritus of Hawk Mountain Sanctuary in eastern Pennsylvania, who first gave me the same advice. I'd grown lazy about identifying the many hawks that approached the lookout at the sanctuary, dropping my binoculars as soon as I had a fix on which raptor I was seeing—which I usually did by recognizing its silhouette alone, while the bird was still at a distance.

"Keep looking as long as you can see the bird," Jim advised the watchers at the lookout. Sometimes a bird identified as a red-tailed hawk might turn out to be an eagle;

sometimes a Cooper's hawk might actually be a peregrine falcon. Only by keeping sight of the bird in binoculars until an unmistakable and unique feature was noted could anyone be absolutely, positively sure of the identification.

I've taken Jim's advice to heart. Even after years of watching birds, I can still be fooled: A flock of white-throated sparrows might have a golden-crowned in their midst. A hummingbird in dim light might be a black-chinned, not an Anna's. And a varied thrush might really be a northern pygmy owl.

Most times, though, identifying a bird at a glance doesn't require so much attention to detail. Most birds are so unique in their looks and habits that it's easy to ID them with just one quick look.

I bet you're already good at identifying some of the birds in your backyard. Mourning dove? Junco? Hummingbird? White-throated sparrow? American goldfinch (well, at least the male)? Chances are, you have 'em nailed.

You already know how those birds look and act, and where the likeliest places are that you'll see them. So when you spot one of these birds, your brain comes up with the right name as if by magic.

It's not magic, but experience, that puts those names on the tip of our tongue. We unconsciously add up every bit of informa-tion we're seeing, sift through it lightning-fast, and presto! Those big, grayish tan birds with the long pointy tails, the ones that are quietly nibbling seeds below the feeder—why, they have to be mourning doves. How do we know? We've recognized their appearance, we know that's their usual place in our yard, we've heard their cooing, and we probably have even registered that they usually show up in pairs or small groups.

In Part One of this book, you'll discover general tips and tricks of bird identification—methods and suggestions that will help you become a better bird-watcher. In Part Two, you'll meet the beautiful birds that keep life interesting in every part of the country. You'll find a "First Impression," the instant information that's a huge clue to pinpointing a species, as well as the finer points that you can also use to narrow it down. And, since I couldn't stop there, you'll also learn about each species' home life and habits, and how to make that bird happy in your own yard.

Learning how to identify what you're looking at only increases the fun of watching birds. As you learn their names, you'll be paying more attention to their fascinating behavior. You'll feel a stronger connection, whether the birds are at your feeder or singing in your tree. And you'll be looking forward to the next visitor that wings its way into your back-yard. I wonder what it will be?

IDENTIFYING BIRDS

How can you figure out who's who among birds when typical field guides show hundreds of pictures that take forever to sort out?

Welcome to bird identification, Sally-style.

In *The Backyard Bird Lover's Field Guide*, I've kept it simple. Instead of sifting through hundreds of "slim chance" birds, you'll find a much more manageable flock—the *most likely backyard birds* in your own geographic region.

You'll learn more about my quick-and-easy approach in Part Two of this book. Go ahead, turn to your region and see what's in store. I'll wait.

Then come back to Part One to discover how identifying birds can bring you health, happiness, and, well, not wealth, I'm sorry to say, but how about a lifetime of delight?

Chapter One

Why Birds?

One of my favorite things in nature is lichens, especially those flat, round patches that decorate rocks. The idea that anything would grow on a rock, turning sunlight into food and very slowly disintegrating that rock, just boggles my mind. So does the incredibly slow growth rate of some lichens, which spread outward so infinitesimally that you can't tell the difference 5 years later.

Finding a lichen I haven't seen before is as big a thrill to me as finding a new seashell on the beach. But finding someone to share that thrill with used to be a little trickier. Now that lichen appreciators can find each other on the Internet, I have others to share my finds with. Still, it's a very small group of enthusiasts.

Thankfully, my other obsessions have a much wider appeal. I have plenty of folks to talk about flowers or butterflies with. And birds? They're the hottest topic of all. In the past 10 years, the birding scene has exploded. Today, more than 50 million of us take part—that's one out of every five people in the United States!

Whether we fill a feeder or take a trip to a hummingbird hot spot, we have plenty of company. Birding is bigger than gardening. Bigger than hunting and fishing combined. I know, I can hardly believe it either. But the "birding industry"—the suppliers of seed, feeders, and all other products or services related to our favorite pastime—assures us it's true.

It's easy to get hooked on birds—just fill a feeder and watch who comes to dinner. Millions of us, of all ages, share the thrill.

Most of us participate in our own backyards, so it's no wonder the pastime tends to fly under the radar. Maybe we should all take up wearing lime green porkpie hats, so we could spot each other.

Speaking of dorky hats, remember when bird-watchers used to be a joke? Cartoons often featured a bunch of folks peering through binoculars, with a mocking punch line aimed at the earnest group.

All you had to do was say, "Yellow-bellied flycatcher," to make your friends burst out laughing.

Okay, so "yellow-bellied flycatcher" still sounds funny. And a bunch of people staring through binocs at the same spot is incongruous enough to cause a giggle (unless you're wondering, "Hey, what are they looking at?").

But nobody's laughing at bird-watchers

Oohing and Aahing

No matter how different we are, we all seem to agree on what's beautiful, what's endearing, or what's repulsive.

Sure, some of those reactions are dictated by culture, and they may change with the times. (Remember when mauve looked good?)

But other things seem to affect us at a visceral level.

Think about a Fourth of July fireworks show, when one of those huge, arching gold fountains rains down overhead. The whole crowd exclaims "Ooh!" in unison.

Beautiful scenery? We agree on that, too. We put it on puzzle boxes and calendars and the picture over the sofa, and we travel to see it. (Hint: It's not a strip mall or a freeway.)

A puppy, colt, lamb, curly-haired toddler? Say "Aww," everyone.

As for gross, there's no need to go into details. We all know what makes us say "Eew!"

I'm convinced that these emotional reactions we seem to share are a big reason why birds have such wide appeal. We simply enjoy watching them as they go about their lives.

Lots of birds fall into the cute or pretty category. Chickadees and fuzzy-headed young birds at our feeder get an involuntary "Aww." Goldfinches, magpies, jays, and other colorful characters make us sit up and take notice. And, like that finale at the fireworks, bluebirds, buntings, tanagers, orioles, and a flock of cardinals in winter are so beautiful, we just have to say "Ooh."

Chickadees are so irresistibly cute that they sell everything from sweatshirts to coffee mugs. Live birds are even better!

anymore, not since we've become an industry all by ourselves.

How big an industry?

Hang onto that seed scoop: Birding brings in $25 billion a year. Yessir, all those bags of seed sure add up. Not to mention the fancy feeders and binoculars and ecotours to Costa Rica.

So just what is it about birds? Why not, say, rocks? Or lizards? Or, for that matter, lichens? Let's take a look.

A PERFECT FIT

Rocks and lizards definitely have their fans. But they miss out on wide appeal for a few simple reasons.

A crystal of clear quartz or a bit of smooth veined turquoise is beautiful to look at. For a few minutes. But no matter how long you watch them, rocks don't do very much. They don't change, unless you have a way longer life expectancy than the rest of us.

Besides, hunting for special rocks is not something you want to share with anyone outside a small, close circle. Rock hounds generally keep quiet about their best finds, instead of letting others in on the discovery. (Anytime you want to share that favorite opal digging spot with me, just give a holler!)

Lizards . . . well, let's just say that for many people, they're an acquired taste. Scales just can't compare to pretty feathers. Lizards aren't often seen basking in the backyard in many areas, either.

Sure, cute little chameleons had a run of popularity there for a while. But most folks never cross the line into putting out a feeder for Gila monsters or raising chickens to tempt a 6-foot iguana.

Birds, on the other hand, have built-in appeal.

Alert and active, bright-eyed birds are a pleasure to watch. They communicate with each other, by song and calls. They're everywhere, in plain sight. And there's no ick factor, like there is with lizards. As a bird-loving friend used to say, "What's not to like?"

Plus, despite that $25 billion figure, you don't have to spend a cent to enjoy them. They're singing right in your own backyard.

Convenience Counts

If your garage is bursting at the seams with tennis racquets, mountain bikes, and all the other apparatus of your outdoor pursuits, you'll appreciate the simplicity of bird-watching.

All you really need are the birds, and they're everywhere.

And maybe a pair of binoculars. Oh, and a metal can for storing seed. But that's it. Unless you want to make your own feeders and houses. Then you'll need a corner for that workbench.

The Birth of Birdfeeders

When the movie *The Graduate* came out in 1967, I was a young teen. I left the theater with a serious crush on Dustin Hoffman. But what I should have paid attention to was the single word of advice he got from an older man in the movie: "Plastics," the fellow said, as if imparting the wisdom of the ages.

You know, maybe it was.

If I'd followed that advice and bought stock in plastics companies way back then, well, let's just say I wouldn't be shopping for cheap deals on sunflower seed.

Speaking of sunflower seed, I'm convinced that the hobby of bird-watching owes much of its amazing growth to plastic. Plastic feeders, to be exact. Red barn-shaped feeders, if we want to narrow it down even further. They were cheap. They were cute, in a country-folksy kind of way. And all of a sudden, in the early 1970s, they were for sale everywhere.

If you remember *The Graduate* (in movie theaters—DVDs don't count!), you probably also remember those feeders. They weren't particularly elegant, but they brought in birds.

That's why I say the boom in bird-watching began with plastic: Feeders could be mass-produced, instead of being sawed and hammered together one at a time. They could carry a tempting low price, just right for that impulse buy near the checkout.

Of course, if you bought a bird feeder, you needed some seed to put in it. Presto, another branch of the industry was born.

Then came another juggernaut: the introduction of the hummingbird nectar feeder, with parts molded from—take a wild guess—yep, plastic. Perky-Pet of Colorado, branching out from its pet-supplies line, made one of the first models. Although another company came up with an earlier model way back in 1950, it was Perky-Pet's reasonably priced and widely available feeder that really started the wave, sometime in the 1970s. The hummingbird feeder was an instant hit because, like the red barn feeder, it worked. Word started to spread, as friends and neighbors enthused about their birds.

Early entrepreneurs started packaging new seed mixes and new seeds. Thistle seed, now called nyjer or niger, arrived on the scene, and soon so did the tube feeders to hold it.

Droll Yankee, Inc., made the first tube feeders in the early 1970s. They were built to last but carried a hefty price tag. Still, once you saw their perches stacked with goldfinches, you wanted one yourself. A Droll Yankee tube feeder in your yard conveyed instant status among those in the know.

Imitations soon arrived, many made from—you guessed it—plastic. Now everyone could have goldfinches!

Success builds on itself. As their feeders attracted birds, folks wanted more—more birds, different birds, more feeders, more foods.

The industry was happy to oblige. Although it stayed relatively small for years, by 1984 birdseed alone was bringing in a cool half-billion bucks. Only 8 years later (1992),

A basin of fresh water is basic to a bird-friendly yard, as this goldfinch attests.

more than $2 billion in birdseed was flying off the shelves.

Yep. Shoulda bought plastics.

Come a Little Bit Closer

Birds are abundant across the country. We don't need to travel to where the birds are. We can just stay home and let them come to us.

Every neighborhood has its birds. No matter where you live, you can just step out the door—or look out a window—and you'll soon see some birds to watch.

You won't have any problem finding a robin to look at. Some birds are perfectly happy to hop about out in the open where we can plainly see them.

Other birds, though, tend to stick to the bushes or trees instead of parading around on the lawn. It takes a lot of patience to get a good look at a chickadee, for instance. Like a lot of birds, chickadees are always on the move, swinging from one branch to another or flitting away before you get a good look.

That's why most of us soon set up a feeder. A tempting tray or tube of seed, plus a block of suet, will quickly coax birds into easy view. Even if they dash in and out at the feeder, we'll still get a better look than if they were in a tree.

Add a birdbath or a fountain, and birds will have another reason to come a little closer. In late winter, you can nail up birdhouses to attract a family. Come spring, you can set out bits of string, cotton, wool, and other materials to entice nesting birds.

Besides putting out food and water and nesting materials for birds, we have another sneaky way to bring them into better view.

Have a Seat

I do a lot of my backyard bird-watching from my sitting spots—a bench under the apple tree, a couple of old wooden chairs out front, the edge of the porch, the back steps. And whenever I go out looking for birds, I spend way more time leaning against a tree or sitting on a comfy rock than I do scrambling through brush or hiking the trails.

Birds are easy to scare, and they'll take cover or slip away if they see an unusual motion or an intruder. But when birds think you're just part of the scenery, you'll get to see more birds, and more interesting behavior.

I could blame my aging joints for my habit of sitting, but really, it's because the bird-watching is better when I'm sitting still. Once I get settled, it takes just a few minutes for the birds to return to their normal activities all around me.

There aren't many outdoor pursuits in which sitting still is a valuable skill. Those of us with creaky knees are grateful!

Watching birds is a great excuse, er, reason, to spend more time sitting in your garden. A young friend adds to the fun.

Put a pair of binoculars to your eyes, and you'll be able to see the faintest stripe at a sparrow's eye, or the color of its beak.

Binoculars aren't strictly necessary, especially if your feeder is near your window. But they do make it easier to see details. And they're indispensable when you branch out beyond the feeder to the fields.

The Other Side of the Fence

It's human nature to want what we don't have. No matter how great the birds are in your own backyard, you'll still find yourself lingering over pictures of birds from other areas.

Maybe it's an indigo bunting you long to see at your feeder, or a bluebird that's your Holy Grail. "Oh, if only we had (bird *x*)," you sigh.

I do it, too.

Just a few days after an out-of-town guest had marveled at the Bullock's orioles and black-headed grosbeaks in my backyard—birds I see every day in summer—I found myself pining for a bird I couldn't have.

I was chatting with a radio show host in southeast Texas, reminiscing about the cypress swamps and the grasslands down there in Big Thicket land.

"Say hi to those cattle egrets for me," I said. "I sure do miss them."

"Cattle egrets? You mean white cowbirds? You miss *them*?"

"Absolutely," I said. "We don't have them up here in the Pacific Northwest."

He couldn't believe it. These small heron relatives are so common down there, no one gives them a second thought. They're just part of the scenery in any cow pasture, totally taken for granted. To a northwesterner, though, they're a bird to yearn for.

That's why you'll find tons of mouth-watering ads in any birding magazine for trips to exotic places—like Costa Rica, Mexico … and New Jersey. Come see sandhill cranes dancing in Wisconsin. Whooping cranes in Texas. Hummingbirds in Arizona, wood warblers in Michigan, hawks in New Jersey. It all sounds so tempting, like living a *National Geographic* magazine article.

Whenever I start feeling deprived by not being able to travel to see special birds, I remind myself of the way "the grass is always greener" syndrome works.

If I lived in the North Woods, where wood warblers are a dime a dozen, I'd be lusting after hummingbirds in Arizona.

And if I had a house in the canyon in Arizona and went through gallons of sugar water a day, I'd probably have the ad for that wood warbler trip taped to my refrigerator.

Whenever I start to feel the grass is greener in other backyards, I remind myself of the first time I saw a Steller's jay. Or an Anna's hummingbird. Or any of the other birds that make birding in the Northwest so special. (Especially if you live somewhere else!)

Steller's jay is a common sight in the West.

Something Different Every Day

The more you watch birds, the more you'll see—and hear. You'll learn their songs and their plumages. You'll note behavior differences and personality types.

Every day brings something new. And just when you think you have a bird figured out, it'll do something that takes you totally by surprise.

The Changing Scene

Whenever I see the first small flock of red-winged blackbirds getting together, I feel a twinge of melancholy. The beginning of flocking behavior, in blackbirds, grackles, starlings, or swallows, means the end of summer. No more long lazy evenings on the deck. Shorter days. And soon the rainy season once again.

As you spend more time watching birds, you'll realize that they follow a yearly pattern in their lives that's timed to the cycle of the seasons. The pattern is just as predictable as a maple flaming red in October.

Here's a quick preview of what you can expect.

◆ Spring will bring incredible migrants stopping by, calling you out the door with unusual songs or thrilling you with a flash of exotic color. Indigo buntings, rose-breasted grosbeaks, tanagers—anything can happen!

◆ Summer slows feeder traffic, because birds are nesting and natural food is at its peak. Now's the time to look for parents carrying food to nests. Add mealworms to your birds' menu, too, to attract the takeout trade.

◆ Late summer brings fledglings to the feeder with their parents. Watch for many birds to take on new colors now, too, as they shift into quieter plumage for fall and winter. Birdsong fades away after nesting; no more dawn chorus.

◆ In late summer to early fall, you'll notice some birds beginning to hang out in small flocks. Some, such as grackles, blackbirds, or starlings, may stick around in flocks that can grow to enormous numbers. Others, such as flickers, robins, and finches, will move along on migration.

◆ Fall means saying goodbye to some favorites, like wrens and tanagers, and hello to other birds passing through or returning for winter. If you live in a mild winter area, you'll be greeting birds that summered up north, like bluebirds and catbirds.

◆ Late fall and winter will be a busy time at your feeder, with dozens of birds hoping for a handout every day.

◆ Some species are reliable friends that you see year-round—jays, house finches, song sparrows, and a handful of others. They're the foundation of your backyard bird club, the charter members who stick around.

Pleasures of the Ordinary

When you watch birds, you never know what you're going to see.

But you *can* count on seeing something interesting.

Some days are "Oh wow!" days. Maybe a storm has blown an oddball bird off course, right into your yard. Maybe a migrating flock has decided to have breakfast in your bushes. Maybe the titmice have brought their fuzzy-headed babies to the peanut-butter feeder.

More often you'll just share "ordinary life" with your birds. Could be you'll happen to notice a cardinal collecting twigs for its nest, or you'll see a song sparrow pulling dead grass from your *Miscanthus* clump for its nest. Maybe you'll see a robin filling its beak with mud at the place where your hose is hooked up. Or a blue jay splashing in your birdbath.

That's the best thing about watching birds. Even the most ordinary bird activities are fascinating to see.

Continuing Education

I learn plenty just by watching birds, but sometimes I get scientific and devise an experiment.

A few years back, I put a pair of orioles to the test. I'd been putting out white strings for them to use in the nest they were building. Sometimes the strings got into a tangle, but I noticed the orioles always managed to get the snarl undone.

Ah, but how clever were they at knots?

First, I tied a tempting piece of string to the branch with a single over-and-under knot, like you do when tying your shoes.

No challenge at all. The male oriole instantly pulled it free.

Okay, double knot. That took him a little longer, but he got that one pretty quick, too.

Triple? Hmm, now he looked confused. After a few minutes he gave up, and the female arrived. She was baffled at first. Then she carefully peered at the knots, her head cocked to one side like she was thinking hard. With a flurry of short, quick jerks at seemingly random spots on the knot, she managed to work it free.

Four knots was too hard a task. Neither bird could tug them loose. Finally, they began shredding the ends of the string and pulling out individual fibers.

Fast-forward 15 years to a new pair of orioles on the other side of the country. It's May of last year, I have just moved to a new place, and I'm wondering how my pair of Bullock's orioles in Washington State compares to its Baltimore relatives back East?

I put out string. One knot, nothing to it.

Two knots: Hey, what's this? The female looks suspiciously toward the house, as if she knows I'm playing a trick on her. But she works it out and triumphantly carries off the string.

Three knots. Uh-oh. No can do. Much chattering, much tugging, no luck.

After two days, I clipped the now very tight knot, loosened the string, and stopped making their lives difficult.

"You know, they sure are pretty, but these

Want a Bullock's or Baltimore oriole? Try a nectar feeder with perches.

orioles aren't as smart as my old ones," I announced to a friend, as we watched the birds drink sugar water from the feeder they visited every morning.

Oh, aren't they?

"Someone's at the door," called the same friend from the kitchen a few days later, "and he has a complaint."

"What? Where?" I asked, not seeing anyone outside the full-length glass door.

My friend pointed to the floor of the deck, just outside the door. There stood the male oriole, on tiptoe, pecking at the glass. "I think he's trying to tell you something."

The nectar feeder was empty.

Hmm. Intelligence test, indeed.

Wonder how fast the last people who lived here figured that out?

50 YEARS OF ENTERTAINMENT

Maybe I'm just easily amused, but I've been watching birds for 50-some years, oops, I mean 39, and it hasn't lost its thrill one bit.

I love being out in the yard on an April morning at the peak of migration, when all my old friends—the vireos, the warblers, the tanagers—are singing "We're back! We're back!"

But the plain old feeder can also keep me entertained for way longer than seems likely. An hour can slip by like nothing when there's a crew of chickadees, nuthatches, and jays coming and going on a winter day. Even house sparrows and starlings are fun to watch.

Not only does watching birds cure boredom, it's also good for your blood pressure. Researchers discovered years ago that feeder-watching takes your mind off your cares and woes, and lowers heart rate and blood pressure.

You can pick up this lifelong hobby at any age. No matter how old you are, or how young you are, birds are fascinating to see.

Watching birds is even more fun when you share it with someone, because you both get to share the thrill of your discoveries. Family and friends—of any age—will love having coffee with the chickadees or spying on the hummingbirds at the hostas.

There's even more good news: You can be a birder on any kind of budget. The only must is a working pair of eyes or ears. Everything else is optional!

Get Equipped

How much did you say that last set of golf clubs cost you? And the bag and shoes? The balls? The little hats for your clubs? Oh, and let's not forget the greens fees.

Or maybe you'd rather run the numbers on mountain biking? Skiing? Fishing?

Face it. Whatever we want to play outside costs money these days. Serious money.

Except birding.

When it comes to watching birds, you don't need the right shoes, the right clothes, the right *anything.*

People have watched and listened to birds for thousands of years using nothing more than their own eyes and ears.

All you need is an interest—you already have that, or you wouldn't be reading this—and a pair of binoculars. And if you're on a Ramen noodles budget, you can hold off on the binocs.

Oh, sure, there are all kinds of high-power spotting scopes and hiking boots and birdcall CDs and other accessories. Somehow, though, I've managed to get to know hundreds of birds without ever owning a $200 pair of waterproof boots or a $2,000 pair of binoculars (though I admit I did drool over a pair of real Irish tweed trousers for a while).

Besides, I think we ought to rough it a bit now and then. I'm not talking about collecting dew for drinking water. But I do think we can survive occasional wet feet. Not to mention you'll be starting out in your own backyard—where dry socks are just a few steps away.

As for those two-grand binoculars? Somehow they keep getting pushed to the bottom of the wish list. Though if you want to put in a good word for me with Santa Claus, that'd be great!

Expand Your Vision

Even the cheapest pair of binoculars, those

Numbers Game

My first binoculars were 7 × 35 powered, one of the standard specs in the world of binoculars.

The first number tells you how much magnification you're getting—the larger the number, the bigger the bird will appear in the binoculars.

In this case, not double or triple or even quadruple your normal vision, but septuple! (I've been waiting for years to use that word.) Seven times better than your natural eyesight: What birder could resist?

Eventually, I moved on to 10-power (decuple!) binoculars, which give me eyesight 10 times better than my own.

Before you rush out and buy the biggest first number you can find, consider this shaky problem. Binoculars will also magnify every tremor and quiver from your hands (better skip that second cup of coffee), the wind, or the vibration of your car if you're in an idling vehicle.

More magnification, more blurring. It's easy to get a good image at 7- or even 8-power. At 10-power, you'll need very steady hands; for 12-power binoculars, better have ice water in your veins. Or high-tech image-stabilizing binocs. Advanced birders often invest in a spotting scope, a telescope that may let you count the scales on that fish a far-off heron is eating.

For backyard bird-watching, 7- or 8-power binoculars will be all you need, unless your "yard" runs to acres.

The second number (35, in the case of those 7 × 35s) is the size in millimeters of the objective lenses, the lenses at the bottom of the binoculars, farthest from your eyes. The bigger the lens, the more light it can admit. So what you see will look brighter, and the color and details of the image—that'd be the birdie—will be easier to make out.

Naturally, there's a trade-off. A bigger objective lens means a heavier pair of binoculars. If you did all of your bird-watching in a shady woods, it might be worth building up your neck muscles so you could lug around a pair with 100-mm lenses. But we usually look at birds in a variety of places, from bright sun to shade. Most birders find that 35 mm or 50 mm lenses work well for them.

$29.99 jobs you can find at any discount store, are a big improvement over unaided eyes. You'll be amazed at the details you can see with them.

When I got my first pair of binoculars, I figured I'd only be using them when I was away from home, to look at birds I didn't know very well. After all, I already was so familiar with my feeder birds that I could recognize them across the yard without binoculars.

Then, one day, I picked up the binocs and took a look at the feeder crowd. It was a revelation. Those white-throated sparrows I knew so well—some of them had a bright yellow patch by their beaks that I'd never noticed with my naked eyes. The woodpeckers had pointy tail feathers as stiff as wire, something I hadn't seen. And bird feet! Those tiny black chickadee toes were simply remarkable. With the binoculars, I could even see the remains of the previous meal on the cardinal's big beak: purple pokeberries, by the looks of it.

When a batch of kinglets came through a few days later, I really appreciated my powerful new "eyes." Instead of sneaking up on the birds as they moved from one tree to another, all I had to do was stand back, lift the binoculars, and look for the little clues that told me which kind of kinglet I was looking at. White bars on the wings and a striped head, hah, that was the golden-crowned. Plainer bird with wide-eyed look—finally I got a clear view at that tiny patch of red on a ruby-crowned's head.

Choosing binoculars is a lot trickier than buying birdseed. What brand? What magnification? Full size or compact? A week's salary or less than a tank of gas? And what if you wear glasses?

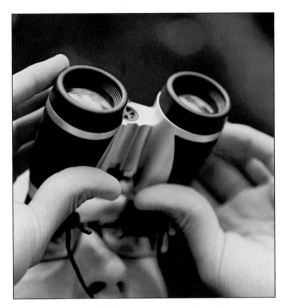

You won't need Popeye's arms to watch birds with lightweight compact binoculars.

You can get as educated as you like, but choosing binoculars still boils down to one question: Are they right for you?

- If the binoculars are too heavy to hold comfortably, it doesn't matter how great their lenses are—quivering muscles will make it all blurry anyway. So choose a pair that you can comfortably hold up to your eyes for minutes (possibly many minutes!) at a time.

- Do the eyepieces adjust to fit the width between your eyes? I've borrowed some that couldn't be closed up enough to fit my not-all-that-close-set eyes.

- If you wear glasses, pull up or twist open the eyecups and try using the binoculars with your glasses on. Comfy?

- Play with the focus knob or wheel. Does it work smoothly and quickly? Is it in easy reach? Does the focus change with a small adjustment, or do you need to turn and turn? You'll be using that wheel a lot when you're looking at birds, so it should be swift, sure, and easy.

- A crisp, clear view is the goal. If the binoculars give you a double image, a wavy spot, an odd colored outline or halo, or streaks of color at the edges of the field of view, or if the view seems distorted in some way, put them back and move on to the next pair.

- Binoculars are status symbols among some birders. Zeiss and Leica, a couple of old-school brands, still get a lot of respect. But the scene is changing rapidly as new manufacturers and models come on the market.

- "Try before you buy" used to be the rule. These days, many folks buy from online or mail-order sources. Wherever you shop, check for a warranty and a reasonable return policy, in case there's a defect in your new binoculars. They should work perfectly from the start.

Some experts tell you to buy the best binoculars you can afford for your first pair. But why should you drop a few hundred bucks on binoculars—or a couple thousand—before you have some experience using binoculars, so that you know which features are important to you?

Binoculars last a long time, unless they've spent a lot of time in the school of hard knocks. I've tried out military-surplus binoculars from World War II and found the image still crisp and bright.

That's why I suggest you start with a perfectly adequate pair of reasonably priced binoculars, which you can buy for less than $50. After you've used them for a while, you'll know which bells and whistles you're hankering for. Then you can invest in a lifetime pair.

How do you decide which kind to buy? Experts' picks and test groups that published their findings in birding magazines used to be the way to go. They're still helpful. But there are so many kinds of binoculars out there that these occasional reviews are always just a sampling.

"What about model ABC," I find myself wondering, "and where's model XYZ?"

On the Internet, that's where. For the first time, we can get an idea of how a particular model works in the real world, by reading users' reviews. Just Google "binocular ratings" to find a vast selection of frank opinions on binoculars of all makes, models, and prices. I often use Amazon.com user reviews for particular models to help me make my decision, too.

Binocular Breakthroughs

Not very long ago, binoculars were big, clunky, metal things that weighed on your neck like a ton of bricks.

Today, you can pick up a pair of compact plastic binoculars small enough to slip in a pocket and light enough that you'll forget they're around your neck. (And you can still get hefty, bigger ones if you prefer.)

Not only have binoculars been downsized, they've also acquired a couple of features that seem like magic: a zoom feature, and a method for practically eliminating vibration in high-power binocs.

Zoom binoculars. Zoom binoculars have something like a zoom lens on a camera: After you zero in on the bird, you can

COMPARING PRICES

You can be a bird-watcher on any budget. The items you might buy to draw in birds for close-up viewing are available at all kinds of prices. Here's how your shopping list might change, depending on how much chicken scratch you can spare.

PINCHING PENNIES	IN MODERATION	SKY'S THE LIMIT
Platform feeder		
Wooden tray homemade from scrap wood. Free	Woodlink Platform Feeder, hanging or pole mounted. Simple wood tray with metal screen bottom. $28.95, www.bestnest.com	Savannah Estate Feeder, white cast resin, plantation-porch motif with fluted pillars, detailed balustrade, and verdigris copper roof, weighs 25 lbs. $485, www.abirdsworld.com
Suet feeder		
Wire suet cage. Plastic-covered wire with latching top and chain for hanging. $3.99, discount store	Squirrel-Proof Suet Haven, wire cage of suet within larger wire cage to exclude squirrels. $23.95, www.duncraft.com	Antique-copper-finish suet feeder with decorative design of two nuthatches on a branch. $29.95, www.bestnest.com
Tube feeder		
Nyjer sock. Plump woven fabric tube already filled with seed for birds to pull through weave. 2 for $4.95, discount store	Droll Yankee Armored Thistle Feeder, tube protected from hungry squirrels by metal bands, with metal feeding ports. $34.99, www.bestnest.com	Royal Masterpiece tube feeder within Victorian-style metal birdcage. $124.95, www.duncraft.com
Birdbath		
Clay plant saucer. $3, discount store	Concrete pedestal-style birdbath. $50, garden center or discount store	Mini Two-Level Cascade Kit, two shallow pools with small waterfall. $180, www.duncraft.com
Nesting box		
Homemade bluebird house from free plans on www.daycreek.com, made from single cedar fence board. $2.50	Eastern Bluebird House, natural wood with 1½" entrance hole and predator-proof extension. $29.95, www.duncraft.com	The Colonial Home, white hand-painted wood with tall, steep, wood-shingled roof with pineapple finial. $349.95, www.abirdsworld.com
Binoculars		
Bushnell Nature View 8 × 40 binoculars. $39, www.amazon.com	Audubon Vector 8 × 42 binoculars. $129.99, www.amazon.com	Leica Ultravid 8 × 42 Rubber Armored Binoculars. $1,695, www.amazon.com
TOTAL COST		
$53.44	$297.83	$2,864.85

make it look bigger in your binocs by zooming in on it.

If you come across binoculars described as, say, 8–12 × 40, you're looking at zoom binocs. With a flick of your finger, that bird in your binoculars will zoom from 8 times bigger to as much as 12 times bigger. It's a nifty feature when you want to check out a fine point or get a better look at a faraway bird.

Image stabilization. Of course we want the most magnification we can get in binoculars. But there's a glitch—the more the image is magnified, the more that tiny tremble of your hands is bumped up, too.

Ta-da! Technology to the rescue!

Canon and Nikon have introduced binoculars that, at the touch of a button, automatically compensate for your shaky grip.

Image Stabilization (IS) is in its infancy, but it's already making a big splash in the

Zero in for a better view with binoculars that have a built-in zoom lens.

birding world. A push of a button stabilizes the image you're looking at, eliminating any blurriness from your trembling hands or a stiff breeze. No more straining to make out a blurry picture, or guessing at a too-small image with lower-power lenses.

With this feature, anyone can use 10-, 12-, even 15-power binoculars and see a crystal clear image of a faraway bird. You can even use binoculars in a moving car, something that used to be impossible. (Try this trick only when you're a passenger!)

I think of IS as sort of like the anti-skip feature on a CD player, which smooths out any jolts to the player so that the music keeps coming through without a hitch. Same deal with this binocular feature: It smooths over any shakiness so that all you see is a constantly steady image. That's huge news for birders.

If it works as well as it's said to, seems like standard high-power binocs may soon be left in the dust (hmm, could that mean bargain closeout sales?). It's hard to stick up for costly classics when this innovation supplies super magnification without blur, in a smaller, lighter pair of binoculars for less money.

So far, only Canon and Nikon offer the feature, using the same technology that's available in their digital cameras. Canon uses the name IS for its method, while Nikon calls its version StabilEyes VR (vibration reduction).

Whatever you call it, it's apparently a wonder. It allows you to look through very high-power lenses, without any of the blurring that would normally occur.

The reviews make my mouth water, but I plan to wait a year or two for the technology to become more established (i.e., cheaper!) before I give it a try.

Besides, my old binocs still work just fine.

If you too can talk yourself out of the latest and greatest, you can find lots of good binoculars for $50 or less. They'll give you years of satisfying use. Move up to $100, and you have even more choices.

If you're looking for a real buy, or if you need to outfit a family, you can find perfectly usable binoculars on eBay for as little as $10, shipping included. You can't beat that!

Well, not unless you happen to hit the right garage sale. Like the one I heard about years ago, when I was watching migrating hawks at a birding hot spot.

It was a friendly, competitive group, and I was getting some good-natured ribbing about the El Cheapos I had slung around my neck. After a while, one of the birders, an out-of-state fellow, proudly offered me a look through his fine binoculars.

Instant surge of envy. They were of legendary quality, with lenses that made mine seem like I was looking through the bottom of a drinking glass.

"Very nice," I said, handing them back before I got too attached.

"Guess what I paid for them," he said.

"Uh, a lot?" seemed a safe answer. They were easily worth a cool $1,000.

I can't remember whether they were Leica or Zeiss, but I do know he was pleased as punch to have found them at a garage sale for—sitting down?—a quarter. Yep, 25 cents.

"Wow, guess the seller didn't know what they were," I said.

"Nope," he chuckled, "not at all. She was a widow getting rid of her husband's stuff. Said she was trying to raise the money to go live with her daughter. Even apologized for not having one of the lens caps."

"Did you tell her?" I asked, hoping he would say he tucked a hundred-dollar bill into her hand.

He gave me an "Are you crazy?" look and pointedly turned his back.

I went back to scanning the sky. Suddenly, my $25 binoculars felt just fine.

Watching Mr. Birder unlock his luxury car a while later, I thought about all the quarters it takes to add up to $1,000.

Guess what? You don't need fancy binoculars to recognize a weasel.

Hitting the Books

The tall bookcase beside my desk is entirely filled with books on identifying birds. Some are tiny, made for children some 60 years ago, with charming drawings and old-fashioned text.

Others are so heavy they could serve as doorstops: *Birds of Ohio,* for instance, totals 671 pages. It's a 1903 edition, dedicated to the author's "first-born son," who's pictured in a short dress and a wide hat, standing in what appear to be his father's big lace-up boots.

You wouldn't lug this one along outside, but you could use it to identify the birds you've seen by comparing them to the book's color photographs of dead, stuffed birds in "lifelike" poses.

As in other old books, the bird descriptions are long and painstaking, practically feather-by-feather. It seems a bit excessive, until you

There's still a little space left on my shelf of field guides, because someday, right after I get those Leicas, I plan to pick up the 1934 first edition of the book that started the whole wave of modern birding: *A Field Guide to the Birds: Giving Field Marks of All Species Found in Eastern North America* by Roger Tory Peterson.

That original book sells for about $3,500 today, but back in 1934, Peterson was lucky to get it published at all.

America was still sunk in the Depression when young naturalist Roger tried to sell his thin little bird book to publishers. With so many people down on their luck, the audience seemed slim. Luckily, Houghton Mifflin Company took a chance on a first printing of 2,000 copies.

Birders had never seen anything like it.

It had hardly any words at all, just a simple drawing of each bird, with—and here's the biggest innovation of all—small arrows pointing to distinguishing features that set the bird apart from its fellows.

To those who were accustomed to pondering paragraphs of feather-by-feather descriptions, in which the most noticeable characteristics were buried in the verbiage, Peterson's book was a revelation.

Now, for the first time, *you could identify birds at a glance.*

That first edition sold out in 1 week.

More than 7 million copies of Peterson's guide, with various revisions, have ended up in birders' hands over the years.

The book has changed over the years. It now has color and more lifelike drawings. But the little arrows are still there, helping you sort out a robin from a towhee, a tree sparrow from a field sparrow.

Battered copies of old Peterson's guides often turn up at library sales, garage sales, and auctions. It's fun to look at them and see how the guide has changed over the years—and how well the older editions still hold up.

A scrub jay checks to make sure this field guide shows him on his good side. Look for a book with "field mark" arrows for fast ID.

realize that the person writing that description was looking at a dead bird: "Birding" was done with a gun back in the old days, so there was plenty of time to examine and describe the resulting specimens at leisure.

Here, take a look at this description from the book:

Adult male: Head black, interrupted by white of chin and white with black stripes of throat; eyelids and a supraloral spot white [*Getting anywhere yet?*]; tail blackish with white terminal spots on inner webs of outer pair of rectrices; wings dusky except on external edges; remaining upper parts grayish slate below [*Guesses, anyone? Anyone?*]; breast, sides, upper belly and lining of wings cinnamon-rufous [*Aha! Now you've got it! It's Robin Redbreast—but we're not done yet ...*]; lower belly and crissum white, touched irregularly with slate; bill yellow with blackish tip; feet blackish with yellowish soles [*Ah, yes, those yellowish soles! A dead giveaway!*]."

I love to page through my old books, but the books I use most often are collected on a shelf in easy reach. These are the field guides—bird books that are small enough to carry in your pocket when you're out in the field. Eastern birds, western birds, birds of the Pacific Coast, birds of Texas, waterbirds, seabirds—they're all here.

You'll definitely want a comprehensive field guide for your own collection, so you can learn more about the birds you're seeing with those new binoculars. Choosing a field guide is a lot like picking out binoculars: Buy the one that feels right to you. To test-drive a field guide, see how easy it is to find a few of the birds that you already know—without using the index. How fast can you find a Canada goose, pigeon, robin, chickadee, woodpecker, sparrow, and hummingbird? That will give you an idea of how easy (or how frustrating) it is to use that particular book.

Check out Recommended Reading, starting on page 309, for a few of my favorites, which you might want to start with.

Chapter Two

Why ID?

Learning the names of our backyard birds is really about learning to notice things. Watching birds is the gateway to a whole new way of seeing. Now we're slowing down and really looking at those birds and what they're doing, instead of giving them just a glance and never really "seeing" them.

A CLOSER CONNECTION

Here's a revealing little quiz: Which of your neighbors do you feel closer to: the ones you've met by name or those whose names you don't know?

Funny, isn't it, how knowing someone's name automatically makes you feel more connected to him or her. It seems to give us permission to get to know each other on a deeper level, instead of staying at arm's length.

When I moved to a small town in Washington State, I quickly became a regular at the little grocery store in town. I'd chitchat with the owner about the weather as he rang up my dog food or chocolate bar. Neither of us quite met the other's eye, although we were pleasant to each other.

After a few weeks of this, I finally stuck my hand out, looked him full in the face, and said, "I'm Sally, by the way."

"Tony," he answered, with a warm handshake.

Since then, I've noticed a definite change in the atmosphere when I go into the store. Now I feel as if there's a friend-to-be on the other side of the counter, no matter how gradually we get to know each other.

It works the same way with birds.

You can pass over a bunch of small brown birds with a casual glance, just like you'd nod to a neighbor you've never met.

Or you can take a closer look, and say "good morning" to the song sparrow, the chipping sparrow, the white-throated sparrow—and, look, there's a fox sparrow; he must be on his way north for nesting. Instantly, you feel as if you've just greeted four friends.

Friends with Feathers

Once you know their names, birds aren't just birds anymore. They're on their way to becoming friends.

Watching your feeder will be more fun when you can put a name to each visitor. I even say it out loud sometimes: "Oh, good morning, chickadees! Hiya, juncos. Howya doin' today, Mr. Towhee?"

Figuring out the names is just the first step to a deeper appreciation of birds. Once you start paying attention to your backyard birds, you'll be amazed at all the things you notice.

Oh, look—it's your friend Mr. Cardinal with his goldfinch and house finch breakfast buddies. Knowing the names makes backyard birds into personal pals.

All you have to do is focus on whatever bird happens to be handy.

Your own eyes are fine if the bird is nearby, but binoculars can make things a lot more interesting.

It doesn't matter what kind of bird you're watching—a robin, a sparrow, a cardinal. Even a plain old starling is fascinating to watch and wonder about.

Once you start really looking at birds, you'll wonder about all kinds of things. Why is that finch crouching and fluttering its wings like it's begging? What is that starling stabbing at in the lawn? Is that chickadee carrying a feather in its beak?

All those whys, whats, and hows are the beginning of a lifetime of learning.

LEARNING FROM NATURE

My son David figured out one of the big secrets to a happy life long before he graduated from college. In fact, I think he was about 6 or 7 years old at the time.

He was completely fascinated by ants then and had just shown me how he could tell the difference between ants that were arriving at the hummingbird feeder (their bellies were black) and ants that were departing the feeder (their bellies were so full of sugar water, they looked like tiny transparent bubbles).

"If I just have something alive to watch," he commented, "I never get bored."

"Isn't it great," I agreed. "And there's always something to watch, no matter where you are."

"And then you can wonder about why. Like why is this ant carrying this stick?"

David asked. "Why isn't he getting sugar water? Fun to think about."

"Sure is," I said. "Let's watch to see what he does next. Maybe that'll tell you why."

Watching what a creature does next may not give us the entire solution—but it's likely to supply the next piece of the puzzle. Meanwhile, without even realizing it, we have a whole new interest.

Anything that we pay attention to becomes more special to us. That's why learning to identify birds will give you a closer connection to them. It will make you feel more connected to nature, too.

What I love best is that no special lessons or practice sessions are called for. All we have to do is open our eyes.

The Worldwide Web

All apologies to the Internet, but it's Mother Nature who should hold the patent on this "worldwide web" thing.

Save the spotted owl? Not without saving flying squirrels, lichens, fungi, and trees.

Every living thing is part of that master plan, from microscopic bacteria and ants to grand old redwoods and African elephants. They're all connected.

Tracking these connections is as much fun as reading a good detective story.

Spotted owls are a hot topic in the Pacific Northwest, where the presence of this endangered species has saved many a stand of grand old trees from the chainsaw. But the owls are just one small strand in an interconnected web that also draws in lichens, fungi, and flying squirrels.

One lichen in the Douglas-fir forests of the Northwest goes by the descriptive name of "tree hair" or "brown beard lichen." It looks like it would fit right in with ZZ Top.

In winter, flying squirrels that live high in the towering trees rely on this lichen for their main food.

In summer, the flying squirrels switch to eating underground fungi (perhaps you've had a taste of truffles yourself?).

Simple enough, so far.

After dining, flying squirrels travel through the forest, depositing spores from those fungi wherever they happen to leave their droppings.

When those spores germinate, the quickly emerging "roots," or *mycelia*, hook up with the roots of trees in a *mycorrhizal association* that benefits the tree in a big way.

No sign of owls yet. But here's where the gee-whiz part comes in:

The tree that those mycelia are helping to nourish provides a home to hundreds, maybe thousands, of creatures. Including—ta-da!—brown beard lichen, flying squirrels, and spotted owls.

Just goes to show how much of the web of life we're still learning about.

Wonder Why?

Here's some more nature lore to learn from birds.

- Why do birds migrate? Birds that depend on insects depart when the weather turns cold in fall. Birds that eat mostly seeds are usually with us year-round.

- Why does the feeder get busy before a storm? You'll notice a big rush at your feeders when a winter storm is on the way. The birds are stocking up because there's likely to be a cold night ahead, and snow or ice will make it harder to find food.

- How do birds know a storm is coming? Birds are sensitive to air pressure changes that herald an approaching storm. Birds stop calling and disappear when severe summer weather approaches. But as soon as the worst has passed, they'll sing the all-clear.

- Why do birds come around when you cut the grass? Mowing the lawn stirs up insects. If you have a large, open lawn, watch for swallows or martins to swoop in for an airborne feast. Small yard? Wrens, robins, and blackbirds will happily check out the pickings your mower leaves behind.

- Why do birds wait until summer to nest? Nesting season is perfectly timed to the peak of caterpillar season. When caterpillars are super-abundant, bird nests are filled with hungry nestlings.

What's an ideal meal to stuff into those gaping beaks? Nice plump caterpillars!

- Where did that little bunch of sunflower seedlings come from? Thank your jays. These birds have a habit of burying the nuts and seeds they carry off from your feeder or from natural sources. Supposedly they come back to eat them later, but I've noticed that they overlook way more than they recollect. You don't suppose they might be planting more food on purpose? I wonder.

- Why do birds sometimes act so agitated? They're passing the word when a strolling cat or other danger is around. Birds don't have an enviable position in the ol' food chain. Eggs, nestlings, adults—every stage of bird life is yummy to some toothed, clawed, or slithery creature. Repeated, insistent chirps are a big clue that a possible bird eater is on the prowl.

Those volunteer sunflower seedlings that pop up all over your yard have been planted by jays. Watch a jay when it leaves your feeder, and you may see it planting the seeds.

Without that tree, there'd be no brown beard lichen for the flying squirrels to eat in winter.

Without the brown beard lichen, there'd be no flying squirrels.

Without the flying squirrels, the tree couldn't hook up with mycelia to bring it nutrients.

Without the flying squirrels, the spotted owl would go hungry.

That's a particularly nifty part of the web. But once you start noticing birds, you'll uncover all kinds of connections, including many simpler ones.

Take goldfinches, for example. You'll discover they nest later than nearly all other birds, waiting until midsummer before they start a family. Midsummer also happens to be when weedy thistles in fields and along roadsides begin to go to seed, their lavender flowers turning to silky tufts.

What do goldfinches line their nests with? Thistledown.

Who eats thistle seed, and drops undigested seeds to start new plants? Goldfinches.

Flickers and ants are another fun duo to watch. Flickers are big, brown woodpeckers that eat mostly ants and also "bathe" in anthills, to get rid of some of the pests that plague them. Sometimes they take an ant in their beak and smear it over their body to deter pests. Or they may perform "passive anting," in which the bird droops its wings over an anthill, fluffs itself up, and lets the ants crawl through its feathers to find lice and other tiny tidbits.

By the way, ever wonder why flickers are brown instead of the more usual black and white? I figure it's because they spend so much time on the ground, eating ants. A brown back blends in better against bare ground; hawks overhead and other predators nearby have a harder time spotting the bird when it's busy anting.

Every day, our backyard birds have something new to teach us. All we have to do is watch. And wonder.

EYES WIDE OPEN

Sooner or later it's going to hit you—you'll realize what you've been missing all these years, simply by not taking notice.

There's no need to feel bad; we all do it. Give yourself a big pat on the back instead. Your eyes are now open!

You never know which bird is going to give the wake-up call, but when it happens, you'll know it.

For me, it was a starling, a bird I'd taken for granted until the day I really *saw* one, and

The first meadowlark you see may seem like a rare bird, until you realize you just haven't noticed them before.

Would You Like That Rare?

Back in the 1970s, "consciousness-raising" was the buzzword. If you became aware of some injustice or other, you'd start noticing that behavior everywhere. Groups held sessions on various topics to help people open their eyes to what was going on around them.

You don't need group therapy for this one. Anything that has a personal connection to you can raise your consciousness.

Just ask any woman who's ever been pregnant. I bet nearly all of us have commented, "Have you noticed how many pregnant women there are these days?"

Or maybe you've bought a new car. Suddenly, you see a lot more of those cars on the highway.

Is it because there are more of those expectant mothers or those cars?

Nope. It's because you're now noticing them. Pregnancy or that kind of car now means something to you.

I see this very human quirk all the time in bird-watchers, too. Friends and family, and sometimes total strangers, often share their bird sightings with me.

I can't tell you how many times one of them has asked, "That must be a rare bird, isn't it?"

Or a variation: "They must be rare around here, aren't they?"

I've done the same thing myself (embarrassing details follow in Chapter 5). So I know that it can be pretty embarrassing to find out that the bird you just saw for the very first time—that "rare" bird—is as common as crabgrass.

"Just watch," I often tell these folks, "Now that you've seen it, you're going to start noticing it all over the place!"

Expecting? Suddenly you'll notice that lots of other women seem to be, too.

noticed the creamy stars sprinkled over its iridescent feathers. Wow! If I'd been missing that with starlings, what else was I missing?

For a country friend of mine, it was a meadowlark that opened her eyes. Betty had lived on a farm her whole life. She'd raised 13 kids, fed cows, cut and baled hay, and cultivated acres of corn.

One early spring day we were driving down the long dirt lane to her house, past the barn and fields she'd spent time in nearly every day of her life, when I happened to see a meadowlark leave the field and alight on a fence post along the road.

I slowed to a stop and handed Betty my battered binoculars.

"These aren't the best," I apologized, "but see if you can get a look at that bird on the post. Just twist that ring in the middle to make 'em focus."

After some fumbling and complaining, I heard her suddenly draw in her breath.

"Ooh," she said, "what in the world is *that*?"

"A meadowlark."

"Now that must be a really rare bird," she said.

Mr. Meadowlark sure looked like a prize, with his big butter yellow chest and bold black necklace. But in these fields, meadowlarks were a dime a dozen.

"Sure is beautiful, isn't he," I said, avoiding the issue.

Betty wouldn't let me off the hook. "But rare, right? All these years, I've never seen one."

"Um, not often seen, anyway," I waffled, "unless you're looking for them."

Her sharp eyes pinned me down. "So they're all over the place, then?"

"Watch the field for a minute," I suggested. "There! See that bird that just flew up? Looks dumpy like a starling, but has white edges on its stubby tail? That's a meadowlark."

We spent the next half-hour or so getting acquainted with the meadowlarks in the field.

As a hardworking farm woman, Betty had never happened to take notice of the birds around her. Her attention had been focused on animals and her own brood, not to mention constant worry about the crops.

Now she had the luxury of being able to spend time looking at birds, and she was instantly hooked. Feeders and birdhouses soon filled the yard around her little house.

When I stopped by at Christmas, Betty hurried me to the feeder window. A multi-

tude of cardinals at the trays and in the snowy bushes made the scene look like a Christmas card.

But the picture-perfect cardinals weren't what Betty wanted to show me.

"Just wait," she said. "Oh good, here he comes!"

It was a meadowlark. Big, bright, and bold as brass, the bird shouldered his way into the tray feeder and began scooping up millet.

Not an uncommon sight in the countryside, especially after snow. But to Betty, a meadowlark will always be something special.

Once your eyes are open to birds, you'll find yourself having a greater appreciation for everything else around you, too. Without even trying, you'll be noticing butterflies, ants, insects, wildflowers, and lots of other things that slipped right by before.

Take a longer look at bunches of birds, and you may spot an oddball in their midst or find out the flock isn't what you'd thought. These are Eurasian tree sparrows, found only near St. Louis.

Have your surroundings changed? Not a bit! You've simply learned to see.

New Bird in Town

Spending the time to figure out the names of your backyard birds means that you'll be quicker to notice new birds.

Recognizing a certain bird quickly becomes automatic. You're training your eyes to discern the differences between species. And you're getting familiar with the posture and habits of each bird.

Once you've sorted out the details on a white-throated sparrow, for instance, you'll quickly notice when a white-crowned sparrow joins the flock.

Without even thinking about it, your eye will go right to the pine siskin mixed in with the goldfinches at the thistle feeder, or to the dark-eyed Oregon junco among the slate-colored juncos.

Pay attention to your first flash of "Hmm, doesn't look right." Often, that fleeting thought means your subconscious is doing a great job of alerting you to something different in the mix. Take a closer look!

COLLECTING BIRDS

Keeping a collection seems to be an ingrained part of the human psyche. Even little kids like to line up their collections of rocks or Matchbox cars. That urge never seems to go away, although the collection may change. Jay Leno has accumulated dozens (Hundreds? Thousands? Can I have that red one?) of classic cars. A fellow I once met had so many pieces of sports memorabilia that he opened a restaurant so he could display it all.

Table for 30?

How many different species of birds might show up in an average backyard over the course of a year? ("Average" meaning a medium-size yard of perhaps 8,000 to 10,000 square feet, with a bird feeder, some shrubs, and a flower bed or vegetable patch.)

Go ahead, take a guess. Five species? Ten? Maybe 15, if you're lucky?

How about 30 or more? That's about average for many backyards.

Add an older shade tree to that mix and the count will go up. Berry bushes or fruit trees? Expect other new friends.

If your yard is within easy flying distance of wild places, or if you live along a major migration route, look for your count to rise dramatically.

I recently moved to a small house on nearly an acre of land. In a few years it'll be bird heaven, but right now that acre is nothing but grass, plus one walnut tree and a couple of apple trees. But still I counted more than 50 different species in or over the yard in my first month! Most are just visiting from nearby wild areas, but they're here every day.

Venture outside your yard, and you might count 100 kinds of birds without too much trouble in any region of the country.

No wonder bird-watching can keep us busy for life!

It's hard to say what will set off that collecting urge. For some of us, it's decorated plates or frog figurines. Others go for first edition books or modern art. Maybe your collection leans toward designer shoes, postcards, or baseball cards. (Have you ever noticed how many mothers mistakenly sold that precious shoe box at a garage sale?)

I'm sure that our collecting urge is why birding has such strong appeal. Seeing a new bird is as much of a thrill as stumbling across a piece of Roseville pottery for your collection—the find is wonderful!

With this collection, you won't need a new set of shelves. Your mom can't sell it at a garage sale. And it doesn't have to cost a penny. All you need is a list.

Starting a list of the birds you've seen seems so innocent, but for many of us, it's the first step to a lifelong passion. Every new bird is an achievement, something to be proud of. There's nothing like constant ego gratification to keep us hooked!

Many birders keep more than one list: A master list of all the birds they've ever seen, plus smaller lists for nesting birds, winter birds, birds at the feeder, or any other category they like.

Keeping a List

Keeping a list of the birds you see is a basic part of birding. Your list can be as casual or as complicated as you like. It may be a simple scribbled list of species on a sheet of paper; official checklists distributed by reputable organizations, such as those in the Peterson guides or used by the National Audubon Society for census-taking; or a computer database with details on sightings. The style of list is up to you and so is its content. You can keep your "Birds I've Seen" list as narrowly focused or as wide open as you like.

Here are some popular birding lists.

The life list. Keep this as your master list, in which you write down every bird you see, no matter where you see it.

Does a kingfisher over your fish pond count as a backyard bird? It's up to you.

The backyard list. Write down every bird you see in your backyard. I find this list just as much fun as the life list, because it's all about my own yard. I include birds that are flying over, too, even though it feels a bit like cheating.

The feeder list. Keep track of who's visited your seed, suet, nectar, and other feeders.

Any other lists that you want to keep. Note the birds that nest in your yard, birds of your state, birds you've seen on certain trips, birds that visit during spring migration, birds that stop by on the fall journey—whatever makes sense to you. It's your collection, so you get to organize it however you like!

Listers

Mention your life list to other birders, and you're likely to get two very different reactions.

Phoebe Snetsinger is tops among listers. She was a birder who shifted into high gear after being diagnosed with melanoma. Instead of having treatment, Phoebe signed up for a birding tour to Alaska. Her cancer went into remission (though it later returned), and she spent the rest of her life "collecting" birds for her list. An heiress who could travel whenever and wherever she wanted, she added birds swiftly, most on guided tours. By 1995, she had hit the rarefied mark of 8,000 species.

Her autobiography, *Birding on Borrowed Time,* is quite a read. Traveling the world on an unlimited budget may sound pretty cushy, but some of Phoebe's experiences were horrifying. And she was a very busy person.

Besides traveling and writing a book, she kept incredibly detailed notes and records—and she managed to have a family. But what is evident throughout her life story is that she never lost the pleasure of watching birds.

On a November morning in 1999, Phoebe was looking for rare birds in Madagascar, off the coast of Africa. She'd added Bird #8,450 to her list that morning, the red-shouldered vanga, a species that had been discovered just 2 years earlier.

To a lister, though, the bird that really counts is the next one. A few hours later, Phoebe Snetsinger was killed in a bus accident while on her way to find #8,451, the Appert's greenbul.

At the time of her death, she had seen more birds than anyone else on earth.

Phoebe Snetsinger: 8,450 birds on her list!

One group will proudly announce the exact numbers of birds on their own life lists, or talk about a super trip when they added new species to their list.

The other group will have, at best, only a rough idea of the number of birds they've seen. Instead of comparing numbers, they'll talk about what the birds they saw were doing, or how beautiful they were.

For bird *listers,* the thrill of the hunt and the satisfaction of adding a new species to the count are the major reasons for birding. Competition plays a big role. More birds on that list give you better bragging rights. Can you measure up? Or do you need another trip to the Rio Grande Valley to add more species to your list?

For bird-*watchers,* the list isn't as important as the pleasure of watching birds, any birds. Sure, it's a thrill to spot a new bird. But it can be just as satisfying to learn more about an old friend.

Naturally, there's plenty of overlap between the two. All of us are interested in birds, for starters. And while listers often look forward to competitive birding marathons such as the Big Day (see "Citizen Science" on page 32), most of them also enjoy watching bird behavior.

Roger Tory Peterson, America's most famous bird-watcher and a lifelong naturalist, was a dedicated lister. His goal was to see half of the birds on Earth in his lifetime. It took him until the mid-1980s, about 10 years before he died at age 88, but he made it.

Sometimes those who aren't listers are belittled as not being "serious birders." That's simply not true. Serious birders fall into both camps. And bird behavior is a science that's every bit as serious as tallying all the species in a given area.

Going to Extremes

For some listers, birding veers into extreme territory. The collecting urge spins out of control. Adding birds to the list becomes an obsession. For some listers, getting to know the birds hardly matters: It's all about adding to the count.

Here's a sample of lister mania, from *To See Every Bird on Earth,* Dan Koeppel's book about his own father's quest: "He got in his car, drove ten hours to the dock where the bird had been seen, stepped out of his car, saw it, and then drove home. Bird Number 6559."

The listing craze is a fairly new phenomenon. It only really got going in the 1970s.

About 10,000 species of birds, give or take a few hundred, are on the Earth. About 800 species of birds can be found in the United States and Canada, not including Hawaii. (The exact number changes as the official list of species is fiddled with and birds are reclassified or new species discovered.)

Listers who've moved to the worldwide category are definitely the most obsessed. Some of them spend hundreds of thousands of dollars to reach remote areas with private guides so they can tick off one more bird.

By the mid-1970s, only 11 birders had tallied 2,500 on their worldwide lists. Thirty years later, 256 had hit that milestone. And among them were a few who had gone much, much further.

Keeping a Bird Journal

I found out just how disorganized I am during a recent move. I was downsizing to a much smaller house, so I was weeding things out by sorting through boxes that had been stored away for many years.

That's when I came across my birding journals. There were maybe a dozen, the oldest dating back to 30 years ago. Some were spiral-bound, others black-and-white composition books, and a couple were beautifully bound journals. But all of them had something in common: Only the first few pages had anything written on them.

That's right. Despite my best intentions, I've never been able to make it a routine to write down daily happenings or musings, week after week.

Each notebook started out with a list. Usually it was an inventory of who was at the feeder, but a few lists were from outings to woods or lakes, and others were from birding trips to other states.

None of the journals continued for more than 3 days, I'm sorry to report. And most petered out after Day 1. I guess I was just too busy watching the birds, or too lazy to make any notes about them.

Still, I had a ball reading through the stack of barely touched notebooks. Wow, was it really 25 years ago that I saw my first blue-winged teal? I still vividly remember that day at Middle Creek Wildlife Refuge in Pennsylvania: Tree swallows and myrtle warblers were eating bayberries off the bushes by the visitors' center. Cedar waxwings were in every juniper tree. Huge swans flew overhead with a rush of wings. And the water was filled with ducks, my teal among them.

None of that was in my journal, though. All I had written was the name of a bird and a date, plus a quick sketch of the teal's head with its trademark crescent moon marking.

My record-keeping on paper may leave a lot to be desired, but at least my sightings are in order in my head.

Learning More

It's way more gratifying to read about a brown thrasher once you know what a brown thrasher is. After you've identified a thrasher, you can read an account of the bird and say, "Yes, yes, I've seen him do that, too," or "Hmm, I'll have to watch for that," or "Now I know where to look for its nest."

Reading is a great way to learn more about our backyard birds. You'll find enough books and magazines about birds and bird-watching to keep you busy for years.

I generally find older books more engaging than most modern ones. The writing is usually more personal and more emotional (okay, florid!) than today's books. Back then, nobody was worried about anthropomorphism, or assigning human emotions or motivations to birds and other animals. Today, many scientists scorn instances of anthropomorphism: "Cheerful chickadee," for instance, would be verboten.

Just try to match this enthusiasm:

> The song of the Goldfinch is, in part, very similar to that of the Canary. It is replete with the lively humor of the bird. One cannot listen to the full song of a characteristic singer without laughing involuntarily at the unmistakable glee with which it is executed. Only the Bobolink can excel the Goldfinch in spontaneity of feeling, and not even he can cram so much pure *fun* into one short musical sentence!
>
> —F. Schuyler Mathews, *Field Book of Wild Birds and Their Music* (1904)

When your eyes get bleary from reading, let the birds themselves be your teacher. I love to read about birds, but I've learned way more just by watching them.

SHARING EXPERIENCES

Birding is a one-size-fits-all hobby. You can tailor it to suit just about any personality.

- If you're feeling like a hermit at heart, you can watch birds all by yourself.

- If you prefer one-on-one or small groups, you can share your pleasure with your family or a small circle of friends.

- If you're a people person, you can connect with all kinds of groups, in person and online.

Sharing with Other Birders

Other collectors usually play it close to the vest when it comes to sharing their finds. They're happy to show you—after the particular item is in their collection. And they're reluctant to disclose a good source. Bird collectors are different. Since no one is actually capturing the bird for his or her collection, most birders don't mind sharing their finds.

When it comes to a rare bird, there is cachet in being the first to find it. But a rare bird is still a thrill for the 100th or 10,000th birder to come along.

That's why group activities are common in birding. You'll find plenty of appealing possibilities.

Birding Groups

The venerable National Audubon Society has chapters in every part of the country. Monthly meetings are usually announced in the newspaper. Members share sightings with each other and learn about conservation.

To find an Audubon chapter near you, check your phone book or Google "Audubon [YOUR STATE]." Or call the news desk of your local newspaper, or a local nature preserve. If all else fails, try the U.S.D.A. extension agent for your county, listed in the blue pages of the phone book.

Audubon is the oldest and best known birders' group. But other groups may also exist in your area. If you live in Kentucky, for instance, you also can check out the Eastern Kentucky Bird Club or the Kentucky Ornithological Society.

You'll find an excellent collection of bird clubs at www.birdingguide.com/clubs/. Just click on your state. As usual, Google is

your friend, too: Search for "bird clubs [YOUR STATE]." You can also keep an eye on information in your newspaper about local meetings.

Citizen Science

Bird-watchers like you and me have contributed our observations to science for hundreds of years. Some of those stories have been found to be a little shaky (swallows burrowing into swamp mud for hibernation? I don't think so!), but anecdotal evidence still forms the basis for our understanding of birds.

The well-respected reference, *The Audubon Society Encyclopedia of North American Birds*, by John K. Terres, for instance, pulls much of its info from a 1900 to 1930 series of books edited by A. C. Bent, which was a collection of hundreds of stories from backyard birders as well as scientists.

Behavioral anecdotes may be my personal favorite, but science also needs cold, hard facts. That's where we come in, yet again! Birders like us have been researching bird populations and distribution patterns for decades. How? Through Audubon's Christmas Bird Count and other regular efforts.

On our end, we're busy marking down what type, how many, where seen, and so on for every bird we spot. That's important data to scientists, who tabulate, collate, and play with those numbers to come up with a yearly picture of American bird life and how it's changing.

Signing up to be part of a bird count is a regular ritual for many bird-watchers. Local counts are part of a national effort. Held on or about the same day, the counts collect valuable data about the distribution and population of birds. Here are the best known.

Audubon Christmas Bird Count. It takes place around Christmastime, which may sound crazy—aren't we all super busy then? Of course. That's why the count provides such a welcome change of pace. Instead of fighting traffic to buy gifts, give yourself (and your family) a gift by spending a day outside looking for birds. It's a great cure for holiday stress. Go to www.audubon.org/bird/cbc/ to find out the details.

Project FeederWatch. Organized by the Cornell Lab of Ornithology, this national count collects data from people with feeders. You won't even have to step outside, except to fill the trays! Go to www.birds.cornell.edu/PFW/.

Breeding bird surveys. These counts will take you outside to look for evidence of nesting birds in an assigned area. Don't worry, you won't have to find the nests! A singing male bird is enough evidence. Ask your local bird club or Google "breeding bird survey [YOUR STATE]."

Great Backyard Bird Count. This one functions as a mid-winter snapshot of bird life in the United States during a particular 4-day period. Birders of any level count birds over the period, then report their highest count for each species at an online site. Collected data is later available for viewing. Check it out at www.birdsource.org/gbbc/.

eBird. This project was developed by the Cornell Lab of Ornithology and the National Audubon Society to track bird populations and distribution, plus other data. You register online and send checklists to eBird's Web site; you can later review your own data or other records. Go to www.ebird.org/.

Big Day. An offshoot of the World Series of Birding (www.njaudubon.org/wsb/), which is held only in New Jersey,

"Big Day" bird counts can raise funds for good causes, with pledges collected for each species on the list.

this count is for anyone who loves listing. Be prepared to be exhausted: You'll be tromping around from before dawn to well after dusk. (Some die-hard participants start with owls at one minute after midnight, and never let up until 24 hours later.) In 2006, a team from East Brunswick, New Jersey, found 88 species in 11½ hours; it was only their second attempt and they expect to do better next year. If you're looking for a good cause to support, consider Earlham College, in Richmond, Indiana, which has produced more ornithologists than any other college in the country. Earlham uses the Big Day as a fundraiser, with money pledged for every species seen. So far, the counts have raised nearly a half-million dollars for the school. Find out more at www.earlham.edu/.

You can find details on all of these counts online. Or you can ask your local chapter of the Audubon Society or other bird club. More watchers are always welcome!

The brown sign that marks a National Wildlife Refuge promises good birding. This one, in arid eastern Washington, has water that draws swans, ducks, geese, and sandhill cranes in spring and fall.

Planning a Vacation?

I'm a big fan of traveling by car because I can explore any place that catches my eye along the way. One of the roadside attractions I always stop for is heralded by a brown sign, often with a silhouette of a flying goose. That's the signature logo for a national wildlife refuge (NWR), public lands that I've learned are always teeming with great birds.

NWRs aren't nearly as crowded as national parks (which are also great for birds) and they're usually traversed by a well-kept dirt road as well as by hiking trails. You'll probably want to get out to stretch your legs for part of your visit. But birding by car is the best way to go: The car works like a blind, so you can approach much closer to birds than you could on foot.

The only drawback about NWRs is that parts of them may be open for hunting in season. Many of these areas serve as a stopping place for waterfowl or other game birds, which are great to look at. But I avoid the refuges during hunting season; personally, I'd rather bird-watch without the background blast of shotguns.

If you'd rather plan ahead, Google "NWR [STATE]" to find out if there are any near your destination. You can also find NWRs listed in AAA tour books, and they're marked on most maps, if your eyes are still up to scanning tiny type. Meanwhile, I keep looking for a bumper sticker that says "I Brake for Brown Signs," but so far, I haven't had any luck.

State and national parks are great places to see birds, too. Ask for suggestions about good spots to bird-watch in the park when you pay the entry fee.

If you prefer more guidance, you can reserve your spot on a birding tour. All kinds of mouth-watering destinations are available. Check the ads in the back of a birding magazine for ideas, or search online. A travel agent can be useful, too. Bird club members are usually brimming with suggestions as well.

Birding hot spots, such as hummingbird-heaven Ramsey Canyon in southern Arizona, offer comfortable inns to relax at while you go birding in the area. You'll meet plenty of like-minded folks to have a friendly conversation with, or to join for an outing at sunrise. Or if you'd rather, you can just kick back on the porch and watch the feeders.

right, and the gray cheeks, and the brownish back and wings. Harris's belly looked whiter than my bird's grayish tan, and the top of its head was black while my bird's was brown. But it had to be Harris's sparrow. Nothing else came close. I had a rare bird!

Excitedly I phoned a nearby bird sanctuary, where the staff had been terrifically encouraging about my fledgling efforts.

"I've got a Harris's sparrow at my feeder," I proudly announced. "Just showed up this morning."

Two birders from the sanctuary came right over. They quickly scanned the scene with their binoculars—once, twice, three times.

Why weren't they seeing it? "Right there," I pointed out.

"That one? The one with the black bib?"

I was ready to go down in the record books. "That's him!"

They seemed to be distinctly unexcited. Were Harris's sparrows more common than I'd thought?

"Got your field guide?" one of the fellows finally asked. I handed it over.

He quickly flipped past all those pages of sparrows I'd pored over. I saw goldfinches go by, and cardinals. Finally he stopped and handed the book back.

"What about this one?" he asked.

Oh. Instant deflation. House sparrow. Not exactly a sighting to trumpet.

The birders were kind. "They do look somewhat alike," they acknowledged. "If the book had had the house sparrow with the other sparrows, you would've seen the difference right away. But he's actually a weaver finch, not a sparrow, so they put him in a different section."

"Any way I might have known that?" I asked, hoping to learn a tip that would help me avoid future shame.

"Practice," they said. "Just keep looking at the pictures and looking up birds. You'll get there."

Focus on Field Marks

I had one more question for the birders from the sanctuary. "How come this house sparrow's bib doesn't look like the picture? It's all spotty, like the bib on a Harris's."

They looked at each other and laughed, as if they'd been down the same path. "There's a lot of variation," they said. "You just learn what to look for. And make sure the field marks match. See that arrow? Harris's has a pink beak. Your bird doesn't."

By the way, this story does have a happy ending. I became an expert in recognizing house sparrows, for one thing. And for another, I did soon sight my rare bird: a tiny

House sparrow plumage can vary, causing a newbie birder to think, "Rare bird!"

heron called a least bittern that showed up at a pond down the road a few weeks later.

Much to their credit, my bird sanctuary pals once again hurried right over. This time, they confirmed it. Only the fifth sighting in the county, they told me.

Smug? Do I seem smug? Heck, 25 years later, I'm still bragging! Oh, and if you want some tips on house sparrow plumage, hey, just let me know.

ID AIDS YOU CAN COUNT ON

Roger Tory Peterson was a genius. But he also was a birder, and he knew how tricky identification could be. So he invented a can't-miss system that was brilliant in its simplicity: field marks.

Field marks are those details of a bird that, taken together, confirm the species without a doubt. Just as important, they're details that you can spot at a glance—once you know to look for them. Every Peterson guide includes arrows pointing to field marks of that species.

Starting in Chapter 6, you'll find an entry called "Details, Details" for each bird, spelling out a few details you can quickly check.

Finding Field Marks Quickly

Field marks are such a simple system; it takes just a few minutes to learn how to look for them. Mostly, it's a matter of where to look and what to watch for.

It'd be great if every bird sat still long enough for us to systematically run through its field marks. But that's not usually the case. So birders train themselves to look fast, since they may only get one glimpse.

Head

Head color and shape are the watchwords. Look for:

◆ Color and shape of beak

◆ A pointy crest, as that of a cardinal or Steller's jay

◆ Raised feathers, a subtler effect than a crest, as often seen on purple finches

Elvis Impersonator?

Field marks are taken so seriously by birders that they've led to some interesting arguments. One of the most notable recently has been the dispute over the identity of "Elvis," the possibly rediscovered ivory-billed woodpecker in an Arkansas swamp.

When the Cornell Lab of Ornithology announced the rediscovery of the ivory-billed in 2005, skeptics immediately surfaced. Code-named "Elvis," the ivory-billed had

been videotaped. Still, it was almost immediately branded an impersonator.

Elvis was actually an abnormal pileated, goes the hypothesis. Supporting evidence? Four of the five ivory-billed field marks, which you can count yourself in Peterson's, weren't seen in the Elvis video. Without those field marks, argue the skeptics, the ID isn't certain.

- A colored cap, like that of a chickadee or tree sparrow

- A colored bib, like that of the house sparrow or Harris's sparrow

- Eye ring, a narrow circle around the eye, often white

- Stripes above, below, or at the eyes

- Pattern on the face

- Eye color

Wings

Wing decoration and sometimes wing shape in flight are clues to look for. Check for these details.

- Wing bars: a horizontal bar or bars of different colors, usually white or yellow, across the wing; take note of how many

- A dab of white, sometimes yellow, on the wing; often called a "pocket handkerchief"

QUICK TIPS

While that bird is in your binoculars, check its field marks in this order: head, wings, tail—and if you still have time—legs. Give the bird a quick once-over, then go back and take a longer look if it hasn't flown away.

- White wing patches seen in flight

- White wing edges seen in flight

- Noticeably pointed wings, usually seen in flight

- Unusually long wings, noted when bird is perched or flying

Tail

Tail details are usually noticed best when the bird takes off or lands. Scan for these possibilities.

- Noticeably long tail

- Noticeably short tail

Wingbars and head stripes are clues that help set a golden-crowned kinglet apart from similar wood warblers.

A female American redstart sports a yellow "pocket handkerchief" and tail spots.

Make a Note

I'm always taken aback by how quickly I forget or mix up the details when trying to ID a batch of birds.

Warblers and sparrows are the worst because they often hang around in flocks of mixed species. It's not unusual to find six or eight kinds of warblers together, or four or five kinds of sparrows, especially during migration time.

When birds are coming through fast and furious, it's all too easy to lose track of the details you do note.

Was the one with the eye ring the same one that had the wing bars? And who had the white tail feathers—the one with the reddish cap or the one with the striped head?

Anytime you're checking details on more than one bird, it makes sense to jot down a few notes on field marks—as you notice them!

◆ Unusually shaped tail, such as the wide keel shape of a grackle

◆ Forked tail, such as a barn swallow or goldfinch

◆ Rounded or square corners of tail

◆ White feathers along edges of tail

◆ White or colored patch on tail

◆ White or colored corners of tail

Legs

Details of legs and feet can help separate very similar birds, or can be an instant clue to ID. Look for:

◆ Noticeably long legs, such as a waterthrush

◆ Noticeably short legs, such as a nuthatch

◆ Color of legs

To ID juncos, look for white tail edges, back and head color, and eye and beak color. This is the red-backed race.

Long legs, bright pinkish in spring, are a big clue to identifying the Louisiana waterthrush.

- Color of feet

- Arrangement of toes, such as the two toes front and two toes back of woodpeckers, or the three-and-one of songbirds

SIZING IT UP

I was so disappointed when I ripped open the package that held my newly ordered field guide to sub-alpine wildflowers. It was so small! It had looked like a normal book online. But in my hand, it was only the size of a small spiral-bound notebook.

That's the same reaction I have to a "bird in the hand." Whenever I see a dead bird, or happen to have the chance to look at a captive, I always exclaim, "It's so small!"

A bird in hand looks surprisingly smaller than the same bird at the feeder or in the yard. Or to put it another way, birds look bigger than they really are. Why? Because there's nothing familiar to compare them to.

The Theory of Relativity

Maybe you've ordered a plant from a catalog that showed a gorgeous close-up of its flowers. Without any background to compare them to, you'd have no way of knowing that the plant was only 3 inches tall.

Same deal with my undersized alpine field guide. If the online photo of the book had included a person's hand, or even a penny, I would've had something familiar against which to judge its size.

Even movie stars can be startlingly short in real life, or so I hear. On the screen, they look 6 feet tall. In person, when we have familiar benchmarks nearby, they suddenly shrink to 5-feet, 6-inches.

It works the same way with birds. Without a familiar reference point in the scene, most of us assume birds are bigger than they actually are.

I remember being stunned when I finally realized how small the shorebirds called "peeps" actually are. I knew that one of the peeps, the least sandpiper, is the smallest shorebird in the world. I'd read the description often enough to be able to rattle off its size: 6 inches.

Yet I still had an entirely inaccurate idea of the size of these birds. On the bare beaches and mudflats where I usually saw them, they didn't look like mini birds at all. I would've sworn they were at least as big as a starling—until a starling happened to land near a small flock of them on a mudflat one day. Either that starling was a relative of King Kong, or peeps are only the size of a sparrow.

Least sandpipers seem much bigger than the sparrow-size birds they are.

A "Handy" Experiment

A few years ago, I was walking down the aisle of Halloween supplies in a local store when an eerie electronic laugh rang out. Apparently I'd set off some sort of motion detector, which had triggered a life-size fake hand to reach out of its plastic coffin. It wasn't exactly my kind of décor, but the thing had possibilities for a science experiment I'd been pondering.

I waited for the after-Halloween clearance sale, then snatched up the hand at a bargain price. A few minutes of brute-force disassembly, and I was the proud possessor of a disembodied pinkish hand and wrist, almost exactly the same size as my own.

Relying on duct tape and florist wire, I managed to secure the appendage to one of my thistle feeders, palm up. With a sprinkling of niger seed, the experiment was ready to begin. For a few minutes, the goldfinches and siskins were leery of this weird new feeder add-on. Not for long. As birds outnumbered perches, a couple of them soon made themselves at home on the hand's fingers.

Oh my gosh! You should see how small a goldfinch is! With the hand as a gauge, I suddenly realized just how big—I mean little—a 5-inch bird really is.

For a week or so, I varied the placement and the treats that the hand held out. It was enlightening to see the actual size of jays, starlings, chickadees, and other friends.

As soon as I removed the "handy" gauge of relativity, though, my unconscious view of the birds came back. I had to try hard to remember how small the chickadee had looked on "my" thumb. Maybe you can find your own plastic Halloween hand for experimenting. Just remember that the eye-opening effect only lasts as long as the visual aid does.

That's why I depend on another system for gauging the size of birds. It's not as exact, but it's a whole lot simpler.

How Big?

Whenever I'm playing the birder version of 20 Questions with someone who's asked me to identify a bird she's seen, I start with one of the most general characteristics: How big was it?

No one I've ever met answers like this: "Uh, I'd figure 10¼ inches head to tail, with a 3-inch beak."

So instead of asking "How big was it?," I ask, "Do you know what a robin looks like?"

Almost everyone says yes.

"Was it bigger than a robin?"

It's funny, but this trick works great.

Try it yourself. You'll find that just having

Gauge the size of an unfamiliar bird by comparing it to your mental image of a robin.

the idea of a robin to compare to the mental image of another bird seems to be enough to give you a pretty good handle on size.

If the bird in question was smaller than a robin, I ask, "Was it about the size of a sparrow?" Seems like a lot more people have a mental image of a robin than they do of a sparrow. Often I hear, "I don't really know how big a sparrow is." If that's the case, I'll switch to a chickadee. Often that will do the trick.

Imaginary Friends

A trio of imaginary birds is a terrific aid to bird-watching.

I've found that a quick and easy way to gauge the size of a new bird is to compare it to one of these three commoners:

- A 5¼-inch black-capped chickadee

- A 6- to 7-inch song or white-throated sparrow

- A 10-inch robin

Become familiar with these birds, and you'll have three excellent benchmarks to draw upon when you're looking at a new bird. Make it a point to watch these three as they move about your yard. Look at each bird

The common grackle is one of a handful of backyard birds that are bigger than a robin.

on the ground, at the feeder, in the shrubs or trees, and in flight. Learn to recognize each of the three from a distance. Meanwhile, your subconscious will be registering how big each of your benchmark birds looks against these different backgrounds.

When a new bird comes along, just picture one of the three nearby. With practice, the best-fitting of your comparison birds will pop up without any prompting. "Hmm, about the size of a robin," you'll think. Or maybe, "Wow, even smaller than a chickadee."

HOW TO AVOID COLOR CONFUSION

The birds in your backyard won't always look like the pictures in this book. Many of these photos show birds at breeding time, when feathers are at their most vivid. And all of them show the birds in ideal light, not in dim shade or bright sun. They've been selected to best show the characteristics of each bird.

QUICK TIP

Fully or mostly albino birds can be most unsettling. When I saw a white bird on the lawn, acting just like a robin, it threw me for a loop. I was accustomed to robins that looked like robins, yet the silhouette and habits were unmistakable. Albinotic birds, which have only some white feathers, can be trickier to figure out. Pay attention to habits, and you'll get it.

How do backyard birds compare in size? Just use the three benchmark birds at the bottom of this page to create a mental image.

OTHER BACKYARD BIRDS	RELATIVE SIZE (size relative to benchmark birds)	ACTUAL SIZE, BEAK TO TAIL
American goldfinch	Smaller than a chickadee	5"
Blue jay	Bigger than a robin	11"
Bushtit	Smaller than a chickadee	4½"
Cardinal	Smaller than a robin	8¾"
Carolina wren	Smaller than a sparrow; bigger than a chickadee	5½"
Common grackle	Bigger than a robin	12½"
Evening grosbeak	Smaller than a robin; bigger than a sparrow	8"
House wren	Smaller than a chickadee	4¾"
Hummingbird	Smaller than a chickadee	3¾"–4¼", depending on species
Mourning dove	Bigger than a robin	12"
Red-breasted nuthatch	Smaller than a chickadee	4½"
Slate-colored junco	About the same as a sparrow	6¼"
White-breasted nuthatch	Bigger than a chickadee; a little smaller than a sparrow	5¾"

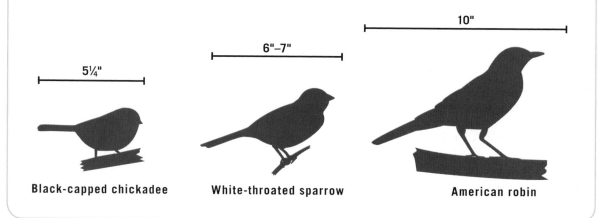

5¼"

Black-capped chickadee

6"–7"

White-throated sparrow

10"

American robin

The red-breasted nuthatch, 4 inches long including beak and tail, is one of our tiniest birds.

What you'll be looking at in your backyard is a lot less perfect.

Gender, age, season, geography, and individual idiosyncrasies can cause enough variations in color to make you doubt your birds' ID.

Gender Differences

Plumage may or may not be different between the genders of a species. In many species, male and female birds look so much alike you'd have to get downright rude to find out for sure. Nearly all sparrow species are perfectly matched pairs. So are jays, chickadees, flycatchers, thrushes, thrashers, catbirds, wrens, and various others.

QUICK TIP

When you see two birds that are obviously interacting but are very differently colored, you're probably watching a male and female or a parent and young. Female or young birds, depending on species, may be greenish, brownish, or streaked.

In other species, you'll notice a slight difference between the sexes. Generally, the female is a slightly less vivid version of the male. You can pick the males out of a flock of robins, for instance, by looking for those birds with the deeper orange chests. Some female wood warblers, too, including the northern parula, look like a faded version of the brighter male.

That leaves the bird species whose genders are markedly different. I hate to generalize because I'm sure I'll overlook somebody, but typically these seem to be the birds with the brightest colors: the cardinal, orioles, tanagers, grosbeaks, crossbills, and on the smaller side, the finches, buntings, wood warblers, and hummingbirds. Males are

A female slate-colored junco is slightly paler and a bit browner than this male.

Young birds look more like their mother than their father. In blue jays, the sexes look alike, so ID of this baby jay is easy.

QUICK TIP

Baby birds often leave the nest before they've become accomplished fliers. They hide in shrubbery or plants for a few days, while the parent bird keeps an eye on them from a distance. If you come across a fledgling in your yard without its parent nearby, you may have a hard time figuring out who this kid belongs to. Listen for an adult bird scolding you: That'll be Mom or Dad. To ID the youngster, back off and look for its parent.

Sorting Out Young Birds

Freshly hatched baby songbirds may be the homeliest creatures on earth. They're naked and blind, and bottom-heavy so that they stay right side up in the nest. They'll soon sprout fluffy down and then their first set of feathers.

When young birds are old enough to leave the nest, they usually display a family resemblance. Baby jays have a few stubby blue wing feathers. Baby goldfinches look something like their mom. In fact in many cases, an immature bird looks more like its mother than its father.

You'll find detailed descriptions of immature birds in comprehensive field guides. Or you can just keep watching, to see which adults your young bird joins up with.

Molting

Most birds change their feathers, or molt, at least partially in fall, after nesting. Some finish the molt in late winter through spring, before breeding.

The process takes place gradually, just a few feathers at a time, over a period of weeks.

Birds that are molting may look funny.

vibrant, with feathers in strong shades of red, orange, yellow, magenta, or blue. Females lean toward the greenish or sometimes brownish side. If you didn't have a field guide, it'd be easy to mistake them for two different species. Rufous-sided towhees and many blackbirds—particularly red-winged and yellow-headed, plus the less showy Brewer's blackbirds—also have so much difference between genders that you may mistake them for other birds altogether.

QUICK TIP

Bird families usually stick together even after the youngsters are flying. Keep watching an immature bird, and you may see it futilely pestering its parents for food, or joining the group when they leave the area.

In their first fall, male rose-breasted grosbeaks look like a warmer-colored version of their streaky brown mama.

QUICK TIP

Pay attention to behavior. When you see a large, young gray bird begging from a smaller adult bird, it's likely that you're watching a young, parasitic cowbird with its unwitting stepparent. Cowbird parents sneak their eggs into the nests of other birds for them to raise.

Their plumage may be splotchy or blotchy, and their wings or tail may have a few gaps.

A chickadee looks like a chickadee year-round. But a few birds, notably goldfinches, look drastically different after the molt, resembling females. Some of the trickiest birds to ID are young male birds—hatched that year—of species in which adult males are brightly colored: tanagers, orioles, grosbeaks, and buntings. "First-year males," the young birds that stop in our yards on their way south in fall and on their way back in spring, look more like their mamas than their daddies. After next year's nesting season, they'll molt again, into adult dress.

Regional Variations

I'll always cherish my Peterson field guide, but *The Sibley Guide to Birds* has supplanted it as my favorite. Not exactly a pocket guide, this 544-pager includes pictures of regional variations in color.

Often these variations in birds are slight. But they can be enough to trip you up on identity. When I first moved to Washington State, I thought I was seeing fox sparrows throughout the white-ash woods along the Columbia River. In spring, they began to sing—like song sparrows!

Sibley confirmed my hunch: Song sparrows in my part of the country are a few shades darker than the same species in my former backyards in the East and Midwest. Instead of a whitish breast streaked with reddish brown, song sparrows in the Pacific Northwest have a gray background for those stripes.

The red-tailed hawk, a common bird that may turn up in your backyard, is famed for color variations. Birds may be light, dark, or somewhere in the middle. The dark form looks like an entirely different species, until you spot that telltale chestnut tail.

QUICK TIP

You can see migration in action by watching the plumage of the birds in your yard. Adult males depart first, followed in a couple of weeks or so by females and juveniles. Keep an eye on plants with fall berries, and you'll see vivid adult male tanagers, orioles, grosbeaks, and others pause first. Later, if your dogwood is suddenly swarming with nondescript birds, look for clues that they're tanagers or grosbeaks in disguise.

In bright sunshine, the neck of a male rock dove, or pigeon, flashes iridescent purple.

Color isn't the only trait that can vary by region. Vocalizations may also be different. The white-breasted nuthatch in the Pacific Northwest looks very similar to birds of other regions. But instead of saying *ank-ank,* he makes a complaining *mew.*

That's why deciding on an ID means taking into account a bird's looks, habits, and voice. If one of them fools you, the others will help you figure it out!

Tricks of the Light

I'm a poor photographer, because I always forget to think about the light. When the exposure is off, the color of the bird is all wrong. It's either much too dark, or way too washed out. And if I happened to snap the shutter when the bird hopped into shade, I

If a bird looks dull and dark without any noticeable color, it may have iridescent feathers that aren't in direct light. Try moving so that your back is to the sun and the bird is ahead of you. (But be sure not to let your shadow fall on the bird.) Buntings and hummingbirds are among the most beautiful iridescent birds; in breeding season, starlings, grackles, doves, and pigeons may also show gorgeous shifting colors.

might not see any iridescent color at all in my subject. But nowadays, with the instant-replay feature of digital cameras, I can retake the photo if I messed up, and if the bird is still there (big if).

Light affects your eyes the same way it does a camera lens. A bird in shade looks darker, and details are obscured. A bird in blasting sun is paler. If light isn't hitting the iridescent feathers of a bird, it'll look dull and dark instead of like a shimmering jewel.

As always, the cure for tricks of the light is to keep watching. With a little luck, the bird will move into a better position, where you can see what it really looks like.

ID Challenges

Some birds are just plain difficult to tell apart, even if you have a lot of experience behind those binoculars. Here's what I look for to pin down those too-close-to-call characters.

Brown Thrushes

Is it a veery or a wood thrush? Or any of the other confusingly close species? Check these traits while the bird is in front of you, then double-check with your comprehensive field guide.

- Color of back—Is it reddish (wood thrush, veery, possibly young Swainson's), brown (hermit, young Bicknell's), or grayish brown (Swainson's, gray-cheeked, Bicknell's, hermit)?

- Breast spots—Are they big and bold and separated by white (wood thrush), do they look muted (veery, young Swainson's), or are they so dense they're almost blurred (interior West race of Swainson's, gray-cheeked, Bicknell's, hermit)? Are they concentrated on the throat and upper breast area, then fade out (veery, Swainson's, gray-cheeked, Bicknell's, hermit), or do bold spots extend down along the wings (wood thrush)?

- Color of tail—Is it distinctly reddish (wood thrush, veery, Bicknell's, hermit)?

- Tail movement—Does the bird raise and lower its tail (hermit)?

- Eye markings—Does the bird have a distinct eye ring (wood thrush, hermit) or "spectacles" (Swainson's)?

Thrashers

The brown thrasher is a cinch to identify— until you see a long-billed thrasher, which is similar enough to make you wonder. The grayer thrashers of the Southwest are even trickier, despite those distinguished beaks. Check these details.

- Color of eye—Is it noticeably light (brown, long-billed, Bendire's, curve-billed, Crissal, LeConte's, sage) or dark (California)?

- Under-tail feathers—What color are the *under-tail coverts,* the feathers in that triangular patch at the base of the bird's tail, behind its legs? If they're white, it's a brown or long-billed thrasher; if they're orangish tan, it's a Bendire's, curve-billed, California, LeConte's, or sage thrasher; if they're dark rusty, it's a Crissal.

- Facial markings—Does the bird have a bold line at its eye, or is that line hard to make out or nonexistent? If it has a dark line, it's a California thrasher; if it has a pale line, it's a sage thrasher. All other species don't have eye lines.

- Breast spots or streaks—Does the breast show any marks, such as round, muted dapples (Bendire's, curve-billed) or streaks (brown, long-billed, sage)?

Warblers

With dozens of species, sorting out wood warblers can be a lifetime hobby. Quickly check these field marks to make it easier. Then consult a comprehensive field guide to see which of the more than 50 North American warbler species you may have.

- Wing bars—How many does it have? How wide are they?

- Tail spots—What color are they? Where are they located?

- Eye markings—Is there an eye ring? An eye stripe?

- Head markings—Are there any other noticeable head markings, such as a cap? A cheek patch?

- Throat color—What color is the throat?

Buntings

There are only a few species of buntings, and still they can be a challenge. Double-check these details and you'll have them mastered—or at least you'll get the males. The uniformly brown females are best identified by certain circumstantial evidence: Which male bunting are they hanging around with?

- Color of breast—Is it the same (indigo) or different (lazuli, varied, painted) than the color of the bird's head and back?

- Wing bars—Can you see any white wing bars on the closed wing? If you do, it's a lazuli bunting.

Bluebirds

All three bluebird species—eastern, mountain, and western—may show up in the same region. Enjoy the treat—and look for these fine points to sort them out.

- Overall color—Is it entirely blue (mountain), with no orange or chestnut? If not, it's an eastern or western.

- Color of breast—Is it orange (eastern or western) or blue (mountain)?

- Color of throat—Is it orange (eastern) or blue (western or mountain)?

- Color of belly—Is it blue (western or mountain) or white (eastern)?

- Color of sides of neck—Are they orange (eastern) or blue (western, mountain)?

- Color of back and above wings—Is any chestnut showing? If yes, it's a western bluebird; if no, it's an eastern or mountain.

Sparrows

Yes, this is the group of birds that causes even seasoned birders to pretend they didn't see its many members. But all it takes is patience—lots of patience—and a comprehensive field guide to sort them out. Try to get a look at these marks while you're looking at the bird, or better yet, snap a few digital pictures that you can pore over later. Consult a comprehensive field guide to pinpoint which of the nearly 50 species of North American sparrows you're looking at.

- Head markings—Is there a cap? Head stripes? Cheek patch? Eye stripes?

- Eye markings—Is there an eye ring? What color?

- Beak color—What color is it? Are both upper and lower halves of the beak the same color?

- Throat color—What color is it?

- Wing bars—Are there any? How many? What color?

- Breast markings—Are there stripes? Streaks? A darker "stickpin" in the center?

- Tail color—Is there any noticeable flash of white tail feathers when the bird flies?

Chapter Five

The Regional Approach

Somehow, despite my best intentions, I still haven't quite managed to make it to Central America to see the resplendent quetzal, a fantastic green, blue, and red bird of the rain forest. The bird of paradise of New Guinea is still waiting for me, too, quivering those extravagant plumes without my binoculars watching.

Those endearing penguins at the South Pole? Maybe someday. As for the "robin redbreast" of England, a small, chubby songbird that shares nothing with our own robin besides a taste for worms, I only recognize it because I met it in *Winnie-the-Pooh* books.

They're great birds, every one. But I haven't felt deprived in the least. (Okay, maybe when I see on TV a bowerbird adding blue—and only blue—objects to its nest, I do have to stop myself from jumping onto a plane to Australia right then and there.)

Our own great big country holds so many wonderful birds that there's been way more than enough to keep me busy for my whole life. Our continent is wildly diverse. We have rolling hills and snow-capped peaks. Flat farmlands and prairies, and at least three distinct kinds of desert. Every kind of water feature you can imagine—from oceans and big rivers on a grand scale, to tiny ponds and brooks.

When I get the itch to travel, all I have to do is visit a different part of the country. I know I'll see different plants, different terrain—and lots of different birds!

WHY REGIONS?

Those exotic places you see on the nature shows are often surprisingly small compared to the United States. You could fit all of Great Britain, including its robin redbreasts, into the state of Oregon. Costa Rica would slip right into West Virginia with room to spare, even with all those quetzal tails. Even New Guinea, with all its marvels, is only twice the size of California.

Check any bird supplies store, and you'll find individual field guides for each of those places. Yet only a handful of states in our own country can lay claim to a field guide focused on that region.

Many birds are generalists, and adapt easily to different conditions, climates, and food. Our friend the American robin is one of them—you'll find it just about everywhere.

On my first trip to the Southwest, where it seemed that every bird I looked at was a new species to me, I was fooled good by a regular old robin. I was sure the brownish gray and rusty red bird I saw hopping about in the desert had to be something special. Straining my eyes, I tried hard to find some detail that would make it something else—a clay-colored robin, perhaps? Nope. It was simply a regular old robin, as at home among the cactus as it was on my lush green lawn back home.

In the "Start Here" chapter, beginning on page 75, you'll find many species that range across most or all of our country. All of the "Start Here" birds are widespread. They're also abundant. And they frequently visit backyards. All of that means you have a good chance of meeting them in your own yard.

Getting familiar with these birds is the basis of becoming a backyard bird-watcher. You probably already know quite a few of them—including that widespread robin.

These birds may not show up in your yard at the same time they visit other parts of the country. Many are seen year-round, but some may stay in your region only to raise a family, or to spend the winter, or to use your yard as a rest stop when they pass through on migration.

That's why I've taken the regional approach in this book. Using a regional approach makes it simpler for you to identify the birds in your own area. And it makes it easy to check out the bird life of other regions so you can dream about that next vacation.

You won't see the same birds in Boston as you do in Minneapolis, or in Seattle, or in Houston, or at Disney World. Sure, there's some overlap—we all get song sparrows, for instance—but there are also dozens of species that tend to stick to certain regions.

Climate and Conditions

Visit New England in January, and you can bet you'll be wearing your warmest winter coat and snuggest hat. Now imagine that you're a ruby-throated hummingbird, and the only down jacket you own is right there on your back. You're not going to be celebrating Christmas in Boston anytime soon; instead, you'll have hightailed it for the sunny South months before.

Climate and weather conditions play a big role in determining which region sees which birds. Here are a few major ways in which the climate in your region may affect birds.

◆ If you live where winters are cold, you're not going to see birds that depend on insects after frost settles in—not unless the birds can ferret out overwintering insects or add other foods to their menu come the cold season. So you'll say goodbye to flycatchers in fall, but you'll still see more adaptable chickadees all winter.

- If your region gets a lot of deep snow, your winter birds are likely to be mostly those species that can find food in the trees, not on the ground. Ground-scratching sparrows—fox, white-throated, white-crowned, and others—will move to areas where seeds are easier to access. But the sparrows will be replaced by juncos, which can switch to finding insects, spiders, or seeds in shrubs, on fallen logs, or in trees, and also are adept at finding small areas where the snow has melted, such as at the base of trees.

- Sheer cold is enough to kill many species of birds. Bluebirds are notoriously susceptible to cold, so they'll winter in warmer regions.

Birds are always surprising the scientists, though, so don't depend on birds to follow the rules. Our feeders and other human changes to the natural landscape may create conditions that are easier for birds to live in.

And bird habits don't always follow rhyme or reason, either. Why do some birds migrate only as far as the South, while other species travel on for hundreds or thousands more miles? No one knows. But we do know that regional differences make an impact on the range and habits of birds.

Habitat and Food

The seasonal divisions you'll find under the "Mark Your Calendar" heading in the individual bird profiles in the regional chapters are based on the species' life cycle. "Winter only" means that you may see the bird on fall migration, during winter, and on spring migration. "Spring to fall" means that you live within its nesting territory; you're likely to see the bird

Cardinals find plenty to eat in snowy regions.

when it arrives on spring migration, then during its nesting season, and finally, after nesting until it leaves on fall migration. "Migration only" means that the bird passes through your area and doesn't linger for long. "Year-round" means just that: You have a chance of seeing the bird at any time of the year.

The climate and geography of your region determine which plants grow there, too. Those plants create the different habitats of the wild land around you—the forests, brush, grasslands, deserts, swamps, and other niches that appeal to various species of birds.

Not only do the plants of a region make a home for birds; they also supply the food that sustains birds in every season. Their food includes seeds, from pinecones to grasses; wild fruits and berries; and the most important by a mile, the teeming thousands of insects that live on those plants.

Page through the regional introductions in this book, and you'll find pictures that show a sampling of the typical landscape of each region. There's such diversity, our regions may as well be separate countries! Swamps draped with Spanish moss; balsam forests gleaming with white birches; stately saguaros: We have enough variety to fill years of pretty picture calendars. And that's just scratching the surface.

Those dramatic differences are easy to see. It's simple to grasp why a bird of the Arizona desert, say, might feel a little out of its league up around the Great Lakes. But less spectacular signs can be equally important in determining the traditional range of a bird.

Many birds are specialists in their food habits, eating only certain kinds of seeds or insects or fruits. And who can say when one of those is the key to hosting a bird species while it's nesting, or simply waving to it when it flies through on April migration? Maybe it's an abundance of grasshoppers that does the trick—and the grasshoppers depend on a grass that only thrives when rainfall is within a certain range. Or maybe the bird needs a plethora of spiderwebs—so a region with drenching downpours that destroy the webs wouldn't work. It's fun to conjecture about why certain species are limited to certain areas. But the truth is that, in many cases, science simply doesn't know what causes a particular species to say, "Here, right here. This is home."

Those skills developed in birds so long ago that we don't even know how it happened. All we can see is the result: Each bird species is perfectly suited to living in its natural habitat.

Going to Extremes

To make a living in places that go to extremes requires specialized behavior and habits—the innate knowledge of how to nest in a cactus, for example, or how to find food when it's 30 degrees below zero.

If you live in a region of extreme climate or conditions, you're likely to see a good number of species that's at home only in your particular region. If you could "transplant" a scissor-tailed flycatcher from the wide-open spaces of its home in Texas to the close quarters of a deciduous woods a few states over, say in Tennessee, that bird would soon be hitching a ride back home. Its body is built for swooping over grasslands to forage, not for finagling its way through forests. Besides, grasshoppers—its mainstay meal—would be few and far between in those Tennessee trees.

You can play the same game with all kinds of specialized birds, from the northern parula of southern swamps to the roadrunner of the Southwest to the crossbills that roam among northern conifers. Although there's some give and take to their habits, many birds from more extreme habitats need a certain kind of niche to be able to put their innate skills to use.

Natural Barriers

You'd think having wings would mean you could travel anywhere you want, but no such luck. Birds are limited in their range by some pretty daunting natural barriers.

One of the biggest was the Great Plains. Those vast prairies of tall grass and short grass acted as a natural stop sign to birds that depended on trees for their food and homes.

As towns and cities sprouted across the Plains, bringing windbreaks and backyard trees, the situation changed—a little. There's still enough open space out there to stop many birds in their tracks.

It works in reverse, too: Many of the birds that developed skills to shine in a grassland setting can't transfer them to a forest. So they stay put, like the dickcissel, or they seek out a downsized version of the Great Plains, like a meadowlark moving into a hay field or pasture across one of those blurred regional boundaries.

Birdlife in these foothill alders is different than birdlife high in the mountains.

Mountains are natural barriers, too, because bird species would have to gradually expand their range up and over. Life at the top is very different from life in the foothills, so most birds stick to a certain level on one side and never make it to the other side.

Blue jays, for instance, are found only east of the Rocky Mountains, except for a scattering of intrepid souls that has made the trip to the far side of the Rockies. The Steller's jay of the West, by the way, has returned the favor. It's been spotted from South Dakota to Florida.

You'll notice that many comprehensive field guides are divided into Eastern and Western versions. That continuous spine of the Rockies is why. Many of the birds in the East are not the same as birds in the West. The barrier of the mountains keeps them separated.

Extended Fingers

Mountains can also function to funnel birds into a region where they wouldn't otherwise occur. Bird life at high elevations often includes species that would never be seen in the lowlands, or that only occur in lowlands during a specific season. Many species nest in the mountains but spend only the winter at lower elevations.

That high-altitude habitat, and the conditions and food that go along with it, is very similar throughout a mountain chain. The slate-colored junco, for example, is only a winter bird from Pennsylvania to Georgia—unless you live in the Appalachians. For that entire stretch of mountains, a long finger extending deeply southward, the slate-colored junco is a year-round species. Instead of moving northward into New England, the species also nests in those cool woodlands

Boundaries are blurred when it comes to birds because habitat, climate, and conditions play such a big role in bird distribution. Start with your own region, but investigate birds of neighboring areas, too.

high up in the mountains. Another mountain inhabitant is the white-headed woodpecker, a bird of the West—the western mountains, that is. It rarely ventures into the lowlands, though it lives year-round in conifer forests in the Sierras and Cascades.

You can clearly see those fingers of mountain habitat extending into other regions in any comprehensive field guide. Once you start paying attention, you'll be quick to spot the differences in range created by the Appalachians, the Rockies, the Sierras, and even the mountains that extend upward from Mexico into the Southwest. More opportunities to see great birds!

THE SEVEN REGIONS

The bird profiles in Part 2 are divided into eight chapters. First comes "Start Here," the common backyard birds shared by most of us across the country. After that, you'll find the seven geographic regions.

I've divided the country into these regions according to attributes that make each unique. Those natural attributes are what make each of the regions home to a wonderful array of interesting birds. As we've talked about, not all species will be unique to just one region; many will overlap into other areas.

In general, the more extreme the climate

and conditions of your region, the more specialized birds you'll see—which means more species that are unique to your region. The Northeast shares many birds with the Midwest and the Southeast. But the Southwest's collection of species includes many unusual, much more restricted birds.

You'll find a detailed description of the characteristics of each region in the regional chapters in Part 2. Here's a quick preview of the regions' most notable features and what kinds of birds you might find there.

The Northeast

The most familiar backyard birds are icons in this region. Here's where you'll enjoy the company of cardinals, black-capped chicka-

Northeast birds are "leaf peepers," too, but it's seeds and insects they seek.

dees, and just about every other bird that shows up on sweatshirts or on those "singing" clocks decorated with birds.

A gentle landscape and relatively moderate climate bring an abundance of nesting birds and many year-round species. A wide variety of habitat, from forest to pasture to seacoast, also boosts the species count. Northern parts of this region, such as Maine, share some species with the Far North.

The Far North

Lucky you—you can enjoy many species that the rest of the country rarely even sees. Those boreal chickadees and fantastic crossbills are simply specialists. They're birds that developed skills to thrive in the challenging conditions of this region.

One of the most extreme regions, this area features deep snow and penetrating cold. That creates specialists among birds, which have learned to exploit any food source they can find. Conifer forests and some deciduous woods sweep across the land. Birds that can extract the seeds of cones have a ready source of food, and so do those species that forage over tree bark and foliage.

The Southeast and South

Hot and steamy in summer, your region is an ideal wintering ground for eastern bluebirds, catbirds, and many other species that are only a seasonal treat elsewhere. The deeper south you go in this region, the more unique birds you'll see. Blue grosbeaks, brown-headed nuthatches, and other winged wonders roam the lush vegetation.

Food is abundant. Insects are often annoyingly plentiful, and berries and small fruits tailor-made for birds grow with wild abandon. In the mountains, more-northern species raise their families in the cooler habitat.

The Midwest

You may not have the endless prairie outside the door of your sod house anymore, but those amber waves of grain aren't a bad substitute. Here's where you'll find vesper sparrows and other interesting grassland birds, species that developed a successful way of life that didn't depend on trees.

Flat and open is the classic picture of the Midwest landscape, but there are also pockets of trees, especially around cities and towns and along rivers and lakes. Those trees shelter some fabulous birds, such as the beautiful orchard oriole, the summer tanager, and a selection of dramatic woodpeckers.

This region is a big one, and its climate changes considerably from the upper to the lower part. That means changes in bird life, too. Species that nest in the northern parts may be year-round or winter friends in the southern area.

Steller's jay is at home in higher elevations.

The West

"Rocky Mountain High" is the theme song for this region, and don't you love it! Those spectacular peaks and endless jagged ridges are the defining feature here. Here's where you'll find many birds that can't scratch out a living on the Midwest Plains, as well as northern birds that live at high elevations.

Like the birds of the Far North, this area includes species that specialize in finding food on conifers, or that shrug off extreme cold. You also can enjoy many birds of lower elevations, such as the black-headed grosbeak and lazuli bunting.

The Southwest and California

California sunshine is too good to resist, unless you live in Tucson or other parts of the Southwest where you have your own sunshiny days. With rain limited to a very small amount each year, the habitat here is comprised of plants that make the best use of a limited resource—and birds that do the same.

As the climate becomes drier, the birds become more specialized, so that each species can exploit some unusual niche in this unusual landscape. You get the lion's share of unique species in this region. How about thrashers with outrageous curved beaks? Wrens that live on spiders they find among the rocks? And hummingbirds that shine like gems in that Southwest sun?

The Northwest

Did somebody say "rain"? Yes indeed. That notorious rain is what makes this region so green and lush and makes the trees grow so tall. After the rainy season, though, the next

6 months are extremely dry. Creeks and waterfalls slow to a trickle or dry up altogether, until the rains come again in fall.

It's a lopsided arrangement, and one that many birds have learned to thrive in. The dim forests are filled with thrushes, band-tailed pigeons, and other birds that like life on the shady side.

The closer to the Pacific Coast, the more rain that falls. Heading east, the land gradually becomes drier, until the dramatic shift from one side of the Cascade Mountains to the other: Because the mountains block the rain, the eastern part of this region is so dry it qualifies as desert. Still, those western forest birds can be found here, thanks to the mountain ranges that pick up again in the eastern part of this region.

BLURRY BORDERS

My son used to have a whole collection of pictures of himself standing proudly beside the "Welcome to … " signs that mark the boundaries between our nation's states. He liked seeing the license plates change, too—a sure sign that he'd entered new territory.

But birds can't read, and state lines hold no significance to them. The only thing they pay attention to is the natural world: the habitat, food sources, climate, and natural features of the land.

When one region fades into another gradually, many bird species are likely to blend, too. That's why the lines on these maps aren't sharp: There's a lot of overlap between the regions.

If you live in the Northeast, for instance, you might see birds from three other regions: the Far North, Southeast and South, and Midwest. All share a blurry boundary with the Northeast.

Remember, too, that changes in elevation can affect which birds you see and when. In early summer, when I haven't seen a junco at my lowland Northwest feeder in months, I like to take a drive way up into the Cascades—until I see that flash of white tail feathers in the trees. Juncos live year-round in the mountains here, but they're a winter-only treat for me.

As I explained earlier, in this book I've divided the country into seven regions, based on their natural features that help determine bird life there. But the blurry edges indicate that birds from neighboring regions may visit, too.

Wherever you see a blurry edge on the map, it's a sign that birds from a neighboring region may also visit in your region. Keep in mind that the likelihood of seeing species from other regions also depends on how close to that blurred boundary you live. If you're clear on the other side of the region, your chances are much slimmer than if you live a hop, skip, and a flap over the line.

No matter how carefully birds are arranged in a bird book, in real life they're not so easy to categorize. The best advice, when it comes to bird-watching, is to *be ready for anything*. You never know who will show up in your backyard!

MEET THE BIRDS

Ready to start matching names to faces? And to speckled breasts, crested heads, flicking tails, characteristic songs, and interesting behaviors? In Part Two, you'll meet more than 140 birds and learn the tricks that will help you identify each one—*at a glance*. Then you can confirm your good guess by checking details of looks, voice, and behavior.

Start with Chapter 6 where you'll make the acquaintance of the most abundant, most widespread backyard species. Regional chapters follow, chockful of birds that are also likely to visit backyards in your particular part of the country. Peruse the profiles for neighboring regions, as well as your own. And if you really want to see how diverse our American birdlife is, let your mouth water by looking at the birds of faraway regions, too. Seasoned birders know that any bird can show up anywhere—even far from its usual haunts.

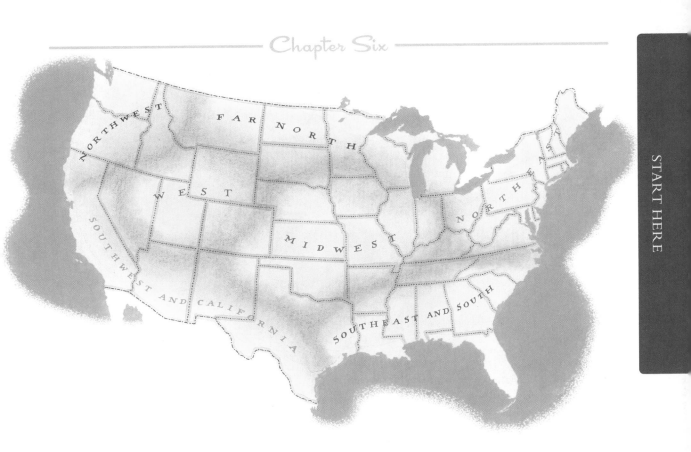

Chapter Six

Start Here

Getting an invitation to a party at a new friend's house is a lot of fun. But walking into a lively room full of people who already know each other can be intimidating. They're chattering away in little groups, smiling and laughing, comparing notes on other folks they know or experiences they've shared. Once I relax and look around, though, I realize I do know some of the guests—there's the fellow I met at the library, the woman I often exchange smiles with at the coffee shop, and the couple who sat next to me at the fund-raiser. Why, they're not all strangers—it's just a room full of friends I haven't yet met.

The birds in this chapter are like the guests at that party. You may expect to find no one but strangers, but I guarantee you'll discover a few familiar faces. If you've been feeding birds or watching your backyard birds for a while, you'll be able to greet many others that you already know. Maybe you haven't learned their names yet. But you soon will, just as I finally was able to put names to the friendly faces I already knew from the library, the coffee shop, and the fund-raiser.

That's why I call this chapter "Start Here." These birds are confidence builders.

Talk to your friends in Massachusetts and

Nebraska, and you can all compare notes on these birds. They're the most widespread of backyard birds. I think of them as our national cast of characters. They range across the entire country or a major part of it, nesting or wintering over huge areas.

You'll see a *lot* of these birds, too. They're abundant, which means you won't wait years for a glimpse at one. Most are well-adapted to life in our backyards, and they're not shy at all about visiting or moving in. They're the birds we're most likely to encounter.

Ready to get the party started?

MEET THE "START HERE" BIRDS

These are the birds you're most likely to see in your yard, no matter where you live. Get a handle on them, and you'll have the basis for a lifetime of bird-watching. Once you have a nodding acquaintance with the "Start Here" birds, you'll find it much easier to notice when a stranger shows up in your yard.

Downy woodpeckers eat suet everywhere.

Everyone knows the American robin.

You'll soon find yourself saying, "Hmm, that gray bird looks just like my juncos, except for that dark head. Wonder if he's some new kind of junco?"

Congratulations! You're a bird-watcher.

Consult a Map

Because these species are so widespread, I haven't included a detailed map of range for each one. You don't actually need a map to get to know these guys. You'll find range descriptions in each species entry.

If you do prefer to see a map, pick up any traditional comprehensive field guide, such as Peterson's or Sibley's. Then you can use it in conjunction with this chapter, to discover exactly who you can expect to see outside your window.

Who's Who

You'll find profiles of 38 species in this section. Of these birds, 22 species are seen in every region of the country. Nearly all of the others are seen in most regions.

Some of these bird species include regional subspecies—birds that share many traits with the species but have some differences in color, song, or habits. You may find such subspecies mentioned in these entries, or you may find full-fledged entries for them in their appropriate regions.

The regions are abbreviated in this chapter and elsewhere. They are:

NE: Northeast

N: Far North

SE: Southeast and South

MW: Midwest

W: West

SW: Southwest and California

NW: Northwest

HOW TO USE THIS CHAPTER

Here's how to use this chapter: Turn to the first page. Read. Look at the picture. Turn to the next page. Repeat.

That's all there is to it. The more often you page through this chapter, the more likely a bird name will spring to mind when that bird shows up in your yard.

You'll see that the birds in this section aren't all to be expected year-round. While some are full-time friends, others stay with us only in certain seasons. If the entry says "year-round,"

Cedar waxwings wander widely to find food.

A song sparrow is likely in most backyards.

it means you can expect to see birds of this species in your yard at any time of year. If the entry says "winter," it means the species is a seasonal visitor that will be around in winter, which in bird land runs from after fall migration until spring migration. So although I may call it "winter," that period may actually be from early fall to early spring.

If the entry says "spring through fall," that means the bird will nest in your region. It goes elsewhere to spend winter, but your backyard may be the place it calls home during spring and summer, until it's time to depart in fall.

No matter what seasons these birds show up in your yard, they're bound to be your most reliable friends. If all you ever saw were the "Start Here" birds, you'd still have a hard time tearing yourself away from your feeder window.

One other note: For each bird you'll find descriptions of wild foods it likes ("Wild

Blue spruce (*Picea pungens*) attracts birds.

Goldfinches seek out pretty cosmos (*Cosmos bipinnatus*) as soon as the first seeds mature. In winter, sparrows glean what the goldfinches dropped.

Menu") and plants you can consider adding to your landscape to attract it ("Plant Picks"). There are also recommendations for stocking your bird feeders ("Feeder Pleasers"), and for other special amenities you might want to offer ("Tricks and Treats").

That's just the beginning, of course. In subsequent chapters, you'll discover even more great birds who call your particular region home.

But that's for later. For now, just "Start Here."

"Start Here" Birds

Here's a list of the birds you'll find in this chapter. The birds are organized by family, according to the checklist of the American Ornithological Union (AOU). You'll find this order also coincides with the arrangement of birds in many more comprehensive field guides, such as Peterson's.

Mourning Dove

First Impression

Big, plump, short-legged, grayish tan bird

START HERE

Mark Your Calendar

Year-round; but in northern parts of states, spring through fall

Details, Details

- Bigger than a robin; 12 inches
- Small head and long tail
- Black spots on wings

Listen Up!

- Easy to imitate, heartbreakingly sad, *ooAH! cooo cooo coo*

Telltale Traits

- Rockets away on loudly flapping wings when startled
- Often in pairs or small group

Look Here

- On ground

Or Here

- In tray feeder
- Perched in trees at dusk to roost at night
- Perched on utility wires

On the Home Front Doves mate for life. But old age for a dove, what with hunting and predators, is only about 2 to 3 years old. The record holder in the wild lived to age 10. • Builds one of the flimsiest nests, a casual collection of sticks that you can see right through • A spruce or pine in the yard is a favorite homesite, but nests in deciduous trees, too • Early nester • Raises more than one family a year

"Like the strokes of a distant bell"

—**Ralph Hoffmann**, *A Guide to the Birds of New England and Eastern New York* (1904)

The voice of the dove is easy to recognize. It's a plaintive cooing that travels far through the mild spring morning air.

Wild Menu: Weed and grass seeds; other seeds, including grain; some insects

Plant Picks: Grow a mixed patch of buckwheat, millet, wheat, and broomcorn for a winter's worth of seeds on the stalk.

Feeder Pleasers
- Millet, milo, cracked corn

Tricks and Treats
- Doves need grit to help digest their food. Buy an inexpensive box of birdcage grit in the pet supply aisle, and pour some on bare ground.

Public Displays of Affection

Doves aren't shy at all about courting in public. They look so romantic as they flirt and cuddle that they've become a symbol of enduring love.

Enduring lust is more like it. It only takes a month from nest to empty nest—and then doves are ready to start the next batch. No wonder they always seem to be kissing and cooing.

Northern Flicker

First Impression
Big, brown woodpecker

Mark Your Calendar
Year-round; but in northern parts of states in this region, spring through fall; winter only in some areas of SW

Details, Details
- Bigger than a robin; 12½ inches
- Shows a big white patch above tail in flight
- Dramatic black swash across breast
- Female lacks "mustache"

Listen Up!
- A fun bird to imitate: a rapid, repeated *wick-a! wick-a! wick-a!*

Telltale Traits
- Often on ground, but does cling to trees like a typical woodpecker
- Strong, fast, undulating flight, except on migration—then flies straight, without bouncy dips
- Colorful, golden or reddish undersides of wings and tail

Look Here
- At feeder

Or Here
- On lawn, eating ants or probing for grubs
- Hammering on a resonant tree, metal rain gutter, or other "drum"

On the Home Front Drills a good-size hole in a dead tree, often snitched by a pair of waiting starlings • Nests in wooden utility poles where trees are scarce • Quickly adopts a nest box

"Few birds combine such charming colors and pleasing contrasts"

—A. C. Bent, *Life Histories of North American Woodpeckers* (1939)

Flickers don't follow the crowd when it comes to color. Unlike most other woodpeckers, they're brown. Bright accents in their wings and on their head, plus a white rump and a bold black breast stripe, add plenty of flash.

Wild Menu: Ants; other insects; fruit

Plant Picks: Elderberries (*Sambucus* spp.), dogwood berries (*Cornus* spp.), Virginia creeper (*Parthenocissus quinquefolia*), other small fruits and berries

Feeder Pleasers
- Suet, peanut butter, and other fat-based foods; mealworms and other insect foods

Tricks and Treats
- Flickers enjoy a good splash in a birdbath. Make sure the edge isn't slippery, so they can get a good grip with their feet when they fly in. Old-fashioned concrete, or a nonslip resin, is a good choice.
- A nest box may also attract starlings; mount it in a woodsy area if you have one.

Isn't That Just Ducky

Whenever I spot a fist-size hole in a dead tree in spring, I keep an eye on it to see who it belongs to. If the tree is in woods, it's usually a flicker residence (starlings tend to take over the holes closer to open space).

But a few times, I've had the thrill of seeing a wood duck emerging from the hole. Some ducks, including the beautiful "woodies" and flashy black-and-white buffleheads, nest high in trees, not near water like you'd expect. They move into an old woodpecker hole to raise their batch of duckies.

Downy Woodpecker

First Impression

Ubiquitous small, black-and-white woodpecker

Mark Your Calendar

Year-round; absent from parts of SW

Details, Details

- As big as a large sparrow; 6¾ inches
- Female lacks red patch on back of head
- W and NW birds have less zebralike striping

Listen Up!

- Keeps in touch with frequent *peek!* contact call
- Staccato *ki-ki-ki-ki-ki-ki,* usually descending in pitch; sounds something like a tiny horse whinnying
- Drums on resonant dead wood

Telltale Traits

- Typical clinging woodpecker posture
- Often hitches around to other side of tree when observed
- Pals around with chickadees, nuthatches, titmice in fall and winter

Look Here

- At suet or seed feeders

Or Here

- On tree trunks or branches
- May visit nectar feeder

On the Home Front Digs out a nest cavity in dead wood • Often nests surprisingly low to ground, about 5 to 6 feet, but can nest to 50 feet • Gratifyingly quick to accept a birdhouse

"When the woodpecker pecks low on the trees, expect warm weather."

—**Old folk saying**

I never remember to note the temperature when I see my downy pecking away, which is probably why I've never noticed any connection between the two. But it's conceivable that movements of insects under tree bark may be susceptible to temperature.

Wild Menu: Insects; fruit; sap

Plant Picks: Common mullein (*Verbascum thapsus*), Virginia creeper (*Parthenocissus quinquefolia*), elderberries (*Sambucus* spp.), mulberries (*Morus* spp.)

Feeder Pleasers

- Suet; mealworms and other insect foods; sunflower seeds; nuts and nut spreads, such as peanut butter or almond butter (mix with cornmeal to make this pricey treat go farther)

Tricks and Treats

- Mount a nest box tailored to these small woodpeckers' size. It will also serve as shelter on cold or snowy winter nights.

Polka-Dotted Zebra

Downies are daily visitors in our backyards, which means that at some point you may happen to find one of their feathers. Late summer to early fall is prime molting season; that's when I often come across a downy woodpecker feather under fruit trees or feeders.

Figuring out who dropped a feather can be tricky. Your downies may have zebra-striped backs, but the feather is likely to look more polka-dotted. Arranged in rows, those dots create the look of stripes.

Blue Jay

First Impression

Big, screaming, blue bird

Steller's Jay

Mark Your Calendar

Year-round, from the Rockies eastward; westward, the Steller's jay takes over

Details, Details

- Bigger than a robin; 11 inches
- Female looks like male

Listen Up!

- Loud and raucous, jays are screamers. You'll soon recognize their harsh, unmusical calls.
- You may occasionally hear a lovely, completely different, very musical phrase that sounds like *too-lee-lee-lee*.

Telltale Traits

- Swoops in to feeding station with loud cries, scattering smaller birds like leaves
- Scoops up several seeds or nuts at once, then goes off to bury them
- Holds nuts or acorns in feet and whacks with bill
- Alerts other birds to danger by screaming and harassing predators in area

Look Here

- At feeder

Or Here

- Silently collecting acorns, walnuts, pecans, or other nuts from backyard trees
- Flying to and from your yard
- At birdbath

On the Home Front Blue jay nests in trees, shrubs, or vines, usually about 15 to 20 feet high • Sings sweet, quiet song to its mate

"Several jays spent the entire day harvesting acorns"

—**William Brewster, "The Birds of the Lake Umbagog Region of Maine" (1937)**

Blue jays and other jays play a big role in keeping trees growing. They plant acorns, pecans, and other nuts by burying them, assuring plenty of trees for the future.

Wild Menu: Nuts, including acorns; fruit; insects; plus frogs, salamanders, snakes, mice, and—sadly—eggs and nestlings of other birds

Plant Picks: Single-headed annual sunflowers (*Helianthus annuus*), corn, oak trees for acorns

Feeder Pleasers

- Nuts, especially peanuts in the shell; sunflower seeds; corn

Tricks and Treats

- You can train jays to come for nuts when you call. Just put nuts out at a certain time every day, call "Here, jays!" and stand nearby until the jays arrive. They'll soon learn when to expect feeding time.
- A simple pedestal birdbath will get attention, but a naturalistic ground-level bath with a dripper will attract more fans.

Gardeners with Smarts

I've noticed that jays are much quicker to snatch up nuts still in the shell from my feeder than they are to grab chopped or hulled nuts. Peanuts, filberts, pecans, English walnuts—whatever I put out, it's the whole nuts still in their shells that jays home in on first.

Do they somehow know that those are the ones that will sprout after they poke them into the soil, ensuring a crop of trees for future generations of jays? Or is it because those nuts keep longest, so the jays know there'll be food during lean times?

Black-Capped Chickadee

First Impression

Active little gray bird with contrasting black head markings

Mark Your Calendar

Year-round

Details, Details

- Chickadee size! 5¼ inches
- Female looks like male

Listen Up!

- Seven different species of chickadees roam the country, and most say some version of the classic *chick-a-dee-dee-dee* of the black-capped.
- Chickadees are talkative, uttering high-pitched, buzzy notes, similar to titmice.

Telltale Traits

- Always in action, moving on, over, and around branches and leaves, in a never-ending quest for food
- Usually in groups
- Often hangs upside down

Look Here

- At feeder

Or Here

- Moving through trees or large shrubs

On the Home Front Often nests in backyards, but is often overlooked • Happily accepts a nest box • Also nests in natural cavities, either abandoned by woodpeckers or dug out by chickadee pair, in decayed branches or stubs • Nests very low, which is why you might miss it—from 1 to about 10 feet tops • The nest is an invitingly cozy collection, thick with moss, feathers, hair, soft plant fibers, and silk cocoons.

"Two days later he would perch on my finger"

—John Woodcock, "A Friendly Chickadee" (1913)

If you have the patience for standing quietly, chickadees are one of the easiest wild birds to hand tame. Nuts are an ideal bribe to bring them to your hand, but you can also try ordinary sunflower seeds.

Wild Menu: Insects; seeds; nuts

Plant Picks: Annual sunflowers (*Helianthus annuus*) and just about any kind of tree or shrub for insects, including oaks (*Quercus* spp.), firs (*Abies* spp.) or other conifers, and redbuds (*Cercis* spp.)

Feeder Pleasers

- Sunflower seeds; chopped nuts; suet, peanut butter, and other nut butters; mealworms and other insect foods

Tricks and Treats

- In late winter, make a collection of soft fibers to offer as nesting material. Short lengths of string, thread, moss, soft feathers, and cotton balls will catch their eye.
- Birdbaths are a hit with this tribe.

Variations on a Theme

The black-capped is the most widespread species, ranging across much of the NE, MW, W, and NW. In the SE, S, and lower MW, it's the look-alike Carolina who entertains you. In the W and SW, look for the mountain chickadee. Coastal W and NW? You get the easy-to-recognize chestnut-backed. Some species overlap, so you might see more than one type in your yard.

Whichever chick-a-dee-dee-dee you host, you'll soon get to be best friends. Just watching these bright-eyed little guys brightens up a winter morning.

84

White-Breasted Nuthatch

First Impression
Odd "tuxedo-clad" gray bird, often clinging in upside-down posture

"Like mirthless laughter"

—Frank Chapman, early American ornithologist, on the song of the white-breasted nuthatch

START HERE

Mark Your Calendar
Year-round; but in some MW regions, winter only

Details, Details
- About sparrow size; 5¾ inches
- Female similar but has paler head
- Stubby tail and long, pointy beak

Listen Up!
- Song is a nasal *whi-whi-whi-whi-whi-whi-whi*—you get the idea.
- Call has regional variations, depending on the subspecies: east of the Rockies, a distinctive *yank-yank*; in the W, a nasal *yidi-yidi-yidi*; Pacific West, a mewling *eeern*
- Talkative like chickadees, with frequent soft, high-pitched notes

Telltale Traits
- Clings to tree trunks with stubby legs, like a woodpecker—but travels upside-down!
- Grab-and-go eating habits at the feeder (except for suet or peanut butter, at which it lingers)
- Flies in undulating swoops

Look Here
- At feeder

Or Here
- Climbing rapidly down tree trunks or main branches, peering intently at bark
- Hammering nuts or seeds into crevices of wood posts, trees, or other hiding places
- With foraging bands of chickadees or kinglets in winter

The "love song" of nuthatches is a monotone trill that gets lost among the music of spring songbirds. But once you start listening for it, you'll hear it often.

On the Home Front Nuthatches are cavity nesters, so they're likely to try a birdhouse. • Put the box up early, in late winter. • Keep your suet feeder filled in summer—parents may bring their young when they leave the nest.

Wild Menu: Insects; nuts; seeds

Plant Picks: Annual sunflowers (*Helianthus annuus*) and nut trees, such as oaks (*Quercus* spp.), hemlocks (*Tsuga* spp.), firs (*Abies* spp.), or other conifers

Feeder Pleasers
- Suet, peanut butter; nuts (chopped last longer); sunflower seeds; mealworms and other insect foods

Tricks and Treats
- Supply a birdhouse.
- Offer soft materials for lining the nest: feathers, moss, cotton balls, and dog hair.

You Talkin' to Me?

He may look like a gentleman in those dapper evening clothes, but the white-breasted nuthatch can show a temper like a barroom brawler. Watch for bullying behavior at the feeder: If another bird gets too close to the food that a nuthatch has its eye on, the nuthatch will instantly flash its wings and spread its tail, while threatening with that wicked-looking beak. Guess who usually gets the goodies?

85

Red-Breasted Nuthatch

First Impression

Tiny, unafraid gray-and-reddish bird that creeps as if it has Velcro feet

Mark Your Calendar

Year-round or winter only

Details, Details

- Smaller than a chickadee; 4½ inches
- Stubby tail and pointy beak
- Female similar to male but paler

Listen Up!

- Used to be described as sounding like a child's tin horn, but since most of us haven't heard that sound for, oh, half a century, just listen for an incessant bleating: a series of repeated *eeen, eeen, eeen* or weak, nasal *yank*s.

Telltale Traits

- Unafraid of people; easy to approach
- Crawls around on trees and branches, often head-down
- Undulating flight

Look Here

- At feeder

Or Here

- Creeping on trunks or branches of trees, often upside down
- On small branches or at cones of firs, hemlocks, other conifers
- With foraging bands of chickadees, or kinglets in winter

On the Home Front Not usually a backyard nester, unless your yard looks like a coniferous forest • Reluctant to use a nest box; offer food instead

"They exhibited no fear"

—Richard Miller, "The red-bellied nuthatch feeding among weeds" (1914)

Tiny red-breasted nuthatches are completely unafraid of us. So it's easy to slowly and quietly walk right up when you see one, and watch whatever it's doing.

Wild Menu: Insects; seeds of conifers

Plant Picks: Annual sunflowers (*Helianthus annuus*), perennial sunflowers (*H. angustifolia, H. maximilianii,* and other spp.), any conifers

Feeder Pleasers

- Suet; insect-enriched suet and other insect foods; sunflower seeds

Tricks and Treats

- Adding a few pines, firs, spruces, or other conifers to your yard will make it inviting.

Thighmaster

Nuthatches move about on tree trunks as easily as woodpeckers, but their style of motion is very different. Woodpeckers have super-stiff tail feathers that they can use to prop themselves up, so they can hitch along, both feet at a time. Nuthatches have to depend on the strength of their legs and feet to cling and get around.

Next time you have both birds in your yard, take a close look and see if you can spot which one is the thighmaster.

Brown Creeper

First Impression

Tiny, brown, mouselike bird spiraling up tree trunk

Mark Your Calendar

Year-round or winter only

Details, Details

- Chickadee size; 5¼ inches
- Mottled back feathers are perfect camouflage against tree bark.

Listen Up!

- You'll have to listen hard to catch the thin, high, lispy notes, which sound very much like the soft calls of the titmice, kinglets, and chickadees it often travels with.

Telltale Traits

- Distinctive habit of creeping up tree trunks
- One or two creepers often join mixed groups of foraging chickadees, titmice, and nuthatches in winter.

Look Here

- On tree trunks

Or Here

- Rarely at feeder

On the Home Front If you think the creeper is well-camouflaged, just try finding its nest: It's hidden behind a piece of bark. • Uses cocoons and silken spider-egg cases to attach a crescent of twigs to back of bark

START HERE

"Like a fragment of detached bark that is defying the laws of gravitation"

—**Winsor Tyler, "Notes on nest life of the brown creeper" (1914)**

The brown creeper is hard to see but unforgettable. Once you spot one of these odd birds spiraling up a tree, you'll have it nailed. The trick is seeing it in the first place!

Wild Menu: Insects; occasionally seeds

Plant Picks: Mature trees

Feeder Pleasers

- Sunflower seeds; may pick at suet or insect foods

Tricks and Treats

- The trick is yours: To spot one of these interesting birds, try to get in the habit of watching for what looks like that moving "piece of bark" on the trunks of trees. Or look for a creeper when it flies from one tree to the base of another, to repeat its upward search for food.

Foraging Friends

In winter, little bands of little birds may include your backyard as part of their foraging territory. Look out bugs, because these birds are all adept at ferreting out insects. Chickadees are the mainstay of the group, with a sprinkling of kinglets, titmice, and nuthatches, and generally a downy woodpecker along for the tour.

Often there's a brown creeper in the mix, too, which is why I get excited when I hear those tiny, soft calls that announce the band of birds is heading my way. It's fun to compare their different foraging styles as they move through.

Carolina Wren

First Impression

Energetic, warm-brown bird with a white eye stripe

Mark Your Calendar

Year-round; not in upper part of country (except NW and NE)

Details, Details

- Small sparrow size; about 5½ inches
- Carolina has warm buff-colored belly; similar Bewick's of western states has grayish white belly
- Male and female look alike

Listen Up!

- Long and varied musical songs
- Harsh, scolding rattle
- Sharp *chip!* when alarmed

Telltale Traits

- Stays hidden in vegetation
- Seems to be always in motion, nervous and quick
- Often cocks tail upward at an angle

Look Here

- In shrubbery, vines, or garden beds

Or Here

- May visit feeder

On the Home Front Bulky nest made of a conglomeration of materials, but well-hidden • May be in cavity or in dense tangle of vines or branches • Usually fairly low, within about 6 feet of ground • May build nests and then not use them for nesting

Bewick's wren

"He comes of his own accord and installs himself . . . wherever it suits his taste."

—**Robert Ridgway**, *Ornithology of Illinois* (1889)

These delightful birds aren't a sure thing, even in the most bird-friendly backyard. So you can feel honored if a wren chooses your backyard as its home.

Wild Menu: Insects; fruit

Plant Picks: Elderberries (*Sambucus* spp.), Virginia creeper (*Parthenocissus quinquefolia*), and other small fruits and berries; hedges, vigorous perennial vines, and shrub groups for cover

Feeder Pleasers

- Mealworms and other insect foods; suet; crumbles of peanut-butter dough (mix peanut butter with flour or cornmeal); doughnuts

Tricks and Treats

- For fast vegetative growth that may attract a wren, it's hard to beat sweet autumn clematis (*Clematis paniculata*) for quick cover in a single season. Grow it on a trellis against your house, garage, or shed for maximum cover.

Ad-Lib Artist

Unlike most songbirds, these wrens don't reliably sing the same song. They mix up the phrases or the notes, like Ella Fitzgerald scat-singing up and down the scale. Plus they make a lot of strange noises—rattles and chatters and trills, often mixed with high, clear notes.

Whenever I find myself straining to figure out who's making those weird noises, I wait for the giveaway: Eventually comes the chirr that announces a wren.

House Wren

First Impression
Small, hyperactive "Jenny wren"

Mark Your Calendar

Spring through fall; winter, too, in southern areas

Details, Details

- Chickadee size or smaller; 4¾ inches
- Male and female look alike: little brown birds, not at all flashy

Listen Up!

- Famed for its long, gurgling, burbling, beautiful song, the avian equivalent of water running over rocks

Telltale Traits

- Busy, busy, busy; always in motion except when singing
- Cocks tail upward frequently
- Male regularly sings from a series of perches, in full view

Look Here

- Constantly hopping about in low, dense cover

Or Here

- Amidst vegetable or flower gardens
- In shrubbery or vines
- If you're lucky, at the feeder

On the Home Front Readily adopts a nest box, although in W, often chooses open woods or woods' edges instead of backyards • It's famed for its selection of oddball homesites. Any object outside with a place to stuff full of twigs and leaves may become a nest site: a boot, a shirt pocket, a scarecrow, an open mailbox.

"There were 637 pieces of food brought"

—Lynds Jones, about house wrens in "Some records of the feeding of nestlings" (1913)

START HERE

House wrens are one of the best friends a gardener could ever ask for. As Jones noted: "161 geometrid larvae, 141 leafhoppers, 112 young grasshoppers," and hundreds more yummy bugs.

Wild Menu: Insects; fruit

Plant Picks: Elderberries (*Sambucus* spp.), raspberries, blueberries, mulberries (*Morus* spp.), and other small fruits

Feeder Pleasers
- May visit a feeder for mealworms and other insect foods or suet

Tricks and Treats
- Wrens love an afternoon at the spa—or should we say, 10 minutes in a birdbath, especially if it has a spray or mister.
- Feathers offered are a hit at nesting time.

The Not-So-Nice Side

House wrens are notoriously aggressive toward other nearby nesting birds, destroying eggs and young with their long, lethal beaks. Back in the 1920s, a spirited campaign was waged to discourage people from putting up wren houses, with magazine articles such as "Down with the House Wren Boxes" (Althea Sherman in the *Wilson Bulletin*, 1925).

By 1948, the little brown birds were being compared to the world scourge of the times: "This Nazi trait has brought them into disfavor ... " tsk-tsked A. C. Bent (*Life Histories of North American Nuthatches, Wrens, Thrashers, and Their Allies*, 1948).

Golden-Crowned Kinglet

First Impression

Tiny, gray-green bird fluttering at branch tips

START HERE

Mark Your Calendar

Winter, most areas; year-round in W and NE; migration only in N

Details, Details

- Smaller than a chickadee; about 4 inches
- Female has paler yellow on crown and doesn't raise head feathers like male

Listen Up!

- Faint, very high-pitched, lisping notes, plus a chickadee-like *chi-chi-chi* chatter

Telltale Traits

- Constantly flicks its wings while moving through branches
- Often hovers at branch tips while feeding
- Joins mixed flocks of chickadees, titmice, nuthatches, and other foragers in winter

Look Here

- Fluttering among and at branches of conifers

Or Here

- Fluttering at foliage of deciduous trees and shrubs
- At apples, crab apples, and other flowering trees, picking off insects at blossoms
- At nectar feeder

On the Home Front Rarely nests in backyards, unless yours is thick with spruces or other conifers • Nests high in a conifer

"A tiny feathered gem"

—**A. C. Bent,** the *Life Histories of North American Birds* **series (late 1800s to mid 1900s)**

You have to look hard to see where the "gem" part of the kinglet comes in. The golden crown is best seen at close range or through binoculars. The male bird's gold deepens to orange at the very top of his head, and he can raise those gem-colored feathers to form a rounded crest.

Wild Menu: Insects; some small fruits

Plant Picks: Short-needled conifers, such as spruce, hemlock, fir; elderberries (*Sambucus* spp.); and flowering crabs (*Malus* cvs.) for insects at flowers

Feeder Pleasers

- May visit nectar or suet feeders; may eat mealworms and other insect foods

Tricks and Treats

- A ground-level birdbath, such as a naturalistic resin style with more than one shallow basin, is ideal; draw them to it with a dripper.

Seasonal Treat

Kinglets retreat to forested places during breeding season, so unless you live near their natural haunts, you may not see them for months at a time.

It's always a fun little surprise to see them again and to renew my acquaintance when they show up in my yard in fall. The birdbath is often a favorite stop—and even there, they can't seem to stop that nervous tic of flicking their wings.

American Robin

First Impression

Alert, gray-brown bird with reddish breast, on lawn

"The harbinger of spring"

—Old folk saying, still well known

Mark Your Calendar

Year-round; but in northern parts of states, spring through fall

Details, Details

- Robin size! 10 inches
- Female looks like a faded version of male

Listen Up!

- Beautiful long, whistled song
- Sharp alarm notes, and concerned— almost clucking—sounds

Telltale Traits

- Pulling worms from ground
- Flipping through leaves to find worms and insects

Look Here

- On lawn

Or Here

- On ground beneath shrubs or trees
- In trees or shrubs
- In birdbath

On the Home Front Maybe the most frequent backyard nester • Builds sturdy cup with mud foundation • Nests at mid-level, in shrubs, roses, on limb or in crotch of trees, or in basket or wreath hanging on house

In many regions, robins are present year-round, but many seek cover in wild areas over winter and act more wary. Then in spring, our backyard robins return to their "regular" habits, hopping about on the grass and raising our spirits.

Wild Menu: Worms; insects; fruit and berries

Plant Picks: Fruits of any kind; loves elderberries (*Sambucus* spp.), mulberries (*Morus* spp.), grapes (*Vitis* spp.), and lots of others; also fond of berries of holly (*Ilex* spp.), dogwood (*Cornus* spp.), and others

Feeder Pleasers

- Rarely visits feeders but may eat mealworms and other insect foods, bread and other baked goods, and chopped and accessible suet

Tricks and Treats

- Give them a bath! Robins will visit your birdbath daily. They also absolutely revel in sprays and misters.

Head-Cock, Bill-Pounce

Have you ever watched a robin's hunting technique? First comes the "head-cock," which scientists have defined as "one eye points to the ground, 3 to 5 cm in front of the bird, along the longitudinal axis of the body. . ." (F. Heppner, 1965) There's more, but it boils down to this: Then the robin spies its prey with both eyes—and nails it with its coup de grace, the "bill-pounce," which is exactly what it sounds like. Down the hatch!

Hermit Thrush

First Impression

Brown bird with speckled breast, nervously flicking tail and wings

START HERE

Mark Your Calendar

Winter in SE and S; spring through fall in W, NE, and parts of N; migration in MW and parts of N

Details, Details

- Robinlike but smaller, only as long as a large sparrow; 6¾ inches
- Female and male look alike

Listen Up!

- A fabled singer, with a haunting, flutelike song

Telltale Traits

- Quickly flicks tail up, then slowly lowers it
- Flicks wings frequently
- Sings at dusk (as well as other times)

Look Here

- In shrubs, especially berry bushes

Or Here

- On the ground, usually near or under vegetation
- Eating berries in fall

On the Home Front Doesn't usually nest in backyards but has been known to nest on golf courses or in cemeteries—areas with big stretches of open land • East of the Rockies, usually nests on ground; west of the Rockies, usually in small trees • Only the female builds the big, bulky nest. • Eggs are beautiful pale blue to turquoise.

"It is the sweetest, ripest hour of the day"

—John Burroughs, on a hermit thrush at dusk, *Wake-Robin* (1887)

The thrushes hold a special place in many bird lovers' hearts. As shadows begin to gather among the trees of the forest, the hermit thrush sings his pure, sweet song.

Wild Menu: Insects; fruit

Plant Picks: Fall-bearing fruits and berries, such as dogwoods (*Cornus* spp.), possumhaw and other native viburnums (*Viburnum* spp.), and spicebush (*Lindera benzoin*)

Feeder Pleasers

- Uncommon feeder visitor; try mealworms or other insect foods and suet

Tricks and Treats

- Plenty of cover: Plant groups of shrubs, and let leaves accumulate beneath them in fall instead of raking them, to provide foraging opportunities.

Far-Flung Hermits

On my first trip to the Southwest, when my neck was aching from looking right, left, up and down at all the new-to-me birds, I spotted a brown bird perched on a rock. It was near a patch of poison oak, in the middle of parched California grasslands.

Hmm, it sure looked a lot like the hermit thrushes I knew from the shady woods back East. It even had the same habit of raising and lowering its tail and flicking its wings.

I opened my field guide to pin down this rare California thrush—and discovered a hermit thrush can turn up anywhere across America!

Northern Mockingbird

First Impression

Slim, large, long-tailed gray bird

Mark Your Calendar

Year-round. Oddly enough, the "northern" mockingbird is absent from the northern tier of states as well as parts of the NW and W.

Details, Details

- Same size as a robin but appears longer; 10 inches
- Female and male look alike

Listen Up!

- Long, musical song; includes imitations of other birds and mechanical sounds

Telltale Traits

- Chases away other birds from feeder
- Quick to harass a snake, cat, or other predator

Look Here

- Singing from a high, conspicuous perch—your chimney?

Or Here

- At feeders—eating or driving off other birds
- At apples, crab apples, and other flowering trees, picking off insects at blossoms
- Eating fruit or berries

On the Home Front Nests in shrubs or trees, usually less than 10 feet off the ground • Raises two or three families a year, and builds a new nest for each • Starts nesting very early, in late winter • Often includes trash—such as paper, foil, plastic—in its nest

"A curious and most interesting performance"

—Alice Bowers Harrington, "Observations on the mockingbird at Dallas, Texas" (1923)

Dancing with the Stars, pshaw. How about dancing with mockingbirds? In courtship, the male and female face each other to perform a series of flashy steps. And to scare off a snake, the male lifts and spreads his wings and tail in an impressive display.

Wild Menu: Insects; fruit

Plant Picks: Roses (*Rosa* spp.) with sprays of small hips, for nesting and winter food; raspberries and other brambles

Feeder Pleasers

- Suet and other fats; mealworms and other insect foods; millet

Tricks and Treats

- Delight your mockingbirds with a birdbath. They're big fans of water.

Quiet! I Need to Sleep!

A mockingbird singing at night may sound romantic, but in reality it can be, shall we say, less than pleasant. Night after night the bird holds forth, usually tuning up well after midnight. Young, unmated males are believed to be the culprits for this behavior.

So how can you make them stop? You probably can't. Instead, try "white noise" to block out the singer: The whir of an electric fan or a soothing recording might save your sanity.

Brown Thrasher

First Impression

Big, reddish brown bird with long tail

Mark Your Calendar

Spring through fall in MW, N, NE; year-round in SE and S; absent in W, NW, and SW, except for strays

Details, Details

- Bigger than a robin; 11½ inches
- Female and male look alike

Listen Up!

- Long, complicated, musical song of repeated phrases

Telltale Traits

- No other bird looks like this!
- "Thrashes" through dead leaves on ground with its bill

Look Here

- On ground, under shrubs

Or Here

- In dense thickets: a hedge, a bramble patch, or a rampant perennial vine

On the Home Front Nests low in shrubs, sometimes on the ground • Young leave the nest only 9 days after hatching—an adaptation that improves survival chances for birds at low levels. • Often nests in backyard shrubs, including forsythia and privet

"Seeks a bit of thick and tangled growth"

—**Althea Sherman, "The brown thrashers east and west" (1912)**

For all their size and eye-catching color, thrashers can be tricky to find. They're skulkers who seek out the densest thicket. Listen for the song, then try to sneak up on the singer.

Wild Menu: Insects; fruit

Plant Picks: Small fruits, especially mulberries (*Morus* spp.) and grapes

Feeder Pleasers

- Was occasional feeder visitor, but now appears more frequently; mealworms and other insect food; suet and other fats

Tricks and Treats

- Provide a birdbath with a nonslip rim and bottom: Thrashers are energetic in the bath.

Feathered Architects

Next time you visit a natural history museum, ask to see a brown thrasher nest. They're often constructed like a series of four nesting baskets: The outside basket is twigs. Inside that is a layer or cup mostly of leaves. Then comes a neat layer of very fine twigs and grass stems. Finally, the inner basket or lining: a cup of clean rootlets, probably from grasses.

All those layers are shaped in place by the female, who pats them down with sideways motions of her feet to help mesh them together.

Gray Catbird

First Impression

A petulant, whining *meeurrr* from the bushes—and it's not Kitty.

"Some of his improvisations are very sweet and musical"

—Charles Townsend, "Mimicry of voice in birds" (1924)

Mark Your Calendar

Spring through fall; winter along extreme southern edge of the United States; year-round along the Atlantic Coast; absent from much of SW, W, and NW

Details, Details

- A little smaller than a robin; 8½ inches
- Solid dark gray with black cap, and reddish brown beneath tail
- Female and male look alike

Listen Up!

- That feline *meow* is unique among birds.
- Also a pretty, musical, whistled song of repeated phrases
- A grating chatter when alarmed
- May mimic other birds

Telltale Traits

- Sings from within a dense bush
- Violently attacks snakes, which often prey upon its nest

Look Here

- More often heard than seen, but may be spotted eating mulberries or other fruit

Or Here

- In patches of raspberries and other brambles
- Foraging on the ground under shrubs

On the Home Front

Builds a bulky nest low to the ground in dense, often thorny shrubs
- One of few birds that quickly recognizes and rejects eggs of parasitic brown-headed cowbird

Poor catbird. Famed for his meow, he's actually an accomplished singer with an ever-changing repertoire. Like the mockingbird, he can mimic other birds or sing his own rambling tune.

Wild Menu: Insects; fruit

Plant Picks: Mulberries (*Morus* spp.), cherries (*Prunus* spp.), blueberries, raspberries, blackberries, and other small fruits; native fruits and berries

Feeder Pleasers

- An unusual but occasional feeder visitor; mealworms and other insect foods; accessible suet

Tricks and Treats

- Occasionally a catbird will linger into winter in cold areas. Pump up its calories by offering chopped suet in a low, open tray feeder or on the ground. Lightly freeze a block of plain suet (or beef fat) to make it easier to chop.

Bye-Bye, Bad Eggs

You'd think birds could easily recognize an egg of a different color laid in their nests. But that's not the case. Of the 220 bird species parasitized by the brown-headed cowbird, scientists say only a dozen have learned to spot the out-of-place eggs.

The gray catbird is one. Only six records are known of catbirds raising baby cowbirds. In experiments with fake cowbird eggs, the catbird gave the bad egg the boot in less than 24 hours.

Cedar Waxwing

First Impression

Elegant, neat, smooth-feathered, grayish-tan bird perched with flock

START HERE

Mark Your Calendar

Year-round in northern third of United States; winter, southern two-thirds. Larger, plumper Bohemian waxwing in northern tier in winter; sporadic visitor elsewhere

Details, Details

- Smaller than a robin but looks much larger than a sparrow; 7¼ inches
- Pointy crest and dashing black mask across eyes
- Trademark dots of red wax on wings
- Female and male look alike

Listen Up!

- Very high, one-note, hissy whistles

Telltale Traits

- Always in a flock or with a partner
- The group flies around together, settling in trees or at food sources.

Look Here

- At berries or other small fruits

Or Here

- In treetops
- Flying, with distinctive high-pitched, single-note, whistling calls

On the Home Front One of the latest birds to nest; often not until July or August • Nests in fork or on branch of trees of many kinds, also in shrubs, high or low • Fashions a bulky cup of twigs, dead leaves, ferns, and other natural materials.

"Few birds care to take life so easily"

—Neltje Blanchan, *Bird Neighbors* (1897)

". . . not to say indolently," continues Blanchan. Placid waxwings are the opposite of peppy chickadees or frenetic warblers: They spend a lot of time just sitting around.

Wild Menu: Fruit; insects

Plant Picks: "People" fruits of any kind, particularly sweet or sour cherries (*Prunus* spp.) and mulberries (*Morus* spp.); berries of holly (*Ilex* spp.), dogwoods (*Cornus florida* and other spp.), mountain ash, and many others

Feeder Pleasers

- Not a feeder visitor

Tricks and Treats

- Waxwings may collect short pieces of string, narrow strips of white cotton cloth, or tufts of natural sheep's wool that you offer. Lay the materials over a branch of a shrub in your yard.

"False Azure"

Cedar waxwings are frequent victims of head-on collisions into windows. Change your perspective when you look at a window from outside and you'll see why a pane of glass can be so deceptive. All you see is a reflection of sky and surroundings. Vladimir Nabokov (famed for *Lolita*) gave an indelible account in his poem, "The Waxwing Slain" (*Pale Fire*, 1962):

I was the shadow of the waxwing slain / by the false azure of the windowpane;
I was the smudge of ashen fluff—and I / lived on, flew on, in the reflected sky.

Common Yellowthroat

Small, quick, secretive, olive-colored bird flashing into low vegetation

Mark Your Calendar

Spring through fall; winter in parts of S, SE, and SW

Details, Details

- Chickadee size; 5 inches
- Male sports a wide black mask
- Both male and female have a yellow throat.
- Female is paler

Listen Up!

- More often heard than seen. Listen for a clear, loud *witchity-witchity-witchity.*
- Also has a short, buzzy *chip!* of alarm.

Telltale Traits

- Hyperactive; darts here and there in bushes, gardens, or overgrown grass
- Stops momentarily to sing, while clutching a flower or grass stem

Look Here

- Low to ground, usually at about 2 to 3 feet, in dense vegetation

Or Here

- In overlooked, overgrown corners of the yard
- In flower gardens
- In vegetable gardens

On the Home Front Nests on or near the ground • Female builds the nest by herself • Very hard to spot the nest, since it's made from dead stems and leaves of surrounding vegetation, so it blends right in • Sometimes built with a roof, instead of as an open cup

"A fine, clear voice"
—**Amos Butler,** *Birds of Indiana*
(1898)

Witchity-witchity-witchity **is an easy way to remember the distinctive song of the yellowthroat, but Butler correctly points out that it's actually closer to** *wit-ti-chee, wit-ti-chee, wit-ti-chee.* **Whichever way they enunciate, yellowthroats say it loudly and often.**

Wild Menu: Insects

Plant Picks: Go for habitat: Try growing ornamental grasses mixed with large, clumping, low-maintenance perennials, such as perennial sunflowers (*Helianthus angustifolia* and other spp.) in an undisturbed corner. The yellowthroat also likes meadows with occasional wild roses or other shrubs.

Feeder Pleasers

- Not usually a feeder visitor; you can try offering mealworms or other insect foods

Tricks and Treats

- May be tempted by a low-level naturalistic birdbath with a dripper

Early Bird

The yellowthroat was one of the first New World birds described in science, and it was Swedish botanist Carolus Linnaeus, the father of genus/species scientific nomenclature, who did the honors.

That original specimen who gave up his life for science (I doubt anyone asked him to volunteer) was collected in 1766 in Maryland. The species was once commonly called the Maryland yellowthroat.

Yellow-Rumped Warbler

First Impression

Small, active, gray/black/yellow/white bird with bright yellow rump patch

Mark Your Calendar

Winter in SE and S; spring through fall in much of W, NW, NE, and N; migration in parts of MW and N

Details, Details

- Between chickadee and sparrow size; 5½ inches
- The myrtle race has a white throat; Audubon's race, a yellow throat.
- Spots of white on outer tail feathers
- Female is not so vivid, and young birds are brownish—but all have the signature yellow rump.

Listen Up!

- High, soft warbling song
- Sharp *chip!* call note

Telltale Traits

- Nervous-jervis! Warblers are constantly on the move, flitting to and fro.
- Sallies out to snatch insects in the air

Look Here

- In trees or shrubs, often at mid-level

Or Here

- Eating bayberries winter to spring

On the Home Front
Does not nest in much of its American range • Nests in conifer forests, on a branch of a conifer; nests high or low • In the SW, nests in mixed forest, sometimes in maples or oaks • Female builds nest while male sings encouragement

Audubon's race

"Wherever bayberries are abundant"

—Ralph Hoffmann, *A Guide to the Birds of New England and Eastern New York* (1904)

Many folks know this bird as the "myrtle warbler," thanks to its love of bayberries, or myrtles (*Myrica* spp.). In winter, bayberry bushes are a magnet for these birds and a good place to approach quietly for a close-up look.

Wild Menu: Insects; berries

Plant Picks: This is one of the few warblers that can digest the wax of bayberries (*Myrica pensylvanica*) and wax myrtle (*M. cerifera*); plant male and female bushes to produce a crop of their fragrant berries. Also try other small berries, including Virginia creeper (*Parthenocissus quinquefolia*).

Feeder Pleasers

- It's becoming a more frequent feeder visitor from fall through late winter. You can try offering mealworms and other insect foods and suet.

Tricks and Treats

- Try a ground-level birdbath with moving water produced by a dripper, Water Wiggler, or mister.

Beach Bums

After a winter storm, I was strolling along a New Jersey beach, just to see what I could see. Lots of pretty shells had washed in, and so had big piles of seaweed.

Those long windrows of kelp and eelgrass were buzzing with small brown flies and other insects—and with myrtle warblers! The birds had forsaken their usual haunts in the bayberry thickets, and like me, they were combing the beach.

Northern Cardinal

First Impression
Bright red bird with pointy crest

Mark Your Calendar
Year-round; absent in W, NW,
and parts of N and SW

Details, Details
- Smaller than a robin; 8¾ inches
- Heavy, conical, orange bill
- Female is reddish gray

Listen Up!
- A great song for beginners at birdsong to learn: *what cheeer! what cheeer!*

Telltale Traits
- Unmistakable appearance
- Often sings from exposed perch
- Pairs often stay together year-round.
- Stays at feeder for minutes at a time, cracking seeds

Look Here
- At feeder

Or Here
- In backyard trees or shrubs

On the Home Front Often uses dense backyard shrubs and roses as homesites • Puts in a good word for "invasive" honeysuckle: cardinals often build nest in tangle of honeysuckle vines (*Lonicera japonica*) • Cardinal nestlings look very much like brown-headed cowbird babies—and the cardinal is a frequent victim of that parasitic species.

"Decidedly social, particularly in the winter"

—**Maurice Brooks, "Notes on the Birds of Cranberry Glades, Pocahontas County, West Virginia" (1930)**

Nothing warms up a winter day like a flock of cardinals. Whether they're perched in a pine tree or at your feeding station, those red birds are simply glorious—especially in snow.

Wild Menu: Seeds; insects; fruit

Plant Picks: Large-headed, stout-stemmed sunflowers (*Helianthus annuus* 'Russian Giant')

Feeder Pleasers
- Sunflower seeds; corn; may eat safflower seeds

Tricks and Treats
- Cardinals often nest in grapevines—and sometimes in grapevine wreaths. Try hanging a wreath on a protected wall of your house, and see if you get any takers. Grapevine bark is used in nest construction, too.

Winter Red

Cardinals in the snow are a popular theme on Christmas cards, and no wonder—it's a beautiful combination. These brilliant red birds gather in groups in winter, feeding and sheltering together. Stock up on sunflower seeds and shelled corn, and you can be their favorite friend all season.

Evening Grosbeak

First Impression
Looks like a giant, darker goldfinch

START HERE

Mark Your Calendar
Winter only in most areas; year-round in parts of W, NW, N, and SW

Details, Details
- Smaller than a robin; 8 inches
- Male's big white wing patches flash as he flies
- Female is gray-green
- Massive, conical bill

Listen Up!
- Distinctive, hard-to-describe calls make an almost constant chatter.

Telltale Traits
- Usually visit in groups
- Eat sunflower seeds steadily for long periods of time
- Often an irregular visitor; plentiful one year, absent or scarce the next

Look Here
- At feeder

Or Here
- In flocks in treetops
- Flying in flocks from place to place

On the Home Front Nest is hard to see: a shallow saucer of loose twigs usually placed high in forest tree • So highly secretive about nesting, and nests so high in trees, that not much is known about it • Watch for birds in winter flocks to begin to pair off as spring approaches.

"Grosspigs"
—Nickname for evening grosbeaks

Better stock up on sunflower seeds if evening grosbeaks descend on your feeders. These "pigs" go through seed like hogs at the trough, cracking one shell after another with their powerful bills.

Wild Menu: Seeds, especially tree seeds; insects; some fruit

Plant Picks: Just keep that sunflower tray stocked for success with grosbeaks. The birds may also eat maple, ash, box elder, and other seeds on your shade trees.

Feeder Pleasers
- Sunflower seeds, and plenty of them

Tricks and Treats
- Try a heater for your birdbath to give grosbeaks a welcome winter spa.

What's That Noise?!

Many years ago, we had a kitchen fire with flames that moved faster than I would've believed possible. We smothered it quickly, but it scared the daylights out of us.

A couple of weeks afterward, I was sound asleep when the faint sound of crackling flames broke into my dreams. Heart pounding, I leaped out of bed and ran downstairs.

No fire, thank goodness. It was just a newly arrived crowd of grosbeaks going through the birdseed.

Rufous-Sided Towhee

First Impression
Big black, reddish, and white "sparrow" scratching on ground

Spotted towhee

Mark Your Calendar

Year-round in most areas; spring through fall in some areas; eastern towhee in eastern half of country; spotted towhee in West

Details, Details

- A little smaller than a robin; 8½ inches
- Female is brown rather than black

Listen Up!

- The call *che-WINK!* is shared by both eastern and western races.
- Calls are distinctive but variable. Once you recognize the timber of its voice, you won't have any trouble recognizing its notes.
- Eastern: also exhorts a buzzy, trilling *drink your teeee!*
- Western: rapid trill with that signature buzzy quality

Telltale Traits

- Scratches vigorously on ground
- Usually shows up singly or as a pair

Look Here

- On ground beneath shrubs

Or Here

- In dead leaves
- Low in dense shrubs or hedges

On the Home Front Nests on ground under bush, or very low in vines or shrubs, to about 5 feet • Builds a cup of twigs, grasses, and rootlets, lined with hair and fine grass • If you get too close to the nest, you'll hear the parents calling *twee* apprehensively.

"Chewink"

—Traditional common name for towhee

That name "towhee" sounds more like *toe-WHEE* when the bird says it himself. It's often preceded by a call that sounds almost exactly like *che-WINK!*

Wild Menu: Insects; fruit

Plant Picks: Plant a hedge or group of shrubs and let fallen leaves accumulate beneath.

Feeder Pleasers
- Millet

Tricks and Treats
- Towhees often visit a birdbath.

Doin' the Hokey Pokey

Watch the legs and feet of a towhee next time you hear one rustling in the dead leaves under your bushes, or spot one going to town beneath the feeder. You'll see they only use a two-footed method for scratching: a quick hop forward, a quick drag back.

No fancy Fred Astaire dance steps here. It looks like they only learned one move from the Hokey Pokey: "You put your both feet in, you put your both feet out."

American Goldfinch

First Impression
Bright yellow and black little bird

Mark Your Calendar
Year-round in a large swath; winter in southern states; spring through fall in northern

Details, Details
- Chickadee size; 5 inches
- Female and male in winter are olive-green

Listen Up!
- High, sweet, twittering, musical song
- Querying call note: *twee?*

Telltale Traits
- Usually in flocks
- Flies in deep dips, often singing *potato CHIP!* (actually, more like *perchick-uh-wee*) along the way

Look Here
- At feeder

Or Here
- In flower garden, eating seeds
- On thistles, dandelions, or other weeds, eating seeds
- In treetops, with the flock

On the Home Front May nest in backyard, usually low in a hedge or shrub • May also nest in a maple or other deciduous tree, or in pines, to about 30 feet high • Watch for goldfinches collecting plant down for their nests about the time that thistles begin to go to seed. • The cup of a nest is so densely woven from plant fibers and so thickly lined with thistledown or other soft materials that it holds water; the parent bird shelters the nest with its wings during showers.

"He stays with a happy company of friends."

—J. H. Stickney, *Bird World: A Bird Book for Children* (1904)

"Perhaps you know some boy or girl who is cheerful and lively all the day and all the year," writes Stickney, as the children's book author extols the goldfinch's supposed virtues. Wonder if that approach would fly with today's middle-schoolers?

Wild Menu: Weed seeds and other small seeds; insects

Plant Picks: Annual sunflowers (*Helianthus annuus*), Sensation cosmos (*Cosmos bipinnatus* 'Sensation'), garden lettuce you let go to seed, and a few choice weeds (dandelions, lamb's quarters, pigweed)

Feeder Pleasers
- Niger seed; sunflower seed; canary seed and finch mix

Tricks and Treats
- Water, water, everywhere—goldfinches can't seem to get enough of a birdbath. Expect to see several "wild canaries" splashing at once.
- Soft nesting materials are often welcomed. Try milkweed fluff, cotton balls, natural tufts of wool, or other soft or downy materials.

Dandelion Appreciation

Goldfinches are just as sunny and yellow as America's most recognized weed, and they're a natural match. Dandelions' little parachute-topped seeds are a big hit with these birds.

I like the look of flowers in my grass, and I like watching goldfinches standing on tiptoe to pluck out their seeds. So I welcome every dandelion that moves in. Call them "goldfinch food," and maybe you, too, can learn to enjoy them.

House Finch

First Impression
Streaky, red-splashed "sparrow" at feeder

Mark Your Calendar
Year-round

Details, Details
- Sparrow size; 6 inches
- Female is streaky gray-brown

Listen Up!
- Sweet, long, warbled song
- *Qweet?* call

Telltale Traits
- Often in small to large groups
- Frequent presence at feeder

Look Here
- At the feeder

Or Here
- In backyard conifers
- In flocks, in trees, or on other perches

On the Home Front Often lives near people, but in W, also in desert and other open spaces; never nests in forests • Frequently nests in hanging baskets, in ivy on walls, or in backyard trees, usually spruce, pine, or palm • The fad for specimen conifers—think suburban brick rancher with blue spruce in front—helped give this once-western species the protected nesting places it needed to spread across the entire country.

"Is it for thee the linnet pours his throat?"

—Alexander Pope (1688–1744), poet, *Essay on Man*

A sweet, pleasing song is always in the air when house finches—once called "linnets"—are around. Males sing year-round, slowing down some in winter but not stopping altogether like many other songbirds. Even the female sometimes sings.

Wild Menu: Buds; seeds; fruit; plus a few insects

Plant Picks: Annual sunflowers (*Helianthus annuus*) and almost any "people" fruit: cherries, peaches, plums, figs, blackberries, strawberries, and more

Feeder Pleasers
- Sunflowers; niger seed; finch mix

Tricks and Treats
- Provide a freshly filled birdbath every day.
- Salt is a hit; try a handful of rock salt in a clay saucer.

Clothes Make the Man

Check out the male house finches at your feeder, and you'll see they show huge variation in the color that washes their head and breast.

Some males are as richly red as strawberry juice, others look faded, and some are even orange to pale yellow.

Females, science has found, go for the guys with the reddest feathers.

Indigo Bunting

First Impression
A brilliant flash of metallic blue

START HERE

Mark Your Calendar

Spring through fall; absent from W, NW, and part of N

Details, Details
- Small sparrow size; 5½ inches
- Female is plain brown

Listen Up!
- *Sweet-sweet-choo-choo-sweet-sweet*—or the more vivid interpretation *fire, fire, where, where, here, here!*
- During nesting season, the male gives a gushing, rippling, joyous song while in flight.
- Sharp *chip!* alarm note

Telltale Traits
- One of the few birds to sing all day, even in heat
- Sings from an exposed perch

Look Here
- At feeder

Or Here
- Singing from a perch, often a utility wire or the tippy-top of a tree
- In brushy, overgrown areas, such as roadsides or old fields
- Eating weed seeds, especially dandelions

On the Home Front Not exactly a model of monogamy: A female may pair with more than one male, and a male may mate with more than one female. • Female raises nestlings by herself • Nests low to ground, usually at 3 feet or less, in shrubs, goldenrod, or other vegetation

"Sang the livelong day"

—**Thomas S. Roberts**, *The Birds of Minnesota* **(1932)**

When there's an indigo bunting in your neighborhood, you'll know it. This is one of the "singing-est" birds in the country, holding forth even in the heat of a summer day, when other birds are silent.

Wild Menu: Seeds; insects; some berries

Plant Picks: Dandelions! Let them go to seed to attract buntings passing through on spring migration.

Feeder Pleasers
- Millet

Tricks and Treats
- If you have a big yard, consider planting a meadow of grasses and rugged perennial wildflowers, such as goldenrods (*Solidago* spp.) and asters (*Aster* spp.), dotted with sumacs (*Rhus* spp.) or wild roses (*Rosa* spp.).

Stay on the Sunny Side

The brilliant blue of a bunting's feathers is nothing more than a trick of the light. Just as the sun makes the sky look blue, hitting it at a certain angle, so does the sun light up a bunting like the rarest of sapphires. In shade, the bunting is just a little dark bird.

Pine Siskin

First Impression

Streaky brown finch that looks a little different at the tube feeder

"Pine Siskins settled on the road to eat the salt"

—Gordon Meade, "Calcium chloride—a death lure for crossbills" (1942)

Mark Your Calendar

Winter in eastern half of country; year-round in much of W and parts of N

Details, Details

- Chickadee size; 5 inches
- Yellow bars on wings
- Noticeable notched tail
- Small, thin, sharp beak
- Female usually doesn't have as much yellow as male

Listen Up!

- What a racket! Noted for its motormouth habit of rapid notes, plus a buzzy *zhreeeee*. Multiply by 50 when a flock descends.

Telltale Traits

- Active little bird
- Generally visits feeder in groups, which explode into flight when disturbed
- Associates with goldfinches—and looks a lot like them at first glance

Look Here

- At tube feeder, eating niger seed

Or Here

- At other seed feeders
- Hanging out in a flock, in a tree near a feeder
- In conifers

On the Home Front

Not a backyard nester
- Nests in conifer forests • The female builds a flattened nest of twigs, rootlets, and grass, lined with soft materials—which she may recycle from an old goldfinch nest.

Crossbills, siskins, and other northern finches have a strong appetite for salt. When a flock settles on a road that's been spread with the stuff to melt snow or ice, they may become victims of passing traffic.

Wild Menu: Seeds, including seeds from conifer cones; buds; insects

Plant Picks: Annual sunflowers (*Helianthus annuus*), weeds, weedy grasses

Feeder Pleasers
- Niger seed; sunflower seed

Tricks and Treats
- Siskins seem to do everything together—they even like group baths. Provide a shallow basin of fresh water.
- Salt is a big hit with flocks of siskins. Try a handful of ice-cream-maker rock salt in a tray feeder.

Call Me Unpredictable

Feast or famine: That's often the way with pine siskins. They're famed for being irregular in their visits to backyards. Some years you'll host dozens, other years only a few—or none at all.

Most of the time they live in conifer forests, and some years, it seems, they just want a change of scenery—or maybe the cone crop failed. Then siskins "irrupt," traveling outside their usual haunts. If they told us they were coming, we could stock up on niger seed.

Slate-Colored Junco

First Impression

Ubiquitous small gray birds with white bellies, on ground

Mark Your Calendar

Winter in most areas; year-round in some parts of W and NE

Details, Details

- Sparrow size, 6¼ inches
- Flash white outer tail feathers when they fly
- Note the pinkish bill.
- Female is paler than male

Listen Up!

- Fast chippering trill, usually a monotone
- Sharp *chip!* alarm note

Telltale Traits

- Often in groups
- Scratches on ground to expose seeds
- Fairly unafraid of humans

Look Here

- On ground beneath feeder

Or Here

- In or at tray feeder
- Under shrubs or hedges
- Scratching for seeds in flower or vegetable gardens

On the Home Front Often nests on ground, in a cavity by a rock, at the foot of a tree, or along a log • May nest in higher places, such as vines on the side of a building or even a hanging basket • Female builds the nest, but male stays near during incubation and warns of intruders

Oregon junco

"Snowbird"

—Traditional common name, still in use

Is it because juncos portend the arrival of winter when they arrive in backyards that they got the name "snowbird"? Or is it because of their snowy underside and a back the color of a gray sky? I vote for the first. What do you think?

Pink-sided junco

Wild Menu: Seeds; insects

Plant Picks: Sow a patch of finch mix or birdseed mix—right from the bag—for juncos to forage in all winter.

Feeder Pleasers
- Millet

Tricks and Treats
- Hold off on cutting back your flower garden until early spring, especially if you grow zinnias (*Zinnia* spp.), bachelor's buttons (*Centaurea cyanus*), and other annuals: Juncos will find cover among the dead stems as they scratch for seeds.

Regional Treats

Not all slate-colored juncos look alike. The species includes several geographic variants, or races. All have dark eyes, a pink bill, and a general gray color. But details are different.

In the W and NW, the striking black hood and rusty brown trim of the Oregon junco add some spice. In the SW and W, you may spot the well-named pink-sided junco. Live in the SW? Watch for the gray-headed junco, which I think would have been better named the rusty-backed—it has a splash of bright rusty red on its upper back.

Song Sparrow

First Impression

Little streaky brown bird scratching or hopping on ground

Mark Your Calendar

Year-round

Details, Details

- Sparrow size; 6¼ inches
- Streaky white breast and distinctly striped head
- Some geographic races, including eastern and midwestern birds, have a distinct darker blotch on the chest, a thickening of their streaks. Juvenile birds, as well as western, northwestern, and southwestern races, may lack this mark.
- Slight color variations geographically: SW birds are ruddier, NW birds are grayer
- Female looks like male

Listen Up!

- Varying gentle songs with musical trills
- Frequent *chip!* alarm note

Telltale Traits

- Scratches on ground with both feet at once
- Usually stays somewhat hidden, in or beneath vegetation
- May remind you of a mouse, fast and secretive

Look Here

- Under feeder, picking up small seeds on ground

Or Here

- At tray feeder
- On ground under bushes
- At low levels, in flower garden, vegetable patch, or shrubbery

"A musician of exceptional ability"

—F. Schuyler Mathews,
Field Book of Wild Birds and Their Music
(1904)

START HERE

And we can enjoy this singer's concerts every day, right in the backyard. The little brown bird is an indefatigable performer, bursting into sweet songs many times a day.

On the Home Front Because song sparrows are so abundant, you have a good chance of enjoying a nesting pair in your own yard.
- Nests on ground or low in shrubs • The nest is surprisingly hard to spot; you may find it by accident when tending your garden.

Wild Menu: Seeds; insects; small fruits

Plant Picks: Strawberries, raspberries, blackberries, blueberries

Feeder Pleasers
- Millet

Tricks and Treats
- Keep that birdbath brimming; song sparrows like a daily splash. Place the bath near a shrub to make the bird feel more at home.

Was That a Moo?

Parent birds work hard dawn to dusk to feed their nestlings. Now imagine trying to feed a baby that's a giant!

That's the predicament of many song sparrows. They're a favorite target of the brown-headed cowbird, which in some regions lays eggs in nearly 20 percent of song sparrows' nests.

You may spot the mismatched, hulking cowbird fledgling when its "parents" bring their family to your feeder. The cowbird will be gray and noisy (but it won't be saying *moo*).

White-Throated Sparrow

First Impression

Streaky brown sparrow with white bib and eye stripe, scratching on ground

Mark Your Calendar

A winter friend in most areas; year-round in northern NE; migrant only in much of MW; absent from much of W

Details, Details

- A large sparrow; 6¾ inches
- Male and female look alike
- Head stripe may be bright white or drab tan
- Yellow spots at bill are worth a close-up view through binoculars

Listen Up!

- This sparrow sings one of the best beloved songs: a quavering, melancholy whistle to the cadence of "*old Sam Peabiddy Peabiddy Peabiddy.*" It's easy to imitate; give it a try.
- Clinking note, as of a chisel striking rock

Telltale Traits

- Usually in groups of a few to several
- May join a group of mixed sparrows and juncos
- Scratches vigorously on ground with both feet simultaneously

Look Here

- Beneath feeder with other sparrows

Or Here

- At tray feeder
- In or under shrubs or hedges
- In flower garden or vegetable patch, scratching for seeds on ground

"I watch eagerly for the arrival of these fall songsters"

—Frank Chapman, *Handbook of Birds of Eastern North America* (1895)

Listen for the plaintive song of this sparrow when fall migrants arrive in your backyard. You might also hear what Chapman calls their "quarrier chorus," a collection of soft *chinks* as the birds settle down together for the night.

On the Home Front Nests only in the very northern states, from Minnesota eastward
- Not usually a backyard nester • Builds nest on ground, often under wild blueberry bush
- Caterpillars are a big part of the nestlings' food.

Wild Menu: Seeds; a smattering of insects; some small fruits

Plant Picks: Scatter a few handfuls of birdseed in late spring to early summer, to grow a self-serve garden for these winter pals.

Feeder Pleasers
- Millet

Tricks and Treats
- White-throats appreciate a sip of water, even in winter. Set out a clay saucer of warm water, or try a birdbath heater. A Water Wiggler device may also keep water from freezing so quickly.

Who's Snoozin'?

Got a dense conifer in your backyard? It may become the Do Drop Inn for white-throated sparrows, juncos, and other winter visitors. These birds gather in communal roosts at dusk, often in a spruce, fir, or juniper. The extra bodies share warmth as they sleep safely among the branches.

White-Crowned Sparrow

First Impression

An elegant, large sparrow with plain gray front and boldly striped head

Mark Your Calendar

Winter, most areas; year-round in parts of W, or spring through fall in other parts of W and NW; migration only, upper MW and NE

Details, Details

- Large sparrow; 7 inches
- Some variation geographically
- Female and male look alike
- Young birds in their first winter have heads striped with brown instead of black, with tan instead of white between stripes.

Listen Up!

- Starts out similar to that of white-throated sparrow, then goes into pretty trills
- Call note: sharp *pink!*

Telltale Traits

- Watch for the bird to raise its head feathers into the crown that gives it its name.
- Scratches with both feet simultaneously
- Usually in small groups or with other sparrows and juncos

Look Here

- On ground or in feeder

Or Here

- In brushy areas, like a casual flower or vegetable garden
- In weedy corners

On the Home Front Mostly nests far to N, except in areas of W • May nest in parking lot shrubbery in W and NW • Often nests near water • A bird of grasslands and brush

"One of the aristocrats of the family"

—Frank Chapman, *Handbook of Birds of Eastern North America* (1895)

It's the crown that does it, plus a habit of perfect posture. White-crowned sparrows have a proud look, especially when they erect their boldly striped head feathers.

Wild Menu: Seeds; some insects; and small fruit

Plant Picks: Weeds! Dandelions are a big favorite. Don't have any weeds or any tolerance for them? Sow a "sparrow garden" of any inexpensive wildflower mix along with a few handfuls of birdseed, and let the plants stand through fall and winter.

Feeder Pleasers

- Millet

Tricks and Treats

- Water, water everywhere: Provide a birdbath, a dripper tube, a water-filled plant saucer on a rock, or a naturalistic "creek."
- Pour birdcage grit on bare ground at your feeding station or in a tray feeder.

Parking Lot Pals

When I moved to Washington State, I was stunned to find these special sparrows nesting in ordinary bushes in the supermarket parking lot. And the library parking lot. And the coffee shop parking lot. And, it seemed, every other parking lot with a few shrubs or trees.

I'm still not quite used to seeing them there. But I am enchanted by hearing their songs as I load my groceries and push my cart into the corral.

109

Chipping Sparrow

First Impression

Tiny, unafraid, streaky brown bird with reddish cap, hopping on ground

START HERE

Mark Your Calendar

Spring through fall in most regions; year-round or winter in SE, S, and parts of SW

Details, Details

- The size of a small sparrow (which it is!); 5½ inches
- Look for that reddish cap and an eye stripe.
- Plain gray breast, unlike similar tree sparrow (larger, with dark spot)
- Female looks like male

Listen Up!

- Long, monotone trill from the trees
- Sharp *chip!* alarm call

Telltale Traits

- Listen for that trill—you'll hear it a lot.
- Not a low-level skulker like most sparrows; often in trees, though it does also forage on the ground

Look Here

- Singing from small backyard trees

Or Here

- At feeder or on ground beneath it
- Foraging for seeds on ground in winter flower garden or vegetable patch
- Singing from a perch, usually moderately high in a tree

On the Home Front Frequent backyard nester • Mostly nests in conifers • Builds in trees or shrubs • Often picks a yew near the house as a nest site

"Who does not know this humblest ... little neighbor that comes hopping to our very doors?"

—**Neltje Blanchan**, *Bird Neighbors* (1897)

Chipping sparrows still come hopping to our doors, so why not get to know these little neighbors? They're common summer residents in town and country, in just about any yard that has at least a small tree and garden.

Wild Menu: Small seeds, especially grass and weed seeds; a few insects

Plant Picks: Weedy grasses, including foxtail grass and crabgrass, are a big hit. Or plant millet or finch mix for a self-serve banquet.

Feeder Pleasers

- Millet

Tricks and Treats

- Chippies eagerly accept horsehair for their nests. Ask at a stable for tail or mane combings.
- Pour a handful of birdcage grit on bare ground below the feeder, or in an open tray feeder.

Finding the Nest

I always like to know where the birds in my yard are nesting. Most are so secretive, it's usually winter before I find out where they raised their family during summer.

But I've had good luck finding chippy nests, because these birds seem to lack any fear of me. Just keep an eye open for a chippy coming and going to the same place day after day. Binoculars will help you see what's happening without taking the chance of disturbing its family.

House Sparrow

First Impression

Big, brown, stocky sparrow with black bib, usually with a bunch of loudly chirping friends

Mark Your Calendar

Year-round

Details, Details

- Large sparrow size; 6¼ inches
- Gray crown and white cheeks
- Female is much drabber and lacks the bib

Listen Up!

- Frequent chirps
- The flock produces a constant chorus of chirping.

Telltale Traits

- Always in a flock
- Frequently squabbles with companions
- Dust baths are a popular activity; look for a few to several birds "splashing" in a dusty spot in your yard.

Look Here

- At the feeder

Or Here

- In a bush near the feeder
- On the ground

On the Home Front Unloved by bluebird fans, due to habit of commandeering nest boxes • Nests in cavity, birdhouse, dense vine, or sometimes in a tree—in spaces that can be completely filled up with leaves and other nesting materials • Often leaves nest materials trailing from entrance of birdhouse

"Too pestiferous to mention"

—H. E. Parkhurst, *The Birds' Calendar* (1894)

A bulletin issued in about 1900 by the Department of Agriculture warned that the progeny of a single pair of house sparrows could amount to precisely 275,716,983,698 in only 10 years! Introduced as "English sparrows," though they actually hailed from Africa, the birds are still abundant but not pestilential. They're common city birds, but not nearly as plentiful as they once were.

Wild Menu: Seeds; insects

Plant Picks: You won't need to do anything special to attract house sparrows. But they'll enjoy a birdseed garden for fall and winter foraging.

Feeder Pleasers

- Millet; any other seed they can crack

Tricks and Treats

- House sparrows relish a good, splashing bath, and they're fun to watch.

Let Me Introduce You

The introduction of new species of birds to America rapidly lost its charm after the population explosion of the house sparrow and the starling. But not all intros met with such "success."

If you're visiting near St. Louis, watch for a bird that looks a lot like a house sparrow, but has a bright reddish brown crown and not much of a bib. That's the Eurasian tree sparrow, introduced in 1870 to "enhance the North American avifauna." Unlike the pushy house sparrow, this one stayed in a relatively confined area and behaved itself.

Common Grackle

First Impression

Big, shiny, long-tailed black bird stalking proudly on ground

Mark Your Calendar

Year-round in many areas; spring through fall in parts of W, N, MW, and NE; absent in parts of W, NW, and SW

Details, Details

- Bigger than a robin; 12½ inches
- Pale yellow eye
- Beautiful blue/purple iridescence on head; bronze iridescence on body and wings
- Wedge-shape tail is distinctive in flight
- Male is more iridescent than female

Listen Up!

- Creaking, grating *kuh-reeez* or other harsh noises

Telltale Traits

- Stalks around, doesn't hop
- Drops wings and bows while *screek*-ing
- Eats eggs and young from other birds' nests so often is pursued by other birds
- May arrive in large flocks during migration

Look Here

- On lawn

Or Here

- At feeder
- Singing from top of conifer
- Scything through leaves for insects

On the Home Front Begins nesting early in season • Usually builds nest in conifer, such as spruce or juniper • Makes a large nest, often with strips of paper, string, and bits of wire

"Squeaking and whistling like creaking sign-boards"

—Ralph Hoffmann, *A Guide to the Birds of New England and Eastern New York* (1904)

Grackles have quite a repertoire of wheezy, mechanical songs—like the repeated creaking of a swinging signboard that needs a drop of oil.

Wild Menu: Seeds; grain; insects; plus other birds' eggs and nestlings, mice, salamanders, fish, and fast-food leftovers

Plant Picks: Your lawn and feeder will be enough of an attraction to lure all the grackles you could possibly want. If you let fall leaves nestle into place below trees and shrubs instead of raking them, you also may be visited by migrating flocks.

Feeder Pleasers
- Millet; cracked corn; sunflower seeds

Tricks and Treats
- Grackles enjoy a birdbath.

Wearing Out Their Welcome

Some backyard bird lovers aren't fond of grackles, because the birds arrive in groups that can clean out a feeder in no time.

Imagine if you were tending a hundred-acre "feeder." In South Dakota, where huge farm fields are planted with sunflowers whose seeds are targeted for our backyard bird feeders, grackles have become huge fans of the stuff. The birds' traditional mixed diet has given way to one that's almost entirely sunflower seeds, eaten from the field. That can put quite a dent in the harvest.

Red-Winged Blackbird

First Impression
Black bird with vivid red shoulders

Mark Your Calendar
Year-round in most areas; spring through fall in parts of NE and N

Details, Details
- A little smaller than a robin; 8¾ inches
- Look closely for the yellowish border below the red epaulets
- Female is streaky brown with yellow tinge on face and throat

Listen Up!
- A screaking *oh-kuh-REE!*
- A sharp *chack!* call note
- Harsh rattle

Telltale Traits
- Often walks about on ground, hopping when necessary to catch up with flock
- Male is usually on visible perch; female generally stays hidden
- Often in groups or flocks
- Males often battle fiercely over females.

Look Here
- At or below feeder

Or Here
- On lawn

On the Home Front May nest in cattails in water; at edges of bodies of water; in dense, grassy, or weedy fields; or in brush • Usually nests in colonies • Nest is large, woven from coarse grasses or cattails and finished with a finer lining • Raises two broods a season

START HERE

"Most effective when seen from in front"

—**Charles Townsend**, *The Birds of Essex County* **(1920)**

The red patches of the male redwing are nearly covered up when he is feeding. But as Townsend says, "when his love passions are excited," the redwing puffs out his gorgeous scarlet epauletes.

Wild Menu: Seeds; insects; some fruit and berries

Plant Picks: Try growing a patch of broomcorn or milo to supply fall and winter food for this species.

Feeder Pleasers
- Millet; cracked corn; birdseed mix; chick scratch; stale bread, corn muffins, and other grain-based products

Tricks and Treats
- You won't need anything but a steady supply of feeder food to keep these birds coming around.

A Cloud of Smoke

When I used to drive home in southern Indiana, I'd often notice what looked like a cloud of smoke on the horizon, far out across the endless flat fields of corn or soybean stubble. The smudge would darken, then dissipate until it was hard to make out, then just as suddenly draw together into a black puff again. Sometimes the "smoke" would veer suddenly in one direction or another, even when there was no wind.

What I was watching wasn't smoke at all, but the cloud made by 30,000 or so far-off red-winged blackbirds. All winter long, they'd range here and there over the farm fields, settling down to feed after a while, then swirling up and regrouping to try another spot.

European Starling

First Impression

Dumpy, waddling, voracious, *screal*-ing, blackish bird

Mark Your Calendar

Year-round

Details, Details

- A little smaller than a robin; 8½ inches
- Female and male look alike
- From fall through winter, the birds acquire a spattering of little "stars" on their bodies—actually the pale tips of their new coat of feathers—and a darker beak.
- From late winter through summer, the birds wear breeding plumage, gleaming with a pretty greenish purple iridescence and lacking their spots. Their beaks also turn yellow.
- It's easy to mistake young starlings for young cowbirds: They're plain, soft gray-brown.
- Often wrongly called grackles, the starling has a much squatter appearance and shorter tail than those svelte, long-tailed birds.

Listen Up!

- A wild array of squeals, squeaks, and hissing chatter
- Also a lovely, liquid, musical song
- Often mimics other birds or mechanical sounds that it hears frequently: Does your garden gate need a drop of oil?
- One of the first birds to begin singing, often in late winter

Telltale Traits

- Usually in flocks, which descend en masse on a likely food source
- Notorious for taking advantage of the hard work of flickers and other woodpeckers, starlings often wait until the other birds have excavated a nest hole, then intimidate them into leaving it. Sometimes all it takes is a lurking pair of starlings to "encourage" the homebuilders to seek another site.

"Even then they do not mean to be a bother"

—**Wilfrid Bronson,** *Starlings* **(1948)**

If starlings were rare birds, we'd probably find them fascinating. But familiarity, in this case, definitely breeds contempt. It's hard to find a starling appreciator, which is why I adore Bronson's little book. The birds do have their good points, if you can look beyond their pest potential. These common birds are tops at destroying many of the six-legged pests that plague our backyards—particularly Japanese beetles.

Telltale Traits—*Continued*

- Often walks about on ground, stabbing into the soil
- In winter, starlings join together in flocks that can number in the tens of thousands.

Look Here

- Scarfing down your feeder foods, especially suet and other soft (and expensive) treats

Or Here

- On the lawn
- In a fruit tree or bush, eating the fruit
- At the birdbath

On the Home Front One of the reasons for starling unappreciation is the birds' habit of commandeering other species' nest holes. Woodpeckers are frequent victims. • Another reason most folks aren't fans of starlings: They often cram their huge, bulky conglomeration of a nest into an opening they create or discover around your house. Under an eave, in a porch ceiling, or in a chimney are prime locations. • The nest itself is a messy affair, spilling over with twigs, straw, grasses, plastic wrap, paper trash, and other flotsam. (At least they recycle.) • Typically several broods a year are raised, so once the first set of fledglings flies the coop, remove the nest and plug up its place.

Wild Menu: Ah! This is where the praise comes in. Starlings eat countless numbers of destructive insects and their larvae, including Japanese beetles and European crane flies. If you're an alfalfa farmer, you may appreciate their position as No. 1 destroyer of the clover weevil. They also eat a lot of fruit, plus weed seeds, grain, and leftovers gleaned from the trash.

Plant Picks: You probably won't want to encourage starlings, but they do love holly berries (*Ilex opaca* and other spp.).

Feeder Pleasers

- Suet, soup bones, meat scraps; any kind of bread products; halved apples, which will provide you plenty of entertainment as the birds pick them completely clean, leaving nothing but the thin peel; softened dog food; millet, birdseed mix, and just about anything else they can get down the hatch. Sunflower seeds are not attractive, although they may be eaten if nothing better is around.

Tricks and Treats

- To keep starlings from swamping your feeders, give them their own diner, away from other offerings. Stock it with the foods they enjoy, and they may stay there instead.
- Starlings are fun to watch splash in a birdbath. A heated birdbath is a huge hit in winter.

Shakespeare, Mozart—and Starlings

The first starlings were released in New York's Central Park by Eugene Schiffelin, a well-meaning and eccentric New Yorker who wanted to import every bird ever mentioned in Shakespeare's plays. Starlings only get one mention in all of the bard's works, in a scheme intended to disturb King Henry IV by repeating the name of a distrusted earl:

> The King forbade my tongue to speak of Mortimer. But I will find him when he is asleep, and in his ear I'll holler 'Mortimer!' Nay I'll have a starling shall be taught to speak nothing but Mortimer, and give it to him to keep his anger still in motion. (*Henry IV*, Part 1, Act 1, Scene 3)

Mozart kept a starling for a pet and was so attached to it that he gave it a funeral when it died, complete with veiled mourners and a procession to its grave.

Whatever your feelings toward starlings, you're likely to see less of them. The species is declining both here and in Europe, for reasons no one yet knows.

115

Brown-Headed Cowbird

First Impression

A unique color combo: black body with brown head

Mark Your Calendar

Year-round in many regions; spring through fall in most of W

Details, Details

- Smaller than a robin, bigger than a sparrow; 7½ inches
- Black feathers are iridescent green in sun
- Female is dull grayish brown all over

Listen Up!

- Quiet, gurgling notes interspersed or followed by high, thin whistle
- Rattling *kkkkk* when alarmed

Telltale Traits

- Usually seen in pairs or flocks
- Males engage in weird poses: drooping wings, puffed chest, stretched neck.
- Female is extremely sneaky when approaching other birds' nests

Look Here

- At or below feeder

Or Here

- Walking on lawn
- Got a horse or other livestock? Look for cowbirds in your barnyard.

On the Home Front Cowbirds are parasitic: The female lays her eggs in other birds' nests for them to raise. • Usually only one cowbird egg is laid in a host's nest. • The eggs are white, speckled with brown. • Many birds don't recognize the eggs as not their own, even if they lay eggs of a completely different size or color.

"Then he would bow or bend his head"

—Herbert Friedmann, *The Cowbirds: A Study in Biology of Social Parasitism* (1929)

Blackbirds, including the cowbird, are famed for odd postures during courtship. Charles Townsend wrote to Friedmann: "A male would look up, puff up feathers, spread wings and tail, and fall on head." *Fall* is right: The bird simply keels over, with head and breast hitting the ground.

Wild Menu: Seeds; insects; small fruits

Plant Picks: Don't encourage these birds if you can help it. You probably can't, since cowbirds eat many of the same foods that songbirds do.

Feeder Pleasers

- Cowbirds will eat just about any seeds or grain you put out for other birds.

Buffalo Bird

Way back when shaggy bison roamed the country in huge numbers, and cattle were much fewer, the cowbird was known as the buffalo bird. Flocks hung out wherever buffalo congregated. The reason for the attraction? Food, just as it is with cattle today.

As they lumber along, grazing beasts stir up millions of insects from the grass. Nimble cowbirds scoot among those heavy hooves to scoop up the insects. You may also spot cowbirds perched on the animals' heads or backs, searching for ticks or other tasty insects.

Northern Oriole

First Impression
A shocking flash of orange

Mark Your Calendar

Spring through fall

Details, Details

- A little smaller than a robin; 8¾ inches
- Baltimore race, the bird in the eastern two-thirds of the country, has a black hood; Bullock's race, the western counterpart, has an orange head with black cap and nape and black throat.
- Bullock's also shows flashy white wing patches, even with wings folded
- Females of both are paler yellow-orange, with drab brown-gray back and wings.

Listen Up!

- Loud, whistled song sounds like short, emphatic sentences
- Rattling *churr* when alarmed

Telltale Traits

- Usually seen in pairs or alone, except at good food sources during migration, particularly in fall
- Males can be pugnacious

Look Here

- Usually in tops of deciduous trees

Or Here

- At flowering trees, picking off insects
- Pulling fibers for nest from plants in flower garden, or collecting string or fibers you supply
- At nectar or fruit feeder
- At birdbath

On the Home Front In winter, when orioles are long gone, the old nests are easy to spot in bare trees

Bullock's oriole

"The herald of spring"

—Alexander Wilson, *American Ornithology* (1832)

Orioles return in spring with a fanfare of robust, whistled songs. Their voices are so distinctive that they can wake you up and pull you to the window to see who's singing.

Wild Menu: Insects; fruit

Plant Picks: Fruits of any kind, particularly sweet or sour cherries, mulberries (*Morus* spp.), and grapes

Feeder Pleasers

- Nectar feeder; halved oranges, pushed onto a spike; grape jelly and other preserves

Tricks and Treats

- Baltimore orioles immediately get busy courting after returning in spring.
- An old white sheet will give you a lifetime supply of thin strips of cloth to offer nesting birds. Keep strips about 6 to 10 inches long.
- Supply a source of fresh water; an old-fashioned birdbath is often popular.

Overdose of Ardor

Male Baltimore orioles are often at war over females. Frequently a third male will attempt to cozy up to a female while her mate is distracted by an interloper. Male orioles are fearless fighters, but they're, um, birdbrained. In my own yard, an ardor-crazed oriole attacked my dog's toy—a stuffed orange and black tiger. Made me laugh, but the hero was proud of himself.

Ruby-Throated Hummingbird

First Impression

Unmistakable tiny buzzing bird with dazzling ruby throat

Black-chinned hummingbird

START HERE

Mark Your Calendar

Spring through fall in eastern half of country; year-round at tip of Florida; black-chinned, the western counterpart, is also spring through fall in most areas

Details, Details

- Tiny! Smaller than a chickadee; 3¾ inches
- Ruby-throated has a green back that shines golden; male, a ruby-colored iridescent throat patch
- Black-chinned, a similar western species, has a purple throat and a significant black chin
- The colorful throat feathers, or "gorgets," look black when not in sunlight.
- Females of both species are green with a whitish belly.

Listen Up!

- Soft, chippering or warbling calls, like whistling through teeth
- A hum from the whirring wings; black-chinned's wings may produce a whistle in flight

Telltale Traits

- Flies like no other bird: backward, forward, and hovering in place.
- Black-chinned often pumps its tail while hovering, as if for balance.
- Both species engage in fly-catching behavior, zooming out from a perch to nab a passing insect, then returning to perch until the next one comes along.
- Ruby-throat can be aggressive, driving away much larger birds from anywhere near a favored food source.
- May also bathe during rain showers by perching with fluffed out feathers.
- Collects small insects from spiderwebs, as well as silken spider egg cocoons and web strands to use in nest-building.

"The old lilac bush by the well was 'swarming' with Hummingbirds"

—Jane Hine, "Observations on the Ruby-Throated Hummingbird" (1894)

During spring migration, hummers often gather in numbers at a flowering shrub or tree. Listen for the hum around lilacs (*Syringa vulgaris*), azaleas (*Rhododendron calendulaceum* and other spp.), weigela (*Weigela florida*), red buckeye and other buckeyes (*Aesculus pavia*, *A. parviflora*, and other spp.), red horse chestnut (*A. × carnea*), and tulip tree (*Liriodendron tulipifera*). Hummingbirds also visit early flowers during spring migration. Look for them nectaring at columbines (*Aquilegia* spp.), especially wild red columbine (*Aquilegia canadensis*), fire pink (*Silene virginica*), sweet William (*Dianthus barbatus*), and the popular groundcover, ajuga (*Ajuga reptans*).

Telltale Traits—*Continued*

- Hummingbirds rarely wallow in a birdbath, but they will eagerly "bathe" in the spray from a garden hose, fountain, or mister. Look for them zipping back and forth through the falling water, or sitting on a perch to catch the spray, then reteating to a dry place to fluff and preen their feathers.
- Frequently visits nectar feeders, but traffic will slow dramatically during nesting season, when hummingbirds become homebodies.

Look Here

- At nectar feeder

Or Here

- Drinking nectar at flowers, especially at red or orange-red blossoms and at tubular blossoms
- Drinking nectar at paloverde tree (black-chinned)
- Drinking nectar at mimosa tree (ruby-throated)
- Hummingbirds spend a lot of time resting their wings. Get in the habit of scanning for the silhouette of the tiny, long-beaked bird perched atop a metal shepherd's crook or the tippy-top of a shrub or trellis. You may also spot one on a slender branch of a young tree, usually in a relatively bare spot where foliage and twigs won't impede takeoffs and landings.

On the Home Front May nest in backyards, but incredibly hard to find—or even to notice • Looks like a knot on a tree limb • Builds a tiny cup about the size of a walnut, of plant down and spider silk; ruby-throat adds lichens to the construction • Black-chinned nests low, from 4 to 8 feet aboveground, often on branch over water or dry creek bed • Ruby-throat also often chooses a site on a branch over water, but builds higher, about 5 to 20 feet up

Wild Menu: Nectar; small insects; small spiders; tree sap

Plant Picks: Salvias (*Salvia* spp.) of any kind, beebalm (*Monarda* spp.) and other mints, trumpet vine (*Campsis radicans*), penstemons of any kind (*Penstemon* spp.), and a host of others

Feeder Pleasers

- Nectar feeder. Be sure your feeder is equipped with a water-filled "ant moat," to prevent a stream of six-legged nectar seekers from draining the feeder (and drowning inside), and with small grids called "bee guards" over the holes, to help deter stinging insects that may harass hummingbirds.

Tricks and Treats

- A misting device, attached to a birdbath or spraying into open air, provides a highly appealing, gentle bath for these birds.

Courtship Capers

In general, male birds of most species impress females by showing they can do it better—whatever "it" happens to be. Those with flashy feathers usually find some way to show off their colors. Others sing their hearts out, or find homesites that a potential mate might like.

With hummingbirds, it's superior flying skills that males use to say "Pick me!"

So how does a bird that can already perform miracles in flight stand out from the crowd? With aerial acrobatics, that's how. Each hummingbird species performs its own "air show," tracing loops, figure eights, and other gymnastics above a female they hope to impress.

The black-chinned and ruby-throated use a similar style of courtship flight: They trace deep U-shapes above the perched female to win her favor, climbing to a height of 15 feet or more, then swinging like a pendulum to and fro. It's jaw-dropping to watch. Focus on the birds in your yard, and you may see it for yourself.

Chapter Seven

Birds of the Northeast

The Northeast is home to an abundance of backyard friends. The number of species found here, and the numbers of individuals, show that this long-settled region is prime bird territory.

Yet a megalopolis and birds just don't seem to go together. From New York to Boston, it sometimes seems like one big gridlocked expressway, dense with subdivisions and people, people, people. It's a major hub of commerce, and it's home to the people who make that commerce run.

Wild things? Good luck to them would seem to be the rule.

Crazy as it seems, though, this intensively settled part of the country is actually heaven for backyard birds.

Cities and towns dating back to the 1700s did change the landscape long ago. But that means that their street trees, city trees, and backyard trees have had plenty of time to grow into grand old specimens. Their leafy boughs create an oasis of green around, over, and among the buildings and roadways.

Next time you fly over the area, take a peek down below. You'll see lots of green— and that's what keeps the Northeast so inviting to birds.

A REAL MIX

The Northeast is densely settled in most parts, although some areas (Hello, Maine! How's it going, upstate Pennsylvania? Good afternoon, northern New Jersey) are still surprisingly wild. They haven't totally paved paradise—yet.

The sprawl from New York City often gets the blame—or credit, depending on how you look at it—for creating the eastern megalopolis. But even today, you can drive out of the city for 45 minutes and end up in a rural, or at least rural-feeling, area.

A big part of the reason for that country feel is the trees.

In the cities, plentiful public parks, old cemeteries, and other open spaces are filled with trees and shrubbery that make birds feel at home.

Chipping sparrows may roost in lilac bushes.

Backyards here are often comparatively large in these days of more typical postage-stamp-size lots. The big yards also are filled with big forsythia bushes, lilacs, and other mature plantings. Those hedges and shrubs

Evening grosbeaks eat maple seeds.

Forsythias may hold a cardinal nest.

are home to cardinals, brown thrashers, and many other backyard birds.

This region is Roger Tory Peterson's old stomping ground. It's also the birthplace of the Audubon Society and the American Ornithological Union (A.O.U.), the organization that keeps the official names and records of American birds nicely straightened out.

THE LAY OF THE LAND

Residential areas new and old share the region with small farms and pastures. Fertile river valleys and lakes created by spring-fed creeks and clear-running streams supply plenty of water year-round, making the region prime bird territory.

Well-weathered mountain ranges, their sharp spines worn to gently rounded slopes, provide totally different habitat for other bird species. Along with good skiing, you'll find nesting juncos, white-throated sparrows, warblers, and other northern birds in the Green Mountains of Vermont, the Poconos of Pennsylvania, the Catskills of New York, and other mountains of this region.

FOOD AND SHELTER

Native trees in the Northeast are a mix of oaks, maples, beeches, and other deciduous types along with some conifers, including the patrician eastern white pine and the eastern hemlock, under siege by woolly adelgids in

There are still plenty of wild places in the well-settled East, and even the cities are green with trees. From the air, it's easy to see the connected corridors of trees along the Connecticut River Valley that provide a safe route for many birds as they move from town to country.

Asters and goldenrod paint fields in fall.

CLIMATE

Four seasons, and what beauties they are! The Northeast is famous for its trilliums, bloodroot, and other spring wildflowers, and for its summer field flowers of asters and goldenrod. In fall, the red maples, sugar maples, and other trees are so spectacular that national bus tours run sight-seeing trips. Winter brings a snowy frosting and scarf-snuggling cold, well below freezing.

Rain is pretty evenly distributed over the seasons, including winter's snow. Summers are humid, often with gusty thunderstorms that can knock a robin's nest right off its branch.

Northerly parts of the region have more intense and longer-lasting cold. But extreme summer heat usually lasts only a few days at a time. Droughts and floods may occur.

Keep a reserve supply of seed in case of ice storms. Your cardinals will thank you.

some areas. All offer plenty of seeds, cones, and insects for birds. Wild cherries (*Prunus* spp.), beach plums (*Prunus maritima*), and other fruit-bearing trees and bushes give birds some variety in their diet. Street-side plantings and backyard trees broaden the menu mix even more. And all of the plants supply nesting places and cover.

Smaller seed-eating birds, including goldfinches and native sparrows such as tree sparrows and field sparrows, find abundant food in the meadows, along roadsides and woods' edges, and in backyards, where dandelions and other weed seeds are often abundant. Farm fields and pastures give ground-dwelling birds, such as grasshopper sparrows, Henslow's sparrows, and meadowlarks, a perfect homesite. And wooden fence posts and old orchards supply the habitat that's most desired by the bird that's most desired—the eastern bluebird.

BIRD LIFE
IN THE NORTHEAST

Birds are abundant in this region, thanks to ample cover and water throughout the area. Most of them spread out to cover other territories besides the Northeast; only a handful is limited to this region.

Many backyard birds, including feeder friends such as blue jays, song sparrows, and downy woodpeckers, are year-round residents in the Northeast. Catbirds, house wrens, and other species stop in just for summer, retreating to warmer regions for winter.

Start Here

Because the Northeast is home to so many widespread species, you'll want to turn back to Chapter 6, "Start Here," to find your most familiar backyard friends.

These are the birds you share with other parts of the country—chickadees, white-breasted nuthatches, tufted titmice, goldfinches, juncos, cedar waxwings, and many others.

Every single one of the "Start Here" birds is happily at home in the Northeast region.

Regional Specialties

You'll find other favorite friends spotlighted in this regional section. Some of these birds also occur in other regions. But every single one of them may turn up in your northeastern backyard.

Be sure to page through the birds of the Far North, too. Many of them pay a brief visit to northeastern backyards as they pass through on migration to and from more northern areas or mountainous parts.

Birds of the Northeast

Here's a list of the birds you'll find in this chapter. Remember to consult the "Start Here" birds, starting on page 79, for the most common birds to be found in the Northeast.

Yellow-Bellied Sapsucker

First Impression
Nondescript woodpecker playing peekaboo around a tree trunk

Mark Your Calendar
Spring through fall

Details, Details
- Slightly smaller than a robin; 8½ inches
- Female has white, not red, throat

Listen Up!
- Mewling or squealing, repeated *clee-ah*
- Sound is peculiar, like a complaining cat

Telltale Traits
- Look for black throat and yellow belly in flight
- Quiet and inconspicuous on migration, but real loudmouths once they get to where they're going
- Drills neat rows of small holes in tree bark and returns frequently to same tree

Look Here
- Usually clinging to trunk or major limb of a living deciduous tree

Or Here
- Males noisily chase each other in mating season in spring, making quite a racket.
- Can be a hog at nectar feeders, drinking sugar water for an hour or longer

On the Home Front Nests in a hole high in a tree • The male bird does most of the excavating of the nest hole and shares incubating duty and those incessant feeding chores.

"Each pair have a 'sugar orchard' of maple or birch, to which they resort constantly to drink the sap"

—**Ralph Hoffmann,** *A Guide to the Birds of New England and Eastern New York* **(1904)**

Sapsuckers drill neat rows of holes in tree trunks and keep them in good working order. They return daily to maintain the holes and to sip the sap and nibble the insects that have accumulated there.

Wild Menu: Sap; insects at sap

Plant Picks: Sapsuckers drill at more than a thousand kinds of trees: Apple, maple, birch, and pine are perennially popular.

Feeder Pleasers
- Nectar feeder; shelled pecans; suet feeder nailed to vertical board or tree

Tricks and Treats
- May use a birdbath

Tapping the Sap

Before you snicker at a sapsucker, consider this: Even our best scientists haven't figured out yet how these birds get tree sap to keep flowing.

Phloem sap is a tree's lifeblood, so the tree quickly stanches the flow. But not so at sapsucker holes, where the sap stays liquid. The latest theory is that sapsucker spit may contain some kind of anti-coagulant that enables the phloem sap to fill the holes that sapsuckers drill.

If it weren't for sapsuckers, ruby-throated hummingbirds couldn't survive so far north, where flowers are few. Their spring arrival is timed to the period of peak sapsucker activity. Bats, flying squirrels, porcupines, warblers, and nuthatches share the sap, too.

Hairy Woodpecker

First Impression

A big "downy woodpecker" with a long, heavy bill

Mark Your Calendar

Year-round

Details, Details

- Almost as big as a robin; 9¼ inches
- Female lacks red patch on head

Listen Up!

- Sharp, loud *peek!*
- Long bursts of very fast drumming with beak on hollow tree or other resonant object

Telltale Traits

- Much rarer than the common downy woodpecker
- Never found on mullein or other weed stalks, unlike downy
- Often flakes off pieces of bark, a giveaway to its location overhead
- Sticks close to mature forests in summer; wanders about in fall and winter and may show up in backyards

Look Here

- On tree trunk or large branch, often of dead wood

Or Here

- At suet feeder

On the Home Front Drills out a hole in dead wood for its nest

"The young when first hatched are repulsive-looking creatures with enormously large heads ... "

—Charles Bendire, *Life Histories of North American Birds* (1895)

Good thing the hairy woodpecker's nest is in a cavity in a tree, hidden from bird-watchers with delicate sensibilities! The big-headed babies soon grow feathers and look like punk rockers when they leave the nest 3 weeks later.

Wild Menu: Insects drilled from wood; acorns and nuts; a small amount of fruit

Plant Picks: Blackberries or raspberries

Feeder Pleasers

- Suet; insect foods; nuts and peanut-butter-based concoctions

Tricks and Treats

- It may take a while before a hairy investigates, but once it does, it'll be a firm fan of mealworms at your feeder.
- Rig up a harness of string or wire and hang a big, meaty bone with marrow intact. A ham bone is perfect for winter woodpecker feeding, if not exactly picturesque.

When in Doubt

I'm always trying to make downy woodpeckers into hairies. Listen—isn't that call a little louder? And the bird a little bigger? And doesn't that beak look thicker than a downy's?

Sorry, but no. What I've learned over the years is a simple guideline: When in doubt, call it a downy. When you see a hairy, you'll know. A hairy woodpecker is so much bigger than a downy (practically robin size!) and its beak is so much stouter, that there's no mistaking it.

It's always a good idea to take a second look at any woodpecker. But when you can't tell immediately whether you're looking at an ultra-common downy or a rarely seen hairy—sorry, but it's probably a downy.

Red-Bellied Woodpecker

First Impression

Big, calm, red-headed woodpecker at feeder

Mark Your Calendar

Year-round

Details, Details

- Almost as big as a robin; 9¼ inches
- Female has red only on back of neck, not top of head

Listen Up!

- Loud, harsh, querulous *quirrrr?*, as if asking, "Where's my food?"
- Steady, medium-speed drumming

Telltale Traits

- Back and wings look grayish from a distance; up close, appear finely black-and-white zebra striped
- Undulating flight, with deep dips
- Often very tame; slow to fly away when you approach

Look Here

- At the feeder eating sunflower seeds or squirrel corn

Or Here

- Clinging to tree trunks or large branches
- Foraging on the ground
- At suet or nectar feeder

On the Home Front Happily accepts a nest box • Also drills out its own home in a dead tree or limb, or in a wooden utility pole or fence post • Often returns to same nest box or cavity the next year • Both parents incubate the eggs and care for the young.

"The drumming and tapping of the busy feathered workmen on a resonant limb is a solace, giving a sense of life and cheerful activity which is invigorating."

—Neltje Blanchan, *Bird Neighbors* (1897)

Unless that resonant woodpecker drumming happens to be on your house, that is. Try a big squirt gun or a spray from a hose to prevent that Swiss cheese look in your siding.

Wild Menu: Insects; seeds; nuts; fruit

Plant Picks: Pecans, oaks, hazels, for nuts; corn or Indian corn; tall, large-headed sunflowers (*Helianthus annuus*); mulberries (*Morus* spp.), elderberries (*Sambucus* spp.), blackberries, raspberries, grapes, and apples

Feeder Pleasers

- Whole ears of dried corn on cob; sunflower seeds; suet and suet-based foods

Tricks and Treats

- Squirrel feeders that hold a fixed ear of corn work great for this big guy to peck at, too.
- Fasten a wire suet cage firmly to a vertical board or tree to give this bird a place to prop its tail to help support its big body.
- May become a nectar drinker

Belly Up!

I'd love to know who first decided this bird's name, because I have a feeling it's someone who didn't like to admit a mistake. The splashy red-decorated head is the first thing you'll notice about this bird. But since there's already a "red-headed woodpecker," this poor bird was named after its red belly—which is really hard to see. As the woodpecker contorts itself at your feeders, you may catch a glimpse of the tiny red-tinged feathers centered low on its belly. If you get a glimpse, then you, too, can say, "Red-*bellied* woodpecker? Ya gotta be kidding me!"

Eastern Phoebe

First Impression

Erect, perched, plain bird with nervously dipping tail

Mark Your Calendar

Very early spring through early fall

Details, Details

- Smaller than a robin and just a little bigger than a sparrow; 7 inches
- Female and male look alike

Listen Up!

- This one's easy: The bird says its own name, except it sounds more like *FEE-we*. The hoarse, whistled song goes like this: *fee-wee-we, FEE-we*. It's repeated over and over and over.
- Also makes a clear, high *chip*

Telltale Traits

- Long, loose tail that's in constant motion: Dip down, raise; dip down, raise—as if tracing and retracing the letter U.
- Sits quietly perched for long stretches, then sallies out after an insect

Look Here

- On a low, conspicuous perch, such as a fence post

Or Here

- Making a nest above a door frame or on a rafter in a shed

On the Home Front The sweet mossy nest, lined with feathers, is saddled to a support, such as a rafter or door frame.• The birds often recycle materials from an old nest; they may also reuse an old nest after some remodeling.

"It is not only fine feathers that make fine birds."

—Aesop

The quietly colored phoebe may not be a glamour queen, but its early spring arrival and its habit of building its nest on the garden shed make it a special friend in the backyard.

Wild Menu: Insects, especially flying insects

Plant Picks: No particular plants attract phoebes. Avoid pesticides: Tent caterpillar moths are a big favorite of phoebes.

Feeder Pleasers

- Doesn't visit feeders

Tricks and Treats

- Buy sphagnum moss at a florist or craft shop. Soak a generous handful in water for several hours, then gently squeeze and shake out some of the excess water. Keep moist and it will begin to green up in a few days. Offer to phoebes and other nest-builders by draping it on a twig.
- A birdbath is welcomed, especially one with a spray or dripper.

Many Happy Returns

Phoebes nested behind John James Audubon's house along the Perkiomen Creek, west of Philadelphia. In 1803, curious if the same birds returned year after year, the famed ornithologist wrote about an experiment he'd tried:

"When they were about to leave the nest, I fixed a light silver thread to the leg of each, loose enough not to hurt the part, but so fastened that no exertions of theirs could remove it. At the next year's season when the Phoebe returned to Pennsylvania, I ... caught several of these birds on the nest, and I had the pleasure of finding two of them had the little ring on the leg."

Great Crested Flycatcher

First Impression

Sudden swooping dash by big grayish and chestnut bird with long tail and loud voice, saying *wheeEEEEP!*

Mark Your Calendar

Spring through early fall

Details, Details

- A little smaller than a robin but seems larger due to its habits; 8¾ inches
- Female and male look the same

Listen Up!

- Raucous voice; a distinctive, loud *wheep* or *kweep* call with a rising tone
- Combination of *kweeps* and *kwips* in an excited chatter

Telltale Traits

- Feisty and irascible—fights with other males, sometimes battling in midair
- Flashes rusty tail and wing feathers in flight
- Raises and lowers head feathers when perched or agitated

Look Here

- Perches alertly on conspicuous treetop branch or other perch, near or in woods or big shade trees

Or Here

- Flying from one perch to another, near or in woods or shady yards
- Eating small fruit in trees

On the Home Front Adopts old woodpecker cavities as nest holes • Called the "snakeskin bird" for habit of tucking a shed snakeskin into its nest

"The wheep bird"
—Old traditional country name

That's a perfect name for this large flycatcher of woodsy places and shaded yards. The birds announce their spring arrival with ringing, musical *wheep* calls. Males seem to be always in a bad mood, yelling loudly while picking fights and threatening others of their kind.

Wild Menu: Insects, especially beetles; fruit

Plant Picks: Wild cherries, mulberries, grapes, blackberries, and raspberries

Feeder Pleasers

- Doesn't usually visit feeders; may be tempted by mealworms or other insect foods

Tricks and Treats

- Great cresteds are quick to make a home in your nest box, if you live near woods or in a neighborhood with plenty of old shade trees. Mount the box about 8 to 12 feet high on a tree, facing an open area. Better to use a too-big box than a too-small one; the birds will stuff it with leaves, grasses, and other filler to set their nest at the right level from the opening.
- May use a birdbath

Too Busy to Wheep

One year, a crop of mulberries on a tree down the road drew all kinds of fruit-eating birds, including fabulous orioles, tanagers, and bluebirds. It was easy to admire them among the greenery. I spent long stretches with my neck craned back, watching the feasting.

I didn't realize great crested flycatchers were there, too, until I caught a familiar flash of long, rusty tail. Sure enough, there were my big noisy friends, eagerly choffing down mulberries without a hoot or holler. I guess their beaks were too full of berries to make a fuss.

Tufted Titmouse

First Impression

Hyperactive little gray bird with pointy head

Mark Your Calendar

Year-round

Details, Details

- Sparrow size; 6½ inches
- Female looks like male

Listen Up!

- Clear, loud, whistled *Pete-o, Pete-o, Pete-o*
- High, thin, lisping notes when foraging in trees

Telltale Traits

- Never sits still for long
- Grasps sunflower seed or nut in feet and pecks with beak

Look Here

- Flying to or from feeder

Or Here

- In trees or sometimes in shrubs, picking off insects
- On ground below trees or feeder, briefly, snatching up bits of nuts or dropped seeds

On the Home Front Often nests near houses
- Builds nest in a natural cavity such as an old woodpecker hole, or in a birdhouse • Lines nest with soft hair • Brings young to feeder soon after they leave the nest

"The woods would be very silent if no birds sang there except those that sang best."

—**Henry Van Dyke, American poet, author, and clergyman (1852–1933)**

The tufted titmouse is a loud and enthusiastic singer, with a limited two-syllable repertoire. Yet his song is always a treat: It signals the end of winter long before the groundhog checks out his shadow.

Wild Menu: Seeds; nuts, including acorns; insects, especially caterpillars; small fruits

Plant Picks: Oaks, pecans, beeches, and other nut trees; mulberries, serviceberries (*Amelanchier* spp.), elderberries (*Sambucus* spp.)

Feeder Pleasers

- Sunflower seeds and chips; chopped nuts; suet, peanut butter, and other fat-based foods

Tricks and Treats

- Stuff a wire suet cage with soft materials for nesting: feathers, dog fur, hairbrush combings, and cotton balls.
- Birdbaths, from simple to elaborate
- Nest boxes mounted about 6 to 20 feet high

Helping Hand

Titmice are loyal feeder friends. And friendly they are—they often fly in to grab a bite while you're standing right there filling the feeder, especially if it's a cold or snowy winter morning.

Like chickadees, titmice are easy to hand tame. Just hold out a handful of whatever they like best at your feeder (nut pieces are usually a good bet), and stand quietly. You may get a taker right away, or it may take several mornings of patience before your new "feeder" is accepted.

Veery

First Impression

Cinnamon brown, robinlike bird with white belly

Mark Your Calendar
Spring through fall

Details, Details
- About the size of a large sparrow but looks like a downsized robin; 7 inches
- Female looks like male

Listen Up!
- The veery says its own name, with some poetic license, of course, in three or four phrases, gently spiraling downward. Most sound like some version of *vreee-uu,* as played on a wooden flute—or a melodious kazoo.

Telltale Traits
- Sings at dusk
- Male often sings from same perch in tree

Look Here
- On ground in shady gardens or woods, especially near streams

Or Here
- At naturalistic water features or birdbath
- At fruit trees and berry bushes in summer
- Flying overhead at night, on migration

On the Home Front Not usually a backyard nester • Nests on ground in its favorite haunts near a stream or in a wet, young woods • Visits backyards near its nesting grounds, or visits during migration

"If you would enjoy it you must bring an ear to hear."

—**Bradford Torrey, on the delights of the veery's song,** *Birds in the Bush* **(1885)**

Fans of the thrush family, which includes the veery, like to debate which of these birds is the best singer. Is it the fabled wood thrush, with its fluting melody? The ethereal hermit thrush? Many vote for the veery, with its haunting, delicate song.

Wild Menu: Insects, including gypsy moth caterpillars; small fruits

Plant Picks: Strawberries, Juneberries (*Amelanchier* spp.), blackberries, dogwood (*Cornus* spp.) berries eaten on fall migration

Feeder Pleasers
- May sample mealworms from a low feeder, but not usually a feeder visitor

Tricks and Treats
- The sound of water may lure the veery during migration. Try a ground-level naturalistic birdbath or constructed stream, with very shallow, nonslip pools for drinking and bathing.

The Woods at Dusk

The dawn chorus of songbirds is justly famous. But if you're rushing around getting kids off to school or yourself off to work in the morning, then you can reserve a seat for the evening performance instead.

Just make yourself comfortable near or in a woods, and listen quietly. Before long, you'll hear the sweet, unearthly voices of thrushes start up all around you. It's an experience you won't forget.

Nashville Warbler

First Impression

Tiny, fast, plain gray and yellow bird with a wide-eyed look

Mark Your Calendar

Spring through fall

Details, Details

- Smaller than a chickadee; 4¾ inches
- Female is similar, not quite identical, but lacks the small dab of red crown feathers that the male wears

Listen Up!

- And hear them you will: When Nashvilles come in, their trilling *seta-seta-seta-seeta-plee-plee-plee* seems to be everywhere.

Telltale Traits

- Distinct white ring around eye
- Has a stubby look due to shorter tail
- Typical active warbler

Look Here

- At catkins of oaks, birches, or other trees, picking off insects

Or Here

- At spring-flowering trees, collecting insects at flowers
- In any tree or shrub, from low levels to very high branches; females forage lower than males

On the Home Front Builds its well-hidden nest directly on the ground under a bush, beside a log, or otherwise disguised • Doesn't usually nest in backyards; prefers undisturbed places

"Nature does nothing uselessly."

—Aristotle, Greek philosopher (384–324 B.C.)

Wood warblers, including the Nashville, are always in motion, because they have a lot of work to do. They're a dead-serious defense for guarding the health of trees. These tiny birds are made for moving quickly through branches and leaves. The sharp beak of a single warbler can nip up hundreds of potential tree eaters every day.

Wild Menu: Insects, including tent and gypsy moth caterpillars

Plant Picks: Birches, firs, oaks, poplars, pussy willows, and many other trees; trees with dangling catkins are a likely choice

Feeder Pleasers
- Doesn't usually visit feeders but may like mealworms

Tricks and Treats
- Offer sphagnum moss in spring; it's a popular nesting material and the birds may accept your handout.

Changing Times

Nashville warblers are fairly common as warblers go, which means you have a good chance of spotting one in your yard. Scientists surmise that's because they can nest in a variety of habitats, from spruce bogs to second-growth woods to overgrown fields. This bird isn't a fan of deep, dark forests. As early settlers cleared the massive eastern hardwood forests, Nashvilles responded with boom years. Even today, soon after areas are logged, Nashvilles are likely to investigate the new territory.

Northern Waterthrush

First Impression

A bobbing, swaying, tail-wagging brown bird walking on the ground with a springy step

Mark Your Calendar

Spring through fall

Details, Details

- Sparrow size but looks like a small thrush; 6 inches
- Streaked white belly and white eye stripe
- Female looks like male

Listen Up!

- Musical, vigorous song, *sweet-sweet-sweet-see-swee,* falling off into a jumble of *chirps* and *chews*
- Call note an emphatic *whik!*

Telltale Traits

- Constantly bobs tail up and down, weaves and dips body
- Seems to have springs in its legs as it walks along; hops over obstacles
- Perches often

Look Here

- In your yard on lawn or under bushes

Or Here

- Near lakes or rivers, often on banks
- In swamps, bogs, or other standing water

On the Home Front Doesn't nest in backyards • Nests in the Far North, from Alaska to Labrador, on the ground, usually in sphagnum bogs or along lakeshores • Nest is hidden amid roots or in stumps • Green moss, twigs, pine needles, and animal hairs are used in construction.

"The world is mud-luscious and puddle-wonderful."

—E. E. Cummings, American poet (1894–1962)

The northern waterthrush agrees wholeheartedly with Cummings. These birds adore muddy banks, swampy pools, and puddle bogs. Give them a log with one end in the water, and it'll become a favorite promenade to stroll along.

Wild Menu: Insects; spiders; snails

Plant Picks: It's not particular during backyard visits; it may show up near shrubs and hedges, or on lawn. Rake additional leaves under your bushes in fall to attract beetles and snails and mimic wild habitat where the bird forages.

Feeder Pleasers
- Uninterested in feeders

Tricks and Treats
- If you're lucky enough to have a small pond or boggy area, place a dead tree limb or log with one end in the water, as an inviting perch.

The Thrush That Isn't

Waterthrushes look a lot like other thrushes at first glance. That brown back, streaky white breast, and habit of walking on the ground all say "thrush." And like thrushes, they're likely to show up in your backyard during migration. But the waterthrushes get their own genus in the wood warbler family, because they're not really thrushes at all.

The ovenbird looks a lot like the waterthrush, but it doesn't have the bobbing and swaying habit.

Scarlet Tanager

First Impression
Brilliant red with black wings

Mark Your Calendar

Spring through fall

Details, Details

- Smaller than a robin; 7 inches
- Male's color can vary from bright red to orange-red
- Female is greenish yellow

Listen Up!

- It has a long, hoarse, slurry song. A good way to find a tanager is to listen for a song from the treetops, then try to locate the singer.

Telltale Traits

- Vivid color and beauty are the best ways to ID a tanager.
- Slinks through tree foliage

Look Here

- High in trees, usually deciduous and especially oaks

Or Here

- At apples, crab apples, and other flowering trees, picking off insects at blossoms
- At your feeder in spring

On the Home Front Usually nests in woods

- Loose, shallow nest attached to tree limb, well out from trunk • Often high up, but may be at eye level

"Seldom conspicuous"

—**A. C. Bent**, *Life Histories of North American Blackbirds, Orioles, Tanagers, and Their Allies* **(1958)**

Despite its brilliant color, the scarlet tanager rarely catches our eye. It stays in the treetops, for one thing, and it moves quietly and smoothly through the branches, without flashing wings or squawking cries.

Wild Menu: Insects; fruit

Plant Picks: Fruits of any kind, particularly sweet or sour cherries and mulberries (*Morus* spp.); early spring flowering trees (crab apples, redbuds); dogwoods (*Cornus* spp.)

Feeder Pleasers

- Millet and other birdseed; chopped suet; mealworms and other insect foods

Tricks and Treats

- A simple saucer of fresh water is welcomed by tanagers on migration. A naturalistic birdbath with trickling water is even more effective.

Watch the Birdie

So much is going on in springtime, when tanagers arrive, that I often forget to watch for them. Besides, they're darn hard to see among all those newly leafed-out branches. Often I find one when I'm casually scanning the trees and spot a dark bird shape against the bright spring sky. A look through binoculars often reveals enough color to say, "Hey, that's a tanager!" Then all I have to do is wait until it moves from a backlighted spot to a place where the sun hits its feathers and turns them fire-engine red. Beautiful!

Rose-Breasted Grosbeak

First Impression

Flashy black and snow-white bird with rosy chest

Mark Your Calendar

Spring through fall

Details, Details

- A little smaller than a robin; 8 inches
- Female is streaky brown

Listen Up!

- Warbling song, similar to robin's
- Squeaky call note; Sibley describes it as "sneakers on a gym floor"

Telltale Traits

- Flashes big white wing patches in flight
- Female looks like an overgrown female purple finch

Look Here

- In shade trees or small trees

Or Here

- At apples, crab apples, and other flowering trees, picking off insects at blossoms
- At feeder

On the Home Front Nests usually fairly low to ground, eye level to about 15 feet • Birches and other small trees are popular nest sites. • Has adapted to nesting in backyards and city parks

"The potato-bug bird"

—Neltje Blanchan, *Bird Neighbors* (1897)

Rose-breasted grosbeaks were once famed for their appetite for potato bugs; they still indulge in our gardens today. Blanchan commended Pennsylvania farmers for recognizing the bird's effort—noting it was "more useful to their crop than all the insecticides known"—and protecting the bird from being shot.

Wild Menu: Insects, including gypsy moth caterpillars and Colorado potato beetle; tree buds; some fruit and seeds

Plant Picks: Mulberries (*Morus* spp.), Virginia creeper (*Parthenocissus quinquefolia*), grapes, maples native to your area for winter seeds

Feeder Pleasers

- Sunflower seeds

Tricks and Treats

- Becoming a regular feeder visitor, so experiment with mealworms and other insect foods
- Birdbaths are popular with migrants.

You Go, Girl!

I'm always leery when I spot two male birds giving each other "the eye" in spring. Battles over a female can be ferocious, and twice I've seen birds (not grosbeaks) actually kill an opponent.

But in the case of the rose-breasted grosbeaks that nested in my front yard, it was the female who took up the attack. When an unattached female arrived and started throwing coy glances toward the already-taken male, the original female didn't take any chances. Instantly she launched into action and fiercely drove the interloper far out of the yard. Then she returned to tenderly reunite with her mate.

Pine Grosbeak

First Impression
Very tame, rosy red bird

Mark Your Calendar
Winter; year-round in northern Maine

Details, Details
- A little smaller than a robin; 9 inches
- Blackish wings with white bars
- Female is greenish and gray

Listen Up!
- Soft, whistled song
- Quiet call notes keep a flock in touch

Telltale Traits
- Hangs around in small groups
- Very calm and easily approached

Look Here
- Eating berries in winter

Or Here
- Quietly perching
- At feeder
- In spruce, pine, or other conifers

On the Home Front Does not nest in NE except in northern Maine • Builds its bulky nest on a limb of a spruce, fir, or possibly a shrub • The open cup is loosely constructed of twigs and roots, with a wonderfully soft inner lining of rabbit fur and grasses—which also provide insulation on those chilly northern nights.

"It seems stupidly tame."

—A. C. Bent, *Life Histories of North American Cardinals, Grosbeaks, Buntings, Towhees, Finches, Sparrows, and Allies* (1968)

Maybe it's the lack of people in their Far North homeland, but pine grosbeaks and other northern birds are exceedingly tame when they periodically pay a visit to other regions. If you move quietly, you can refill the sunflower seeds while they sit at the feeder.

Wild Menu: Tree seeds, seeds from conifer cones, weed seeds; tree buds; also fruit and insects

Plant Picks: Junipers (*Juniperus* spp., with berries), barberries (*Berberis* spp.), American bittersweet (*Celastrus scandens*), mountain ashes (*Sorbus* spp.), many others

Feeder Pleasers
- Sunflower seeds

Tricks and Treats
- Pine grosbeaks are a great reason to have a reserve bag of sunflower seeds on hand: Winter flocks may number 100 or more birds!

Just Moping Around

In Newfoundland, home to that breed of big, black, seafaring dogs and hordes of pine grosbeaks, these sedate birds go by the name of "mopes." That means someone who just sits around, and sitting motionless is something pine grosbeaks do a lot.

But when they're eating, pine grosbeaks are great fun to watch, because they feed for much longer stretches than most birds do. That's because they're equipped with an extra-large *gular pouch,* which they can stuff full when they find a good food source—a nifty survival trick in a harsh climate.

Red Crossbill

First Impression

Very tame, rosy red birds that twist and turn upside down like parrots—and get a load of that beak!

Mark Your Calendar

Winter; year-round in Maine

Details, Details

- The size of a big sparrow; 6¼ inches
- The similar white-winged crossbill has two flashy white bars on black wings.
- Female is grayish green

Listen Up!

- Mechanical trilling song, often sung in chorus by flock
- Thin, weak call notes

Telltale Traits

- Travels in groups
- Uses beak and feet like parrot to crawl on branches
- Very approachable

Look Here

- Extracting seeds from conifer cones with that remarkable bill

Or Here

- At feeder
- In trees

On the Home Front Crossbills nest only in the northern parts of this region. • The nest is built in a pine, cedar, spruce, or other conifer, and cozily lined with moss, feathers, and fur. • Parents feed nestlings for weeks after they fledge, until their beaks cross into the shape that allows them to efficiently extract seeds from cones.

" . . . everything in nature is lyrical in its ideal essence, tragic in its fate, and comic in its existence."

—George Santayana, philosopher, essayist, poet (1863–1952)

Did someone say comical? Take a gander at the beak on the red crossbill, and you may think you're looking at Nature's sense of humor. Not so. It may look funny to us, but it's actually a serious tool for slipping between the scales of a pinecone and extracting the nutritious seeds.

Wild Menu: Seeds of conifer cones; also other tree seeds and buds; insects

Plant Picks: Any conifer native to your area; pines (*Pinus* spp.) are fast-growing

Feeder Pleasers
- Sunflower seeds; suet and other fat-based foods

Tricks and Treats
- Even in the dead of winter, birds enjoy fresh water. Invest in a heater for your birdbath, or set out a shallow container of warm water for a short-term solution.
- If you live in nesting territory, offer soft materials such as feathers or a scrap from an old fur coat.
- Crossbills, like other northern finches, are huge fans of salt. Try some rock salt in an open tray feeder.

Here Today, Gone Tomorrow

If somebody invites you to come over and see the flock of crossbills in her backyard, drop everything and get going! These birds are sporadic wanderers; there's no guarantee they'll be at the same place tomorrow. And when one leaves, the whole flock picks up and goes. A chance to admire these oddballs is worth putting other responsibilities off 'til tomorrow. Errands will wait, but the crossbills might not. Oh, and don't forget your camera.

American Tree Sparrow

First Impression

Small brown bird with reddish cap and dark spot on breast

Mark Your Calendar

Winter

Details, Details

- Sparrow size, of course; 6¼ inches
- Female looks like male
- Reddish stripe at eye (an "eye line")

Listen Up!

- Talks with others in a musical twitter, *teedle-eet, teedle-eet*
- High, sweet, warbling song not usually heard in winter

Telltale Traits

- Often in small flocks
- Bounding, zigzagging flight when crossing open space—hard for predators to follow

Look Here

- In feeder or on ground beneath it

Or Here

- Hanging on stems, eating weed seeds and grass seeds in garden beds
- Scratching for dropped seeds on the ground in flower beds or brushy places

On the Home Front A winter visitor only
• Nests way up North, near Santa Claus's homeland • Despite the name of "tree sparrow," the birds build their nests on the ground in the tundra.

"I once had a sparrow alight upon my shoulder for a moment, while I was hoeing in a village garden ... "

—Henry David Thoreau (1817–1862)

He continues: " ... and I felt that I was more distinguished by that circumstance than I should have been by any epaulet I could have worn." Maybe this winter a tree sparrow will sit on *your* shoulder?

Wild Menu: Seeds of weeds, grasses, and sedge; some insects

Plant Picks: Plant a few handfuls of finch mix or white proso millet to make these little guys happy all winter long. They'll clean off the seeds of any weeds you may've missed, too.

Feeder Pleasers

- Millet, by a mile
- Finch mix

Tricks and Treats

- A heated birdbath is the ultimate tree sparrow spa. An electric birdbath heater will pay you back with entertainment all winter long.

The Winter Chippy

You'll soon learn to glance at the breast of your sparrow visitors to verify the dark spot or "stickpin" that marks the plain breast of the tree sparrow. Without that dot, this little bird looks almost the same as its summertime cousin, the chipping sparrow, a favorite friend in the backyard.

But chipping sparrows ("chippies" for short) leave town when winter rolls in. That leaves the feast of seeds in your yard to the tree sparrow, or "winter chippy."

Field Sparrow

First Impression

Small brown bird with blank, wide-eyed look

"There is not a sprig of grass that shoots uninteresting to me."

—**Thomas Jefferson, American naturalist, gardener, and US president from 1801 to 1809**

Mark Your Calendar

Spring through fall; year-round in southerly part of region

Details, Details

- Small sparrow size, what else? 5¾ inches
- Pink bill
- Reddish cap and white eye ring; no dark spot on breast
- Female looks like male

Listen Up!

- Plaintive *see-a, see-a, see-a, see-a, wee, wee, wee, wee*
- Sharp, short *chip!* of alarm

Telltale Traits

- Vigorous scratcher on ground
- Often in flocks of mixed sparrow species

Look Here

- On ground beneath feeder, or in tray feeder

Or Here

- Scratching elsewhere in your yard for seeds, in flower beds or vegetable garden
- Hanging on weed or grass stems to reach seeds

On the Home Front Nests in thicket or thorny bush, usually in field but possibly in backyard • Well-made cup of dead grasses is placed on or near ground • Once called "huckleberry bird" for habit of nesting in those bushes

What's so special about a sparrow? Everything! Once you begin looking at birds, you'll find out that every species, even the commonest sparrow, can keep you fascinated for hours. There's not a single boring creature under the sun.

Wild Menu: Insects; weed and grass seeds

Plant Picks: A scattering of millet seed in your vegetable garden or flower bed will give you hours of fun, watching field sparrows and other sparrows at the stalks. No need to buy special seed; just plant some of your birdseed.

Feeder Pleasers

- Millet; canary seed and other small seeds

Tricks and Treats

- Like other winter sparrows, the field sparrow appreciates a warm bath on a cold day. Check out a heater for your birdbath.
- Nests are often lined with horsehair from the animal's mane or tail. Ask at a nearby stable for the currycomb leavings if you don't have your own trusty steed.

Bird Barometer

The number of sparrows at your feeder is a quick clue to the weather. Field sparrows and others will arrive in force at your feeder just before a snow or ice storm sweeps in. Apparently they can feel the change in air pressure, or perhaps some other clue alerts them to stock up in case food might soon be in short supply.

After a snow, field sparrows won't wait for you to clear off the feeders. They'll scratch deep holes to reach buried seed in a tray or on the ground. I once watched a field sparrow taking turns with a larger fox sparrow in the little clearing they'd managed to make after a snow—it only had room for one bird at a time.

Purple Finch

First Impression

Small raspberry-red bird with alert look

Mark Your Calendar

Year-round

Details, Details

- The size of a sparrow; 6 inches
- More intense all-over color and stouter than a house finch
- Female is streaky brown with distinctive light eye stripe

Listen Up!

- Fast, rising and falling, warbled song
- Call note is a sharp metallic *tick!*

Telltale Traits

- Can raise head feathers for an almost crested effect
- An erratic wanderer; some years may bring many, other years only a few

Look Here

- At tray or tube feeder

Or Here

- In trees

On the Home Front Nests in spruces and other conifers, often high aboveground • Often adds bits of shed snakeskin to nest • Nest lined with hair, wool, or other fine fibers

"Eats many of the seeds of the most destructive weeds"

—**Edward Forbush,** *Useful Birds and Their Protection* (1913)

Snifflers of America, rejoice! Ragweed seeds are a favorite of the purple finch. Small finches (and their cousins, the sparrows) do a gargantuan job of destroying future weeds. As with everything in nature, it's always a matter of balance.

Wild Menu: Seeds of trees and weeds; tree buds; some berries

Plant Picks: Red maple (*Acer rubrum*), birch (*Betula* spp.), conifers, sunflowers (*Helianthus annuus*), raspberries or blackberries

Feeder Pleasers

- Sunflower seeds; finch mix

Tricks and Treats

- Northern finches, of which this is one, are fond of salt—and also of the mortar used in brickwork. Put a small handful of rock salt into an open tray feeder, or set up a salt block.
- Purple finches usually retreat to the woods to raise their families. But if your yard is nearby, or has large conifers that might be considered for nest sites, try offering soft materials, such as tufts of natural wool, for lining.
- Birdbaths are popular year-round with purple finches.

Lover's Dance

A tango looks tame compared to the male purple finch's courtship dance routine.

When ardor grabs hold, the male flutters his wings vigorously while hopping and contorting. He thrusts out his breast, cocks his tail up, raises his crest feathers, and sings a love song, often while holding out a bit of nesting material to his beloved—just to help her get the hint, I suppose. Eventually, he's so overcome that he flies up, comes back down, and poses with drooping wings, tail propped, and head tilted to the sky.

Who could resist?

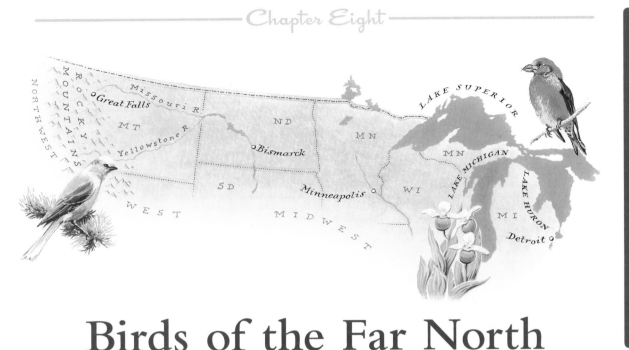

Birds of the Far North

So you live in the land of cold, snowy winters? Lucky you! Your region is home to many fabulous birds, including redpolls and tundra species that move in when they need a respite from homelands even farther north.

You get to see a whole other world of birds that other people only dream about. Meanwhile, birds such as crossbills, which folks in milder climes can only hope to host during an irregular irruption year, are yours to enjoy as nesters and summer residents.

WATER, WATER EVERYWHERE

This region is swimming in water. There are the Great Lakes, for starters, then countless smaller and shallower lakes formed by gla-

ciers. Freshwater marshes called "prairie potholes" dot the landscape in some areas, too. And you can't go far without finding a river, stream, or creek.

Add Heat and Wait

Summers are warm here. Add that heat to all that water, and you have the perfect breeding ground for one of the North's most famous "assets"—insects.

Millions of insects live in the water when immature, spending months creeping around on the bottoms of ponds and lakes. When warm weather comes, they emerge from the water, hatching into airborne hordes of black flies, mosquitoes, and the notorious no-see-ums.

Those insects make us slap and swear,

especially when we forget the repellent. But birds have another reaction: Yum!

A Bounty of Birds

Those tiny bugs bring hordes of birds into this region. Tiny wood warblers, svelte wax-wings, and many other species flock to the feast of winged insects. Toss in the caterpillars and other bugs among the branches of the region's many trees, and you have ideal habitat for insect-eating birds and their nesting families.

Room to Stretch

The northern tier of states is sparsely populated compared to many other regions of the United States. Cities are few and generally far

Snow can be frequent, deep, and drifting.

Canada or gray jays may visit your yard.

between. Homesteads are generously sized, with acres of elbow room. Small towns dot the landscape, and cows graze on the lush grass of dairy farms. Countless clear blue lakes and ponds, from "pothole"-size to acres-wide, are dotted across the land, many of them fringed by wild rice and rushes.

Why are there so few people in such an idyllic place?

Winter, in a word.

COLD CALLS THE TUNE

You'll need your mittens and your warmest coat when you live in the North. Winter is the defining quality of this region, where snow comes early and stays late. You're probably used to a thermometer that reads below zero, and so are your birds.

A challenging climate calls for specialized birds. In the North, you'll enjoy species that can make the most of conditions that would leave less well-adapted birds begging for mercy.

Here's where cold-hardy birds, including boreal chickadees and Canada jays, are thoroughly at home. Their diet and their dense feathers make them able to withstand the worst Mother Nature can dish out.

Although you'll find many of the familiar friends of the "Start Here" chapter in this region, you'll also see other wonderful birds that you can call your own.

THE LAY OF THE LAND

Fragrant balsam firs and other conifers thrive in this region, filling forests big and small, and springing up fast on any open patch of ground. Elegant white birches gleam against the dark-needled evergreen boughs.

Tree seeds—including a bounty of conifer cones—provide many a meal for nuthatches, crossbills, and other northern birds. Their big advantage is that these seeds stay above the snow, unlike weed and grass seeds.

In fall, the woods come alive with the foliage of golden birches, flaming maples, and other deciduous trees. In spring, if you're

Lakes and ponds provide abundant insects for birds of the North. So do the forests.

lucky, you may come across a knee-high patch of drop-dead-gorgeous pink lady's slippers (*Cyprideum acaule*).

Forests are one big feature of the North. But water is just as important.

Parts of the Far North are promoted as vacation hot spots: The turbulent water of the Wisconsin River at the Dells, the canoeing areas of Boundary Waters in Minnesota, and other places draw visitors from many miles away.

Even avian vacationers get into the act. To birds of the extreme North, up near the Arctic Circle, the Far North must feel like Hawaii. In some winters, those extreme northern species, such as Bohemian waxwings, pine grosbeaks, and redpolls, show up here in huge numbers.

Showy ladyslipper orchids glow in the woods.

INSECT HEAVEN

All those lakes and creeks for canoeing make the North a haven for water lovers. Don't forget to count insects among those fans. Many bugs spend part of their lives underwater, emerging into the air as hungry adults.

The North is famous for its swarms of pesky insects, including mosquitoes. In Roseville, Minnesota, you can take in the "Bluegrass Buzz," a festival that celebrates music *and* mosquitoes.

In other, more heavily populated regions, and in places with big agriculture, pesticide use is common. But in the wide-open North, pesticide use is relatively restrained. That's another reason why the region is a haven for insects—and the birds that eat them.

Many migrant birds, especially tiny wood warblers, are thick in the North. The insects they depend upon are wildly abundant here—*slap! slap!*

BIRD LIFE IN THE NORTH

Birds are abundant in this region.

Some backyard birds, including feeder regulars such as blue jays and downy woodpeckers, are year-round friends here.

Others, including the song sparrow and American goldfinch, are only warm-weather friends in the *brrrr!* North. In other regions, these birds are at home year-round.

Bird populations may shift from year to year in this region, because so many species depend on tree seeds—one of the few bird foods that remains accessible above deep snow. When the cone crop is slim, many birds depart southward. That's when bird lovers in other regions look out their window and exclaim, "Oh, look! Pine grosbeaks!"

Include evergreens for shelter in your yard.

Familiarize yourself with those common and abundant "Start Here" birds to get to know your most basic backyard friends. These are the birds you share with other parts of the country—chickadees, white-breasted nuthatches, tufted titmice, goldfinches, juncos, cedar waxwings, and many others. Then dive into the regional specialties here.

Regional Specialties

You'll find other favorite friends spotlighted in this regional section. Some of these birds also occur in other regions. But every single one of them may turn up in your northern backyard.

Be sure to page through the birds of the Northeast, Midwest, and West, too. Many of them pay a brief visit to northern backyards as they pass through on migration to and from more southern areas.

Start Here

The North shares many of the birds in Chapter 6, "Start Here," with other regions.

Birds of the Far North

Here are the birds you'll find in this chapter. Remember to consult the "Start Here" birds, starting on page 79, for the most common birds to be found in the Far North.

Black-Backed Woodpecker

First Impression
Medium-size black woodpecker

Mark Your Calendar

Year-round

Details, Details

- Robin size; 9½ inches
- Glossy black has blue sheen in right light.
- Male has bright yellow patch on crown
- Only has three toes; the bird lacks the second back toe.
- Resembles the three-toed woodpecker, but back is solid black instead of barred

Listen Up!

- Loud, sharp, *peek!* call
- Has a "scream-rattle-snarl" warning call. Easy to imagine!
- Long bouts of drumming with beak, starting slow but accelerating

Telltale Traits

- Flakes off bark as well as digs into wood
- Tame and easy to approach
- Awkward climber; may hop on ground
- Flies with typical woodpecker style: a wing flap followed by a bound

Look Here

- In irruption years, may show up in backyard or visit feeder

Or Here

- On conifers
- Foraging on logs
- On burned trees; listen for their calls.

On the Home Front Nests relatively high, in live or dead trees, especially conifers

"One bird will annually destroy 13,675 of these grubs"

—**Foster Beal, "Food of the Woodpeckers of the United States" (1911)**

Black-backed woodpeckers are eating machines when it comes to the larvae of wood-boring beetles. They help keep forests from being overwhelmed by wood eaters.

Wild Menu: Mostly larvae of wood-boring and other beetles, and a few other insects; acorns; small fruits

Plant Picks: During irruption, may visit a backyard conifer

Feeder Pleasers
- Try mealworms or suet

Tricks and Treats
- Plant a conifer native to your area.

Safety Glasses?

This woodpecker is one of the hardest-pecking birds around. Most woodpeckers keep their tails propped against the tree while pecking, but this guy gives such a strong whack that its tail actually lifts up for even more leverage.

Got a headache already? Not the woodpecker, which has special head bones that absorb the shock. The black-backed woodpecker does take one precaution: It closes its eyes when whacking wood, which helps protect them from flying splinters.

Hairy Woodpecker

First Impression

A big "downy woodpecker" with a long, heavy bill

Mark Your Calendar

Year-round

Details, Details

- Almost as big as a robin; 9¼ inches
- Female lacks red patch on head

Listen Up!

- Sharp, loud, *peek!*
- Long bursts of very fast drumming with beak

Telltale Traits

- Less often seen than the common downy woodpecker
- Never on mullein or other weed stalks, unlike downy woodpecker
- Often flakes off pieces of bark, a giveaway to its location overhead
- Sticks close to mature forests in summer; wanders about in fall and winter and may show up in backyards

Look Here

- On tree trunk or large branch, often of dead wood

Or Here

- At suet feeder

On the Home Front Drills a cavity high or low; excavation takes 1 to 3 weeks • The cavity is used for roosting, too: In Minnesota, the winter temperature inside averaged a whopping 37.4°F to 42.8°F warmer than the temperature of the tree surface outside.

"They utter a soft 'puirr, puirr'"

—Charles Bendire,
Life Histories of North American Birds (1895)

Baby woodpecker voices are the best clue to locating a nest hole. When you hear their unusual noises, try to track them down. But don't disturb them, or you'll miss out on the fun of watching the family grow up and leave home.

Wild Menu: Insects drilled from wood; acorns and nuts; a small amount of fruit

Plant Picks: Blackberries or raspberries

Feeder Pleasers

- Suet; mealworms and other insect foods; nuts and peanut-butter-based concoctions

Tricks and Treats

- It may take a while before a hairy investigates, but once it does, it'll be a firm fan of mealworms at your feeder.
- Rig up a harness of string or wire and hang a big, meaty bone with marrow intact. A ham bone is perfect for winter woodpecker feeding, if not exactly picturesque.

Telltale Tapping

Sometimes I don't know which I depend on more—my eyes or my ears. Listening has led me to many a woodpecker I never would've noticed just by looking. Even the big hairy is surprisingly well camouflaged against bark.

Listen for repeated tapping—much softer than drumming—and you may find a hairy, downy, or even a chickadee working away. Listen for the patter of something falling to the ground, and you're likely to track down a hairy at work, flaking off pieces of bark.

Gray Jay

First Impression

Tame, curious, large gray bird, like a giant chickadee

Mark Your Calendar

Year-round

Details, Details

- Bigger than a robin; 11½ inches
- Male and female look alike
- Plumage varies in different areas; head may be dark or whitish

Listen Up!

- Soft, whistled notes, not at all like a typical jay's screeches and squawks
- When alarmed or squabbling, the "jay-ness" comes out in a harsh rattle.

Telltale Traits

- Delightfully tame
- Hangs out in small groups
- Curious; investigates anything out of the ordinary, probably in hopes of food

Look Here

- At feeder—or on your hand

Or Here

- Nearby! They flock to people to see what's going on, and often follow us through the woods.

On the Home Front Nests very early, when it's still cold and snowy • Nests on branch of conifer, near trunk, at low to high levels • Breaks off dead twigs from branches for nest material; doesn't pick them up from ground

"The boldest of all our birds"

—Manly Hardy (now, *there's* a name!), *Life Histories of North American Birds* (1895)

Gray jays will be your best friends forever—if you give them a bite to eat now and then. They'll eat out of your hand with very little coaxing. Or off of your hat, or from your picnic plate, or out of your lunch bag, or anywhere they can find accessible edibles.

Wild Menu: Carrion and small rodents; caterpillars and other insects; wild fruit; and just about anything else they can get down their gullets

Plant Picks: Conifers native to your area for cover, and oaks (*Quercus* spp.) or Virginia creeper (*Parthenocissus quinquefolia*) for food

Feeder Pleasers

- Suet; meaty soup bones; bread and other scraps; dog food

Tricks and Treats

- Offer facial tissues and cotton puffs for nest materials; the birds may take them right from your hands if they happen to be building nearby.

King-Size Comforter

Brrr! There's nothing like a downy quilt on a cold winter night! Within minutes, the air from your body is trapped between the feathers, and you feel as if you're floating in a cozy cloud.

The same principle keeps gray jay babies from freezing—in fact, it keeps them snug and warm. Mama jay stuffs silken moth cocoons into the chinks between the twigs that form the foundation of her nest. Then she builds a deep, insulating cup of feathers or fur inside it. One nest that was dissected and inventoried contained 437 feathers, mostly those of ruffed grouse—a fine substitute for an expensive eiderdown quilt!

Boreal Chickadee

First Impression
> A gray and brown (not black), super-friendly chickadee

"Chick-chick"
—Old common name in parts of Canada

Mark Your Calendar
Year-round

Details, Details
- Chickadee-dee-dee size; 5½ inches
- Female and male look alike

Listen Up!
- Wheezy, distinctive call, not the classic; says *yesterdaaay* or *fee-lay-dee* in a chickadee voice
- Also a clear trill and a single, sharp, *dee!* note

Telltale Traits
- Like the typical chickadee: swinging from branch tips, flitting through foliage
- Always on the move
- But usually in a small group of like members; doesn't often pal around with other species like the black-capped chickadee does

Look Here
- At feeder

Or Here
- Branch tips and among foliage of conifers
- At conifer cones, often high up in balsam firs or other trees

On the Home Front Uses both conifers and deciduous trees • Usually nests low, less than 10 feet aboveground • One week after leaving the nest, fledglings are already adept at hanging from branch tips like their parents.

Tamest of all the chickadees, this friendly little mite is a favorite with northerners. Old timers (and some folks today) call it the chick-chick or fillady. The names reflect the calls the little bird frequently makes.

Wild Menu: Insects; conifer cone seeds; other seeds

Plant Picks: Any native conifer; annual sunflowers (*Helianthus annuus*)

Feeder Pleasers
- Suet; sunflower seeds; mealworms and other insect foods; peanut butter and other fats

Tricks and Treats
- Offer nesting materials, such as sphagnum moss, deer fur, rabbit fur, or any other soft materials, in a clean wire suet cage.

Saving for a Snowy Day

Winters are long in the North Woods, but this little bird has adopted a way to get through most of the lean times: It hides food in nooks and crannies, to retrieve later.

Even insects it has caught and killed are put aside for a snowy day. Most are the caterpillars of moths and butterflies, but researchers have even found the birds setting up a stash of aphids.

Like other birds of this region, boreal chickadees are an irruption species: Sometimes they move south, especially when the conifer crop is scanty and the pantry is bare.

Ruby-Crowned Kinglet

First Impression

Tiny, hyperactive, grayish bird with wide-eyed look, fluttering at branches

Mark Your Calendar

Spring through fall in some areas; migration only in others

Details, Details

- Smaller than a chickadee; 4¼ inches
- Distinct whitish eye ring
- Female lacks the male's ruby crown

Listen Up!

- Song is a lively melody of high, clear, whistled notes, falling in pitch near the end
- Call note is a husky *jit,* easy to recognize

Telltale Traits

- Always in motion; even more nervous in habit than golden-crowned kinglet
- Tame and easily approached
- Constantly flicks wings
- Often forages as part of a mixed flock of chickadees and others
- Jerky, undulating flight

Look Here

- Fluttering at branch tips of conifers

Or Here

- Among foliage of any trees or shrubs, often at eye level or low to ground
- May visit nectar feeder

On the Home Front Nests mid-level to high in conifers, especially spruce • Builds a deep, narrow, hanging nest; only the tail tip of the female is visible when she's in it

"One of our most brilliant songsters"

—**A. C. Bent,** *Life Histories of North American Thrushes, Kinglets, and Their Allies* **(1939)**

This is one of our tiniest birds, but with one of the loudest voices. Bradford Torrey described it in 1885 as "a prolonged and varied warble, introduced and often broken into, with delightful effect, by a wrennish chatter."

Wild Menu: Insects

Plant Picks: Any native short-needled conifer, or any native small tree, evergreen or deciduous, will host the insects these birds seek.

Feeder Pleasers
- A rare visitor, but try mealworms or other insect foods; may visit nectar feeders

Tricks and Treats
- Avoiding pesticides is the best thing you can do for tiny kinglets. No extra inducement is needed when your yard has insects to offer.

Migration Music

Fabulous birds are everywhere during spring migration, and I'm constantly swinging my binoculars and craning my neck to see who's singing now. With so many birds to look at—rose-breasted grosbeaks! scarlet tanagers! orioles!—it's easy to let kinglets slip by.

Except for their voice. When I hear that remarkable song, I automatically think it must come from a bigger bird, and I start scanning for the singer in the treetops. After way too long, I remember, "Oh, right, it's a *kinglet!*" And there he'll be, right under my gaze, pouring out his heart as beautifully as any "famous" songbird.

Swainson's Thrush

First Impression

Quiet olive-brown robinlike bird with speckled breast, on ground

Mark Your Calendar

Spring through fall in some areas; migration only in others

Details, Details

- Smaller than a robin; 7 inches
- Look for pale eye ring to distinguish from similar thrushes
- Female and male look alike

Listen Up!

- A long song of repeated phrases, in typical fluting thrush style. One transcriber suggests *whip-poor-will-a-will-e-zee-zee-zee*, rising at the end, and adds helpfully, "sometimes with an extra *a-will*."
- Piping call note sounds like a spring peeper.

Telltale Traits

- Often on ground, but also in shrubs and treetops
- Moves around on ground in long, bouncy hops
- May sing at night

Look Here

- On ground

Or Here

- At berry bushes

On the Home Front Usually nests in shrubs or in young spruce or other conifers, beneath taller trees • Seeks out delicate, lacy, skeletonized leaves to use in the lining of its mossy, grassy cup • Female is very wary when approaching the nest, giving nervous *whit* calls.

"These birds easily escape observation"

—**Frank Chapman**, *A Handbook of the Birds of Eastern North America* (1924)

Plant its favorite berry bushes and you may get to be friends with this quiet-colored thrush. By the way, Chapman, one of America's premier ornithologists, dedicated his handbook in this way: "to my mother, who has ever encouraged her son in his natural history studies."

Wild Menu: Berries; insects; snails

Plant Picks: Blackberries and raspberries; for migrants, shrubs and trees with fall-ripening berries, including spicebush (*Lindera benzoin*), flowering dogwood (*Cornus florida*), shrubby native dogwoods (*Cornus* spp.), and many others

Feeder Pleasers

- Doesn't usually visit feeders, but it may like mealworms and other insect foods

Tricks and Treats

- Offer moss for nest building.
- May visit a birdbath, particularly one near the ground

Love at First Song

Seems like every bird lover has a favorite thrush. For me, it's the Swainson's, which I often think of by an earlier name, the olive-backed thrush.

It was twilight on a soft spring day when a sweet, plaintive, spiraling song rose from the ravine I was following. Soon I heard a faint, fluting echo, equally sweet and mellow, then another and another. Swainson's thrushes were all around, making magic in the gathering dusk. That was it—I was in love.

Eastern Bluebird

First Impression

Unbelievable blue that takes your breath away

Mark Your Calendar
Spring through fall

Details, Details
- Smaller than a robin, as big as a large sparrow; 7 inches
- Female is duller, looks faded

Listen Up!
- Sweet, gurgling, whistled *tru-a-ly, tru-a-ly!*
- Brief, husky, *chew* call note that seems to keep birds in touch

Telltale Traits
- Travels in short, slow, fluttering swoops from one perch to another
- Often glides from low perch to ground with wings spread, to catch insects

Look Here
- Perched near or in open areas, often near the edge of a woods or orchard

Or Here
- In golf courses, cemeteries, large parks, or pastures, or on roadsides
- At apples, crab apples, and other flowering trees, picking off insects at blossoms
- At feeders or birdbaths

On the Home Front Nests in natural cavity or nest box • The female alone builds the nest. You may see a male carrying nesting material, but this "nest demonstration display" actually hinders the female's progress. • Nest is often made entirely of grasses or pine needles

"Somewhere there's a bluebird of happiness"

—From the song "Bluebird of Happiness," recorded by Art Mooney & His Orchestra (1948)

Happiness, indeed. Introduced at Radio City Music Hall, the song produced a best-selling record for Mooney and friends. Bluebirds seem to be irresistible, no matter what they're selling.

Wild Menu: Insects; fruit and berries

Plant Picks: Flowering trees; small fruits, including mulberries, serviceberries (*Amelanchier* spp.), winterberry and evergreen hollies (*Ilex* spp.), Virginia creeper (*Parthenocissus quinquefolia*), flowering dogwood (*Cornus florida*)

Feeder Pleasers
- Mealworms and other insect foods; accessible suet, peanut butter mixed with cornmeal, and other fat-based foods

Tricks and Treats
- The sound of trickling water is a big draw.
- Put up a roost box for bluebirds to stay at night.

Enemy No. 1: Jack Frost

Cold weather is the culprit in many bluebird deaths. Thousands of these pretty birds have died due to extreme cold, which may swoop in after the birds come back in spring.

Just as bad are spring snowstorms and ice storms, which prevent the birds from eating. You can help in tough times by keeping your feeder stocked with high-fat foods, such as peanut butter and finely chopped suet, so bluebirds don't waste precious calories to forage.

Bohemian Waxwing

First Impression

Plump, sleek, taupe bird, very tame, one of a flock

Mark Your Calendar

Winter, all areas except W near Canadian border, where it's year-round

Details, Details

- Smaller than a robin; 8¼ inches
- Get out your binocs! Like the cedar waxwing, this bird is beautiful in every detail. Look for the white wing patches and rusty patch under the tail that set it apart from the similar cedar waxwing.
- Female looks like male

Listen Up!

- Trilled *screee* calls similar to cedar waxwing

Telltale Traits

- Almost always in flocks, small or large
- Very tame
- May be mixed with a flock of cedar waxwings; check for a bigger bird in their midst
- Wanders sporadically in winter
- Expert at fly-catching: flying from a perch to nab an insect, then returning to perch

Look Here

- At berry bushes, eating berries

Or Here

- At feeder
- Perched with a flock in a tree
- Fly-catching from a perch

On the Home Front Nests far to the N, from Canada to Alaska • Usually nests near lake or stream, in swampy areas, or near beaver ponds

"The very incarnation of peace and harmony"

—Neltje Blanchan, *Bird Neighbors* (1904)

Unexpected and unpredictable, Bohemian waxwings may descend upon your city or backyard in winter, in flocks great or small. Windows are a danger to these gentle Northland birds, which aren't accustomed to the deceptive reflections of the glass.

Wild Menu: Fruits; buds; insects, including many mosquitoes

Plant Picks: Fruits and berries that linger into winter, including hollies (*Ilex* spp.), junipers (*Juniperus* spp.), hawthorns (*Crataegus* spp.), mountain ashes (*Sorbus* spp.), crab apples (*Malus* cvs.)

Feeder Pleasers
- Dried fruit, raisins, possibly apples cut in half

Tricks and Treats
- Plant a mixed hedge to pack lots of fruits and berries into your yard.

Friendly One in the Family

If you approach cedar waxwings slowly and quietly, they may let you walk right up to the bush where they're feeding. But their Bohemian cousins make cedar waxwings look like snobs. Like many birds of the Far North, Bohemians are unbelievably tame.

The very first one I saw, mixed in a flock of cedar waxwings scarfing down mountain ash berries, came right to my hand when I held out a branch of berries. The next one landed on my head when I was filling the feeders!

Bay-Breasted Warbler

First Impression

Quick, pretty little bird boldly marked with rusty brown

Mark Your Calendar

Migration in most of region; spring through fall along northern tier near Canadian border

Details, Details

- Chickadee size; 5½ inches
- Two noticeable white wing bars and white corners of tail, visible in flight
- Female is greenish with a flush of rusty red along sides

Listen Up!

- Short, high, thin, monotone trill: *tee-te, tee-te, tee-te, tee tee tee*
- Typical warbler call note: a sharp *chip!*

Telltale Traits

- Active, darting movements amid foliage
- Rarely see more than one at a time, usually among other warbler species
- Tame and unsuspicious; will allow you to approach—but most likely will have moved on before you can do so

Look Here

- Usually in treetops of deciduous trees, moving quickly through foliage

Or Here

- With a "wave" of other warblers, often in a group that includes blackpoll warblers

On the Home Front Nests in very northern edge of region, then northward into Canada
- Builds fragile nest on limb of spruce, balsam fir, or other dense conifer

"Little Chocolate-Breasted Titmouse"

—Name bestowed upon the bay-breasted warbler by Alexander Wilson in *American Ornithology* (1832)

No matter what you call it, this pretty little bird is always a treat to see. In *The Warblers of North America* (1907), Frank Chapman described this species as "among the rarer Warblers the mere sight of which is stimulating."

Wild Menu: Insects; it's a major eater of spruce budworms

Plant Picks: Spruces and other conifers host its natural insect foods, but it may visit any tree in your yard during migration.

Feeder Pleasers

- Not a feeder visitor

Tricks and Treats

- Trees, to provide a safe corridor for travel and plenty of snacking on the go, are all you need to boost your chances with this little guy.

Happy Family

If you could watch a family of bay-breasted warblers at home, you'd see some heartwarming behavior. The pair of birds is devoted to their nest and to each other. While the female sits on her eggs, the male serenades her from a nearby treetop—and sometimes she sings back to him. During heavy rain and on hot days, the female stands in the nest, shielding her babies with outstretched wings.

Blackburnian Warbler

First Impression

A tiny, active bird with a vivid orange head and throat, quickly moving through foliage

Mark Your Calendar

Spring through fall in many areas; migration only in others

Details, Details

- Chickadee size; 5 inches
- Body is streaky black and white, with white lower belly
- Female is yellower instead of deep orange

Listen Up!

- Super-high wheezy notes that sound as if they should be on a secret "dogs only" whistle—*tsi-tsi-tsi* and so on
- Typical warbler *chip* call note

Telltale Traits

- Striking color is the best clue.
- Like most warblers, constantly in motion, gleaning insects as it moves through trees

Look Here

- Often in hemlocks

Or Here

- Hopping through foliage of conifers or deciduous trees
- Foraging with a mixed group of chickadees, kinglets, and other small birds

On the Home Front

Builds nest in conifers, especially hemlocks or occasionally spruces
- Dense cup of twigs, rootlets, fibrous lichens, and soft materials

"The hemlock warbler"

—John James Audubon, on the female Blackburnian, in *Birds of the Connecticut Valley in Massachusetts* (1937)

Warblers were tough for early ornithologists to get a handle on—the birds traveled so far, the sexes looked so different, and their plumage and habits changed from one season to another. Audubon thought the female was a different species and called it the hemlock warbler. "Blackburnian" is for a Mrs. Blackburn, a patron of ornithology who collected stuffed birds.

Wild Menu: Insects

Plant Picks: Hemlocks, other conifers any deciduous trees

Feeder Pleasers

- Not a feeder visitor

Tricks and Treats

- Many warblers appreciate a birdbath during their travels in spring and fall. A mister, drip tube, or other device that creates the sound of moving water may help draw them in.

Sit Tight!

Years ago, I was lucky enough to find a nest of Blackburnian warblers in a gracious old hemlock tree, within easy reaching distance. The female seemed unperturbed by my presence and stayed sitting on her nest. After several days of observing her, I couldn't resist and reached out a finger to gently stroke her back. She didn't even flinch.

"Never before have I seen a bird harder to flush or more loath to leave the nest," noted R. C. Harlow, cited in *Ecology* (October 1958). Harlow took a slightly different approach than I did: He reported hitting the female several times with small twigs before she flew off. But even after that, he noted, she returned immediately to her eggs.

Black-Throated Green Warbler

First Impression

Tiny, active bird with striking black throat and snowy belly, combing the trees with similar greenish yellow birds

Mark Your Calendar

Spring through fall in many areas; migration only in others

Details, Details

- Smaller than a chickadee; 5 inches
- Bright yellow face
- Large white corners of tail
- Female is paler and has black only on sides of throat, not in center

Listen Up!

- Short, high buzzes, sounding like "trees, trees, murmuring trees"
- Sharp *chip!* call note

Telltale Traits

- Male is tireless singer; when these guys are in your area, you'll know it
- Behaves like most other warblers: fast and active, moving quickly amid foliage
- Males and females are strongly territorial and may attack other trespassing warblers during nesting season.

Look Here

- Usually hopping quickly through foliage

Or Here

- Flying from one tree to another
- Hopping on ground
- Perched and singing

"Trees, trees, murmuring trees"

—Traditional transliteration of the species' song

Despite their name, warblers are no great shakes as singers. Most have high, wheezy little voices without much melody. Birders use handy phrases to try to sort them out.

On the Home Front Gets down to business soon after arriving in spring • Female chooses a site, usually in a conifer, close to trunk and low to ground • The well-built cup is a pretty thing, with white birch bark woven among twigs held together by spider silk. • Nestlings are so loud you can hear them from hundreds of feet away.

Wild Menu: Insects, including many caterpillars

Plant Picks: Conifers and deciduous trees, especially insect-rich trees such as spruces and other conifers, birches, willows, oaks

Feeder Pleasers

- Not a feeder visitor

Tricks and Treats

- May visit a naturalistic ground-level birdbath basin with a pump or trickling tube

Tiny Target

Black-throated green warblers are tiny birds, only 5 inches from beak tip to tail tip. Yet, like many warbler species, they're a frequent target of the parasitic brown-headed cowbird.

At 7½ inches long, the cowbird is much larger than an adult warbler—and its babies are bigger, too. Yet the cowbird often deposits an egg into a warbler nest.

And the pint-size adoptive parents obligingly raise the giant without ever seeming to wonder, "Hey, why is Junior so big?"

Canada Warbler

First Impression

Striking black necklace on bright yellow breast of a small gray bird moving quickly through low foliage

Mark Your Calendar

Spring through fall in many areas; migration only in others

Details, Details

- About chickadee size; 5¼ inches
- Yellow spectacle-effect eye ring
- Female has only a faint necklace and lacks black "whiskers" of male

Listen Up!

- One of the better singers among warblers: a long, loud, clear song of varied notes
- Sharp *chip!* call note

Telltale Traits

- Cocks tail and flicks wings constantly when foraging
- Feeds mostly in flight, instead of scouring foliage like many other warblers

Look Here

- Foraging through branches of rhododendron and other understory shrubs, low to ground

Or Here

- Fly-catching for insects

On the Home Front Not a backyard nester
- Nests in dense cover, including mossy, ferny places, thickets, or rhododendrons • Builds bulky cup of leaves, grass, and bark on or near ground • Like many warblers, reluctant to flush from nest when disturbed • Parasitized by brown-headed cowbird

"Listen to that beak snap!"

—Mary Roth, my mother, watching Canada warblers fly-catch for insects in her yard

Most warblers pick insects off branches, but Canada warblers take to the air, chasing down zigzagging mosquitoes and other fast fliers. Listen hard, and you can hear the wind rushing through their wings as they dash and dart after prey—and the snap of their beak when they snatch it.

Wild Menu: Insects, including many mosquitoes

Plant Picks: Native shrubs, great for harboring yummy insects, are always a likely pick.

Feeder Pleasers
- Not a feeder visitor

Tricks and Treats
- You won't need anything but bountiful bugs to bring this warbler in.

Sphagnum Specialist

Whenever I find myself stepping on springy, spongy sphagnum moss in a moist northern forest (wet sneakers, anyone?), I start looking for Canada warbler nests. Haven't had any luck so far, no doubt because they're well hidden, often between the roots of a tree that keeled over, or tucked into a mossy lump that looks just like every other mossy lump.

Sphagnum wetlands and bogs are a likely locale for nesting pairs, so keep your eyes open for these little birds where the skunk cabbage grows.

Mourning Warbler

First Impression

Tiny gray bird with gray hood and yellow belly

Mark Your Calendar

Spring through fall in many areas; migration only in others

Details, Details

- About chickadee size; 5¼ inches
- Dark face
- Female has a paler gray hood and face

Listen Up!

- Short, churring song that sounds something like, *"Kiss me Charlie, Charlie, Charlie"*
- *Chip!* call note

Telltale Traits

- Creeps around in brush like a wren, giving you only teasing glimpses
- Males often sing from a conspicuous perch

Look Here

- Near or on ground

Or Here

- Low in shrubs or brush
- Singing from top of bush or small tree

On the Home Front Not a backyard nester

• Nests on or near the ground • Well-concealed in dense vegetation, such as horsetail (*Equisetum* spp.), blackberries, or ferns • Like other warblers, parasitized by brown-headed cowbird • Family groups remain together for weeks after young birds leave the nest.

"Its song is a paean of joy"

—**Edward Forbush**, *Birds of Massachusetts and Other New England States* (1929)

As active as any other warbler, this species gets its name from its coloring, which suggests the once traditional wearing of black crepe by the grief-stricken. But as Forbush wrote, "It seems as happy and active as most birds."

Wild Menu: Insects

Plant Picks: Shrubs and shade gardens

Feeder Pleasers

• Not a feeder visitor

Tricks and Treats

• A ground-level birdbath with moving water of some sort may attract all kinds of interesting warblers on migration.

Sneaky Skulker

It's hard to remember to look down when there's so much going on in the trees above during migration. But when you see flocks of mixed warblers moving through your trees in spring, take a look lower down, too. Watch for a quick glimpse of this shy skulker, who sometimes seems like he's playing hide-and-seek with us, hopping in and out of view.

Scarlet Tanager

First Impression
Brilliant red with black wings

Mark Your Calendar
Spring through fall

Details, Details
- Smaller than a robin; 7 inches
- Female is greenish yellow

Listen Up!
- Long, hoarse, slurring song

Telltale Traits
- Vivid color and beauty are the best ways to ID a tanager.
- Slinks through tree foliage

Look Here
- High in trees, usually deciduous and especially oaks

Or Here
- At apples, crab apples, and other flowering trees, picking off insects at blossoms
- At your feeder in spring

On the Home Front Usually nests in woods
- Loose, shallow nest attached to tree limb, well out from trunk • Often high up, but may be at eye level

"The appointed guardian of the oaks"

—Edward Forbush,
Useful Birds and Their Protection (1907)

Scarlet tanagers and oak trees go together like red and green for Christmas. Oak trees harbor plentiful insects, including many resting moths, a favorite of tanagers. The birds often use oaks as nest sites, too.

Wild Menu: Insects; fruit

Plant Picks: Fruits of any kind, particularly sweet or sour cherries and mulberries (*Morus* spp.); early-spring-flowering trees (crab apples, redbuds); flowering dogwood (*Cornus florida*)

Feeder Pleasers
- Millet and other birdseed; chopped suet; mealworms and other insect foods

Tricks and Treats
- A simple saucer of fresh water is welcomed by tanagers on migration. A naturalistic birdbath with trickling water is even more effective.

Branching Out

Spectacular scarlet tanagers seem to have a split personality when it comes to filling their bellies. In the wild, they eat almost entirely insects and fruit. In all my years of exploring and observing, I've never once seen one of these birds nibbling at seeds in their natural haunts. But in the backyard, these beautiful birds broaden their menu to include birdseed! Sure, they love mealworms and suet, too, just as you'd expect. But, at least during spring migration, they gobble down millet and seed mix with gusto.

Red Crossbill

First Impression
Strawberry red, very tame bird—and get a load of that beak!

Mark Your Calendar
Year-round; in some areas, winter only

Details, Details
- The size of a sparrow; 6¼ inches
- Dark wings—but that bill is the only detail you'll need
- Female is grayish green
- The similar white-winged crossbill, also an erratic wanderer, has two white bands across its wings.

Listen Up!
- Mechanical clicking or trilling song, often sung in chorus by flock
- Thin, weak call notes

Telltale Traits
- Travels in groups
- Uses beak and feet like a parrot to crawl on branches
- Very approachable

Look Here
- At conifer cones

Or Here
- At your feeder
- In trees

On the Home Front Depending on when the conifer crop ripens, the birds nest anytime from December to September! • Well-concealed nest is placed in a spruce, pine, or other conifer • Makes good use of nearby materials, including conifer twigs, lichens, and conifer needles.

"Capricious little visitors"

—Neltje Blanchan, *Bird Neighbors* (1897)

Crossbills can't be taken for granted. Their movements are unpredictable, so they may show up in your backyard every day in winter—or not! Enjoy them when you can.

Wild Menu: Seeds of conifer cones; also other tree seeds and buds; insects

Plant Picks: Pines, spruces, larches, firs, and other conifers

Feeder Pleasers
- Sunflower seeds

Tricks and Treats
- Crossbills are greatly fond of salt. Offer a handful of rock salt in your feeding tray when crossbills arrive.

The Legend of the Crossbill

Crossbills and Christianity? According to an old German legend that American poet Longfellow turned into verse, the bird tried its hardest, but without success, to pull the nails from the Crucifixion cross. Because of its efforts, the crossbill became stained with blood.

"In the groves of pines it singeth / Songs, like legends, strange to hear"

—"The Legend of the Crossbill," by Henry Wadsworth Longfellow, in *Longfellow's Poetical Works* (1893)

FAR NORTH

Pine Grosbeak

First Impression
Very tame, rosy red bird

Mark Your Calendar
Winter

Details, Details
- A little smaller than a robin; 9 inches
- Blackish wings with white bars
- Female is greenish and gray

Listen Up!
- Soft, whistled song
- Quiet call notes keep a flock in touch.

Telltale Traits
- Hangs around in small groups
- Very calm and easily approached

Look Here
- Eating berries in winter

Or Here
- Perched quietly for long periods of time
- At feeder
- In spruce, pine, or other conifers

On the Home Front
Not a backyard nester
- Nest is well-hidden in dense branches of conifers, usually about eye level or lower
- Like many other northland birds, this one builds its nest out of whatever's close at hand: conifer twigs, rootlets, and grasses, lined with needles, lichen, and a few feathers. • Parents feed young birds a yummy regurgitated paste of vegetable matter and insects.

"They persistently gourmandize"
—Neltje Blanchan, *Bird Neighbors* (1897)

Slow-moving pine grosbeaks feature a special adaptation of a throat pouch, which allows them to eat way more at one time than other birds can. Then they sit around digesting. See if you agree with Blanchan, who wrote, "[I]f the truth must be confessed, they appear to be rather stupid and uninteresting."

Wild Menu: Tree seeds, seeds from conifer cones, weed seeds; tree buds; fruit; insects

Plant Picks: Junipers (*Juniperus* spp.) with berries, barberry (*Berberis* spp.), American bittersweet (*Celastrus scandens*), mountain ash (*Sorbus* spp.), many others

Feeder Pleasers
- Sunflower seeds

Tricks and Treats
- Pine grosbeaks are a great reason to have a reserve bag of sunflower seeds on hand: Winter flocks may number 100 or more birds!

Boring? Maybe

But brightening up a winter day, definitely. Even Neltje Blanchan, who seems to have had a low opinion of the birds because of their gluttonous ways and lack of activity, gave them credit for making the winter scene a lot cheerier: "They visit us at a time when we are most inclined to rapture over our bird visitors." Got those sunflower seeds ready?

Common Redpoll

First Impression

Little, plump, streaky bird splashed with red on throat and head

Mark Your Calendar

Winter

Details, Details

- Chickadee size; 5¼ inches
- A small black bib
- Female lacks wash of pinkish red on breast; has only red patch on forehead

Listen Up!

- Constantly "talking" in trilling, tinkling notes
- Listen for the distinctive *churrrrr* when the flock flies from place to place

Telltale Traits

- Acrobatic and active
- Exuberant birds, with lilting, bounding flight
- A redpoll or two may mingle among your other finches; or you may be visited by a small or large flock of only redpolls.

Look Here

- At the feeder

Or Here

- Gleaning seeds from weeds and grasses
- Deep in a hole in the snow, dug to reach buried seeds
- Hanging acrobatically at branch tips in birches or other trees

On the Home Front Not a backyard nester
- Well-built nest is made from fine twigs woven with rootlets and grasses, and lined with a thick layer of feathers or other soft material.

"Restlessness is certainly one of the chief characteristics of the redpoll in the open."

—**A. C. Bent,** *Life Histories of North American Cardinals, Grosbeaks, Buntings, Towhees, Finches, Sparrows, and Allies* (1968)

Watch redpolls in your garden and you'll see that the flock is almost constantly moving. At the feeder, though, redpolls feed calmly for many minutes at a time.

Wild Menu: Seeds; buds; some insects

Plant Picks: Birches (*Betulus* spp.); any plants with seeds remaining in your garden, such as seed-rich annual bachelor's buttons (*Centaurea cyanus*), cosmos (*Cosmos bipinnatus*), and zinnias (*Zinnia* spp.); also weeds and grasses

Feeder Pleasers

- Niger and finch mix; black oil sunflower seeds

Tricks and Treats

- Like other northern finches, redpolls appreciate an offering of salt.
- Fresh water is always welcome; try providing a heated birdbath.

Take a Closer Look

Even after years of feeding birds, I'm surprised by how often redpolls slip in without my noticing right away. A few redpolls can easily blend right in among goldfinches, house finches, and pine siskins at my feeders.

The big difference? These birds don't fly away when I come outside to restock feeders. They're so tame—especially when there's snow on the ground—that I sometimes have to shoo them away so I can refill the seed tube.

American Tree Sparrow

First Impression

Small, streaky brown bird with reddish cap and dark spot on breast, scratching on ground

Mark Your Calendar

Winter

Details, Details

- Sparrow size, of course! 6¼ inches
- Female looks like male
- Reddish stripe at eye ("eye line")

Listen Up!

- Talks with others in a musical twitter, *teedle-eet, teedle-eet*
- High, sweet, warbling song not usually heard in winter

Telltale Traits

- Often in small flocks
- Bounding, zigzagging flight when crossing open space—hard for predators to follow

Look Here

- In feeder or on ground beneath it

Or Here

- Hanging on stems, eating weed seeds and grass seeds in garden beds
- Scratching for dropped seeds on the ground in flower beds or brushy places

On the Home Front Not a backyard nester

- Usually nests on ground in tundra, often in clump of grass near small tree or shrub
- Female gathers nesting material from the general vicinity of the nest and builds nest alone • Nest is kept cozy with an inner ring of fine grass almost half an inch thick, lined with a layer of feathers—usually ptarmigan
- Both parents feed young.

"Winter chippy"

—An old name

Tree sparrows look a lot like chipping sparrows, another common backyard bird. But there's one big difference—that dark dot in the middle of their breast. It's often called a "stickpin," and it's the key to telling the species apart. Of course, by the time tree sparrows move into your yard for the winter, chipping sparrows are long gone.

Wild Menu: Seeds of weeds, grasses, and sedges; some insects

Plant Picks: Plant a few handfuls of finch mix or white proso millet to make these little guys happy all winter long. They'll clean off the seeds of any weeds you may've missed, too.

Feeder Pleasers

- Millet, by a mile; finch mix

Tricks and Treats

- A heated birdbath is the ultimate tree sparrow spa. An electric birdbath heater will pay you back with entertainment all winter long.
- Got any lemming fur? How about a snowshoe hare pelt? Put them, or any other fur, out for nesting material possibilities.

Waste Not, Want Not

Tree sparrows are adept at ferreting out stray seeds. And that's another great reason not to hurry to clean up your garden.

These loyal winter friends appreciate the cover of those dead standing stems, whether they're annuals, perennials, or those weeds that sneaked their way in. Let them stand, and all winter long, you'll see tree sparrows searching for seeds on and below them.

Fox Sparrow

First Impression

Big, plump, rusty sparrow with heavily streaked or speckled breast

Mark Your Calendar

Migration only, but still a treat!

Details, Details

- A big sparrow; 7 inches
- Much geographic variation in color and song; some are redder, grayer, or thicker-billed
- Female looks like male

Listen Up!

- With 18 subspecies divided into at least four distinct groups, fox sparrows show a lot of variation in song. The group of this region is the red or Taiga fox sparrow, which sings a rich, melodious, whistled song.

Telltale Traits

- Scratches vigorously on ground; can dig a hole through several inches of snow to reach seeds
- Secretive when not at feeder; stays concealed in brushy areas
- Usually arrives singly at feeder

Look Here

- On ground beneath feeder

Or Here

- In or at feeder
- Scavenging seeds from a winter garden or weeds

On the Home Front Not a backyard nester

- Nests on ground, in low bushes, or in small trees

"In their search for food they make the snow fly"

—A. C. Bent, *Life Histories of North American Cardinals, Grosbeaks, Buntings, Towhees, Finches, Sparrows, and Allies* (1968)

The big fox sparrow is a powerful and determined digger who scratches vigorously to uncover seeds buried in the snow. Often the bird will scratch for buried seeds instead of eating at leisure in the feeder.

Wild Menu: Seeds; insects; fruits

Plant Picks: Fall-ripening berries may catch the eye of migrants. Try elderberries (*Sambucus* spp.), burning bush and other euonymus (*Euonymus* spp.), eastern red cedar (*Juniperus virginiana*), pokeweed (*Phytolacca americana*).

Feeder Pleasers
- Millet

Tricks and Treats
- A birdbath is often welcomed.

Snow Removal Service

Fox sparrows are great at digging through snow to reach the seeds below. They use their feet like little snow scoops, clawing the snow out of the way. In minutes, they can excavate a surprisingly deep hole.

One morning, after a 6-inch snow, I looked out and saw some smart white-throated sparrows taking advantage of an energetic fox sparrow's efforts. While Foxy dug away, the white-throats gathered behind him, where the excavated snow was piling up, and methodically picked out every bit of millet the fox sparrow was unearthing.

Clay-Colored Sparrow

First Impression
Small sparrow with plain breast and striped head

Mark Your Calendar
Spring through fall

Details, Details
- A small sparrow; 5½ inches
- Strongly striped head; markings become less distinct once breeding season is over
- Similar to tree sparrow, but without the eye ring that gives that bird its typical wide-eyed look
- Also looks a lot like chipping sparrow; look for the reddish cap of the chippy
- Female looks like male

Listen Up!
- Rasping, monotone buzzy notes: *zhee zhee zhee*
- Sharp *chip!* alarm note

Telltale Traits
- Hops on ground
- Hangs out in flocks unless nesting
- Often in large flocks, sometimes with other species, such as Brewer's sparrows in the western part of this region

Look Here
- At feeder

Or Here
- In shrubs, hedges, and brushy places
- In garden, eating seeds

On the Home Front
Nests are usually built low, in snowberry shrubs (*Symphoricarpos albus*). • The nest is made of grass, fine twigs, rootlets, and lots of hair. • More than a third of nests may be parasitized by brown-headed cowbirds.

> *"Shrub cover may be a more important factor"*
>
> —J. A. Dechant, "Effects of management practices on grassland birds: clay-colored sparrow" (2004)

Although this species is often considered a grassland bird, researchers have shown that it prefers areas with shrubs among the grass. Western snowberry and silverberry are its favorites in the wild and in the backyard.

Wild Menu: Seeds; insects

Plant Picks: Flowers with many small seeds, including sweet alyssum (*Lobularia maritima*), cockscomb (*Celosia* spp.), amaranth (*Amaranthus* spp.), and others; also weeds and weedy grasses, such as foxtail (*Setaria* spp.)

Feeder Pleasers
- Sunflower seeds; cracked corn; millet

Tricks and Treats
- Plant shrubs to provide cover to make this sparrow feel at home. Native western snowberry (*Symphoricarpos occidentalis*) and American silverberry (*Elaeagnus commutata*) are perfect candidates.

The Hand of Man

This sparrow has greatly benefited from human activities—or in this case, the cessation of certain human activities. In olden days, the northern prairie frequently was burned, either by natural or man-made fires. Regular blazes prevented shrubs and trees from gaining a foothold.

Then setting fires was stopped. The grassy prairie grew up into shrubs, creating ideal habitat for the clay-colored sparrow, which expanded its range to take advantage of it.

Purple Finch

First Impression
Small raspberry-red bird with alert look

Mark Your Calendar
Year-round, spring through fall, winter only, or migration only, depending on location

Details, Details
- The size of a sparrow; 6 inches
- More intense all-over color and stouter than a house finch
- Look for the raised feathers on the head, which give the bird an alert look that's different from a house finch.
- Female is streaky brown with distinctive light eye stripe

Listen Up!
- Fast, rising and falling, warbled song
- Call note is a sharp, metallic *tick!*

Telltale Traits
- Can raise head feathers for an almost crested effect
- An erratic wanderer; some years may bring many, other years only a few

Look Here
- At tray or tube feeder

Or Here
- In trees
- At fruit trees, eating buds or blossoms

On the Home Front Nests in spruces and other conifers • Often adds bits of shed snakeskin to nest • Nest lined with hair, wool, or other fine fibers

"One of the most delicious songsters"

—Neltje Blanchan, *Bird Neighbors* (1897)

Called a purple linnet in olden times, this pretty species is quite the vocalist. Often I only get to enjoy the purple finch as a winter visitor, so I miss out on his long, warbling song. If you live where he nests, you may be fortunate enough to hear his full, rich melody.

Wild Menu: Seeds of trees and weeds; occasionally tree buds or flowers; some berries

Plant Picks: Red maple (*Acer rubrum*), birches (*Betula* spp.), conifers; sunflowers (*Helianthus annuus*); raspberries or blackberries

Feeder Pleasers
- Sunflower seeds; finch mix

Tricks and Treats
- Northern finches, of which this is one, are fond of salt—and also of the mortar used in brickwork. Put a small handful of rock salt into an open tray feeder, or set up a salt block.
- Purple finches usually retreat to the woods to raise their families. But if your yard is nearby, or has large conifers that might be considered for nest sites, try offering soft materials, such as tufts of natural wool, for lining.
- Birdbaths are popular year-round with purple finches.

Christmas Present

Growing Christmas trees for sale is big business in the North. Truckloads are cut and shipped to points hundreds of miles away, or mail-ordered across the country.

One year, the Christmas tree we bought held a bird nest like I'd never seen before. After some research, I figured out that the cup of twigs and sticks, lined with animal hair and fur, probably had belonged to a purple finch—who had raised its family in Minnesota or points north. We felt especially honored.

Yellow-Headed Blackbird

First Impression
Unmistakable! Big black bird with striking yellow hood

Mark Your Calendar
Spring through fall

Details, Details
- Smaller than a robin; 9½ inches
- Male flashes white wing patches in flight
- Female is much less dramatic but still has yellow tinge

Listen Up!
- Or maybe you should cover your ears—a menagerie of squawks, squeeps, rattles, shrieks, and clacks, plus a noise like a chainsaw

Telltale Traits
- Sight alone is enough to positively ID this dramatic bird
- Usually in flocks
- Nervous tail flicks

Look Here
- At feeder

Or Here
- In marshes with cattails or other reeds
- In winter, turns to grain fields for food. Huge flocks "roll over" fields, the birds in back moving to front as the field is scoured of waste grain.

On the Home Front Not a backyard nester, unless you have a large, reed-fringed pond • Nests in colonies, in a marsh • Nests are built within a clump of reeds, and woven from reeds.

"Xanthocephalus xanthocephalus"
—Scientific name of yellow-headed blackbird

Xantho means yellow; *cephalus* means head. Why repeat the word as both genus and species epithet? No doubt because once just isn't enough to emphasize what an astounding bird this is!

Wild Menu: Weed seeds; grain; aquatic insects

Plant Picks: Your feeder will keep these birds content.

Feeder Pleasers
- Sunflower seeds; cracked corn

Tricks and Treats
- A birdbath or water feature may attract a yellow-headed splasher.

What's That Noise?

We were watching our local colony of nesting yellow-heads when all of a sudden, they simultaneously began making a peculiar harsh rattle. All the usual cacophony halted instantly. No birds were then visible, but the cattail marsh buzzed with this unsettling call.

What could it be, we wondered. Then we sighted a Cooper's hawk—a bird eater—flying through. One of the blackbirds had spotted it when it was still far off and raised the alarm. Scientists call that the "hawk alarm call," and note that it's given only by males.

Chapter Nine

Birds of the Southeast and South

The Southeast and South share many bird species with the Northeast and the Midwest. But you also get some species that are mainly at home in the mild climate of your region, such as the charming little brown-headed nuthatch. And you get to enjoy the company of hummingbirds, bluebirds, and many other beloved birds in winter, long after they've retreated from less hospitable regions.

Everyone from chickadees to flamingos is at home here. Gracious old cities, brand-spankin'-new suburbs, small and large farms, and plenty of woods—plus lots of water—supply habitat for a hugely varied population of birds.

Plants grow like mad in this kind of climate, which is great news for gardeners and birds. Insects flourish spectacularly well, too, which is another boon to birds.

THE LAY OF THE LAND

Long, steamy summers, mild winters, and abundant rain make this region a nearly tropical paradise in some places. The farther south, the more extreme the steam heat, until it becomes subtropical. Coastal marshes and Spanish-moss-draped sloughs are part of the scenery, too, as the highlands relax into plains as they near the sea. The sandy beaches of the Atlantic and the Gulf of Mexico add another element to the region.

Yet, in other parts of this area, you might think you were in New England. The southern Appalachian Mountains pass through several states in this region, providing homes for forest birds. Piney woods and stands of magnificent deciduous trees, such as tulip poplar, sycamore, and sweet gum, plus a plethora of oaks, dominate other parts of the landscape.

Pine cones provide seeds for nuthatches.

FOOD AND SHELTER

That immense diversity of habitat means an equal variety of plant life—and that means food choices galore for birds. Wood warblers can thrive on the myriad of insects in the trees, while gnatcatchers flit after gnats in the swamps, and sparrows feast in the fields. Nuthatches and woodpeckers can patrol tree bark for bugs, while tanagers take care of those insects found in treetop foliage. For every niche in this varied landscape, there's a bird ready to take advantage of it.

Trees are rich in insects and insect larvae, a real draw for woodpeckers. Bayberries (*Myrica pensylvanica*) and wax myrtles (*M. cerifera*) supply fall and winter food for tree swallows, waxwings, and yellow-rumped warblers. Swamps offer even more choices, with swarms of mosquitoes and gnats ready for feasting upon.

Rampant growth means plenty of shelter, too. Evergreens are abundant here, and not only conifers: This region is home to spectacular live oaks, magnolias, laurels, and other broad-leaved evergreens, too—all of them adding to the possibilities of year-round cover for backyard birds.

Dense undergrowth of various heights supplies cover that appeals to thrushes, blue

Woodsy streams thread through the Appalachians.

grosbeaks, vireos, and sparrows. Vines are another big part of the southern landscape, and birds make good use of them, too. Curtains of ghostly Spanish moss (*Tillandsia usneoides*) supply protection, when birds are moving from place to place or looking for a nesting site.

CLIMATE

Hot, humid summers seem a small price to pay for winters that often are so mild that you can get by with just a sweater against the nighttime chill. More northerly areas in this region and mountainous locations are much colder, of course, with occasional opportunities for sledding or making a snowman.

In some parts of the region, flowers bloom year-round—and so hummingbirds stay, too. Strong summer storms and drenching rains are common, which can spell trouble for robins' nests and others that may topple from their supporting branches. Occasional ice storms can swoop in, wreaking havoc on trees still carrying a burden of leaves.

This area is winter vacationland for many northerners—including those with feathers. The brown thrasher, eastern bluebird, gray catbird, and oriole leave their summer homes in the more northern states to winter here.

BIRD LIFE IN THE SOUTHEAST AND SOUTH

Birds are abundant in this region. Most of them spread out to cover other territories besides this one. While this region gets bragging rights for its many fabulous wading birds, such as wood storks and flamingos,

that's not true for birds that visit backyards. Only a handful of backyard bird species are limited to this region.

Nearly all migrants swarm through this region on their way to points north in spring, or when they're retracing their flight in fall. Other species stick around much longer. Many backyard birds, including feeder friends such as cardinals, song sparrows, and downy woodpeckers, are year-round residents in the Southeast. White-crowned sparrows, white-throated sparrows, fox sparrows, and vesper sparrows are here all winter, while chipping sparrows remain all year.

Bayberries (*Myrica* spp.) are bird favorites.

Start Here

Because the Southeast and South are home to so many widespread bird species, you'll want to turn to Chapter 6, "Start Here," to find your most familiar backyard friends.

These are the birds you share with other parts of the country—chickadees, white-breasted nuthatches, tufted titmice, gold-finches, juncos, cedar waxwings, and many others.

Every single one of the "Start Here" birds is happily at home in the Southeast and South.

Regional Specialties

You'll find other favorite friends spotlighted in this regional section. Some of these birds also occur in other regions. But every single

Blue grosbeaks may be in shrubs in this region.

one of them may turn up in your southeastern backyard.

Be sure to page through the birds of the Northeast and Midwest regions, too. Many of them are also at home in your region. Flip through the birds of the Far North, too, because in order to reach those haunts, they'll have to pass through your area during migration.

Birds of the Southeast and South

Here's a list of the birds you'll find in this chapter. Remember to consult the "Start Here" birds, starting on page 79, for the most common birds to be found in the Southeast and South.

Red-Bellied Woodpecker

First Impression

Big, calm, red-headed woodpecker at feeder

Mark Your Calendar

Year-round

Details, Details

- Almost as big as a robin; 9¼ inches
- Female has red only on back of neck, not top of head

Listen Up!

- Loud, harsh, querulous *quirrrr?* as if asking, "Where's my food?"
- Steady, medium-speed drumming with beak

Telltale Traits

- Back and wings look grayish from a distance; up close, finely black-and-white zebra striped
- Undulating flight, with deep dips
- Often very tame; slow to fly away when you approach

Look Here

- At the feeder eating sunflower seeds or squirrel corn

Or Here

- Clinging to tree trunks or large branches
- Foraging on the ground
- At suet or nectar feeder
- In citrus or other fruit trees

On the Home Front Excavates a cavity in a dead tree, dead limb, or wooden fence post for a nest site; may accept a nest box • In southern areas, often raises more than one brood

"I frequently found oranges that had been riddled by this woodpecker"

—Benjamin Mortimer, "Notes on habits of a few birds of Orange County, Florida" (1890)

Once called the "orange sapsucker," the red-bellied woodpecker may add some "Florida sunshine" to its diet when the fruit is on the tree or on the ground. An opportunistic feeder, the bird will also sample grapefruits, mangoes, and even nectar from banana flowers.

Wild Menu: Insects; seeds; nuts; fruit

Plant Picks: Pecans or oaks for nuts; mulberries (*Morus* spp.); citrus in mild-winter areas; field corn or Indian corn; tall, large-headed sunflowers (*Helianthus annuus*)

Feeder Pleasers

- Whole ears of dried corn on cob; sunflower seeds; suet and suet-based foods

Tricks and Treats

- Squirrel feeders that hold a fixed ear of corn work great for this big guy to peck at, too.
- May become a nectar drinker

Love Your Hat!

When I was a kid, I spent many an afternoon poking into forgotten corners of my father's secondhand store. In one room, crammed to the ceiling with antique clothing, I came across stacks of hatboxes. I expected to find fantastic creations, but instead I found raw materials for making hats a hundred years ago. Birds, to be exact. I dropped the box in horror. Onto the floor tumbled glossy wings of purple martins, white egret plumes—and the striking black-and-white backs of red-bellied woodpeckers, which were once slaughtered wholesale for their feathers.

Red-Headed Woodpecker

First Impression

A breathtaking bird! Bold white and black patches with a vivid crimson head

Mark Your Calendar

Year-round

Details, Details

- A little smaller than a robin; 9¼ inches
- Female looks like male
- Juvenile has brown head

Listen Up!

- Rattles, *chirr*s, and makes a loud, wheezy *queeer queeer queeer*
- Doesn't usually excavate into wood for insects; does drum weakly on occasion

Telltale Traits

- Fly-catches! The bird flies from a perch after an insect, then returns to eat it.
- Usually seen alone or in pairs; after nesting, may forage in family groups
- Not a rare bird in general, but "locally common" in some parts of its range
- Stores acorns, nuts, and sometimes grasshoppers to eat later

Look Here

- Fly-catching from a utility pole, fence post, or tree

Or Here

- Flying across an open area
- On ground beneath trees, eating nuts
- Eating fruit or berries in bushes or trees
- Scavenging corn in farm field

On the Home Front Nests in dead trees or utility poles, near the top • May reuse same cavity for several years or excavate a new one below it

"Strongly contrasted blotches of black, white, and crimson flashing in the sunlight"

—Spencer Trotter, *Life Histories of North American Woodpeckers* (1939)

You'll never forget your first sighting of this fabulous bird, whether it's flying across a field, clinging to a tree, or contentedly eating corn at your feeder. It's perfectly gorgeous.

Wild Menu: Insects; fruit and berries; corn; nuts and acorns

Plant Picks: Cherries, grapes, mulberries; corn; oak trees for acorns; pecan trees for nuts; crab apples and other flowering trees for insects

Feeder Pleasers

- Dried corn on the cob, pushed firmly onto a spike; nuts; suet

Tricks and Treats

- Got any weathered wooden posts around? Install them as inviting perches for fly-catching.

The Shores of Gitche Gumee

Why does the red-headed woodpecker have a red head? In Longfellow's classic poem "Hiawatha," there is a climactic scene in which the hero slays a great and evil magician. Hiawatha receives advice from a woodpecker, who tells him that the only place the evil one can be mortally wounded is at the roots of his long hair. Hiawatha releases the arrows, and the magician falls. In gratitude, the hero daubs the woodpecker's head with blood.

Pileated Woodpecker

First Impression
Humongous "Woody Woodpecker"

Mark Your Calendar
Year-round

Details, Details
- As big as a crow; 16½ inches
- The cartoon character Woody Woodpecker was drawn from the pileated woodpecker.
- Big, strong beak
- Watch for big white patches on the wings, and even bigger white patches underneath, when the bird flies.
- "Pileated" means "crested"—that pointy tuft of feathers on the head.
- Female is similar to male but lacks the red forehead and red mustache

Listen Up!
- Hollers *awoik! awoik!* in a ringing voice
- Sounds very similar to the flicker, but louder and slower

Telltale Traits
- Often pecks at logs as well as dead trees
- Pries off long strips of dead wood to reveal its favorite food, carpenter ants
- Flies like a crow, with deep wing beats
- Noisy; can be heard from far away
- Can raise and lower that red crest

Look Here
- At your suet feeder

Or Here
- Clinging to tree trunk
- Hammering at dead trees, logs, or stumps, looking for ants
- Flying across open space or swooping from tree to tree

"Easily located by the half-bushel of big fresh chips scattered about on the ground"

—George Simmons, *Birds of the Austin Region* (1925)

For all their size, pileated woodpeckers are often easy to overlook. Watch for wood chips: the remains of their excavating. Look up, and you may spot the big-beaked bird itself.

On the Home Front May nest in backyard or even accept a nest box • Usually excavates its nest hole high up in a dead decaying tree

Wild Menu: Insects, mostly carpenter ants and wood-boring beetle larvae; fruit and berries

Plant Picks: Hackberry (*Celtis occidentalis*), sassafras (*Sassafras albidum*), blackberries or raspberries, shining sumac (*Rhus copallina*), Virginia creeper (*Parthenocissus quinquefolia*), flowering dogwood (*Cornus florida*), persimmon (*Diospyros virginiana*), and other berried plants

Feeder Pleasers
- Suet, served in a stationary feeder that supplies a sturdy place to get a grip and prop a big tail

Tricks and Treats
- Keep that old stump in your yard to attract ants. This big woodpecker may be close behind.

Pileated by Phone

Is there a bird you're yearning to see, but which, for some reason, you never quite catch? For one of my friends, that bird was the pileated woodpecker.

One day, as he was talking to his father on the phone, his dad broke in: "A giant woodpecker just landed on the tree right outside the window!" Yep, it was a pileated. My friend tried not to whimper while his dad described every detail with gusto.

Brown-Headed Nuthatch

First Impression

Acrobatic plain gray bird with brown cap, often poised upside down

Mark Your Calendar

Year-round

Details, Details

- Smaller than a chickadee; 4½ inches
- Female looks like male

Listen Up!

- Says *cha-cha-cha* or *cah-cah-cah,* and sometimes a conversational twitter of *pit-pit.*

Telltale Traits

- Creeps up and down trees, looking for insects
- Often hangs head-down from a bunch of pine needles, alertly looking for insects
- Picks off flakes of bark, making a pattering sound below as the flakes fall

Look Here

- At your feeder

Or Here

- On tree trunks, fence posts, or even buildings
- Hanging like a tiny, drab parrot from a cluster of needles on a pine branch
- Flying from one tree to another
- Tilt your neck way back: These little birds often stay high in pines. Listen for their calls, then track them down with binocs.
- At a nest box or nest hole, fairly low to ground

On the Home Front Digs out a cavity or recycles a woodpecker hole • May use a nest box • Most nests are at lower than 10 feet aboveground

"Its favorite haunts are in the pines"

—**A. C. Bent,** *Life Histories of North American Nuthatches, Wrens, Thrashers, and Their Allies* **(1948)**

This nuthatch spends much of its time on or about loblollies, long-leaf, and other pine trees. It's often so high up it's hard to see—except at nesting time, when oddly enough, it makes its home close to eye level.

Wild Menu: Insects

Plant Picks: Pines native to your area, such as loblolly (*Pinus taeda*) or long-leaf (*Pinus palustris*)

Feeder Pleasers

- Suet feeder, including insect-enriched suet; sunflower seeds; peanuts and other nuts

Tricks and Treats

- Mount a birdhouse at about 4 to 8 feet high (ideally on a pine tree), and you may be able to see utterly adorable baby nuthatches being fed by their parents. Chickadees or titmice might become tenants instead, though.

Tool Time

The tiny brown-headed nuthatch has a remarkable habit that sets it apart from most other species: This bird often uses a tool when feeding.

This bird's daily grub consists of insects hiding on trees, often under the bark. To get at these tidbits, the nuthatch has been seen using a flake of bark to pry off another piece of bark. It makes for better leverage, I suppose, because the bark chip is wider than the bird's sharp little bill. Like they say, the right tool makes the job faster and easier.

Blue-Gray Gnatcatcher

First Impression

An active mini-mockingbird with up-tilted tail, in the branches overhead

Mark Your Calendar

Spring through fall in most areas; year-round along Gulf Coast and in Florida and Deep South

Details, Details

- Smaller than a chickadee; 4½ inches
- Male is blue-gray during breeding season; pale gray otherwise; female is similar
- Whitish belly and noticeable white eye ring
- Watch for the distinctive white edges of the black tail; they show best in flight.

Listen Up!

- A constant barrage of thin, very high, lisping or buzzy notes, generally *zee-u, zee-u, zil, zeet, zee-e*, sometimes with a mewing tone like a catbird. It's so distinctive you won't confuse it with any other sound.

Telltale Traits

- Look for that nervous tail—rising, lowering, twitching from side to side.
- Often cocks tail up, like a wren
- Highly active, always in motion, constantly searching foliage or flitting about
- In winter, gnatcatchers hang out with all kinds of great birds, from kinglets to cardinals—enough to keep your binoculars busy for an hour or more.

Look Here

- Fly-catching, by flying out from a branch to nab a gnat or other insect in mid-air

Or Here

- Flitting among branches of trees

"It tends to maintain an upright position"

—**A. C. Bent**, *Life Histories of North American Thrushes, Kinglets, and Their Allies* (1949)

Unlike chickadees and kinglets, which may contort themselves into acrobatic postures to reach a morsel among the leaves, this gnatcatcher species gleans its insects without ever hanging from twigs.

On the Home Front

Builds its pretty nest far out on a branch, near the tip; look just above halfway up the tree • Builds a strong cup of delicate materials

Wild Menu: Insects, including plenty of—can you guess?—gnats!

Plant Picks: Oaks (*Quercus* spp.), which apparently host a myriad of gnatcatcher-approved insects

Feeder Pleasers

- Not a feeder visitor

Tricks and Treats

- The best inducement for a gnatcatcher will be the insects in your yard. Avoid using insecticides to make sure your little pals have plenty to eat.

Roaming with Friends

A friend and I headed south for the warm sunshine of the Gulf one winter. In Georgia, we pulled off the highway to stretch our legs. Naturally, I headed for the trees beside the gas station, to see what I could see. As I stepped close, I could hear the familiar high-pitched *zee-zee* calls of a band of little birds: chickadees, check; titmice, yep; kinglets, hello little guys. But, wait, what was that familiar voice? Cheerfully calling *zee-e-e-e*, blue-gray gnatcatchers were also part of the little band. Welcome to a winter haven!

Eastern Bluebird

First Impression

Unbelievable blue that takes your breath away

Mark Your Calendar

Year-round

Details, Details

- Smaller than a robin, as big as a large sparrow; 7 inches
- Orange-red throat and breast; white belly
- Female is duller, looks faded

Listen Up!

- Sweet, gurgling, whistled, *tru-a-ly, tru-a-ly!*
- Brief, husky call note that seems to keep birds in touch: *chew*

Telltale Traits

- Travels in short, slow, fluttering swoops from one perch to another
- Often glides from low perch to ground with wings spread, to catch insects

Look Here

- Perched near or in open areas, often near the edge of a woods or an orchard

Or Here

- In golf courses, cemeteries, large parks, or pastures, or on roadsides
- At apples, crab apples, and other flowering trees, picking off insects at blossoms
- At feeders or birdbaths

On the Home Front Eagerly accepts a birdhouse, but will face stiff competition from house sparrows • Very early nester, so mount boxes in late winter • Nesting may fail if late snow, ice, or freeze arrives; birds will try again.

"They are gathered sociably in companies of half a dozen or more"

—**Winsor Tyler**, *Life Histories of North American Thrushes, Kinglets, and Their Allies* **(1949)**

When you see one bluebird in your yard, you're probably soon going to see more. Bluebirds usually flock together in family groups. In winter, the families may join together to make much bigger flocks. Got that mealworm feeder ready?

Wild Menu: Insects; fruit and berries

Plant Picks: Flowering trees; small fruits, including mulberries (*Morus* spp.), serviceberries (*Amelanchier* spp.), bayberry (*Myrica* spp.), sumac (*Rhus* spp.), winterberry and evergreen hollies (*Ilex* spp.), Virginia creeper (*Parthenocissus quinquefolia*); flowering dogwood (*Cornus florida*)

Feeder Pleasers

- Mealworms and other insect foods; suet, peanut butter mixed with cornmeal, and other fat-based foods, in an accessible feeder

Tricks and Treats

- The sound of trickling water is a big draw.
- Put up a roost box so bluebirds can stay cozy at night.

Foraging Friends

Some birds band together into small flocks of mixed species in wintertime and forage together in their feeding territory. Each species in the group seeks food in a slightly different way and in a different place, so they don't compete with one another.

In winter, look for bluebirds roaming in open places, such as cornfields, cotton fields, or sugarcane fields, as well as your own backyard. Watch for warblers, too, when you notice bluebirds: Their winter foraging friends include palm warblers, myrtle warblers, and pine warblers. No one knows why they hang out together. Maybe they just like the company!

Wood Thrush

First Impression

Rusty robinlike bird with boldly spotted breast

Mark Your Calendar

Spring through fall; migration only on the Florida peninsula

Details, Details

- Smaller than a robin; 7¾ inches
- Female looks like male

Listen Up!

- The flutist of the woods: languid, liquid, *ee-oh-lay, ee-oh-lay*
- Like other thrushes, a short, terse call note when alarmed

Telltale Traits

- Sings in late afternoon and at dusk
- Often sings when rain is on its way

Look Here

- On ground in woodsy areas or shade garden near woods

Or Here

- Eating small fruits or berries, especially in summer or on fall migration
- At naturalistic low-level water feature or birdbath

On the Home Front Unless your yard adjoins a woods, you're unlikely to host nesting wood thrushes. • Well-hidden nest is similar to robin's, usually saddled on a branch or tucked in a crotch at eye level or above • Keep cats indoors if you live in thrush territory; their depredations contribute to the declining numbers of these storied singers.

"Beryl green"
"Pale sulphite green"
"Nile blue"

—Descriptions of the color of wood thrush eggs

How about "robin's egg blue"? Whatever name you call them by, thrush eggs are pretty things. All thrushes, including the robin and bluebirds as well as the wood thrush, lay greenish blue or blue eggs.

Wild Menu: Insects; small fruits and berries

Plant Picks: Mulberries (*Morus* spp.), serviceberries (*Amelanchier* spp.), elderberries (*Sambucus* spp.), dogwoods (*Cornus* spp.), spicebush (*Lindera benzoin*)

Feeder Pleasers

- May eat mealworms and other insect foods from low feeder

Tricks and Treats

- If you live near a thrush woods, tear strips of white cloth about ½ inch wide and 6 inches long and lay them in a shady garden. The birds may weave them into their nests.
- Coax thrushes with a birdbath equipped with a dripper or moving water.

The Better to See You With

Next time you're lucky enough to spot a wood thrush, take a close look with binoculars at its eyes. See how big they are? The bird's eyes are larger than most similar size birds, a trait emphasized by their white eye ring. Dr. Arthur A. Allen, a dean of American ornithology, theorized in 1934 that the wood thrush sticks to the shady side, staying in woodsy places, because its eyes are so large that too much sunlight makes the bird uncomfortable ("The Veery and Some of His Family," *Bird-Lore*).

Palm Warbler

First Impression

Tiny greenish yellow bird with eye-catching reddish brown cap, flicking tail up and down

Mark Your Calendar

Winter, along Gulf and Atlantic Coasts and Florida; inland, migration only

Details, Details

- Small sparrow size; 5½ inches
- This species comes in two different variations: brown or yellow forms or races.
- "Yellow" birds have a rich yellow breast heavily streaked with reddish brown in breeding season; when not in breeding season, they are dull yellowish brown with no cap or streaky breast.
- "Brown" birds are much duller, being brownish with a brownish white belly, but they still wear that noticeable reddish cap.
- Female and male look alike

Listen Up!

- A weak, buzzy trill
- Sharp *chick!* call note

Telltale Traits

- When you watch this bird constantly raising and lowering its tail, you'll see why it's such a great clue to identification.
- Often in small groups, especially during migration

Look Here

- On the ground. Look hard: They're tricky to see against dead leaves.

Or Here

- In flower or vegetable gardens
- In brush along fences
- Flitting through shrubbery
- In palmetto clumps

"A prominent feature of winter bird life in Florida"

—**Arthur Howell**, *Florida Bird Life* (1932)

This warbler often sticks to low levels or the ground, instead of taking to the tall treetops like many other warbler species. In winter, the birds are a regular sight in backyards and city parks, as well as along roadsides and on grassy or weedy open ground.

On the Home Front Nests far, far to the North • Nests in sphagnum peat bogs, generally at the foot of a short conifer • It's a mystery to science about which bird does the building, how long it takes, and other details.

Wild Menu: Insects; some small fruits

Plant Picks: Bayberries (*Myrica* spp.) and raspberries, for winter berries; groups of shrubs or hedges, palmettos (*Sabal* spp.), and willows (*Salix* spp.) for good foraging possibilities

Feeder Pleasers

- Not usually a feeder visitor; try mealworms

Tricks and Treats

- The usual insects in your yard are enough.

Poinsettias and Palms

Flocks of 50 or more seemed to be everywhere in the old days, but palm warblers are still common in their winter range. On a trip to the Deep South one winter, I enjoyed watching a flock of these birds inspect the yellow centers of big red poinsettias for insects. Of course, to a northerner, the poinsettias themselves were jaw-dropping—blooming outside at Christmastime!

186

Northern Parula

First Impression

A plump, *cute*, blue, yellow, and white little bird flitting through foliage

Mark Your Calendar

Spring through fall; also winter in Florida peninsula

Details, Details

- Smaller than a chickadee; 4½ inches
- Rusty and black band across upper breast
- White wing bars show up well in flight.
- Snow white belly
- Admire the fine points with binoculars—if you can focus on this active little guy.
- Female is paler version of male

Listen Up!

- Unmusical buzz that rises in pitch, punctuated by a sharp note at very end
- Call note: a sharp *chip!*

Telltale Traits

- Forages more like a chickadee and nuthatch than like the typical fluttering wood warbler: It often hangs head down to reach the underside of leaves; creeps along branches; or clings to trunk.
- Often with mixed flocks of other warblers

Look Here

- In any backyard tree or shrub, gleaning insects

Or Here

- In Spanish moss (*Tillandsia usneoides*), where its bright feathers blend in
- In deciduous trees

"Small, dumpy, and short-necked"

—**David Allen Sibley, in my favorite comprehensive field guide,** *The Sibley Guide to Birds* (2000)

Dumpy?! A stubby tail, compact shape, and plump breast make this an adorable little bird—it looks more like a baby bird instead of the usual sleek warbler.

On the Home Front Usually picks a homesite in swamps, where Spanish moss grows • The nest is a bowl hollowed out of the surrounding moss or lichen.

Wild Menu: Insects, including many spiders

Plant Picks: Spanish moss is a natural draw for this bird, if you live where it thrives. Otherwise, any backyard tree not sprayed with pesticides may catch its attention.

Feeder Pleasers
- Not a feeder visitor

Tricks and Treats
- You won't need anything other than trees and shrubs with insects.

PAR-you-luh, Please

I've called this bird the *pa-ROO-luh* warbler my whole birding life. Wrong on two counts: pronunciation and that word "warbler." "Parula," properly accented on the first syllable, is a Latin word that means "little titmouse." Our friend the tufted titmouse belongs to the genus *Parus*; "parula" is the diminutive of that word, indicating smaller size. That's why the official common name of this bird doesn't include the word "warbler." If we said "northern parula warbler," we'd really be saying "northern little titmouse warbler."

Prothonotary Warbler

First Impression
Small, vivid, golden yellow bird

Mark Your Calendar
Spring through fall

Details, Details
- About chickadee size; 5½ inches
- Blue-gray wings and some snowy white under the tail add nice contrast.
- Female very similar to male

Listen Up!
- Most warblers don't have a melodic song, but this one will catch your ear. It sings a series of rising notes: *tsweeet tsweeet tsweeet tsweeet*. The song fades into the background, though, because it never changes.
- A sharp *chip!* call note

Telltale Traits
- Constantly on the move, examining crevices or hopping over logs to pick insects from hiding places
- Clings to tree trunks like a nuthatch to extract insects

Look Here
- At a nest box in your yard

Or Here
- In trees or shrubs in your yard with flocks of other warblers during migration
- In swamps

On the Home Front Nests in a cavity • Eagerly accepts a nest box • Often uses an old downy woodpecker hole in dead snag or branch of live tree • Cypress knees are a favorite homesite.
• Fills hole with plenty of moss before adding other materials, including fishing line

"What a name to saddle on the Golden Swamp-Bird!"

—Aaron Bagg and Samuel Eliot, Jr.,
Birds of the Connecticut Valley in Massachusetts (1937)

"Wrongly compounded in the first place, wrongly spelled, wrongly pronounced!" the authors fumed. All because a certain papal official—"first notary" or *protonotary*—wears a yellow hood. Still, whatever you call this bird, or however you pronounce its name, it's still a beauty, gleaming like a yellow flame in the dim swamps.

Wild Menu: Insects

Plant Picks: Bald cypress trees (*Taxodium distichum*), sweet gum (*Liquidambar styraciflua*), or any other native tree of your area, for best insect possibilities

Feeder Pleasers
- Not usually a feeder visitor; you might try mealworms

Tricks and Treats
- Mount a small birdhouse—wren or chickadee size works well—in a shady spot to attract nesting pairs.

The Voice of the Swamp

Early ornithologists had to do quite a bit of bushwhacking back in the old days. Often it was hard to tell when their next step would bring them blundering into a swamp.

William Brewster (1851–1919), a cofounder of the American Ornithological Union, didn't stay behind his desk for long. At the age of 27, he wrote about slogging through the Southeast. The prothonotary warbler was abundant, he wrote, and useful: The male's song was as good an indicator as frogs' croaking for where the explorers should watch out for water.

Summer Tanager

Vivid, rosy red bird, without a crest—usually being chased by another

Mark Your Calendar
Spring through fall

Details, Details
- Smaller than a robin; 7¾ inches
- Note absence of black wings. The scarlet tanager, which has black wings and tail, also appears in backyards in the S and SE.
- Female is greenish yellow, sometimes with tinges of red-orange

Listen Up!
- A short, musical song of hurried phrases, repeated after a pause
- Call sounds like *chicky-chucky-chuck*

Telltale Traits
- Your best chance of spotting one is in spring when the males return. They chase each other, sing constantly, and very actively establish territories.
- Forages alone in mid- to upper levels of trees, usually deciduous
- Skilled at fly-catching
- Moves through foliage very deliberately and slowly
- Despite its color, it's very inconspicuous.

Look Here
- Usually in deciduous trees

Or Here
- Chasing other males or a female
- Flying after wasps or other winged insects

On the Home Front Usually nests high in trees • Only the female gathers nest material and builds the nest.

"Tangers in uncountable abundance"

—Francis Weston, *Life Histories of North American Blackbirds, Orioles, Tanagers, and Allies* (1958)

Weston was describing the summer tanagers that piled up on the Gulf Coast when stormy weather in spring prevented the birds from continuing their migration flight inland. Look for a swarm of tanagers in city parks, street trees, or your own backyard in April, if heavy rain, fog, or north winds prevail.

Wild Menu: Insects, especially bees and wasps; fruit and berries

Plant Picks: Fruits of any kind, particularly bite-size mulberries (*Morus* spp.) and blackberries. To attract tanagers, bluebirds, and other fabulous fruit eaters, you might try letting a plant of the common pokeweed (*Phytolacca americana*) grow in your yard.

Feeder Pleasers
- Not usually a feeder visitor, but may eat bananas; you might try mealworms, too.

Tricks and Treats
- Add a drip tube or mister to your birdbath and you may manage to see summer tanagers freshen their feathers.

Bee Eaters

Not my kind of a meal, but summer tanagers eagerly eat bees and wasps, to such an extent that they've become pests around beehives. Next time you come across a paper wasp nest (*Polistes* spp.), make it a habit to look for tanagers. Not only have the birds been seen snatching flying wasps from the colony, they've even been noted pecking through a wasp nest to get at the plump larval grubs inside.

Blue Grosbeak

First Impression

A dark, nothing-special, sparrow size bird hopping about on the ground—until it moves into the sun and reveals its deep, rich, cobalt blue

Mark Your Calendar

Spring through fall; migration only in South Florida

Details, Details

- The size of a big sparrow; 6¾ inches
- Big, heavy bill
- Cinnamon wing bars and a big bill set this species apart from the similar indigo bunting.
- Female is grayish brown
- Juvenile females are warm reddish brown; juvenile males are blotched with blue.

Listen Up!

- Rarely sings at midday, unlike the similar-looking indigo bunting
- Long, warbling song with a quiet quality that doesn't grab attention
- Metallic *zink* call note

Telltale Traits

- Flies low, from one shrub to another
- Often forages on ground

Look Here

- Hopping on ground, often beneath shrubs, looking for food

Or Here

- Singing from within a shrub
- Perched in the top of a bush or small tree
- Foraging in flocks on plowed fields

"The female never acquires much blue"

—Jonathan Dwight, Jr., "The Sequence of Plumages and Moults of the Passerine Birds of New York" (1900)

The male blue grosbeak is easy to confuse with the male indigo bunting. The female grosbeak also looks a lot like the female bunting. Both are brown, but the female blue grosbeak has tinges of blue on her wings.

On the Home Front Nests usually not more than 8 feet aboveground, in small trees, shrubs, brambles, or vines • May nest in backyard

Wild Menu: Insects; grain; weed seeds; fruit

Plant Picks: Plant shrubs in groups, or add a hedge or a patch of blackberries to supply the cover these birds crave.

Feeder Pleasers
- Millet; birdseed mix

Tricks and Treats
- Often incorporates shed snakeskins and other unusual, soft, or crinkly materials into its nest: cotton, rags, newspaper, string, cellophane, and plastic snack wrappers. Try an offering of these or similar materials at nesting time.

Let's Get Together

Blue grosbeaks aren't abundant birds. But they gather together after nesting, at first in small groups, but then in larger ones as other families join in. These flocks roam about, foraging in grain fields and sometimes backyards, until it's time to pack up and leave on fall migration. I used to mentally say "blackbirds" when I saw such a flock—until the day I lifted my binoculars because something just didn't seem quite right. I was stunned to see that every one of them was a blue grosbeak.

Painted Bunting

First Impression
Unbelievable parrotlike colors—red and blue and lime green

Mark Your Calendar
MW, spring through fall; may stray to other areas

Details, Details
- Small sparrow size; 5½ inches
- Female is yellowish green
- Not until fall of its second year does the male bird acquire its full, stunning plumage. Until then, males look like females.

Listen Up!
- Sweet, high-pitched, tinkling, melodic song
- Low *chip!* alarm call

Telltale Traits
- Acts like a sparrow, foraging in grassy or weedy places
- Male sings from exposed, elevated perch, to about 30 feet high
- A "scrapper": Male birds fight viciously with each other over females and territories, sometimes to the death.

Look Here
- At feeder

Or Here
- Eating seeds of foxtail grass or other weeds, while clinging to the stems
- Singing from top of bush

On the Home Front May nest in an appealing, shrubby backyard • Nests in low vegetation, usually less than 6 feet from ground

"The nonpareil"

—French for "without an equal"; traditional name for this bunting in the South

You won't believe your eyes the first time you see a painted bunting. It looks just too outrageous to be true. Each blotch of color is clearly defined, so that the bird looks like Joseph's coat-of-many-colors.

Wild Menu: Seeds, especially grass and weeds; grain; some insects

Plant Picks: Scatter a few handfuls of birdseed mix or finch mix in a sunny patch of soil, cover lightly, and keep your fingers crossed for buntings.

Feeder Pleasers
- Millet; birdseed mix; sunflower seeds; cracked corn

Tricks and Treats
- Don't be too fussy a weeder, and your payoff could be painted buntings—they seek out weedy grasses, especially foxtail grass, as well as dock, pigweed, and other common weeds.
- Add more birdbaths, fountains, or water features of any kind for drinking and bathing.

Aggressive Beauty

I first met painted buntings one April, when the males had just returned to the Augusta, Georgia, area from their winter vacation. I felt lucky to spot three of the birds, each already singing lustily from its claimed territory. Their colors were simply amazing.

When the females arrived a few days later, those gorgeous birds began to fight like junkyard dogs. I shooed apart two birds joined in battle because males have been known to fight to the death. But as soon as I stepped away, they returned to the fray.

Field Sparrow

First Impression

Small brown bird with blank, wide-eyed look

Mark Your Calendar

Year-round; winter only in some parts of Deep South

Details, Details

- Small sparrow size, what else? 5¾ inches
- Pink bill
- Reddish cap and white eye ring; no dark spot on breast
- Female looks like male

Listen Up!

- Plaintive *see-a, see-a, see-a, see-a, wee, wee, wee, wee*
- Sharp, short *chip!* of alarm

Telltale Traits

- Vigorous scratcher on ground
- Often in flocks of mixed sparrow species

Look Here

- On ground beneath feeder, or in tray feeder

Or Here

- Scratching elsewhere in your yard for seeds, in flower beds or vegetable garden
- Hanging on weeds or grass stems to reach seeds

On the Home Front Nests in thicket or thorny bush, usually in field but possibly in backyard • Well-made cup of dead grasses is placed on or near ground • Ground nests are usually close to a shrub or tree. • Raises several broods a season, making a new nest each time

"Can be closely imitated by anyone willing to practice"

—Arthur A. Allen, *The Book of Bird Life* (1930)

Field sparrows have a simple song that's easy to mimic. Whistling back to a singing male bird often lures the bird in, to investigate the intruder—which will give you a better look at the bird.

Wild Menu: Insects; weed seeds and grass seeds

Plant Picks: A scattering of millet seed in a corner of your vegetable garden or flower bed will give you hours of fun, as you watch field sparrows eating seeds from the stems. There's no need to buy special seed; just plant some of your birdseed.

Feeder Pleasers

- Millet; canary seed and other small seeds

Tricks and Treats

- Like other winter sparrows, the field sparrow appreciates a warm bath on a cold day. Check out a heater for your birdbath.
- Nests are often lined with horsehair from the animal's mane or tail. Ask at a nearby stable for the currycomb leavings if you don't have your own trusty steed.

Slow in Summer

You've probably noticed that birds are abundant at your feeders in fall, winter, and early spring. But suddenly their traffic drops off. What's happened? Nothing but natural behavior.

As field sparrows and other feeder birds disperse to breeding territories, they tend to stick close to their nest area as they search for food. And that might not include your feeding station. They also switch to eating more insects in summer, and bugs are also what they usually feed their babies. Don't worry, though, the birds will be back come fall.

Vesper Sparrow

First Impression

Nondescript streaky grayish brown sparrow, with white outer tail feathers

"Shows white outer tail-feathers"

—**Arthur A. Allen,**
The Book of Bird Life
(1930)

Mark Your Calendar

Winter only in most parts of this region; spring through fall in upper tier of states in this region

Details, Details

- Sparrow size; 6¼ inches
- Brown streaks may show against a tan or white background.
- White eye ring
- Male and female look alike

Listen Up!

- Two long, low whistles give way to pretty, musical trills, something like the song of a song sparrow.
- Sharp *chip!* alarm note

Telltale Traits

- Walks or runs on ground
- "Grass sparrow" and "grass finch" are old names reflecting its habit of hanging out in fields, meadows, and pastures.
- Male sings from highest available perches within nesting territory, not on ground

Look Here

- At feeder

Or Here

- In grassy areas
- Singing from fence post, tree, or other elevated perch

The vesper sparrow and song sparrow look a lot alike, but the vesper has white feathers on the outside edges of its tail. It's also a grayer bird than the song sparrow, which is a warmer brown color.

On the Home Front Not a backyard nester
- The female alone builds the nest, at the base of a plant or by a clump of crop residue. • The nest is a woven cup of grasses and other plants, camouflaged among the vegetation.

Wild Menu: Insects, especially grasshoppers; seeds; grain

Plant Picks: Try planting a prairie or meadow to entice a vesper sparrow to your yard.

Feeder Pleasers
- Millet; birdseed mix; might like mealworms

Tricks and Treats
- Provide a low-level birdbath.

Tail Betrayal

I was exploring an old farm road in South Carolina without my binoculars when I noticed a bunch of sparrows on the ground ahead of me. As I drew closer, they ran ahead of me, then immediately returned to feeding on the ground. I took several more steps; the same thing happened.

Squinting to see better, I focused on one of the birds facing me. Song sparrows, I decided, going by the streaky breast with a "stickpin" spot. Even the sweet snatches of song sounded like those of song sparrows. Then my dog came bounding up from behind, and the birds instantly flushed. White tail feathers! It was my introduction to vesper sparrows.

Fox Sparrow

First Impression

Big, plump, rusty sparrow with heavily streaked or speckled breast

Mark Your Calendar

Winter only; only rarely spotted along the coast and on Florida peninsula

Details, Details

- A big sparrow; 7 inches
- Much geographical variation in color and song; some are redder, grayer, or thicker-billed. The fox sparrow in this region is the red or Taiga race; it's a beautiful rusty-red bird.
- Female looks like male

Listen Up!

- With 18 subspecies divided into at least four distinct groups, fox sparrows show a lot of variation in song. The group of this region is the red or Taiga fox sparrow, which sings a rich, melodious, whistled song.

Telltale Traits

- Scratches vigorously on ground; can dig a hole through several inches of snow to reach seeds
- Secretive when not at feeder; stays concealed in brushy areas
- Usually arrives singly at feeder

Look Here

- On ground beneath feeder

Or Here

- In or at feeder
- Scavenging seeds from a winter garden or weeds

"They scratch lustily for their food amongst fallen leaves"

—**A. C. Bent**, *Life Histories of North American Cardinals, Grosbeaks, Buntings, Towhees, Finches, Sparrows, and Allies* (1968)

Fox sparrows certainly do have a passion for scratching—you'll often hear one rustling in the leaves before you see it. The big sparrow forages with fervor among the fallen leaves beneath shrubs and hedges.

On the Home Front Not a backyard nester in this region • Other subspecies nest in the United States, but the red fox sparrow group nests far to the north, from Canada to Alaska. • Nests on ground, in low bushes, or in small trees

Wild Menu: Seeds; insects; fruits

Plant Picks: Weeds are wildly popular in winter, especially smartweeds (*Polygonum* spp.), ragweed, lamb's quarters, and other plants we usually get rid of rather than encourage. If you have a discreet place for a weedy patch, the sparrows will flock there.

Feeder Pleasers
- Millet

Tricks and Treats
- A birdbath is often welcomed.

Here Today, Gone Tomorrow

Migrant visitors are a delightful surprise in the backyard, but I'm especially fond of those temporary guests who come immediately to the feeder, where I'll spot them first thing in the morning.

I also like birds who stick out like a sore thumb, so you know you've got someone different. The fox sparrow fills the bill on all counts, plus he's a beauty to see against fall colors or an early snow.

Boat-Tailed Grackle

First Impression

Huge, beautifully iridescent blackbird with exaggeratedly long tail, stalking about on ground

Mark Your Calendar

Year-round along the Gulf and Atlantic Coasts and in Florida; absent in other areas

Details, Details

- Way bigger than a robin: male, 16½ inches; female, 14½ inches
- Gulf Coast birds have dark eyes; Atlantic Coast birds, north of Florida, have light eyes.
- Female is brown, not iridescent black
- Boat-tailed grackle gleams with greenish blue iridescence; similar great-tailed grackle leans toward purple-blue

Listen Up!

- Loud, piercing "wolf whistle" calls
- Also a variety of rattles, *churrs*, and other rasping, guttural noises

Telltale Traits

- Unmistakable by sight alone—except in Louisiana, where this species overlaps with the similar great-tailed grackle, once considered a subspecies of the boat-tailed
- Watch for weird display postures, with up-tilted head, spread wings, and ruffled feathers.

Look Here

- On lawn

Or Here

- At feeder

"Clarinero"

—Name for male boat-tailed grackle in Mexico

This species of grackle ranges into Mexico and Central America. *Clarinero* means "trumpeter" in Spanish; it's an appropriate name for these powerful vocalists.

On the Home Front Pairs begin nesting as early as February. • Nests in colonies, usually in a marsh, and often where alligators are present

Wild Menu: Just about anything it can get into its beak: fish, shrimp, crabs, frogs, snails, crayfish; small birds, nestlings of other marsh birds (including herons and red-winged blackbirds); insects; grain

Plant Picks: Just food in the feeder

Feeder Pleasers
- Millet; birdseed mix; cracked corn

Tricks and Treats
- A big, sturdy birdbath may be welcomed.

Not Very Neighborly

Gators may seem like the creature to be wary of in the swamp, but many marsh birds are opportunistic when it comes to eating—and they have a taste for meat.

Although ibises are much bigger than boat-tailed grackles, ibis eggs and their newly hatched young are suitable for a grackle's gullet. Black vultures and fish crows also lick their lips—er, beaks—over the poor ibis's family. Even the fish that an ibis catches aren't safe—the boat-tailed grackle often grabs fish right out of the ibis's bill.

Brewer's Blackbird

First Impression

Glossy blackbird with pale yellow eyes walking on ground

Mark Your Calendar

Winter only in some parts of this region; not at all or only as strays in other parts

Details, Details

• A little smaller than a robin; 9 inches
• Part of this bird's Latin name means "blue head," referring to its iridescence: blue to purple on head and breast, green on body.
• Female is dull gray-brown with dark eye

Listen Up!

• Squeaks, trills, and whistles
• Harsh *check!* call note

Telltale Traits

• Walks on ground
• Head jerks forward with every step
• Holds back end of body and tail raised up when feeding on ground

Look Here

• Walking about on ground beneath feeder

Or Here

• Walking on lawn or other open areas
• In fall and winter, in large mixed flock with other blackbirds and starlings

On the Home Front
Not a backyard nester
• Nests in colonies • A colony often nests near water, in a variety of habitats, including willow thickets, wet meadows, and swamps. • Usually nests low to ground, at about 3 to 5 feet, but may also nest on ground or at higher level

> *"Walking and feeding on pad-lily* (Nymphaea) *leaves, even one leaf serving to hold up a bird"*
> —Frank Richardson, "Water surface feeding of blackbirds" (1947)

In sloughs and other quiet waters where water lilies grow, Brewer's blackbirds often walk about, perfectly at home, on the wide, flat leaves held at the water's surface. Watch closely and you may see them catching newly emerged damselflies and other aquatic insects.

Wild Menu: Insects; seeds and grain; occasionally fruit

Plant Picks: Try planting a patch of milo (sorghum) and let it stand in winter to attract visits from Brewer's blackbirds.

Feeder Pleasers
• Birdseed mix; millet

Tricks and Treats
• Blackbirds are fond of bathing. Provide a birdbath, and for an extra treat, a mister so they can loll in the spray.

Pretty Posers

Blackbirds of all sorts are fascinating to watch, because some of their communication is done by dramatic physical posturing. The "ruff-out" display of the Brewer's blackbird is done mostly by males, as part of courtship. The bird fluffs out all the feathers of its head, neck, and breast, while partly fanning and drooping its wings and spreading its tail. When the ruffing is at its peak, the bird lets loose with a *squee* or other harsh noise. Then he immediately goes back to normal. The whole sequence only lasts for a couple of seconds, but it's a great show.

Rufous Hummingbird

First Impression
A flash of iridescent copper and orange

Mark Your Calendar

An occasional stray in fall or winter, but seems to be expanding its range and becoming more frequently sighted

Details, Details

- Tiny! 3¾ inches, and a good part is beak
- Female is iridescent green with a dab of orange-red on throat

Listen Up!

- Buzzy sounds and variations of *zee-chew-chew-chew*
- Male dives from a great height, producing a stuttering *v-v-v-vroooom*

Telltale Traits

- Unmistakable: He hovers! He buzzes! He goes backward, forward, sideways!
- Pugnacious personality

Look Here

- At nectar feeder

Or Here

- At flowers, especially red or red-orange blossoms or tubular-shape ones
- Perched on a slender twig or other raised spot, often at top of young tree or shrub

On the Home Front Nests in the Pacific Northwest, not in this region • The nest is well-camouflaged; it looks exactly like a knobby bit of a lichen-covered branch. • The tiny cup, about the size of a Ping-Pong ball cut in half, is made of plant down and bits of bark and moss, held together with spider webs and lichens.

"The pugnacity of these birds is the most prominent characteristic"

—William Kobbé, "The Rufous Hummingbirds of Cape Disappointment" (1900)

Kobbé was writing about the hummingbirds he saw on the coast of Washington, a hundred years ago. Today, that same personality trait is evident even in birds who make the long trek across the country to the Southeast.

Wild Menu: Nectar; insects

Plant Picks: "Hummingbird flowers": tubular blossoms, especially in red or orange-red, which bloom in your area during fall or winter. Scarlet milkweed (*Asclepias curassavica*), Hong Kong orchid (*Bauhinia × blakeana*), and powderpuff (*Calliandra haematocephala*) are three possibilities for wintertime hummingbird flowers.

Feeder Pleasers
- Nectar feeder

Tricks and Treats
- A mister or garden sprinkler may attract bathing hummers.

Chicken or Egg?

Or, in this case, hummingbird or hummingbird feeder? No one really knows why in recent years rufous hummingbirds have been spotted far outside their usual western range. Is it because people have put out more nectar feeders? Are there more nectar feeder watchers? Or is it a real shift in the migration pattern for the species?

I vote for "all of the above." I think that as we hummingbird fans hang more feeders, the birds find more to support them in the off-season. And maybe they say, "Hey, why should I fly all the way to Central America when I can just *laissez les bon temps roulez* in New Orleans?"

Common Ground Dove

First Impression
Small, ruddy dove on ground

Mark Your Calendar

Year-round

Details, Details

- The length of a large sparrow, but much plumper; 6½ inches
- Stocky and short-necked, it looks as if its shoulders are hunched.
- Female is paler
- Also look for the larger (13-inch) Eurasian collared dove, with black collar at the back of its neck, and the white-winged dove (11½ inches), with a strip of white outlining the edge of its folded wing.

Listen Up!

- A series of rising *woot, woot*s that gave it its nickname of "moaning dove"

Telltale Traits

- Very tame; lets you approach very closely
- Won't fly until you almost step on it
- Spends most of its time on the ground
- Walks briskly with head nodding

Look Here

- On the ground

Or Here

- At the feeder
- Perched on fence or in tree
- In tobacco fields

On the Home Front Nests nearly year-round
- Builds its casual nest on the ground or in a low shrub, vine, fence, or stump

"Oh that I had wings like a dove!"
—**Psalms LV.6**

Doves have long, pointed wings built for fast flying. But this species seems to be reluctant to use them. The ground dove is almost always seen walking about on the ground, not flapping through the air.

Wild Menu: Seeds, especially weeds and grain; insects; small berries

Plant Picks: Plant a patch of birdseed by scattering handfuls of inexpensive seed mix. Let the plants stand to provide seed all fall and winter.

Feeder Pleasers
- Millet; birdseed mix; cracked corn

Tricks and Treats
- Doesn't need any extra enticement to visit

Double the Doves

The South is home to several kinds of interesting doves, who will happily raise their families right in your backyard. Since doves feed their young "pigeon milk," which they produce from food they've eaten themselves, the time of nesting isn't dependent on, say, a boom crop of caterpillars. So doves tend to nest just about all year.

Look out also for the Eurasian collared dove, which may nest in cabbage palm (*Sabal palmetto*), magnolias (*Magnolia* spp.), ficus (*Ficus* spp.), black olive (*Bucida bucera*), eastern red cedar (*Juniperus virginiana*), live oak (*Quercus virginiana*), and other trees. White-winged doves, which often visit backyards, prefer to nest in colonies in woodlands.

Northern Bobwhite

First Impression
A flock of plump, streaky brown "footballs" scuttling through

Mark Your Calendar
Year-round

Details, Details
- About the same length as a robin, but much plumper; 9¾ inches
- Stubby tail
- Female is streakier, with tan rather than white face markings
- The scaled quail, with quiet gray plumage, ranges through the lower western part of this region.

Listen Up!
- Clear as a whistle: *bob-WHITE!*
- The flock (called a covey) talks quietly with soft, low calls.

Telltale Traits
- A secretive bird; you'll hear bobwhites much more often than you'll see them
- Always in a covey, except when nesting
- Walks and runs over the ground
- Flies only when absolutely necessary; prefers to run away

Look Here
- On ground at feeder

Or Here
- In brushy fields or prairie plantings
- Foraging amid standing stems from last year's garden

On the Home Front The male and female build a ground nest together, weaving an arch of weeds and grasses overhead to conceal it.

Feed Store Finds

"They sometimes become very tame"

—J. H. Stickney, *Bird World* **(1898)**

Bobwhites and other quail are creatures of habit. Once they discover that your feeding station holds a reliable feast, they're likely to become regulars. And, as Stickney writes, they may "come shyly into the barnyard or about the house for food."

Wild Menu: Seeds; grain; insects; berries; fruits

Plant Picks: A birdseed patch, mixed with corn and milo, supplies cover and food.

Feeder Pleasers
- Cracked corn; birdseed mix; millet

Tricks and Treats
- Provide a ground-level birdbath, such as a naturalistic molded resin type, with a drip tube

I'm a big fan of "feed stores," those country places where you can pick up a 100-pound sack of grain, a fly swatter, or any other staples you might need. I often stumble across a product I never knew existed, but definitely want to try. One of my best finds was a poultry waterer—basically, an overturned jar in the center of a saucer that automatically refills when needed. Works great for bobwhites, if you can live with an object that definitely looks utilitarian. You can also buy one online at www.lehmans.com.

— Chapter Ten —

Birds of the Midwest

The region we call the Midwest was once home to such vast grasslands that early travelers could get lost for days. The grass was waist- or shoulder-high, and there were no landmarks to help you get your bearings. No mountain peaks cracked the horizon, and deep forests were mostly to the east and west.

Farm fields dominate the region now, with crops flourishing in the deep, fertile soil the prairies left behind. Those huge fields mean lots of open space—and birds that are adapted to that kind of habitat.

It's the plaintive whistled notes of the meadowlark and the sweet trills of ground-hugging sparrows that are the signature songs of many parts of this region, although you'll also find sweet-voiced thrushes and other forest birds in pockets of woods in the Midwest. In backyards with big shade trees, orioles and tanagers are often fixtures.

Many of the backyard birds of this region will look familiar to backyard bird-watchers in many parts of the country. That's because dozens of the most common and most widespread species are just as at home here as they are in other regions.

WILD WEATHER

The Midwest has a geography all its own. Travel here from the East or West, and you'll notice that mountains and hills gradually give way to gentle slopes, then to land that's so flat you can see forever. From the air, you can easily spot the Midwest, too: It's a vast crazy quilt of green corn, golden wheat, blue-gray oats, and other crops, stitched together by roads and decorated with far-flung farmhouses and occasional towns. Skyscraper cities are here, too, but they quickly give way to wide open spaces on their outskirts.

Wind is a constant in this region. With few landforms to impede its movement, the wind—from soft, breezy caress to laundry-whipping gust—is a part of life here. Windbreaks of hedges and trees shield yards and gardens, especially in rural areas. Humidity is part of midwestern living, too. Summers can be mighty muggy.

Productive fields cover what once was prairie.

Storms are simply a fact of life in the Midwest. When warm air from the South hits that cold air sweeping down from the North, wild weather is the result. Crashing thunderstorms, towering lightning, and tornadoes blow through in spring and summer. Blizzards or icy cold can blast in with little warning in winter.

Those storms can sweep birds off course by a few miles or by hundreds of miles. Keep an eye out for oddballs, which can show up far outside their usual range or customary habitat. On a smaller scale, summer storms can also disrupt bird life by dislodging nests from trees, or by downing trees, nests and all. That's sad to see, but bird parents will usually quickly get busy on replacement nests.

You'll want to plant trees and shrubs and other plants in your yard to soften the blow of weather extremes for your bird friends. Food sources help, but cover is just as vital. Deciduous trees offer summer shade and nesting sites, while conifers and broad-leaved evergreens help keep birds cozy in winter. If your yard is exposed to open fields, you'll want a hedge or windbreak; include some evergreens in it for a four-season wind shield.

Include scattered groups of evergreens or

Electrical storms are common in the Midwest and can disrupt bird activities.

single specimen evergreens in your yard, too, for shelter in unpredictable weather. They'll offer extra safety when storms roll in.

THE LAY OF THE LAND

Like other regions of the United States, the Midwest is a mix of cities, towns, and country land. But the rural areas are huge, with fields of soybeans, wheat, corn, and other crops as far as the eye can see. Most of our grain is raised here—and a lot of our birdseed!

Streams and rivers water the land, but drought cycles often occur every few years. Sparrows and other birds teem along every watercourse, from ponds to lakes to rivers, wherever they can find a bit of brush for cover. The grasslands and farm fields are also full of birds accustomed to that kind of a life. These are often ground nesters, such as meadowlarks, or birds that form gigantic flocks, such as blackbirds of various kinds.

The Midwest is well-known for being flat, but you'll find plenty of rolling hills, too, as well as sandstone bluffs, shale outcroppings, and other changes in elevation. Still, it's not exactly the nosebleed section of the US: The highest point in Indiana, where I lived for a decade, is only 1,257 feet above sea level. Stand there on Hoosier Hill—the exact highest point is tucked in a little thicket—and you'll feel the wind coming across miles of openness.

The Midwest grows acres of sunflowers for oil, snacks, and birdseed.

FOOD AND SHELTER

Midwesterners are proud of their prairie heritage. Fabulous grasses, as high as your ears, whisper and sing as they rustle in the breeze. In summer and fall, the grasses are splashed with confetti colors from tall, bright wildflowers. Many of the prairie flowers belong to the composite or daisy family, which means they're chock-full of seeds for any birds nearby or passing through.

I learned a lot about the wonderful prairie plants when I lived in the Midwest. But what really took me by surprise were the glorious trees, and the huge colonies of spring wildflowers blooming beneath them.

Some parts of this region are dotted with gorgeous forests, nearly totally deciduous in nature. Guess what that means? Yep, fall colors that will take your breath away. Flaming sugar maples are as good as any in Vermont, and they're bolstered by scarlet oak, coppery beech, golden hickory, and purple ash leaves.

Oh, and don't forget one of the trademark trees of the Midwest: the sweet gum (*Liquidambar styraciflua*), whose leaves look burnished deep red from a distance, but are actually a spectacular mix of red, orange, honey gold, and maroon—often on the same leaf! They're so incredible, I used to wear them as jewelry, by simply pinning a leaf to my sweater.

Those deciduous trees produce tons of acorns and seeds for jays, titmice, nuthatches, and other birds; they also supply shelter and

Maturing soybeans dominate the view, but hedgerows and field edges hold many birds. Little patches of woods hold wonderful spring wildflowers.

Purple spikes of *Liatris* punctuate a prairie.

Thrushes and bluebirds seem to be partial to deciduous hollies, such as winterberry (*Ilex verticillata*) and spicebush (*Lindera benzoin*).

The deciduous woodlands are home to another well-kept secret of this region: the unbelievable spring wildflower show. Immense colonies of dense mayapple (*Podophyllum peltatum*), or vast sky-blue stretches of wild sweet William (*Phlox divaricata*) or knee-high Virginia bluebells (*Mertensia virginica*), are just a few of the dozens of species that make spring a delight.

Although the wildflowers don't supply much food for birds, they do make spring bird-watching a pleasure that's hard to beat anywhere in the country. Don't forget to keep an eye out for the delectable mushrooms called morels, too!

Every spring, I looked forward to spending a long day in the woods, welcoming back spring migrants and admiring wildflowers, then coming home with my sack of loot—a mess of morels to dip in cornmeal batter and fry up to hot, juicy perfection.

CLIMATE

The Midwest gets four seasons, but they're not always evenly distributed. Intense cold and intense heat mark the seasonal extremes in winter and summer, but spring and fall can be glorious.

Winters are long, especially in the upper Midwest, where snow and cold may seem to last forever. Ice storms are more the order in the lower part of the region, though they can occur anywhere. Snow and ice may make it impossible for birds to find food, so your feeders can be a literal lifesaver in winter.

nest sites to scarlet and summer tanagers, thrushes, and many other shade-loving species. In winter, finches pry apart the seeds of tulip trees (*Liriodendron tulipifera*), box elders (*Acer negundo*), and other big trees, while titmice and chickadees work at the seedpods of smaller redbud trees (*Cercis canadensis*).

Shrubs and small trees are a hit with many birds in this region, whether they're the lilac in your backyard or the spicebush (*Lindera benzoin*) in the woods. They supply cover and places to move about safely, and they also serve as a handy diner. Insects on foliage, flowers, or bark, plus any fruits or berries or seeds, add variety to the birds' menu.

In fall, berried shrubs are a huge draw for birds. Look for migrating rose-breasted grosbeaks and tanagers to gather at dogwood trees (*Cornus* spp.); native dogwood shrubs, such as silky dogwood (*Cornus amomum*); and native viburnums, including arrowwood (*Viburnum dentatum)* and other species.

A drought will bring birds to your birdbath.

By the time summer rolls around, you may find yourself wishing for another taste of that winter weather! The air is hot and humid in summer, and 90°F days can set in even while the daffodils are still blooming. Seasonal dry stretches and even drought occur fairly often. A birdbath or water feature in your yard will be popular with birds during dry times, and may even pull birds from surrounding fields.

Spring is famous as tornado season, and most midwesterners are used to taking sensible precautions. A weather radio that broadcasts important alerts is a common fixture in midwestern homes.

One way you'll know when the threat of bad weather has passed is to listen to the birds. When the black clouds move on, you'll hear birds singing again as they come out of their storm shelters.

BIRD LIFE IN THE MIDWEST

Birds are abundant in this region, thanks to plenty of wide open spaces, plus inviting backyards in farms, small towns, and cities. Roadsides and scattered patches of woods support thriving bird life, too.

Large expanses of open land encourage grassland birds, such as meadowlarks, dickcissels, scissor-tailed flycatchers, buntings, and kingbirds. Once, they were the natural inhabitants of the vast, grassy prairies that covered this area. Now, they live in or along farm fields and other open land. Not all grassland birds will come into backyards, but many, including sparrows, blackbirds, and quail, have expanded their horizons to include a welcoming backyard.

With its bounty of grasses, prairie wildflowers, and grain crops, seed-eating birds are in heaven here. You'll notice an abundance of seed-eating species such as black-

Grasslands support all kinds of wildlife as well as seed-eating birds.

Summer tanagers are a seasonal treat.

birds and native sparrows in this region. And you can easily tempt them to your yard by planting a garden of seed-rich sunflowers (*Helianthus annuus*), millet, and other bird-seed plants. Birds will find plenty to pick at in your flower or vegetable garden, too, over fall and winter.

Birds that usually stick to open fields often show up in backyards in fall or winter, wherever there's a welcoming handout of seeds on the stem or in the feeder. When I lived in the Midwest, I hosted meadowlarks every winter—at my in-town feeder.

Some backyard birds, including feeder friends such as blue jays, song sparrows, and downy woodpeckers, are year-round residents in the Midwest.

Other species are more of the fair-weather variety. They return reliably each spring to raise their families and spend the summer. But winter vacation? No thanks, they say, as they flock south. As soon as the days grow shorter, they're off for a more hospitable climate. Insect eaters such as summer tanagers, scissor-tailed flycatchers, and orioles, for instance, are only seasonal pleasures instead of year-round friends.

A few unusual species can really liven up a winter day in the Midwest. This is vacation land for some of the super-hardy birds of the Far North, including Lapland longspurs, red-breasted nuthatches, and tree sparrows.

Upper and Lower Midwest

This region covers a wide area from north to south, which means that the seasonal aspects of bird-watching may be different for some species.

In the more southerly part of the region, say, Oklahoma, chipping sparrows may stick around all year. While you're enjoying those chippies at Christmas, your friends in Iowa are looking forward to the return of "their" birds next spring.

Other species, such as the vesper sparrow, may be present in summer in the northern parts of the region and in winter only in the southern sections. And some only pass through the lower Midwest on their way to nesting grounds in the upper part of this region.

You'll find general range and seasonal info for each species in this chapter. But you may also want to check a more comprehensive field guide, such as Peterson's or Sibley's, to pinpoint birds' ranges in your particular area.

Start Here

Like other regions, the Midwest is home to many common and widespread species of backyard birds. That's why you'll want to begin your tour of midwestern bird life by turning to Chapter 6, "Start Here." That's where you'll find many familiar backyard friends that you may already know by name, such as the cardinal, chickadee, goldfinch, and robin.

These are the birds you share with other parts of the country. You'll also find white-breasted nuthatches, tufted titmice, juncos, cedar waxwings, and many others who are happy to pay a visit to your backyard.

Every single one of the "Start Here" birds is happily at home in the Midwest region. You'll see some of these species more often than others. But if you keep looking, eventually you may get to know them all.

Regional Specialties

"Start Here" birds are just the beginning! In this chapter, which spotlights birds of the Midwest region, you'll meet other interesting friends. Some of these birds also occur in other regions. But every single one of them could turn up in your midwestern backyard.

Because of your location smack-dab in the middle of the country, you're likely to see birds whose ranges are to your east or west, too, as well as your regulars. Strong storms—and you know all about those!—may carry them astray into your region. Or they may just be wandering.

Paging through the other regional sections will help you get acquainted with possible travelers. Then, if they do turn up in your backyard, you'll find it's more like saying hello to a new friend for the first time than trying to identify a stranger.

Be sure to page through the birds of the Far North region, too (Chapter 8). Many of them pay a brief visit to midwestern backyards as they pass through on migration to and from more northern areas or mountainous places.

Birds of the Midwest

Here are the birds profiled in this chapter. Remember to consult the "Start Here" birds, starting on page 79, for the most common birds to be found in the Midwest.

Red-Headed Woodpecker

First Impression

A breathtaking bird! Bold white and black patches with a vivid crimson head

Mark Your Calendar

Spring through fall in part of region; year-round in other areas

Details, Details

- A little smaller than a robin; 9¼ inches
- Female looks like male
- Juvenile has brown head

Listen Up!

- Rattles, *chirr*s, and a loud, wheezy *queeer queeer queeer*
- Doesn't usually excavate into wood for insects; does drum, weakly, on occasion

Telltale Traits

- Fly-catches! The bird flies from a perch after an insect, then returns to eat it and wait for another one.
- Usually seen alone or in pairs; after nesting, may forage in family groups
- Not a rare bird in general, but locally common: in some parts of its range, it's easy to spot; in other areas, it's absent
- Stores acorns, nuts, and sometimes grasshoppers to eat later

Look Here

- Fly-catching from a utility pole, fence post, or tree

Or Here

- Flying across an open area
- On ground beneath trees, eating nuts
- Eating fruit or berries in bushes or trees
- Scavenging corn in farm field

"A bird of the open country"

—A. C. Bent, *Life Histories of North American Woodpeckers* (1939)

Most woodpeckers stick close to the woods. Look for this drop-dead-gorgeous bird winging across fields or hollering from a utility pole out in the open.

On the Home Front Nests in dead trees or in wooden utility poles, high up near top • May use a nest box • Male does most of excavation

Wild Menu: Insects; fruit and berries; corn; nuts and acorns

Plant Picks: Cherries, grapes, mulberries (*Morus* spp.), and other fruits; corn; oak trees for acorns; pecans for nuts; crab apples and other flowering trees for insects

Feeder Pleasers

- Dried corn on the cob, pushed firmly onto a spike; nuts; suet

Tricks and Treats

- Got any weathered wooden posts around? Install them as inviting perches for fly-catching in your yard. You can also try "planting" a new wood post; the taller, the better.

Cavity Karma

Birds that nest in cavities can get pugnacious when it comes time to lay claim to a nest hole. The bird that dug it doesn't always get to enjoy its new home! Starlings are famed for snitching holes from woodpeckers. Great crested flycatchers may also usurp the holes for their own use.

Before you start feeling too sorry for red-headed woodpeckers, keep in mind that this species may use the same tactics to steal a nest hole from red-bellied woodpeckers.

Red-Bellied Woodpecker

First Impression

Big, calm, red-headed woodpecker at feeder

Mark Your Calendar

Year-round; absent from western part of this region

Details, Details

- Almost as big as a robin; 9¼ inches
- Female has red only on back of neck, not top of head
- Tiny, hardly noticeable patch of red-tinged feathers on lower belly

Listen Up!

- Loud, harsh, querulous *quirrrr?*
- Steady, medium-speed drumming

Telltale Traits

- Back and wings look grayish from distance; up close, appear finely black-and-white zebra striped
- Undulating flight, with deep dips
- Often very tame; slow to fly away when you approach

Look Here

- At feeder eating sunflower seeds or corn

Or Here

- Clinging to tree trunks or large branches
- Foraging on ground
- At suet or nectar feeder

On the Home Front Excavates a cavity in a dead tree, usually deciduous, often in woods • May adopt a nest box • Breeding activity begins very early; in Illinois, breeding begins in late winter, with nesting as early as March.

"Drinking the sweet sap from the troughs in sugar camps"

—**Charles Bendire, describing the diet of this species,** *Life Histories of North American Birds* (1895)

Red-bellieds have a definite sweet tooth. One of these big birds may appropriate a nectar feeder, clinging in an acrobatic position while it guzzles the feeder dry.

Wild Menu: Insects; seeds; nuts; fruit

Plant Picks: Pecan or oak trees for nuts; field corn or Indian corn; tall, large-headed sunflowers (*Helianthus annuus*); mulberries (*Morus* spp.)

Feeder Pleasers

- Whole ears of dried corn on cob; sunflower seeds; suet and suet-based foods

Tricks and Treats

- Squirrel feeders that hold an ear of corn fixed in place work great for this big guy to peck at, too.
- Fasten a wire suet cage firmly to a tree or post to give this bird a place to prop its tail.
- May become a nectar drinker

Easier Excavating

Get in the habit of looking for dead limbs and snags in your yard and neighborhood, and you may spot a woodpecker nest hole. Often you'll spot more than one, with the older ones at top and the freshest-looking one at bottom.

There's a reason for this: fungus. Wood-decaying fungi usually enter at the top of a stub, carried into the wood by rain. As the fungi break down the wood, they make digging easier for woodpeckers. As the fungi work their way down the dead snag, so do the woodpeckers, excavating the softening wood underneath last year's hole.

Scissor-Tailed Flycatcher

First Impression

Pale gray bird with outrageously long, skinny tail, usually perched

Mark Your Calendar

In upper MW, an occasional stray; in lower MW, spring through fall

Details, Details

- From tip to tip, the flycatcher measures 10 inches—but that tail is 6 inches all by itself! Bird's body is about sparrow size.
- Female has a shorter tail than male, but it's still notably long
- Tail is deeply forked, easily visible in flight
- Look for salmon-colored undersides of wings and sides of body in flight.

Listen Up!

- Series of rapid, twittering notes
- Calls *ko-peek*!

Telltale Traits

- Opens and closes tail in flight, like a pair of scissors
- Perches for hours, sallying forth to snatch insects from the air or on the ground
- Swoops to ground from perch, or dashes out into air, returning to same perch
- Can hover in mid-air
- Sometimes hops on ground

Look Here

- On perch near open space

Or Here

- On ground, capturing grasshoppers or other insects
- In flight across open land
- Eating fruit or berries

"Most fantastic of feathered sky-dances"

—Herbert Brandt, *Texas Bird Adventures* (1940)

Like an exotic bird-of-paradise, this all-American species uses his fantastic feathers to wow the female in a courtship extravaganza that lasts for weeks.

On the Home Front May nest in backyard in small tree or shrub

Wild Menu: Insects, especially grasshoppers, crickets, wasps, and beetles; some fruit

Plant Picks: Try a meadow or prairie planting with posts for perching.

Feeder Pleasers
- Hulled sunflower chips; insect-enriched suet

Tricks and Treats
- Avoid pesticides to ensure grasshoppers.

Sky Dancer

John Terres, in the *Audubon Society Encyclopedia of North American Birds* (1980), notes that the male scissor-tail makes a remarkable courtship flight. First the flycatcher flies to about 100 feet high, until he's just a dot against the blue sky. Then he plunges down partway and zigzags, while vocalizing in a cackle that sounds like rapid hand clapping.

Hold your applause, though, because the best is yet to come. Climbing straight up again, he then goes into a series of backward somersaults that show off his incredible tail. Watch for the show when you're in scissor-tail country in May or June.

Eastern Bluebird

First Impression

Unbelievable blue that takes your breath away

Mark Your Calendar

In upper MW, spring through fall; in lower MW, year-round

Details, Details

- Smaller than a robin, as big as a large sparrow: 7 inches
- Female is duller, looks faded

Listen Up!

- Sweet, gurgling, whistled *tru-a-ly, tru-a-ly!*
- Brief, husky call note that seems to keep birds in touch: *chew*

Telltale Traits

- Travels in short, slow, fluttering swoops from one perch to another
- Often glides from low perch to ground with wings spread, to catch insects

Look Here

- Perched near or in open areas, often near the edge of a woods or an orchard

Or Here

- In golf courses, cemeteries, large parks, or pastures, or along roadsides
- At apples, crab apples, and other flowering trees, picking off insects at blossoms
- At feeders or birdbaths

On the Home Front Early nester, even in upper Midwest • Cavity nester • Prefers a site in open area or at edge of woods, not in forest • Only the female incubates and broods young, but the male pitches in when it's mealtime.

"Cows use the box to scratch their backs"

—**Thomas Musselman, on why he had to mount 200 nest boxes (near Quincy, Illinois) *outside* of fences, "Three Years of Eastern Bluebird Banding and Study" (1935)**

Finding just the right spot for a bluebird box can be a matter of trial and error—or frustration, thanks to house sparrows claiming the box. Why not start a trail like Musselman's on a rural road where bluebirds can live in peace?

Wild Menu: Insects; fruit and berries

Plant Picks: Flowering trees; small fruits, including mulberries (*Morus* spp.), serviceberries (*Amelanchier* spp.), winterberry (*Ilex verticillata*) and evergreen hollies (*Ilex* spp.), Virginia creeper (*Parthenocissus quinquefolia*); dogwood (*Cornus* spp.)

Feeder Pleasers

- Mealworms and other insect foods; accessible suet, peanut butter mixed with cornmeal to form a crumbly dough, and fat-based foods

Tricks and Treats

- The sound of trickling water is a big draw.
- Put up a roost box so bluebirds can stay cozy.

Shaking Out the Sheets

Female bluebirds are good housekeepers, according to evidence from video cameras placed inside nest boxes. They even shake out their nests, with a motion that scientists call "tremble-thrusting." The female pokes her beak deep into the nesting material and, with a rapid trembling motion, shakes her entire nest. According to the evidence on camera, this helps shake loose parasitic larvae from the bedding.

Summer Tanager

First Impression

Vivid rosy red bird, without a crest

Mark Your Calendar

Spring through fall in some parts of this region; only a stray in northern and western areas

Details, Details

- Smaller than a robin; 7¾ inches
- Note its absence of black wings. The scarlet tanager, which has black wings and tail, also appears in backyards in the MW.
- Female is greenish yellow, sometimes with tinges of red-orange

Listen Up!

- A short, musical song of hurried phrases, repeated after a pause
- Call sounds like *chicky-chucky-chuck*

Telltale Traits

- Your best chance of spotting one is in spring when the males return. They chase each other, sing constantly, and actively establish territories.
- Forages alone in mid- to upper levels of trees, usually deciduous
- Skilled at fly-catching
- Moves through foliage slowly

Look Here

- Usually in deciduous trees

Or Here

- Chasing other males or a female
- Flying after wasps or other airborne insects

On the Home Front Usually nests high in trees
- Female gathers nest material and builds nest

"The summer redbird"

—Traditional name

The cardinal is more often called "redbird," but the name certainly applies to this species, too. Unlike the cardinal that resides year-round, the "summer redbird" is gone before the autumn leaves change color.

Wild Menu: Insects, especially bees and wasps; fruit and berries

Plant Picks: Fruits of any kind, particularly mulberries (*Morus* spp.) and blackberries. To attract tanagers, bluebirds, and other fabulous fruit eaters, let a plant of the common poke-weed (*Phytolacca americana*) grow in your yard.

Feeder Pleasers

- Not usually a feeder visitor, but has been reported to eat an offering of bananas; may like mealworms, too.

Tricks and Treats

- Add a drip tube or mister to your birdbath and you may see summer tanagers freshen up.

Taking Inventory

In the 1950s, researchers in the Midwest disassembled a summer tanager nest to take a detailed inventory of what it was made from. The materials weren't what you might expect. Instead of being gathered from treetops, they'd been collected from fields or roadsides. The base was constructed entirely of panicles of white vervain (*Verbena urticifolia*), a common, easily overlooked, weedy wildflower. The second layer was made of at least 46 pieces of a grass called *Bromus japonicus*. And the soft inner layer was woven from 215 fine stems of muhly grass (*Muhlenbergia schreberi*).

Blue Grosbeak

First Impression

A dark, nothing-special, sparrow size bird hopping about on the ground—until it moves into the sun and shows its deep, rich, cobalt blue coloring

"A very diligent singer in the early morning hours"

—Henry Nehrling, *Our Native Birds of Song and Beauty* (1896)

Mark Your Calendar

Spring through fall

Details, Details

- The size of a sparrow; 6¾ inches
- Cinnamon wing bars and a big bill set this species apart from the indigo bunting.
- Female is grayish brown
- Juvenile females are warm reddish brown; juvenile males are blotched with blue.
- Look close to see the big, heavy bill.

Listen Up!

- Long, warbling song with a quiet quality that doesn't grab attention
- Metallic *zink* call note

Telltale Traits

- Flies low, from one shrub to another
- Often forages on ground

Look Here

- Hopping on ground, often beneath shrubs

Or Here

- Singing from within a shrub
- Perched in the top of a bush or small tree
- Foraging in flocks in plowed fields

On the Home Front Nests usually not more than 8 feet up, in small trees, shrubs, brambles, or vines • May nest in backyard • The female provides most of the food for the young in the nest.

But, continues Nehrling, "I have rarely heard its lively strain during noontide." That helps set this species apart from the very similar and much more abundant indigo bunting, who's famed for singing during the heat of the day.

Wild Menu: Insects; grain; weed seeds; fruit

Plant Picks: Plant shrubs in groups or add a hedge or a patch of blackberries to supply the cover these birds crave.

Feeder Pleasers
- Millet; birdseed mix

Tricks and Treats
- Often incorporates shed snakeskins and other unusual, soft, or crinkly materials into its nest: cotton, rags, newspaper, string, cellophane, and plastic snack wrappers. Try offering these or similar materials at nesting time.

Bring on the Blue

Blue grosbeaks are easy to confuse with indigo buntings, but they have their own behavior that sets them apart. Indigo buntings don't hang out in flocks, although you may see several of them feeding in the same place during migration. Blue grosbeaks are more social.

After the young birds leave their parents, they form small flocks that forage together. When the parents are finished raising their second brood, that batch of birds joins the flock, too. Look for them in grainfields and grasslands. They'll look black—like a flock of cowbirds—until you take a closer look with binoculars.

Rose-Breasted Grosbeak

First Impression
Flashy black and snow-white bird with rosy chest

Mark Your Calendar
Spring through fall in some areas of the region; migration only in others

Details, Details
- A little smaller than a robin; 8 inches
- Female is streaky brown

Listen Up!
- Warbling song, similar to robin's
- Squeaky call note; Sibley describes it as "sneakers on a gym floor"

Telltale Traits
- Flashes big white wing patches in flight
- Female looks like an overgrown female purple finch

Look Here
- In shade trees or small trees

Or Here
- At apples, crab apples, and other flowering trees, picking off insects at blossoms
- At feeder

On the Home Front Nests in a wide variety of habitats, including deciduous, mixed, and coniferous woodlands, overgrown fields and pastures, roadsides, along railroads, city parks, and of course in backyards • Nests usually less than 20 feet from ground • Makes a loose, open cup, often so thinly constructed that eggs can be seen right through the bottom of it.

"Within a stone's throw of brick buildings"

—**A. C. Bent,** *Life Histories of North American Cardinals, Grosbeaks, and Allies* **(1968)**

Bent noted that in the 50 years since he was a boy, this bird that formerly nested far from human dwellings "learned to find sanctuary ... closer to the haunts of man in our towns, villages, and suburban grounds."

Wild Menu: Insects, including gypsy moth caterpillars and Colorado potato beetles; tree buds; some fruit and seeds

Plant Picks: Elderberries (*Sambucus* spp.), mulberries (*Morus* spp.); Virginia creeper (*Parthenocissus quinquefolia*); grapes; maples native to your area for winter seeds

Feeder Pleasers
- Sunflower seeds

Tricks and Treats
- It's becoming a regular feeder visitor, so offer mealworms and other insect foods.
- Birdbaths are popular with migrants.

Ever-Lovin' Elderberries

I didn't know I had rose-breasted grosbeaks nesting in my Pennsylvania yard years ago until I spotted a male grosbeak flying to and from my patch of elderberry bushes. Through binoculars, I could see the bird's beak was splashed with purple juice from the berries. More exciting, he was carrying berries in that beak—and that meant there were nestlings nearby! Sure enough, the birds had a nest in a young red maple that I walked beneath several times a day. I'd never even been aware that a family was getting started there. Did they choose the nest site because of the berries nearby? Or just by a happy coincidence? They never told.

Painted Bunting

First Impression

Unbelievable parrotlike colors—red and blue and lime green

Mark Your Calendar

Lower MW, spring through fall; may stray to other areas

Details, Details

- Small sparrow size; 5½ inches
- Female is yellowish green
- Not until fall of the second year does the male bird acquire its full stunning plumage. Until then, males look like females.

Listen Up!

- Sweet, tinkling, melodic song
- Low *chip!* alarm call

Telltale Traits

- Acts like a sparrow, foraging in grassy or weedy places
- Male sings from exposed, elevated perch
- A "scrapper": Male birds fight viciously with each other, sometimes to the death.

Look Here

- At feeder

Or Here

- Eating seeds of foxtail grass or other weeds, while clinging to the bending stems
- Singing from the top of a bush

On the Home Front Not usually a backyard nester • Nests in low vegetation, usually less than 6 feet aboveground • Makes a well-woven, deep cup of plant fibers and stems

"The most common cage bird they have"

—Edward Wilson, noting the common practice of keeping this species as a pet, *American Ornithology* (1832)

Wilson also noted that "Many of them have been transported to Europe." Audubon commented on the practice, too, describing how the birds were trapped when attracted by a live or stuffed bunting decoy, and remarking that "Few vessels leave the port ... without taking some Painted Finches."

Wild Menu: Seeds, especially grass and weeds; grain; some insects

Plant Picks: Scatter a few handfuls of birdseed mix or finch mix in a sunny patch of soil.

Feeder Pleasers

- Millet; birdseed mix; sunflower seeds; cracked corn; chick scratch (a crushed grain mixture available at farm feed stores)

Tricks and Treats

- Don't be too fussy a weeder. Painted buntings seek out weedy grasses, as well as dock, pigweed, and other common weeds.
- Add more birdbaths, fountains, or water features of any kind for drinking and bathing.

Caging Nature

When I was a little girl, my mom kept canaries. One day, the pet shop we visited had new birds for sale: beautiful creatures that the sign called "painted buntings." My mom couldn't resist those colors; even though the birds were extremely nervous, so she took one home to join the canaries. Within a few days, it had calmed down and learned the routine.

The bunting lived to a ripe old age of 12. Years later, I was looking through my first field guide when I stopped, stunned. There was my mom's painted bunting—a wild songbird of the lower Midwest and South. It must have been trapped in the wild, not raised in an aviary like her singing canaries. No wonder the poor thing had been so frantic.

Dickcissel

First Impression

A prettier, yellow-splashed house sparrow; or a miniature meadowlark!

Mark Your Calendar

Spring through fall

Details, Details

- Same size as house sparrow: 6¼ inches
- From the front, the dickcissel bears a surprising first-glance resemblance to the meadowlark, thanks to a dramatic black V on its upper chest.
- Use binoculars to see its yellow facial markings.
- Female is paler and lacks black V at throat

Listen Up!

- All together now: *dik-dik-dik-SISSEL! dik-dik-dik-SISSEL!*
- Actually, that *sissel* may sound more like *siss-siss-siss*, with sibilant emphasis.
- Call note, a quick *check*

Telltale Traits

- Forages on or near ground
- Often turns up among house sparrows
- Sings incessantly in nesting season

Look Here

- At the feeder or on ground beneath it

Or Here

- On ground, in nearby open land, such as overgrown pastures or weedy fields
- Low to ground, on brushy roadsides or in shrubby areas of your yard

On the Home Front Usually nests in old fields or prairie, low but not on ground

"What's with that name?"

—Bird-watchers who first hear about the dickcissel

There's a simple explanation for the name of this bird: That's exactly what its song sounds like—the syllables *dick-sis-sel* repeated over and over and over, from dawn to dusk, throughout breeding season.

Wild Menu: Seeds; grain; insects, including many grasshoppers and cankerworms

Plant Picks: Bluestem (*Andropogon* spp.), switchgrass (*Panicum virgatum*), and other prairie grasses and wildflowers will make this species feel at home.

Feeder Pleasers

- Millet; birdseed mix; cracked corn and chick scratch (a crushed grain mixture available at farm feed stores)

Tricks and Treats

- Occasionally a dickcissel will linger long into fall, even winter. That's when it's likely to show up at your feeder.

Hello, My Name Is . . .

In my early days as a bird-watcher, I glanced at a letter posted on the wall of the visitor's center at Hawk Mountain in Pennsylvania. It remarked on a sighting of a dickcissel, in what seemed to be a joking tone. Years later, after I had moved from Pennsylvania (where dickcissels don't exist) to Indiana (where they are common), I was walking along a field when I heard what I thought was a new kind of grasshopper or other insect. From every side, I heard the same song: three quick *dik-dik-dik* syllables, ending with a sibilant burst of *sss-sss-sss*—dickcissels, holding forth on all sides. I never snickered at their name again.

217

Harris's Sparrow

First Impression

A very big, white- or gray-bellied sparrow with a black bib and head

Mark Your Calendar

Most areas, winter only; in northern part of this region and a few other areas, only seen on migration

Details, Details

- Our biggest sparrow; 7½ inches
- Look for the dramatic black facial markings of adult birds.
- A lot of variation in plumage: belly, for instance, may be white or gray
- Note adult's pink bill.

Listen Up!

- Single, plaintive, whistled note, repeated several times; similar to white-throated sparrow's whistle, but all on same pitch
- Sudden *week!* alarm call
- Winter flocks make a wide variety of calls.

Telltale Traits

- Kicks and scratches on ground
- When alarmed by a person, flies up into trees instead of seeking low cover
- When alarmed by a hawk, takes shelter in low cover, instead of up in trees.
- May visit singly, in pairs, in flocks, or mixed in a flock of other sparrows

Look Here

- At feeder or beneath it

Or Here

- Scratching in flower or vegetable garden
- In hedges, shrub groups, overgrown corners, and other brushy places

On the Home Front Nests *waaaay* up near Arctic Circle • Nests on ground, in scraped-out depression under small shrub

"The only North American songbird that breeds exclusively in Canada"

—The National Audubon Society Watchlist

The Midwest is the winter home of this big, pretty sparrow, which nests in remote boreal forest edges and tundra. Because its Canadian summer home is so hard to reach, the nesting habits of this species were not discovered until 1931.

Wild Menu: Seeds; grain; insects; snails

Plant Picks: Scatter a few handfuls of birdseed mix to grow a patch for winter foraging. Let flower garden stalks stand, so sparrows can seek seeds on or under them.

Feeder Pleasers

- Millet; birdseed mix; cracked corn and chick scratch (a crushed grain mixture available at farm feed stores); accessible suet; leftover bread

Tricks and Treats

- For a high-calorie winter warm-up, toss crumbled, stale doughnuts and cornmeal with chopped suet.
- Puddles from melting snow are favorite spots for a bath. Try a low-level basin with a heater for backyard visitors.

Sharing Lessons

Harris's sparrows can create dissension at your bird feeder. Often they act aggressively, chasing other birds away. Cut down on the competition by supplying chicken scratch and millet in a low tray feeder or directly on the ground, away from other feeders.

Lark Sparrow

First Impression

Big, slender sparrow with white-cornered tail

Mark Your Calendar

Spring through fall

Details, Details

- Sparrow size; 6½ inches
- Dramatic white corners of tail, like towhee
- Whitish or pale breast with black spot in center
- Striking head pattern in chestnut, gray, white, and black—like the patches of a Harlequin
- Female looks like male
- Immature birds show a distinct but less bold version of the head pattern.

Listen Up!

- A pretty song, full of liquid trills, with the occasional rattling note—often sung in flight
- Alarm call, a sudden *chewp!*

Telltale Traits

- Spends a lot of time on ground or lawn
- Forages on ground with much scratching
- Frequent singer from ground, fence post, trees, and wires, or in air
- The male struts like a turkey to court the female, with his tail spread to show off its white corners.

Look Here

- On the ground, usually scratching for food

Or Here

- Foraging in vegetable or flower garden
- Foraging on lawn
- Singing from a perch or in the air

"Conspiculously edged with white"

—Ralph Hoffmann, on the tail of the lark sparrow, *Birds of the Pacific States* (1927)

Sparrows can be tricky to tell apart, so any flashy markings are a big help. With this species, watch for the conspicuous white-edged bottom and sides of its tail in flight.

On the Home Front Nests low to or on ground, often hidden by overhanging branch

Wild Menu: Seeds, especially of grasses; insects, particularly grasshoppers

Plant Picks: Tolerate a few weedy grasses, such as foxtail, in your garden, or sow millet. Your lawn is inviting to these birds.

Feeder Pleasers

- Doesn't often come to feeders during breeding season, but may on migration. Offer millet, birdseed mix, or chick scratch (a crushed grain mixture available at farm feed stores).

Tricks and Treats

- A birdbath, especially one low to the ground, may be welcomed during drought.

Recycled Nests

No one knows why, but this species has a penchant for "recycling" the nests of other birds as its homesites. Nests of scissor-tailed flycatchers, western kingbirds, thrashers, and especially mockingbirds are often sought out—sometimes while the original owner is still in residence!

Those owners can get mighty aggressive defending their real estate. If you spot one chasing a sparrow, you may be seeing the home-front defense in action.

Vesper Sparrow

First Impression

Nondescript, streaky brown sparrow—with white outer tail feathers

Mark Your Calendar

Spring through fall in upper MW; migration only or winter in most of lower MW

Details, Details

- Sparrow size; 6¼ inches
- Brown streaks may show against a tan or white background.
- White eye ring
- Male and female look alike

Listen Up!

- Two long, low whistles give way to pretty, musical trills, something like the song of a song sparrow.
- Sharp *chip!* alarm note

Telltale Traits

- Walks or runs over the ground
- "Grass sparrow" and "grass finch" are old names, reflecting its habit of hanging out in fields, meadows, and pastures.
- Male sings from highest available perches within nesting territory, not on ground

Look Here

- At feeder

Or Here

- In grassy areas
- Singing from an elevated perch

On the Home Front Not a backyard nester
- The female alone builds the nest, placing it at the base of a plant or by a clump of crop residue.

"Two or three long, silver notes of peace and rest, ending in some subdued trills and quavers"

—John Burroughs, *Wake-Robin* (1871)

"Vesper" means "of or pertaining to the evening," and that's what gave these birds their name. Although vesper sparrows also sing at other times, it's after sunset, when most birds have ceased singing, that you can really appreciate their pretty song.

Wild Menu: Insects, especially grasshoppers; seeds; grain

Plant Picks: Try a prairie planting or meadow to entice a vesper sparrow to your yard.

Feeder Pleasers
- Millet; birdseed mix; chick scratch (a crushed grain mixture available at farm feed stores); maybe mealworms

Tricks and Treats
- Provide a low-level birdbath.

After-Dinner Treat

Vesper sparrows range across almost the entire country, according to the maps in field guides. Yet many folks still miss out on the pleasures of vesper sparrows. They sing at what has become, in modern life, one of our busiest times of the day. We're eating dinner, or helping with homework, or watching kids or grandkids at school events.

If your calendar is jam-packed, why not pencil in "vesper sparrows, twilight" on a few dates in spring and summer? Once you catch this romantic concert, you'll never forget it.

Field Sparrow

First Impression

Small brown bird with blank, wide-eyed look

Mark Your Calendar

Spring through fall in upper Midwest; year-round in lower; absent in extreme western part of this region

Details, Details

- Small sparrow size, what else? 5¾ inches
- Pink bill
- Reddish cap and white eye ring; no dark spot on breast
- Female looks like male

Listen Up!

- Plaintive *see-a, see-a, see-a, see-a, wee, wee, wee, wee*
- Sharp, short *chip!* of alarm

Telltale Traits

- Scratches vigorously on ground
- Often in flocks of mixed sparrow species

Look Here

- On ground beneath feeder, or in tray feeder

Or Here

- Scratching elsewhere in your yard for seeds, in flower beds or vegetable garden
- Hanging on weeds or grass stems to reach seeds

On the Home Front Not usually a backyard nester; as its name says, prefers old fields with scattered shrubs—but keep looking! • Female builds early nests on or near ground, often in grass clumps or below shrubs

Field sparrows may seem like ordinary little brown birds at the feeder, but they have an unusual and charming habit of breaking into song on bright nights in nesting season.

Wild Menu: Insects; weed seeds and grass seeds

Plant Picks: A scattering of millet birdseed on a patch of your vegetable garden or flower bed will give you hours of fun, as you watch field sparrows and other sparrows eating seeds off the stems.

Feeder Pleasers

- Millet; canary seed and other small seeds

Tricks and Treats

- Like other winter sparrows, the field sparrow appreciates a warm bath on a cold day. Check out a heater for your birdbath.
- Nests are often lined with horsehair from the animal's mane or tail. Ask at a nearby stable for currycomb leavings if you don't have your own trusty steed.

Cowbird Culture

Parasitic brown-headed cowbirds are common in the Midwest, and that's bad news for field sparrows, as they're frequent victims. The cowbird sneakily lays its own eggs in the sparrow's nest, passing off parenting chores to the poor field sparrow.

In one Iowa study, nearly 80 percent of nests were parasitized by cowbirds. That doesn't necessarily mean boom times for cowbirds, however: Once the field sparrow discovers the foreign eggs, it often deserts its nest—even if it has already laid its own eggs.

Bobolink

First Impression

Flock of startling black-and-white birds flying across a field, singing tinkling, joyous songs

Mark Your Calendar

Upper MW, spring through fall; lower MW, migration only

Details, Details

- The size of a large sparrow; 7 inches
- Sometimes called the "skunk blackbird," thanks to its black-with-white feathers
- Female looks like a sparrow, gray-brown with streaky back and wings
- After breeding season, the male loses his dramatic colors and turns to a warm tan version of the female

Listen Up!

- A warbling, bubbling song that sounds like *"bob-o'-link, bob-o'-link, spink, spank, spink"*
- Also a low *chuck* call

Telltale Traits

- Walks slowly over ground, grabbing bites of food as it goes
- Male sings while flying, constantly warbling; flies low, almost hovering
- When not nesting season, birds stick together in flocks

Look Here

- In grassy fields

Or Here

- In cultivated fields, especially hay fields for nesting and grainfields when foraging
- Possibly at your feeder; look closely at those "sparrows" in case they're bobolinks not in breeding plumage.

"Robert of Lincoln is gayly drest"

—American poet William Cullen Bryant (1794–1898), "Robert of Lincoln"

As for that gay dress, here are the details: "Wearing a bright black wedding-coat; White are his shoulders and white his crest." Bryant was a little off. Maybe he didn't use binoculars to see that the bobolink has no white crest, but a large straw-colored patch on the back of his head.

On the Home Front Usually nests in fields; many nests destroyed by farm machinery

Wild Menu: Insects; seeds; on southward migration and in winter, eats grain

Plant Picks: Acreage with hay and crops attract bobolinks, but your best bet is your feeder.

Feeder Pleasers
- Millet or birdseed mix

Tricks and Treats
- Go for a ride in the country in spring and look for bobolinks. They're a delight to watch.

Made in the Shade

On a summer day in the Midwest, temperatures regularly climb into the nineties or above. Cattle and horses in a pasture gather under a tree, and farmers do the same when it's time to take a break. Parent birds keep their precious babies out of the strong heat of the sun also. They start by building their nest in a shady location, usually beneath an overarching plant. If the sun's rays still peek through, the parents shade their nestlings by crouching over the nest with wings spread like a parasol.

Meadowlark

First Impression

Dumpy, waddling, streaky brown bird with a glorious yellow chest marked by a broad black V

Mark Your Calendar

Spring through fall in upper part of this region; year-round in lower part

Details, Details

- A bit smaller than a robin; 9¼ inches
- Both the eastern and western meadowlarks are in this region. They look very much alike.
- Yellow breast is paler when not in breeding season
- White outside feathers on tail, in flight
- Female and male look alike
- Reminiscent of starling body shape and walking style

Listen Up!

- Eastern: clear, slurred, simple whistle of a few syllables, with hint of melancholy
- Western: lives up to the name "lark," with its rich, clear, gurgling, whistled song; notes descend toward end

Telltale Traits

- Busily walks about on ground
- Sings from clump of tilled soil, hillock of grass, fence post, or other perch
- Generally flies low, often in flock

Look Here

- On ground in grassy places

Or Here

- At feeder, especially in winter or during migration

"The very spirit of the boundless prairie"

—**A. C. Bent,** *Life Histories of North American Blackbirds, Orioles, Tanagers, and Allies* **(1958)**

The clear, piercing whistle of the meadowlark carries over a long distance. It's so distinctive that despite almost endless variation in its song, its voice is instantly recognizable as the soul of the prairie.

On the Home Front Nests in old fields, pastures, meadows • Its interesting roofed nest is almost impossible to find, as it's woven right into surrounding grasses.

Wild Menu: Mostly insects; some seeds and grain

Plant Picks: Plant native prairie grasses and wildflowers, such as Indian grass (*Sorghastrum nutans*) and bluestems (*Andropogon* and *Schizachyrium* spp.), with perennial sunflowers (*Helianthus* spp.), silphiums (*Silphium* spp.), or others, to create a bit of grassland for this bird to forage in.

Feeder Pleasers
- Birdseed mix; cracked corn; millet

Tricks and Treats
- In fall, set up a ground-level feeder to attract migrating or winter-territory meadowlarks.

Meat on the Menu

Meadowlarks have a song that's ethereal, but their eating habits can be really down to earth. Like other members of the Blackbird family, they occasionally engage in a meal of meat. I've seen meadowlarks eating what they could from roadkill. Horned larks, abundant in open land, have an unfortunate habit of gathering along roads—and waiting until the very last second to take flight. Driving through Oklahoma after a snowstorm one year, I saw some pragmatic meadowlarks putting dead horned larks to good use.

Brewer's Blackbird

First Impression

Glossy black bird with pale yellow eyes walking on ground

Mark Your Calendar

Likely visitor but it may be migration only, nesting, winter only, or year-round

Details, Details

- A little smaller than a robin; 9 inches
- Part of this bird's Latin name means "blue head," referring to the iridescent blue to purple on its head and breast, and green on its body.
- Female is dull gray-brown, not shiny, with dark eye

Listen Up!

- Squeaks, trills, and whistles
- Harsh *check!* call note

Telltale Traits

- Walks on ground
- Head jerks forward with every step
- Holds back end of body and tail raised up when feeding on ground

Look Here

- Walking about on ground beneath feeder

Or Here

- Walking on lawn or in other open areas
- In fall and winter, in large mixed flock with other blackbirds and starlings

On the Home Front Nests in colonies, often near water, in a variety of habitats, from fields to swamps • Usually nests low to ground, about 3 to 5 feet up, but may also nest on ground or at higher level

"Satin bird"

—**Old common name**

The name "Brewer's blackbird" tells us nothing about this bird; Audubon named it that in honor of his friend, Dr. Thomas Brewer of Boston, a fellow ornithologist. On the other hand, the old name of "satin bird" fits this species perfectly: The male's glossy feathers gleam like candlelight on a long satin cape.

Wild Menu: Insects; seeds and grain; occasionally fruit

Plant Picks: Try planting a patch of milo (sorghum) to attract summer to winter visits from the Brewer's blackbird.

Feeder Pleasers
- Birdseed mix; millet

Tricks and Treats
- Blackbirds are fond of bathing. Provide a birdbath, and for an extra treat, a mister that they can loll under.

Building Supply

I always enjoy trying to figure out what old bird nests I come across are made of. In southern Indiana, where soybean fields are a fixture, I happened across many Brewer's blackbird nests. Often the cup was constructed of familiar material: pieces of dried soybean stems, with empty seedpods dangling here and there like festive decorations.

Yellow-Headed Blackbird

First Impression
Unmistakable! Big black bird with striking yellow hood

Mark Your Calendar
Spring through fall in most parts of this region; migration only in some lower MW areas

Details, Details
- Almost as big as a robin; 9½ inches
- Male flashes big white wing patches in flight
- Female is much less dramatic but still has yellow tinge

Listen Up!
- A cacophony of squawks, *squeeps*, rattles, shrieks, and clacks, plus a noise like a chainsaw

Telltale Traits
- Sight alone is enough for positive ID
- Usually in flocks
- Nervous tail flicks

Look Here
- At feeder

Or Here
- In marshes with cattails or other reeds
- Stalking about on lawn in flock
- In winter, in grainfields. Huge flocks "roll over" fields, birds in back moving to front as they scour field for wasted grain.

On the Home Front
Not a backyard nester, unless you have a large, reed-fringed pond • Nests in colonies, in marsh • The male selects a breeding territory, then females in his harem build nests within it.

"A wail of despairing agony"

—**William Leon Dawson, on the love song of the male yellow-headed blackbird,** *The Birds of California* **(1923)**

This species' courtship has been described as "more spectacular than beautiful," and weird sounds are certainly part of it.

Wild Menu: Weed seeds; grain; aquatic insects

Plant Picks: Your feeder will keep these birds content.

Feeder Pleasers
- Sunflower seed; cracked corn

Tricks and Treats
- A birdbath or water feature may attract a yellow-headed splasher.

Wails and Shrieks

Yellow-headed blackbirds nest in many places in this region, and it's well worth looking for a colony near your neighborhood, if only to get an earful of their incredible vocalizations. No other bird has so many weird sounds up its sleeve. And talk about loud!

William Leon Dawson wrote his description of the male's love song in the 1920s, but it's apt today. "When you have recovered from the first shock, you strain the eyes in astonishment that a mere bird, and a bird in love at that, should give rise to such a cataclysmic sound."

Orchard Oriole

First Impression

Reddish chestnut bird with black hood singing from shade tree as he hops from twig to twig

Mark Your Calendar

Spring through fall

Details, Details

- A little larger than a sparrow; 7¼ inches
- No other male bird has this unusual coloring.
- Female is yellow-green with gray wings
- White wing bars

Listen Up!

- A rich, musical, warbled song that sounds something like this: *look here, what cheer, what cheer, whip yo, what cheer, wee yo*
- Song is different from that of Baltimore or Bullock's orioles; sounds more like a robin

Telltale Traits

- Constantly hops from twig to twig in foliage, even when singing
- Often obscured by leaves, but not shy

Look Here

- In deciduous trees

Or Here

- At apples, crab apples, and other flowering trees, picking off insects at blossoms
- In city parks, golf courses, or cemeteries with scattered trees, or along shaded streets
- Near streams, rivers, and other water

On the Home Front May nest in backyard
- Usually nests low, in small trees • The nest is an open pouch of grass suspended from a fork near the tip of a branch.

"A gentle, friendly, and sociable bird"

—A. C. Bent, *Life Histories of North American Blackbirds, Orioles, Tanagers, and Allies* (1958)

Nowadays, describing birds in terms of human characteristics is frowned upon by scientists. But Bent hit this bird's personality right on the mark, no matter what language he used. This species, he wrote, "lives in perfect harmony with many other birds ... and seems to enjoy human environments."

Wild Menu: Insects, mainly; plus a bit of fruit

Plant Picks: Shade trees for nest sites and insects; also mulberries (*Morus* spp.), cherries, strawberries, raspberries, and grapes

Feeder Pleasers
- Not usually a feeder visitor; may visit a nectar feeder

Tricks and Treats
- A birdbath may appeal, especially one with trickling water.
- Offer nesting materials in spring: cotton balls, tufts of natural wool, snippets of yarn, and other soft bits.

Birding by Ear

The spring chorus of birdsong can sound like a confusing mess when you first begin trying to sort out the singers. But if you spend a little time each day listening and looking, you may soon find yourself admiring a lovely orchard oriole through your binoculars.

Listen for a musical song that seems to move slowly through the foliage, instead of coming from the same place. Then focus your glasses on the singer. It's not tricky, because sooner or later the bird will slip into view. All it takes is a bit of patience.

Northern Bobwhite

First Impression

A flock of plump, streaky brown "footballs" scuttling through

Mark Your Calendar

Year–round

Details, Details

- About the same length as a robin, but much plumper; 9¾ inches
- Stubby tail
- Female is streakier, with tan rather than white face markings
- The scaled quail, another football–shape bird but with gray plumage, ranges through the lower western part of this region.

Listen Up!

- Clear as a whistle: *bob-WHITE!*
- The flock (called a covey) talks quietly with soft, low calls.

Telltale Traits

- Secretive birds; you'll hear bobwhites much more often than you see them
- Always in a covey, except when nesting
- Walks and runs over the ground
- Flies only when it needs to make a fast getaway; prefers to run

Look Here

- On ground at feeder

Or Here

- In brushy fields or prairie plantings
- Foraging amid standing stems from last year's garden

On the Home Front The male and female build their nest together, often weaving an arch of weeds and grasses overhead. • Nest on ground • May nest in backyard, in undisturbed corner

"He seeks the home, garden, farm, and field"

—Edward Forbush, *A History of the Game Birds, Wild-fowl, and Shore Birds of Massachusetts and Adjacent States* (1912)

Forbush had other praise to bestow on the bobwhite: "He is the friend and companion of mankind; a much needed helper on the farm; a destroyer of insect pests and weeds; . . . and, last as well as least, good food, a savory morsel, nutritious and digestible."

Wild Menu: Seeds; grain; insects; berries; fruits

Plant Picks: A birdseed patch, mixed with corn and milo, will supply all–important cover as well as months' worth of food.

Feeder Pleasers

- Cracked corn and chick scratch (a crushed grain mixture available at farm feed stores); birdseed mix; millet

Tricks and Treats

- Provide a ground-level birdbath, such as a naturalistic molded resin type, with a drip tube for extra coaxing power, and bobwhites may become regular visitors to your spa.

Overdose of Ardor

In spring, that *bob-WHITE!* call can be a cry of battle. If another male dares to answer, the birds may advance on each other, calling as they go. Whenever I hear bobwhites trading insults, I try to sneak up on the scene. A few times, I've seen the actual clash, in which the "cute little birds" rush at each other with beating wings and claws and tearing beaks, like a couple of dueling roosters. In all cases, one of the birds gave up quickly and made his getaway.

Chapter Eleven

Birds of the West

The West has some of the most spectacular scenery in America, with high mountain ranges, flower-filled flatlands, and sunsets that set the sky on fire. This region is wildly diverse, with those staggering mountains yielding to sagebrush, and dense, well-watered forests giving way to arid scrub. Yet to birds, the scene all makes sense.

Many of the species in this area, from woodpeckers to hummingbirds, treat it as one world, but with seasonal homes. In spring, many birds move to cooler, higher elevations to raise their families. In fall, the "vertical migration" changes direction, and nesting birds of the mountains retreat downward to lower elevations, where the cold isn't quite as brutal and food can still be easily found.

THE LAY OF THE LAND

This region is the most wildly diverse of all of the seven regions in this book. Aromatic sagebrush flatland, cut by canyons, leads to gentle foothills, then upward to the high mountains of the Rockies.

Blizzards are common in the long, harsh winters of this region. But summers are pure delight. They're relatively cool and short, although it can be hot at times. Spring brings fantastic spreads of wildflowers, and autumn gilds the scenery with glowing aspens.

Big cities and their suburbs are here, but there are still plenty of wide open spaces. Occasional towns and ranches, from mini-size to huge working spreads, add another twist to the habitat available for birds. Native plants are popular in backyards here; they're so well adapted to the rigorous conditions.

FOOD AND SHELTER

Conifers, aspens, and other trees of this region harbor a host of insects on their foliage, and in and under their bark. That's a real draw for nuthatches, chickadees, and wood-peckers, among the most dedicated guardians of the trees.

In the sagebrush country, where trees are mostly absent except for junipers (*Juniperus* spp.) and other small trees, dryland birds such as quail, native sparrows, and thrashers find a home. These birds live on or near the ground, so they're well suited to the open sagebrush country. Wildflowers abound in this region, all of them well-adapted to the challenging climate. Explore the possibilities of growing penstemons (*Penstemon* spp.), native perennial flowers that are magnets for hummingbirds.

Also plant fruits and berries; their water content makes them a real treat for many birds of this area. Native shrubs are your best choice, because the birds already know and love them. Try buffaloberry (*Shepherdia argentea*), golden currant (*Ribes aureum*), wax currant (*R. cereum*), or any others that catch your eye. You'll find other suggestions in the following profiles of individual birds. If your locally owned nursery doesn't have a good

Mmm, smell that sagebrush! Drier parts of the West, where trees give way to plants that can thrive with little water, also bring a change in birdlife. Quail and sparrows stay low among the cover.

selection of natives, ask around. The West is full of passionate gardeners who have learned how to work with their climate instead of struggle against it.

CLIMATE

Brrr! Winters are extreme in the western mountains. Even in the foothills, snows fall deep and often. The deserts in this area get their share of snow, too. And wind is a fact of life. Folks don hooded parkas and face masks to protect themselves from frigid air and blowing snow. All the more reason to add an extra metal trash can full of emergency supplies of birdseed. Running out feels awful when your birds are facing a blizzard. Weather can swing dramatically in this region, with temperatures dropping like a rock as fast-moving fronts roar through. It can be 70°F one day—and snowing the next!

Spring comes earlier to lower elevations, while mountains are still sleeping under snow. Eventually the warming air melts the white stuff, and waterfalls and rivulets course and drip off every slope.

Summer is fabulous in the mountains, with meadows of wildflowers, sometimes called mountain "parks," creating staggering sweeps of color. Lower down, summer brings the dry season, and the early wildflowers soon give way to brown and gray. This is a fairly dry climate, with most of the precipitation from fall through spring; summers are dry, and humidity is low. Cyclical droughts can be a problem, too. Those are good reasons to include several birdbaths in your backyard, with at least one of them at ground level.

Westerners take pride in their hardiness, and the birds are pretty tough, too. Birds in

Black-headed grosbeaks are common.

this region seem to follow two paths to thrive in this climate: Either they adapt to the conditions, like the rosy finches that call from rocky cliffs even in winter, or they move lower down in cold weather and range higher up in warm seasons, like the hummingbirds.

BIRD LIFE IN THE WEST

Birds are abundant in this region, with some species seen only in the mountains, some in the deserts, and a good number adjusting to life both high and low. Most species are found in neighboring regions, too, because similar terrain and habitat are found elsewhere.

The elevation at which you live will affect the birds you see in your backyard—and when you see them. Steller's jays, broad-tailed hummingbirds, and other species move up the mountains in spring and down in late summer to fall. So depending on where your homestead is on their journey, you may enjoy them as nesting birds, winter residents, or only as passersby.

Because of all the variation in western terrain, you may want to invest in a comprehensive field guide with detailed range maps for each bird species. That way you can see at a glance whom you can expect, and when they'll be arriving.

Start Here

Even though the West is home to many birds that would never be seen in the East, it also harbors a lot of familiar friends. Turn to Chapter 6, "Start Here," to find many of your loyal backyard friends, the birds you share with other parts of the country—chickadees, white-breasted nuthatches, tufted titmice, goldfinches, juncos, cedar waxwings, and many others.

Regional Specialties

The West is where the bird life changes. Eastern species thrive also across the Midwest. But once you hit those mountains, it's time for a change. The birds here are very different from eastern birds.

Suddenly there's the vivid western tanager, flickering like a flame in the conifers. Striking black-headed grosbeaks take over from the rose-breasted ones found eastward. Grassy fields are full of lazuli buntings instead of the indigo species. Just about everywhere you look, you'll find unique birds that never cross the Great Plains.

Be sure to page through the birds of the Far North, Northwest, and Southwest and California regions, too. Those regions are your neighbors, and many of their birds also range into your territory.

Birds of the West

Here are the birds you'll find in this chapter. Remember to consult the "Start Here" birds, starting on page 79, for many other common birds in the West.

Lewis's Woodpecker

First Impression

A large black woodpecker with a pale collar, gliding across an open area between trees

Mark Your Calendar

Depending on location: year-round, winter only, spring through fall, or migration

Details, Details

- Bigger than a robin; 10¾ inches
- Worth finding in binoculars: Its black feathers have a green sheen, and its red face and deep pink-red belly are beautiful.
- Female looks like male

Listen Up!

- Harsh *churr, churr, churr*
- Sudden *yick!* alarm call

Telltale Traits

- Flight almost looks like slow motion
- Glides or soars, without flapping wings
- Often fly-catches from perch, swooping out after passing insects
- Stores acorns and nuts in caches, often in a crevice of a utility pole or a fissure in bark
- May perch on utility wires
- Battles with other woodpeckers over stored food
- Pair remains together year-round

Look Here

- On a prominent perch in a tree or on a post, flying out to catch insects

Or Here

- In oaks, collecting acorns
- In flocks in winter, in oak groves or nut tree orchards
- Gliding from perch to ground to catch grasshoppers, crickets, and other insects

"My acquaintance with this exotically brilliant woodpecker began in the mountains of Colorado"

—**Johnson Neff**, *A Study of the Economic Status of the Common Woodpeckers* (1928)

This beautiful bird can be considered a pest in apple orchards. But after analyzing the contents of hundreds of stomachs of these woodpeckers, Neff concluded that the bird actually eats more harmful insects than it does apples.

On the Home Front May accept a nest box if you live near open Ponderosa pine forests, its typical breeding habitat • The male usually does most of the excavating of a nest hole.

Wild Menu: Insects; nuts; acorns; fruit

Plant Picks: Oaks (*Quercus* spp.), English walnut trees (*Juglans regia*), grapes, apples

Feeder Pleasers

- Doesn't usually visit feeders; try offering English walnuts in the shell, or whole corn

Tricks and Treats

- Has been reported to use nest boxes

Tending the Store

Unlike birds that store their food still in the shell, Lewis's woodpecker cracks open every bit it gets its beak on. Nuts and acorns are shelled before storage, with the ready-to-eat nut meats and acorn pieces tucked into its cache. In winter, the birds visit their larder daily, spending hours turning the pieces so that they get some air and mold doesn't set in.

White-Headed Woodpecker

First Impression

No mistaking that clownish white face on a solid black body

Mark Your Calendar

Year-round, in mountains

Details, Details

- Almost robin size; 9¼ inches
- Look for a red patch on head.
- White patches in wings add an accent when the wings are folded. They look flashy in flight.
- Female lacks red on head
- Feathers are often smeared with the sticky pitch of the pines the birds forage in.

Listen Up!

- Sharp, emphatic *chick!* may be repeated rapidly
- A rattling, metallic call that sounds like a chisel dropped on a concrete floor
- Occasionally drums on wood, but not as much as many other woodpecker species

Telltale Traits

- Frequently fly-catches its food, flying out from perch to snatch passing insects
- Flakes off scales of conifer bark with its bill to get at insects underneath
- Extracts seeds from conifer cones
- Often forages at base of conifers

Look Here

- At birdbath

Or Here

- In conifers, especially Ponderosa pine, but also sugar pine, sequoia, and Douglas fir
- When you visit the Sequoia National Forest in northern California

"A crowbar instead of a hammer"

—**James Merrill, "Notes on the Birds of Fort Klamath, Oregon" (1888)**

Most woodpeckers are "hammerheads"—they get their food by drilling it out of wood with their strong beak and skull. But the white-headed uses finesse instead of brute strength. It slips its beak under flakes of bark and lifts them off, as if prying with a crowbar.

On the Home Front Not a backyard nester
- Nests in dead pine stumps • Often excavates several holes in same stump • Makes its home at varying heights, from about 4 to 25 feet high, but usually about 8 feet aboveground

Wild Menu: Conifer seeds, mostly those of Ponderosa pine; bark beetles and other insects

Plant Picks: Ponderosa pine (*Pinus ponderosa*), for future supplies of cones and insects

Feeder Pleasers
- Not usually a feeder visitor; keep that suet block up, just in case

Tricks and Treats
- Water! This woodpecker loves a good drink and frequently visits birdbaths and other water features.

Clever Camouflage

Pine trees often have broken stubs of branches that can look white from a distance when the light hits them just right. They'll then cast a shadow that makes the area beneath look black. Are you sensing a connection? Yep, despite its dramatic plumage, the white-headed woodpecker is superbly camouflaged. Its head becomes just another branch stub, and its body a shadow. Only those falling flakes of bark give it away.

Clark's Nutcracker

First Impression

A big, bold, gray bird with black wings

Mark Your Calendar

Year-round; generally at higher elevations

Details, Details

- Significantly bigger than a robin; 12 inches
- Classy color scheme of pale gray body accented with black wings and tail, with white edges
- Female and male look alike

Listen Up!

- Betrays its connection to the jays as soon as it opens its mouth: harsh squawks, a guttural *charr, char-r-r-r,* and various yelps and rattles
- Also some musical tooting notes
- An unusual noise is made by its wing feathers when the bird checks a deep dive, such as one down into a canyon: The wind creates a sudden roar against them.

Telltale Traits

- Big and bold; very tame and curious
- Noisy and boisterous
- Often in flocks
- Flies straight or undulating; also prone to sudden deep dives into canyons
- Often hops or walks on ground
- Hammers at trees to extract larvae

Look Here

- At the feeder

Or Here

- Near you, hoping for a handout
- Fly-catching from a perch
- In trees, eating conifer cone seeds, acorns, or berries
- Foraging on ground

This big gray bird shares many traits with a similar big gray bird, the gray jay, who also goes by the name "camp robber." Both are clever and daring, and quick to take advantage of any unattended edibles.

On the Home Front Not a backyard nester
- Nests high up in mountains, at 6,000 to 8,000 feet elevation • Builds a huge nest of sticks and bark strips, lined with grasses and pine needles • Usually nests in a juniper or pine, often very high up, in dense branches where the nest is sheltered

Wild Menu: Insects, including butterflies; fruit; acorns; seeds from pinecones; any scraps it can get its beak around

Plant Picks: Just keep that feeder stocked and the nutcracker will be your new best friend.

Feeder Pleasers
- Sunflower seeds; chick scratch (a crushed grain mixture available at farm feed stores); suet; nuts; any fat-based recipes you can think of or find for sale in bird supply stores; meat scraps

Tricks and Treats
- Carry a pocketful of nut meats with you; you may be able to tempt these birds to take them from your open palm.

Building Supply

If you do any snowshoeing or cross-country skiing in the high country in late winter, you may get to see Clark's nutcrackers collecting materials to build their nests. Juniper twigs are a favorite; the birds wrench them off trees with quick jerks and some help from the sharp edges of their beaks. The construction process takes a while, because the nest needs to be big and thick for insulation from the cold.

Black-Billed Magpie

First Impression

Big, exotic, black-and-white bird with super-long tail

Mark Your Calendar

Year-round

Details, Details

- Almost twice as long as a robin; 19 inches
- Watch for the flash of iridescence on those black feathers in sunlight.
- Shows big white wing patches in flight
- A black bill separates this species from the yellow-billed magpie of California.
- Female and male look alike

Listen Up!

- Rapid *shack-shack-shack*
- Various nasal notes

Telltale Traits

- Conspicuous and brash
- Walks about with tail slightly raised
- That extravagant tail seems to be always twitching when the bird is on the ground.
- Hops when in a hurry
- Often in flocks
- Unmistakable in flight (except where range overlaps yellow-billed magpie)

Look Here

- Strutting about on ground

Or Here

- At feeder
- Patrolling for leftovers at trash cans and in parking lots

On the Home Front Both male and female work on constructing the 2- to 4-foot durable nest made of heavy, often thorny sticks.

- A canopy of thorny sticks also covers the top.

"Magpies were very numerous during the buffalo days"

—Frank Farley, "Changes in the Status of Certain Animals and Birds during the Last Fifty Years in Central Alberta" (1925)

Magpies followed on the heels of the buffalo hunters, waiting around for their share of any leftovers at the kill. Lewis and Clark also noted the birds' voracious appetites, commenting that they snatched the meat even while it was being dressed after a hunt.

Wild Menu: Insects, including grasshoppers, beetles, ants, and others; acorns; grain; berries; food scraps; carrion

Plant Picks: A grapevine may attract the birds.

Feeder Pleasers

- Meat scraps; suet; magpies prefer meat but will also eat bread and other baked goods.

Tricks and Treats

- Magpies are intelligent birds who quickly learn your routine. Feed them at the same time every day, and they'll soon be waiting for their treat.
- A sturdy birdbath can be a big hit.

Who's Inside?

Knock at a magpie's door, and you never know just who might answer. Those giant-size nests, with all their thorny protection, are too good to waste, so other birds often make use of them when the magpie family departs. In Colorado, I came across a nest that had been claimed by a pair of kestrels (small falcons). Sharp-shinned hawks, mourning doves, grackles, and even ducks and herons have also been known to set up housekeeping in magpie nests.

Scrub Jay

First Impression

Big, noisy, bluish gray bird with whitish gray belly

Mark Your Calendar

Year-round; absent from some northern parts of region; mostly at lower elevations

Details, Details

- Bigger than a robin; 11½ inches
- In the right light, blue can be striking
- Has no crest
- Female and male look alike

Listen Up!

- A harsh, scolding cry of *cheek-cheek-cheek!*
- Also a rising note that sounds like a question: *quay-feeeee?*
- Other grating calls, including *ker-wheek!*
- A very quiet, private, and decidedly musical "whisper song" sung to its mate

Telltale Traits

- Loud, bold, and intelligent
- Also can be secretive and quiet
- Often hops about on ground
- Usually in small groups
- Look for it in shrubs (the "scrub" from which it gets its name).

Look Here

- At your feeder

Or Here

- In oak trees or nut trees
- On the ground
- In shrubs or hedges
- Burying nuts or acorns
- At the birdbath

"Nests with white, black, bay, and sorrel linings"

—**William Dawson, on colors of horsehair used in scrub jay nests,** *The Birds of California* (1923)

"The lining varies delightfully," Dawson noted, "but is largely dependent upon the breed of horses or cattle on the nearest ranch." He recounted how one jay "pitched out" the existing lining of its nest when coal-black horsehair became available.

On the Home Front May nest in backyard
- Makes a well-concealed, bulky nest of twigs, lined with rootlets • Builds low to the ground, from 2 to 12 feet or so

Wild Menu: Acorns, nuts, corn, fruit; insects, including wasps and bees; scorpions, snails, mice, snakes, lizards, and frogs

Plant Picks: Plant giant sunflowers (*Helianthus annuus* 'Russian Giant') for these jays

Feeder Pleasers
- Nuts and peanuts, in the shell; sunflower seeds; suet

Tricks and Treats
- A freshly filled birdbath may be popular.

Peanut Gallery

Jays bury nuts and acorns, which may be why these birds are much more strongly attracted to nuts in the shell than seeds at the feeder—as long as they're crackable. Peanuts in the shell are such a draw that, with some patience, you can tame the birds to take them from your hand. I've had good luck by first setting a few peanuts about 10 feet away from me, and standing quietly until the birds retrieved them. Then, over several days, I gradually move the nuts nearer to me until the jays will come within arm's length to get their treat. Finally, they'll take them right from my hand. Try this after a snowstorm, when the birds are hungriest.

Steller's Jay

First Impression
Striking black and blue bird with big crest

WEST

Mark Your Calendar
Year-round; usually at elevations up to 3,500 feet

Details, Details
- Bigger than a robin; 11½ inches
- Accent of small, light stripes on forehead.
- Female and male look alike

Listen Up!
- Like most jays, the Steller's has a repertoire of harsh calls, plus a gentle, musical song
- A loud, harsh *shaack! shaack! shaack!*
- Occasionally chortles *klook, klook, klook*
- May scream shrilly like a red-tailed hawk

Telltale Traits
- Loud and conspicuous
- May also be quiet and secretive
- Often raises the alarm when it spots a person walking in the woods
- Often visits singly, instead of in a group

Look Here
- At your feeder

Or Here
- Hopping or flitting upward around a tree
- Foraging on the ground
- Burying nuts or acorns

On the Home Front
May nest in backyard
- Builds bulky cup of sticks and leaves, lined with rootlets or evergreen needles

"Streaks on forehead paler blue or bluish white"

—**Robert Ridgway,**
The Birds of North and Middle America Part III
(1904)

The Steller's jay of the West is a geographic race that is slightly different in looks from the Steller's jay of the Pacific Coast. Its twin forehead streaks are whitish blue, instead of cobalt blue.

Wild Menu: Acorns; nuts; conifer seeds; insects; frogs; small snakes

Plant Picks: Plant Douglas firs or other conifers native to your area. Try annual sunflowers with big seed heads (*Helianthus annuus* 'Russian Giant').

Feeder Pleasers
- Nuts and peanuts, in the shell; sunflower seeds; suet

Tricks and Treats
- In cold weather, chop up a block of suet into half-inch pieces and scatter it in a tray feeder.

Fruit Eaters?

Have you ever seen Steller's jays eat fruit? I haven't. Not in my yard, which is packed with serviceberries (*Amelanchier* spp.), elderberries (*Sambucus* spp.), cherries, and every other tempting bird fruit or berry I can squeeze in. Not in the wild, either. Bird lover friends who I've checked with say they, too, have never seen a Steller's eat fruit.

Yet "wild or cultivated fruit" often shows up on published lists of this bird's diet. If you've ever witnessed a Steller eating fruit, I'd love to hear about it. Because the only reports I could find, after determined digging, was an anecdotal account of apples damaged by the jays during a severe drought—a possible reason why Steller's jays might peck at fruit.

Mountain Chickadee

First Impression

Small, lively, acrobatic gray and white bird with black-striped head

Mark Your Calendar

Year-round; absent in some areas. Lives at high elevations, often 8,000 to 10,000 feet, especially in nesting season; in fall and winter, many move lower

Details, Details

- Chickadee size! 5¼ inches
- From fall through early spring, shows distinctly striped head
- As feathers become worn, the white stripe is less distinct, and the black stripes may blend to look like the head of the black-capped species, also common in this region.
- Female and male look alike

Listen Up!

- Says *chick-a* in the familiar way, then adds its own slower, descending tones to the *fee-bee-bay* that follows
- Also high, thin calls, like a black-capped

Telltale Traits

- The typical chickadee—swinging from branch tips, flitting through foliage
- A great little acrobat, always in motion
- If disturbed at nest or nest box, hisses and flutters its wings to scare away intruder

Look Here

- At feeder

Or Here

- Branch tips and among foliage of conifers
- At conifer cones, often high up in lodge-pole pines, spruces, firs, or other trees
- In fall and winter, look in oaks, cotton-woods, and willows as well.

"They may be met with almost anywhere in the forested mountains."

—**Florence Merriam Bailey**, *Birds of New Mexico* (1928)

And you may have to look way, way up to get a glimpse of these active little guys that often forage high up in the conifers. Listen for their little voices, then be patient as they move to a lower spot.

On the Home Front May use a nest box in your backyard, if you live in the mountains
- Usually uses an existing hole in a dead tree

Wild Menu: Insects; conifer cone seeds, other seeds

Plant Picks: Any native conifer

Feeder Pleasers
- Suet; sunflower seeds; peanut butter and other fatty foods; may eat mealworms and other insect foods

Tricks and Treats
- Offer nesting materials, such as fur, tufts of natural fleece, snippets of angora wool, or any other soft materials, in a clean wire suet cage.

Ups and Downs

Tasty insects are everywhere in the mountain forests in summer. Caterpillars munch the conifers, ants work away, and a menagerie of other six-legged meals scurries about. No wonder so many bird species in this region, including the mountain chickadee, take to the mountains to raise their families. In fall, when insects wane and the weather cools, those birds forsake the forests and move to the valleys and foothills, where food is plentiful.

Plain Titmouse

First Impression

Very plain, small gray bird with crested head

Mark Your Calendar

Year-round; only the juniper titmouse is found in this region

Details, Details

- About sparrow size; 5¾ inches
- Both juniper and oak titmice are plain gray birds; the oak species has a brownish tinge.
- Female looks like male

Listen Up!

- The juniper titmouse, the bird found in this region, gives a rapid trill, fairly loud.
- The oak titmouse also trills, but has clear, whistled notes in its refrains, too.
- Both species can sound a lot like chickadees, which are close relatives. Listen for their raspy *tschick-a-dee* call.

Telltale Traits

- Actively in motion in the branches of trees, picking off insects
- Moves from branch to branch
- Flies with shallow undulating dips
- Often sings from a perch

Look Here

- At feeder

Or Here

- In junipers
- In pinyon-juniper woods

On the Home Front Happily moves into a nest box • The nest box or cavity is lined with soft, cozy grass, moss, fur, and feathers.

"This is indeed a plain titmouse"

—**A. C. Bent,** *Life Histories of North American Jays, Crows, and Titmice* **(1946)**

Actually it's *two* plain titmice. The species has been recently divided into the oak titmouse and the juniper titmouse. They look almost alike, but live in different habitat and have different voices.

Wild Menu: Insects; acorns; pine seeds and other seeds

Plant Picks: Oaks (*Quercus* spp. native to your area); pines, especially pinyon (*Pinus edulis*); junipers (*Juniperus scopulorum, J. osteoperma,* and other spp. native to your area)

Feeder Pleasers

- Sunflower seeds; suet; chopped nuts

Tricks and Treats

- Offer soft materials at nesting time: wool tufts, bits of fuzzy yarn, feathers, and anything else you can round up.

Together Forever _____

Wedding anniversary greeting cards could easily feature titmice as a symbol of a long-lasting union. These plain-Jane birds almost always keep the same mate year after year. And they often return to the same place to raise their family. In 1936, John Price, who studied the family relationships of the plain titmouse, noted: "There was only one case of 'divorce' where a bird took a new mate while its former mate was still known to be living." (*Condor,* Vol. 38). Guess that independent thinker must have had a mighty good reason.

Bushtit

First Impression

Tiny gray bird flying out of bush with high, thin calls; then another bird, and another, and another, and another . . .

Mark Your Calendar

Year-round; absent from northern part of this region

Details, Details

- One of our smallest birds, even smaller than a chickadee; 4½ inches
- Long tail
- Often looks fluffed-up
- One of the most unusual variations of gender: the male has dark eyes, the female, pale eyes

Listen Up!

- A constant stream of thin, high-pitched, *tsit-tsit-tsit* calls
- The calls are a great clue to the impending arrival of a flock of bushtits. When you hear them, look around for the bitty birds.

Telltale Traits

- Constantly on the move, foraging rapidly through the foliage of bushes and small trees, then traveling on to the next
- Often travels with mixed group of chickadees and kinglets in winter
- Tame around people and gentle to each other; no sign of squabbling in their flock

Look Here

- Moving in a flock from one group of bushes in your yard to the next

Or Here

- At the birdbath
- Flying through or over your yard in a talkative flock

"Intensely gregarious disposition"

—**Robert Woods, correspondence quoted in** *Life Histories of North American Jays, Crows, and Titmice* (1946)

You'll never see a bushtit all by its lonesome self. These tiny birds stick together, roaming the bushes in big flocks.

On the Home Front The nest is a long, loose, hanging sack, suspended from a tree or bush.
- It may take a month and a half before the nest is built and egg-laying starts. • Builds in deciduous or evergreen trees

Wild Menu: Insects, especially scale insects; spiders

Plant Picks: Fruits of any kind, particularly sweet or sour cherries, mulberries (*Morus* spp.), grapes

Feeder Pleasers
- Suet, especially suet enriched with insects

Tricks and Treats
- Bushtits love their baths. Keep a birdbath brimming, and you may see the whole bunch lining up at once.

Home Helpers

Bushtits are such sociable birds that they even help each other around the nest. Unmated birds or females whose nests have failed may help to raise another pair's brood. More than one of these helpers, which scientists call "supernumeraries," may help out at a single nest—a nest might have as many as six adults caring for the children. Good thing the birds build those hanging "socks" so strong: At night, everybody piles in to sleep together!

241

Mountain Bluebird

First Impression

An incredible turquoise blue bird—or a sky blue bird when not in breeding plumage

Mark Your Calendar

Spring through fall in northern part of this region; year-round southward

Details, Details

- Bigger than a sparrow; 7¼ inches
- Female is gray with pale blue wings; may have red tinge on breast, similar to female western bluebird

Listen Up!

- Sings mostly in early morning
- Clear, short, warbling song, similar to that of its cousin, the American robin
- Also a quiet, conversational warble, and a nasal *pew* call

Telltale Traits

- More often seen in the air than other bluebird species
- Fluttery flight
- Often hovers while foraging
- Often perches on a post or other lookout

Look Here

- At the nest box

Or Here

- In open areas
- On a fence post
- On utility wires

On the Home Front Welcomes a nest box; mount it within 6 feet of the ground in an open, grassy area • Often uses same place next year; builds new nest atop old one

"Ranges up to the highest meadows"

—Joseph Grinnell and Tracy Storer, *Animal Life in the Yosemite* (1924)

This gorgeous bluebird lives in pristine mountain meadows and clearings at just below timberline—but it also ranges all the way down into the foothills, and is often spotted around ranch buildings.

Wild Menu: Mostly insects; some fruit, including mistletoe berries

Plant Picks: Try bite-size berries, such as native currants (*Ribes* spp.) and elderberries (*Sambucus* spp.).

Feeder Pleasers

- Mealworms; suet in an accessible feeder; commercial or homemade "bluebird food" (mix cornmeal and peanut butter into a crumbly dough)

Tricks and Treats

- Invest in a bluebirds-only feeder to keep other birds from gobbling up those mealworms. An outer cage of wire, similar to a suet feeder, keeps out bigger starlings.
- A heated birdbath is a big draw on chilly days.

Catch the Concert

Folks used to argue over whether the mountain bluebird actually sang or not. I haven't heard its song, but I don't feel too bad: Even one of the most well-versed authorities on birdsong, Aretas A. Saunders, who wrote about birdsong back in the early 20th century, reported, "In all my experience with this species in Montana, I never heard it sing."

If you live in the West, you can find out for yourself. The current consensus is that this species does warble away early in the morning. Listen up, and see if you agree.

Western Bluebird

First Impression
Gentle blue bird with chestnut-orange breast and back patches

Mark Your Calendar
Migration only in some areas; spring through fall in others; year-round in southern part of region

Details, Details
- The size of a big sparrow; 7 inches
- Female is much paler blue-gray with faded orange; wings flash vivid blue in flight

Listen Up!
- A low, whistled, *f-few! f-few!*
- Occasionally, a short burst of chattering

Telltale Traits
- Like other bluebirds, a calm bird that often sits perched
- In pairs during nesting season; in flocks at other times, especially during winter
- Flies out from perch to nab insects in air
- Swoops from perch and flutters over grass when foraging

Look Here
- At the feeder

Or Here
- At the nest box
- On a rock or fence post perch
- Fluttering to the ground after an insect
- On wires

On the Home Front Another good reason to put up a nest box! • Early nester; begins when nights are still below freezing • Also nests in natural cavities, old woodpecker holes, or a crevice of a building • Usually raises two broods

"I awoke in the darkness at 4:20 a.m. to find a bluebird already singing"

—Winton Weydemeyer, "Singing of the Mountain Bluebird and the Western Bluebird" (1934)

You'll have to be quite an early bird yourself to beat this bluebird to the punch. In late April, when nesting season is in full swing, males begin serenading long before sunrise.

Wild Menu: Mostly insects; fruit in winter, including mistletoe berries

Plant Picks: Elderberries (*Sambucus* spp.) are favored; also encourage native junipers (*Juniperus* spp.) for their eventual berries. Butterfly gardens may attract butterfly-eating bluebirds.

Feeder Pleasers
- Mealworms and other insect foods; accessible suet; commercial or homemade bluebird food (mix cornmeal and peanut butter into a crumbly dough)

Tricks and Treats
- Get your nest box up early. By the end of winter, the pairs are already house shopping.
- Bluebirds are a great excuse to go ahead and try a heated birdbath. A daily bath is welcome, even in winter.

Kiss Me Quick

Hang a ball of mistletoe at Christmas, and you continue a long tradition of inviting a romantic kiss. But mistletoe can be a destructive partner to the lodgepole and other native pines (*Pinus* spp.) and other trees upon which it grows. This unusual plant siphons off nutrients from the tree to which it's attached.

Mountain bluebirds play a big role in spreading mistletoe. They feast on the berries, then fly to a nearby perch to sit and digest.

Western Tanager

First Impression

A brilliant flash of red-orange, yellow, and black in the trees

Mark Your Calendar

Spring through fall

Details, Details

- Smaller than a robin; 8 inches
- Fancy wing bars—one yellow, one white—in flight or perched
- Male has black tail
- Male's red almost disappears in fall
- Female is drab gray-green with yellowish head, breast, and belly, and gray wings

Listen Up!

- Low, warbling song, somewhat similar to robin, but huskier
- Frequent *pit-ick* call note

Telltale Traits

- One of the most vivid birds of the region
- Forages for insects among the foliage
- Often easily visible when it flies from one tree to another, or fly-catches from a tree

Look Here

- At feeder

Or Here

- Foraging in mature conifers
- At the birdbath

On the Home Front May occasionally nest in backyards with conifers • Often nests in trees along an edge—bordering a road, a meadow, or other opening • Usually picks a Douglas fir (*Pseudotsuga menziesii*), western hemlock (*Tsuga heterophylla*), or other conifer as a homesite

"They were at first found feeding on early cherries"

—W. Otto Emerson, "A Remarkable Flight of Louisiana Tanagers" (1903)

Cherries are still a draw for western tanagers, more than a hundred years after Emerson noticed the "remarkable flight" of what were once called Louisiana tanagers.

Wild Menu: Insects; fruit

Plant Picks: Try planting a sweet or sour cherry tree to bring tanagers to your own backyard.

Feeder Pleasers

- Cracked corn; millet and birdseed mix; suet; dried fruit, plus halved oranges

Tricks and Treats

- Keep a birdbath brimming and you may see a tanager take its bath.

That's Some Flycatcher!

True flycatchers are drab green birds. Not so the western tanager, who adopts the same technique. If the light is right, this bird will look like a living flame as it sallies out from a tree to snatch a termite or other flying insect, then swoops back to its perch.

I've seen tanagers spend hours at this activity. They start in the morning near the top of a tree, because insects are most active higher up early in the day. Then the birds work their way downward, with frequent pauses to perch and sing. By later afternoon, they're fly-catching from the lowest branches.

Black-Headed Grosbeak

First Impression

A small flock of vivid orange-and-black birds at the feeder, tame and chubby, and showing flashy white wing patches when they fly

Mark Your Calendar

Spring through fall

Details, Details

- Smaller than a robin; 8¼ inches
- Flashy white wing patches when the male flies
- Strong, conical beak for cracking seeds
- Female is streaky dark brown with buff breast and pale belly
- Striking striped head on females and juvenile birds

Listen Up!

- A pretty warbled song of clear, whistled notes with trills, similar to a robin
- Also a sharp *spick!* call note

Telltale Traits

- Very tame; isn't afraid of people
- Often in a small flock, except when nesting
- Shares habits with its eastern counterpart, the rose–breasted grosbeak

Look Here

- At feeder

Or Here

- Foraging in shrubs or trees
- Singing from top of tree
- Flying across open space, with those wing patches flashing
- Eating fruit

"Grosbeaks come back with glorious songs"

—Joseph Grinnell and Tracy Storer, *Animal Life in the Yosemite* (1924)

Loud, sweet singing is the main occupation of male grosbeaks when they arrive on nesting grounds. All day long, they sing from tall perches, claiming a territory as their own.

On the Home Front
Often nests in backyards
- Breeds from subalpine mountainsides to desert areas, where it seeks out bushes and trees along rivers • Builds nest in outer branches of small trees or shrubs

Wild Menu: Insects; fruit

Plant Picks: Elderberries (*Sambucus* spp.), cherries, blackberries, and raspberries

Feeder Pleasers
- Sunflower seeds

Tricks and Treats
- Fond of taking a bath; adores a sprinkler or mister

Gentlemen Before Ladies

Ever wonder where the girls are when you look at your feeder in spring? Migrant songbirds, like the black-headed grosbeak, return to nesting grounds on a schedule that depends on their gender. First come the males, resplendent in spring finery. About a week to 10 days later, the females arrive. Juveniles—birds that hatched from last year's nests—are last on the scene.

That extra time gives males the chance to establish territories, so they have a home territory ready and waiting when the ladies arrive. When it's time to leave in fall, the order is reversed: Males go first, females next, and the kids bring up the rear.

Red Crossbill

First Impression

Strawberry red, very tame bird—and get a load of that beak!

Mark Your Calendar

Year-round; in some areas, winter only

Details, Details

- Sparrow size; 6¼ inches
- Dark wings—but that bill is the only detail you need
- Female is grayish green

Listen Up!

- Clicking or buzzy phrases, not melodic, sounds like *kimp kimp kimp*

Telltale Traits

- Contorts itself like a parrot, clinging and twisting to reach pinecones

Look Here

- At conifer cones

Or Here

- At your feeder

On the Home Front Unlike that of nearly all other birds, the time of nesting is determined by when the conifer crop ripens. The birds begin nesting anytime from December to September! • Well-concealed nest is placed in a spruce, pine, or other conifer • Parents feed nestlings for weeks after they fledge, until their beaks cross into the shape that allows them to efficiently extract seeds from cones.

"Can be approached with care"

—John Terres, *The Audubon Society Encyclopedia of North American Birds* (1980)

The intriguing crossbills (both red and white-winged) often allow you to sneak up for a closer look. As long as you're quiet and don't make any alarming, sudden moves, you'll be able to stand near enough to watch them use those fantastic bills to extract seeds from pinecones.

Wild Menu: Seeds of conifer cones

Plant Picks: Pines, spruces, larches, firs, and other conifers

Feeder Pleasers
- Sunflower seeds

Tricks and Treats
- Greatly fond of salt. Offer a handful of ice cream maker salt in your feeding tray when crossbills arrive.

Lap It Up

I haven't had many visits from crossbills, but I'll never forget the flock that spent a few weeks at my place, cleaning off every berry from a hedge of Tatarian honeysuckle bushes. The birds were fascinating to watch, especially since they let me stand just 2 feet away.

But the most jaw-dropping moment was when the flock descended to a "bubbling spring" birdbath I'd set up in the yard. Gathering alongside, each bird maneuvered its head so that its bill was sideways to the water. Then it used its tongue to lap up the water, a drop or two at a time.

Pine Grosbeak

First Impression
Very tame, rosy red bird

Mark Your Calendar

Year-round or winter only; absent from some areas

Details, Details

- A little smaller than a robin; 9 inches
- Blackish wings with white bars
- Juvenile birds may be rusty chestnut instead of the color of Hawaiian Punch.
- Female is gray with greenish head

Listen Up!

- Soft, whistled song
- Quiet call notes keep a flock in touch

Telltale Traits

- Hangs around in small groups
- Very calm and easily approached

Look Here

- Eating berries in winter

Or Here

- Quietly perching
- At feeder
- In spruce, pine, or other conifer

On the Home Front Not a backyard nester
- Nest is well-hidden in dense branches of conifers, usually about eye level or lower
- Like many other Northland birds, this one builds its nest out of whatever's close at hand—conifer twigs, rootlets, grasses—and lines it with needles, lichen, and a few feathers.
- Parents feed young birds a yummy regurgitated paste of vegetable matter and insects.

"Rather stupid and uninteresting"
—Neltje Blanchan,
Bird Neighbors (1897)

Pine grosbeaks spend a lot of time just sitting around. Are they lazy? Nope, just digesting. When they find a good source of food—not a sure thing in winter—they take advantage of it, filling their special throat pouch with as much as they can.

Wild Menu: Tree seeds, seeds from conifer cones, weed seeds; tree buds; also fruit and insects

Plant Picks: Spruces native to your area, including Englemann spruce (*Picea engelmanii*), alpine fir (*Abies lasiocarpa*), mountain ash (*Sorbus* spp.)

Feeder Pleasers
- Sunflower seeds

Tricks and Treats
- Pine grosbeaks are a great reason to have a reserve bag of sunflower seeds on hand: Winter flocks may number 100 or more birds!

Lily Lovers

As snows begin to melt, sunny yellow glacier (also called avalanche) lilies (*Erythronium grandiflorum*) come alive, pushing up at the edge of the retreating snow, right through the white stuff. Within a day or two of the snow's retreat, showy colonies of hundreds of these pretty flowers are in full bloom, bordering the snowbanks. The flowers fade quickly, ripening into seed capsules—which pine grosbeaks seek out for food. Talk about a taste of spring!

Lazuli Bunting

First Impression

A sparrow-size turquoise "bluebird," singing its heart out and shining like a living jewel

Mark Your Calendar

Spring through fall

Details, Details

- Smaller than a sparrow, only a bit bigger than a chickadee; 5½ inches
- Iridescent plumage, like that of the closely related indigo bunting
- Two highly noticeable white wing bars will quickly tell you this isn't a bluebird.
- Female is warm brown, with a buff breast

Listen Up!

- A fast, clear, high-pitched, warbling, *see-see-see-sweert-sweert-sweert* song that lasts long
- Also a sharp *pick!* call note

Telltale Traits

- Sings frequently, all day long
- Male moves from one perch to another around his territory to sing
- Males chase each other in spring.
- After nesting, birds congregate in groups.

Look Here

- At your feeder

Or Here

- Singing from the highest perches available
- Foraging in brushy corners of the yard
- In thickets, hedges, and clumps of bushes

On the Home Front Usually not a backyard nester • Builds nest low to ground, usually within 3 feet • Well-hidden in dense, shady shrubs of many kinds

"A considerable flock of lazuli buntings "

—Arthur Fuller and B. P. Bole, "Observations on Some Wyoming Birds" (1931)

Once the kids have left home, buntings gather in small groups to flock and forage. Males continue to sing after nesting is finished, long into summer. Watch how the male bunting changes color in the light; as feathers are exposed at various angles, their shades shift from blue to blue-green. The species is named for the gemstone lapis lazuli, but there are a lot more turquoise tones in those feathers than there are deep, clear blue ones.

Wild Menu: Seeds; insects

Plant Picks: Tolerate some weedy grasses, such as wild oats (*Avena barbata*) or needlegrass (*Stipa* spp.), in your yard, and lazulis may arrive to glean seeds. Native currants (*Ribes* spp.), which soon grow into a thicket, are a favorite hangout.

Feeder Pleasers
- Millet

Tricks and Treats
- May visit a birdbath

Keep an Eye on the Sky

A bird perched in plain view at the tippy-top of a tree makes an inviting target for predators, especially those with wings. Singing male lazuli buntings often get dived upon by sharp-shinned and Cooper's hawks. The hawks may spot the singing bird from above, or zero in on its voice from a perch. Either way, the attack seems to come out of nowhere. If the male bunting doesn't have his wits about him, there may be nothing remaining to mark his territory but a sad little puff of blue feathers where he was perched seconds before.

Rosy Finch

First Impression

A flock of brown and pink sparrows

Mark Your Calendar

Winter only, except high in the mountains, where found year-round

Details, Details

- Sparrow size; 6¼ inches
- Wing feathers are pale or translucent in flight.
- All adults have a sharply conical little black beak, with a pale area where it joins the head; juveniles have a yellow bill.

Listen Up!

- They have a husky whistled song of a few notes. Mostly, they use a buzzy *chew* call.
- *Chip!* alarm call

Telltale Traits

- Exceedingly tame
- Very social birds, in flocks except when nesting
- Usually on ground
- Undulating flight, in sweeping curve
- Long wings allow easy flight even in stiff mountain winds.
- When one bird gives the *chip!* call and flies, all the rest take off with it.

Look Here

- In feeder or on ground beneath it

Or Here

- Foraging on ground, especially near patches of snow
- Foraging for insects in conifers
- Investigating weeds protruding from snow

"As characteristic of the mountaintops as the rocks and the perpetual snow"

—A. C. Bent, *Life Histories of North American Cardinals, Grosbeaks, Buntings, Towhees, Finches, Sparrows and Allies* (1968)

Rosy finches are part of the winter scene in the West, eagerly visiting feeders and backyards from the mountains to the foothills, lowlands, and even the deserts. But for breeding season, the birds withdraw to the highest mountaintops.

On the Home Front Possibly the highest-altitude-nesting bird in North America • Nests on mountaintops in the Rockies and other mountains, in a crevice on a cliff.

Wild Menu: Seeds; some insects; some bits of green vegetation

Plant Picks: An open area will make these birds of windswept places feel at home. A spread of birdseed is all you need.

Feeder Pleasers
- Millet; birdseed mix; sunflower seeds

Tricks and Treats
- A birdbath, especially a heated one, may attract several customers.

Pack Your Bags

A few species of birds in extremely cold conditions feature a unique adaptation that allows them to survive in harsh weather. It's a *gular pouch*, an expandable food storage area off the throat. When rosy finches come across an abundance of food, they can stuff their pouches full to the brim, to be digested later when pickin's aren't as plentiful.

This feature also allows them to carry a generous helping of food from long distances for their nestlings, without having to make exhausting return trips.

Yellow-Headed Blackbird

First Impression

Unmistakable! Big black bird with striking yellow hood

Mark Your Calendar

Spring through fall

Details, Details

- A little smaller than a robin; 9½ inches
- Male flashes big white wing patches in flight
- Female is much less dramatic but still has yellow tinge

Listen Up!

- Or maybe you should cover your ears—a cacophony of squawks, *squeeps,* rattles, shrieks, and clacks, plus a noise like a chainsaw

Telltale Traits

- Sight alone is enough to positively ID this dramatic bird.
- Usually in flocks
- Nervous tail flicks

Look Here

- At feeder

Or Here

- In flocks on lawn
- In marshes with cattails or other reeds
- In winter, this bird turns to grainfields for food: Huge flocks "roll over" fields, the birds in back moving to the front as they scour the field for wasted grain.

"Poured out his grotesque love notes"

—**A. C. Bent,** *Life Histories of North American Blackbirds, Orioles, Tanagers and Allies* **(1958)**

The voice of the yellow-headed blackbird is as attention-getting as its showy colors. You won't have to listen hard to find these birds—their repertoire of weird calls is loud!

On the Home Front Not a backyard nester, unless you have a large, reed-fringed pond • Nests in colonies, in a marsh • The male selects a breeding territory, then the females in his harem build nests within it. • Nests are built within a clump of reeds, and woven from reeds.

Wild Menu: Weed seeds; grain; aquatic insects

Plant Picks: Your feeder will keep these birds content.

Feeder Pleasers
- Sunflower seed; cracked corn

Tricks and Treats
- A birdbath or water feature may attract a yellow-headed splasher.

Social Climbers

Yellow-headed blackbirds nest together in a colony in a marsh. But when it's time for the young to leave the nest, they're on their own. The big, gawky babies can't fly yet, so they take a pragmatic approach—they climb out. Grasping a marsh reed in one foot, then in the other, they make their way upward until it bends under their weight. Then they reach out and make a grab for the next reed. Baby blackbirds look pretty silly climbing around, but it's serious business: One misstep and they can land in the water. At the least, they could get a thorough soaking; at the worst, they could become a mouthful for a hungry fish.

Broad-Tailed Hummingbird

First Impression
A zippy little green guy with a rosy red throat

Mark Your Calendar
Spring through fall; absent from some areas

Details, Details
- Significantly smaller than a chickadee; 4 inches, and that includes the bill!
- Focus your binoculars to find the white eye ring and the white stripe from eye to chin.
- All-green back
- Rusty chestnut patch on outside tail feathers near body
- Female lacks red throat; hers is grayish

Listen Up!
- In normal flight, the male's wings make a high trilling sound.
- During a dive, the male's wings buzz loudly.
- Various high-pitched twittering sounds

Telltale Traits
- Unmistakably a hummingbird: hovers, zips forward, back, up, down
- Often hovers in front of a flower

Look Here
- At nectar feeder

Or Here
- At flowers
- Flying through spray of sprinkler
- Perched on a twig

On the Home Front May nest in your backyard—but good luck finding that tiny, camouflaged cup! • May freshen up last year's nest by adding new material on top

"As the country begins to dry up, these Hummingbirds retire to higher altitudes"

—**Charles Bendire**, *Life Histories of North American Birds* **(1895)**

Like many birds of the West, hummingbirds spend time at lower altitudes when they return from migration. They follow the bloom of wildflowers up the mountains to their nesting grounds.

Wild Menu: Nectar; small insects; spiders

Plant Picks: How about some Rocky Mountain plants for *the* Rocky Mountain hummingbird? Native and cultivated varieties of penstemons (*Penstemon* spp.) are perfect. So are native columbines (*Aquilegia* spp.). Want a little variety? Add salvias (*Salvia* spp.) of any sort.

Feeder Pleasers
- Nectar feeder

Tricks and Treats
- Attach a mister to your birdbath, or put it on a timer and spray from a tree, shrub, or post.

Pretty Chilly

Western weather is famous for its unpredictability. Hummingbirds wait until the flowers are blooming to begin nesting, but even that may not be long enough. If a cold spell sets in after the eggs are laid, hatching may be delayed because the female may go into a state of torpor, or slowed metabolism, during cold nights. That unique adaptation enables hummingbirds to weather cold temperatures without ill effects. But less body heat from Mom means a slowdown in egg development.

Chapter Twelve

Birds of the Southwest and California

This region has a beauty all its own. Spectacular rocks and canyons form the backdrop for plants that you'll see nowhere else in the country—stiff-armed saguaro, spiny sticks of brilliant red ocotillo (*Fouquieria splendens*), thorny bushes and trees, and other plants built to survive in this demanding climate.

This is America's desert. Its vast area of land is as lacking in water as other parts of the country are awash in it. Still, plenty of plants and birds have found a niche to thrive in here, and so have people.

THE LAY OF THE LAND

The desert isn't just one kind of desert. This region features three main types of desert—the Sonoran, the Chihuahuan, and the Mojave—which vary even further within themselves.

Mountain ranges, including the Sierra Madre, the Chisos, the Guadalupe, and others, rise within the deserts in some areas, creating "sky islands" of cooler, slightly wetter microclimates of coniferous forests.

Birds live everywhere in the desert, but

253

Vast spreads of fast-growing wildflowers, like these California poppies (Eschscholtzia californica), color springtime in the arid Southwest.

people usually stick close to the cities, where the rigorous climate is tempered by creature comforts such as water on demand and air conditioning. That leaves lots of open space for wild things.

FOOD AND SHELTER

It's 110°F in the shade? Better seek shelter from that brutal sun.

But just what's providing that shade? A rock, a scrubby small tree, a bush—not a shade tree with a dense canopy of big, lush leaves.

Shade trees are rare in this region, except for the cottonwoods along rivers and imported species such as palms and eucalyptus. Instead, you'll find hundreds of native plant species with gray leaves, woolly leaves, tiny leaves, leathery leaves, or other adapta-

tions designed to conserve water in the face of the ferocious summer heat. Thorns are popular, too, to prevent these plants from being eaten by desert animals. Shrubby plants and small trees are widely scattered, with plenty of open space between them, because with less than 10 inches of rain a year, there's not enough water to support dense groves or solid thickets.

Birds of this region know how to make use of any scrap of shade. They select nest sites that provide some relief from the sun, often at the foot of or within the branches or leaves of desert plants. Rocks cast shade, too, so birds often nest or rest beside them.

The particulars of the plants depend on the type of desert. The saguaros of the hot Sonoran yield to yuccas and agave in the Chihuahuan. The extremely dry Mojave, which includes Death Valley, is spotted by

Joshua trees (*Yucca brevifolia*) and other adapted yuccas. The chaparral areas of California are anchored by scrub oaks (*Quercus* spp.) and dense with shrubs adapted to that Mediterranean climate—and to periodic wildfires.

The American deserts are famed for their fantastic sweeps of color when their wildflowers bloom. Most of these are annual species, which can cram their life cycle into a very short span of time—just enough to take advantage of the winter rains. They spring up fast as soon as the rains begin, and blossom in just a matter of weeks. Then they set seed for next year and fade away. Those abundant seeds are a bounty for many desert birds, especially native sparrows and goldfinches.

Insects are just as plentiful in the desert as in more moderate climates, but like the plants, they're adapted to the heat and dryness. Beetles scuttle about, armored scale insects coat the branches, and spiders live in every nook and cranny. All make bountiful bird food!

Yuccas, agaves, and other perennial desert plants and shrubs provide another important food source: nectar. The desert is full of nectar flowers, so no wonder it's also full of hummingbirds. Orioles of this region depend on nectar, too, along with insects and fruit.

Speaking of fruit, that's another important food for birds of this region. Large, juicy fruits of saguaro, prickly pear, and other cactuses are prime bird food. Their high water content gives curve-billed thrashers and other birds a drink whenever they take a bite of pulp.

The stout arms of saguaro cactus provide a place for nesting cavities and perching spots for owls, woodpeckers, and other birds.

The lovely white-winged dove is common in wild brushy areas and in backyards.

Choose native plants for your yard; you won't have to baby them in this challenging climate. Investigate the possibilities of penstemons (*Penstemon* spp. and cultivars) and salvias (*Salvia* spp. and cultivars); any of them will be a hit with hummingbirds. Grevilleas (*Grevillea* spp. and cultivars), red-hot pokers (*Kniphofia* spp. and hybrids), and other plants from countries of similar climate, especially Africa and Australia, also thrive here; you'll find plenty of them at nurseries.

Most birds in this region are *xerophilous,* adapted to thriving without needing a daily drink of water. Instead, they obtain moisture from cactus fruits, nectar, or other foods they eat. Native plants with fruits and berries are popular with orioles, thrashers, and other fruit eaters; try any offered by your local nursery.

Still, you'll have great results if you put a birdbath in your xeric garden for these xerophilous birds: Most of them are quick to indulge in water if it's offered. Your birdbath may wind up being more popular than your feeding station. Set a basin on the ground, too, for quail and other ground-level birds.

BIRD LIFE IN THE SOUTHWEST AND CALIFORNIA

Fabulous birds flourish in these conditions of extreme heat and scanty water. Most of them are unique to this region, perfectly adapted to desert life. You'll see an abundance of

Pines provide tasty seeds for a host of appreciative birds.

Prolific flowers provide nectar for butterflies and hummingbirds, plus a banquet of insects and seeds for other birds.

thrashers, for instance, with extra-long beaks that they use adeptly when foraging among cactus thorns.

Some common American birds also scratch out a living here. The first time I visited the Southwest, I had to check and recheck a field guide before I could convince myself that the robin I saw hopping around in the desert really was a robin. I was sure it had to be some exotic species that had a subtle difference. But nope: It was a plain old robin.

You'll have to look a little harder to see many of the birds of this region. Many species, such as the California towhee, are colored to blend in with the landscape. Other species, though, including the vivid black-and-yellow Scott's oriole, stand out like neon signs against the landscape's subtle hues.

While bird-watchers in wetter regions of the country are straining their eyes to see songbirds far overhead in the foliage, you can enjoy watching birds right at eye level or lower. Most species in this region live at ground level or low to medium heights, because tall trees are scarce, except near water. Irrigated farming areas and riversides attract many birds, which may spill over into nearby backyards.

Start Here

Even though the Southwest and California region is home to many birds that would never be seen in other regions, it also harbors a lot of familiar friends. Turn to Chapter 6, "Start Here," to find many of your loyal backyard friends, the birds you share with other parts of the country—goldfinches, juncos, cedar waxwings, and many others.

Regional Specialties

Desert birds are distinctly different from the list of species found in any other region. The acorn woodpecker busies itself stuffing acorns into holes like marbles into a Chinese checkerboard. The tiny pygmy nuthatch roams the pines. Shrubs are decorated with the round, thorny nests of the verdin, a chickadee-like bird with a beautiful yellow head. Cactus wrens and California thrashers duke it out for nesting territories and sitting space at the feeder. Just about everywhere you look, you'll find unique birds that never leave their desert home. Many species native to Mexico or Central America reach the northern extent of their range in this region, including fantastic hummingbird species. That's why southern Arizona, New Mexico, and Texas are famed birding hot spots. Lucky you—you live in the thick of it!

If you live near the borders of this region, be sure to page through the birds of the West, Northwest, and Midwest regions, too. Those regions are your neighbors, and many of their birds may range into your territory.

This ash-throated flycatcher has recycled a former woodpecker home in a large cactus.

Birds of the Southwest and California

Here are the birds profiled in this chapter. Remember to consult the "Start Here" birds, starting on page 79, for other common birds in the Southwest and California.

Acorn Woodpecker

First Impression

Black woodpecker with clownish pale yellow face and shocking light eyes in black cheeks

Mark Your Calendar

Year-round; absent from parts of this region

Details, Details

- A little smaller than a robin; 9 inches
- Male has a red cap, over onto back of neck
- Flashy white rump and wing patches visible in flight
- Female has a smaller amount of red on head

Listen Up!

- Highly vocal, with all sorts of raucous sounds
- Often calls *ja-cob, ja-cob* or *whack-up, whack-up*
- Also high, nasal calls
- Drums in short stretches, picking up speed

Telltale Traits

- Always in a small group, from two or three birds to about 15
- Frequently drills holes for storing acorns and fills them, or is tending its stores

Look Here

- At suet feeder

Or Here

- At utility poles or trees, looking after its cache of acorns
- At oak trees, collecting acorns
- At almond or other nut trees
- Fly-catching from a perch

On the Home Front Not usually a backyard nester • Excavates nest hole in living or dead cottonwoods or willows, or utility poles

"A solid 'mass' of acorns, totalling, say, some 20,000"

—**William Dawson,** *The Birds of California* (1923)

The acorn woodpecker doesn't seem to have an off switch: The bird drills and stuffs so many holes with acorns that it can't possibly ever eat them all. Many go to waste.

Wild Menu: Acorns; nuts; insects in summer

Plant Picks: No surprise here: Plant an oak tree, or an almond, pecan, or English walnut.

Feeder Pleasers

- Suet; sunflower seeds; nuts; may become a regular at nectar feeder

Tricks and Treats

- These birds can sure guzzle the sugar water from your hummingbird feeder. Try securing a nectar feeder to a post, so that it doesn't swing under the bird's weight. This convenience may wean it away from your hummingbird feeder. Once the bird is in the habit of using it, gradually switch to a weaker sugar solution (one part sugar to six or eight parts water).

Skewed Instinct

I first met acorn woodpeckers in Arizona, where a group of these birds was busy tending to its stores. Most of them were inserting acorns—pointy end first—into the perfectly sized holes they'd drilled, but one woodpecker had something else in its beak. I couldn't tell from a distance what it was. Quietly, I moved closer, keeping my binoculars focused on the bird. At last I saw: This guy was storing pebbles! For years I've wondered why.

Gila Woodpecker

First Impression

A "bald" woodpecker with a zebra coat

Mark Your Calendar

Year-round, mostly in southern Arizona; absent from much of this region

Details, Details

- A little smaller than a robin; 9¼ inches
- Finely patterned black-and-white back and wings; soft tan head and belly
- Male has a red crown
- Female looks like male but lacks red crown

Listen Up!

- Perhaps the noisiest woodpecker, constantly carrying on
- Makes harsh laughing sounds
- Shrill *pit!* calls and rasping *churr*s

Telltale Traits

- Extremely bold and vocal; you can't miss this bird, because he'll be complaining loudly somewhere nearby
- Highly aggressive
- Threatens and chases others of its kind—and any other bird that comes close; even attacks large thrashers
- Pecks at dead or living trees
- Undulating flight

Look Here

- At feeder

Or Here

- In or on saguaro cactus, often pecking at it
- Flying across open space, calling loudly
- Carrying corn or other food to a post or tree to peck at it

"Afraid neither of being seen nor being heard"

—M. Gilman, quoted in *Life Histories of North American Woodpeckers* (1939)

Perhaps Gilman had spent a little too much time around the birds, as he continued, "All his talk at us has a distinctly 'colicky' tone and one feels like giving him something to whine about."

On the Home Front If you have saguaro in your backyard, you may host a nesting pair.
- May also accept a nest box • Drills a cavity

Wild Menu: Ants and other insects; saguaro fruits; mistletoe berries

Plant Picks: Saguaro cactus is the first choice for this bird.

Feeder Pleasers
- Suet; a quail block—a compressed block of seeds and grain available at feed stores and wild bird supply stores; birdseed mix; dry dog food; nectar; meat scraps and meaty bones

Tricks and Treats
- Old books mention this species' fondness for watermelon, so why not give it a try? Cut it into fist-size chunks, with rind intact, and let the birds pick them clean.

Recycling

Trees are scarce in the Sonoran desert, so woody saguaros are a prime target of Gila and other woodpeckers. Once I saw a female launch itself straight out from a new hole, as if she'd hit the button on an ejector seat.

Woodpecker holes are prime real estate for cavity-nesting birds who can't drill their own. I spotted a cactus wren entering a hole, carrying insects for its babies. A kestrel perched atop another cactus with a nest hole, nervously flicking its tail as it watched me. But the best was last: A tiny elf owl, like a cute little stuffed toy, peered out of a hole, its big yellow eyes glaring fiercely at me. It was so utterly adorable, I wanted to slip it into my pocket.

Vermilion Flycatcher

First Impression

Small, glowing red bird with grayish black wings and tail

Mark Your Calendar

Spring to fall in the southern part of this region; absent or an occasional stray in other areas

Details, Details

- Sparrow size; 6 inches
- Notice how its red body shows when the bird lifts its wings in flight—beautiful!
- Dark stripe extends backyard from eye
- Take a close look at that tiny thin beak.
- Female is light gray with a streaky white breast and lovely salmon-pink on lower belly to tail

Listen Up!

- Male sings an ecstatic courtship song, *pit-pit-pit pit-a-see!*, while rising in flight
- A sharp *peet!* call note

Telltale Traits

- Relatively tame
- Like tanagers, this bright bird can be surprisingly hard to see in trees.
- Spends much of time perched, often conspicuously
- Flies out from a perch after insects

Look Here

- Flying from one perch to another, often from the tip of a tall stem to a shrub or tree

Or Here

- Perched at tip of plant or weed stem
- Fly-catching from perch

"Butterfly-like"

—Edward Gifford, on the courtship flight of the vermilion flycatcher, *Proceedings of the California Academy of Science* (1919)

The vermilion flycatcher sings ecstatically during his slow, fluttery courtship flight. At times he hovers like a floating ball of vermilion, with breast and head feathers fluffed to show their blinding red color.

On the Home Front

Not usually a backyard nester • Usually nests near a stream or other water • Builds a soft little nest deep in a forked branch of a willow, cottonwood, or other tree

Wild Menu: Insects, including many bees

Plant Picks: Scattered shrubs, small trees, and flowers with tall stems that make good perches

Feeder Pleasers

- Not a feeder visitor

Tricks and Treats

- Feed this flycatcher's predilection for bees by planting flowers such as agastache (*Agastache* spp.), lupines, sunflowers, chamise (*Adenostoma fasciculatum*), and phacelia (*Phacelia* spp.).

Missed Opportunity

I always wondered why I saw so many excellent photographs of vermilion flycatchers, until I went hunting the bird myself. This species usually sticks to the trees along irrigation ditches or roadsides, so I thought I'd have to search there. But as soon as I walked behind my motel outside of Tucson, I spotted a flicker of burning red. Soon the flycatcher perched on a slim, bare branch, just above eye level.

I was stunned to see that it stayed put as I sneakily approached. In fact, I felt kind of silly taking one baby step after another, because the bird seemed totally undisturbed by my presence. If only I'd had a camera, I, too, could've taken one of those jaw-dropping shots.

Ash-Throated Flycatcher

First Impression

An alertly perched taupe bird that flashes a startling cinnamon tail in flight

Mark Your Calendar

Spring through fall; year-round in extreme southern parts of range

Details, Details

- Bigger than a sparrow but smaller than a robin; 8½ inches
- Resembles great crested flycatcher of eastern half of United States
- Wings as well as tail show cinnamon color in flight
- Pale yellow belly
- Female looks like male

Listen Up!

- A vocal bird whose frequent, distinctive calls quickly become familiar
- Loud *quirrr, quirrp* calls, similar to the great crested flycatcher
- Also loud *hip, hip, ha-wheer* or *che-hoo! che-hoo!*
- Often makes soft, low *ha-whip* calls

Telltale Traits

- Flicks tail up and down and sometimes sideways
- Usually engaged in fly-catching

Look Here

- Perched conspicuously on a low tree or bush to nab passing insects

Or Here

- At nest box
- Fly-catching over a flower garden or flowering shrub
- Flying across open space

"In the boom of a gasolene engine shovel"

—**Wilson Hanna, describing a nest that moved up and down, "Odd Nesting Site of Ash-Throated Flycatcher" (1931)**

Like the house wren, the ash-throated flycatcher has a penchant for choosing unusual nesting sites—exhaust pipes, the legs of pants on a clothesline, an empty mailbox, and other cavities.

On the Home Front Often accepts a nest box mounted about 4 to 10 feet high in quiet area
- Nests in woodpecker holes and other natural cavities, as well as in oddball sites

Wild Menu: Insects, including bees, wasps, dragonflies, mantids, and cicadas; cactus fruit

Plant Picks: Flower gardens are popular hangouts for this bird because of all the insects they attract. Flowering shrubs, such as woolly butterfly bush (*Buddleia marrubifolia*), as well as the fruits of saguaro, cardon, and organ-pipe cactuses are favored; or try elderberries.

Feeder Pleasers
- Not a feeder visitor

Tricks and Treats
- Offer a wire basket stuffed with nesting materials, including tufts of sheep's wool; 4-inch pieces of string or yarn; and short, narrow strips of cloth.

Not a Drop to Drink

Even in the heat of summer in its arid range, the ash-throated flycatcher ignores a tempting birdbath. Juicy fruit, swallowed whole, seems to supply the moisture the bird needs.

In a study in 1977, at a spring in an oak-madrona woodland in California, out of 45 species of birds observed, 21 never came for a drink—and the ash-throated flycatcher was one.

Pinyon Jay

First Impression

A noisy flock of big, plain, light blue birds

Mark Your Calendar

Year-round, although flocks may come and go as they move about in search of food

Details, Details:

- About the size of a robin; 10½ inches
- Looks squat and chubby compared to longer-tailed jays
- Crestless
- Female and male look alike
- The similar scrub jay, also in this region, has a much longer tail and a pale belly.

Listen Up!

- Constantly calls in flight, a soft *hoy-hoy-hoy*
- Harsh *karee-karee-karee* or *kree-kree-kree* calls, rising in pitch
- Also various buzzy, trilling, rattling calls

Telltale Traits

- Usually in a flock, sometimes very large
- Several birds may act as sentries, while the rest of the flock feeds.
- Spends a lot of time on the ground, foraging for food and caching seeds
- Unearths its cached seeds even when buried under snow

Look Here

- At the feeder

Or Here

- On the ground
- Foraging in pine trees
- Perched in other trees
- At the birdbath

"Our most gregarious bird"

—**A. C. Bent**, *Life Histories of North American Jays, Crows, and Titmice* (1946)

Noisy and restless, pinyon jays roam about the foothills in flocks. In the wild, flocks can build to 100 or more birds, but much smaller groups visit backyards.

On the Home Front May nest in backyards
- Builds a bulky nest in pinyon pines (*Pinus edulis*), junipers, and oaks, usually from 3 to 20 feet aboveground

Wild Menu: Pinyon pine seeds and other seeds; juniper and other berries; acorns; plus lizards, snakes, insects, and small mammals

Plant Picks: Pines, especially pinyon (*Pinus edulis*), ponderosa (*Pinus ponderosa*), and Jeffrey (*Pinus jeffreyi*); also oaks. For a faster food crop, try planting tall annual sunflowers.

Feeder Pleasers
- Sunflower seeds; pine nuts in the shell

Tricks and Treats
- Pinyon jays will drink from a birdbath, but they're not fond of bathing there.
- Provide a bare, dusty area in your yard and you may see these birds, and others, take dust baths.

Nuts about Pine Nuts

Pinyon pines have big, meaty seeds that are a hit with wildlife and people alike. They're still a staple for native Americans, as they've been for thousands of years. In years when the cones yield a bumper crop, Navajos may collect a million pounds. The nuts are high in fat, protein, and carbohydrates—a single nut supplies about 20 calories! Collecting nuts isn't easy, because they have to be pried out of the cones. Shelling them is even harder. Many folks use a rolling pin to crack the hard brown hulls without smashing the delectable nut meat inside.

Plain Titmouse

First Impression

Very plain-colored, small gray bird with crested head

Mark Your Calendar

Year-round; oak titmouse along coast; juniper titmouse in most of rest of region

Details, Details

- About small sparrow size; 5¾ inches
- The oak titmouse and the juniper titmouse live in different habitats and have different voices.
- Both juniper and oak titmice are plain gray birds; the oak species has a brownish tinge.
- Female looks like male

Listen Up!

- Juniper titmouse gives a rapid loud trill
- Oak titmouse also does a trill, but has clear, whistled notes in its refrains, too
- Both species can sound a lot like chickadees. Listen for the raspy *tschick-a-dee* call.

Telltale Traits

- Actively in motion in the branches of trees, picking off insects
- Moves from branch to branch
- Flies to the next tree with shallow undulating dips
- Often sings from a perch

Look Here

- At feeder

Or Here

- In junipers
- In pinyon–juniper woods

"A high, clear whistle"
—**Ralph Hoffmann**, *Birds of the Pacific States* (1927)

The trademark *Peter, Peter* whistle of the tufted titmouse is echoed by this western counterpart. Taxonomists recently separated the plain titmouse into two species, oak and juniper, partly because the juniper titmouse doesn't have the whistle in its vocal repertoire.

On the Home Front Happily moves into a nest box • The juniper species nests in stumps or crevices of old, gnarled junipers; the oak titmouse seeks out an existing cavity or digs its own hole in soft, decayed wood, usually in—guess what?—oaks.

Wild Menu: Insects; acorns; pine seeds and other seeds

Plant Picks: Oaks (native to your area); pines, especially pinyon (*Pinus edulis*); junipers (native to your area)

Feeder Pleasers
- Sunflower seeds; suet; chopped nuts

Tricks and Treats
- Offer soft materials at nesting time: wool tufts, bits of fuzzy yarn, feathers, and anything else.

Mini Cop

Like crows and jays, the plain titmouse, which looks like a miniature crested jay, shares the habit of serving as the alarmist when danger is near. It raises an outcry when it spots an owl or hawk, a wandering cat, or sometimes a person walking in its territory.

One year, when I was traveling with our cats (in travel crates), I found out how insistent this small bird can be. We were stopped at a campground, with our caged kitties temporarily set on the picnic table. The cats were justifiably complaining, and a pair of curious plain titmice came to investigate. Perched overhead, they kept up a chatter that drew other birds to see what was going on. Thanks to our felines, we enjoyed some great bird-watching!

Verdin

First Impression

Little gray bird with yellow face at the nectar feeder

Mark Your Calendar

Year-round; absent from some of this region

Details, Details:

- Smaller than a chickadee; 4½ inches
- Upper parts are ashy or brownish gray; pale below
- Warm chestnut shoulder patch

Listen Up!

- A whistling *tseet-tsoor-tsoor*
- Several variations of loud call notes, including a rapid *chip chip chip*

Telltale Traits

- A busy and active little bird
- Behavior similar to a chickadee, but it doesn't hang upside down
- Highly vocal
- Joins mixed flocks of sparrows, juncos, gnatcatchers, and warblers

Look Here

- At the nectar feeder

Or Here

- At flowers, searching for insects
- Often in trees or bushes; rarely on ground
- At clumps of mistletoe
- Prefers desert scrub and brushy areas with thorny trees or bushes

On the Home Front May nest in a large, naturalistic backyard that opens to wild space, in acacias (*Acacia* spp.), paloverde (*Cercidium floridum*), or mesquite (*Prosopis* spp.) • Nest is often at end of a low branch

"So strongly is it built that it is difficult to tear one apart"

—Herbert Brandt, *Texas Bird Adventures in the Chisos Mountains and on the Northern Plains* **(1940)**

The ball-shape nests of verdins are a familiar sight throughout their range. The determined Brandt noted that heavy gloves were necessary to handle the nests because "the multitude of thorns will effectively repel bare hands."

Wild Menu: Insects; nectar; and a sampling of small fruits

Plant Picks: A flower garden may be a popular foraging place. Thorny native shrubs such as mesquite (*Prosopis velutina* and other spp.) and small trees will also welcome this bird.

Feeder Pleasers

- Nectar

Tricks and Treats

- Gather as many kinds of soft materials as you can to offer for nesting in early spring. Feathers are always popular.

Sleeping Spaces

Once you start looking for verdin nests, you'll see lots of them dotting the small trees and bushes. Are there that many brooding birds in such a small area? Nope. Many of those nests are roosting nests built for sleeping.

The tiny birds use the same strong nest construction to create a safe space to spend the night. Those thorny twigs help keep out snakes and other bird-eating predators.

Bushtit

First Impression

Tiny gray bird flying out of a bush with high, thin calls; then another bird, and another, and another, and another . . .

Mark Your Calendar

Year-round; absent from a few small parts of this region

Details, Details

• One of our smallest birds, even smaller than a chickadee; 4½ inches
• Long tail
• Often looks fluffed-up
• An unusual variation of gender: males have dark eyes, females have pale eyes

Listen Up!

• A constant stream of thin, high-pitched *tsit-tsit-tsit* calls
• The calls are a great clue to the impending arrival of a flock of bushtits. When you hear them, look around for the bitty birds.

Telltale Traits

• Intensely gregarious; always in a flock
• Constantly on the move, foraging rapidly in bushes and small trees
• Often travels with mixed group of chickadees and kinglets in winter
• Tame around people and gentle to each other; no sign of squabbling in flock

Look Here

• Moving in a flock from one group of bushes in your yard to the next

Or Here

• At the birdbath
• Flying in a talkative flock
• At the suet feeder

"An individual bird ... takes temporary leadership, and is followed to a new location"

—**Robert Miller, "The Flock Behavior of the Coast Bush-Tit" (1921)**

Miller surmised that it was "the hunger instinct" that caused one bird of the flock to suddenly take off for a new foraging place. No one really knows. Maybe these tiny birds just have wanderlust?

On the Home Front The nest is a long, loose, hanging sack, suspended from a tree or bush.
• Builds in deciduous or evergreen trees

Wild Menu: Insects, especially scale insects; spiders

Plant Picks: Unsprayed shrubs and trees of any kind

Feeder Pleasers
• Suet, especially suet enriched with insects

Tricks and Treats
• Bushtits love their baths. Keep a birdbath brimming, and you may see the whole bunch lining up at once.

Disappearing Act

Bushtits occur in the Northwest and West regions, too. Every few days, a flock of about 40 of these tiny gray mites sweeps into my yard in Washington State. The entire flock plays follow the leader from one shrub to another, then stops off at the suet feeder to fill their beaks. A few minutes later, perhaps with a last pit stop at the birdbath, they're gone again. All told, they may spend 10 minutes, tops, in my acre yard. With these fast-action birds, you'll want to "Catch 'em while you can!"

Pygmy Nuthatch

First Impression

Itty-bitty, short-legged, big-headed bird clinging to tree trunk

Mark Your Calendar

Year-round in some areas; absent in others

Details, Details

- Smaller than a chickadee; 4¼ inches
- Long, thin, pointy beak
- Dark eye stripe divides brownish top of head from white chin and cheek
- Small light patch at back of neck
- Female and male look alike

Listen Up!

- High, repeated peeping: *pip-pip-pip*
- A variety of *chip*s and squeaky calls

Telltale Traits

- Incessantly vocal; you'll hear them when they come around
- Sticks tight to bark as it sidles along tree branches and trunk
- Probes crevices with its long beak to extract or whack at hiding insects
- May scour bark headfirst or upside down
- Travels in small family flocks
- Often travels in winter with chickadees, titmice, and other small birds

Look Here

- At the feeder

Or Here

- Hitching down the bark of a pine tree
- Moving slowly in an incessantly peeping flock through the branches of tall pines
- Playing follow the leader as they move from one tree to another
- Usually in or around pines and pine forests

"Gray midgets"

—**Irene Wheelock**, *Birds of California* (1904)

Scientists measure length from tip of beak to tip of tail, and for this species that's just a smidgen more than 4 inches. Factor in that long beak and you have one tiny bird!

On the Home Front May nest in backyard
- Often accepts a nest box • Digs a hole or uses an old woodpecker home in wooden post or dead branch or top of dead pine • Nests at widely varying levels, from just above your head to over 60 feet high. • Lines its nest cavity with individual scales of pinecones, leaves, and soft materials, including fur and feathers

Wild Menu: Insects; seeds of pinecones

Plant Picks: Tall, big-headed annual sunflowers (*Helianthus annuus*) are a good start; add native pines, such as ponderosa (*Pinus ponderosa*) to your yard for additional temptation.

Feeder Pleasers
- Suet; sunflower seeds; chopped nuts

Tricks and Treats
- Mount a nest box, which the little birds may also use for nighttime shelter.

Room for One More?

Like many other cavity-nesting birds, pygmy nuthatches also seek out cozy "indoor" places to sleep at night. During nesting season, parent birds pile in with their kids. In winter, the entire flock may try to squeeze into the same cavity.

One evening in New Mexico, I watched 22 of these birds enter a bluebird nest box, one after the other. Made me wonder how they arranged themselves in there. Were they all clinging to the rough wooden walls? Or did late arrivals end up on top of the early birds?

Cactus Wren

First Impression

A big, bold, brown bird with a speckled belly and a striking white eye stripe

Mark Your Calendar

Year-round; absent in northern areas

Details, Details

- A little smaller than a robin; 8½ inches
- Looks more like a thrush or small thrasher than a wren
- Coastal birds have whitish underparts; inland, a subspecies shows peachy flanks and lower belly
- Tail has white outer corners
- Female and male look alike

Listen Up!

- Noisy and loud
- This bird doesn't look like a wren, and it doesn't sound like one either. Instead of an ecstatic bubbling song, it has a low, throaty, croaking quality to its voice.
- Also rapidly repeats a single note
- May give jaylike squawks

Telltale Traits

- Tame and curious; unafraid of humans
- Often sings atop spiny cactuses
- Most active in morning; perches or forages in shade during hot afternoons
- Grasps a leaf in beak and lifts up, peering intently for insects on underside

Look Here

- Perched on top of a cactus

Or Here

- At the feeder
- Hopping about on the ground
- At the birdbath

"The birds could plainly be heard rattling about inside"

—Joseph Grinnell, on cactus wrens amid dead fronds of date palm, "Midwinter Birds at Palm Springs, California" (1904)

Cactus wrens make the most of plants within their range. Although the birds usually stay close to ground level, they may forage anywhere that insects are abundant.

On the Home Front Often nests in a specimen cactus in a backyard • Cholla and prickly pear are favorite nesting sites.

Wild Menu: Mostly insects; some fruit, including that of saguaro

Plant Picks: Specimen cholla or prickly pear cactus (*Opuntia* spp.) for perching, nesting, and fruits; elderberries for summer food

Feeder Pleasers
- Dry dog food; suet; halved oranges and chunks of watermelon (with rind); try mealworms and other soft foods, too.

Tricks and Treats
- Provide a birdbath for an occasional drink or bath. This xerophilous species can also get along fine without drinking any water at all, thanks to the juicy cactus fruit it eats.
- Maintain a dusty area—near a shrub is an inviting spot—so the birds can take dust baths.

Get Out! No, You Get Out!

Cactus wrens and curve-billed thrashers seem to be sworn enemies. Both nest in the same kind of habitat and both resent sharing it. During nesting season, cactus wrens attempt to drive off any curve-billed thrashers they spy, and vice versa. Despite the difference in size (cactus wrens are about 2½ inches smaller), they seem pretty equally matched, with each species succeeding at times in ousting the other.

Curve-Billed Thrasher

First Impression

Big, drab, grayish tan bird with an outrageous downward curved beak

Mark Your Calendar

Year-round; absent from parts of this region

Details, Details

- Larger than a robin; 11 inches
- Focus your binoculars on that orange eye.
- Faintly speckled breast
- Female looks like male

Listen Up!

- You'll often hear a sharp, two-note, *whit-wheet!* whistle, given by both sexes. It's loud and startling!
- The male's warbled song of musical phrases sounds a lot like the brown thrasher's. Each phrase is repeated two or three times, then there's a short pause before it's on to the next paired phrases. The song itself is very varied, but usually includes *quit-quit* and *weet-weet* phrases.

Telltale Traits

- Runs rapidly or hops across the ground
- Flies low and fast from one bush to another
- Tosses aside leaves and debris with its bill
- Digs holes a few inches deep with that beak
- Often hides in shrubbery

Look Here

- Perched on a cholla cactus

Or Here

- On the ground
- Beneath shrubs
- At the feeder or the birdbath

"Like water running through a sieve"

—Herbert Brown, "The Habits and Nesting of Palmer's Thrasher" (1888)

Watching a curve-billed thrasher (once called Palmer's thrasher) slip smoothly through the branches and among the spines of a cholla cactus is amazing. The viciously spiny cactus is usually so quick to jab its barbed spines into any passerby that it's called "jumping cactus."

On the Home Front May nest in backyards
- Usually nests in cholla cactus, 3 to 5 feet aboveground • Builds nest of thorny twigs lined with grass • Competes with cactus wren for nest sites and territory

Wild Menu: Insects; cactus fruit

Plant Picks: Fruits of any kind, particularly sweet or sour cherries, mulberries (*Morus* spp. and cvs.), and grapes

Feeder Pleasers
- Mealworms; suet; millet, milo, and birdseed mix; nuts

Tricks and Treats
- Keep a birdbath brimming for this bird.

Thrashers Galore

Thrashers are hard to identify. Six species of similar thrashers, including Bendire's, curve-billed, California, Crissal, LeConte's, and possibly the long-billed, plus the thrush-like sage thrasher, occur in the Southwest. It takes practice to sort them out where ranges overlap. That's if you get to see them at all—most species are notorious skulkers. They stay in dense brush, coming out to forage on the ground, where their drab colors blend right into the background.

One good way to track down thrashers is to listen for a singing bird. They may sing from within a tangle of branches, but often they move to a conspicuous perch to pour out their long and varied songs. Check the details to figure out which species is doing the singing.

Hepatic Tanager

First Impression

A soft red, slinky bird in the treetops

Mark Your Calendar

Spring through fall in mountain forests; migration only in some areas; absent in some parts of region

Details, Details

- Smaller than a robin; 8 inches
- Note the brightness of the red (sometimes red-orange) on the bird's crown and throat, compared to the dull red body.
- Female is grayish with yellow-orange forehead and breast

Listen Up!

- A slow melodic song, full of pauses
- Also a low *chup* call note
- A rising *tweet* in flight

Telltale Traits

- Slow and deliberate
- Fairly tame birds

Look Here

- Foraging in pines or oaks

Or Here

- At feeder
- Fly-catching after passing insects
- At birdbath

On the Home Front Not usually a backyard nester, unless your backyard is in or very near a pine-oak forest • Builds a loose, open saucer of stems, grasses, and—for a unique and charming touch—flower stems with flowers still on them • Nests in branch fork in pines and oaks

A Step Ahead of Science

"Slow and deliberate in their movements"

—A. C. Bent, *Life Histories of North American Blackbirds, Orioles, Tanagers, and Allies* (1958)

These beautiful tanagers move slowly and quietly through the treetops and branches of pines and oaks, gleaning insects. The only way to find them there is to look up!

Wild Menu: Insects; some fruit

Plant Picks: Pines native to your area, such as pinyon (*Pinus edulis*) or Jeffrey (*P. jeffreyi*); grapes or cherries

Feeder Pleasers

- Mealworms and other insect foods; halved papaya and other fruits

Tricks and Treats

- Provide a pedestal-type birdbath or other water source.
- Hepatic tanagers are fond of butterflies and moths, just in case you need another reason to plant a butterfly-attracting garden.

Official data about the hepatic tanager shows a lot of gaps, including its diet and bathing habits. Yet backyard bird-watchers have snapped photos of this bird at their feeders. And I saw one take a bath when my family was camping in the Chiricahua Mountains of Arizona. As soon as we pulled into the campsite, birds were already gathering. When I filled a frying pan with water, we suddenly drew a crowd. A bright yellow-and-black Scott's oriole alighted on the pan while I was carrying it. I can take a hint—I filled the skillet and set it nearby. Our next customer was a hepatic tanager, who exuberantly splashed nearly all the water out of the pan. Finally, he yielded to the oriole and went off to fluff and preen.

California Towhee

First Impression

Drab grayish brown bird scratching on ground

"Striking together two silver dollars"

—**Richard Hunt, on metallic sound of California towhee, "Evidence of Musical Taste in the Brown Towhee" (1922)**

Mark Your Calendar

Year-round in western California

Details, Details

- About robin size; 9 inches
- Use binoculars to see orangish eye color.
- Look for the pretty orangish color where the tail joins the body.
- Short, sparrowlike bill
- Female looks like male
- Similar canyon towhee has a reddish cap and a necklace of short, dark streaks and spots; Abert's towhee of Southwest is another look-alike, with dark face

Listen Up!

- A series of sharp, metallic clinks, *chink-chink-chink-ink-ink-ink,* picking up speed into almost a trill, and often ending with a drawn out, lower *chinnnnk*
- Also a sharp, high *chink* call note

Telltale Traits

- One of the most common backyard birds
- Tame around people in backyards; much shier in the wild
- Almost always on the ground, either in the open or under a bush or parked car
- Reminiscent of a big sparrow
- Scratches at ground with feet, hopping forward and dragging back

Look Here

- At feeder

Or Here

- Foraging on ground or under shrubs

Short on silver dollars? Then try to imagine the rhythm of this towhee's song: Hunt said it's like a golf ball dropped on a hard surface and "allowed to bounce itself motionless."

On the Home Front May nest in backyards

- Builds a bulky nest in a dense shrub or tree

Wild Menu: Seeds, especially weeds; some insects

Plant Picks: Scatter a few handfuls of birdseed mix; towhees will forage among the plants' standing stems all fall and winter.

Feeder Pleasers

- Millet; birdseed mix

Tricks and Treats

- Rein in your weeding habit, and you'll make towhees happy. They eagerly seek out seeds of pigweeds (*Amaranthus* spp.), knotweeds (*Polygonum* spp.), filaree (*Erodium cicutarium*), and others.

Home-Court Advantage

Without flashy colors or bold markings, the many species of drab-colored southwestern birds can be tough to identify—for visitors, that is. When you live with these birds, you get to know their voices and habits, which are major clues to sorting out the species.

Geography factors in, too: If you live in L.A., you're not likely to have an Abert's towhee scratching in your backyard. Visitors, though, will have to constantly consult their field guides, to see when they're leaving one species' stomping ground and moving into another's territory.

Lesser Goldfinch

First Impression
A smaller, darker goldfinch

Mark Your Calendar

Year-round in southern and coastal parts of region; spring through fall in rest

Details, Details

- Smaller than a chickadee; 4½ inches
- Smaller than American goldfinch
- Big white patches show in wings and tail in flight.
- Unlike American goldfinch, doesn't change plumage colors for winter
- Male's black cap extends farther back than that of American goldfinch
- Female is duller and lacks the black cap
- Lawrence's goldfinch also shows up in some parts of this region, usually foraging in weeds under oaks. It's a gray bird with a black face and yellow splashes on breast, wings, and tail.

Listen Up!

- Canarylike song of varied, rising notes
- A plaintive, high, clear, *te-yeee* or *tee-ee* call

Telltale Traits

- Gregarious birds, usually in flocks except in nesting season
- Undulating flight
- Often sing and call on the wing

Look Here

- At the birdbath

Or Here

- At the feeder
- In gardens or weedy corners, eating seeds
- Perched with the flock in a treetop
- Flying with the flock in dipping, rising flight

"Especially fond of the seeds of the wild sunflower"

—**Alfred Gross**, in A. C. Bent's *Life Histories of North American Cardinals, Grosbeaks, Buntings, Towhees, Finches, Sparrows, and Allies* (1968)

Sunflowers grow wild in this region, reverting to a shorter, widely branching form with seed heads just a couple of inches across. Goldfinches visit the plants as soon as the seeds start to ripen.

On the Home Front May nest in backyard
- Female builds a dainty cup of plant fibers and grasses, lined with thistledown and feathers

Wild Menu: Weed seeds, especially thistle

Plant Picks: Weed seeds are dear to this bird's heart, so tolerate a few if you can. Or plant a meadow garden with native grasses and flowers.

Feeder Pleasers
- Niger seed; millet and finch mix

Tricks and Treats
- Water draws this species like a magnet. Any birdbath may attract them
- They're fond of salt; offer a scant handful of table salt in an open tray feeder.

The Indiana Connection

New Harmony, Indiana, where I used to live, was once a Utopian community full of scientists and freethinkers, including Thomas Say, a 19th-century American naturalist responsible for describing many species of wildlife for the first time—including the coyote and a firefly.

On an 1819 expedition to the Rocky Mountains, Say and companions collected a specimen of the lesser goldfinch. His description was published and made official in 1923.

Lark Bunting

First Impression

A dramatic black-and-white sparrow

Mark Your Calendar

Year-round in southern part of region; spring through fall in eastern and northern parts; migration only or occasional stray in other areas; absent in some parts

Details, Details

- The size of a big sparrow; 7 inches
- When it's in breeding plumage, look for the male's white wing patches and white tail tip.
- Outside of breeding season, the male is heavily streaked with black face and pale blue beak.
- Female is grayish brown with streaky white breast and dark stripe on throat

Listen Up!

- A rich, pretty, warbled song of musical trills, interspersed with high, metallic rattling noises
- Low, soft, *hoo-ee* call note

Telltale Traits

- Not usually a backyard bird, but a vivid presence in surrounding open land
- In huge flocks, from hundreds to thousands of birds, except during nesting season
- The flock moves like a rolling wheel, with birds at the rear continuously fluttering to the front. When they find food, the wheel stops and the birds eat their fill.

Look Here

- In open areas

Or Here

- In arid land, grassy areas, or brushy places
- Singing from a fence post

"Habitat loss due to urbanization"

—Diane Neudorf, on threats to species, *Lark Bunting* (Calamospiza melanocorys): *A Technical Conservation Assessment* (2006)

City sprawl can cause more than traffic jams. Although there are plenty of lark buntings, scientists are watching the species for the impact human activities have upon it.

On the Home Front Not a backyard nester

- Builds nest on ground, at foot of sagebrush (*Artemisia* spp.), shrubs, or clump of weeds

Wild Menu: Seeds, especially weed seeds; in summer, grasshoppers and other insects

Plant Picks: If you have a backyard big enough to suit this freewheeling species—and that means many acres—you won't have to plant anything to draw it in.

Feeder Pleasers

- Not usually a feeder visitor

Tricks and Treats

- Spring migration is the best time to observe a flock with males in full breeding plumage.

Living Up to the Lark

In March or April, the male lark buntings leave the massive wintering flock and move northward to nesting grounds. On this trek, the male birds—in beautiful, fresh breeding plumage—are suddenly gripped by the urge to sing, and what a show they put on! One by one, male birds suddenly rise up from the ground into the air, pouring out an ecstatic song. Because they're still in a flock, there may be dozens to hundreds of males doing the same thing at once. It's an incredible spectacle, both to see and to hear.

Scott's Oriole

First Impression

A beautiful song coming from a big, slim, striking yellow-and-black bird

Mark Your Calendar

Spring through fall; absent in a few areas

Details, Details

- About the size of a robin; 9 inches
- Male has dramatic black hood, with bright yellow belly and shoulders
- Female is much paler, has dull greenish head, and variable amounts of black on head or breast

Listen Up!

- Rich, musical song of whistled notes
- Female sings softly near the nest
- Also a quick, harsh *jerk!*

Telltale Traits

- Usually seen singly or in pairs
- Constantly singing
- Cling to stems of flowers to get nectar

Look Here

- At nectar feeder

Or Here

- At fruit feeder
- At flowers
- Climbing quietly along branches through foliage, peering for prey
- At birdbath

On the Home Front May nest in backyards
- Often attaches its nest to the drooping, dead leaves of *yuccas*, near where they join the plant
- Builds a cup-shape nest; not as pendulous as those of other oriole species

"Few birds sing more incessantly"

—**William Scott,** "On the Breeding Habits of Some Arizona Birds" (1885)

You'll probably hear this bird before you see it. Scott noted, "At the earliest daybreak, even when the sun is at its highest, and during the great heat of the afternoon, its very musical whistle is one of the few bird songs that are ever present."

Wild Menu: Insects, especially butterflies; fruit; nectar from flowers

Plant Picks: Aloes (*Aloe* spp.), ocotillo (*Fouquieria splendens*), red-hot pokers (*Kniphofia* spp.), yuccas (*Yucca* spp.); figs, peaches, apricots, or cactuses.

Feeder Pleasers
- Nectar feeder; halved oranges or grapefruits; mealworms; suet, especially with insects

Tricks and Treats
- Flowers are key to the heart of Scott's oriole—and not just because of their nectar. The bird may visit your blooms to pluck butterflies.

Mastering Monarchs

Everyone knows that monarch butterflies are poisonous. Everyone but Scott's orioles, that is: On their wintering grounds in Mexico, the birds eat plenty of them. The secret? Not all monarchs have the same concentration of toxins. In 1979, monarch experts William Calvert, Lee Hedrick, and Lincoln Brower (*Science*) found that Scott's orioles flew repeatedly into the colonies to peck at the butterflies. Often, an oriole would release a butterfly without eating it—probably because its bad taste indicated a higher level of toxins.

Hummingbirds

First Impression

Tiny, zippy, unmistakable birds with brilliant iridescent color

Mark Your Calendar

Spring through fall, migration, or year-round, depending on where you live and on the species of hummingbird

Details, Details

- Itty-bitty birds, from 3¼ inches to about 5 inches, including the long bill
- This region is hummingbird heaven. Depending on where you live, you might spot Allen's, Anna's, black-chinned, broad-billed, broad-tailed *(shown above)*, calliope, Costa's, magnificent, rufous, or white-eared hummingbirds, plus a selection of Mexican species that occasionally stray northward.

Listen Up!

- Various twitterings, chips, and high, thin, squeaky calls

Telltale Traits

- Unique ability to fly frontward, backward, up, or down, or to hover
- So fast you may only hear the buzz as one goes by
- Hover at flowers
- Often perch on slim twigs or other places where takeoff is unimpeded by vegetation

Look Here

- At nectar feeder

Or Here

- At flowers
- Perched in shrubs or small trees, or on garden ornaments

"By the first of July ... the Hummingbirds are found in countless thousands at higher elevations"

—Joseph Grinnell, *Birds of the Pacific Slope of Los Angeles County* (1898)

Hummingbirds follow the flowers. Many species leave lower elevations by late June, when flowers stop blooming, and head for the mountains, where flowers are then in full glory.

On the Home Front May nest in backyards
- Hummingbird nests are tiny cups built of spider silk, plant down, lichens, and other bits of materials.

Wild Menu: Nectar; insects

Plant Picks: Hummingbird flowers! Check your local nursery for native perennials, annuals, and shrubs.

Feeder Pleasers
- Nectar feeder

Tricks and Treats
- Supply a garden ornament at least 5 feet tall—such as a trellis or hanging basket holder—made of metal less than ½ inch in diameter. If the very top is slender enough for their tiny feet, your backyard hummingbirds may make it a prime perching spot.
- Misters and sprinklers are popular with hummingbirds, who bathe in the spray.

Green Flowers

Red and red-orange flowers are tops for hummingbirds, bringing in the birds like a beacon. But in the dry-as-a-bone desert, a flower of another color is also a standout: tree tobacco (*Nicotiana glauca*). This greenish-yellow flowered South American perennial blooms from April to September, providing a feast to hummingbirds. It's easy for the birds to zero in on the plant because it stays green in the dry season. The plant sticks out like a green thumb.

White-Winged Dove

First Impression

A soft taupe-gray dove with a black "pen mark" on the side of its face and a long white crescent along the edge of its folded wings

Mark Your Calendar

Spring through fall in southern parts of this region; year-round in a few small extreme southern areas; absent in other parts

Details, Details

- Bigger than a robin; 11½ inches
- In flight, look for bold white wing patches separating the dark wing feathers from the pale body.
- Use binoculars to admire the blue ring around the orange-red eye.
- Tail has white band at tip
- Female and male look alike

Listen Up!

- Monotonous, repeated hooting call, with the same rhythm as that of barred owl: *who cooks for you*
- Other slow, deep, cooing sounds

Telltale Traits

- Usually on ground
- Fast, direct flier; wings make clapping sound on takeoff
- Gather together in large flocks after nesting

Look Here

- On the ground in open areas

Or Here

- At the feeder or birdbath
- In gardens, eating weed seeds

"At times, 3,000 to 4,000 visible in flight"

—**John K. Terres,** *The Audubon Encyclopedia of North American Birds* **(1980)**

A gregarious bird, this dove often feeds and travels in huge flocks. Watch for groups of a few thousand during spring migration, as the birds move northward from wintering grounds in the tropics.

On the Home Front May nest in backyards
- Nests in various trees and shrubs, including citrus, mesquite (*Prosopis* spp.), and tamarisk or salt cedar (*Tamarix aphylla*), and in cactus

Wild Menu: Seeds, especially wild sunflowers and grain, plus weed seeds, especially doveweed (*Murdannia nudiflora*); cactus fruit

Plant Picks: Scatter a handful of black oil sunflower seed or milo among garden beds.

Feeder Pleasers
- Sunflower seeds; birdseed mix; cracked corn; millet and milo

Tricks and Treats
- Water is a big draw. A ground-level basin or saucer is best.

Decimating Doves

The passenger pigeon, now extinct, garners all the publicity when it comes to having been hunted to extermination. But other species of doves and pigeons, including this one, were killed off by the tens of thousands in the old days. From the early 1870s to the 1920s, settlers saw millions of white-winged doves; by 1930, the species was declining fast. Hunting continued, though, and as recently as 1968, three-quarters of a million doves were harvested in Arizona alone. Today, the daily hunting limit for these doves is much less than the 50 birds it was just a few decades ago, and the population is stable.

California Quail

First Impression

A flock of grayish brown "footballs" with bobbing black topknots

Mark Your Calendar

Year-round; the similar Gambel's quail is found year-round elsewhere in this region

Details, Details

- Robin length but much plumper; 10 inches
- Feather patterns are striking and elegant.
- Black face boldly marked with white
- Breast feathers have a distinctive thin, dark rim, creating an effect like overlapping scales.
- Female has a grayish face lacking bold pattern, and an abbreviated topknot
- Gambel's quail, also in this region, is a similar species but has a plain tan breast

Listen Up!

- Repeated calls of *whee-hee-hoo*
- Also various other calls, including gurgling noises and a single crowlike *caw*

Telltale Traits

- Almost always in a flock, except during nesting season
- Follows a regular schedule, showing up at about the same time each day
- Usually walks from place to place
- Only flies if forced by being chased

Look Here

- At feeder

Or Here

- At birdbath
- On ground

"A very perfect model of a husband and father"

—W. Leon Dawson, on the monogamous California quail, *The Birds of California* (1923)

Was it the "loose" attitudes of the Roaring Twenties that caused Dawson to expand on his theme? "Even in domestication, with evil examples all about and temptresses in abundance, the male quail is declared to be devoted to a single mate."

On the Home Front Frequent backyard nester
- Ground-level nests are well-hidden under a shrub or hedge or beside a rock.

Wild Menu: Seeds; insects; small green leaves

Plant Picks: Try buckwheat for a quail-attracting crop. These birds will also find plenty to eat naturally in your yard.

Feeder Pleasers
- Birdseed or cracked corn; a quail block, a compressed block of seeds sold at wild bird supply stores

Tricks and Treats
- Give quail a ground-level basin or pool.

Set Your Watches

I was visiting a friend in southern California one afternoon, when she stood up and said, "Let's take our iced tea and go out to the garden. The quail should be here any minute." "How do you know?" I asked. "Easy," she said. "The covey always comes to feed an hour after sunrise and an hour before sunset." We had just settled ourselves onto her garden bench when there was a sudden movement under the hedge. Like clockwork, there they came, one bird scuttling along after the other in single file. They headed for her garden pool first, where they drank as if they hadn't seen water in weeks. Then they ambled over to the feeding station and settled in for supper.

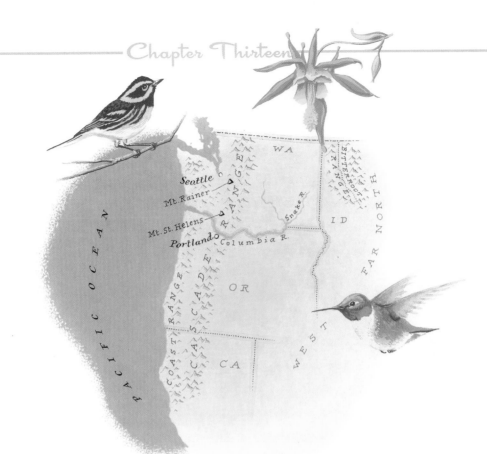

Chapter Thirteen

Birds of the Northwest

The Northwest is marked by mountain ranges that run north and south through the region. Major cities, including Seattle, Spokane, and Portland, are located here, but there's still plenty of wild land. Small towns, originally built around local logging or mining companies, dot the landscape. Orchards, wineries, and cattle pastures are common sights in some places. There's a diversity of landscape, from desert sagebrush to deep, dark, moss-draped forests, from mountain forests and alpine meadows to wild, crashing ocean waves pounding the rocky coastline.

MOUNTAINS ARE THE BACKBONE

Mountain ranges are the defining factor of the Northwest. Their effect on the weather greatly determines the climate and character of each part of this region, because mountains can block rain or channel winds and snow.

Look on a topographical map, and you'll see that the illustration above is just the beginning of the story. On a topo map, the Northwest looks like a piece of badly crumpled

NORTHWEST

Steller's jay is at home in higher elevations.

paper that's been roughly smoothed out again. These mountains are rugged, with steep slopes and deep, forested canyons.

Meet the Mountains

In the north are the Olympic Mountains—tall, jagged peaks that form an unbroken sweep against the sky where Puget Sound cuts far inland from the Pacific Ocean. Some areas, including Tacoma and Seattle, are dripping wet. Other places that fall in the "rain shadow" of mountain ranges that block moisture, such as the town of Sequim on the Olympic Peninsula, receive such a diminished amount of rain that lavender farms are big business.

Along the Northwest coast, where moisture rolls off the ocean unimpeded, the climate is mild and wet. Flowers bloom all winter, and hummingbirds are an everyday sight. Summers can be cool and foggy, and winters are rainy much of the time.

On the east side of the Coast Range, between it and the Cascade Mountains, wide, fertile valleys are home to plenty of people and a thriving agricultural industry. Grass seed, peppermint, raspberries, and other fruit are the mainstay crops. As you leave the valley and move into the foothills, moss-covered big-leaf maples, Douglas firs, and western red cedars dominate the scene, with a tangled understory of evergreen salal (*Gaultheria shallon*) and waist-high sword ferns. Bird life changes gradually as treetop species take over from the blackbirds and sparrows of the lowlands.

East of the Cascades and Rockies, where the mountains have blocked the rainfall coming from the coast, the climate is much drier. Sagebrush and desert plants flourish, trees are shorter and of different species, and rocky outcrops break through the dry grasslands. Birds are almost entirely different here, with dryland and grassland species suddenly replacing the tanagers and grosbeaks of the wet forests.

The mountains themselves add even more variety to the natural life of this region. Conifers dominate their forested slopes until high altitude thins the trees. Some peaks, including the volcanoes Mount Rainier, Mount Saint Helens, and Mount Hood, offer their own kind of very-high-altitude habitat. Mountain goats cling to rocky precipices, golden eagles cruise the heights, and alpine meadows are ablaze with flowers and butterflies during short summers.

Birding is big in this region, because there's so much variety. A day trip can quickly take you to entirely different surroundings than you have at home.

LEGENDARY RAIN

Living with the Northwest's rain is a point of pride for many northwesterners. Others become seasonally depressed when the gloom rolls in during fall, and some move here only to leave again after a few years of what seemed like never-ending rain.

The big secret, though, is that the rain only lasts part of the year. In summer, the climate is about as good as it gets. One pleas-ant, sunny day follows another, with barely a sprinkle or even a cloud.

Rain, Rain, Come to Stay

Those mountains, plus its proximity to the Pacific Ocean, make much of the Northwest a mighty rainy place. Lush green forests carpeted in moss so thick you can't hear your own footsteps are nature's reward for the months of rain that soak the region each year.

West of the Cascades, the climate has two main seasons: rainy and dry. (East of the Cascades is a different story, which we'll get to a bit farther on in this chapter.)

The rainy season usually begins in earnest in late October. Look at the 5-day forecast now and you'll see there's a rain cloud for almost every day, with only an occasional picture of the sun; just a couple of weeks before, the opposite was true.

By the time November gets a good start, the sun is a rare sight. I often joke with friends that the forecasters put a picture of the sun in their weekly predictions just to keep us all sane. As long as there's some hope of sunshine, the rain seems to be more easily endured.

Most of the time, the rain is light. You soon get used to going about any outdoor activities you choose, even if it's raining. Besides, those hundred-foot trees in the forests do an excellent job of catching most of the falling droplets while you walk under them. Only once in a while do you get a cold trickle down your neck when you nudge a branch!

The first time we cut a Christmas tree in the national forest—a ritual for many folks in this region—I was stunned by how heavy the 6-foot tree was. A few good shakes dislodged most of that weight: It was water collected

Thick moss covers trees and forest floor.

among the needles of the sweet little fir.

As for boots, I generally don't bother. The thick layer of conifer needles and decomposing logs underfoot, blanketed with moss, soaks up water like a sponge. In fact, if you break off a piece from a rotting log in the rainy season, you can squeeze clear, cold water out of it.

I do miss the sunshine in the Northwest, but I also love a dim, rainy day in the woods. Winter wrens burst into song on all sides, tiny kinglets and chickadees forage through the trees overhead, and if I'm lucky, I'll catch a glimpse of a lovely varied thrush.

Rain, Rain, Go Away

By April, rain is usually beginning to dwindle in the Northwest, and by May, the skies are mostly sunny. Because the winters are mild west of the Cascades, flowers bloom earlier. That means that your bed of beautiful bearded iris or even roses is likely to be turned into mushy petals by rain. As for daffodils, I quickly learned to plant only single, strong-stemmed varieties: The fluffy types end up on the ground, thanks to the weight of spring rains.

Some years have rainy springs, others dry. But by June, it's sunny almost every day. Temperatures are moderate, and gardens grow like crazy. Don't be too envious, though, because by July, plants are starting to look like they could use a drink. Backyard grass, velvety green right through winter, goes dormant in summer. Now the birdbath becomes the hot spot in the yard, as chickadees, finches, buntings, and black-headed grosbeaks take turns at the water.

Summer is also the time when the snow melts in the mountains, and hundreds of sub-alpine wildflowers flood the meadows with color. It's my favorite time of year—a feast of flowers! I always see plenty of birds then, too, including nesting juncos, warblers, and thrushes in the mountains.

DIFFERENT ON THE DRY SIDE

Northwest rain doesn't accurately depict the climate once you venture east of the mountains. In the "rain shadow" areas, moisture is scarce, so plant life and bird life are totally different. So is the climate. Instead of a wet and dry season, the central and eastern parts of the Northwest have four distinct seasons: cold, often snowy winters; brief springs; hot, parched summers; and autumns that can change to winter in a heartbeat.

Thunderstorms, a rare event on the west-

On the dry side of the mountains, pines and grasslands replace lush, mossy forests.

ern side of the mountains, are taken in stride here. And wind is a fact of life. In winter, it sweeps down from Canada; in summer, it sweeps up from the Southwest deserts with a desiccating effect.

Instead of the lush, easy life of the western-side birds, where food is plentiful year-round, birds in the eastern parts of the Northwest have to work hard for a living. In this area a well-stocked feeder and a reliably filled bird-bath are great inducements for lazuli buntings, lesser goldfinches, and other birds to visit your yard.

THE LAY OF THE LAND

Towering firs, spruces, hemlocks, and cedars create forests big and small in the western part of this region. Alders spring up in any patch of open ground. East of the mountains, pines and junipers take over, and the trees become sparser and finally give way to sagebrush and shrubs.

Tree seeds—including a bounty from conifer cones—provide meals for chickadees, nuthatches, and other northwestern birds. Insects abound, too, nourishing orioles, tanagers, and hunting hordes of tiny bushtits.

A myriad of streams, rivers, and waterfalls in the western part of the region provide a bounty of other insects. In the grasslands, there's even more on the menu, including grasshoppers, ants, and plenty of other delectable critters. Plus the bark and dead wood of all those northwestern trees supply more feeding places for woodpeckers, nuthatches, brown creepers, and other birds adapted to gleaning bark or pecking into wood.

Fruit eaters such as cedar waxwings and tanagers find plenty to sing about here. Along with miles of cherry orchards and vineyards, the Northwest is filled with berry-bearing shrubs and wild fruit trees. Blackberries are the most common, and most notorious: They fill many an opening, gone wild from an introduced species. There's such a huge crop of blackberries that many go uneaten, even those berries that linger into the depths of winter. At higher elevations, huckleberries (*Vaccinium* spp.) and currants (*Ribes* spp.) provide abundant fruit for varied thrushes and hermit thrushes.

BIRD LIFE IN THE NORTHWEST

Birding is a popular pastime in this region, but it often isn't easy. Many species are hard to find in the dense vegetation. And many spend most of their lives high in the treetops. I soon learned their songs and calls, so that I wouldn't have to spend so much time craning my neck trying to get a bead on whoever was singing far above me. When I returned to the East for a visit, I was surprised by how easy the birding seemed to me. Finding a scarlet tanager in an oak tree—which for me was once a frustrating challenge—was now much easier, compared to finding a singing Townsend's warbler in the dark branches of a 150-foot fir.

Many birds occur singly in the Northwest, and roam relatively large territories. It often takes some looking to spot even a single individual. The number of songbird species isn't as great as I was accustomed to in other places: There are no thrashers, mockingbirds, or catbirds at every corner. Instead of dozens of warbler and vireo species, there's only a scant handful. Did I mention there are no blue jays? Well, maybe a rare stray now and then.

But I'm not complaining. There are fabulous Steller's jays and engaging scrub jays. Enough sparrows to keep you busy with binoculars year-round. And I still get shivers every time I hear a varied thrush's eerie whistle at twilight, or listen to the liquid trill of a winter wren. Whatever Northwest habitat you live in, you'll find plenty of birds to make life interesting.

Start Here

The Northwest shares many of the birds in Chapter 6, "Start Here," with other regions.

Familiarize yourself with those common and abundant "Start Here" birds to get to know your most familiar backyard friends. These are the birds you share with other parts of the country—chickadees, white-breasted nuthatches, American goldfinches, juncos, cedar waxwings, and many others. Then get to know the regional specialties here.

Regional Specialties

You'll find other favorite friends spotlighted in this regional section. Some of these birds also occur in other regions. But every single one of them may turn up in your northwestern backyard.

Be sure to page through the birds of the Far North, Midwest, and Southwest, too. Many of them also range across the border into northwestern backyards.

Birds of the Northwest

Here are the birds profiled in this chapter. Remember to consult the "Start Here" birds, starting on page 79, for many other common birds in the Northwest.

Pileated Woodpecker

First Impression
Humongous cartoon character Woody Woodpecker

"The large red-crested woodpecker"

—Mark Catesby,
The Natural History of Carolina, Florida, and the Bahama Islands (1731)

You can pronounce "pileated" as either "pie-lee-ated" or "pill-ee-ated." It simply means crested—and what a crest this big bird has!

Mark Your Calendar
Year-round in some parts of this region; absent from some areas

Details, Details
- As big as a crow; 16½ inches
- Big, strong beak
- Watch for big white patches in the wings, and even bigger white patches underneath when the bird flies.
- A pointy tuft of feathers on the head
- Female is similar to male but lacks the red forehead and red mustache

Listen Up!
- Hollers *awoik! awoik!* in a ringing voice
- Sounds very similar to the flicker, but louder and slower
- Drums on resonant surfaces, long and loud

Telltale Traits
- Often pecks at logs as well as dead trees
- Pries off long strips of dead wood to get at carpenter ants
- Often flakes off bark
- Flies like a crow, with deep wing beats
- Noisy; can be heard from far away
- Can raise and lower that incredible red crest

Look Here
- At your suet feeder

Or Here
- Clinging to tree trunk
- Pecking at dead trees or dead limbs
- Flying or swooping from tree to tree

On the Home Front Not usually a backyard nester • Pair shares territory all year

Wild Menu: Insects, mostly carpenter ants and wood-boring beetle larvae, with a sampling of spruce budworm and other delicacies; nuts; small amount of berries

Plant Picks: None

Feeder Pleasers
- Suet, served in a stationary feeder

Tricks and Treats
- In this region, carpenter ants and termites are abundant, thanks to all that decaying wood.

The Postman Rings Twice

For all their size, pileateds are easy to overlook. Watch for a pile of wood chips at the base of a tree, then look up. If you're lucky enough to discover a current nest cavity, watch for the parents' "shift change." Both birds take turns keeping their young ones cozy. When the relief parent is arriving, it calls on its way to the nest to alert the sitting bird, who will often peek out and give a soft *chuck*. When the returning bird comes in for its landing, the one in the hole often gives a few soft tap-tap-taps before flying out.

Lewis's Woodpecker

First Impression

A large black woodpecker with a pale collar, gliding across an open area between trees

NORTHWEST

Mark Your Calendar

Varies depending on specific location; might be year-round, winter only, spring through fall, or migration only

Details, Details

- Bigger than a robin; 10¾ inches
- Its black feathers have a green sheen, and its red face and deep pink-red belly are beautiful.
- Female looks like male

Listen Up!

- Harsh *churr, churr, churr*
- Sudden *yick!* alarm call

Telltale Traits

- Unusually slow flight, almost looks like slow motion
- Glides or soars at times, without flapping
- Often fly-catches from perch, swooping out after passing insects
- Stores acorns and nuts in caches, often in crevice of utility pole or fissure in cottonwood bark, for winter feeding
- May perch on utility wires
- Battles with other woodpeckers over stored food
- Pair remains together year-round

Look Here

- On a perch in a tree, especially a pine; or on a post, flying out to catch insects

"Such enormous appetites I was glad to give them their liberty"

—**Charles Bendire, who kept a few young woodpeckers captive,** *Life Histories of North American Birds* **(1895)**

Grasshoppers were a favorite of his captives, reported Bendire, noting that his charges "climbed everywhere over the rough walls of my house."

Or Here

- In oaks, collecting acorns
- In flocks in winter, in oak groves or nut tree orchards
- Gliding from a perch to the ground to catch grasshoppers, crickets, and other insects

On the Home Front May accept a nest box if you live near open Ponderosa pine forests, its typical breeding habitat

Wild Menu: Insects; nuts; acorns; fruit
Plant Picks: Oaks (*Quercus* spp.), English walnut trees (*Juglans regia*); grapes and apples
Feeder Pleasers
- Doesn't usually visit feeders, but offer it English walnuts in the shell or whole corn
Tricks and Treats
- Has been reported to use nest boxes

"Utility" Poles

Not quite what their makers had in mind, but poles with utility indeed! Those tall wood poles are a utilitarian favorite of Lewis's woodpeckers. The poles often split open some shallow cracks as they age, creating inviting fissures that are just the right size for stuffing full of acorns. One summer, when grasshoppers were extra plentiful, I spotted one of these woodpeckers parking its extra insects in a utility pole. The pretty bird crammed dozens of grasshoppers into the cracks, securing them with well-placed beak taps.

Red-Breasted Sapsucker

First Impression
Odd calls that lead to a blackish woodpecker with a red head and breast

Mark Your Calendar

Year-round

Details, Details

- A little smaller than a robin; 8½ inches
- The only woodpecker in this region with a red head and breast
- The red is not as flashy as that of many woodpeckers.
- Watch for the white wing patches and white rump, especially in flight.
- Male and female look alike

Listen Up!

- A grab bag of odd, nasal calls: most often, a mewing or squealing *neeah*
- To keep in touch, a pair of birds gives hoarse *wik-a wik-a* calls.
- May also make a *geert* sound
- Much less vocal in winter

Telltale Traits

- Tapping and drumming sounds are a surefire sign that a woodpecker is nearby.
- Moves up and down tree trunks in herky-jerky movements on short legs
- Often stays on same tree for hours

Look Here

- On the trunk or limbs of living trees, sometimes not far from ground

Or Here

- Tapping or drumming on stumps or dead trees, sometimes at very top of tree

> *"67 species of fruit, forest, and ornamental trees"*
>
> —Johnson Neff, tallying the targets of this species, in "A Study of the Common Woodpeckers in Relation to Oregon Horticulture" (1928)

With that kind of variety, your backyard may have trees that red-breasted sapsuckers will investigate for sap potential.

On the Home Front Digs out a cavity in a dead tree or in a dead snag of a living tree

Wild Menu: Sap; ants and other insects; tree fruit, seeds, and inner bark

Plant Picks: May sample elderberries (*Sambucus* spp.) and huckleberries or blueberries

Feeder Pleasers
- Not usually a feeder visitor

Tricks and Treats
- Apple trees are favorites of this sap-seeking bird.

Going Down?

It gets cold in them thar hills, so in fall, many sapsuckers move down from their summer homes at high elevations in the mountains. If you live in lower areas, especially near a river or other water, winter will be your prime time for hosting these red-tinged birds.

Keep an eye out for their calling card: rows of small, closely spaced holes drilled into the trunks of trees in your yard. Scan those trees every time you're outside. These birds can be mighty quiet when they're on a tree, and it's surprisingly easy to overlook them entirely. On a rainy winter day, they blend right into the mossy bark.

Scrub Jay

First Impression

Big, noisy, bluish gray bird with whitish gray belly

Mark Your Calendar

Year-round; mostly at lower elevations; absent from some northern parts of this region; Steller's jay usually at higher elevations than scrub, but often overlap

Details, Details

- Bigger than a robin; 11½ inches
- The Pacific race has a distinct blue necklace across its breast and whiter underparts than the interior race.
- Female and male look alike

Listen Up!

- A harsh, scolding cry of *cheek-cheek-cheek!*
- A questioning: *quay-feeeee?*
- Other grating calls, including *ker-wheek!*
- A very quiet, private, and decidedly musical "whisper song," sung to its mate

Telltale Traits

- Loud, bold, and intelligent
- Also can be secretive and quiet
- Often hops about on ground
- Usually in small groups
- Look for it in shrubs (the "shrub" from which it gets its name)

Look Here

- At your feeder

Or Here

- In oak trees or nut trees
- On the ground beneath shrubs
- In shrubs or hedges
- Burying nuts or acorns

"The flat-headed jays"

—**Harry Swarth,** *The Pacific Coast Jays of the Genus* **Aphelocoma** (1918)

In the eastern United States, where the only jay species wears a jaunty crest, a "flat head" would look odd. In the West, jays come in crested and crestless species.

On the Home Front Nests in trees, sometimes in blue elder (*Sambucus caerulea*) and other shrubs, sometimes in dense vines, such as wild grape

Wild Menu: Huge variety: nuts, fruit, insects, snails, mice, snakes, frogs

Plant Picks: Plant giant sunflowers for seeds.

Feeder Pleasers
- Nuts and peanuts, in the shell; sunflowers; suet

Tricks and Treats
- A freshly filled birdbath may attract jays.

The Peanut Gallery

Scrub jays quickly learned that my appearance in the yard means one very important thing: the possibility of a treat. Like a cat hearing a can opener, they fly in from blocks away as soon as I come outside. The tamest among them swoop within a few feet to watch me with bright black eyes. Easy to grasp what they're thinking: "Peanuts! We want peanuts!" How do they know what's in my lumpy pocket? I trained them, by tossing them the treats every time I came outside. And they trained me, to always bring peanuts in the shell along.

Chestnut-Backed Chickadee

First Impression

Little brown, black, and white bird, never sitting still

Mark Your Calendar

Year-round in some parts of this region; absent from others

Details, Details

- Small chickadee size, of course; 4¾ inches
- The only chickadee with a chestnut-colored back
- Black cap and throat
- Male and female look alike

Listen Up!

- These little cuties don't sing a whistled song but they are fairly vocal.
- Listen for a higher, thinner variation of the classic call, sounding like *kiss-a-dee*.
- Also a buzzy trill similar to the chipping sparrow's and a *tsidi-tsidi-cheer-cheer*

Telltale Traits

- More common in rural or forested areas
- Often upside down on branches
- Always on the move, searching leaves and branches for caterpillars and other insects
- In winter, often part of a flock of nuthatches, kinglets, and other chickadee species

Look Here

- At the feeder

Or Here

- In conifer trees; possibly deciduous trees
- In shrubs and hedges

"Old familiar friends in more richly colored garments"

—**A. C. Bent,** *Life Histories of North American Jays, Crows and Titmice* **(1946)**

Gray and white with a black-trimmed head is the typical garb of most chickadee species. This one takes it up a notch with a pretty, rusty brown back and sides.

On the Home Front Nests in cavities—including, maybe, that nest box in your backyard
- Prefers nest boxes that face east to southeast, probably because they warm up faster

Wild Menu: Insects; seeds; buds

Plant Picks: Native conifers in your yard will make these little guys feel at home.

Feeder Pleasers
- Suet; sunflower seeds; nuts

Tricks and Treats
- If you live within nesting territory, a wire suet cage stuffed with wool, feathers, and other soft materials may draw nest-building birds.

Variations on a Theme

With some practice, it's pretty easy to peg a birdcall as that of a chickadee. But figuring out which species is which is for the advanced class! These birds sound very similar, even when they're saying *chick-a-dee*. Some species are more sibilant, others change the tempo, others say more *dee-dees*, and this one raises the pitch. Still, no matter how tricky they can be to sort out, the same suet and sunflowers will satisfy all species—and bring them in where you can identify them by color instead of calls.

Bushtit

First Impression

Tiny gray bird flying out of bush with high, thin calls; then another bird, and another, and another, and another . . .

Mark Your Calendar

Year-round; absent from northern part of this region

Details, Details

- Even smaller than a chickadee; 4½ inches
- Long tail
- Often looks fluffed-up
- An unusual variation of gender: The male has dark eyes, the female, pale

Listen Up!

- A constant stream of thin, high-pitched *tsit-tsit-tsit* calls
- When you hear their calls, look around for a flock of the bitty birds.

Telltale Traits

- Intensely gregarious; always in a flock
- Constantly on the move, foraging rapidly through the foliage of bushes and small trees, then traveling on to the next
- Often travels with mixed group of chickadees and kinglets in winter
- Tame around people and gentle to each other; no sign of squabbling in flock

Look Here

- Moving in a flock from one group of bushes to the next in your yard

Or Here

- At the birdbath
- Flying through or over your yard in a talkative flock

"There are always a few stragglers hurrying along"

—A. C. Bent, *Life Histories of North American Jays, Crows and Titmice* (1946)

Gregarious bushtits travel in a flock that moves, mostly as one, from one bush or tree to the next. But there always seem to be a few who aren't paying attention and must rush to catch up.

On the Home Front The nest is a long, loose, hanging sack, suspended from a tree or bush.
- The birds are strongly attached to their flock.

Wild Menu: Insects, especially scale insects; spiders

Plant Picks: Unsprayed shrubs and trees

Feeder Pleasers
- Suet, especially suet enriched with insects

Tricks and Treats
- Keep a birdbath brimming, and you may see the whole bunch lining up at once.

It's a Marvel

Orioles are famous for their fabulous hanging nests, but the little bushtit does an even more marvelous job. The pair actually makes its fabric out of spider silk with some pieces of vegetation. The birds add to it until it stretches across a branch fork or other gap. Then the female sits in it, causing it to stretch downward. While the male adds bits of moss, lichens, and other material to the outside, the female keeps stretching the nest until it forms a long, loose sack, shaped like a gourd—but looking more like a mossy green sock!

Varied Thrush

First Impression

A fancy robin with a dark necklace

Mark Your Calendar

Year-round; many move to higher altitudes for nesting, lower elevations for winter

Details, Details

- About the same size as a robin; 9½ inches
- Long-necked, short-tailed, with a plump tummy
- Back may appear grayish, black, or deep blue
- Use binoculars to admire the orange trim on head, throat, belly, and wings.
- Female is paler and has gray breast band

Listen Up!

- An extended, single-note, buzzy whistle
- Also a short *vree* trill, or a harsh *churr* note

Telltale Traits

- Very shy and usually difficult to approach
- Spends a lot of time on ground or near it
- Usually moves a short distance at a time, either by hopping or flying
- Rarely seen far from cover
- May be aggressive at feeder, driving off other birds

Look Here

- At the feeder

Or Here

- In shady, dark areas, in, under, or near shrubs and trees
- Often associates with robins, so take a good look at those birds in your backyard
- At the edge of a forested area

"Where spruce trees and alders and crowding ferns contend for a footing"

—**William Dawson, on where varied thrushes are found,** *The Birds of California* **(1923)**

Apparently Dawson must've spent at least one winter in the famously rainy Northwest. His description continues: ". . . and where a dank mist drenches the whole with a fructifying moisture."

On the Home Front Not usually a backyard nester • Usually nests in mature forests

Wild Menu: Worms; berries; seeds; slugs; snails; fruit; insects; nuts, especially acorns

Plant Picks: Blueberries, blackberries; manzanita and bearberry (*Arctopstaphlyos* spp.); toyon (*Heteromeles arbutifolia*)

Feeder Pleasers

- Millet and birdseed mix; accessible suet

Tricks and Treats

- May use a birdbath, if it's near shelter

Not Quite Harmony

The eerie and strangely beautiful song of the varied thrush is as unique as its plumage. Unlike other thrushes, which sing complicated melodies, this songbird has an exceedingly simple song. It's a slightly buzzy whistle on one pitch, held for about 2 seconds. After a long pause, it whistles again—but on a different pitch. Pause, then another whistle, again on a different pitch, and so on for the entire concert. Because the notes sound similar yet are different tones, you could easily be fooled into thinking there's more than one varied thrush in the vicinity.

Swainson's Thrush

First Impression

Quiet olive-brown robinlike bird with speckled breast, on ground

Mark Your Calendar

Spring through fall in some areas; migration only in others

Details, Details

- Smaller than a robin; 7 inches
- In the western part of this region, this thrush shows more russet than olive coloring on its back and head; that russet-backed race gives way to the interior race, a drab olive-brown bird.
- Look for its "spectacles": the pale eye rings with pale lines from eyes to beak, to distinguish it from the similar hermit thrush.
- Female and male look alike

Listen Up!

- A long song of repeated phrases, in typical fluting thrush style; one transcriber suggests *whip-poor-will-a-will-e-zee-zee-zee*, going up at end
- Piping call note sounds like spring peeper

Telltale Traits

- Often on ground, but also in shrubs and treetops
- Gets around on ground in long, bouncy hops
- May sing at night

Look Here

- At berry bushes

Or Here

- On ground

"They sang almost continuously through the night"

—Wilfred Osgood, "Biological Investigations in Alaska and Yukon Territory" (1909)

Many thrush species are famed for occasionally singing at night, but usually you'll hear only a few phrases, not an hours-long concert. Osgood's observations were made in summer in Alaska, where "nights" are light enough for walking, fishing—or birds singing.

On the Home Front Nests in many different trees and shrubs • The female builds a cup of grasses, stems, and twigs.

Wild Menu: Berries; insects; snails

Plant Picks: Blackberries and raspberries, twinberry (*Lonicera involucrata*)

Feeder Pleasers

- Doesn't usually visit feeders, but it might like mealworms and other insect foods

Tricks and Treats

- Offer moss for nest building.
- May visit a birdbath, particularly one near to ground

Twice as Nice

Wild cherries and chokecherries (*Prunus* spp.) in the Northwest are a favorite food of the Swainson's thrush. The bird nibbles off the flesh of the small fruit, then drops the pit to the ground. Each visit may result in dozens of dropped pits—a bonanza to some creatures below.

I once came across an old bird nest being used as a pantry by one of those creatures. When I peered into the pretty, mossy nest to see how it was constructed, a bright-eyed deer mouse looked up at me from atop its treasure trove of cherry pits.

Townsend's Warbler

First Impression

Black and yellow on a small, fast-moving bird

Mark Your Calendar

Spring through fall in some parts of this region; winter only along much of coast; migration only in some areas

Details, Details

- Chickadee size; 5 inches
- Bold black markings on head and throat
- Back is olive green
- Two white wing bars
- Female is paler version of male

Listen Up!

- A persistent singer; listen for *weez weez weez zeee* or *swe swe swe zee*
- A sharp *chip!*

Telltale Traits

- Highly energetic
- Very territorial; male aggressively chases other males during nesting season
- May join a mixed flock of chickadees, nuthatches, and kinglets in winter

Look Here

- At suet feeder

Or Here

- Quickly moving through foliage of trees or shrubs during migration
- Singing while foraging or from perch in tall conifer
- At birdbath

On the Home Front May be a backyard nester if you have large spruce or fir trees • Can be hard to observe because it nests at 60 feet or higher

"Incessantly repeated . . . comes the song of the Townsend warbler"

—Walter Taylor and William Shaw, *Mammals and Birds of Mount Rainier National Park* (1927)

This wood warbler's song is one of the signature sounds of the great Pacific Northwest forests. It filters downward from the tops of the immensely tall trees, where the little birds flit amid the foliage.

Wild Menu: Insects

Plant Picks: Douglas fir (*Pseudotsuga menziesii*)

Feeder Pleasers

- Suet; peanut butter; mealworms; possibly nectar

Tricks and Treats

- Try a trickling, naturalistic birdbath to tempt this pretty little bird.

Sweet Stuff

Got a hummingbird feeder? Some house finches, woodpeckers, and several species of wood warblers, among others, have learned to help themselves to a sip of sugar water.

This warbler already has a predilection for sweet stuff. On wintering grounds in Mexico and Central America, Townsend's warblers are often seen visiting trees that are infested with colonies of scale insects. Like aphids, scale insects excrete a sticky-sweet substance known as honeydew. It's so desirable that the warblers fight over it.

Wilson's Warbler

First Impression

Tiny, active yellowish green bird with black beret

Mark Your Calendar

Spring through fall in forested areas; anywhere in this region during migration

Details, Details

- Smaller than a chickadee; 4¾ inches
- Even without binoculars, you can catch the black button eye and black cap on that yellow face.
- Female has duller, browner cap than male

Listen Up!

- A bright, hurried, staccato twitter rising in pitch
- Also a *chip* call note

Telltale Traits

- Restless and quick-moving
- Often jerks its tail
- Flutters, almost hovering in midair, when chasing insects

Look Here

- Foraging in shrubs or hedges

Or Here

- In willows and other trees, usually within about 15 feet from ground
- Often near water
- In rhododendrons or blackberry thickets

On the Home Front Usually nests in forests or swamps, but may nest in wooded backyard
- Builds nest on or near ground

"A flash of sunny gold"

—A. C. Bent, *Life Histories of North American Wood Warblers* (1953)

The Wilson's warbler has an olive green back, tail, and wings, but it's that flash of bright yellow underparts that you'll notice as the bird moves quickly through the bushes.

Wild Menu: Insects

Plant Picks: Blackberry patch; also shade gardens with sword ferns (*Polystichum munitum*) and rhododendrons (*Rhododendron* spp.)

Feeder Pleasers
- Not usually a feeder visitor, but you can try offering mealworms

Tricks and Treats
- Warblers are a great reason to invest in a recirculating pump for your birdbath; a gentle liquid gurgling may entice them.

Sit Tight

Like many warblers, the female Wilson's often stays on the nest when a human approaches. Since the nest is well-hidden by foliage, the chances are better you'll overlook it if she just sits tight. Ornithologists call a bird like this a "close sitter"; it's a trait shared by many species of wood warblers.

If you're lucky enough to notice a nest, that sit-tight habit will give you a good opportunity to get a close look at Mama. If you blunder into a nest by accident, the female bird may flutter pitifully on the ground, pretending she has a broken wing. It's all an act to distract you from that precious cup of eggs or babies. Back off a few paces and stand quietly, and she'll soon return to her nest.

Yellow Warbler

First Impression
A vivid dash of yellow among the willows

Mark Your Calendar

Spring through summer; one of the earliest fall migrants

Details, Details

- Chickadee size; 5 inches
- Vivid rusty red streaks on breast
- Female is duller colored, with muted olive-streaked breast

Listen Up!

- Bright, high-pitched *sweet sweet sweet sweeter than sweet* or s*weet sweet sweet I'm so sweet*
- Also *chip* call

Telltale Traits

- Forages in shrubs and plants relatively close to ground
- Like most warblers, a fast, restless little bird
- Males are very territorial and chase and fight with other males in breeding season.

Look Here

- Got any willows? They're magnets for this bird.

Or Here

- Foraging in gardens, hedges, or shrubs
- In brush along fences
- At the birdbath

On the Home Front May nest in backyards, but usually nests in wild places with thickets and trees • Generally builds nest on ground or from about 3 to 7 feet up, though some may be higher • Makes beautiful, deep cup of fibers with many soft materials

"Nor does it mind our company in the least"

—**A. C. Bent,** *Life Histories of North American Wood Warblers* (1953)

It's tricky to get close enough to most wood warblers to snap a picture, but yellow warblers are a much easier subject. They seem to have no fear of people, and will allow you to approach closely.

Wild Menu: Insects

Plant Picks: Willows, including pussy willows (*Salix* spp.); also substantial bushy plants, such as hibiscus (*Hibiscus moscheutos* and other spp.) and elderberries (*Sambucus* spp.)

Feeder Pleasers
- May visit for mealworms

Tricks and Treats
- Consider a naturalistic ground-level birdbath, with a trickling dripper to catch this bird's attention.

Cover Up

This tiny, pretty bird is a frequent target of the parasitic brown-headed cowbird, which lays its eggs in the warbler's nest. One of the few birds that seems to recognize the difference between the cowbird's much larger, brown-speckled white eggs and its own small, pale bluish, spotted eggs, this warbler often cuts its losses. When it spots cowbird eggs, it covers up the cowbird eggs and its own eggs by building another nest bottom over them. Then it begins its egg-laying process all over again.

Black-Headed Grosbeak

First Impression

A small flock of vivid orange-and-black birds at the feeder, tame and chubby, and showing flashy white wing patches when they fly

Mark Your Calendar

Spring through fall

Details, Details

- Smaller than a robin; 8¼ inches
- Male flashes eye-catching white wing patches in flight
- Note the strong, conical beak, built for cracking seeds.
- Female is streaky dark brown with buff-colored breast and pale belly
- Striking striped head on females and juvenile birds

Listen Up!

- A pretty warbled song of clear, whistled notes with trills, similar to a robin's
- Also a sharp *spick!* call note

Telltale Traits

- Very tame; isn't afraid of people
- Often in a small flock, except when nesting
- Shares many habits with its eastern counterpart, the rose-breasted grosbeak

Look Here

- At feeder

Or Here

- Foraging in shrubs or trees
- Singing from top of tree
- Flying across open space, with those wing patches flashing
- Eating fruit

"It eats a considerable quantity of orchard fruit"

—Foster Beal, "Birds of California in Relation to the Fruit Industry" (1910)

Birds were once classed as either friend or foe by weighing the cultivated crops they ate against the pest insects in their diet. Beal recommended that the black-headed grosbeak not be killed despite its taste for fruit, because it is "an active enemy of insect pests."

On the Home Front Nests low, from as little as 3 feet aboveground to about 20 feet
- Usually makes home near creek or river

Wild Menu: Insects; fruit

Plant Picks: Elderberries (*Sambucus* spp.), cherries, blackberries, raspberries

Feeder Pleasers
- Sunflower seeds

Tricks and Treats
- Fond of taking a bath; adores a sprinkler

A Cup of Moss

As a born-and-bred easterner, I had quite an adjustment period before the dim, damp conifer forests of the Northwest felt like home. After a few years, though, I found it perfectly normal that every surface in a Northwest forest is swathed in moss. In fact, I've become a fan of it.

When I spy an unusually lush ball of moss within arm's length, I can't resist touching it. Sometimes, instead of inches of springy moss, I discover a surprise beneath the green carpet: an old bird nest, often that of a black-headed grosbeak. Like any other stationary object in these wet woods, an unused nest soon is covered by luxuriant moss.

Lazuli Bunting

First Impression

A sparrow size, turquoise "bluebird," singing its heart out and shining like a living jewel

Mark Your Calendar

Spring through fall

Details, Details

- Smaller than a sparrow, only a bit bigger than a chickadee; 5½ inches
- Iridescent plumage, like that of the closely related indigo bunting
- Two highly noticeable white wing bars will quickly tell you that this isn't a bluebird.
- Female is soft, warm brown, with a buff-colored breast

Listen Up!

- A fast, clear, high-pitched warbling *see-see-see-sweert-sweert-sweert* song that lasts long
- Also a sharp *pick!* call note

Telltale Traits

- Sings frequently, all day long
- Male moves from one perch to another around his territory to sing
- Males chase each other in spring.
- After nesting, birds congregate in groups.

Look Here

- At your feeder

Or Here

- Singing from the highest perches available
- Foraging in brushy corners of the yard
- In thickets, hedges, and clumps of bushes

Buntings are indefatigable singers. The male lazuli bursts into song frequently, all day long, except when he's caring for the fledglings of the first brood while his mate is sitting on the second nest.

On the Home Front May nest in backyards that open to wild places • Builds nest close to ground, within 3 feet • Just about any shrub will do.

Wild Menu: Insects; seeds, especially grass seeds

Plant Picks: Sow a patch of bluegrass seed or lettuce seed in an open area near a shrub. Let it go to seed, and you may see a flash of lapis blue in your own yard.

Feeder Pleasers
- Millet; finch mix

Tricks and Treats
- A well-stocked feeder is the best temptation.
- May visit a birdbath

A Bit of a Stretch

The invasive reed canary grass (*Phalaris arundinacea*) is highly unpopular with people, but a big hit with the avian population. The grass stems are long and flexible, so it takes ingenuity for the birds to bring those seeds to their beaks. I once watched lazuli buntings cling to a stronger weed nearby, then s-t-r-e-t-c-h to reach the grass seeds. As soon as they pulled out a seed, though, the stem moved out of reach again. Finally one bird wised up: He inched his way up the stem, bending it as he went. By the time he reached the seed head, it was touching the ground. He pinned it down with one foot and ate at lesiure.

Purple Finch

First Impression

Small raspberry-red bird with alert look

Mark Your Calendar

Year-round along coast; winter only farther inland; absent from part of this region

Details, Details

- The size of a sparrow; 6 inches
- More intense all-over color and stouter than a house finch
- Look for the raised feathers on the head, which give the bird an alert look that's different from a house finch.
- Female is streaky brown with light eye stripe; muddier facial pattern in this region than in purple finches elsewhere

Listen Up!

- Fast, rising and falling, warbled song
- Call note is a sharp metallic *tick!*

Telltale Traits

- Can raise head feathers for an almost crested effect
- An erratic wanderer; some years may bring many, other years only a few

Look Here

- At tray or tube feeder

Or Here

- In trees
- At fruit trees, eating buds or blossoms

On the Home Front Nests may be at just about any height, all the way to 50 feet aboveground.
- Usually tucked among the dense branches of a conifer • The dense cup of twigs and roots has a fine lining of grasses, plant fibers, and hair.

"They bathe in brooks with the temperature below freezing point"

—Edward Forbush, *Birds of Massachusetts and Other New England States* (1919)

Purple finches are water lovers, whether they show up in the Northwest or in New England. Supply a birdbath in winter and you're likely to see these pretty birds reveling in the bath.

Wild Menu: Seeds of trees and weeds; occasionally tree buds or flowers; some berries

Plant Picks: Conifers; raspberries or blackberries; ash trees (*Fraxinus* spp.) for seeds

Feeder Pleasers
- Sunflower seeds; finch mix

Tricks and Treats
- Put a small handful of rock salt into an open tray feeder, or set up a salt block.
- If your yard is near a forest or has large conifers that might be considered for nest sites, try offering soft materials, such as tufts of natural wool, for lining.
- Birdbaths are popular year-round with purple finches.

Savoring Seeds

Ash tree seeds are held in small, elongated, flat pods that grow in dangling clusters. When I was a kid, we called the pods "bananas," and served them at our dolls' tea parties.

I haven't had a doll tea party in ages, but I do enjoy watching purple finches eat their share of these seeds right in the trees. Oregon white ash (*Fraxinus latifolia*) is common along the mighty Columbia River in my part of the Northwest. In spring, cedar waxwings gather in the trees to eat the pollen-dusted flowers. In winter, I search the bare silhouettes of the trees to spot small flocks of purple finches, busily working at the persistent dangling seeds.

Lesser Goldfinch

First Impression
A smaller, darker goldfinch

Mark Your Calendar

Year-round in some areas, mostly along coast; spring through fall in other areas; absent in some parts of this region

Details, Details

- Smaller than a chickadee; 4½ inches
- Smaller than American goldfinch
- Big white patches show in wings and tail in flight.
- Unlike the American goldfinch, this species doesn't change plumage colors for winter.
- Male's black cap extends farther back than American goldfinch, which has only black forehead
- Female is duller version and lacks black cap

Listen Up!

- Canary-like song of varied, usually rising notes
- A plaintive, high, clear *te-yeee* or *tee-ee* call

Telltale Traits

- Gregarious birds, usually in flocks except in nesting season
- Undulating flight
- Often sing and call on the wing

Look Here

- At the birdbath

Or Here

- At the feeder
- In gardens or weedy corners, eating seeds
- Perched with flock in treetop
- Flying with flock in dipping, rising flight

"Captured only by using water as bait"

—**Ernest Clabaugh, on catching this species for banding, "Methods of Trapping Birds" (1930)**

Lesser goldfinches live in arid areas as well as more moderate climes, but all find water irresistible. A birdbath is an even bigger attraction than a feeder, in all seasons.

On the Home Front May nest in backyard
- Female builds dainty cup of plant fibers and grasses, lined with soft stuff such as thistledown and feathers

Wild Menu: Weed seeds, especially thistle

Plant Picks: Weed seeds are dear to this bird's heart, so tolerate a few if you can. Or plant a meadow garden with native grasses and flowers.

Feeder Pleasers
- Niger seed; millet and finch mix

Tricks and Treats
- Water draws this species like a magnet. Any birdbath may attract them, but they'll find it faster if you add a dripper they can hear.
- Like other finches, they're fond of salt; try a scant handful of ordinary table salt in an open tray feeder.

A Little Off

You'll probably do a double take when you spot your first lesser goldfinch. The birds look and act a lot like their bigger cousin, the American goldfinch, and even their voices have a similar querying quality. But something is just a little off.

When I saw my first birds of this species at my birdbath, it was the small, almost flattened-looking head of the male that first caught my eye. Then I noticed the dark back that gave the bird its old name of "green-backed goldfinch." Since the American goldfinches were still in sunny yellow, it was easy to figure out that this bird was something else.

Golden-Crowned Sparrow

First Impression

A bunch of streaky brown birds with striped heads topped with yellow, busily feeding on ground

Mark Your Calendar

Winter only from coast to east of mountains; absent in some parts of this region

Details, Details

- A big sparrow; 7¼ inches
- During breeding season, males and females sport a bright yellow crown bordered by dramatic black stripes.
- Head markings are less distinct when not nesting

Listen Up!

- Sweet, whistled notes in a minor key, to the tune of *"Three Blind Mice"*

Telltale Traits

- Almost always in loose flocks
- Sings frequently, even in winter
- Picks up seeds from ground
- Raises head feathers when excited
- Unlike many sparrows, golden-crowneds often fly up into tree when disturbed, instead of diving for bushes

Look Here

- In or below feeders

Or Here

- In trees, shrubs, and hedges
- In flower gardens
- Eating seedlings and new grass sprouts

On the Home Front Not a backyard nester
- Nests from British Columbia to Bering Sea

"Young birds are particularly tame and unsuspicious"

—Harry Swarth, "Birds and Mammals of the Skeena River Region of Northern British Columbia" (1924)

The same trait holds true in the Lower 48. In fall, when golden-crowned sparrows flock to feeders within their range, it's easy to approach them quietly without causing alarm. Got your camera ready?

Wild Menu: Seeds, insects, buds, flowers, and young seedlings

Plant Picks: It may eat buds and flowers of calendula (*Calendula officinalis*), or pansies (*Viola* × *wittrockiana*); also eagerly eats newly planted lawn grass and sprouts of fall-planted garden peas.

Feeder Pleasers
- Millet; birdseed mix

Tricks and Treats
- Let some birdseed sprout beneath your feeder; golden-crowned sparrows may nibble on it.

What's That You Say?

It's easier to remember a bird's song if you can translate it into English. The cardinal's *what cheer,* the brown thrasher's *hoe it hoe it, cover it up, cover it up,* and the white-throated sparrow's *old Sam Peabiddy* are quick clues to remember when you hear the actual bird. They can also give you a fun peek into the past.

Looking for the mother lode in Alaska a century ago was exhausting work with pick and shovel. Maybe that's why to the ears of goldminers, the golden-crowned sparrow seemed to be singing *I'm so weary.* Discouraged miners suggested another variation: *no gold here.*

Lincoln's Sparrow

First Impression

A song sparrow that looks different

Mark Your Calendar

Winter only along the coast; spring through fall in most other parts of this region

Details, Details

- Small sparrow size; 5¾ inches
- Smaller than the similar song sparrow
- Black streaking on buff-colored breast may merge into a spot, like on the song sparrow
- Use binoculars to look for the buff-colored cheeks, breast, and sides.
- Male and female look alike

Listen Up!

- A musical, bubbly song that bursts forth like that of a wren
- A *chip* call of communication or alarm
- Buzzy *zeet* or *zrr-zrr-zrr* notes during breeding season

Telltale Traits

- A skulker; very secretive
- Usually stays low to ground in heavy cover; rarely far from shrubs or trees
- Chases moths and plucks their wings before eating
- Often scratches on ground, kicking both feet backward, to uncover insects and seeds
- Sometimes with flocks of other sparrows

Look Here

- On the ground under your feeder among other sparrows

Or Here

- Beneath or in dense shrubs or hedges
- In trees
- In bramble patches

"Tom's Finch"

—Name bestowed by John James Audubon, in honor of his companion, young Tom Lincoln, who shot the specimen, "Macgillivray's Finch," *Ornithological Biography* (1834)

To get a close-up look at birds, early naturalists depended on guns rather than binoculars. "Tom's Finch" (name later changed to Lincoln's sparrow) is an elusive bird that flits from one bush to another.

On the Home Front Not a backyard nester, unless your backyard is many acres in size; seeks undisturbed location • Nests on ground

Wild Menu: Seeds; insects

Plant Picks: Think thick cover for this bird: dense hedges, groups of tight-knit shrubs, and patches of blackberries and raspberries.

Feeder Pleasers
- Millet; birdseed mix

Tricks and Treats
- A well-stocked feeder near sheltering bushes will help this shy bird feel at home.

Check and Double-Check

Like the lesser goldfinch and other more unusual backyard visitors, Lincoln's sparrow can be easily overlooked. A lone bird often joins a flock of mixed sparrows to scratch for seeds. Sad but true, sparrows are one of the regular visitors that we often take for granted. Take a few minutes to look carefully at each bird in a bunch under the feeder—with binoculars. You may be surprised at who's dining.

Dark-Eyed Junco (Oregon Race)

First Impression

A striking black hood and a flash of white tail feathers

Mark Your Calendar

Year-round; absent from some areas in nesting season

Details, Details

- Sparrow size; 6¼ inches
- Rust-tinged brown back and cinnamon sides
- Male and female have white belly and white outer tail feathers
- Female is paler version of male

Listen Up!

- Both male and female sing
- Song is a short trill; you'll often hear it in feeder birds in early spring
- Sharp *chip!* or buzzy *tzeet* calls

Telltale Traits

- Usually on or near ground
- Often in flocks
- Often scratches at leaf litter to uncover seeds and bugs

Look Here

- Under or in the feeder

Or Here

- Beneath shrubs
- In winter, on the lawn or in flower or vegetable gardens
- Singing from a tree in spring

On the Home Front Retreats to conifer forests in mountains in nesting season; may be a backyard nester in those areas • Usually builds nest on ground, in natural cavity near rock or tree, or sometimes among roots of a wind-fallen tree

"There is not an individual in the Union who does not know the little Snow-bird"

—John James Audubon, *The Birds of America* (1831)

Juncos, or snowbirds as many folks still call them, are common across the country. In the Northwest, the most familiar race is the Oregon junco, which sports a dramatic black hood.

Wild Menu: Seeds; in nesting season, insects; may eat snow for moisture in winter

Plant Picks: Juncos are prone to panic attacks: They dive for the nearest bush when they get scared. Scattered shrubs and hedges of any kind will give them safe hiding places. Tolerate a few weeds in your yard if you can, too; juncos eagerly eat weed seeds.

Feeder Pleasers

- Millet; birdseed mix

Tricks and Treats

- Supply a birdbath, and juncos will visit frequently.
- Wait until spring to cut back the dead stems in your gardens, so juncos can forage there all winter.

Going Up

Oregon juncos leave my lowland yard in April. I generally forget all about them until my first foray into the mountains to see the wildflowers at higher altitudes. As soon as the road starts to seriously climb, I see juncos flitting about along the edges or twittering from the bushes.

It always takes me a second to say, "Oh, right, juncos!" Then I start watching for singing males and nesting pairs—maybe the same birds that will flock to my yard again in fall.

Western Tanager

First Impression

A brilliant flash of red-orange, yellow, and black in the trees

Mark Your Calendar

Spring through fall

Details, Details

- Smaller than a robin; 8 inches
- Use binoculars to admire those fancy wing bars when birds are in flight or perched.
- Male has black tail
- Male's red almost disappears in fall
- Female is drab gray-green with yellowish head, breast, and belly, and gray wings

Listen Up!

- Low, warbling song, somewhat similar to robin's, but huskier
- Frequent *pit-ick* call note

Telltale Traits

- A visual standout: one of the most vivid birds of this region
- Forages for insects among the foliage
- Often easily visible when it flies from one tree to another, or fly-catches from a tree or other perch

Look Here

- At feeder

Or Here

- Foraging in mature conifers
- At the birdbath

On the Home Front May occasionally nest in backyards with conifers, if you live near forest

"The sales of the fruit which was left did not balance out the bills paid out for poison and ammunition"

—W. Otto Emerson, quoting correspondence from H. A. Gaylord, "A Remarkable Flight of Louisiana [now western] Tanagers" (1903)

Early orchardists despised these beautiful birds because they gobbled the cherries from their trees. Growers killed the birds by the hundreds when they descended on their orchards. I often wonder how many of these birds we'd see today if they hadn't been killed wholesale back in the old days.

Wild Menu: Insects; fruit

Plant Picks: Plant a sweet or sour cherry tree to attract tanagers—and be prepared to share the crop!

Feeder Pleasers

- Cracked corn; millet and birdseed mix; suet; dried fruit, plus halved oranges

Tricks and Treats

- Keep a birdbath brimming and you may get to see a tanager take its bath.

Living Flames

Seeing a tanager makes it a red-letter day in my book because the birds aren't plentiful. One glorious May day, I was visiting Catherine Creek, a wildflower area on the dry side of the mountains in Washington. I was studying a purple flower when a sudden flicker of yellow and red caught my eye.

Coming up the hill through the gnarled oaks was a flock of western tanagers. Not the hundreds I've read about in the old days, but at least a dozen. They moved rapidly through the oak branches over my head, picking off insects at the flowering oak catkins. Occasionally, one of the birds would dart out into the air after a flying insect, its vivid colors flashing like flames. It took just seconds for the birds to pass, but it was a sight I'll remember forever.

Rufous Hummingbird

First Impression
A flash of iridescent copper and orange

Mark Your Calendar
Spring through fall

Details, Details
- Tiny! 3¾ inches, and a good part is beak
- Female is iridescent green with a dab of orange-red on throat

Listen Up!
- Buzzy sounds and variations of *zee-chew-chew-chew*
- Male dives from a great height, producing a stuttering *v-v-v-vroooom*

Telltale Traits
- Unmistakable: He hovers! He buzzes! He goes backward, forward, sideways!
- Pugnacious personality

Look Here
- At nectar feeder

Or Here
- At flowers, especially red or red-orange blossoms or tubular-shaped blossoms
- Perched on slender twig or other raised spot, often at top of young tree or shrub

On the Home Front Often nests in backyards, but nest is almost impossibly hard to find • Makes tiny and well-camouflaged nest that looks exactly like knobby bit of lichen-covered branch • The tiny cup, about the size of a Ping-Pong ball cut in half, is made of plant down and bits of bark and moss, held together with spiderwebs and lichens.

"Hot tempered in the extreme"

—**Henry Henshaw, "List of Birds Observed in Summer and Fall on the Upper Pecos River, New Mexico" (1886)**

You'll see vicious battles when rufous hummingbirds seek the same nectar feeder or flower. The males will often perch nearby even when they're not drinking, so they can zoom out and drive away any competition.

Wild Menu: Nectar; insects

Plant Picks: "Hummingbird flowers," which have tubular blossoms, especially in red or orange-red: Start with red-flowering currant (*Ribes sanguineum*) and salmonberry (*Rubus spectabilis*) to catch the attention of spring migrants. Columbines (*Aquilegia formosa* and other spp.) and penstemons (*Penstemon* spp.) are popular; so are salvias (*Salvia* spp.), red-hot pokers (*Kniphofia* spp.), and honeysuckles (*Lonicera* spp.).

Feeder Pleasers
- Nectar feeder

Tricks and Treats
- A mister or garden sprinkler may attract bathing hummers.

Can't We Just Get Along?

Every time I see a photo of several hummingbirds sharing a feeder, I wonder if there's something I'm doing wrong. That's just not the scene at *my* feeder. Once in a while a male and female will dine side by side. But two males? Or a crowd? Never.

Turns out it isn't my behavior, but the habits of the hummingbird species I've hosted that make the difference. Some species are just more willing to share than others. And my usual birds, the rufous hummingbirds, are the most temperamental of the bunch.

Anna's Hummingbird

First Impression
Tiny, zippy bird with neon pink head and throat

Mark Your Calendar

Year-round within about 100 miles of the coast; spring through fall only in inland northern California; absent elsewhere in this region. Eastward in this region, watch for the smaller, purple-throated calliope hummingbird, from spring through fall.

Details, Details

- Smaller than a chickadee, but one of the larger hummingbirds: 4 inches
- Female has small iridescent pink-red patch in center of throat

Listen Up!

- Rapid twittering when chasing another hummer
- Thin, high, squeaky *screetch screetch screetch*
- Listen for explosive, single *TEWK!* at the bottom of a male's courtship dive: The sound is so loud and so odd it may take you a while to believe it came from that tiny hummer.

Telltale Traits

- A typical hummingbird, with all the incredible flying skills of its family
- Often perches on thin tip of tree, skinny branch, or garden ornament

Look Here

- At nectar feeder

Or Here

- At flowers
- On a slender perch, often singing
- Up in the air overhead during courtship
- At a mister or sprinkler

"He will use the same perch almost constantly"

—A. C. Bent, *Life Histories of North American Cuckoos, Goatsuckers, Hummingbirds and Their Allies* (1940)

Keep an eye out for perched hummingbirds when you're out in the yard. The male often chooses a perch where he's silhouetted against the sky.

On the Home Front Often a backyard nester, but tiny nest easy to entirely overlook • Builds very small cup of lichens, plant down, and spider silk on branch

Wild Menu: Nectar; plus a bigger proportion of insects than most hummingbirds

Plant Picks: Tubular "hummingbird flowers," especially in red or orange-red: red-flowering currant (*Ribes sanguineum*), salmonberry (*Rubus spectabilis*), columbines (*Aquilegia* spp.), penstemons, salvias, honeysuckles (*Lonicera* spp.), and many others

Feeder Pleasers
- Nectar

Tricks and Treats
- Water, especially a mister or sprinkler that the bird can fly through, are a hit in all seasons. If you use a handheld nozzle, hummers in your yard may show up to flit through the spray.

Thanks for the Flowers!

Old field guides on my shelf show I have no chance of seeing an Anna's hummingbird in my backyard, yet the birds are here year-round. Because of global warming? Nope. Because of gardens. Anna's hummingbird once lived only in parts of California. As civilization spread, and people's backyards sprouted flowers, Anna's changed their ways. When bird lovers added nectar feeders, these hummers became even more widespread.

Band-Tailed Pigeon

First Impression

What are those pigeons doing way out here in the forest?

"Recovered from former decimation"

—John Terres, *Encyclopedia of North American Birds* (1980)

Mark Your Calendar

Year-round; absent from some areas in this region; usually above 2,000 feet elevation except in some coastal areas

Details, Details

- Bigger than a regular pigeon; 14½ inches
- Male and female look alike
- Subtly colored in shades of gray and rosy gray, with white crescent on back of neck
- Eyes are dark; bill and legs are yellow
- Wide band at tip of tail is much paler gray than rest of tail, easily visible in flight

Listen Up!

- Similar to other pigeons and some owls, a deep, mellow *who-whoo who-whoo who-whoo*
- Also guttural and nasal calls
- Their wings make a loud flapping noise when the birds take off.

Telltale Traits

- Usually in small flocks
- Fast, direct flight
- Perches and feeds in trees and on ground
- Sometimes hangs upside down while feeding in trees

Look Here

- Feeding on fruit in your yard

Or Here

- May visit feeders

On the Home Front Not usually a backyard nester • Typically nests in heavily forested areas • Makes a loose platform of twigs and sticks

Like the passenger pigeon of the eastern half of the country, the band-tailed was once hunted excessively in the West. Luckily, the slaughter stopped before these birds were completely wiped out.

Wild Menu: Grain; seeds; fruit; acorns and other nuts; flowers of trees; occasionally insects

Plant Picks: Native red or blue elderberries (*Sambucus callicarpa, S. racemosa, S. caerulea*). Manzanita (*Arctostaphylos columbiana*), salal (*Gaultheria shallon*), and junipers may attract a feeding flock.

Feeder Pleasers

- Hazelnuts in the shell; corn; birdseed mix

Tricks and Treats

- If you see band-tails nearby, scatter a few handfuls of rock salt and birdcage grit in a tray feeder.
- When acorns are abundant, collect some for the feeder; these pigeons swallow them whole.

Picture Window

My son got to know a small flock of band-tailed pigeons quite well one summer. Outside his bedroom window of our house on the coast of Oregon grew several big bushes of native red elderberries, and a single bush of later-ripening blue elder. Once the pigeons had spotted them, the birds were daily visitors. Though bulky, they were remarkably agile as they climbed around on the twigs. When a branch bent beneath their weight, they moved down it like tightrope walkers to reach the berries at the tip. They drove our indoor cats crazy!

Mountain Quail

First Impression

Tiny chickens with topknots, running through the brush

Mark Your Calendar

Year-round; at high altitudes during summer nesting season; descend lower in winter

Details, Details

- Larger and plumper than a robin; 11 inches
- Sides are striped with vertical white bars
- Head plume is long and straight, not curled like other quail
- Male and female look alike
- California quail, also in this region, have curled topknots and different markings.

Listen Up!

- Male and female make soft clucking, wheezing, and whistled calls
- Male also gives a loud, crowing *QUEEark!*

Telltale Traits

- Very secretive and elusive, always in or near dense shrubs
- Usually walks or runs
- When startled, may explode into flight
- Likes to dust bathe

Look Here

- Scuttling across open space between bushes or hedges

Or Here

- In nearby brushy areas
- In a variety of wild habitats, from fir forests to sagebrush stands near aspens

On the Home Front The mountain quail is so elusive that its home life hasn't been extensively studied. • Nests on ground, often on steep hillsides, against log or beneath bush

"As a lonely mountaineer he is not half known"

—John Muir, on this "very handsomest and most interesting of all American partridges," *The Yosemite* **(1920)**

The mountain quail is a secretive bird that usually sticks to the mountains. If your yard borders a wild habitat and your style is naturalistic, you may see them occasionally.

Wild Menu: Fruits; seeds; acorns; seeds from conifers; leaves; buds; flowers

Plant Picks: A dense cover of shrubs is a must. If your yard is part of a quail's territory, smooth sumac berries (*Rhus glabra*) may help coax the bird into view.

Feeder Pleasers

- If you see a quail at your feeder, it's most likely a California quail scarfing down the cracked corn. Mountain quail aren't feeder visitors.

Tricks and Treats

- If you have a natural or naturalistic creek on your property, watch for a covey drinking.

Grazers

Mountain quail sample any vegetable matter in their path. As the covey moves like a flock of grazing animals, the birds nibble along the way. A nip of a leaf there, a bite of seeds here, a few buds from that bush, some fallen conifer seeds, the seed heads of flowers. Bulbs of wildflowers are scratched up, and even mushrooms may be fair game. It's a varied diet that changes according to the kind of habitat a particular flock adopts.

RECOMMENDED READING

Thousands of books about birds have been published over the years, so choosing those you like best is a matter of personal taste. Most of the books and publications I cited in this book are from my personal collection of field guides, old books, and journals. I've found them at used-book shops, library sales, flea markets, yard sales, and on the Internet. They still turn up, more often than you might expect, and usually at reasonable prices. The hunt is part of the fun!

Traditional Field Guides

Visit a bookstore to see the many comprehensive field guides that are available. These chunky, pocket-size books (okay, big pockets!) are made to take along on outings; most have sturdy bindings and wipe-clean covers. Choosing a field guide is a matter of personal preference; some have photos, others have illustrations; some are limited to particular areas, others cover the entire country. I like field guides that include a range map next to each species' picture, rather than maps grouped at the back of the book; that way, I can tell instantly whether that bird is likely in my area.

These traditional field guides are highly popular with bird lovers.

Sibley, David Allen. *The Sibley Guide to Birds*. New York, NY: Knopf, 2000.

Robbins, Chandler S., Bertel Brun, Herbert S. Zim, and Arthur Singer. *Birds of North America: A Guide To Field Identification, Revised and Updated* (Golden Field Guide from St. Martin's Press). New York: St. Martin's Press, 2001.

Peterson, Roger Tory. *A Field Guide to Eastern Birds*. 5th edition. Boston: Houghton Mifflin, 2002

Peterson, Roger Tory. *A Field Guide to Western Birds*. 3rd edition. Boston: Houghton Mifflin, 1998

The Bent Books

The "Bent books" are my favorite series about birds. I first encountered this 20-volume series (published between 1919 and 1968) in the Kutztown State College library, in eastern Pennsylvania, when I was 16; they formed the basis of my education in bird life and lore, and I still draw from them today. Just last spring, while watching a pair of courting and nesting Virginia rails in a swamp, I thought, "Wonder what Bent has to say about this?" and pulled out his book when I reached home. Reading a Bent book is almost as good as sharing stories with a fellow bird-watcher.

Arthur Cleveland Bent collected hundreds of anecdotes and sifted through published material to fill each volume with a lifetime of learning about the bird species of

North America. The many volumes were published by the Smithsonian Institution; most were reprinted by Dover. They are out of print, but you can still find many reasonably priced copies on the Internet or at used-book shops and other sources.

Look for A. C. Bent, *Life Histories of North American Woodpeckers*, and other "*Life Histories of ...*" books (Smithsonian Institution or Dover reprint; various publication dates).

You can also find some Bent books online at www.birdsbybent.com/; excerpts appear on Web sites (search for the name of the bird you're interested in, plus the name "Bent").

The Treasure Hunt for Old Books

Back in the dark ages before the Internet, the only way you could track down an old book was by asking a bookshop to send out postcards to other shops, expressing interest. It was often a months-long process with disappointing results. Today, you can simply go online and track down a copy of just about any book you might be looking for in a matter of minutes.

My favorite book finder is AbeBooks, www.abebooks.com, a clearinghouse Web site that lists tens of thousands of books and other publications offered by booksellers around the world, any of which you can purchase. You can browse by category (Warning: Can be addictive!) or search for a specific book. Each seller describes the condition of its book or publication and lists its price, so you can choose a volume that enhances your library and fits your budget. Back issues of ornithological journals, such as the *Auk*, are available for as little as $1 apiece, plus shipping.

The auction site www.ebay.com also includes listings for interesting old bird books and journals.

Booksellers often list out of print books on www.amazon.com; just search for the book by name, then click on "Used & New."

If you do an online search for the title you're looking for, you're likely to find other sources that offer the book. Happy hunting!

Scientific Journals

The *Auk* is the journal of the American Ornithologists' Union (AOU). Founded in 1883, the AOU is devoted to the scientific study of birds, although many of the earlier issues of the journal include anecdotes contributed by amateur bird-watchers. The first issue of the *Auk* was published in 1884, and it's still being published today. Anyone who likes birds can join the AOU; an annual membership costs $80 (student rate, $26).

www.aou.org
American Ornithologists' Union
1313 Dolley Madison Blvd.
Suite 402
McLean, VA 22101
(703) 790-1745

The *Condor* is the journal of the Cooper Ornithological Society (COS), founded in 1893; the *Condor* has been published since 1899 and is still going strong today. COS is dedicated to the scientific study of birds and their conservation, and encourages membership for anyone who enjoys birds. Fees are similar to those of the AOU. You can join the COS via its Web site or through the Ornithological Societies of North America (OSNA; see opposite page).

www.cooper.org
Cooper Ornithological Society

Joining the Ornithological Societies of North America (OSNA) opens the door into the world of serious birders. This umbrella organization gathers together various bird-focused organizations to make it easier to manage memberships and publications. It was founded in 1979 by the AOU, the COS, and the Wilson Ornithological Society. Today it also handles membership services for the Association of Field Ornithologists, the Raptor Research Foundation, and the Waterbird Society, along with its original three. Join any of these organizations through OSNA, and you'll receive the *Ornithological Newsletter,* published six times a year. It's chock-full of news and opportunities for bird-watchers who want to, or already have, made birding part of their life's work. You'll find info about volunteer and paid field assistant positions, for which helpers are needed outdoors ("in the field"), plus news about research grants, scientific meetings, and other members.

www.osnabirds.org
OSNA Business Office
5400 Bosque Blvd., Ste. 680
Waco, TX 76710
(254) 399-9636

SOURCES

I often say I wish I could meet each one of you because I have a feeling we're kindred spirits. Since there's nothing I like more than talking with friends about birds, plants, and nature, I've created a place where we can do just that. Just stop in at my Web site, www.sallyroth.com. You'll find pictures from my own backyard, stories that I couldn't squeeze into this book, news about upcoming projects, and plenty of ideas for making your own place a real haven for birds, butterflies, and other wild creatures. You'll also find a place on the Web site where you can ask questions, share your own discoveries, or just enjoy talking to like-minded folks about birds, gardening, and nature. See you there!

Also, check out the sources below for bird supplies and plants for all regions of the country.

Supplies

Look for bird feeders, nest boxes, and birdseed at nearby wild bird supply stores. Discount stores and even supermarkets also carry a selection of products. Craft sales and bazaars often have handmade feeders and houses.

Online, try these Web sites. All offer a wide variety of supplies and temptations for the backyard bird lover.

Duncraft
102 Fisherville Rd.
Concord, NH 03303
(888) 879-5095
www.duncraft.com
Online, phone, mail order, printed catalog also available free upon request

BestNest
4750 Lake Forest Drive, Suite 132
Cincinnati, OH 45242
(877) 562-1818 or (513) 232-4225
www.bestnest.com
Online catalog only; online or phone orders

Wild Birding World
The Kayes Group, Inc.
PO Box 3326
Mesquite, NV 89027
(845) 834-3215
www.wildbirdingworld.com
Online catalog only; online or phone orders

www.abirdsworld.com
(877) 725-1965
Online catalog only; online or phone orders

www.Amazon.com
Online only

Plants

All of the plants I've recommended in this book's regional bird profiles are widely available in those regions. If you're hunting for bird-approved plants, start with your local nurseries and garden centers. Independently owned nurseries usually have staff members who know plants and can help you find what you need. Many stock a selection of native species. Prices may be lower at garden centers, but the selection is usually not as good and the staff not as knowledgeable. Don't see what you're looking for? Just ask; they may be able to order it for you. You can also order plants online; just search for the plant by name.

You can find an excellent selection of native plants and other bird-appealing plants, including wildflowers, grasses, shrubs, trees, and vines, at trustworthy mail-order suppliers, too. Here's a very small sampling to whet your appetite.

Northeast

Tripple Brook Farm
37 Middle Rd.
Southampton, MA 01073
(413) 527-4626
www.tripplebrookfarm.com
Hundreds of fabulous plants—I need a bigger yard!—including native viburnums and many, many other natives

North and Midwest

Hamilton's Native Nursery & Seed Farm
16786 Brown Rd.
Elk Creek, MO 65464
(417) 967-2190
www.hamiltonseed.com
Seeds and plants of native grasses, prairie flowers, shrubs, and trees, plus other great finds

Southeast and South

Woodlanders, Inc.
Bob McCartney
1128 Colleton Avenue
Aiken, SC 29801
(803) 648-7522
www.woodlanders.net
One of the older native plant specialists (since 1979), Woodlanders offers bird-attracting natives for Southern regions. Call for a catalog; no online shopping—yet.

West

Blake Nursery
316 Otter Creek Rd.
Big Timber, MT 59011
(406) 932-4195
www.blakenursery.com
Specializes in plants for western gardens, including a terrific selection of hardy Montana natives that will thrive elsewhere in the West, too—or give that western touch to an eastern garden.

Northwest, West, and Southwest

Forestfarm
990 Tetherow Rd.
Williams, OR 97544-9599
(541) 846-7269
www.forestfarm.com
Plant addicts, beware: One look at this chunky, jam-packed catalog and you're sunk. An unbelievably vast selection of thousands of plants, including natives from across America. Lots of favorite plants in my gardens have come from Forestfarm—even when I lived in Pennsylvania.

PHOTO CREDITS

© Wally Bauman/Alamy: page 239

© Mark Belko/Alamy: page 42 *(top)*

© Blickwinkel/Alamy: page 268

© Rick and Nora Bowers/Alamy: page 290

© Gay Bumgarner/Alamy: page 2

© Gary W. Carter/Alamy: pages vii, 83 *(blue jay)*, 112

© Chao-Yang Chan/Alamy: page 26

© Jim Cole/Alamy: page 52

© Bruce Coleman Inc./Alamy: page 275

© Corbis Premium Collection/Alamy: pages 85, 224

© Danita Delimont/Alamy: pages 34, 101 *(Eastern)*, 109, 301

© Peter Forsberg/Alamy: page 25

© franzfoto.com/Alamy: page 296

© William Leaman/Alamy: pages 36, 43, 53 *(top)*, 183, 210, 221, 267, 298

© Clive Limpkin/Alamy: page 46 (left)

© Oyvind Martinsen/Alamy: page 48

© Mike Mckavett/Alamy: page 247

© Mira/Alamy: page 10

© David Osborn/Alamy: page 24

© Malcolm Schuyl/Alamy: page 259

© Stock Connection Distribution/Alamy: page 209

© SuperStock/Alamy: page 101 *(inset)*

© Terry Wall/Alamy: page 227

© Chris Wallace/Alamy: page 244

© Deborah Allen: page 186

© David Boyle/Animals Animals: pages 8, 238

© Mark Chappell/Animals Animals: pages 214, 271

© Alan G. Nelson/Animals Animals: page 4

© Marie Read/Animals Animals: pages 212, 215, 222

© AP Images: page 29

© Linda Freshwaters Arndt: page 140

© Ron Austing: pages 83 *(inset)*, 84, 89, 92, 98 *(myrtle)*, 130, 135, 164, 171

© Cliff Beittel: page 87

Courtesy of Kevin Burke/Earlham College: page 33

© Mark Bolton/Corbis: page xvi

© Joe McDonald/Corbis: page 18

© Norbert Schaefer/Corbis: page 7

© Tom Stewart/Corbis: page 3

© Richard Day/Daybreak Imagery: pages viii, 21, 81, 91, 95, 96, 103, 106 *(dark-eyed)*, 127, 128,

© Barbara Gerlach/DRK Photo: page 305

© Donald M. Jones/DRK Photo: page 246

© Tom and Pat Leeson/DRK Photo: page 22

© Digital Vision/Getty Images: page 16

© Image Source/Getty Images: page 13

© Photographer's Choice/Getty Images: page 38

© Steve Greer Photography: page 86

© Russell C. Hansen: page 118 *(ruby-throated)*

© Janet Horton: pages 45 *(right)*, 80, 111, 250

© Bill Leaman/The Image Finders: page 126

© Peter LaTourrette: front cover, page iii

© Tom and Pat Leeson: pages ix, 82, 97, 99, 102, 106 *(top inset)*, 117 *(Baltimore)*, 161, 179, 181, 187, 226, 236, 237, 243, 265, 285, 304

© Kitchin and Hurst/Leeson Photo: pages 131, 245

© Steve Maslowski: pages 6, 180

© Charles W. Melton: page 248

© Jerry Mercier: page 110

© Matthias Breiter/Minden Pictures: page 153

© Tim Fitzharris/Minden Pictures: pages 134, 288

© Christo Baars/Foto Natura/Minden Pictures: page 234

© Dietmar Nill/Foto Natura/Minden Pictures: page 166

© Thomas Mangelsen/Minden Pictures: page 159

© Michael Quinton/Minden Pictures: pages 155, 169

© Tom Vezo/Minden Pictures: pages 165, 190, 233, 286, 292, 295

© Aflo/Nature Picture Library: page 197

© Wegner/ARCO/Nature Picture Library: page 23

© Niall Benvie/Nature Picture Library: page 28

© John Cancalosi/Nature Picture Library: page 269

© Laurent Geslin/Nature Picture Library: page 49

© Rolf Nussbaumer/Nature Picture Library: pages x, 294

© Tom Vezo/Nature Picture Library: page 53 *(bottom)*

© Dave Watts/Nature Picture Library: page 118 *(inset)*

© David Welling/Nature Picture Library: page 198

© Sandra Nykerk: page 93

© John W. Bova/Photo Researchers, Inc.: page 45 *(left)*

© Steve Maslowski/Photo Researchers, Inc.: pages 46 *(right)*, 184

© Steve and Dave Maslowski/Photo Researchers, Inc.: pages 157, 273

© Anthony Mercieca/Photo Researchers, Inc.: pages 299, 300

© Rod Planck/Photo Researchers, Inc.: page 235

© James Zipp/Photo Researchers, Inc.: pages 188, 193, 216, 249

© Marie Read: pages 132, 191

© Johann Schumacher Design: pages 138, 139, 262

© Brian E. Small: pages 47 *(left)*, 182, 213, 218, 266, 274, 293

© David Stuckel: page 113

© Gerald D. Tang: page 199

© G. Bailey/Vireo: pages 133, 141

© R. Bannick/Vireo: page 287

© A. and J. Binns/Vireo: pages 51 *(right)*, 154, 251

© R. and N. Bowers/Vireo: pages 35, 98 *(inset)*, 192, 223, 264, 270, 272

© R. Crossley/Vireo: page 167

© R. Curtis/Vireo: pages 156, 189

© R. and S. Day/Vireo: page 58

© S. Fried/Vireo: page 145

© J. Fuhrman/Vireo: page 152

© W. Greene/Vireo: page 105

© J. Heidecker/Vireo: pages 51 *(left)*, 90

© S. Holt/Vireo: pages 116, 263

© J. Jantunen/Vireo: page 142

© S. J. Lang/Vireo: page 57 *(top)*

© G. Lasley/Vireo: pages 106 *(bottom inset)*, 241

© G. McElroy/Vireo: pages 42 *(bottom)*, 59, 137, 144, 160, 168, 172, 220

© A. Morris/Vireo: page 173

© P. Moylan/Vireo: page 55

© R. Nussabaumer/Vireo: page 117 *(inset)*

© R. Royse/Vireo: page 136

© S. and S. Rucker/Vireo: page 88 *(inset)*

© H. P. Smith/Vireo: pages 302, 306

© K. Smith/Vireo: page 242

© B. Steele/Vireo: pages 162, 163, 219, 240

© T. Vezo/Vireo: page 60

© D. Wechsler/Vireo: page 196

© J. Wedge/Vireo: page 94

© J. R. Woodward/Vireo: page 47 *(right)*

© Walt Anderson/Visuals Unlimited: page 256 *(bottom)*

© Gerry Bishop/Visuals Unlimited: page 176 *(bottom)*

© Rick and Nora Bowers/Visuals Unlimited: pages 77 *(top)*, 256 *(top)*

© Gay Bumgarner/Visuals Unlimited: page 72

© John Cornell/Visuals Unlimited: pages 114, 194, 195

© Gerald and Buff Corsi/Visuals Unlimited: page 252

© Dr. John D. Cunningham/Visuals Unlimited: page 307

© Derrick Ditchburn/Visuals Unlimited: pages 70, 289, 291

© Robert W. Domm/Visuals Unlimited: page 122 *(bottom left)*

© Chuck Doswell/Visuals Unlimited: page 202 *(bottom)*

© Wally Eberhart/Visuals Unlimited: pages 122 *(top)*, 148 *(top)*

© Bruce Gaylord/Visuals Unlimited: page 123

© Barbara Gerlach/Visuals Unlimited: pages 206 *(bottom)*, 255

© John and Barbara Gerlach/Visuals Unlimited: pages 100, 150, 225

© Adam Jones/Visuals Unlimited: pages 54, 65, 74, 78 *(bottom)*, 104, 124 *(top)*, 174, 205, 257, 278

© Dick Keen/Visuals Unlimited: page 206 *(top)*

© Steve Maslowski/Visuals Unlimited: page 41, 57 *(bottom)*, 76, 88 *(Carolina wren)*, 108, 122 *(bottom right)*, 124 *(bottom)*, 129, 158, 170, 178, 185, 217, 231, 258, 276

© Joe McDonald/Visuals Unlimited: pages 77 *(bottom)*, 148 *(bottom)*

INDEX

Boldface page numbers indicate illustrations. <u>Underscored</u> references indicate boxed text.

USDA PLANT HARDINESS ZONE MAP

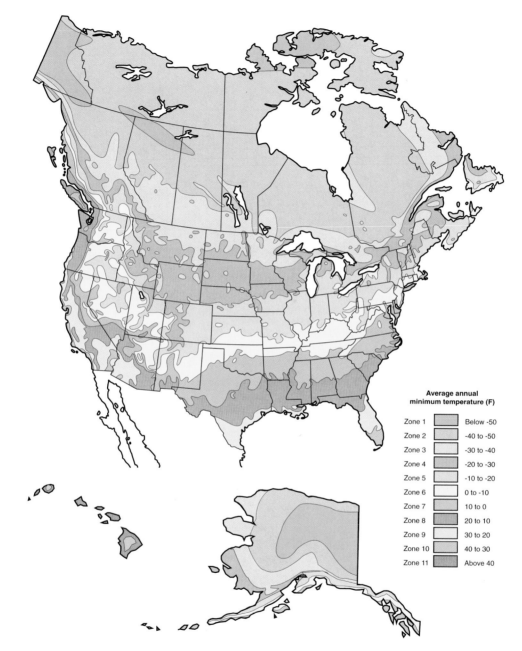

Average annual minimum temperature (F)

Zone	Temperature
Zone 1	Below -50
Zone 2	-40 to -50
Zone 3	-30 to -40
Zone 4	-20 to -30
Zone 5	-10 to -20
Zone 6	0 to -10
Zone 7	10 to 0
Zone 8	20 to 10
Zone 9	30 to 20
Zone 10	40 to 30
Zone 11	Above 40

This map is recognized as the best indicator of minimum temperatures available. Look at the map to find your area, then match its pattern to the key at right. When you've found your pattern, the key will tell you what hardiness zone you live in. Remember that the map is a general guide; your particular conditions may vary.